CompTIA® Linux+™ Certification (2009 Objectives)

CompTIA® Linux+™ Certification (2009 Objectives)

Part Number: 085039
Course Edition: 1.0

NOTICES

HELP US IMPROVE OUR COURSEWARE

Your comments are important to us. Please contact us at Element K Press LLC, 1-800-478-7788, 500 Canal View Boulevard, Rochester, NY 14623, Attention: Product Planning, or through our Web site at **http://support.elementkcourseware.com**.

CompTIA® Linux+™ Certification (2009 Objectives)

About This Course

The *CompTIA® Linux+*™ certification course, developed to cover CompTIA's 2009 objectives, builds on your existing user-level knowledge and experience with the Linux operating system, to present fundamental skills and concepts that you will use on the job in any type of Linux career.

The *CompTIA® Linux+*™ certification course can benefit you in two ways. If your job duties include Linux troubleshooting, installation, or maintenance, or if you are preparing for any type of Linux-related career, it provides the background knowledge and skills you will require to be successful. In addition, it assists you if you are preparing to take the CompTIA® Linux+™ certification examination, 2009 objectives (Exam Code: XK0-003), in order to become a CompTIA® Linux+™ Certified Professional.

Course Description

Target Student

This course is intended for entry-level computer support professionals with basic knowledge of computer hardware, software, and operating systems, who wish to increase their knowledge and understanding of Linux concepts and skills to prepare for a career in Linux support or administration, or to prepare for the CompTIA® Linux+™ certification, 2009 objectives (Exam Code XK0-003). A typical student in the CompTIA® Linux+™ Certification course should have at least 6 to 12 months of Linux experience.

Course Prerequisites

To ensure your success, we recommend you first take the following Element K course or have equivalent knowledge:

- *CompTIA® A+® Certification: A Comprehensive Approach for 2009 Objectives*

How to Use This Book

As a Learning Guide

Each lesson covers one broad topic or set of related topics. Lessons are arranged in order of increasing proficiency with *Linux+ Certification*; skills you acquire in one lesson are used and developed in subsequent lessons. For this reason, you should work through the lessons in sequence.

We organized each lesson into results-oriented topics. Topics include all the relevant and supporting information you need to master *Linux+ Certification*, and activities allow you to apply this information to practical hands-on examples.

You get to try out each new skill on a specially prepared sample file. This saves the time taken for typing and allows you to concentrate on the skill at hand. Through the use of sample files, hands-on activities, illustrations that give you feedback at crucial steps, and supporting background information, this book provides you with the foundation and structure to learn *Linux+ Certification* quickly and easily.

As a Review Tool

Any method of instruction is only as effective as the time and effort you are willing to invest in it. In addition, some of the information that you learn in class may not be important to you immediately, but it may become important later on. For this reason, we encourage you to spend some time reviewing the topics and activities after the course. For additional challenge when reviewing activities, try the "What You Do" column before looking at the "How You Do It" column.

As a Reference

The organization and layout of the book make it easy to use as a learning tool and as an after-class reference. You can use this book as a first source for definitions of terms, background information on given topics, and summaries of procedures.

Course Icons

Icon	Description
	A **Caution Note** makes students aware of potential negative consequences of an action, setting, or decision that are not easily known.
	Display Slide provides a prompt to the instructor to display a specific slide. Display Slides are included in the Instructor Guide only.
	An **Instructor Note** is a comment to the instructor regarding delivery, classroom strategy, classroom tools, exceptions, and other special considerations. Instructor Notes are included in the Instructor Guide only.
	Notes Page indicates a page that has been left intentionally blank for students to write on.
	A **Student Note** provides additional information, guidance, or hints about a topic or task.
	A **Version Note** indicates information necessary for a specific version of software.

Course Objectives

In this course, you will acquire the skills needed to install and support one or more distributions of the Linux operating system, and learn information and skills that will be helpful as you prepare for the CompTIA® Linux+™ certification examination, 2009 objectives (Exam Code: XK0-003).

You will:

- identify basic Linux concepts and perform basic Linux tasks.
- manage user and group accounts.
- manage partitions and the Linux filesystem.
- manage various files in Linux.
- work with Linux permissions and ownership.
- print files.
- manage packages.
- manage kernel services.
- work with the Bash shell.

- manage jobs and processes.
- manage system services.
- configure Linux services to provide users with network connectivity.
- configure basic Internet services.
- implement measures to secure Linux.
- manage hardware associated with Linux machines.
- troubleshoot Linux system issues.
- install the Linux operating system.
- configure the GUI.

Course Requirements

Hardware

- 2 GB of memory or higher
- A processor with 2.7 GHz capacity or higher
- DVD R/W drive (Boot capable)
- Floppy disk drive
- Generic keyboard and mouse
- Sound and display cards (VGA - 256 color 800x600)
- Two Network Interface Cards (NICs) for srvA and one NIC for srvB
- Generic Monitor
- 80 GB hard disk
- Printer with parallel port

● Printer with USB port

Software

● A licensed copy of Red Hat Enterprise Linux 5 for the instructor and students.

● A copy of the Red Hat Enterprise Linux 5 Rescue CD for the instructor and for each student.

● A copy of Debian 5 for the instructor and students.

Class Setup

Classroom Network Connectivity

1. For each student and instructor, set up an independent network consisting of two systems.

2. Label the instructor system as **srvA** and **srvB.** The **srvA** server is assigned the IP address 192.168.0.2 and the **srvB** server is assigned the IP address 192.168.0.3.

3. Label the students system as **Student X—srvA** and **Student X—srvB,** where X is the student number. Assign the IP addresses, 192.168.0.4 and 192.168.0.5, for Student1—srvA and Student1—srvB. For the remaining students, assign even numbers for srvA and odd numbers for srvB.

4. On each system, install Red Hat Enterprise Linux 5.3.

5. Synchronize the system time on each network.

Installing Red Hat Enterprise Linux 5.3 on srvA

To install Red Hat Enterprise Linux 5 on srvA:

1. Insert Red Hat Enterprise Linux CD 1 in the DVD-RW drive.

2. On the Red Hat Enterprise Linux 5 page, to install or upgrade an existing system, press **Enter.**

3. On the Welcome to Red Hat Enterprise Linux Server page, select **Skip** and then press **Enter.**

4. On the Red Hat Enterprise installation page, click **Next.**

5. On the Language Selection page, in the language selection list box, verify that the **English (English)** option is selected and click **Next.**

6. On the Keyboard Configuration page, in the Keyboard selection area, verify that **U.S. English** is selected and click **Next.**

7. At the **Installation Number** dialog box, enter the installation number provided with the Red Hat Enterprise Linux 5 CDs.

8. To install Red Hat Enterprise Linux 5, choose **Install Red Hat Enterprise Linux Server** and click **Next.**

9. On the disk partitioning setup page, from the partition layout drop-down list, select **Create custom layout** and click **Next.**

10. Delete the existing partitions.

11. Partition the hard disk according to the table and click **Next.**

Type	Mount Point	Size
swap		Twice the RAM size (1024 MB)
ext3	/	20000 MB

12. On the Boot Loader Configuration page, click **Next.**
13. On the Network Configuration page, configure network parameters.
    - Click **Edit.**
    - In the **Enable IPv4 support** section, in the **Edit Interface** dialog box, select the **Manual configuration** option.
    - In the **IP Address** text box, type *192.168.0.2* and in the **Prefix(Netmask)** text box, type *255.255.255.0*
    - Uncheck the **Enable IPv6 support** option and click **OK.**
    - In the text box beside the **manually** option, type *srvA* and click **Next.**
    - In the **Error With Data** message box, click **Continue** two times.
14. On the time zone selection page, in the selected city drop-down list, verify that the **America/New_York** option is selected and click **Next.**
15. On the set root password page, in the **Root Password** text box, type *p@ssw0rd* and press the **Tab** key.
16. In the **Confirm** text box, type *p@ssw0rd* and click **Next.**
17. On the Software Selection page, in the **Include Support** section, check the **Software Development** and **Web server** options.
18. In the **Customize** section, select the **Customize now** option and click **Next.**
19. In the first list box, select the **Servers** option, and in the adjacent list box, check the **DNS Name Server, FTP Server,** and **Network Servers** packages.
20. In the first list box, select the **Desktop Environments** option, and in the adjacent list box, check the **KDE (K Desktop Environment)** package.
21. In the first list box, select the **Base System** option, and in the adjacent list box, check the **System Tools** package and click **Next.**
22. On the about to install page, click **Next** to start installation.
23. In the **Required Install Media** dialog box, click **Continue** to continue installation.
24. At the **Change CDROM** prompts, enter the respective RHEL 5 CDs.
25. On the Congratulations page, click **Reboot** to reboot the system.
26. On the **Welcome** page, click **Forward.**
27. On the License Agreement page, verify that the **Yes, I agree to the License Agreement** option is selected and click **Forward.**
28. On the **Firewall** page, from the **Firewall** spin box, choose **Disabled** and click **Forward.**
29. In the message box, click **Yes.**
30. On the **SELinux** page, from the **SELinux Setting** spin box, choose **Disabled** and click **Forward.**
31. In the message box, click **Yes.**

32. On the **Kdump** page, click **Forward.**

33. On the **Date and Time** page, set the current date and time and click **Forward.**

34. On the **Choose Server** page, click **Forward.**

35. On the **Set Up Software Updates** page, select the **No, I prefer to register at a later time** option and click **Forward.**

36. In the Red Hat network connection dialog box, click **No thanks, I'll connect later.**

37. On the **Finish Updates Setup** page, click **Forward.**

38. On the **Create User** page, create an user account, named *jsmith*, with Full Name as *Joyce Smith* and password as *myp@$$w0rd*

39. In the confirmation dialog box, click **Continue.**

40. On the **Sound Card** page, click **Forward.**

41. On the **Additional CDs** page, click **Finish.**

42. In the confirmation dialog box, click **OK** to reboot the system.

43. At the GUI Login screen, press **Ctrl+Alt+F1** to switch to the first terminal. Log in as *root* in the CLI with the password as *p@ssw0rd*

44. Type useradd eric and press **Enter** to create a new user account for Eric.

45. Type passwd eric and specify *myp@$$w0rd* as the password.

46. Type useradd robert and press **Enter** to create a new user account for Robert.

47. Type passwd robert and specify *myp@$$w0rd* as the password.

Install Debian Linux 5 on srvA as the Second Operating System (Dual Boot)

To install Debian Linux 5 on srvA as the second operating system (Dual Boot):

1. Insert the Debian Linux CD-01 into the CD-ROM/ DVD drive and reboot the system.

2. On the **Installer boot menu** page, select the **Graphical install** option and press **Enter.**

3. On the **Choose language** page, in the **Choose a language** section, verify that **English** is selected and click **Continue.**

4. On the **Choose language** page, in the **Choose a country, territory or area** section, verify that **United States** is selected and click **Continue.**

5. On the **Select a keyboard layout** page, in the **Keymap to use** section, verify that **American English** is selected and click **Continue.**

6. On the **Configure the network** page, observe that the network autoconfiguration failed message is displayed. Click **Continue** to manually configure the network.

7. On the **Configure the network** page, in the **Network configuration method** section, select the **Configure network manually** option and click **Continue.**

8. On the **Configure the network** page, in the **IP address** text box, enter *192.168.0.2* as the IP address. Click **Continue.**

9. On the **Configure the network** page, in the **Netmask** text box, verify that 255.255.255.0 is the subnet mask and click **Continue.**

10. On the **Configure the network** page, in the **Gateway** text box, verify that 192.168.0.1 is the gateway address and click **Continue.**

11. On the **Configure the network** page, in the **Name server addresses** text box, verify that 192.168.0.1 is the name server address and click **Continue.**

12. On the **Configure the network** page, in the **Hostname** text box, enter *srvA* as the host name. Click **Continue.**

13. On the **Configure the network** page, in the **Domain name** text box, enter *localdomain* as the domain name. Click **Continue.**

14. On the **Configure the clock** page, verify that **Eastern** is selected and click **Continue.**

15. On the **Partition disks** page, in the **Partitioning method** section, select the **Manual** option and click **Continue** to define a partition of size 20 GB.

    a. Select the **FREE SPACE** and click **Continue** to define a new partition.

    b. In the **How to use this free space** section, select the **Create a new partition** option and click **Continue.**

    c. In the **New partition** size text box, type *20.0 GB* to define the partition size and click **Continue.**

    d. In the **Type for the new partition** section, select the **Primary** option and click **Continue.**

    e. In the **Location for the new partition** section, select the **Beginning** option and click **Continue.**

    f. In the **How to use this partition** section, select the **Ext3 journaling file system** option and click **Continue.**

    g. In the **Mount point for this partition** section, select the **/ - the root file system** option and click **Continue.**

    h. In the **Partition settings** section, select the **Done setting up the partition** option and click **Continue.**

16. After defining the partitions, verify that the **Finish partitioning and write changes to disk** option and click **Continue.**

17. In the **Write the changes to disks** section, select **Yes** to write the changes onto disks.

18. Create a new user account.

    a. On the **Set up users and passwords** page, in the **Root password** text box, type *p@ssw0rd* as the password and then in the **Re-enter password to verify** text box, retype the password to confirm.

    b. In the **Full name for the new user** text box, type *jsmith* and click **Continue.**

    c. In the **User name for your account** text box, type *Joyce Smith* and press **Enter.**

    d. In the **Choose a password for the new user** text box, type *myp@$$w0rd* as the password.

    e. In the **Re-enter password to verify** text box, renter *myp@$$w0rd* as the password to confirm.

19. On the **Configure the package manager** page, verify that the **No** option is selected to skip scanning another CD or DVD.

20. On the **Configure the package manager** page, select **No** to skip using a network mirror.

21. If necessary, participate in the package usage survey.

22. On the **Software selection** page, and click **Continue** to accept the default collections of software.

23. If necessary, on the **Configuring xserver-xorg** page, select the desired video modes and click **Continue.**

24. On the **Install the GRUB boot loader on a hard disk** page, install the GRUB bootloader to the master boot record.

25. On the **Finish the installation** page, select the **yes** option to set the clock to UTC. Click **Continue.**

26. On the **Finish the installation** page, remove your CD-ROM disc and then click **Continue** to reboot your system.

27. On the GUI screen, log in as *jsmith* with *myp@$$w0rd* as the password.

28. Choose **System→Administration→Login.**

29. Enter *p@ssw0rd* as the root password.

30. In the **Login Window Preferences** dialog box, select the **Security** tab.

31. In the **Security** section, check the **Allow local system administrator login** check box. Click **Close** to save the changes.

32. Choose **System→Log Out jsmith** to log out of the system.

33. Log in as root.

34. In the **This session is running as a privileged user** message box, click **Continue** to ignore the warning message.

35. Choose **Applications→Accessories→Terminal** to launch the terminal window.

36. In the **Terminal** window, type `gedit /boot/grub/menu.lst` to open the file in the gedit editor.

37. Change the line that reads "default 0" as **default 3** to set Red Hat Enterprise Linux 5.3 as the default operating system. Save and close the file.

38. Choose **System→Shut Down.** In the **Shut down this system now** message box, click **Restart** to restart the system.

39. Observe that the system boots the Red Hat Enterprise Linux 5.3 operating system.

Install Windows Vista Business Edition on srvB

To install Windows Vista Business Edition:

1. Boot your computer with the DVD containing Windows Vista Business Edition.

2. In the **Install Windows** window, click **Next** to continue the setup.

3. Click the **Install now** button.

4. In the **Product key** text box, type the product key of your software and click **Next** to continue.

5. Accept the license agreement and click **Next** to continue.

6. On the **Which type of installation do you want** screen, select **Custom (advanced).**

7. On the **Where do you want to install Windows** page, create a new partition, C with a capacity of 10 GB. Format the partition as NTFS.

8. Select the C drive partition to install Windows Vista and click **Next** to continue.

9. The computer will automatically restart after a few minutes. Remove the DVD before the system restarts.

10. After finalizing the setup, the computer will restart once again.

11. In the **Type a user name** text box, enter an account name of User##, where ## is a unique number between 1 and 10—adjust the range accordingly for the number of students in the class. Name the instructor's user account, User100.

12. In the **Type a password** text box, type *p@ssw0rd*

13. In the **Retype a password** text box, retype the password to confirm the login details.

14. In the **Type a password hint** text box, type *p@ssw0rd* and click **Next** to continue.

15. In the **Type a computer name** text box, type a computer name. For the instructor's computer, name the computer, Computer100. For student computers, name each as Computer##, where ## is a unique number between 1 and 10—adjust the range accordingly for the number of students in the class.

16. Click **Next** to continue.

17. On the **Help protect Windows automatically** screen, click **Use recommended settings.**

18. Specify your time and date settings.

    ■ From the **Time zone** drop-down list, select your time zone.

    ■ In the **Date** section, select the date.

    ■ If necessary, modify the system time.

19. Click **Next** to continue.

20. On the **Select your computer's current location** screen, click **Work.**

21. On the Thank you screen, click **Start** to start working with Windows Vista.

22. In the **Password** text box, type *p@ssw0rd* and press **Enter.**

Activate Windows Vista

1. Choose **Start→Control Panel→System And Maintenance.**

2. Click **System.**

3. In the **Windows Activation** section, click **Activate Windows Now.**

4. If prompted, click **Continue.**

5. In the **Windows Activation** dialog box, click **Activate Windows Online Now.**

6. On the **Activation was Successful** page, click **Close.**

Installing Red Hat Enterprise Linux 5.3 on the System srvB as the default operating system (Dual boot)

To install Red Hat Enterprise Linux 5 on the System srvB:

1. Insert Red Hat Enterprise Linux CD 1 in the DVD-RW drive.

2. On the Red Hat Enterprise Linux 5 page, to install or upgrade an existing system, press **Enter.**

3. On the Welcome to Red Hat Enterprise Linux Server page, select **Skip** and then press **Enter.**

4. On the Red Hat Enterprise installation page, click **Next.**

5. On the Language Selection page, in the language selection list box, verify that the **English (English)** option is selected and click **Next.**

6. On the Keyboard Configuration page, in the Keyboard selection area, verify that **U.S. English** is selected and click **Next.**

7. At the **Installation Number** dialog box, enter the installation number provided with the Red Hat Enterprise Linux 5 CDs.

8. To install Red Hat Enterprise Linux 5, choose **Install Red Hat Enterprise Linux Server** and click **Next.**

9. On the disk partitioning setup page, from the partition layout drop-down list, select **Create custom layout** and click **Next.**

10. Partition the hard disk according to the table and click **Next.**

Type	Mount Point	Size
swap		Twice the RAM size (1024 MB)
ext3	/	20000 MB

11. On the Boot Loader Configuration page, rename **Other** to *Windows* and click **Next.**

12. On the Network Configuration page, configure network parameters.
   - Click **Edit.**
   - In the **Enable IPv4 support** section, in the **Edit Interface** dialog box, select the **Manual configuration** option.
   - In the **IP Address** text box, type *192.168.0.3* and in the **Prefix(Netmask)** text box, type *255.255.255.0*
   - Uncheck the **Enable IPv6 support** option and click **OK.**
   - In the text box beside the **manually** option, type *srvB* and click **Next.**
   - In the **Error With Data** message box, click **Continue** two times.

13. On the time zone selection page, in the selected city drop-down list, verify that the **America/New_York** option is selected and click **Next.**

14. On the set root password page, in the **Root Password** text box, type *p@ssw0rd* and press **Tab.**

15. In the **Confirm** text box, type *p@ssw0rd* and click **Next.**

16. On the Software Selection page, in the **Include Support** section, check the **Software Development** and **Web server** options.

17. In the **Customize** section, select the **Customize now** option and click **Next.**

18. In the first list box, select the **Servers** option, and in the adjacent list box, check the **DNS Name Server, FTP Server,** and **Network Servers** packages.

19. In the first list box, select the **Desktop Environments** option, and in the adjacent list box, check the **KDE (K Desktop Environment)** package.

20. In the first list box, select the **Base System** option, and in the adjacent list box, check the **System Tools** package and click **Next.**

21. On the about to install page, click **Next** to start installation.

22. In the **Required Install Media** dialog box, click **Continue** to continue installation.

23. At the **Change CDROM** prompts, enter the respective RHEL 5 CDs.

24. On the Congratulations page, click **Reboot** to reboot the system.

25. On the **Welcome** page, click **Forward.**

26. On the License Agreement page, verify that the **Yes, I agree to the License Agreement** option is selected and click **Forward.**

27. On the **Firewall** page, from the **Firewall** spin box, choose **Disabled** and click **Forward.**

28. In the message box, click **Yes.**

29. On the **SELinux** page, from the **SELinux Setting** spin box, choose **Disabled** and click **Forward.**

30. In the message box, click **Yes.**

31. On the **Kdump** page, click **Forward.**

32. On the **Date and Time** page, set the current date and time and click **Forward.**

33. On the **Choose Server** page, click **Forward.**

34. On the **Set Up Software Updates** page, select the **No, I prefer to register at a later time** option and click **Forward.**

35. In the Red Hat network connection dialog box, click **No thanks, I'll connect later.**

36. On the **Finish Updates Setup** page, click **Forward.**

37. On the **Create User** page, create an user account, named *jsmith*, with Full Name as *Joyce Smith* and password as *myp@$$w0rd*

38. In the confirmation dialog box, click **Continue.**

39. On the **Sound Card** page, click **Forward.**

40. On the **Additional CDs** page, click **Finish.**

41. In the confirmation dialog box, click **OK** to reboot the system.

42. At the GUI Login screen, press **Ctrl+Alt+F1** to switch to the first terminal. Log in as *root* in the CLI with the password as *p@ssw0rd*

43. Type `useradd eric` and press **Enter** to create a new user account for Eric.

44. Type `passwd eric` and enter *myp@$$w0rd* as the password two times to set and confirm the password.

45. Type `useradd robert` and press **Enter** to create a new user account for Robert.

46. Type `passwd robert` and specify *myp@$$w0rd* as the password two times to set and confirm the password.

Installing the Course Data Files on srvA and srvB in Red Hat Enterprise Linux 5.3

1. Copy the 085039Data folder and extract the contents from 085039data.zip to the /root directory.

2. Create a folder named rhelsource in the /root/085039Data/Managing_Packages directory.

3. Copy the contents of RHEL 5 Disc 1 into the rhelsource folder.

4. Copy the contents of the Server folder in the other four RHEL 5 CDs into the /root/ 085993Data/Managing_Packages/rhelsource/Server folder.

5. On the message box that appears, click **Skip.**

For the Instructor

Copy the 085039Data folder from the course CD-ROM to the / directory of your system. Extract the compressed file to the / directory. View the contents of the 085039Data folder.

List of Additional Files

Printed with each activity is a list of files students open to complete that activity. Many activities also require additional files that students do not open, but are needed to support the file(s) students are working with. These supporting files are included with the student data files on the course CD-ROM or data disk. Do not delete these files.

1 Familiarizing Yourself with Linux

Lesson Time: 2 hour(s)

Lesson Objectives:

In this lesson, you will identify basic Linux concepts and perform basic Linux tasks.

You will:

- Identify the key events in the history and development of Linux.
- Enter basic shell commands.
- Access help in Linux.
- Start and stop Linux.

Introduction

You may have experience using the Linux environment, or you may be ready to learn Linux for the first time. In either case, it is good to have an understanding of how Linux was developed and where it is today. In this lesson, you will identify important elements in the history and development of Linux, and perform basic Linux tasks.

When Linux was first available, it was not readily accepted by businesses. But today, it is rapidly gaining acceptance in the corporate world, especially for website activities. Linux is also increasingly used on desktops as a viable alternative to various versions of Microsoft Windows for businesses and individuals alike. By learning the origin of Linux and familiarizing yourself with its basic functions, you will become a confident Linux user.

This lesson covers all or part of the following CompTIA Linux+ (2009) certification objectives:

- Topic B
    - Objective 2.1
    - Objective 4.6
    - Objective 5.1
- Topic C
    - Objective 2.1
- Topic D
    - Objective 2.6

TOPIC A

Review the History and Development of Linux

Operating systems vary greatly from manufacturer to manufacturer. Irrespective of your knowledge about the Linux environment, a basic understanding of its roots will be beneficial to you. In this topic, you will identify key events in the history and development of Linux.

Over the past few years, Linux has gained ground rapidly in the competitive operating system market. Linux is widely preferred for web servers and Internet systems. Many individuals and organizations have accepted it as a desktop and server alternative because of its high security, low cost, and ease of licensing. By learning about the basics of Linux and its development cycle, you will understand and appreciate its benefits.

Open Source Software

Definition:

Open source software enables users to access its source code and gives them the right to modify it. Open source licensing ensures that free and legal redistribution of the software is possible. Although the software can be modified and improved by individual users, the integrity of the author's code is preserved by ensuring that modifications to the original source code are redistributed only as patches.

Example:

Figure 1-1: *Linux is an open source operating system.*

The Need for Open Source

In the early days of computing, many programmers freely shared new software they developed with other users, along with the source code, which enabled users to modify and improve the software. However, with the introduction of restrictive licensing practices by big companies, operating systems and utility programs could not be legally copied by users, and users no longer had access to the source code. This made it impossible for users to create their own customized versions of the software. Some programmers, therefore, disliked the concept of closed source and proprietary software. Richard Stallman, then working at MIT's Artificial Intelligence labs, was one such programmer who wanted to create an alternative. Some examples of open source software are Linux, Perl, PHP, Python, and OpenOffice.

Free Software vs. Open Source Software

Although most of the free software is also open source, the terms are not interchangeable. Open source is a development methodology in which anyone can access the source code, though it is possible to prevent any modification of the code by means of a special licensing agreement. Free software focuses on ethical issues of protecting a user's freedom, where there are no restrictions on how the user runs a program, or how frequently the user is allowed to copy and share the program.

The GNU Project

GNU's Not Unix (GNU) is a comprehensive computer operating system composed entirely of free software. The *GNU project* was started by Richard Stallman in 1984, as an initiative to produce a source for free and open software. Stallman wrote much of the GNU software himself, including the GNU C compiler (gcc) and the emacs text editor. Later, several programmers worked together to develop more utilities that are compatible with the GNU utilities.

 Richard Stallman chose the recursive acronym "GNU's Not Unix" to show that though GNU was like the free version of *Unix* in its design, it did not contain any code from Unix. Note that the "G" in GNU is included in the pronunciation of the term: "guh-NOO."

The Free Software Foundation

FSF is a nonprofit organization founded by Richard Stallman in 1984 to promote the development of free software. It advocates the movement against the monopoly of copyrighted, proprietary software by ensuring the availability of all software to users without any restrictions on use, distribution, or modification.

Free software refers to users' rights rather than cost, and so free software may be sold at a price. Free software must not be confused with freeware, which is software that is available free of cost. Freeware may sometimes include even proprietary software offered on a demo basis. For an online source, see **http://www.fsf.org**.

Copyleft

Definition:

Copyleft is the method of ensuring that all original works, and their derivative works, are kept free and open. The term "copyleft" is used to define a concept that is essentially the opposite of "copyright". Richard Stallman proposed this concept to create a licensing arrangement under which software can be freely used, modified, and copied by others. The Free Software Foundation (FSF) recommends that all free software be copylefted and released under General Public License (GPL).

Example: GNU Utilities

The GNU utilities released under GPL are copylefted because they cannot be copyrighted by anyone who modifies them.

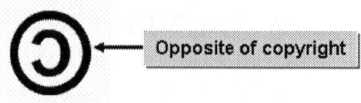

Figure 1-2: The copyleft symbol.

GPL

GPL is a licensing agreement that effectively enforces public ownership of software released under it. GPL states that a programmer holds the copyright to a specific piece of software. This prevents the software from being placed in the public domain, where anyone can modify it and then copyright the modified version. The software is then subjected to a licensing agreement that allows it to be freely used, modified, and copied. Anyone who modifies the code and distributes it to others must provide the open source code that includes their modifications, making it freely available under the terms of GPL. Copyleft is a principle or standard of which GPL is an implementation. There are three versions of GPL.

Version	Date of Release
GPLv1	January 1989
GPLv2	June 1991
GPLv3	June 2007

The Linux Operating System

The *Linux* operating system is a complete, open source operating system that combines GNU utilities and the Linux *kernel*. The kernel is the central core of the Linux operating system that manages all the computer's physical devices. The Linux kernel was developed by Linus Torvalds in 1991, while he was a student at the University of Helsinki. A year later, Torvalds released Linux kernel 1.0 under GPL. The Linux commands closely resemble those found in other Unix-type operating systems. Many programs written for other operating systems run on Linux.

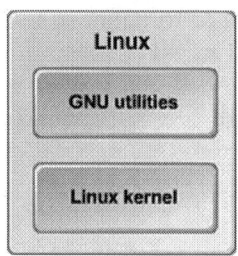

Figure 1-3: Linux is a combination of GNU utilities and the Linux kernel.

Origin of the Linux Kernel

Linus Torvalds, a student at the University of Helsinki in Finland, independently developed a Unix-like operating system kernel in 1991 for his own use, inspired by another system called Minix. He posted his creation on the Internet and asked other programmers to help him further develop it. At that point, Linux could already run Unix utilities such as bash, gcc, and gnu-sed. Until Torvalds agreed to release Linux under GPL, the GNU project was not a complete operating system and the kernel itself was incomplete as an operating system without utilities.

Linux Timeline

The following table outlines important dates in the development of Linux.

Year	Linux-Related Events
1984	Richard Stallman launched the GNU project.
1989	GNU and GPL were released.
1991	Linus Torvalds developed a Unix-like operating system called Linux (version .02).
1992	Linux kernel 1.0 was released under GPL, and S.u.S.E. and TurboLinux were founded.
1993	Red Hat was founded, the Debian project began, and Slackware was first released.
1994	Caldera Inc. was founded.
1995	Red Hat Linux 4.0 was released.
1996	The penguin (Tux) was suggested as the mascot for Linux and Linux kernel 2.0 was released.
1997	Red Hat Linux 5.2 and Debian 1.3 were released.
1998	MandrakeSoft was founded and Debian 2.0 was released.
1999	Red Hat Linux 6.0 and SuSE 6.3 were released.
2000	Red Hat Linux 7.0 and Caldera OpenLinux eDesktop 2.4 were released.
2001	Linux kernel 2.4, SuSE 7.2, Debian 2.23r, Slackware 8.0, Caldera OpenLinux Server, and Workstation 3.1 were released.
2002	GNOME 2.0 was released.
2003	Linux kernel 2.6 and Fedora were released.
2004	The GNU project celebrated its 20th anniversary, and GNOME 2.6 and the first official version of Ubuntu Linux were released.
2005	Red Hat Enterprise Linux 4 was released. Mandrake Linux was renamed as Mandriva Linux.
2007	Red Hat Enterprise Linux 5 and Red Hat Enterprise Linux 5 Update 1 (5.1) were released.
2008	Linux kernel 2.6.28 and Red Hat Enterprise Linux 5 Update 2 (5.2) were released.
2009	Red Hat Enterprise Linux 5 Update 3 (5.3) and Linux kernel 2.6.29 were released.

Uses of Linux

Linux is mainly used on servers, workstations, and desktops.

Use	Description
Server	Used as a web server, to host websites, and as a file server, to provide file access for multiple clients. Also used to control and secure network traffic.
Workstation	Designed for a business environment geared toward programmers.
Desktop	Focused on home users who run office and graphics applications and games.

Other Uses of Linux

The Linux operating system is very versatile. It can be used as a:

- Domain name server
- Routing server
- Database server
- Software development platform
- Parallel processor
- Gateway server

Benefits of Linux

Being an open source operating system, Linux is continually evolving with the support of its user base. The benefits of Linux are increasing daily. Some of these include:

- Low cost
- Easy licensing
- Increased likelihood of bug detection
- Better performance and stability
- Ability to be easily customized
- Increased security
- Compatibility of software across different versions
- Smaller file sizes and reduced use of system resources

Drawbacks of Linux

As with any operating system, Linux has some drawbacks. Some of these include:

- Limited number of mainstream applications.
- Possible lack of comfort in believing that a single vendor can provide support.
- The operating system is free, but the cost of teaching employees how to use it can be significant.

Comparing Linux with Other Operating Systems

In many ways, Linux is the same as other operating systems. It has a Graphical User Interface (GUI), and you can use it to edit documents, browse the Internet, and play games. Where Linux stands out is in its stability and reliability. Linux can run on almost all hardware such as Macintosh, PC, and even Mainframe.

Linux Distributions

Since its creation, Linux has evolved into hundreds of distributions, also called distros, each tailored to their designers' needs. If you are a beginner, you will find it easier to choose one of the mainstream distributions because of their simplified installations. Some common distributions are:

- Red Hat Enterprise Linux
- Fedora
- SUSE Linux Enterprise
- openSUSE
- Debian
- Mandriva
- Ubuntu
- Mint

Internet Reference for Common Linux Distributions

You can refer to common Linux distributions in the following Internet sites:

- Red Hat Enterprise Linux—**www.redhat.com**
- Fedora—**http://fedoraproject.org**
- Debian—**www.debian.org**
- SUSE Linux Enterprise—**www.novell.com/linux**
- openSUSE—**www.opensuse.org**
- Mandriva—**www.mandriva.com**
- Ubuntu—**www.ubuntu.com**
- Mint—**www.linuxmint.com**

Software Acquisition

There are two ways of obtaining Linux software: purchasing it from a local computer outlet or downloading it from a website. While it is convenient to purchase Linux software from a store, downloading it is also practical over a broadband connection.

Comparing Distributions and Their Packaging Solutions

Linux distributions are similar to each other and each has its own strengths and weaknesses. The software packaged with each distribution can make a huge difference in how Linux works for you. Although you can always download or purchase missing components, the software package is easier to use if the components have already been tested and compiled together to work with your distribution.

ACTIVITY 1-1
Reviewing the Development of Linux

Scenario:
Your manager, Linda, asked you to conduct research on the benefits and disadvantages of utilizing Linux in a business environment. She specifically wants to know about the basic concepts of open source software and compare the features of various Linux distributions.

1. **Which of these statements about open source software are true? Select all that apply.**

   a) Its source code is accessible by all.

   b) Users have the right to modify and redistribute it.

   c) It is always available at zero price.

   d) It cannot be updated.

2. **Which of these statements apply to Linux? Select all that apply.**

   a) Increased security

   b) Proprietary in nature

   c) Customizable

   d) Easy licensing procedure

   e) High cost

3. **True or False? Software released under GPL can be modified and copyrighted by any user.**

   ___ True

   ___ False

4. **What are the advantages of Linux? Select all that apply.**

   a) Enables software to be customized.

   b) Comes with strong single-vendor support.

   c) Increases the likelihood of bugs being detected because of increased numbers of programmers who can view code.

   d) Fosters a community among users and a sense of shared responsibility for the software.

5. **What are the potential disadvantages of using Linux? Select all that apply.**

   a) Licensing Linux is a difficult task and requires large amounts of money.

   b) Limited number of mainstream applications are available.

   c) Possible lack of comfort in believing that a single vendor can provide support.

   d) Mainstream Linux distributions come complete with a set of games and office, network, and graphics applications.

---

6. **True or False? There are a limited number of Linux distributions and that is why users have trouble when deciding which distribution to use.**

   __ True

   __ False

---

7. **True or False? Because of Linux's simple licensing terms, IT administrators do not have to spend a lot of time monitoring the number of installations or tracking licenses.**

   __ True

   __ False

TOPIC B
Enter Shell Commands

Now that you understand the origin of Linux, you should learn its basics so that you can use it. The Linux shell prompt is where you enter commands. In this lesson, you will learn about the shell and enter shell commands.

Learning to enter shell commands will allow you to interact directly with the Linux operating system. You will be able to utilize Linux commands to perform various tasks. In its formative stages, Linux was operated solely through the command line interface using shell commands. With the addition of the GUI, tasks have become easier, but a lot of power and flexibility still resides in knowing the shell commands.

The Command Line Interface

The *Command Line Interface (CLI)* is a text-based interface for the operating system, where a user typically enters commands at the *command prompt* to instruct the computer to perform a specific task. A *command line interpreter,* or command line shell, is a program that implements the commands entered in the text interface. The command line interpreter analyzes the input text provided by the user, interprets the text in the concept given, and then provides the output.

Figure 1-4: A CLI screen.

The Graphical User Interface

The Linux *Graphical User Interface (GUI)* is a collection of icons, windows, and other on screen graphical elements that help users interact with the operating system. The desktop menu provides access to the GUI applications available on the Linux desktop. There are different GUI implementations such as K Desktop Environment (KDE) and GNU Object Model Environment (GNOME).

Figure 1-5: A GNOME desktop.

The following table lists the uses of common desktop menu categories in the GNOME GUI.

Desktop Menu Category	Used To
Accessories	Access applications for performing work-related tasks such as creating text documents and presentations or using a calculator.
Internet	Access applications for performing tasks on the Internet such as web browsers, email clients, instant messengers, or web editors.
Sound & Video	Access applications for viewing movies and listening to sound files or CDs.
System Tools	Access options for changing the settings on the Linux system.
Help	Access help on Linux.

Shells

Definition:

A *shell* is a component that interacts directly with users. It also functions as the command interpreter for the Linux system. The shell accepts user commands and ensures that the kernel carries them out. The shell also contains an interpretive programming language.

The various shells available in Linux are described in the following table.

Shell	Description
Bash	This is the default Linux shell. It provides the flexibility of the C shell in a Bourne shell-type environment. Use the command bash to open the Bash shell.
Bourne	This is the original Unix shell developed by Steve Bourne at Bell Labs, and is available on all Linux systems. Use the command sh to open the Bourne shell.
C shell	This was developed by Bill Joy at Berkeley and was designed to support C language development environments. It was also designed for more interactive use, providing several ways to reduce the amount of typing needed to complete a job. Use the command csh to open the C shell.
Korn	This shell is a combination of the C and Bourne shells. It uses the features of the C shell but the syntax of the Bourne shell. Use the command ksh to open the Korn shell.

Example:

Figure 1-6: A blank shell prompt.

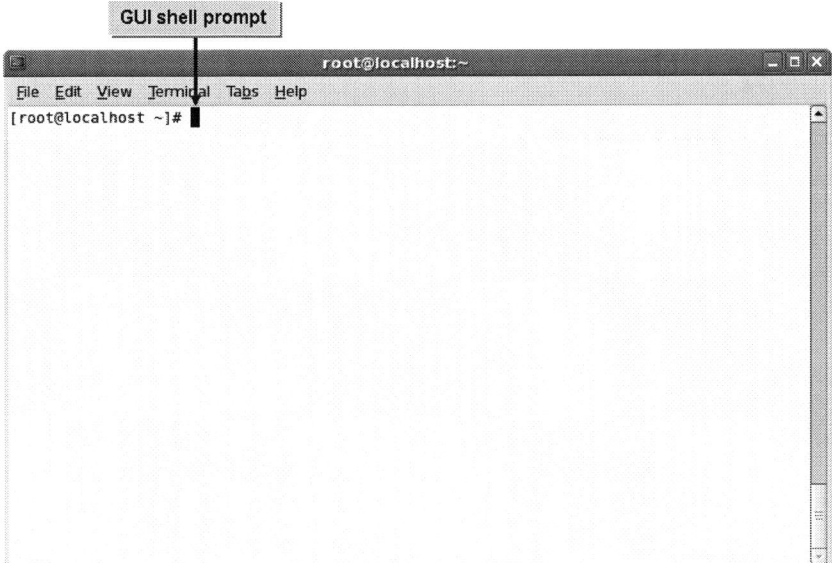

Figure 1-7: The shell prompt in the GUI terminal window.

Opening Multiple Shells

You can have several shells open at the same time, with different processes or programs running in each shell. For example, to open a second Bash shell, enter `bash` at the command prompt. To open a C shell, enter `csh`. To close a shell, either enter `exit` or press **Ctrl+D**.

Determining the Current Shell

The `echo` command enables you to determine the shell that is established at the login. To determine the current shell, enter `echo $SHELL`, where `$SHELL` is the environmental variable name that holds the name of the current shell.

View a File One Page at a Time

To view a file one page at a time, simply type the `more` command in front of the file you want to open. For example, if you want to read the /etc/passwd file, type `more /etc/passwd`.

The head and tail Commands

The `head` command displays the first 10 lines of each file. The `tail` command displays the last 10 lines of each file. These commands are useful when you only need to see the beginning or the end of a file. For example, you can check recent log entries by viewing the last 10 lines of a log file.

Virtual Terminals

A *terminal* or *console* is a computer interface for text entry and display, where information is displayed as an array of preselected characters. Linux supports six virtual terminals in the CLI mode, which provide a text terminal with a login prompt to the shell. You can choose among these six terminals by using the key combination of **Ctrl+Alt+F1–F6.** You can be logged in to multiple virtual terminals at the same time.

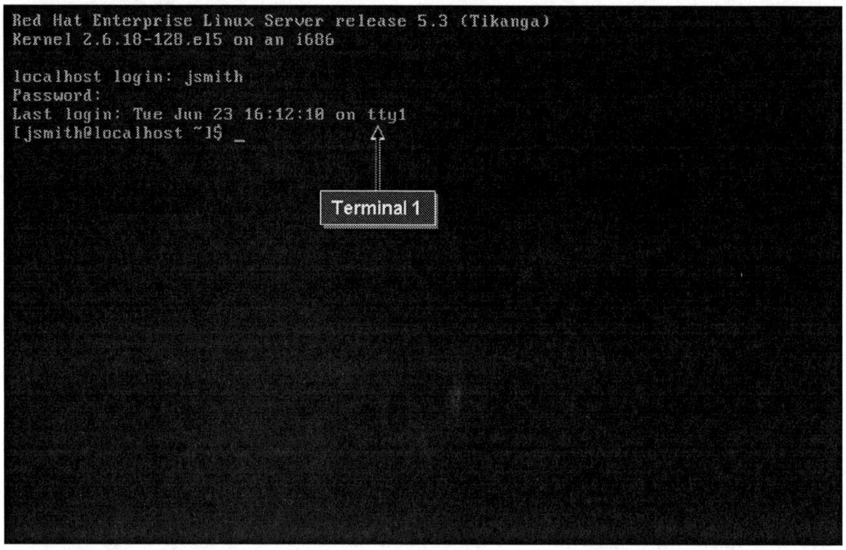

Figure 1-8: Terminal 1 with the user jsmith logged in.

Shell Commands

The generic format for a shell command is `command -option argument`. After typing your command, the shell responds by performing a specific action that is associated with that command. Linux is case sensitive, so you must enter commands in the required case.

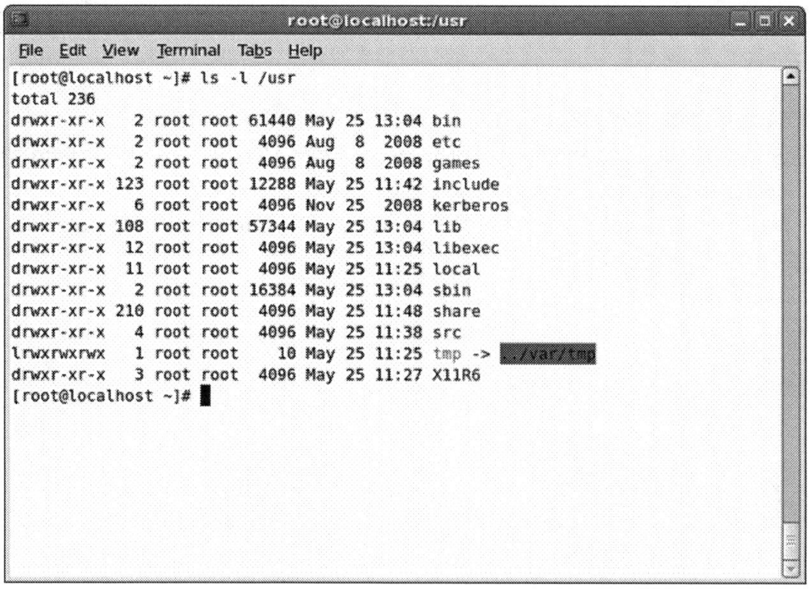

Figure 1-9: The ls command displays the list of files in the usr directory.

Argument

An *argument,* also called command line argument, is usually a file name or directory name that indicates the files on which the command will operate. It is used as an input by some commands in Linux. Arguments can be files, directories, commands or even a command switch. For example, ls *{file name},* ls *{directory name},* and ls -l.

Command History

Sometimes, commands can become quite long. You can access previously entered commands that are stored in the History file by using the **Up Arrow** and the **Down Arrow** keys.

The Tab-Completion Feature

Some commands have long names containing version number information, weird spellings, or capitalizations. This can make it difficult to correctly enter the commands on the first try. In such a case, you can make use of the tab-completion feature. To use this feature, enter the first few characters of the command and then press the **Tab** key. If there is only one match, the rest of the file name is displayed. If you press the next letter of the file name you want and press the **Tab** key again, the complete file name should come up. If the system still cannot differentiate between the commands, it will beep again, and you have to enter additional characters or press the **Tab** key two times to view all available options.

Issuing More Than One Command

You can issue more than one command before pressing **Enter**. Place a semicolon (;) between the commands and they will be issued one after the other.

The date Command

The date command displays the current date and time set on a system. You can use the hyphen (-) or the colon (:) between the different fields of the date for a clear output.

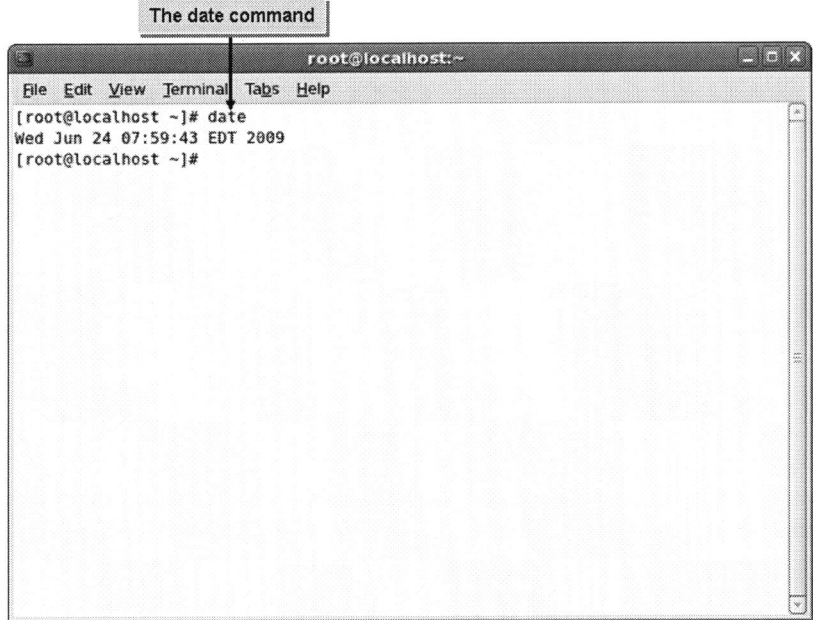

Figure 1-10: Viewing the current date using the date command.

Syntax

The syntax of the date command is date +[format], where *FORMAT* is the string of characters that are used to display the different fields of the output.

Characters Used with the date Command

The characters that are used to display the different fields of the date command are listed below.

Character	Description
%d	Displays the current day of the month (01 to 31).
%D	Displays the date in the format mm/dd/yy, where mm is month, dd is day, and yy is year.
%H	Displays the current hour in the 24-hour format (00 to 23).
%l	Displays the current hour (1 to 12). This option does not display A.M. or P.M. after the hour.
%m	Displays the current month of the year (01 to 12).
%M	Displays the current minute (00 to 59).
%r	Displays the time in the 12-hour format, i.e. hh:mm:ss [A.M. or P.M.].
%R	Displays the time in the 24-hour format, i.e. hh:mm. This option does not display the seconds.
%S	Displays the seconds (00 to 60).
%T	Displays the time in the 24-hour format, i.e. hh:mm:ss. This option displays the seconds also.
%y	Displays the last two digits of the current year.
%Y	Displays the current year in four digits (yyyy).

The cal Command

The cal command displays the calendar for any month or year. If you do not specify the month or year with the cal command, it will display the calendar of the current month. You can display the calendar of a specific month in a year by specifying the month and the year after the cal command. The year must be specified in the yyyy format. The command cal 09 will display the calendar for the year 9 A.D. and not for the year 2009.

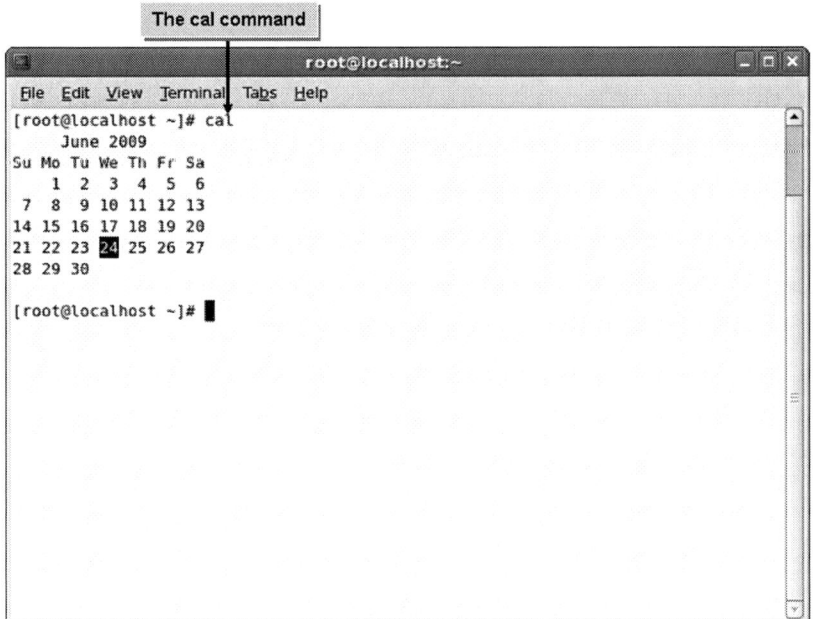

Figure 1-11: Viewing the calendar of the current month using the cal command.

Syntax
The syntax of the cal command is cal *{month}* *{year}*.

Options for the cal Command
Some options for the cal command include:

Option	Description
-m	Displays Monday as the first day of the week.
-j	Displays the Julian dates.
-y	Displays the current year's calendar.

The uptime Command

The uptime command displays the time from when a system started running. The output of the uptime command gives information about the current time, how long the system is running, and how many users are currently logged in.

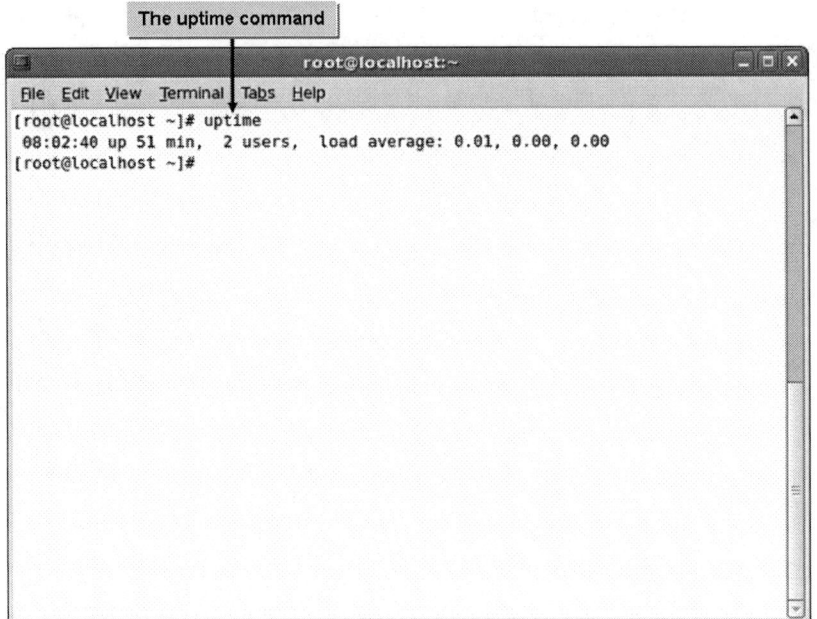

Figure 1-12: Using the uptime command to view the time from when the system started running.

Load Average

The last field of the uptime command output displays the system's load averages for the last 1 minute, 5 minutes, and 15 minutes. This information can be used to check whether the system is busy.

The who Command

The who command is used to determine the details of users currently logged in to a system. The output of the who command includes the user name, the name of the system from which the user is connected, and the time since the user is connected.

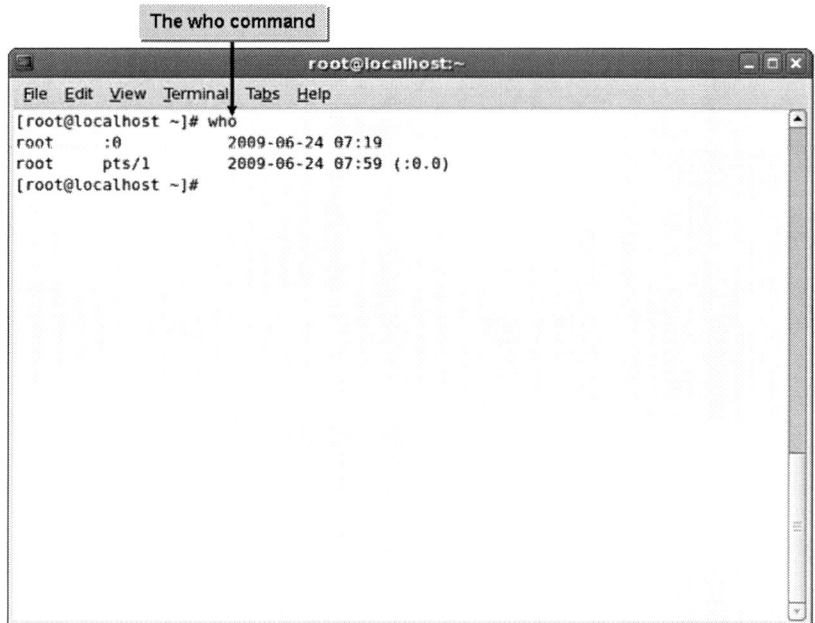

Figure 1-13: Displaying user details using the who command.

The who Command Options

The -i option can be used to see how long users have been idle. A dot indicates that the users were active up to the last minute, old indicates that the users have been inactive for over 24 hours, and anything between 2 minutes and 23 hours 59 minutes shows the length of time they have been idle. The am i option displays information only for the user who runs the command. The output is preceded by the host name.

The whoami Command

The whoami command is used to display the user name with which you are currently logged in to the system. Sometimes, you may need to log in to a system and switch among different users, and you may not be sure with which user you are currently logged in. In such instances, you can use the whoami command to know your current user name.

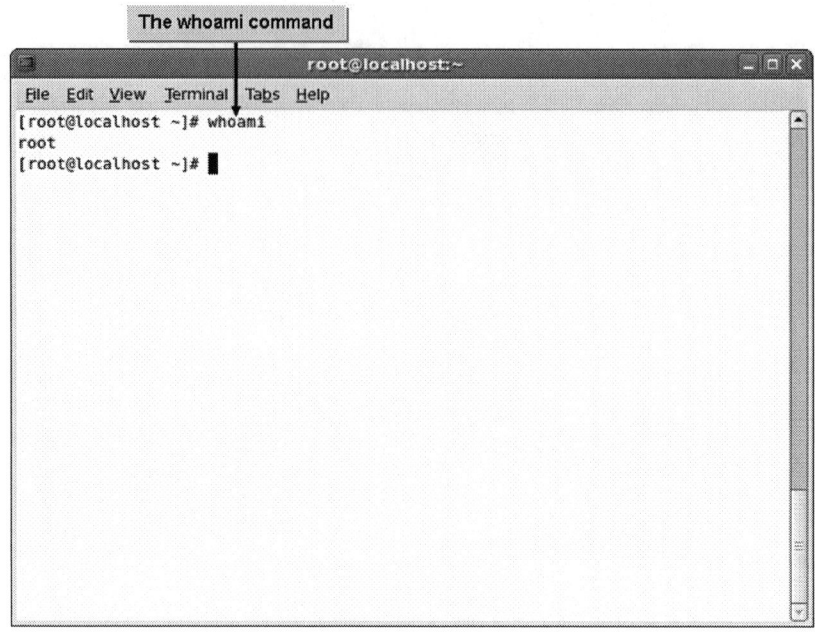

Figure 1-14: Displaying the user name using the whoami command.

The hostname Command

The hostname command is used to display the host name of the system you are currently logged in to. When you log in to different systems using the same terminal, you can use the hostname command to identify the system on which you are presently running the commands.

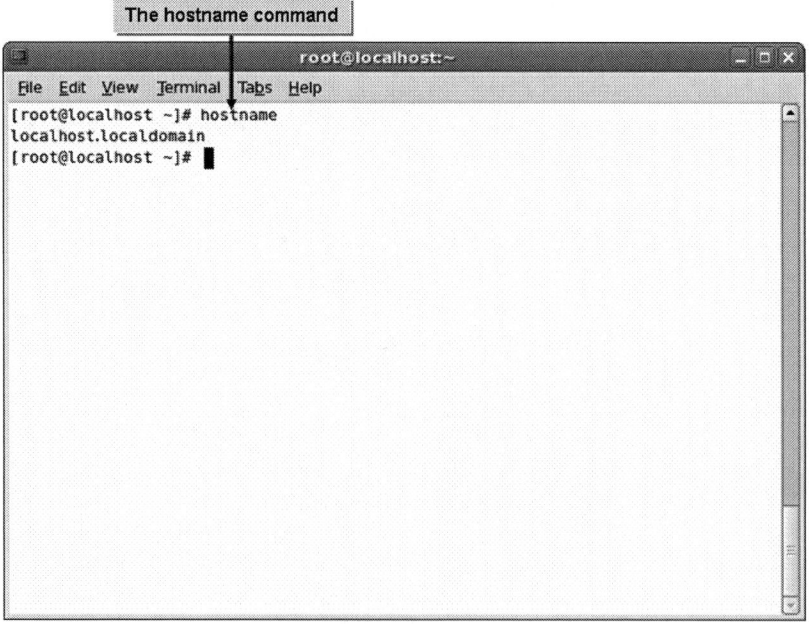

Figure 1-15: Viewing the hostname of the Linux system using the hostname command.

The w Command

The w command is primarily used to display the details of users who are currently logged in to a system and their transactions. The first line of the output displays the status of the system. The second line of the output displays a table with the first column listing the users logged in to the system and the last column indicating the current activities of the users. The remaining columns of the table show different attributes associated with the users.

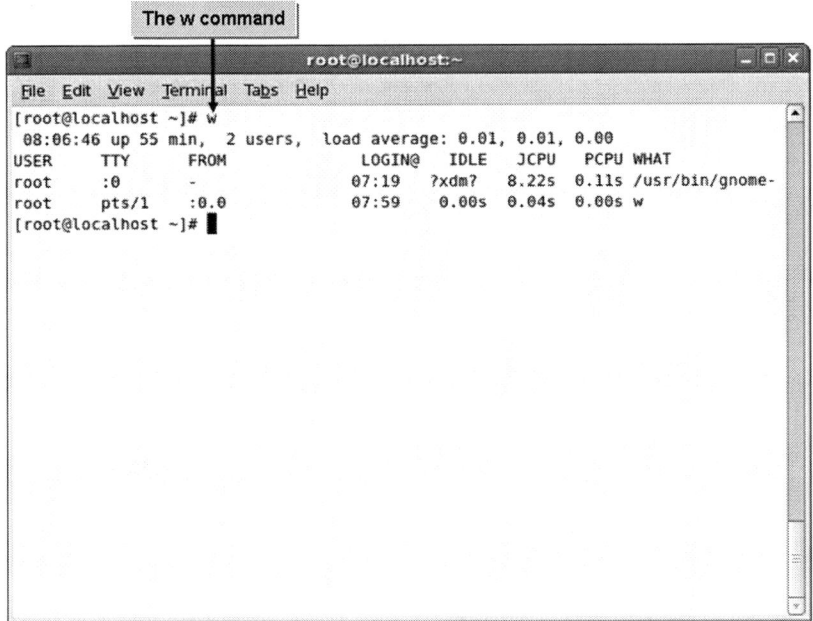

Figure 1-16: *Viewing user details using the w command.*

The last Command

The last command displays the history of user log in and log out, along with the actual time and date. It also has options that enable you to filter users who have logged in through a specific terminal. For example, last 1 will display the details of users who logged in using the first terminal. The last command retrieves the information from the /var/log/wtmp file.

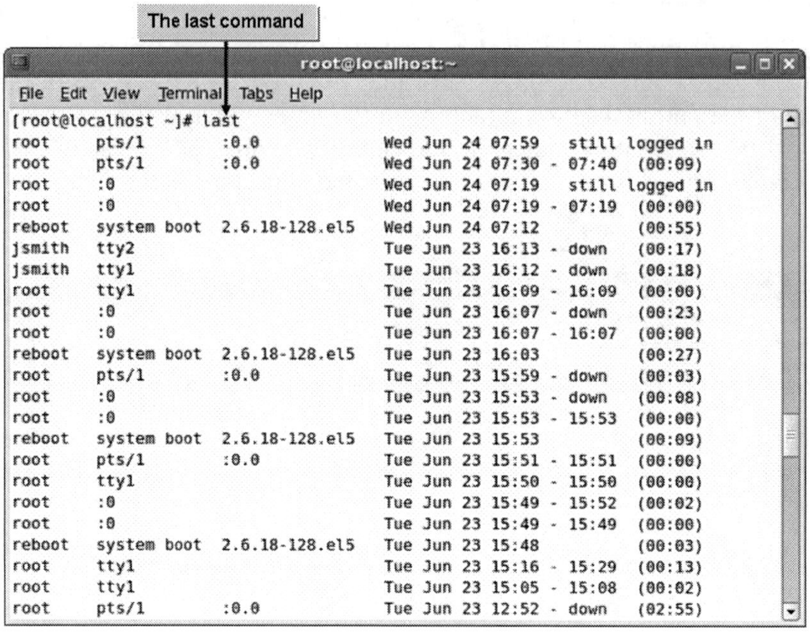

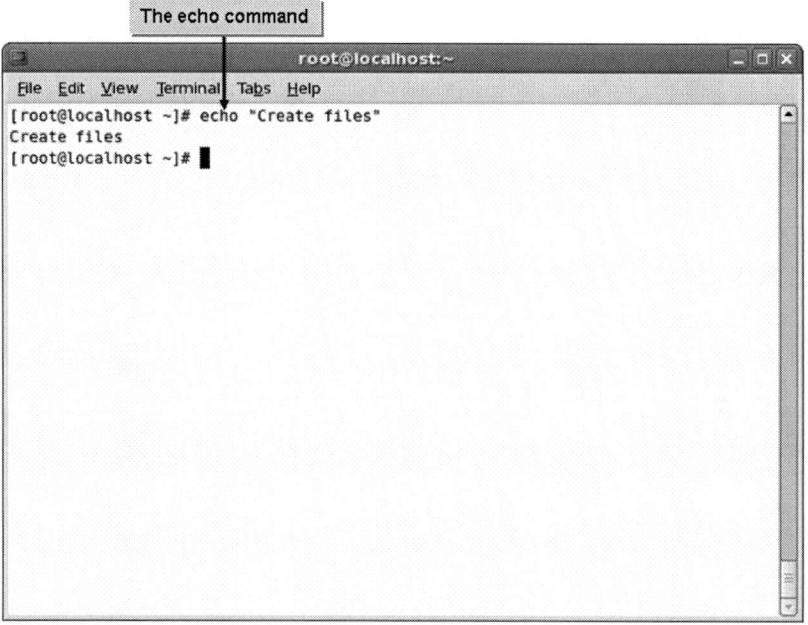

Figure 1-17: Viewing the history details of user logins.

The echo Command

The echo command is used to display a line of text on the terminal. It is useful for programmers writing shell scripts because it can be used to display additional information. The text that needs to be displayed should be inserted after the echo command. You can also use the echo command to display the value stored in a variable by specifying the variable name after the echo command.

Figure 1-18: Displaying text using the echo command.

Syntax

The syntax of the echo command is echo *{"string"}*.

The sleep Command

The sleep command is used to pause system activities for a specified time. The sleep *{time}* command hangs up the prompt for the number of seconds specified by the value of the variable *time*.

Figure 1-19: Pausing activities using the sleep command.

The cat Command

The cat command displays, combines, and creates text files. This command is frequently used to read small text files.

 The name of the cat command is a short form of the word concatenate.

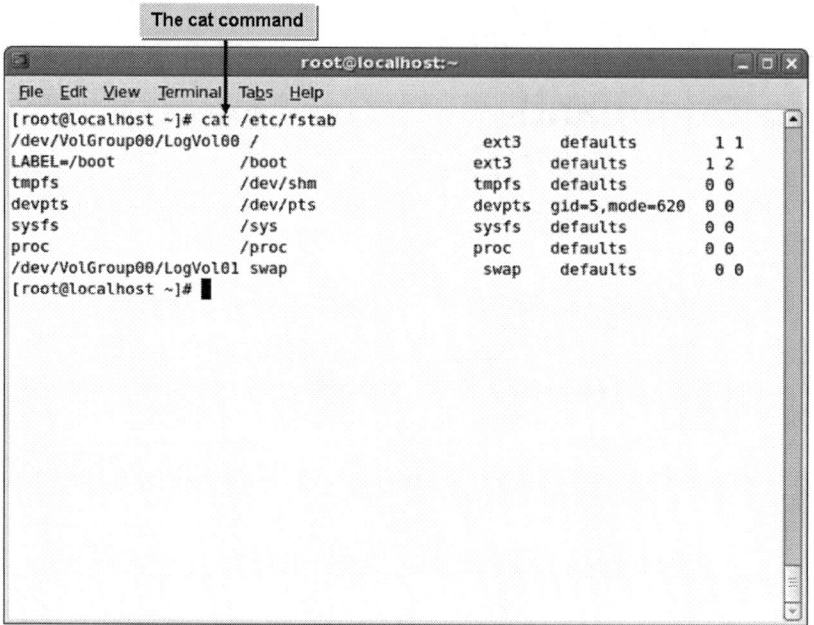

Figure 1-20: The cat command displaying a text file.

The `cat` command options are described in the following table.

Option	Description
-n	Precedes the output with its respective line number.
-b	Numbers the lines, excluding the blank lines.
-u	Omits to buffer the output. (The default output is buffered.)
-s	Omits to display results for nonexistent files.
-v	Displays nonprinting characters as visible characters, other than tabs, new lines, and form-feeds.
-e	Prints a $ character at the end of each line, prior to the new line.
-t	Prints tabs as ^I and form-feeds as ^L.

Syntax

The syntax of the `cat` command is `cat [command options] {file name}`.

The which Command

The which command is used to verify whether a user has the right to execute a command. The which command displays the complete path of the command by searching the directories assigned to the *PATH variable*. For example, on entering which cat, the following output is displayed: /bin/cat

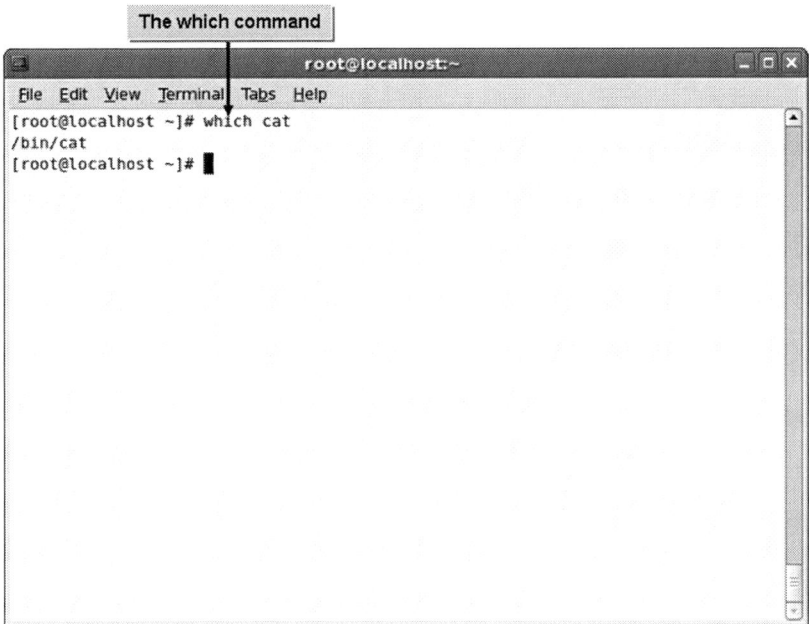

Figure 1-21: The which command displays the complete path of the command.

How to Enter Shell Commands

Procedure Reference: Log in to Your System

To log in to your system:

1. Log in to the GUI of the system.
   a. In the **Username** text box, enter the user name.
   b. In the **Password** text box, enter the password of the user.
2. Log in to the CLI of the Linux system.
   a. Press **Ctrl+Alt+F1** to switch to the first terminal.
   b. To log in to the system, enter the user name.
   c. Enter the password.

Procedure Reference: Monitor User Logins

To monitor user logins:

1. Log in as root.
2. Monitor user logins in the system.
   - Enter w to display the login information about the connected users and the processes associated with those users.
   - Enter who to display the users who are currently logged in to the system.

Procedure Reference: Check the System Date and Calendar Using Commands

To check the system date and calendar:

1. Log in to the CLI of the Linux system.

2. Enter the `date` command to view the date details.

   ● Enter `date` to check the current date and time on the system.

   ● Enter `date +%m-%d-%y` to view the date in the month-date-year format.

   ● Enter `date +%r` to view the current time in the hour-minute-second [AM or PM] format.

3. Enter the `cal` command to view a specific calendar.

   ● Enter `cal` to display the current month's calendar.

   ● Enter `cal {month} {year}` to view a specific month's calendar.

   ● Enter `cal [option]` to display the calendar in a specific format.

 In addition, in the GUI, you can choose **System→Administration→Date & Time** to view the system date and time in the **Date/Time Properties** dialog box.

4. If necessary, enter the `clear` command to clear the terminal screen.

Procedure Reference: Display the System Information Using Commands

To display the system information:

1. Enter a suitable command to view specific system information.

   ● Enter `uptime` to check the duration since the system is running.

   ● Enter `last` to display the history of logins.

   ● Enter `lastb` to display the history of bad logins on the system.

   ● Enter `hostname` to display the host name of the system you are currently logged in to.

   ● Enter `whoami` to display the user name with which you are currently logged in.

ACTIVITY 1-2

Using Basic Commands

Before You Begin:

1. The Red Hat Enterprise Linux 5.3 server is set up and configured to use the GNOME GUI.

2. The system is booted and the GUI login screen is displayed.

Scenario:

You have been provided with a Linux system at your workstation and are required to work as a team along with your colleagues who will also access your system from their systems. After logging in to your system, you decide to check the details of the users who are connected to your system to update yourself with the usage of your system.

 Whenever the instruction states "enter *command*", you are required to type the command and press **Enter**.

What You Do	How You Do It
1. Log in to the GUI as jsmith.	a. In the **Username** text box, type *jsmith* and press **Enter** to log in to the system.
	b. In the **Password** text box, type *myp@$$w0rd* and press **Enter** to log in to the system.
2. Log in to the first terminal as jsmith.	a. Press **Ctrl+Alt+F1** to switch to the first terminal.
	b. Type *jsmith* and press **Enter** to log in to the first terminal.
	c. Type *myp@$$w0rd* and press **Enter**.
	d. At the command line, enter **date** to view the current date and time of the system.
	e. Observe that the current date and time of the system is displayed.

3. Log in to the fifth terminal as eric.

    a. Press **Ctrl+Alt+F5** to switch to the fifth terminal.

    b. Type *eric* and press **Enter** to log in to the fifth terminal.

    c. Type *myp@$$w0rd* and press **Enter.**

    d. Enter `date` to view the current date and time of the system.

    e. Observe that the current date and time of the system is displayed.

4. Log in to the sixth terminal as robert.

    a. Press **Ctrl+Alt+F6** to switch to the sixth terminal.

    b. Type *robert* and press **Enter** to log in to the sixth terminal.

    c. Type *myp@$$w0rd* and press **Enter.**

    d. Enter `cal` to view the calendar for the current month.

    e. Observe that the calendar of the current month is displayed.

5. View the list of users who are currently logged in to the Linux system.

    a. Press **Ctrl+Alt+F1** to switch to the first terminal.

    b. Enter `who` to view the list of users who are currently logged in to the Linux system.

    c. Observe the list of user names displayed in the first column of the command output.

6. Display information about users currently logged in to the Linux system.

    a. Enter `w` to display information about users currently logged in to the Linux system.

    b. Examine the **USER** and **WHAT** columns to check the names of users logged in currently and obtain information about what each user is doing.

    c. Enter `clear` to clear the terminal screen.

ACTIVITY 1-3
Using System Commands

Before You Begin:
You have logged in as jsmith in the first terminal of the CLI.

Scenario:
After viewing the details of the users connected to your system, you decide to check the details of the system, the duration for which the system is running, and the system date and time.

What You Do	How You Do It
1. Check the name of your Linux system.	a. At the command line, enter **hostname** to check the name of your Linux system.
	b. Observe the hostname of your system.
	c. Enter **clear** to clear the terminal screen.
2. Check how long the system has been running and the current date and time.	a. Enter **uptime** to check how long the system has been running.
	b. Observe that the first column of the command output displays how long the system has been running.
	c. Enter **date** to check the current date and time of your system.
	d. Observe the displayed date and time.
3. Check the current calendar.	a. Enter **cal** to view the calendar for the current month.
	b. Observe the calendar for the current month. Enter **cal** *<year>* to view the calendar for the current year.
	c. Observe the calendar for the year. Enter **clear** to clear the terminal screen.

TOPIC C
Get Help Using Linux

Now that you are familiar with the Linux shell, you may want to begin using commands in your system. However, you may need assistance with the various commands available. In this topic, you will familiarize yourself with the help and support options offered by Linux.

By learning about Linux support options, you can increase your access to information about the Linux environment. Doing so will help you support your implementation of Linux. The information provided in the Linux documentation will enable you to easily troubleshoot problems you encounter.

Linux Documentation

Definition:

Linux documentation is the material that provides information on various Linux commands and blocks of code. Some Linux documentation is available in electronic format and some in print format. Linux documentation is available from sources such as manual pages, online resources, published works, Usenet newsgroups, and mailing lists.

Example:

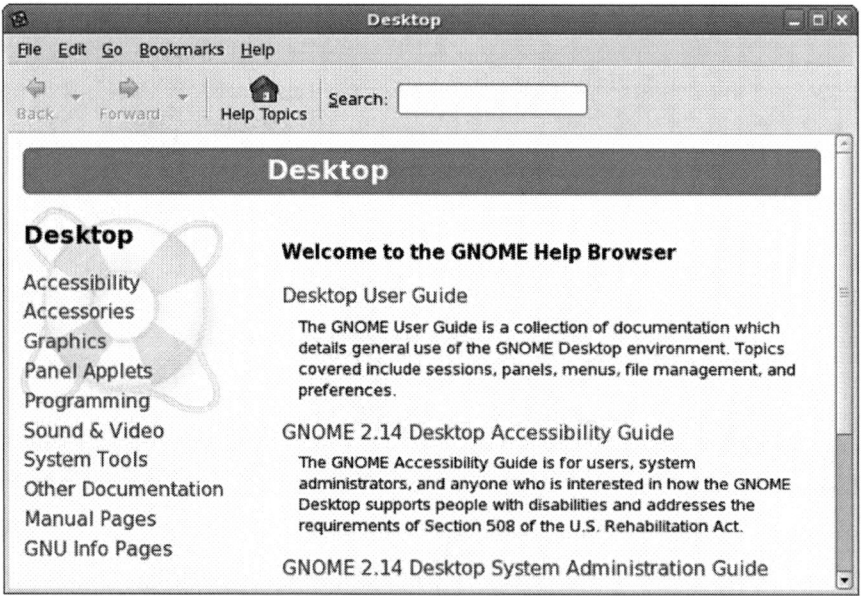

Figure 1-22: Built-in Linux help in the GUI.

System Documentation

System documentation is the term given to the collection of documents that list the system requirements; its functioning capabilities, limitations, design specifications; the internal workings of the system; and the steps for maintaining the system.

Manual Pages

The Linux *manual pages,* or man pages, contain the complete documentation that is specific to every Linux command; they are presented in simple ASCII text format. The man page for a specific command is displayed using the man command. The man pages are available on the system by default. They usually include information such as the name of the command, its syntax, a description of its purpose, the options it supports, examples of common usage of the command, and a list of related commands.

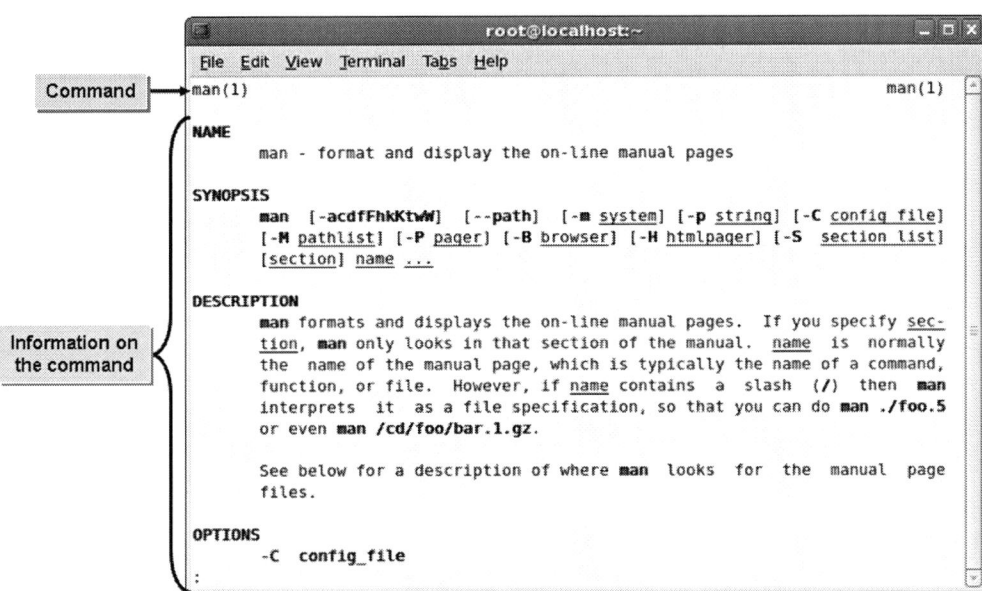

Figure 1-23: Viewing information on the manual pages.

Syntax

The syntax of the man command is man *topic*.

The man Command Options

The man command supports different options. Some of the frequently used options are listed here.

Option	Description
-a	Finds all entries matching the query.
-D	Displays debugging information.
-f	Displays a short description of the command along with the man pages/sections.
-h	Displays help options for the man command.
-k	Lists all manual pages/sections containing the keyword along with their location.
-K	Searches for the specified string on all pages.
-t	Formats the man pages to enable printing.

Man Page Sections

Man pages for a single command may be listed under several sections. All the available manual page sections for a particular command can be listed using the `whatis` command. When a command has more than one section listed, it means that documentation for the same command is available from more than one source. These sections are identified by the number displayed beside the command, for example, `fsck (8)`.

Various man page sections are given in the table below.

Section Number	What It Contains
1	General commands
2	System calls
3	C library functions
4	Special files (usually found in /dev)
5	File formats and conventions
6	Games and screensavers
7	Miscellaneous
8	System administration commands and daemons

Keys to Navigate Through Linux Man Pages

You can navigate through the Linux man pages using a number of keys. The functions of different keys are given in the following table.

Key	Used To
Home	Move to the beginning of the man page.
End	Move to the end of the man page.
Page Up	Scroll up the page progressively.
Page Down	Scroll down the page progressively.
N	Move to the next occurrence of the search term.
P	Move to the previous occurrence of the search term.
Q	Quit and return to the shell prompt.

The apropos Command

The `apropos` command is generally used when a user does not know which command to use to perform a certain action. It can be used with a keyword to display a list of the manual pages containing the keyword along with their man page sections. The `apropos` command searches a regularly updated database called the whatis database for the specified string and returns all matching entries.

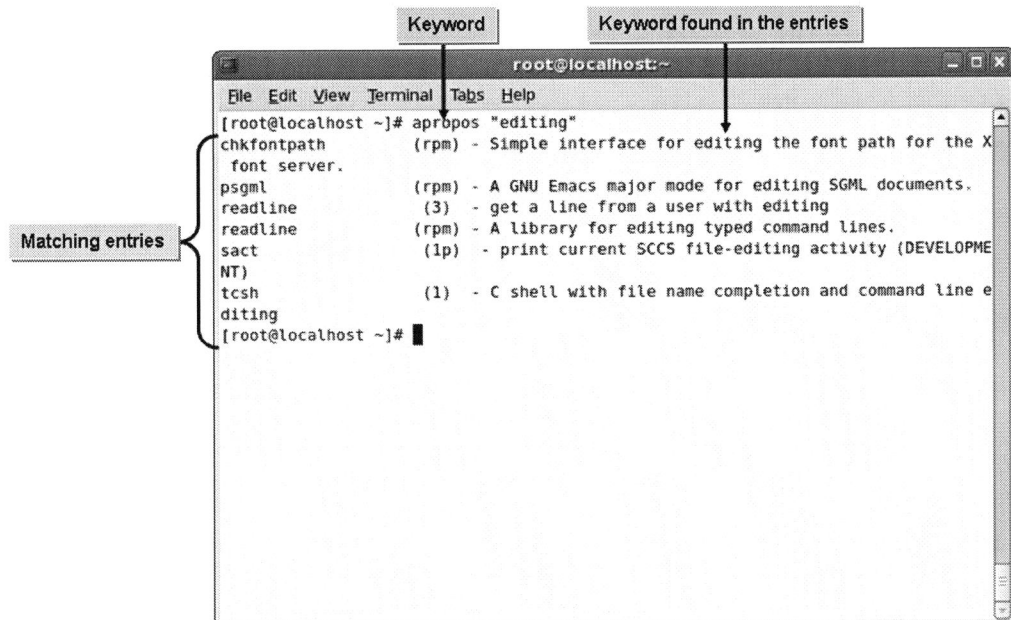

Figure 1-24: Searching for help using the apropos command.

Syntax

The syntax of the `apropos` command is `apropos keyword`.

Other Built-In Help Options

In addition to the `man` and `apropos` commands, Linux offers other built-in options for help.

Help Option	Description
`whatis`	Displays a short description of the command along with the man pages/sections matching the exact command. This command searches a regularly updated database for documentation. The syntax of this command is `whatis command`.
`info`	Displays info pages containing additional or recent information about a command. The syntax of this command is `info command`.
`command --help`	Displays a quick summary of the usage of a command and a list of arguments that can be used. This feature can be used with most commands in Linux. The syntax of this command is `command -options`.

The /usr/share/doc Directory

The /usr/share/doc directory contains documents installed on the system, describing in detail certain aspects of configuring or using Linux.

HOWTOs

HOWTO documents may be installed on your system, usually under the /usr/share/doc directory. The HTML version of the files can be displayed in any web browser, including the text-based Lynx browser. The text files can be viewed through any text editor or by using the display commands such as cat, more, or less. HOWTOs can be found on most systems and can also be found on the web at **http://linuxdocs.org/HOWTOs/HOWTO-INDEX/howtos.html** and other sites.

HOWTOs are comprehensive documents, much like FAQs, but generally not in question-and-answer format. However, many HOWTOs contain an FAQ section at the end. There are several HOWTO formats available: plain text, PostScript, PDF, and HTML. In addition to the HOWTOs, there are a multitude of mini-HOWTOs on short, specific subjects.

Getting Help from Info Pages

To display info pages, enter info, with or without options and arguments. By itself, the command info will display the help file on how to work with info pages. Entering info [topic] will display the info page for the specified topic. The command info --help displays a brief help description.

When the info page is displayed, any text with an asterisk (*) in front of it is a link. Move your cursor (using the arrow keys) to the text, and then press **Enter** to access the linked info page. To return to the previous document, type **U** and then type **D** to return to the top of the page. Type **Q** to return to the command prompt.

LUGs

A good source of information for Linux users and developers is Linux User Groups, or LUGs. These can be virtual (based on the web) or there may be a group of people who meet in your neighborhood. The virtual ones sometimes take the form of a message board with a question-and-answer database.

Online Help

The Internet is the best place to get documentation for any distribution of Linux. There are dedicated websites and online forums that help Linux users with specific distributions or Linux in general. Documentation for commercial distributions is available in their respective official websites. These include the release notes of different versions and updates, the deployment guide, the installation guide, and the virtualization guide. For example, the Red Hat documentation can be accessed from the URL, **www.redhat.com/docs/manuals/enterprise**.

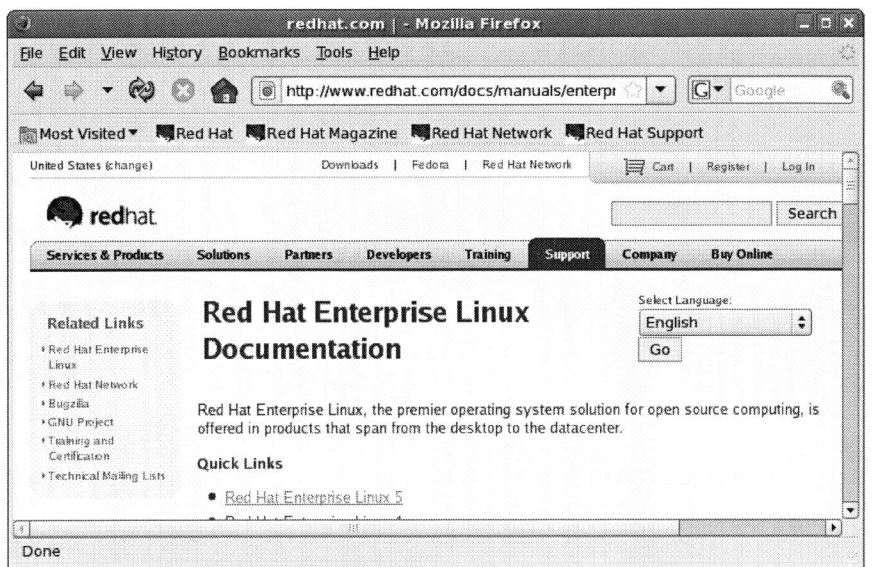

Figure 1-25: *The Red Hat online documentation.*

How to Access Help in Linux

Procedure Reference: View Linux man Pages

To view Linux man pages:

1. At the command line, enter man *[command]*, where [command] is the command you want to view a man page for.

2. View the list of command options available for the command.

3. Close the man page for the specified command.

Procedure Reference: Display the man Page for a Command

To display the man page for a command:

1. Log in as a user.

2. Enter man *[section] {command}* to display the man page for a specific command under a specific section.

3. Navigate through the man pages.

    ●   Use the **Up Arrow** or **Down Arrow** key to navigate within a page.

    ●   Use **Page Up** or **Page Down** to navigate through several pages.

    ●   Search for some specific topic in the man pages as required.

        a. Enter **/search string** to search though the man page for the specified string.

        b. If necessary, type n to locate the next occurrence of the string in the man page.

4. Press **Q** to close the man page.

Procedure Reference: Use the whatis Command

To use the whatis command:

1. Log in as a user.

2. Enter makewhatis to build the whatis help database.

3. Enter whatis command to display the man page sections and a short description of the specified command.

4. Enter man [section] {command} to view the man page for the specified command under the specified section.

5. Press **Q** to close the man page.

Procedure Reference: Find the Relevant man Pages Using the apropos Command

To find the relevant man pages using the apropos command:

1. Log in as a user.

2. Enter apropos keyword to search the keyword in the whatis database and display the matching man page sections for the specified keyword.

3. Enter man [section] {command} to display the man page for a specific command under a specific section.

4. Press **Q** to close the man page and return to the command prompt.

Procedure Reference: Display the Info Documents of a Command

To display the info documents of a command:

1. Log in as a user.

2. Enter info command to read the info documents for the specified command.

3. Navigate through the info pages.

   ● Use the **Up Arrow** or **Down Arrow** key to navigate within a page.

   ● Use **Page Up** or **Page Down** to navigate through several pages.

   ● Type n or p to move to the next or previous page, respectively.

   ● Type s to search for a particular string on the info pages.

   ● Use the **Tab** key to go to the next link.

4. Press **Q** to close the info page.

Procedure Reference: Display the Options of a Command

To display the options of a command:

1. Log in as a user.

2. Enter command --help to display the command syntax and a list of options.

3. Enter command -options to use the necessary option to execute the required task.

ACTIVITY 1-4

Identifying Linux Documentation Types and Uses

Before You Begin:
1. Press **Ctrl+Alt+F5.**
2. Type `logout` and press **Enter** to log out eric from the fifth terminal.
3. Press **Ctrl+Alt+F6.**
4. Type `logout` and press **Enter** to log out robert from the sixth terminal.
5. Press **Ctrl+Alt+F1.**

Scenario:
Your manager, Linda, is having trouble understanding certain commands. She knows that there are several types of support documentation available, but is unsure of how to use them. She also heard that a large part of the hidden cost involved with implementing Linux is a result of limited support. She would like you to submit a report on the different types of Linux documentation and their uses. You decide to explore the available help options.

What You Do	How You Do It
1. Display the manual for the `gzip` command.	a. At the command line, enter **man gzip**
	b. Press the **Spacebar** to continue reading through the man page.
	c. Press **Q** to return to the command line.
2. Build the `whatis` database.	a. Enter **logout** to log out **jsmith.**
	b. Enter **root** to log in as **root.**
	c. At the password prompt, enter **p@ssw0rd**
	d. Enter **makewhatis** to build the `whatis` database.
3. Search through the man pages for the word "zip."	a. Enter **apropos zip**
	b. Observe that the output lists all the instances where the keyword "zip" is found.

4. View the list of locations where the keyword is found in the man pages.

   a. At the command line, enter **whatis gzip**

   b. View the results.

   c. Enter **clear** to clear the terminal screen.

5. **True or False? It is common practice to write a detailed report of exactly what is installed and changed on each Linux system in your environment.**

   __ True

   __ False

6. **What are the additional help options that may be installed on your Linux system?**

   a) --help

   b) helpme

   c) HOWTO

   d) Textinfo

7. **In what formats are HOWTOs available?**

   a) PostScript

   b) Email

   c) PDF

   d) HTML

ACTIVITY 1-5

Getting Help Using Linux Manual Pages

Before You Begin:
You have logged in as root in the CLI terminal

Scenario:
Your organization supports customers around the world and you may have to support different customers with varying time zones. To achieve this, your system time should correspond to the time on the clients' systems. You are unsure about the procedure to change the system date and time. You decide to browse the manual pages to find more help.

What You Do	How You Do It
1. Find the man page for the `date` command.	a. Enter **whatis date** to see the relevant man pages for the `date` command with various sections.
	b. Enter **man 1 date** to see the man page of the `date` command under section 1.
2. Search through the man page.	a. Enter **/FORMAT** to move to the first instance of the text "FORMAT."
	b. Enter **/** to navigate to the next instance of the text "FORMAT."
	c. Enter **/** to view the different formats allowed for the date command.
	d. Press **Q** to close the date man page.

3. View the info page.

    a.   Enter **info date** to view the complete info document for the `date` command.

    b.   Press **/** and enter ***Examples*** to navigate to the text "Examples."

    c.   Press **/** and press **Enter** to navigate to the next instance of the text "Examples."

    d.   Press **Enter** to view examples of the `date` command.

    e.   Observe the first three examples of the `date` command.

    f.   Press **Q** to close the info page.

    g.   Enter **clear** to clear the terminal screen.

TOPIC D
Start and Stop Linux

You now understand how to access documentation and log files in the shell. But you cannot access the shell or even troubleshoot system problems without knowing how to start and stop your system. In this topic, you will start and stop the Linux system.

We all expect our operating systems to load and run the necessary processes at boot time. There are occasions, however, when you, as a Linux administrator, may want to start, stop, or restart the system manually. The ability to manage these essential services will help you perform maintenance and upgrades on your system.

Services

Definition:

A Linux *service* is an application or set of applications that perform tasks in the background. Services running on a Linux system range from basic services to server services. Services can be broadly classified as critical services and noncritical services. Critical services are the core services that are vital for the functioning of the Linux system. Noncritical services are services that are initiated by applications installed on the system.

Example:

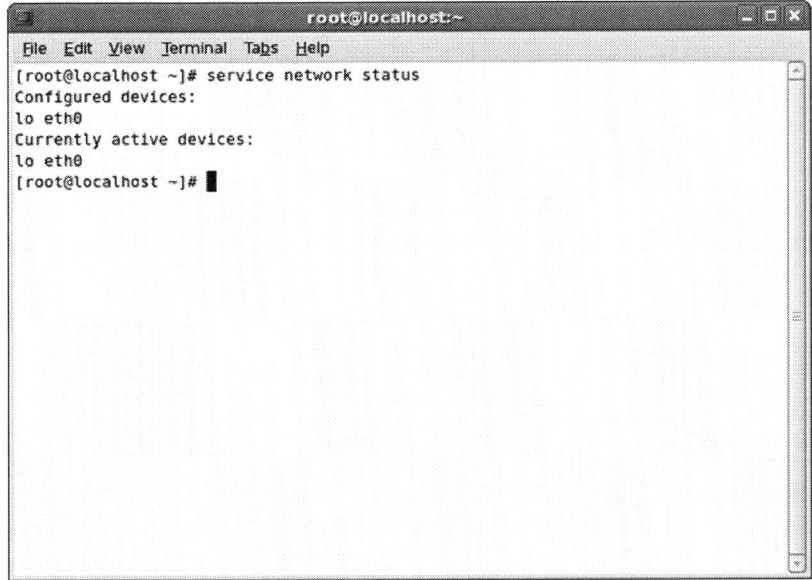

Figure 1-26: The network service displaying its status.

Daemons

Definition:

A *daemon* is a program that runs in the background without the need for human intervention, often handling commands delivered for remote command execution. It lies dormant until an event triggers it into activity. Some daemons operate at regular intervals. Most daemons are started when the system boots. Daemons are started either by the operating system, by applications, or manually.

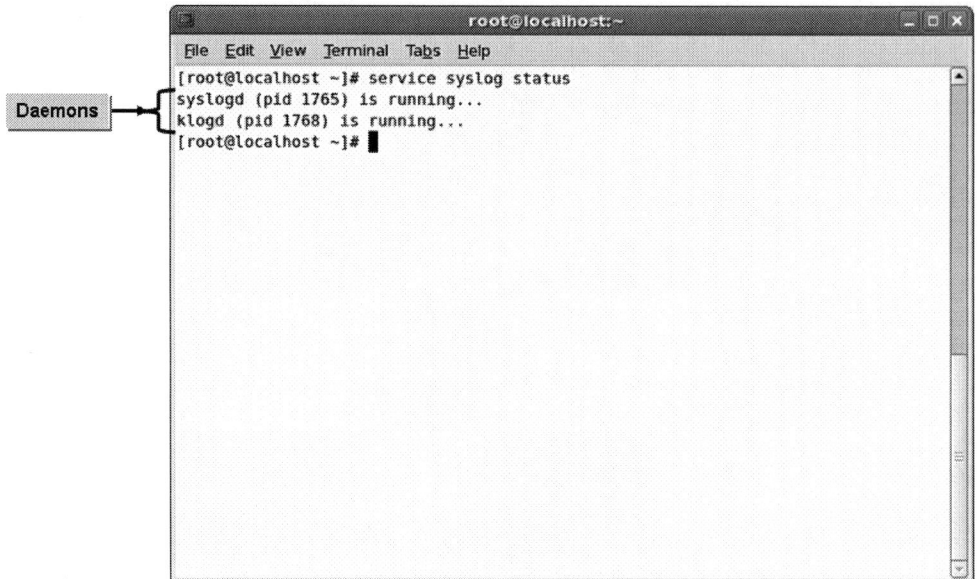

Figure 1-27: Daemons running in the background for the syslog service.

Example: The lpd Daemon

The Line Printer daemon, or `lpd`, controls the flow of print jobs to a printer. It works in the background and sends the output to the printer without affecting other processes that the user is working on at that time.

Init Runlevels

Init is used to set the *runlevel* of your system. The runlevel specifies the group of processes that can exist. Init creates processes at system boot time from a script in the /etc/inittab file. You can change the current runlevel by using the `telinit` command. The *init* man page says, "Init is the parent of all processes."

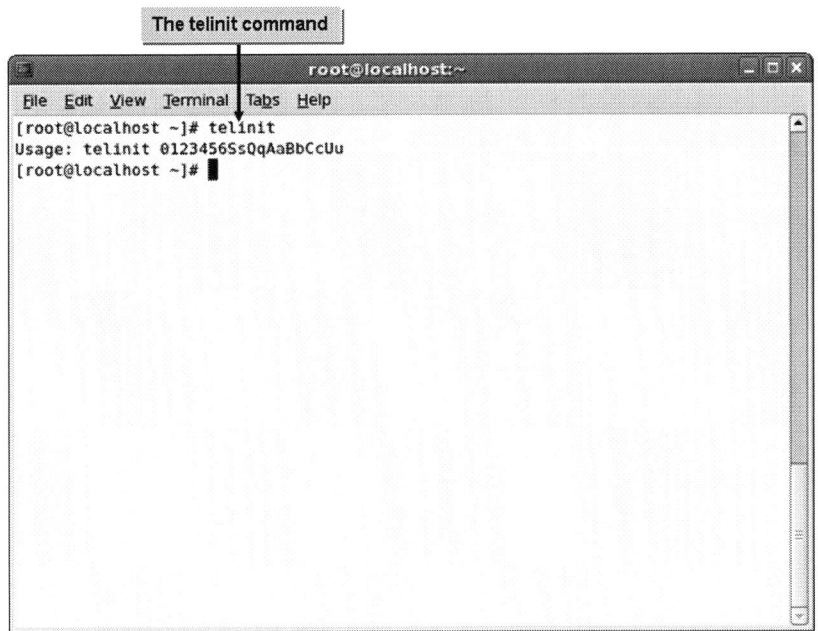

Figure 1-28: *The different runlevels that can be specified with the telinit command.*

Init Runlevels Table

The following table describes the processes that can run at each init level.

Init Level	Description
0	Halts the system
1	Single-user mode
2	Multiuser mode without networking
3	Multiuser mode with networking
4	User configurable
5	Used for GUI (X11 multiuser mode)
6	Reboots the system

System Booting

During the installation of Linux, the *bootloader* you choose will be put on the *Master Boot Record (MBR)*. GRand Unified Bootloader (GRUB) and Linux Loader (LILO) are the Linux bootloaders that load and start the kernel. Only one bootloader can be used on a system.

System Shutdown

The *shutdown command* is used to shutdown a system. This closes files and performs other tasks necessary to safely shutdown the system. It warns all users that the system is going to shutdown and that no one can log in after the command is issued. After certain installations or removal of hardware, it is necessary to shutdown the Linux system.

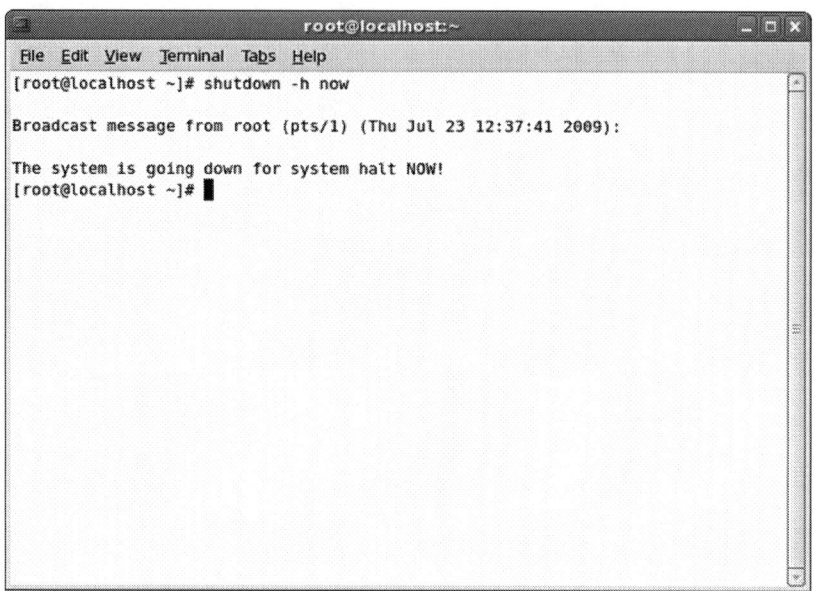

Figure 1-29: *Shutting down a Linux system.*

Shutdown Command Options

When you need to restart your Linux system, you should use the `shutdown` command with the appropriate options. The syntax of the `shutdown` command is `shutdown [-t seconds] [-options] time [warning message]`.

The `-t` option specifies how many seconds to wait before changing to another runlevel. The other options are listed in the following table.

Option	Used To
-k	Send warning messages to everyone, but does not really shutdown the system.
-r	Reboot the system after shutdown. Upon reboot, if you are using a boot manager to load various operating systems, you can switch to another operating system or log in to Linux.
-h	Halt the system after shutdown. At this point, you can safely turn off the power.
-n	Shutdown the system without invoking init. It is recommended not to use this option.
-f	Skip the filesystem check on reboot.
-F	Force the filesystem check on reboot.
-c	Cancel a shutdown in progress. This option does not use the time parameter, but can use the warning message option.

How to Start and Stop Linux

Procedure Reference: Manage Runlevels from a Shell

To manage runlevels from a shell:

1. At the command prompt, bring up your current runlevel.
2. Switch to runlevel 1.
3. Verify that you are at runlevel 1.
4. Exit back to runlevel 3.

Procedure Reference: Manage Runlevels from a Configuration File

To manage runlevels from a configuration file:

1. Edit the /etc/inittab file to start at runlevel 1.
2. Restart the computer.
3. Verify that you are in runlevel 1.
4. Edit the /etc/inittab file to start at runlevel 3.
5. Restart the computer.

ACTIVITY 1-6
Starting and Stopping Linux

Before You Begin:
You have logged in as root in the CLI.

Scenario:
You are given the task of managing the implementation of Linux at your company. To begin, you must learn to start and stop your Linux system and familiarize yourself with various runlevels.

What You Do	How You Do It
1. Examine various runlevels.	a. At the command line, enter **more /etc/inittab**
	b. Press the **Spacebar** two times to continue.
	c. Observe the contents of the /etc/inittab file displayed on the monitor.
	d. Enter **runlevel** to determine your current runlevel.
	e. Observe your current runlevel.
2. Switch to the single-user mode.	a. At the command line, enter **telinit 1**
	b. Observe that the services of previous runlevel are stopped and runlevel 1 service has started.
	c. Enter **runlevel** to verify that you are in single-user mode.
	d. Observe that the command shows 1 S, for single user 1.
	e. Enter **exit** to return to the default runlevel, which is runlevel 5.
	f. Press **Ctrl+Alt+F1** to switch to the first terminal of the CLI.
	g. At the login prompt, enter **root**
	h. At the password prompt, enter **p@ssw0rd**

3. Restart the Linux system.

  a. At the command line, enter `shutdown -r now`

  b. Observe that the services are stopped and processes are killed before restarting the system.

  c. Press **Ctrl+Alt+F1** to switch to the first terminal of the CLI.

  d. Log in to the system as *root* with the password as *p@ssw0rd*

Lesson 1 Follow-up

In this lesson, you identified basic Linux concepts and performed basic Linux tasks. These skills can assist you in supporting Linux users and machines.

1. **What are the advantages of open source software over licensed software?**

2. **What are the advantages of using Linux?**

2 | Managing User and Group Accounts

Lesson Time: 1 hour(s), 15 minutes

Lesson Objectives:

In this lesson, you will manage user and group accounts.

You will:

- Create user and group accounts.
- Configure user profiles.
- Manage user accounts.

Introduction

You are now familiar with the history of Linux, its shells, and its help and support options. This basic knowledge is a good starting point, but there is more to learn. Before users can take advantage of the operating system, user accounts need to be created. You will also have to create group accounts to manage the users. In this lesson, you will manage user and group accounts.

One of the benefits of Linux is its multiuser capabilities. By creating and modifying users and groups, you can further tailor the Linux environment to the needs of your organization. You will also be able to provide individualized services to users after creating an account for them.

This lesson covers all or part of the following CompTIA Linux+ (2009) certification objectives:

- Topic A
  - Objective 5.1
- Topic B
  - Objective 5.1
- Topic C
  - Objective 5.1

TOPIC A
Create User and Group Accounts

In this lesson, you will manage user and group accounts. The first step in managing them is to create the accounts you need. In this topic, you will create user and group accounts.

As a Linux+ administrator, you will be required to create user and group accounts on a regular basis. By creating user accounts, you will enable users to access the Linux system. Group accounts enable you to group users with similar functions together. This will considerably reduce the time and effort you invest in monitoring and managing user activities.

User Accounts

Definition:

A *user account* is a collection of information that defines a user on a system. It is the representation of a user on a computer. User account information includes the user name and password for the user to log in to the system, groups to which the user belongs to, and rights and permissions that the user has, to access the system and its resources. When an account is created, it is assigned a unique number that is called *User ID (UID)*.

Example:

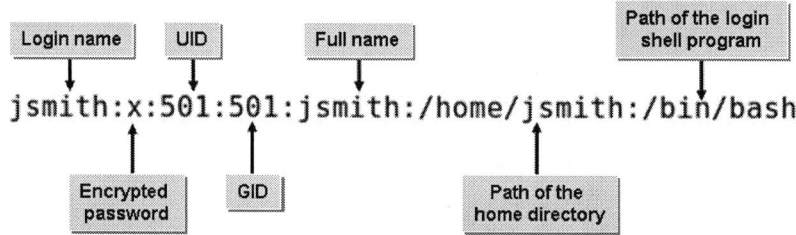

Figure 2-1: The format in which the user account information is stored by a system.

The useradd Command

The useradd command is used to add a new user. You need to specify the user name along with the command to create a new user account. Special user accounts are required to run processes associated with certain services. For example, ntp is a user account that is used to run the NTPD service.

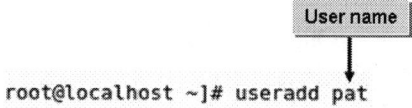

Figure 2-2: A new user added using the useradd command.

The `adduser` file is a script file that performs the same functions as the `useradd` command.

Special User Accounts

In special user accounts, the UID value for the users will be less than the default UID value, which is 500. Such special users will not have a home directory. You can create a special user account using the `useradd -r Special user name` command.

User Accounts

Linux allows you to add user accounts by directly editing the password file. However, this is not recommended because you may damage your system if you accidentally leave something out or alter existing user accounts. If the system is damaged, nobody will be able to log in—not even the root user. In such a case, you will have to reinstall your system and redefine the user accounts.

Default User Accounts

Numerous user accounts are created by default upon system installation. Some of the main user accounts are:

● root

● bin

● daemon

● ftp

● sshd

● nfsnobody

● apache

● squid

The Role of the Root

Every Linux system has at least one system administrator whose job is to maintain the system and make it available to users. This user is the root. The root user can perform any task on the Linux system without restrictions. System administrators are also responsible for adding new users to the system and for setting up their initial environment.

Passwords

A password is an entity that allows the Linux system to authenticate a user. Generally, when user accounts are created without passwords, they can be easily misused. For this reason, when you create a user account, you should immediately set a password for the user. In Linux, if a password is not set for the user account, the account gets locked automatically. This is to help prevent unauthorized access to the system.

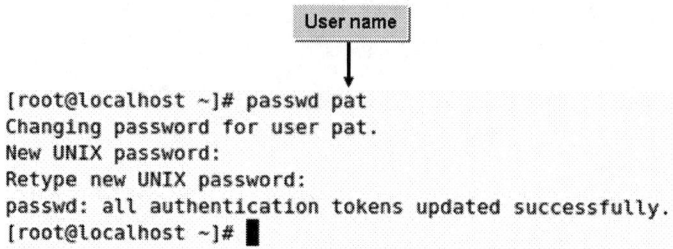

```
[root@localhost ~]# passwd pat
Changing password for user pat.
New UNIX password:
Retype new UNIX password:
passwd: all authentication tokens updated successfully.
[root@localhost ~]# █
```

Figure 2-3: Setting password for the user "pat."

 You can change the password of your user account using the `passwd` command. You cannot change the password for any other user account because the password command does not allow you to specify any other user name. Only the root user can change the password for other users by specifying the user name with the `passwd` command.

Syntax

A root user can create a password for a user by entering `passwd [user name]`, where `[user name]` is the name of the user for whom the password is set.

Bad Password Message

If you enter an alphanumeric password, you may get a bad password message stating that it is based on a dictionary word. The password will still be assigned even though the message is displayed. You will probably need to change it to a more secure password.

The /etc/passwd File

When you add a new user, information about the user is saved in the /etc/passwd file.

There are various fields in the /etc/passwd file.

Field	Description
User name	Stores the user name with which the user logs in to the system. It is recommended to limit user names to eight alphanumeric characters.
Password	Stores the password that is assigned to the user in an encrypted form.
User ID	Stores the unique number that is assigned to each user. Linux tracks users by the UID rather than the user name.
Group ID	Stores the unique number that is assigned to each group. Users can be members of one or more groups.
Full name	Stores the real name of the user.
Home directory	Displays the default directory where the user is placed after logging in.
Login shell	Displays the default shell that is started when the user logs in.

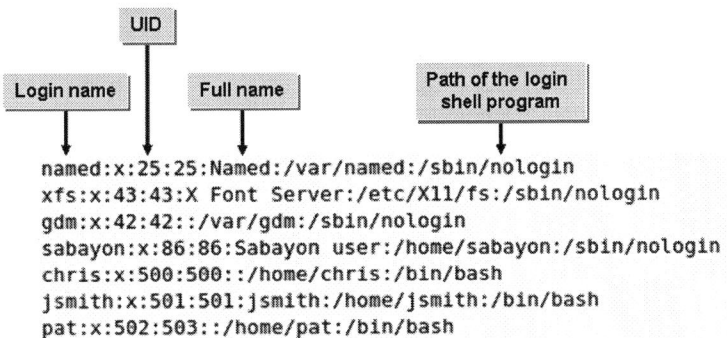

Figure 2-4: *The contents of /etc/passwd file.*

Shadow Passwords

Each user's password is stored and encrypted in the /etc/passwd file. This file needs to be readable, which makes copies of users' encrypted passwords easily obtainable. You can overcome this problem, by using shadow passwords. Shadow passwords store the encrypted passwords in a separate highly protected file, the /etc/shadow file, which makes it difficult to decipher passwords. This file contains the encrypted passwords and the account or password expiration values. The /etc/shadow file is readable only to the root user. Similarly, the /etc/gpasswd file stores the encrypted passwords for groups.

The /etc/shadow File

The /etc/shadow file contains the following information:

- username: The user name.
- passwd: The encoded password.
- last: Number of days since the password was last changed.
- may: Number of days before which the password may be changed.
- must: Number of days after which the password must be changed.
- warn: Number of days pending before which the password will expire.
- expire: Number of days after which the password will expires and the user account will be disabled.
- disable: Number of days since Jan 1, 1970, that the user account has been disabled.
- reserved: A reserved field.

The id Command

The `id` command is used to display UID and group ID (GID) information. Entering the command with no options displays information about the user who is currently logged in. You can also specify a user name as an option to display ID information about a specific user.

The finger Command

The `finger` command is used to display information about users, including login name, real name, terminal name, write status, idle time, login time, office location, and office phone number. Some of these fields may be blank if no information was included when the user account was created. You can also view information about a specific user by entering `finger [user name]`.

Groups

Definition:

A *group* is a collection of system users having the same access rights. Every user must be a member of a group. Users can also be members of more than one group. Group membership is used to limit access to files and system resources. The `groupadd` command allows you to add a group.

Example:

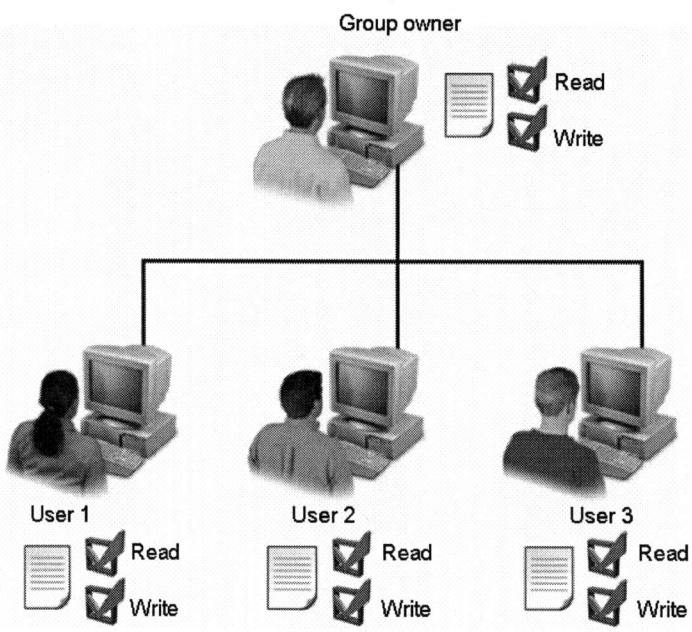

Figure 2-5: A group of users with their permissions.

Standard Groups

The following table lists the standard groups set up by the installation process.

Group	GID	Default Member
root	0	root
bin	1	root, bin, and daemon
daemon	2	root, bin, and daemon
sys	3	root, bin, and adm
adm	4	root, adm, and daemon
tty	5	None
disk	6	root
lp	7	daemon and lp
mem	8	None
kmem	9	None
wheel	10	root
mail	12	mail

Group	GID	Default Member
news	13	news
uucp	14	uucp
man	15	None
games	20	None
gopher	30	None
dip	40	None
ftp	50	None
nobody	99	None
users	100	None

User Private Groups

A *User Private Group (UPG)* is a unique group that is created by default whenever a new user account is created. This is the primary group of the new user account. Only the new user is a member of this group.

The /etc/group File

The *etc/group file* contains a list of groups, each on a separate line. Each line consists of four fields for attribute definition, separated by colons. The /etc/group file is also termed as the *group database*.

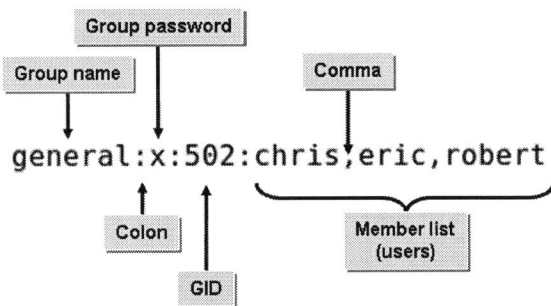

Figure 2-6: An example of an entry in the /etc/group file.

The following table lists the different fields and their usages.

Field	Description
Group name	Stores the name of the group.
Group password	Stores the password of the group in an encrypted form.
GID	Stores the group identifier; similar to a UID for groups. The default GID value is 500.
Members	Stores the names of the members of the group separated by commas.

How to Create User and Group Accounts

Procedure Reference: Create a User Account

To create a user account:

1. Log in as root in the CLI.
2. At the command prompt, enter useradd {user name} to add a new user.
3. Enter passwd {user name} to set a password for the user.
4. Confirm the password.
5. If desired, use the newly created user name and password to log in to the system.

 While creating a user with the useradd command, a user private group with the same name is also created.

Procedure Reference: Create a Group Account

To create a group account:

1. Log in as root in the CLI.
2. At the command prompt, enter groupadd {group name} to add a new group.
3. Verify that the group was created by viewing the /etc/group file.

ACTIVITY 2-1
Creating User and Group Accounts

Before You Begin:

1. You have logged in as root in the CLI of srvA.

2. The first terminal is displayed.

Scenario:

Two new employees joined your company and their user accounts need to be created. Also, there has been a major reorganization in your company. Your manager will like you to create departmental groups according to the new structure.

User account details:

- User name for the new account: chris

- Password for chris: myp@$$w0rd

- User name for the new account: pat

- Password for pat: myp@$$w0rd

- New groups to be created along with their GID numbers: IT_Support (544), Customer_ Support (545), Programming (546), and Design (547)

What You Do	How You Do It
1. Add two new users chris and pat	a. At the command line, enter **adduser chris** to add a new user.
	b. Enter **passwd chris** to change the password for the user.
	c. Enter *myp@$$w0rd* to assign the new password.
	d. Enter *myp@$$w0rd* to confirm the password.
	e. Observe that the password is updated successfully.
	f. Enter **adduser pat** to add another user.
	g. Enter **passwd pat** to change the password for the user.
	h. Enter *myp@$$w0rd* two times to assign the new password.

2. Add user groups IT_Support, Customer_Support, Programming, and Design with the GID numbers specified.

   a. Enter **groupadd -g 544 IT_Support** to add a new group.

   b. Enter **groupadd -g 545 Customer_Support** to add the second group.

   c. Enter **groupadd -g 546 Programming** to add the third group.

   d. Enter **groupadd -g 547 Design** to add the fourth group.

3. Check that the users' accounts and groups are created.

   a. Enter **tail /etc/group** to view the group accounts on your system.

   b. Observe that the newly added groups are displayed and have been added to the list of groups.

   c. Observe that the user accounts have a default group created with the same name as the user.

   d. Enter **tail /etc/passwd** to view the user accounts.

   e. Observe that the newly added users are displayed and have been added to the list of users.

   f. Enter **clear** to clear the terminal screen.

TOPIC B
Configure User Profiles

Now that you can create user and group accounts, the next step is to configure user profiles. Each user connected to a system requires a distinct identity to differentiate one user from another. In this topic, you will configure user profiles.

All users connected to the system require customized settings for their system. Further, there may be files to be shared in common by default. By configuring user profiles, every user can be given a distinct identity. This differentiates one user from another.

User Profiles

Definition:
A *user profile* is a set of options, preferences, bookmarks, and other user items that characterize a user. User profiles define settings such as network resources, data, attributes, and permissions that the system assigns to a user. These settings are retained for every session. The user can specify a name for the user profile. Otherwise, the profile will be called "Default User." Each user can create several user profiles for business or personal use.

 If you do not specify a name for the user profile, the system will label it as "Default User."

Example:

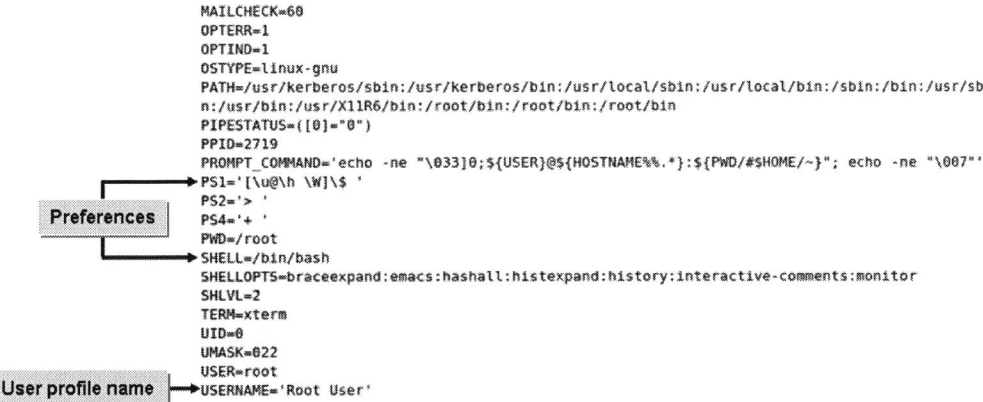

```
MAILCHECK=60
OPTERR=1
OPTIND=1
OSTYPE=linux-gnu
PATH=/usr/kerberos/sbin:/usr/kerberos/bin:/usr/local/sbin:/usr/local/bin:/sbin:/bin:/usr/sbi
n:/usr/bin:/usr/X11R6/bin:/root/bin:/root/bin:/root/bin
PIPESTATUS=([0]="0")
PPID=2719
PROMPT_COMMAND='echo -ne "\033]0;${USER}@${HOSTNAME%%.*}:${PWD/#$HOME/~}"; echo -ne "\007"'
PS1='[\u@\h \W]\$ '
PS2='> '
PS4='+ '
PWD=/root
SHELL=/bin/bash
SHELLOPTS=braceexpand:emacs:hashall:histexpand:history:interactive-comments:monitor
SHLVL=2
TERM=xterm
UID=0
UMASK=022
USER=root
USERNAME='Root User'
```

Preferences

User profile name

Figure 2-7: The list of values set for the root user profile.

Modifying Default Options
You can modify default options while configuring a user profile. Some commonly modified options include:

- PS1—This variable stores information about the primary prompt; the prompt that is displayed on login. This variable may or may not be modified.

- PS2—This variable stores information about the secondary prompt.

- PATH—This variable stores information about the search paths for commands. You can modify the PATH if you want to use commands that are not stored in the standard directories.

Hidden Files and Directories

Some files and directories in the system are hidden. The `ls` command lists all files, except hidden files. To display all files, including hidden ones, the `ls -a` command is used. The names of hidden files and directories start with a period. You can also add a period to the names of directories to hide them. Hidden files are usually those files that require minimal editing.

The Profile File

When a user logs in and starts a new Bash session, several commands need to be typed to customize the user's session. It will be tedious to type these commands every time the user logs in. Therefore, these commands are saved in a special executable file from where Bash will run the commands every time the user logs in. This file is called a *profile file* because it contains the commands that are used to tailor the session according to the requirements of the user. Individual profile files for every user are available at the ~/.bash_profile file, and changes to this file affect the user's customized settings.

Global User Profiles

Definition:

A *global user profile* is a set of options, preferences, bookmarks, stored messages, attributes, permissions, and other user items that users have access to, on whichever system they log in to. Global user profiles are stored on the server. Each time a user logs in, data in the global profile is copied to the local system. While the user is logged in, any changes made to the settings affect only the local copy of the profile.

Example:

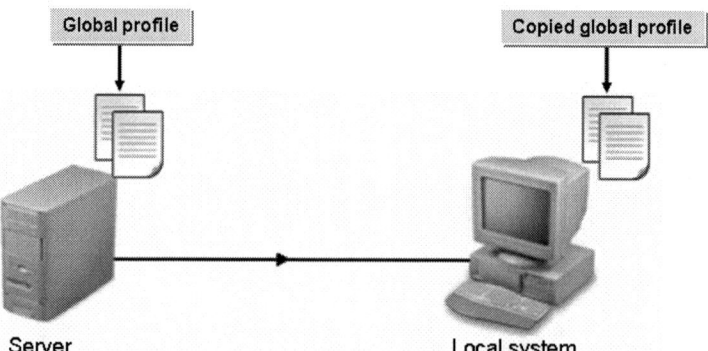

Figure 2-8: A global user profile allows the user to access any system connected to the server in which the profile is saved.

Skel Directories

Definition:

When a new user account is created, the *skel directory* stores a copy of the files and directories that are placed in the home directory of the new user. The skel directory path is /etc/skel. This ensures that all new users begin with the same settings. Modifications made to the skel directory affect only the new users.

 Skel is derived from the word "skeleton," which implies a basic folder structure.

Example:

Skel directory

```
[root@localhost ~]# ls -a /etc/skel
. .. .bash_logout .bash_profile .bashrc .emacs .mozilla .zshrc
[root@localhost ~]#
```

Figure 2-9: Default files in the skel directory.

Managing the /etc/skel Files

By default, the hidden files for configuring a user's environment are stored in the skel directory. These include .bash_profile, .bashrc, .screenrc, and others. If there are other files that you would like to include in new user accounts, you can add those files to this directory. The files will then be copied to the new users' home directories when new users are created.

How to Configure User Profiles

Procedure Reference: Maintain skel Directories for New User Accounts

To maintain skel directories for new user accounts:

1. Log in as root in the CLI.
2. Enter cd /etc/skel
3. Enter gedit .bash_profile
4. Make the necessary changes, such as changing PS1, PS2, or the PATH variable for a new user account.
5. Save and close the file.

The Gedit Editor

Gedit is a simple yet powerful GUI-based text editor used in the GNOME desktop. In the GUI environment, you can use the gedit {file name} command to open a specific file. Alternatively, you can choose **Applications→Accessories→Text Editor** to launch the gedit application and use the GUI components to open a specific file.

Procedure Reference: Delegate Files to New Users

To delegate a file to a newly created user by default:

1. Log in as root in the CLI.

2. Enter cd /etc/skel

3. Enter mv /[location of the file]/[file name] .[file name] to move the file as a hidden file.

4. Verify that the files have moved as hidden files.

   a. Create a user.

   b. Log in as the new user.

   c. Enter cat .file name to view the file that was placed in the /etc/skel directory.

ACTIVITY 2-2
Configuring User Profiles

Data Files:

Desktoppolicies.txt

Before You Begin:

1. You have logged in as root in the CLI of srvA.

2. The first terminal is displayed.

3. At the command line, enter
   `cp /085039Data/Managing_Users_and_Groups/* /root.`

4. Enter `clear` to clear the terminal screen.

5. Switch to the GUI.

6. Log in as root.

Scenario:

You are assigned the task of creating user accounts and configuring user profiles for employees in a startup company. Based on the new company's policy, all new user accounts should be provided with the Desktoppolicies.txt manual, and the user's command prompt should display the company name along with the user name.

The Desktoppolicies.txt file is located in the root directory.

The company name is "OGC Products."

User account details:

● User name for the account to be created: newuser

● Password for the newuser: myp@$$w0rd

What You Do	How You Do It
1. Move the Desktoppolicies.txt file as a hidden file.	a. Choose **Applications→Accessories→Terminal.**
	b. In the **root@localhost** window, enter `cd /etc/skel` to switch to the skel directory.
	c. Enter `ls -al` to view the hidden files.
	d. Enter `mv /root/Desktoppolicies.txt .Desktoppolicies.txt` to move the Desktoppolicies.txt file as a hidden file.

2. Display the user name along with the company name at the command prompt.

a. Enter `gedit .bash_profile`

b. Press **Ctrl+End** to move to a new line at the end of the file.

c. Type **PS1=" [OGC Products/ \u] "** and press **Enter** to change the primary prompt.

d. Save the file and close the **gedit** window.

e. Clear the terminal screen.

3. Assign the Desktoppolicies.txt file to the **newuser** account.

a. Enter `useradd newuser` to add the newuser account.

b. Enter `passwd newuser` to set a password for newuser.

c. Enter **myp@$$w0rd** to assign the password.

d. Enter **myp@$$w0rd** to confirm the password.

4. Check that the file has been moved.

a. Press **Ctrl+Alt+F1** to switch to the first terminal.

b. Log out **root.**

c. Log in as **newuser.**

d. Observe that the company name is displayed.

e. Enter `cat .Desktoppolicies.txt` to verify that the file has been moved.

f. Observe that the contents of the file are displayed on the screen indicating that the file was moved.

g. Log out of the **newuser** account.

TOPIC C
Manage User and Group Accounts

You created user and group accounts and even configured user profiles. Your next step will be to manage user and group accounts on an ongoing basis. This will enable you to efficiently organize your Linux environment. In this topic, you will manage user and group accounts.

Once a user or group account is created, there are many tasks that need to be performed to maintain that account. As a system administrator, you will be required to maintain the accounts and passwords of numerous users. This is achieved by effective management of user and group accounts.

The userdel Command

The `userdel` command allows you to modify the system account files, deleting all entries that refer to the login of an existing user. However, it will not allow you to remove an account if the user is currently logged in. You must kill any running processes that belong to an account before deleting the account.

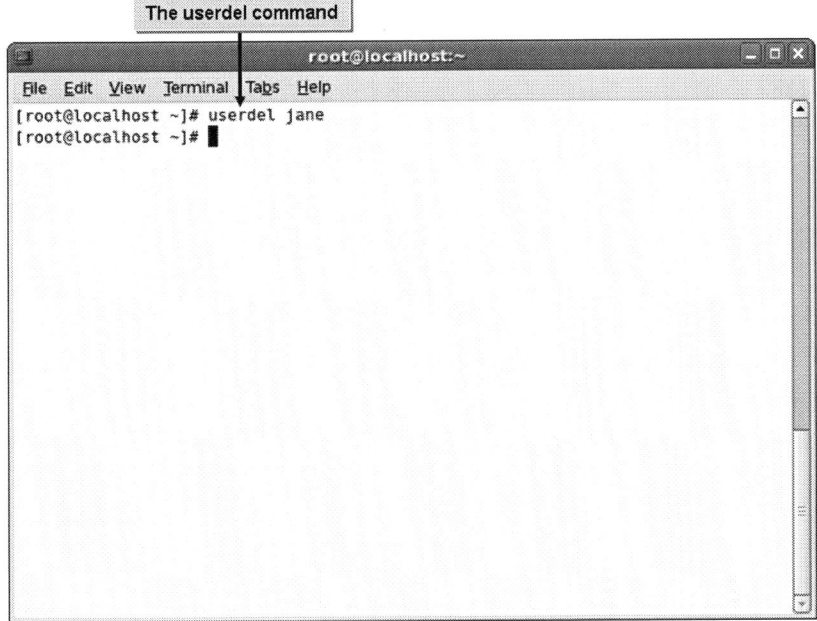

Figure 2-10: The userdel command is used to delete an unused user account.

The -r Option

The `-r` option will delete the files in the user's home directory, along with the home directory itself. Files located in other filesystems will have to be searched for and deleted manually.

The usermod Command

The usermod command has options that enable you to modify various user account parameters. You can change a user's name, default groups, UID, or passwords.

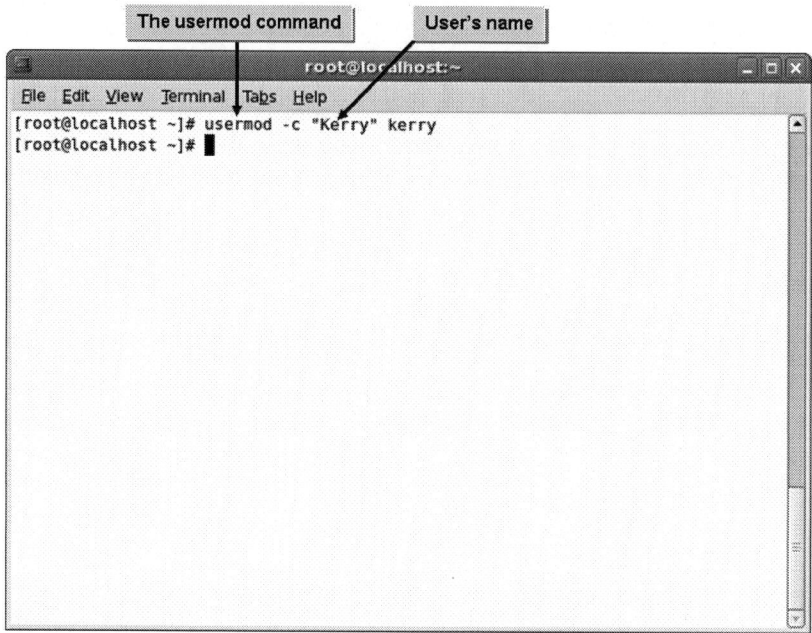

Figure 2-11: The usermod command is used to add more information about the user.

Some of the common usermod command options and their descriptions are given in the following table.

Option	Allows You To
usermod -l {new login}{login}	Modify the login name of the user.
usermod -c "comment" login	Modify the user's full name, office address, and contact numbers in the password file. Alternatively, you can use the chfn user name command to modify the details.
usermod -f {number of days} {login}	Modify the number of days for a password to expire and to disable the account permanently.
usermod -u {new unique user ID} {login}	Modify the numerical value of a user's ID, which has to be unique.
usermod -d {new login directory} login	Modify the user's default login directory.
usermod -L user name	Lock the password and suspend the user account temporarily.
usermod -U user name	Unlock the password.
usermod -e yyyy-mm-dd user name	Change the expiration date for the user account.

The lock Command

The `lock` command is used to temporarily prevent a user from logging in to a Linux system. This is done by disabling the user's password using the `passwd -l` command. The user's login is usually locked as a security measure, to prevent unauthorized usage when the user is unavailable.

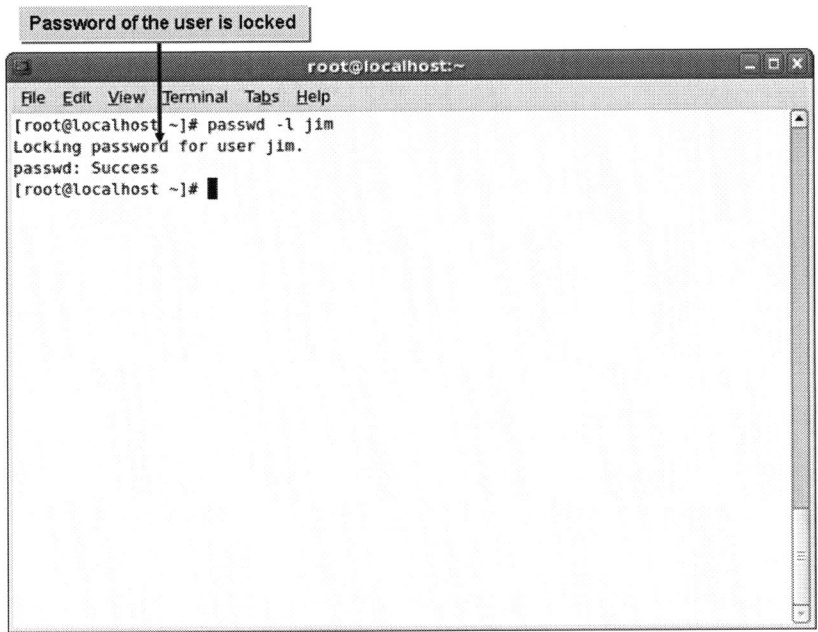

Figure 2-12: The passwd -l command is used to lock the user's password.

Temporarily Suspending User Access

If you need to prevent logging in to a system through an account, but don't want to delete it, you can edit the /etc/shadow file and replace the existing encrypted password with an asterisk. Be sure not to delete the colons on either side of the password because it could corrupt the file. Then, to reactivate the account, remove the asterisk and assign a new password to the user account.

Group Management

Groups, like users, are identified by a system with a unique number known as GID. In Linux, users can be members of one primary group and multiple supplemental groups. The `groupdel` and `groupmod` commands are useful in managing groups.

Command	Description
groupdel	Allows you to delete a group from the system.
groupmod	Allows you to change the group's name and the numerical value of the group's ID by modifying the system account files.

Group Account with GID

To add a new group to the system with a name of print_users and a GID of 700, you will enter `groupadd -g 700 print_users` at the command line.

Adding Users to a Group

As with users, the group file can be directly edited to add groups. You can use the `groupadd` command to add users instead of editing the group file.

How to Manage User and Group Accounts

Procedure Reference: Change a User's Home Directory

To change the home directory of a user:

1. Log in as root in the CLI.
2. Enter `mkdir /{Name of the directory}` to create a directory.
3. Enter `mkdir /{name of the directory}/{user name}` to create a directory for the specified user.
4. Enter `chown {user name}:{user name} /{name of the directory}` to change the ownership of the directory.
5. Enter `usermod -d /{name of the directory}/{user name} {user name}` to set the user's new home directory.

The mkdir Command

The `mkdir` command allows you to create new directories. The syntax of the command is `mkdir {directory name}`.

The chown Command

The `chown` command is used to change the user or group that owns one or more files or directories.

Procedure Reference: Modify User Settings in the CLI

To modify user settings in the CLI:

1. Log in as root.
2. Enter `usermod [command options] {user name}` to modify user settings.

Procedure Reference: Modify User Settings in the GUI

To modify user settings in the GNOME GUI:

1. Log in as root in the GUI.
2. Choose **System→Administration→Users and Groups** to open the **User Manager** window.
3. Modify user settings as desired.
   - Click **Add User** to add a new user.
   - Double-click a user name to modify user settings.
   - Select a user and click **Delete** to remove the user account.

Procedure Reference: Remove User Accounts

To remove user accounts:

1. Log in as root.

2. Enter `userdel [command options] {user name}` to delete user accounts.

Procedure Reference: Manage Default Password Aging Information

To manage default password aging information:

1. Log in as root.
2. Enter `gedit /etc/login.defs` to open the /etc/login.defs file.
3. Manage the password aging information.
    - Modify **PASS_MAX_DAYS** to control the maximum number of days a password may be used.
    - Modify **PASS_MIN_DAYS** to control the minimum number of days allowed between password changes.
    - Modify **PASS_MIN_LEN** to control the minimum password length.
    - Modify **PASS_WARN_AGE** to control the number of days to issue warnings before a password expires.
4. Save and close the file.

Procedure Reference: Set or Change Password Aging Information

To set or change password aging information:

1. Log in as root.
2. Enter `chage [command options] {user name}` to change the password aging information of the specified user.

Procedure Reference: Modify and Delete Groups

To modify or delete groups:

1. Log in as root.
2. Manage the groups.
    - Use the `groupmod -g {group name}` command to change the GID.
    - Use the `groupdel {group name}` command to delete a group.

ACTIVITY 2-3
Configuring a New User Account

Before You Begin:
1. Log in to the CLI terminal as root.
2. In the first terminal, modify the /etc/skel/.bash_profile file and remove the last line starting with PS1.
3. Enter `clear` to clear the terminal screen.

Scenario:
You are working as a junior system administrator, and your organization has hired a new network administrator on contract. You will need to create a user account for the new recruit based on the following details:

- User name for the new account: netadmin1
- Password for the netadmin1 user: myp@$$w0rd
- The netadmin1 user account needs to be valid until July 2011.
- The /home/users/netadmin1 directory should be set as the default home directory for the netadmin1 user.

What You Do	How You Do It
1. Create a user account named netadmin1.	a. Enter **`useradd netadmin1`** to create a user.
	b. Enter **`passwd netadmin1`** to set a password for the new user.
	c. Enter ***myp@$$w0rd*** to assign the password.
	d. Enter ***myp@$$w0rd*** to confirm the password.
	e. Enter **`logout`** to log out of the **root** account.

2.	Log in to the system using the new user account details.	a.	Log in as **netadmin1.**
		b.	Enter **pwd** to view the default home directory.
		c.	Observe that /home/netadmin1 is the default home directory for **netadmin1** user.
		d.	Log out of the **netadmin1** account.
3.	Set the expiration date for the new user account.	a.	Log in as **root.**
		b.	Enter **usermod -e {year}-07-31 netadmin1** to set July 31 of the next year as the expiration date for the **netadmin1** user account.
4.	Change the home directory of the netadmin1 user.	a.	Enter **mkdir /home/users** to create a parent directory.
		b.	Enter **mkdir /home/users/netadmin1** to create a home directory.
		c.	Enter **chown netadmin1:netadmin1 /home/users/netadmin1** to change the ownership of the directory.
		d.	Enter **usermod -d /home/users/netadmin1 netadmin1** to change the default home directory of the **netadmin1** user to /home/users/netadmin1.
		e.	Log out of the **root** account.
5.	Check that the home directory of the netadmin1 user has changed.	a.	Log in as **netadmin1.**
		b.	Enter **pwd** to view the new home directory.
		c.	Observe that the home directory has changed to /home/users/netadmin1.
		d.	Log out of the **netadmin1** account.

ACTIVITY 2-4

Managing Group Accounts

Before You Begin:

1. Log in to the CLI terminal as root.

2. On the terminal, create two groups named Finance and Marketing.

3. Enter `clear` to clear the terminal screen.

Scenario:

You are assigned the task of changing the GID for the finance department so that it matches the department number. In addition, you need to remove the marketing group from the system because the work of the marketing department will be outsourced to another company from now on.

What You Do	How You Do It
1. Change the GID to match the finance department number, 555.	a. Enter `groupmod -g 555 Finance` to alter the GID of the finance department.
	b. Enter `tail -20 /etc/group` to verify that the change was made.
	c. Observe that the GID of the finance department has been changed.
2. Delete the user group, Marketing.	a. Enter `groupdel Marketing`
	b. Enter `cat /etc/group | less` to verify that the **Marketing** group was deleted.
	c. Press the **Spacebar** till you reach the end of the file to verify that the **Marketing** group is no longer listed.
	d. Press **Q** to quit the display.
	e. Clear the terminal screen.

Lesson 2 Follow-up

In this lesson, you created and managed user and group accounts. This will help you efficiently organize and maintain a Linux environment with numerous users.

1. How is organizing users into groups useful to you?

2. Why is it essential to configure a user profile?

3 Managing Partitions and the Linux Filesystem

Lesson Time: 2 hour(s), 30 minutes

Lesson Objectives:

In this lesson, you will manage partitions and the Linux filesystem.

You will:

- Create partitions.
- Navigate through the Linux filesystem.
- Manage a Linux filesystem.
- Maintain Linux filesystems.

Introduction

You are now familiar with user and group accounts in Linux. Besides user and group management, another major Linux component that you will need to manage is the filesystem. In this lesson, you will create partitions on the hard disk and navigate, manage, and maintain the Linux filesystem.

Data organization facilitates efficient resource management and faster retrieval of information. Data organization is done by sorting data into filesystems. The Linux filesystem is part of what sets Linux apart from other operating systems. Understanding the structure and workings of the filesystem will assist you in storage, management, and troubleshooting of data.

This lesson covers all or part of the following CompTIA Linux+ (2009) certification objectives:

- Topic A
  - Objective 1.2
  - Objective 1.3
  - Objective 1.4
  - Objective 2.7
- Topic B
  - Objective 1.5
  - Objective 1.6

- ■ Objective 2.1
- ● Topic C
  - ■ Objective 1.4
  - ■ Objective 2.4
  - ■ Objective 2.7
- ● Topic D
  - ■ Objective 2.7

TOPIC A
Create Partitions

Before you work with the Linux filesystems, you should partition the hard disk of your system. Proper partitioning of the hard disk will ensure that users have enough space to store their data. In this topic, you will create and manage disk partitions.

The hard disk is the most critical component for data storage in any system. Without effective disk partitioning, data on the disk will be unorganized and cluttered. Improper disk partitioning may lead to a system crash. As a Linux+ administrator, it is your responsibility to ensure that the disks are partitioned properly such that users have enough space to store their data in an efficient manner.

Filesystems

Definition:

A *filesystem* is a method that is used by an operating system to store, retrieve, organize, and manage files and directories on mass storage devices. A filesystem maintains information, such as the date of creation and modification of individual files, their file size, file type, and permissions, and it provides a structured form for data storage. A filesystem by itself does not interpret the data contained in files, because this task is handled by specific applications. Filesystems vary depending on several parameters, such as the purpose of the filesystems, the information they store about individual files, the way they store data, and data security.

Example:

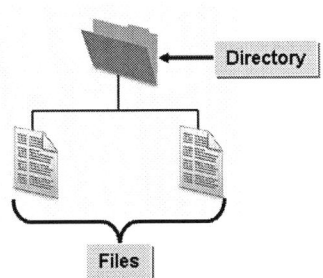

Figure 3-1: Files are stored in directories.

Filesystem Labels

Filesystem labels are assigned to filesystems for easy identification. The labels may be up to 16 characters long and can be displayed or changed using the `e2label` command.

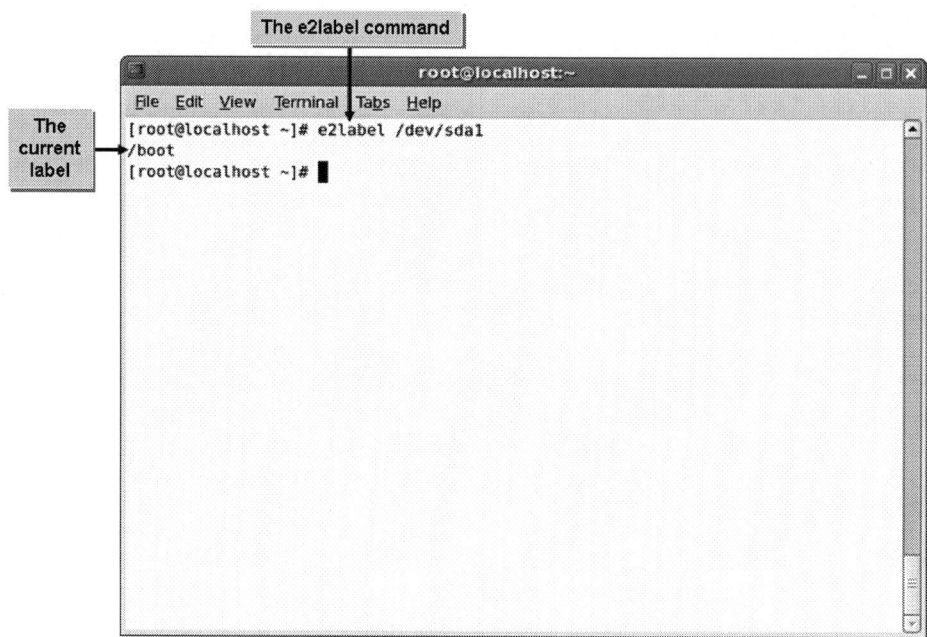

Figure 3-2: An example of a filesystem label.

Syntax

The syntax for setting filesystem labels is `e2label /dev/{device name}{partition number}`. They can also be set using the `tune2fs -L volume label` command.

Filesystem Types

Linux supports many filesystem types. Some common filesystem types are described in the following table.

Filesystem Type	Description
ext2	This used to be the native Linux filesystem of some of the previous releases. It is still supported in the current releases of Linux.
ext3	This is an improved version of ext2 and is the native Linux filesystem now. In case of an abrupt system shutdown, ext3 is much faster in recovering data and ensures data integrity. You can easily upgrade your filesystem from ext2 to ext3.
reiserfs	This can handle small files efficiently. It handles files smaller than 1K and is faster than ext2. If appropriately configured, it can store more data than ext2.
vfat	This is a 32-bit filesystem and supports long file names. It is compatible with the FAT filesystem of Microsoft Windows XP and Microsoft Windows NT.

Filesystem Type	Description
XFS	This is a 64-bit, high-performance journaling filesystem that provides fast recovery and can handle large files efficiently.
JFS (Journaled File System)	This is a 64-bit journaling filesystem that is fast and reliable. It is better equipped to handle power failures and system crashes.
swap	This is not a true filesystem, but rather is a portion of the hard disk that is used in situations when Linux runs out of physical memory and needs more of it. Linux pushes some of the unused files from RAM to swap to free up memory.
ISO 9660	This is a filesystem standard defined by the International Standardization Organization (ISO), also called as CDFS (Compact Disc File System). Linux allows you to access DVD's and CD's that use this filesystem.

Access Other Filesystems

Linux allows you to access other filesystems and mount them when required. However, you cannot install Linux on these filesystems.

Filesystem	Description
FAT	The FAT (File Allocation Table) filesystem is compatible with different operating systems, including all versions of Windows, MS-DOS, and UNIX. It is primarily used for formatting floppy disks.
NTFS	NTFS (NT File System) is the recommended filesystem for Windows-based computers. NTFS provides many enhanced features over FAT or vfat, including file- and folder-level security, file encryption, disk compression, and scalability to very large drives and files.

Partitions

Definition:

A *partition* is a section of the hard disk that logically acts as a separate disk. Partitions enable you to convert a large hard disk to smaller manageable chunks leading to better organization of information. A partition must be formatted and assigned a filesystem before data can be stored on it. Partitions are identified using a partition table, which is stored in the boot record. The partition table can contain entries for a maximum of four primary partitions. Partitions can be classified into primary and extended partitions. The size of each partition can vary, but cannot exceed the total free space of the hard disk.

Example:

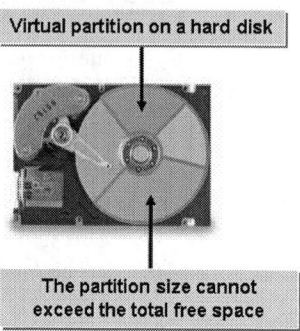

Figure 3-3: Partitions on a hard disk.

Hard Disk Size Specification

Before proceeding with the installation process, you need to plan the hard disk layout based on your requirements. Each partition has a recommended size specification. The following table lists the recommended size specification for partitions.

Partition	Recommended Size
/	Minimum 1 GB.
/boot	100 MB.
swap	Double the RAM size.
/var	Minimum 250 MB. If the possibility of the installation of many applications exists in the future, allocate the appropriate size.
/home	Varies based on the number of users.

Disk Partitioning

Most operating systems, including Linux, use disk partitions. Data of different types can be stored in separate locations on the hard disk. The partition size can be specified by a user. However, the filesystem size must be considered before specifying the partition size. Disk partitioning enables the user to separate system files from user accessible ones. Corrupted partitions do not affect the other partitions, and they can be recovered separately.

Partition Types

There are three types of partitions: primary, extended, and logical. Functioning of the hard disk depends on the types of partitions on it. The recommended protocol for partitioning a hard disk is three primary partitions and one extended partition with any number of logical partitions within.

Each partition has a set of specific features. The three types of partitions are described in the table.

Partition Type	Description
Primary	A maximum of four primary partitions are allowed. The swap filesystem and the boot partition are normally created in a primary partition.
Extended	There can be only one extended partition, which can be further subdivided. This partition type does not contain any data and has a separate partition table.
Logical	A logical partition is created within an extended partition. There is no restriction on the number of logical partitions, but it is advisable to limit it to 12 logical partitions per disk drive.

The fdisk Utility

Definition:

An *fdisk* is a menu-driven utility program that is used for creating, modifying, or deleting partitions on a disk drive. Using `fdisk`, a new partition table can be created, or existing entries in the partition table can be modified. The `fdisk` utility understands the DOS and Linux type partition tables. Depending on the partition table created, the DOS FDISK or the Linux fdisk program is invoked. The `fdisk` utility also allows you to specify the size of partitions.

Example:

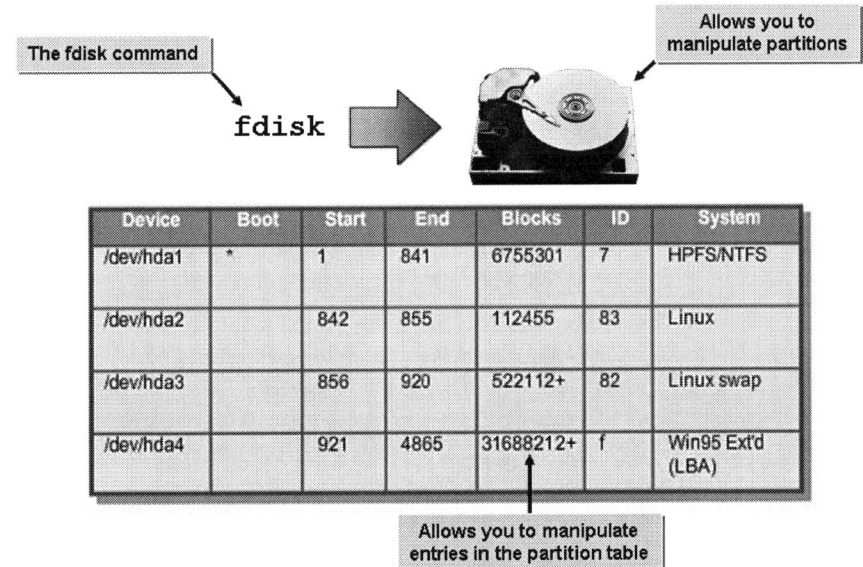

Figure 3-4: A partition table created with the fdisk utility.

Syntax

The syntax of the `fdisk` utility is `fdisk [option] {device name}`.

The fdisk Utility Options

The `fdisk` utility provides various options for partitioning disks according to the requirements of users. Some of the `fdisk` options are described in the following table.

Option	Enables You To
-b *sector size*	Specify the number of disk sectors.
-H *heads*	Specify the number of disk heads.
-S *sectors*	Specify the number of sectors per track.
-s *partition*	Print the partition size in blocks.
-v	List the `fdisk` version.
-l	List partition tables for devices.

The fstab File

The *fstab* file is a configuration file that stores information about storage devices and partitions and where and how the partitions should be mounted. The fstab file is located in the /etc directory. It can be edited only by a root user. The fstab file consists of a number of lines—one for each filesystem.

Each line in an fstab file has six fields, which are separated by spaces.

Field	Description
Device or partition name	Specifies the name of the device or filesystem that has to be mounted.
Default mount point	Indicates where the filesystem has to be mounted.
Filesystem type	Specifies the type of filesystem used by the device or partition.
Mount options	Specifies a set of comma-separated options that will be activated when the filesystem is mounted.
Dump options	Indicates if the `dump` utility should back up the filesystem. Usually, zero is specified as the `dump` option to indicate that `dump` can ignore the filesystem.
fsck options	Specifies the order in which the `fsck` utility should check filesystems.

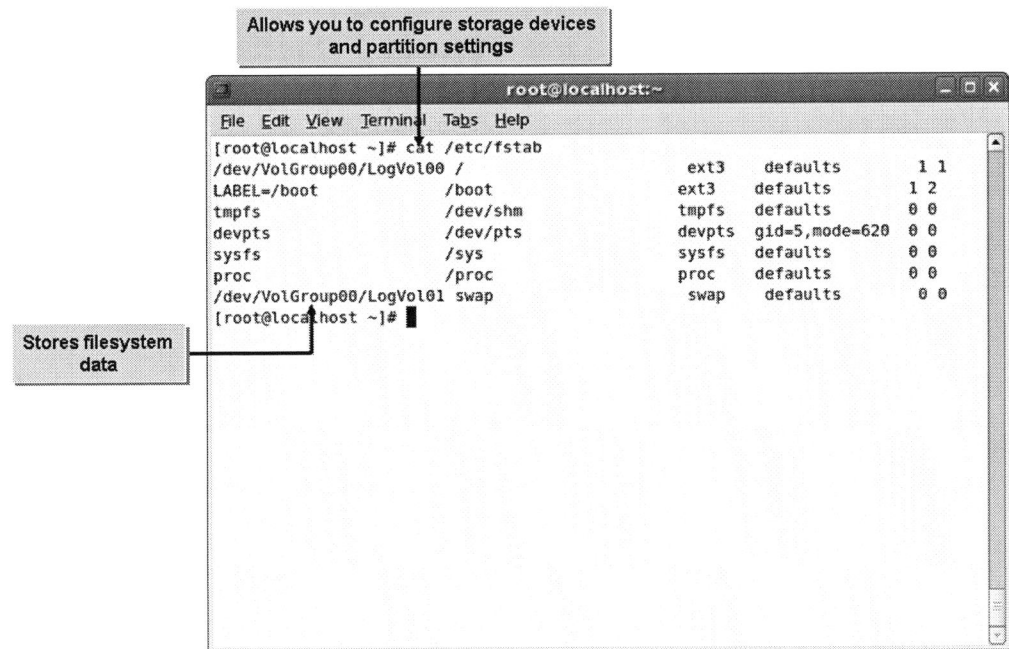

Figure 3-5: The /etc/fstab file contains partition and filesystem settings.

The mkfs Command

The *mkfs command* is used to build a Linux filesystem on a device, which is usually a hard disk partition. The following table lists some options of the mkfs command and their description.

Option	Allows You To
-v	Produce *verbose* output, where the output message will keep changing constantly as the program is processing.
-V	Produce verbose output, including all filesystem specific commands that are executed.
-t fstype	Specify the type of filesystem to be built.
fs-options	Pass filesystem specific options to the filesystem builder.
-c	Check the device for bad blocks, before building the filesystem.
-l file name	Read the list of bad blocks from a specified file.

Building New Linux Filesystems Using the mkfs Commands

The mkfs commands are used to build a new Linux filesystem. The different mkfs commands are given in the following table.

If You Need To Build	Use This `mkfs` Command
An ext2 filesystem	`mkfs.ext2 /dev/hdaPartition number` or `mke2fs /dev/hdaPartition number`
An ext3 filesystem	`mkfs.ext3 /dev/hdaPartition number`
A reiserfs filesystem	`mkfs.reiserfs /dev/hdaPartition number`
A vfat filesystem	`mkfs.vfat /dev/hdaPartition number`
An XFS filesystem	`mkfs.xfs /dev/hdaPartition number`
A JFS filesystem	`mkfs.jfs /dev/hdaPartition number`

The mke2fs Utility

The *mke2fs utility* is used to create both ext2 and ext3 filesystems. It has various options. Some of the options are listed below in the following table.

Option	Enables You To
`-b block size`	Specify the size of the block in bytes.
`-c`	Check the device for errors in the blocks, before creating the filesystem.
`-f`	Specify the fragment size in bytes.
`-j`	Create a journaled ext3 filesystem.
`-M`	Set the directory that was last accessed for the filesystem to be mounted.
`-V`	Print the version number of the `mke2fs` utility.

Syntax

The syntax of the `mke2fs` utility is `mke2fs [options] {filesystem name}`.

Device Recognition by MBR

Device recognition is performed by MBR at system startup, by recognizing the hard disk and all the partitions on it. The MBR has two main components that help it to detect any devices that are connected to the system.

Component	Description
The Master Partition Table	Contains the list of partitions on the hard disk. Technically, the hard disk can have many partitions. The four partitions displayed in the partition table are known as primary partitions. All other partitions are linked to these primary partitions. The table displays the partition id, its starting cylinder, and the number of cylinders occupied by the partition.
The Master Boot Code	Contains the program for loading the operating system on the hard disk. This program is loaded to initiate the boot process.

The Cylinder

The *cylinder* is the aggregate of all tracks that reside in the same location on every disk surface. On multiple-platter disks, the cylinder is the sum total of every track with the same track number on every surface. On a floppy disk, a cylinder comprises the top and corresponding bottom tracks.

Partition Management

Partition management is the process of creating, destroying, and manipulating partitions to optimize system performance. Effective partition management enables you to keep track of the data in the partitions and avoid data overflow. Various utilities, such as sfdisk, partprobe, and GNU parted, are available for partition management.

The sfdisk Utility

The *sfdisk utility* is used to manipulate partitions. This utility manages partitions by listing the number of partitions and their sizes, checking the partitions, and repartitioning a storage device.

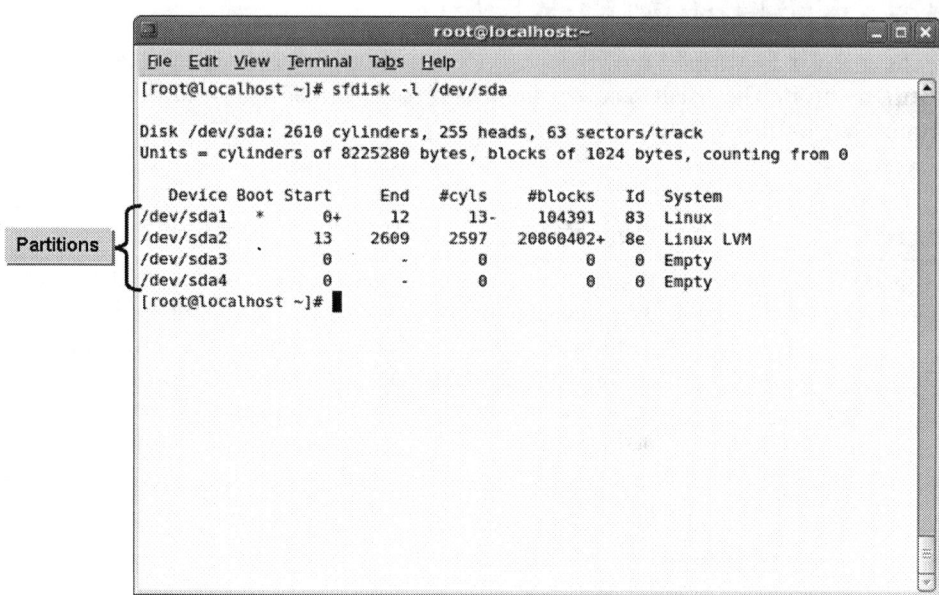

Figure 3-6: *Listing partitions on the hard disk using the sfdisk utility.*

There are various options available in the `sfdisk` utility to manage partitions.

Option	Enables You To
`-s`	List the partition size.
`-l device`	List partitions on all hard disks.
`-V device`	Check for consistency in all partitions.
`device`	Repartition hard disks. However, if the code is wrongly entered, it may lead to loss of data.
`-i`	Set numbers for all cylinders in the hard disk.
`-A number`	Activate the partition indicated by the partition number.

Syntax

The syntax of the `sfdisk` utility is `sfdisk [options] device`.

The GNU Parted Utility

The *GNU Parted utility* is also used to manage partitions. It is particularly useful when creating partitions on new hard disks. It can be used to create, destroy, and resize partitions. This utility is generally not used for resizing ext3 partitions.

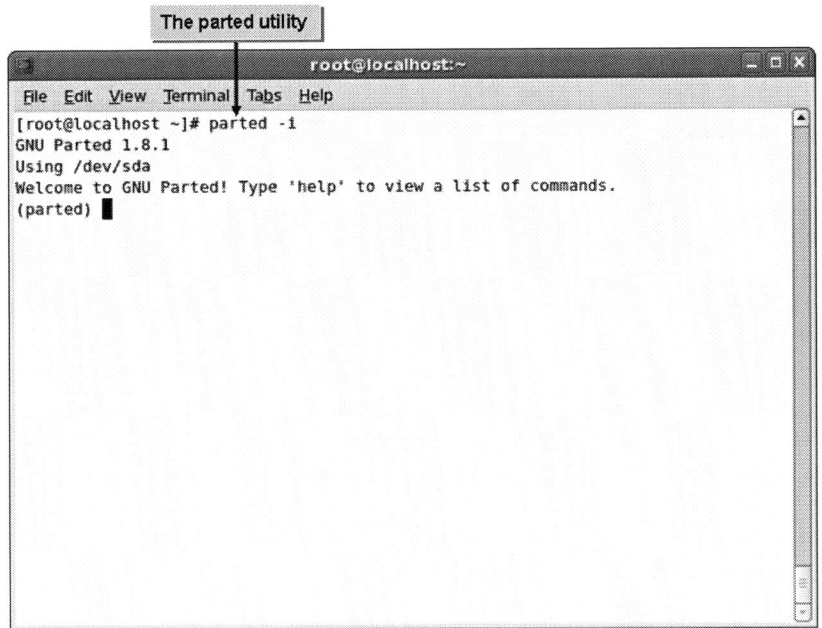

Figure 3-7: *The welcome screen of the GNU Parted utility.*

A number of options are available in the GNU Parted utility.

Option	Enables You To
-h	Display a help message.
-v	Display the version of GNU Parted.
-i	Configure `parted` to ask for user input.
-s	Stop `parted` from asking for user input.

Syntax

The syntax of the `parted` utility is `parted [option] device {command [argument]}`.

The partprobe Program

The *partprobe* program is used to update the kernel with changes in the partition tables. The program first checks the partition table and if there are any changes, it automatically updates the kernel with the changes.

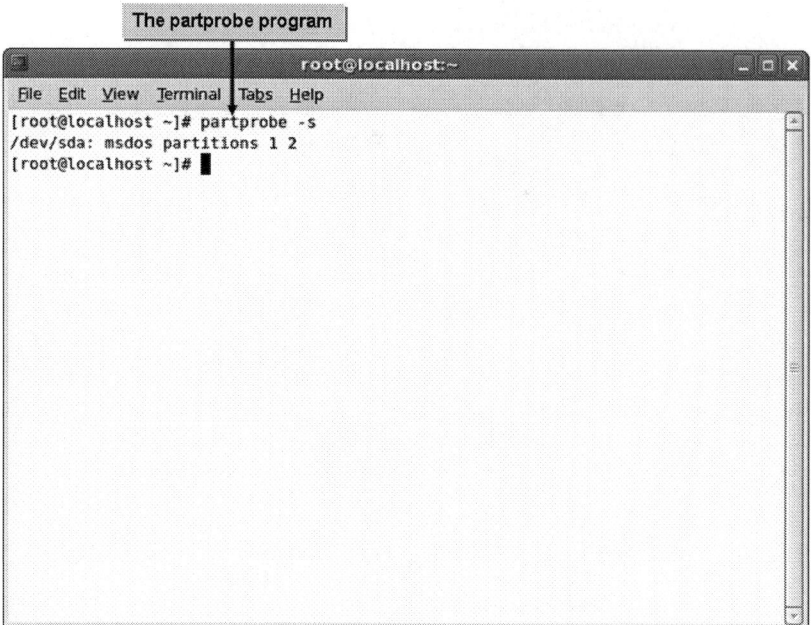

Figure 3-8: *Using the partprobe utility to display the storage devices and their partitions.*

The `partprobe` program has several options.

Option	Enables You To
-d	Cancel any updates.
-s	Display the storage devices and their partitions.
-v	Display the version of the `partprobe` program.

Syntax

The syntax of the `partprobe` utility is `partprobe [options] [devices...]`.

How to Create Partitions
Procedure Reference: Create a Primary Partition

To create a primary partition:
1. Log in as root.
2. Enter fdisk /dev/{device name} to partition the disk.
3. Enter n to create a partition.
4. Create a primary partition.
   a. Enter p to create a primary partition.
   b. To accept the default starting point of the partition, press **Enter.**
   c. Specify the partition size.
      - To accept the default partition size, press **Enter.**
      - To specify a custom partition size.
         - Enter **+[Required size]** to specify the partition size in blocks.
         - Enter **+[Required size]K** to specify the partition size in kilobytes (KB).
         - Enter **+[Required size]M** to specify the partition size in megabytes (MB).
5. Enter w to write the partition table on the disk.
6. Enter partprobe or reboot the system to update the partition table.
7. Enter sfdisk -l /dev/{device name} to list the partition table.

Procedure Reference: Create an Extended Partition

To create an extended partition:
1. Log in as root.
2. Enter fdisk /dev/{device name} to begin disk partitioning.
3. Enter n to create a partition.
4. Create an extended partition.
   a. Enter e to create an extended partition.
   b. To accept the default starting point of the partition, press **Enter.**
   c. To accept the default partition size, press **Enter.**
   d. Enter n to create a logical partition within the extended partition.
   e. To accept the default starting point of the partition, press **Enter.**
   f. Specify the partition size.
      - To accept the default partition size, press **Enter.**
      - To specify a custom partition size.
         - Enter **+[Required size]** to specify the partition size in blocks.
         - Enter **+[Required size]K** to specify the partition size in kilobytes (KB).
         - Enter **+[Required size]M** to specify the partition size in megabytes (MB).
5. Enter w to write the partition table on the disk.
6. Enter partprobe or reboot the system to update the partition table.
7. Enter sfdisk -l /dev/{device name} to list the partition table.

Procedure Reference: Apply Labels to a Partition

To apply labels to a partition:

1. Log in as root.

2. At the command prompt, enter e2label /dev/{device name}{Partition number} {label name} to apply a label to the partition.

3. Enter e2label /dev/{device name}{Partition number} to view the applied or associated label.

4. If necessary, enter mount LABEL={label name} {mount point} to mount the partition using its label.

ACTIVITY 3-1
Creating Partitions

Before You Begin:

1. On srvA, you have logged in to CLI as root.

2. At the command line, enter `mkdir /morning /evening` to create two directories.

3. Clear the terminal screen.

Scenario:

Your organization has a support team that works in two shifts. One employee uses a system in the morning shift and the same system is used by another in the evening shift. Both need to have separate partitions mounted according to the details given here:

- The logical partitions, **sdb5 and sdb6,** need to be mounted on /morning and /evening directories, respectively.

- Login name for the root user: root

- Password for the root user: p@ssw0rd

You also need to ensure that these partitions are easily identified for maintenance. The labels that need to be applied to the partitions and used for mounting them are:

- For the morning shift: Mrng

- For the evening shift: Evng

What You Do	How You Do It
1. Create an extended partition.	a. Enter `fdisk /dev/sdb` to begin the disk partitioning process.
	b. Enter `n` to create a new partition.
	c. Enter `e` to create an extended partition.
	d. Press **Enter** to accept the default starting point of the partition.
	e. Enter *+15000M* to specify the size of the partition.

2.	Create two logical partitions within the extended partition.	a.	Enter **n** to create a new partition.
		b.	Press **Enter** to accept the default starting point of the partition.
		c.	Enter **+1024M** to specify the size of the partition.
		d.	Repeat the steps from (a) to (c) to create another logical partition of size 1024M.
		e.	Enter **w** to write the partition table on the disk.
3.	Set logical partitions for the ext2 filesystem.	a.	Enter **mkfs.ext2 /dev/sdb5** to create an ext2 filesystem on /dev/sdb5.
		b.	Enter **clear** to clear the terminal screen.
		c.	Enter **mkfs.ext2 /dev/sdb6** to create an ext2 filesystem on /dev/sdb6.
		d.	Enter **clear** to clear the terminal screen.
4.	Verify that the two new partitions have the ext2 filesystem.	a.	Enter **parted** to run the GNU Parted utility.
		b.	Enter **select /dev/sdb** to select the sdb partition.
		c.	At the **(parted)** prompt, enter **print** to view the list of existing partitions.
		d.	Observe that the partitions five and six have **ext2** filesystem.
		e.	Enter **q** to quit from the parted utility.
		f.	Enter **clear** to clear the terminal screen.

5.	Apply labels to the partition.	a.	Enter `e2label /dev/sdb5` to view the existing label of the **/dev/sdb5** partition.
		b.	Observe that there is no label set for the **/dev/sdb5** partition.
		c.	Enter `e2label /dev/sdb5 Mrng` to apply a new label **Mrng** to the partition.
		d.	Enter `e2label /dev/sdb6` to view the existing label of the **/dev/sdb6** partition.
		e.	Observe that there is no label set for the **/dev/sdb6** partition.
		f.	Enter `e2label /dev/sdb6 Evng` to apply a new label **Evng** to the partition.
		g.	Enter `clear` to clear the terminal screen.
6.	Verify the labels applied to the partitions.	a.	Enter `e2label /dev/sdb5` to verify that the partition label for **/dev/sdb5** has changed.
		b.	Observe that the label is set as Mrng for the **/dev/sdb5** partition.
		c.	Enter `e2label /dev/sdb6` to verify that the partition label for **/dev/sdb6** has changed.
		d.	Observe that the label is set as Evng for the **/dev/sdb6** partition.
7.	Mount the partitions using their labels.	a.	Enter `mount LABEL=Mrng /morning` to mount the **/dev/sdb5** partition using its label.
		b.	Enter `mount LABEL=Evng /evening` to mount the **/dev/sdb6** partition using its label.
		c.	Enter `mount` to verify that the partitions have been mounted using their labels.
		d.	Observe that the partitions /dev/sdb5 and /dev/sdb6 are mounted on /morning and /evening directories.
		e.	Enter `clear` to clear the terminal screen.

TOPIC B
Navigate Through the Linux Filesystem

Now that you have partitioned your hard disk in a proper and efficient manner, it is time to move around the filesystem. In this topic, you will navigate through the filesystem.

Navigating through the filesystem will allow you to access, create, and delete files and directories. While being able to navigate through the filesystem in the GUI environment may be easier, the CLI will give you more control over the workings of the Linux system.

Filesystem Hierarchy

Linux comprises regular files that include text files, executable files or programs, input for programs, and output from programs. Besides these, the Linux filesystem consists of other types of files.

These file types are described in the following table.

File Type	Description
Directories (d)	Contains the lists of all files.
Special files	Includes system files. These files are in the /dev format. These can be *block special files* (b) or *character special files* (c). Block special files are large files that are used for data storage. Character special files are small files that are used for streaming of data.
Links (l)	Makes a file accessible in multiple parts of the system's file tree.
Domain sockets (s)	Provides inter-process networking that is protected by the filesystem's access control.
Named pipes (p)	Allows processes to communicate with each other, without using network sockets.

The file Command

The `file` command is used to determine the type of file. The syntax of the command is `file [option] {file name}`.

The Filesystem Hierarchy Standard

The *Filesystem Hierarchy Standard (FHS)* is a collaborative document that specifies a set of guidelines for the names of files and directories and their locations. The important advantages of FHS include compatibility between the systems that are FHS compliant and restriction on users changing the /usr partition that contains common executable files.

 The complete documentation of FHS is available at **http://www.pathname.com/fhs/**.

Standard Directories

The Linux operating system comprises directories that enable you to organize user files, drivers, kernels, logs, programs, and utilities, into different categories. In Linux, / represents the `root` directory, which is the topmost directory, and all other directories are subdirectories under it.

Some of the standard root directories are described in the following table.

Directory	Description
/boot	Stores the files necessary to boot the Linux operating system. The /boot partition must be present in the first sector of the hard disk, from which the system boots. For example, the /boot/grub/menu.lst file.
/bin	Stores essential command line utilities and binaries. For example, the /bin/ls file.
/dev	Stores hardware and software device drivers. It maintains filesystem entries that represent the devices connected to the system. For example, the /dev/sda1 driver.
/etc	Stores basic configuration files. For example, the /etc/samba/smb.conf file.
/lib	Stores shared program libraries required by the kernel, command line utilities, and binaries. For example, the /lib/libc.so.6 file.
/sbin	Stores binaries that are used for completing the booting process and also the ones that are used by the root user—the administrator. For example, the /sbin/ifconfig file.
/usr	Stores small programs and files accessible to all users. For example, the /usr/share/doc file.
/var	Stores system log files, printer spools, and some networking services' configuration files. For example, the /var/log/messages file.
/tmp	Stores temporary files. For example, the /tmp/filename.tmp file.

Directory	Description
/opt	Stores files of large software packages. These packages normally create a subdirectory bearing their name under the /opt directory and then place their files in the subdirectory. For example, the /opt/nessus file.
/mnt	Is the mount point for temporarily mounting data from locations such as floppy disks, CDs, DVDs, and network partitions.

/usr Subdirectories

The /usr directory contains some important subdirectories.

Subdirectory	Description
/usr/bin	Includes executable programs that can be executed by all users.
/usr/local	Includes custom build applications that are stored here by default.
/usr/lib	Includes object libraries and internal binaries that are needed by the executable programs.
/usr/lib64	Serves the same purpose as /usr/lib except that it is meant only for 64-bit systems.
/usr/share	Includes read-only architecture independent files. These files can be shared among different architectures of an operating system.

File Naming Conventions

A file name is a string of characters that identify a file. By using the right combination of characters in file names, you can ensure that the files are unique and easy to recognize.

Guidelines

File names can:

- Be in any case, but they are predominantly in lower case.
- Contain any character except the forward slash (/) because it is used to represent the root directory.
- Use alphanumeric characters, underscores, hyphens, and periods.
- Never begin with a hyphen.
- Have spaces between characters, but this is not recommended.

audit_file.txt

Figure 3-9: *A sample file named using the appropriate conventions.*

Example: Naming Files Appropriately

Jim created a text file with some auditing information. He used the naming convention followed in Linux and named the file audit_file.txt. He ensured that all the letters in the file name are in lower case. In addition, the name has an underscore instead of a space.

Creating File Names with Space

You can create file names with spaces between characters by including a backward slash \ along with a space in the file name. For example: `touch Audit\ File.txt` will create a file named Audit File.txt.

File Browsers

In Linux, you can navigate through a filesystem using a file browser. The default file browser on GNOME desktops in Red Hat and Fedora distributions is the Nautilus browser. This browser operates in two modes.

Mode	Description
Spatial	This is the default mode that enables you to open a particular window at exactly the same position on the screen by remembering the last position. Each folder or directory that you select is opened in a new browser window.
Browser	This is the mode that enables you to display the selected folder in the same window. You need to modify the preferences in the **Computer** window.

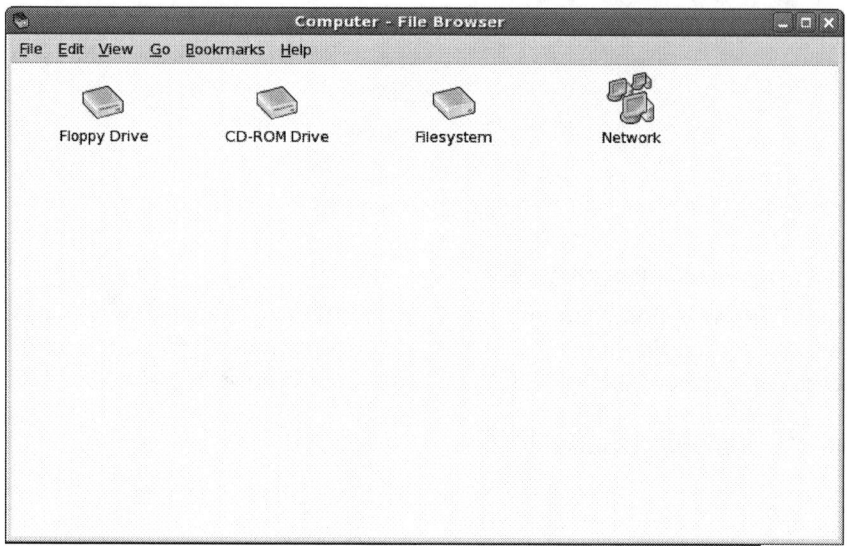

Figure 3-10: *The Nautilus file browser.*

The Home Directory

The *home directory* is where you are placed when you log in to the system. In Linux, by default, every user, except the root user, is assigned a specific directory in /home. In many shells, including Korn, C shell, and Bash, the tilde character (~) represents your home directory. A user can create subdirectories and files within this directory. As soon as the user logs in to the system, control is automatically transferred to the user's home directory. The home directory of the *root user* is **/root**. The root user can access all files and resources on the system.

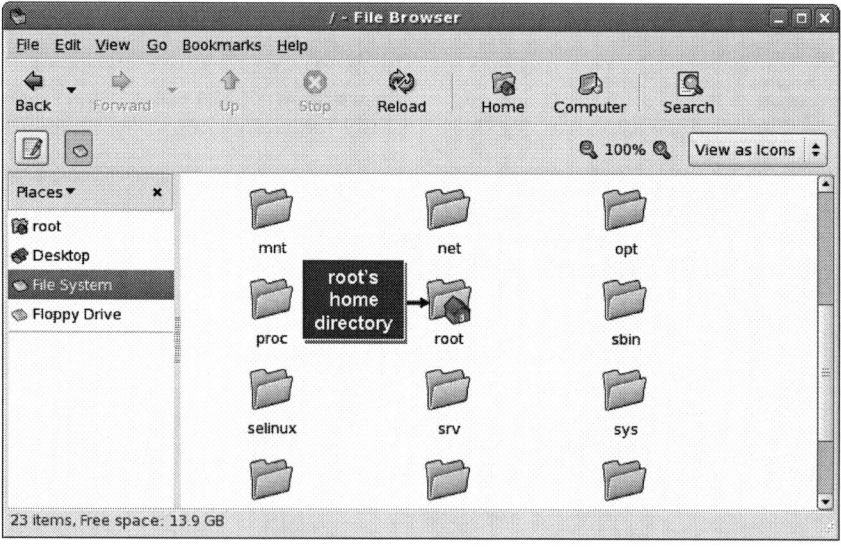

Figure 3-11: *The home directory of the root user.*

The Current Working Directory

The *current working directory* is the location on the system which you are accessing at any point of time. For example, when you log in to a system, you are placed in your home directory. So, your current working directory is your home directory. The current working directory can be listed in shorthand with a period (.).

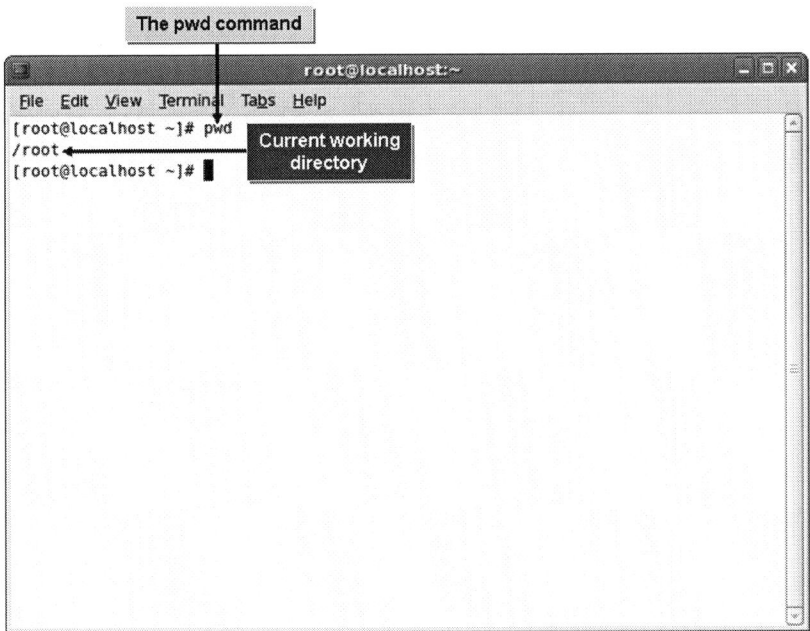

Figure 3-12: Viewing the current working directory using the pwd command.

The pwd Command

When you navigate through a filesystem, you may need to know your current working directory. The *pwd command* displays your current working directory relative to the root directory. It displays the full path name.

The Parent Directory

The *parent directory* is one level above your current working directory. All directories, except the root directory, have a parent directory. You can use the double period notation to switch to the parent directory.

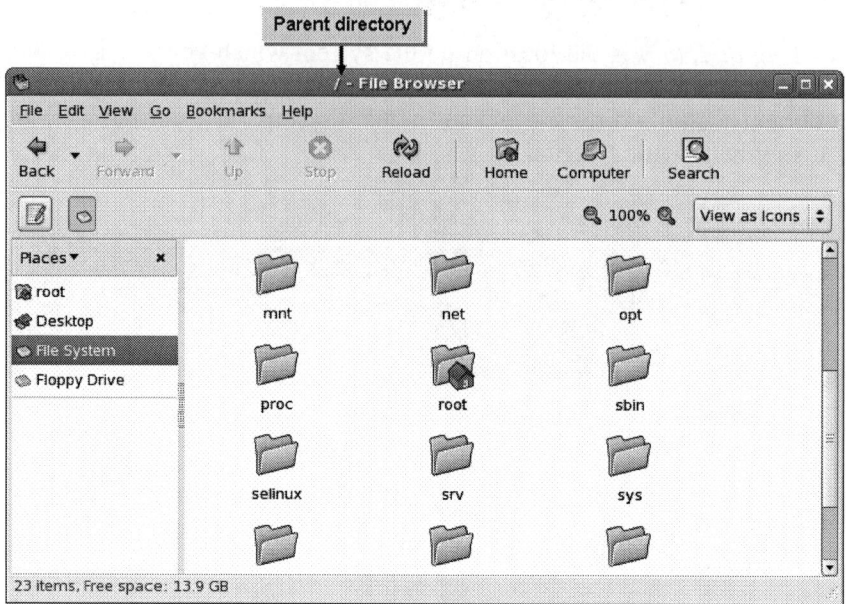

Figure 3-13: The root (/) directory is the parent directory for all other directories.

Paths

Definition:

A *path* specifies a location in the filesystem. It begins with the root directory, the directory at the top of the directory tree, and ends with the directory or file you want to access.

You can refer to a particular file by providing a path to the specific directory that contains the file. For example, the directory jsmith contains a subdirectory work, which contains the file mywork. To refer to that file, use the following path name: `/home/jsmith/work/mywork`. Notice that the forward slash (`/`) character is used to separate items in the path. The slash that precedes jsmith represents the root directory, from which the path to the file mywork begins.

Example:

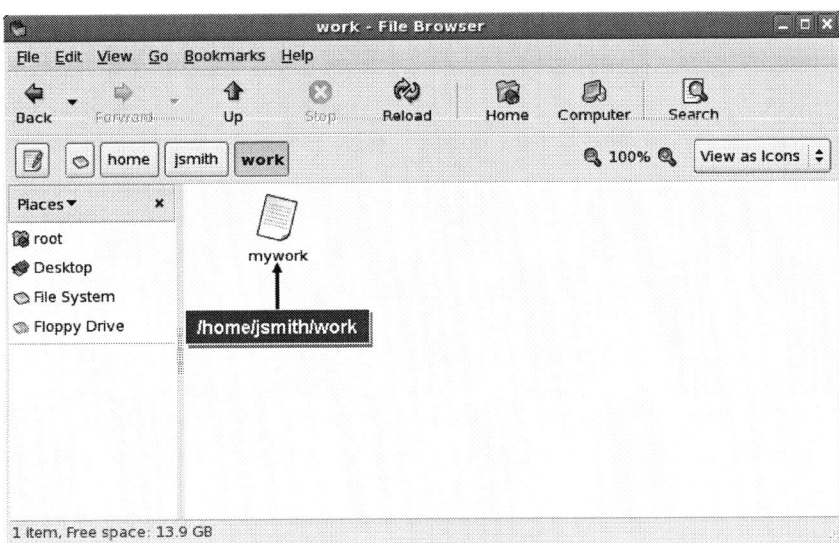

Figure 3-14: The path to the file mywork.

Absolute and Relative Paths

Paths are of two types—absolute and relative. *Absolute paths* refer to the specific location, including the domain name, irrespective of the working directory or combined paths. These paths are usually written with reference to the root directory, and therefore start with a forward slash. Paths that do not begin with a forward slash are called relative paths. A *relative path* is the path relative to the current working directory; therefore, the full absolute path need not be included. These paths can contain the period [.] and double period [. .], which are indications for the current and parent directory.

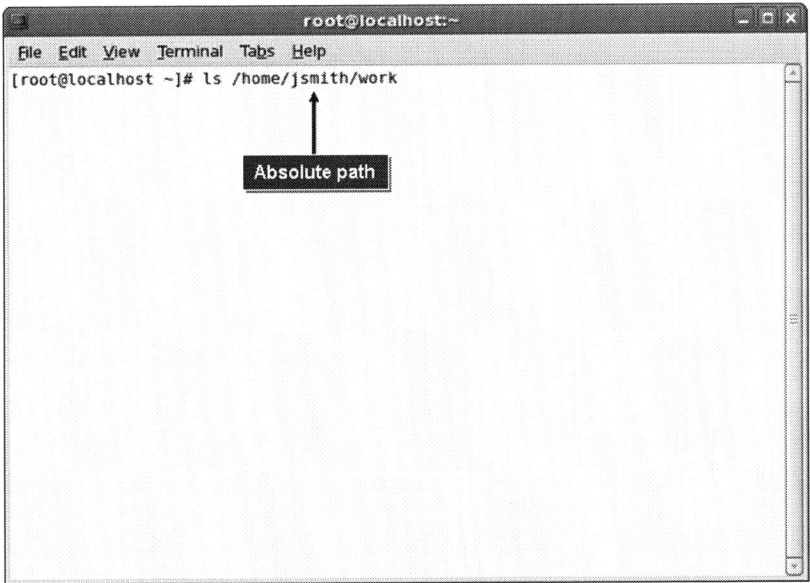

Figure 3-15: Listing files in a directory using the absolute path.

Basic Filesystem Commands

There are some basic filesystem commands that will allow you to modify files and display information within the Linux filesystem.

Command	Enables You To
cd	Traverse the directory structure. There are several ways to specify the path name of the directory you need to switch to. The syntax of the *cd* command is cd *{Absolute or Relative path}*.
ls	List the files in the current working directory. This command displays only the file name when the command is run without any options. However, it can be used to list information such as size, file type, and permissions by running the command with the respective options. The syntax of this command is ls *[command options] [Absolute or Relative path of the directory]*.
mv	Move files and directories from one directory to another, or renames a file or directory. The syntax of this command is mv *{Absolute or Relative path}/{file or directory name} {Absolute or Relative path}/{new file or directory name}*.
cp	Copy a file. The syntax of this command is cp *[command options] {Absolute or Relative path of the file or directory to be copied}/{file or directory name} {Absolute or Relative path of the destination}*.
rm	Delete files or directories. The syntax of this command is rm *[command options] {Absolute or Relative path of file or directory}/{file or directory name}*.
touch	Change the time of access or modification time of a file to the current time. In addition, the touch command creates an empty file if the file name specified as an argument does not exist. The syntax of this command is touch *{file name}*.
mkdir	Create a directory. The syntax of this command is mkdir *{directory name}*.
rmdir	Delete directories. The syntax of this command is rmdir *{directory name}*.
pushd	Add a directory at the top of a stack of directories or rotate a stack of directories. The syntax of this command is pushd *[option] {directory name}*.
popd	Remove entries from a stack of directories. When no option is specified, it removes the top directory from the stack. The syntax of this command is pushd *[option]*.

The -v Option

-v is a command option that can be used with the basic file management commands. This option explains the running of the command to produce the desired output, in a verbose manner.

ls Command Options

The `ls` command options are described in the following table.

Option	Description
-l	Displays a long list including permissions, number of hard links, owner, group, size, date, and file name.
-F	Displays the nature of a file, such as * for an executable file and / for a directory.
-a	Displays all files present in the directory, including the files whose names begin with a period (.).
-R	Recursively displays all subdirectories.
-d	Displays information about symbolic links or directories rather than the link's target or the contents of the directory.
-L	Displays all files in a directory including symbolic links.

Changing the Current Directory

There are times when you need to move out of your home directory into another directory in the filesystem. In such situations, you can use the `cd` command to change directories. The `cd` command enables you to traverse the directory structure. There are several ways to specify the path name to the directory that you wish to make your working directory:

- The `cd` command without a path name takes you to your home directory, irrespective of your current directory.

- The `cd [path name]` command takes you to the path name specified. The path name can be the full path name (from the root down to the specified directory) or the relative path name (starting from your current working directory).

- The `cd ~/[path name]` command takes you to the specified directory, relative to your home directory. (Remember to replace `~/[path name]` with `$HOME`, if necessary.)

How to Navigate Through the Linux Filesystem

Procedure Reference: Change Directories

To change directories:

1. Log in as a user in the CLI.

2. Enter pwd to view the present working directory.

3. Enter cd *{Absolute or Relative path of the target directory}* to change to the target directory.

4. If necessary, enter pwd to verify if you have changed to the target directory.

Procedure Reference: List Files and Directories

To list files and directories:

1. Log in as a user in the CLI.

2. Enter the ls *[command options]* command to list the files and directories.

Procedure Reference: Work with Files and Directories Using the Nautilus Browser in the Spatial Mode

To work with files and directories using the Nautilus browser in the spatial mode:

1. Log in as a user in the GUI.

2. Double-click the **Computer** icon on the desktop.

3. Double-click the desired directory to open it.

4. Double-click the desired file in the directory.

5. Press **Ctrl+Shift+W,** if necessary, to close all parent windows.

6. Click the **Close** button to close the Nautilus browser.

Procedure Reference: Work with Files Using the Nautilus Browser in the Browser Mode

To work with files using the Nautilus browser in the browser mode:

1. Log in as a user in the GUI.

2. From the menu bar, choose **Application→System Tools→File Browser.**

3. Double-click the desired file or directory either in the right pane or in the left pane to view it.

4. Close the Nautilus browser.

Procedure Reference: Set the Nautilus Browser to Open Always in the Browser Mode

To set the Nautilus browser to open always in the browser mode:

1. Log in as user in the GUI.

2. Double-click the **Computer** icon on the desktop.

3. In the **Computer** window, choose **Edit→Preferences.**

4. In the **File Management Preferences** dialog box, select the **Behavior** tab.

5. In the **Behavior** section, check the **Always open in browser windows** check box and click **Close.**

6. Close the **Computer** window.

7. Double-click the **Computer** icon to open the Nautilus browser in the browser mode.

ACTIVITY 3-2
Changing Directories

Before You Begin:
You have logged in as root in the CLI.

Scenario:
You have been hired as a junior administrator in an organization and provided administrative access to your Linux system. However, as the superuser, you do not have a specified directory in /home to work in. You therefore decide to switch to the home directory and work with files.

What You Do	How You Do It
1. Switch from the /root directory to the /home directory.	a. Enter **pwd** to view the current working directory.
	b. Observe that the current working directory is **/root.**
	c. Enter **cd /home** to change to the home directory.
	d. Enter **pwd** to view the current working directory.
	e. Observe that the current working directory is now changed to **/home.**
2. List the files in the directory.	a. Enter **ls -a** to list all the files in the **/home** directory.
	b. Observe the listed files in the directory.
	c. Enter **clear** to clear the terminal screen.

ACTIVITY 3-3
Using the Nautilus Browser to View File and Directory Content

Before You Begin:

1. You have logged in as root in the first terminal.

2. Switch to the GUI.

3. You have logged in as the root user.

4. Close the terminal window.

Scenario:

A new employee needs assistance on basic filesystem navigation and usage in the GUI. You decide to demonstrate the usage of the Nautilus browser by navigating through file content.

What You Do	How You Do It
1. Open directories using the Nautilus browser in the Spatial mode.	a. Double-click the **Computer** icon on the desktop.
	b. In the **Computer** window, double-click the **Filesystem** directory.
	c. Observe that the directory opens in a different window, and view the contents of the directory.
	d. Close the **/** directory window.

2. Set the Nautilus browser to open in the browser mode and view directory content.

a. In the **Computer** window, choose **Edit→ Preferences.**

b. In the **File Management Preferences** dialog box, select the **Behavior** tab to change the behavior of the browser window.

c. In the **Behavior** section, check the **Always open in browser windows** check box and click **Close** to enable the windows to open in browser mode.

d. Close the **Computer** window.

e. Double-click the **Computer** icon on the desktop to verify the changes made.

f. Observe that the Nautilus browser opens in the browser mode.

g. In the left pane, double-click the **File System** directory to view the contents of the **/** directory.

h. Observe the contents of the directory.

i. Close the browser window.

TOPIC C
Manage the Filesystem

Now that you can navigate through the Linux filesystem, it is time to learn how to manage it. In this topic, you will manage the Linux filesystem.

Managing the Linux filesystem will allow you to customize the system to suit your requirements. Also, you will be able to organize files and directories, mount additional drives, and use recordable media for backups or storage.

Filesystem Management Tasks

While managing a filesystem in Linux, you will perform the following tasks:
- Back up files and directories.
- Mount and unmount filesystems.
- And, create swap space on a disk partition.

Burning Discs

While managing your filesystem, you may have to back up some data in discs. Linux allows you to burn CDs and DVDs with GUI-based programs, which guide you through the burning process as well as from the CLI. To burn a disc from the CLI:

1. Create a directory and copy the files you would like to burn.
2. Make an ISO image of the files using the `mkisofs` command.
3. And, burn the CD using the `cdrecord` command.

 You must have a CD or DVD writer installed on your system to be able to burn discs.

ISO Image

An *ISO image* or *disk image* is an archive file format for files that are to be written to optical discs like CDs and DVDs. It is a standard defined by the International Organization for Standardization (ISO) and has a file extension of .iso.

Mount Points

Definition:

A *mount point* is an access point to information stored on a local or remote storage device. The mount point is typically an empty directory on which a filesystem is loaded or mounted, to make the filesystem accessible to users. If the directory already has some contents, they become invisible to the users until the mounted filesystem is unmounted.

 You can use the /etc/fstab file to list the filesystem to be mounted and unmounted when the Linux system boots and shuts down, respectively.

Example:

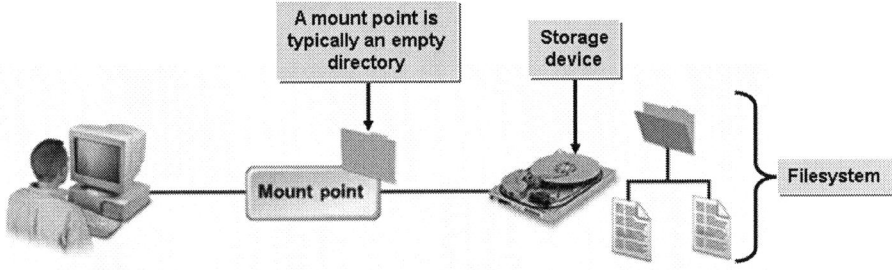

Figure 3-16: The process of mounting a filesystem.

Mount

In Linux, a filesystem cannot be accessed directly. It has to be associated with a directory to make it accessible to users. This association is brought about by loading, or in other terms mounting, the filesystem in a directory by using the `mount` command. After using the filesystem, it needs to be disassociated from the directory by unloading or unmounting the filesystem using the `umount` command.

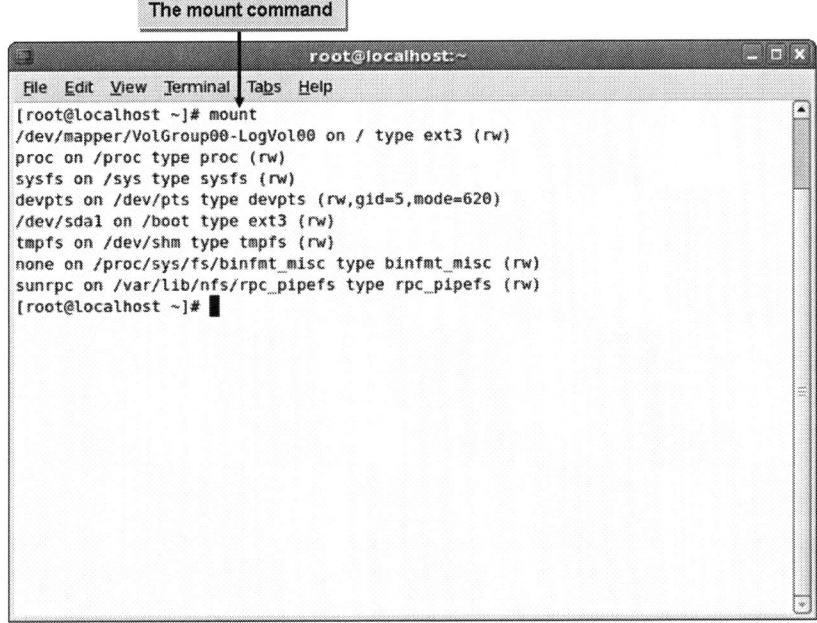

Figure 3-17: A list of currently mounted filesystems.

Mount Options

There are various mount options that you can specify for a filesystem.

Option	Enables You To
auto	Specify that the device has to be mounted automatically.
noauto	Specify that the device need not be mounted automatically.
nouser	Specify that only the root user can mount a device or a filesystem.
user	Specify that all users can mount a device or a filesystem.
exec	Allow *binaries* in a filesystem to be executed.
noexec	Prevent binaries in a filesystem from being executed.
ro	Mount a filesystem as read-only.
rw	Mount a filesystem with read and write permissions.
sync	Specify that input and output operations in a filesystem should be done synchronously.
async	Specify that input and output operations in a filesystem should be done asynchronously.

Binaries

Binaries are source codes that are compiled into executable programs, or are assembled so that they are readable by the computer system. Binaries are encoded so that they can be transmitted over the Internet. In addition, binaries can be pictures, word processing files, or spreadsheet files. Some binaries may contain viruses that can harm the system.

Swap Space

Definition:

Swap space is a partition on the hard disk that is used when the system runs out of physical memory. Linux pushes some of the unused files from the RAM to the swap space to free up memory. Usually, the swap space equals twice the RAM capacity.

Example:

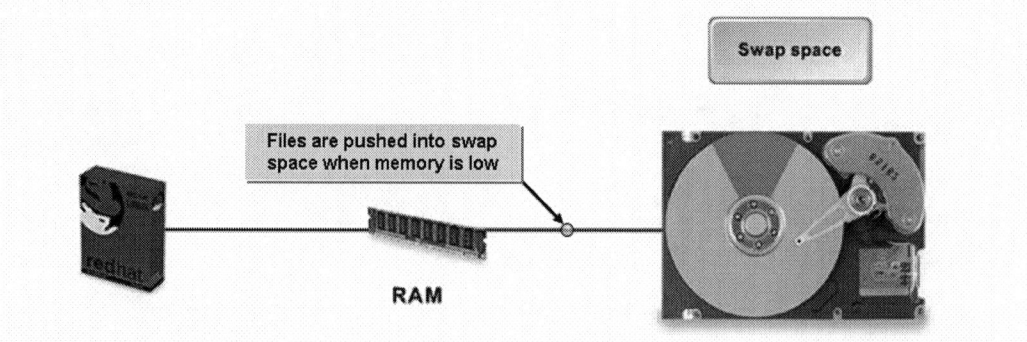

Figure 3-18: Swap space being created on a hard disk.

Swap space is of three types.

Swap Type	Description
Device swap	Device swap space is configured when you partition the hard disk. It is used by the operating system to run large applications.
Filesystem swap	Filesystem swap space is configured primarily when you install Linux. It is utilized by the operating system as an emergency resource when the available swap space runs out.
Pseudo-swap	Pseudo-swap space allows large applications to run on computers with limited RAM.

Swap Files

Swap files are created for storing data that is to be transferred from a system's memory to a disk. It is dynamic and changes in size when data is moved in and out of the memory. It is used as a medium to transfer data from the RAM on to the hard disk.

Swap Partitions

A swap partition is an area of virtual memory on a hard disk to complement the physical RAM in the computer. Swap partitions are created by Linux because they perform better than swap filesystems.

The mkswap Command

The *mkswap command* is a system administration command that is used to create swap space on a disk partition. It provides options to perform various tasks.

Option	Enables You To
-c	Verify that the device is free from bad sectors before mounting the swap space.
-f	Force a swap partition of an area larger than the permissible limit.
-p	Set the page size to be used by the mkswap command.
-L label	Activate the swap space using labels applied to partitions or filesystems.

Syntax

The syntax of the mkswap command is mkswap [option] device {size}. The device argument of mkswap is generally a disk partition, such as /dev/hda2 or /dev/sdb3, but it can also be a file.

Swap Partition Management Commands

A number of commands are used to manage swap partitions. The most important commands are the swapon command and the swapoff command.

Command	Description
swapon command	It is used to activate a swap partition on a specified device. It provides a number of options for specifying devices.
swapoff command	It is used to deactivate the swap space on devices.

The swapon and swapoff Command Options

Some of the frequently used swapon and swapoff command options are given in the following table.

Option	Description
swapon -e	It is used to skip devices that do not exist.
swapon -a	It is used to activate all the swap space.
swapoff -a command	It is used to deactivate all the swap space.

How to Manage the Filesystem

Procedure Reference: Create a Mount Point

To create a mount point:

1. Log in as root.
2. Enter mkdir {mount point} to create a mount point.
3. Enter chown {user name} {mount point} to set the user as the owner of the mount point.
4. Enter chgrp {group name} {mount point} to set the group as the owner of the mount point.

The chgrp Command

The chgrp command is used to change the group ownership of one or more files or directories.

Procedure Reference: Mount a Filesystem

To mount a filesystem:

1. Log in as root in the CLI.
2. Enter mount [command options] /dev/{device name}{Partition number} {mount point} to mount the specified device on the specified mount point.
3. Enter mount {mount point} to verify that the filesystem is mounted on the specified mount point.

Procedure Reference: Mount Filesystems at Startup

To mount filesystems at startup:

1. Log in as root in the CLI.

2. Enter `vi /etc/fstab` to open the /etc/fstab file.

3. Type `* {device or partition name} {mount point} {filesystem type} {mount options} {dump options} {fsck options}` to add an entry for the new filesystem.

4. Save and close the file.

5. Reboot the system to mount the filesystem automatically, or enter `mount -a` to reload the mount table with recent changes from the /etc/fstab file.

6. Verify that the filesystem has been automatically mounted at startup.

    a. Log in as root.

    b. Enter `mount` to mount all filesystems.

Procedure Reference: Unmount a Filesystem

To unmount a filesystem:

1. Log in as root in the CLI.

2. Unmount a filesystem.

    ● Enter `umount [command option] /dev/{device name}{Partition number}` to unmount the filesystem.

    ● Or, enter `umount [command option] {mount point}` to unmount the filesystem.

Procedure Reference: Manage Filesystems

To manage filesystem:

1. Log in as root in the CLI.

2. Enter `fuser {mount point}` to display the details about the processes using the filesystem.

3. Enter `fuser -km {mount point}` to kill all processes using the filesystem.

4. Enter `umount {mount point}` to unmount the filesystem.

 The filesystem cannot be unmounted while it is being used by another process.

Procedure Reference: Manage Swap Partitions

To manage swap partitions:

1. Log in as root in the CLI.

2. Enter `mkswap /dev/{device name}{Partition number}` to create a swap partition.

3. Type `/dev/{device name}{Partition number} swap swap {mount options} {dump options} {fsck options}` to add the partition entry to the /etc/fstab file.

4. Enter

    `swapon {device name}`

    to activate the swap partition.

5. Enter

    `swapoff {device name}`

    to deactivate the swap partition and convert it into a standard Linux filesystem.

Procedure Reference: Format a Partition with a Filesystem

To format a partition with a filesystem:

1. Log in as root in the CLI.
2. Format a partition with a filesystem.

    ● Enter `mkfs -t {filesystem type} /dev/{device name}{Partition number}` to create the specified filesystem on the specified partition of the device.

    ● Or, enter `mke2fs [command options] /dev/{device name}{Partition number}` to create an ext2 filesystem on the specified partition of the device.

ACTIVITY 3-4
Mounting Filesystems

Before You Begin:

1. You have logged in as root in the GUI.

2. Switch to the CLI.

3. At the command line, enter `useradd netadmin2` to create the user netadmin2.

4. Enter `passwd netadmin2` to set the password for netadmin2.

5. At the **New UNIX password** prompt, enter *myp@$$w0rd* to set the password for netadmin2.

6. Confirm the password by retyping the same password at the prompt.

7. Enter `umount /dev/sdb5` to unmount the /dev/sdb5 partition.

8. Enter `umount /dev/sdb6` to unmount the /dev/sdb6 partition.

9. Enter `cd /root` to change to the root directory.

10. Enter `clear` to clear the terminal screen.

Scenario:

There is a meeting at your office. A couple of users want to have their systems moved to the conference room so that they can access their files during the conference. You find that there are multiple systems to be moved, and this will take a lot of time. Therefore, you decide to take the required files from the users and load them on the system in the conference room in separate partitions, so that the users can access their files.

Use the following user and partition details to mount the filesystems:

● User name: netadmin1, Partition size: 1 GB, Mount point: /admin1, User and group owner of /admin1: netadmin1

● User name: netadmin2, Partition size: 1 GB, Mount point: /admin2, User and group owner of /admin2: netadmin2

What You Do	How You Do It
1. Create mount points for users.	**a.** Enter **mkdir /admin1**
	b. Enter **chown netadmin1 /admin1** to set the **netadmin1** user as the owner of /admin1 mount point.
	c. Enter **chgrp netadmin1 /admin1** to set the **netadmin1** group as the owner of /admin1 mount point.
	d. Create a mount point, /admin2, and assign user ownership and group ownership to netadmin2 by following the steps from (a) to (c).
	e. Enter **clear** to clear the terminal screen.
2. Mount and verify the filesystem.	**a.** Enter **mount -a /dev/sdb5 /admin1** to mount the filesystem for netadmin1.
	b. Enter **mount**
	c. Observe that the line **/dev/sdb5 on /admin1 type ext2 (rw)** is displayed, indicating that the filesystem is mounted.
	d. Enter **mount -a /dev/sdb6 /admin2** to mount the filesystem for netadmin1.
	e. Enter **mount**
	f. Observe that the line **/dev/sdb6 on /admin2 type ext2 (rw)** is displayed, indicating that the filesystem is mounted.
3. Create an entry in the fstab file to mount the /dev/sdb5 and /dev/sdb6 filesystems when the system boots.	**a.** Enter **vi /etc/fstab** to open the fstab file.
	b. Press **Shift+G** to go to the last line.
	c. Press **O** to switch a new line in the insert mode.

 The insert mode allows you to insert text by typing.

d. Type **/dev/sdb5 /admin1 ext2 defaults 0 0** and press **Enter** to mount the /dev/sdb5 filesystem when the system boots.

e. Type **/dev/sdb6 /admin2 ext2 defaults 0 0** to mount the /dev/sdb6 filesystem when the system boots.

f. Press **Esc.**

g. Save and close the file.

h. Enter **clear** to clear the terminal screen.

i. Enter **mount -a** to update the fstab file.

4. Check that the specified filesystem mounts when the system boots.

a. Enter **reboot** to reboot the system.

b. Press **Ctrl+Alt+F1** to switch to the CLI.

c. Log in as **root** in the CLI of the Linux system.

d. Enter **mount** to verify that the filesystems are mounted at the specified mount points on boot.

e. Observe that the partitions **/dev/sdb5** and **/dev/sdb6** are mounted into the **/admin1** and **/admin2** directories, respectively.

f. Enter **clear** to clear the terminal screen.

TOPIC D
Maintain the Filesystem

After managing a Linux filesystem, it is important to learn how to keep it up and running. In this topic, you will maintain the Linux filesystem.

Maintaining the Linux filesystem will assist you in troubleshooting and general maintenance of your system. If a power outage or other unplanned shutdown occurs, you will need to know how to verify the data integrity of your local drives.

Filesystem Maintenance Tasks

Maintaining a filesystem in Linux, involves the following tasks:

- Checking the integrity of the filesystem.
- Managing the size of partitions.
- Removing temporary files.
- And, performing system recovery.

Local Storage Devices

There are different types of storage devices in Linux. Each device has a particular use associated with it.

Device	Description
Hard disk	An internal device that can store large amounts of data. It can be accessed quickly.
Floppy drive	A removable medium that can store smaller amounts of data. It cannot be accessed as quickly as a hard disk.
Tape drive	A device that is used to store large amounts of data on a magnetic tape. Tape drives can be internal or external. External tape drives are portable, whereas in internal tape drives only the tape is removable. Data is accessed sequentially in a tape drive.
USB drive	A small, portable, storage device that is used to store files that need to be carried around.
CD-R(W)	A removable optical disc that stores 650-700 MB of data. It can be accessed faster than other removable storage media.
DVD-R(W)	A removable optical disc that stores 4.5 GB (or more) of data. It can be accessed faster than other removable storage media.

Journaling Filesystems

A *journaling filesystem* is a method that is used by an operating system to quickly recover after an unexpected interruption, such as a system crash. Journaling filesystems can remove the need for a filesystem check when the system boots. By using journaling filesystems, the system does not write modified files directly on the disk. Instead, a journal is maintained on the disk. The journaling filesystem process involves the following phases:

1. The journal describes all the changes that must be made to the disk.

2. A background process makes each change as and when it is entered in the journal.

3. If the system shuts down, pending changes are performed when it is rebooted.

4. Incomplete entries in the journal are discarded.

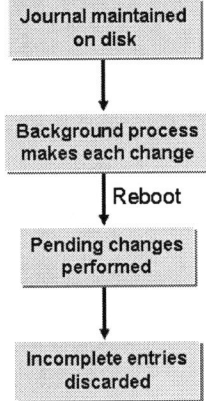

Figure 3-19: Stages in the journaling process.

Performance Issues with Journaling

A journaled filesystem works well with small files and small drives. With the growth of file and drive sizes, performance will suffer. Some of the reasons for poor performance include:

● Filesystem recovery time after a power failure or improper shutdown.

● Bitmap method of tracking the filesystem.

● Wasted space and fragmentation.

The fsck Command

The *fsck command* is used to check the integrity of a filesystem. *Filesystem integrity* refers to the correctness and validity of a filesystem. Most systems automatically run the fsck command at boot time so that errors, if any, are detected and corrected before the system is used. Filesystem errors are usually caused by power failures, hardware failures, or improper shutdown of the system.

The fsck command
executed in the single-user mode

```
Telling INIT to go to single user mode.
INIT: Going single user
INIT: Sending processes the TERM signal
INIT: Sending processes the KILL signal
sh-3.2# fsck /dev/sda1
fsck 1.39 (29-May-2006)
e2fsck 1.39 (29-May-2006)
/dev/sda1 is mounted.

WARNING!!!  Running e2fsck on a mounted filesystem may cause
SEVERE filesystem damage.

Do you really want to continue (y/n)? yes

/boot: recovering journal
/boot: clean, 33/26104 files, 15271/104388 blocks
sh-3.2# _
```

No errors in
the filesystem

Figure 3-20: Checking the integrity of a filesystem from the single user mode.

Syntax

The syntax of the `fsck` command is `fsck -t {filesystem type} [options].`

Repair Filesystems

You can use the `fsck -r /dev/{filesystem}` command to repair a filesystem. The command will prompt you to confirm your actions. If you are simultaneously checking multiple filesystems, you should not use this option because it allows you to repair only a single filesystem at a time.

The tune2fs Utility

The *tune2fs utility* helps tuning parameters associated with a Linux filesystem. Using this utility, a journal can be added to an existing ext2 or ext3 filesystem. If the filesystem is already mounted, the journal will be visible in the root directory of the filesystem. If the filesystem is not mounted, the journal will be hidden. The `tune2fs` utility is available with most Linux distributions.

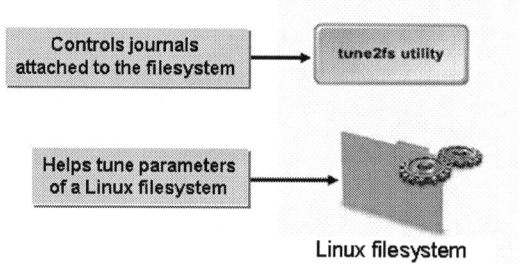

Figure 3-21: The tune2fs command is used to manage filesystems.

Syntax

The syntax of the `tune2fs` command is `tune2fs [options] {device name}`.

The dumpe2fs Utility

The *dumpe2fs utility* is primarily used for managing an ext2-based filesystem. It dumps the status of the ext2 filesystem on to the standard output device and prints the block group information for the selected device.

The `dumpe2fs` utility has various options.

Option	Enables You To
-x	Print a detailed report about block numbers in the filesystem.
-b	Print the bad blocks in the filesystem.
-f	Force the utility to display the filesystem status irrespective of the filesystem flags.
-i	Display filesystem data from an image file created using the `e2image` utility.

Syntax

The syntax of the `dumpe2fs` command is `dumpe2fs [options] {block size} {device name}`.

How to Maintain the Filesystem

Procedure Reference: Configure ext2 Filesystems

To configure ext2 filesystems:

1. If you already have a mounted drive with an existing filesystem:
    a. Back up all data on the drive to removable media or another drive.
    b. Unmount the drive using the `umount` command.
    c. Configure the ext2 filesystem using the `mkfs -t` command.
2. If you have an empty drive:
    a. Configure the ext2 filesystem using the `mkfs -t` command.
3. Mount the drive using the `mount` command.
4. Update the /etc/fstab file to reflect the changes that were done to the filesystem.

Procedure Reference: Configure ext3 Filesystems

To configure ext3 filesystems:

1. If you have a drive with the ext2 filesystem:
    a. Unmount the drive using the `umount` command.
    b. Convert the filesystem using the `tune2fs -j <partition>` command.

2. If you already have a mounted drive with an existing filesystem other than ext2:

    a. Back up all data on the drive to removable media or another drive.

    b. Unmount the drive using the `umount` command.

    c. Configure the ext3 filesystem using the `mkfs -t` command.

    d. Mount the drive using the `mount` command.

3. If you have an empty drive:

    a. Configure the ext3 filesystem using the `mkfs -t` command.

    b. Mount the drive using the `mount` command.

4. Update the /etc/fstab file to reflect the changes that were done to the filesystem.

Procedure Reference: Configure reiserfs Filesystems

To configure reiserfs filesystems:

1. Verify that you have a kernel version later than 2.4.16.

2. If you already have a mounted drive with an existing filesystem:

    a. Back up all data on the drive to removable media or another drive.

    b. Unmount the drive using the `umount` command.

    c. Configure the reiserfs filesystem using the `mkreiserfs` command.

    d. Mount the drive using the `mount` command.

    e. Update the /etc/fstab file to reflect the changes that were done to the filesystem.

3. If you have an empty drive:

    a. Configure the reiserfs filesystem using the `mkfs -t reiserfs` command.

    b. Mount the drive using the `mount` command.

    c. Add the drive to the /etc/fstab file.

Procedure Reference: Manage Local Filesystems

To manage local filesystems:

1. Switch to the single-user mode.

2. Check the filesystem using the `fsck` command.

3. Return to the multiuser mode after the check is complete.

ACTIVITY 3-5

Maintaining the Linux Filesystem

Before You Begin:

1. You have logged in as root in the CLI.

2. Enter `telinit 3` to switch to runlevel 3.

3. Press **Enter** to continue in the new runlevel.

4. Enter `clear` to clear the terminal screen.

Scenario:

Due to a thunderstorm, there was a brief power outage overnight and the Linux systems were not shutdown properly. The systems need to be checked for consistency. Using the `fsck` command, verify the drive and data integrity of the hard disk.

What You Do	How You Do It
1. Run the `fsck` command on the local filesystem.	a. Enter **telinit 1** to switch to single-user mode.
	b. Enter **fsck /dev/sdb1**
	c. At the warning prompt, press **Y** and then press **Enter.**
	d. Observe that the message displays "clean", which indicates that there is no error in the filesystem.
	e. Enter **telinit 3** to switch to runlevel 3.

2. At which runlevel can you perform disk maintenance without damaging the disks?

    a) Runlevel 0

    b) Runlevel 1

    c) Runlevel 3

    d) Runlevel 5

3. True or False? You can run the e2fsck command to perform a disk check on a mounted filesystem.

    ___ True

    ___ False

ACTIVITY 3-6

Configuring the ext3 filesystem

Before You Begin:

1. The Linux system is running in runlevel 3.
2. Log in as root.
3. Enter `telinit 5` to switch to the GUI.
4. Switch to the first CLI terminal.
5. Press **Enter** to continue.
6. Enter `clear` to clear the terminal screen.

Scenario:

Two users complain that they lost data due to improper shutdown of the system. You run the disk check utility and verify that the disk is not corrupt. Further, you decide to convert the existing filesystem to a journaling filesystem to ensure that data will not be lost even if the system is accidentally turned off.

What You Do	How You Do It
1. Unmount the /dev/sdb5 and /dev/sdb6 partitions.	a. Enter **mount** to view the mounted partitions.
	b. Observe that the two partitions, **/dev/sdb5** and **/dev/sdb6,** are mounted automatically.
	c. Enter **umount /dev/sdb5** to unmount the /dev/sdb5 partition.
	d. Enter **umount /dev/sdb6** to unmount the /dev/sdb6 partition.
	e. Enter **mount** to view the mounted partitions.
	f. Observe that the two partitions, /dev/sdb5 and /dev/sdb6, are not listed indicating that they have been unmounted.

2.	Convert the **/dev/sdb5** and **/dev/sdb6** partitions to the ext3 filesystem.	a.	Enter `tune2fs -j /dev/sdb5` to convert the partition to the ext3 filesystem.
		b.	Observe the details displayed during the conversion of the filesystem.
		c.	Enter `tune2fs -j /dev/sdb6` to convert the partition to the ext3 filesystem.
		d.	Observe the details displayed during the conversion of the filesystem.
		e.	Enter `clear` to clear the terminal screen.
3.	Verify that the two new partitions have the ext3 filesystem.	a.	Enter `parted` to start the **GNU Parted** utility.
		b.	Enter `select /dev/sdb` to select the /dev/sdb partition.
		c.	At the **(parted)** prompt, enter `print` to view the list of existing partitions.
		d.	Observe that the partitions 5 and 6 have the **ext3** filesystem.
		e.	Enter *q* to quit from the parted utility.
		f.	Enter `clear` to clear the terminal screen.

4. Modify the partition entries in the fstab file to mount the ext3 filesystems on when the system boots.

a. Enter **vi /etc/fstab** to open the fstab file.

b. Navigate to the line containing the "/dev/sdb5" entry and place the cursor on the number 2 in "ext2."

c. Press **I** to switch to the insert mode.

d. Type **3** and press **Delete.**

e. Press the **Down Arrow** key and the **Left Arrow** key to navigate to the line containing the "/dev/sdb6" entry and place the cursor after the number 2 in "ext2."

f. Type **3** and press **Delete.**

g. Press **Esc.**

h. Save and close the file.

i. Enter **clear** to clear the terminal screen.

j. Enter **mount -a** to update fstab entries.

k. Enter **reboot** to reboot the system.

5. Check that the specified filesystem mounts when the system boots.

a. Press **Ctrl+Alt+F1** to switch to the CLI.

b. Log in as **root** in the CLI of the Linux system.

c. Enter **mount** to view the mounted partitions.

d. Observe that the two partitions, /dev/sdb5 and /dev/sdb6, have ext3 as the filesystem.

e. Enter **clear** to clear the terminal screen.

OPTIONAL ACTIVITY 3-7

Formatting and Creating a Filesystem on a Floppy Disk

Scenario:
A user wanted to transfer files from one system to another, without getting into the hassle of setting up network shares and sending the data over the network. You decide to show the user how to format a floppy disk to transfer the files.

What You Do	How You Do It
1. Determine the size of the floppy disk and the correct `fdformat` command to use.	a. Enter **man fdformat**
	b. Find the **fd0h1440** entry.
2. Format the floppy disk.	a. Insert a blank floppy disk in the floppy disk drive.
	b. Enter **fdformat /media/floppy** to format the floppy disk.
3. Create a filesystem on the floppy disk.	a. Enter **mkfs /media/floppy**
	b. Enter **mount /media/floppy** to mount the floppy disk.
	c. Enter **ls /media/floppy** to verify that the filesystem was created.
	d. Verify that there is a lost+found directory listed.

Lesson 3 Follow-up

In this lesson, you created partitions and filesystems on the hard disk. Knowledge of the filesystem structure assists you in navigating, managing, and maintaining filesystems efficiently.

1.   **When do you think formatting a partition is necessary? Why?**

2.   **Is the ext3 filesystem better that the ext2 filesystem? How?**

4 Managing Files in Linux

Lesson Time: 2 hour(s), 15 minutes

Lesson Objectives:

In this lesson, you will manage various files in Linux.

You will:

● Create a text file in Linux.

● Locate files within the Linux filesystem.

● Manage links to a file.

● Back up files and restore files.

● Manage database using MySQL.

Introduction

You have a basic understanding of the Linux filesystem. Now, it is time to learn how to manipulate the files and directories within Linux. In this lesson, you will manage various types of Linux files.

As a Linux administrator, you should keep your files well organized on your system. Learning how to create, edit, locate, link, back up, and restore files will help you tailor the system to your needs.

This lesson covers all or part of the following CompTIA Linux+ (2009) certification objectives:

● Topic A
  ■ Objective 2.1
● Topic B
  ■ Objective 2.1
  ■ Objective 2.3
● Topic C
  ■ Objective 2.1
● Topic D
  ■ Objective 1.8
  ■ Objective 2.4
● Topic E
  ■ Objective 3.7

TOPIC A
Create and Edit Files

You have a good understanding of the Linux filesystem types. Now, you can move on to creating and editing files. In this topic, you will create and edit files.

Working with text files is a basic and routine task for most users. Consider a scenario where you may need to submit a report on your current project. You will require an application, such as a text editor, to create the report. The text editor will allow you to create and edit text files with ease. You can also use a text editor to create and edit configuration files, which will allow you to customize your system.

Text Editors

Definition:

A *text editor* is an application that allows you to view, create, or modify the contents of text files. It was originally created to write programs, but is now being used even to edit ordinary text files. Text editors work on different modes such as the command mode and the insert mode. There are various types of text editors that are compatible with Linux such as Vim, gedit, and nano. However, text editors do not always support the formatting options that word processors provide. Text editors may work either in the CLI or GUI.

Example:

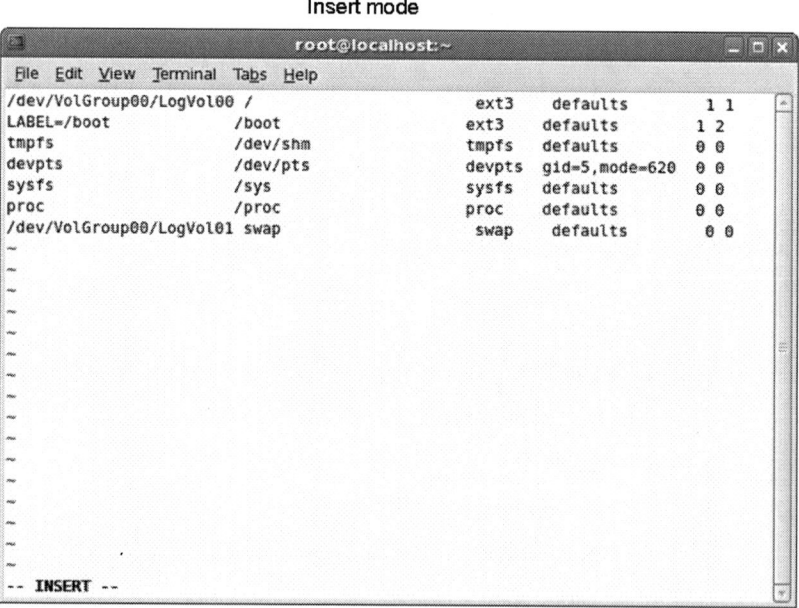

Figure 4-1: The Vim text editor in the insert mode.

Command mode

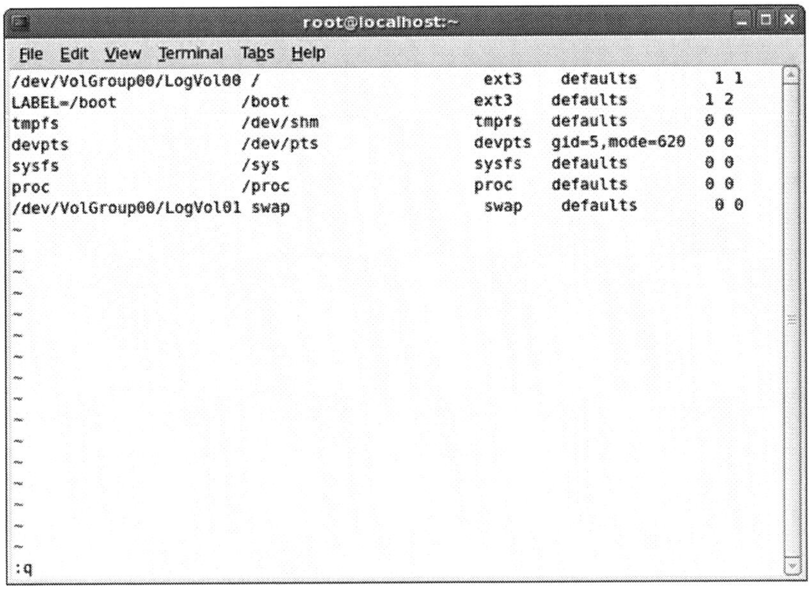

Figure 4-2: *The Vim text editor in the command mode.*

List of Text Editors

There are many text editors that are compatible with Linux.

Text Editor	Description
Vim	The *Vi* IMproved, or VIM, text editor is the default text editor in Linux. It is widely used in programming and for processing simple text files. It is a powerful editor that optimizes speed by employing simple keystrokes to perform complex text editing.
Emacs	A flexible, powerful, and popular text editor used in Linux and Unix. It offers numerous features such as content-sensitive editing modes and support for various languages. It can be easily customized.
Gvim	The graphical version of the Vim editor.
KWrite	A flexible GUI-based text editor used in KDE.
gedit	A simple yet powerful GUI-based text editor used in the GNOME desktop.
nano	A small, user-friendly text editor that evolved from the Pico text editor.

Emacs

Emacs is derived from "Editor MACroS". It was written by Richard Stallman.

KDE

KDE is an alternative GUI desktop for Linux. It provides basic desktop functions, applications, tools, and documentation for developers to write applications for the system.

The vim Command

The `vim` command invokes the Vim editor. However, the `vi` command may also be used for this purpose because it automatically redirects the user to Vim. When entered without a file name as an argument, the `vim` command opens a welcome screen by default. To open a file, the syntax `vim` *file name* is used. If the file does not exist, Vim creates a file by the name specified and opens the file for editing. Vim supports multiple files being opened simultaneously.

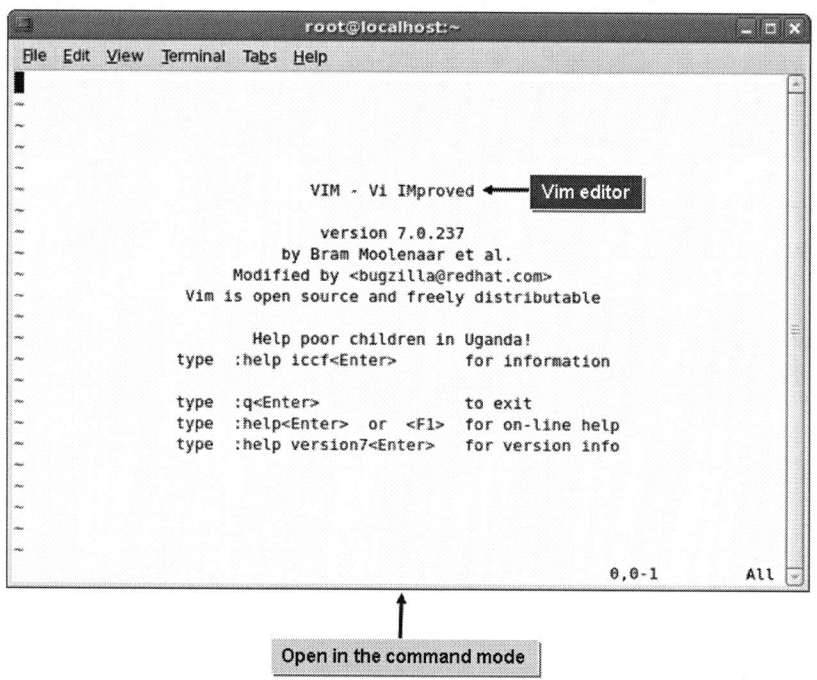

Figure 4-3: *The introductory screen of Vim.*

Vim Modes

Vim is a modal editor and its different modes decide the functionality of various keys.

Some of the common modes in Vim are listed here.

Mode	Description
Insert	Allows users to insert text by typing.
Execute	Allows users to execute commands within the editor.
Command	Allows users to perform different editing actions using single keystrokes.
Visual	Allows users to highlight or select text for copying, deleting, and so on.

Switch Modes

You can switch between the different modes of Vim. The command mode is the default mode of Vim. You can switch from the command mode to any other mode by using a single keystroke.

Some of the keys to switch modes are listed here.

Key	Function
i	Switches to the insert mode and inserts text to the left of the cursor.
A	Switches to the insert mode and adds text at the end of a line.
I	Switches to the insert mode and inserts text at the beginning of a line.
o	Switches to the insert mode and inserts text on a new line below the cursor.
O	Switches to the insert mode and inserts text on a new line above the cursor.
v	Switches to the visual mode to enable selection, one character at a time.
V	Switches to the visual mode to enable selection, one line at a time.
:	Switches to the execute mode to enable users to enter commands.
Esc	Returns to the command mode.

The Execute Mode Commands

In the command mode, when the : operator is entered, a small command prompt section appears at the bottom-left of the editor. This indicates that the user is in the execute mode and can run commands supported by Vim.

Some commands supported by Vim are listed below.

Command	Function
`:w file name`	Saves a file with a file name if it is being saved for the first time.
`:q`	Quits when no changes have been made after the last save.
`:q!`	Quits ignoring the changes made.
`:qa`	Quits multiple files.
`:wq`	Saves the current file and exits.
`:!{any Linux command}`	Executes the command and gets the result in the Vi interface.

The Vim Help Options

A major source of built-in documentation for Vim can be accessed using the `:help` command. To find topic-specific help, you can add the necessary topic as an argument. To quit the help manual, you can use `:q`. The `vimtutor` command helps first time users learn the basics of Vim by allowing them to practice Vim commands and shortcuts.

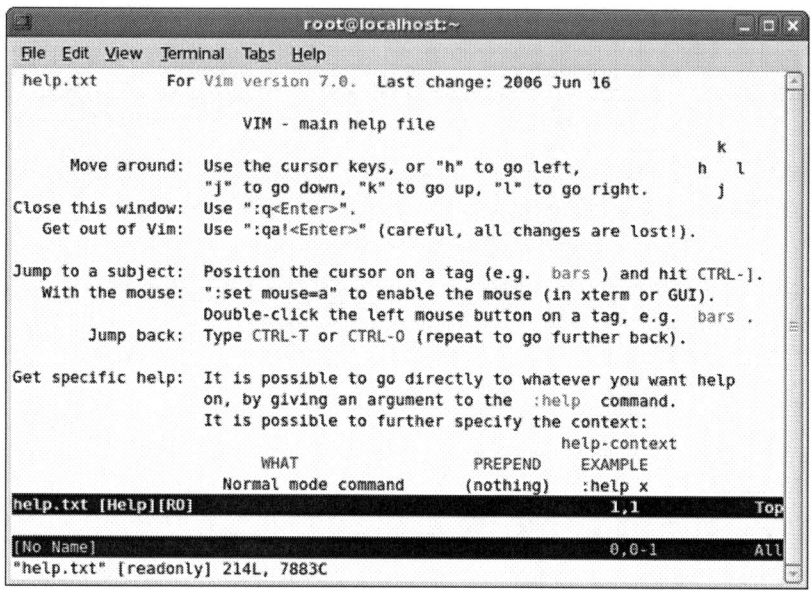

Figure 4-4: *Viewing the help file using the Vim text editor.*

Motions

Motions are single-key shortcuts that are used to navigate through files in the command mode. These keys position the cursor anywhere within a document. They can be used for moving the cursor through characters, words, lines, or even huge blocks of text.

Navigation Key	Used To
H	Move left one character.
J	Move down one line.
K	Move up one line.
L	Move right one character.
^	Move to the beginning of the current line.
$	Move to the end of the current line.
W	Move to the next word.
B	Move to the previous word.
E	Move to the end of the current word or to the end of the next word if you are already at the end of the word.
Shift+L	Move the cursor to the bottom of the screen.
Shift+H	Move the cursor to the first line of the screen.

Navigation Key	Used To
(Line number) Shift+G	Move the cursor to the specified line number.
GG	Move the cursor to the first line of the file.
Shift+G	Move the cursor to the last line of the file.

Navigation Using the Arrow Keys

In addition to using the **K, J, H,** and **L** keys to navigate through the editor, you can also use the **Up, Down, Left,** and **Right Arrow** keys. The conventional navigation keys such as **Home, End, Page Up,** and **Page Down** also work in Vim.

Editing Operators

Editing operators in the command mode are powerful tools that can be used to manipulate text with simple keystrokes. They can also be used in combination with motions to edit multiple characters.

Some of the frequently used editing operators are listed here.

Editing Operator	Used To
x	Delete the character selected by the cursor.
d	Delete text.
dd	Delete the current line.
p	Paste text on the line directly below the cursor.
P	Paste text on the line directly above the cursor.
/[text string]	Search through the document for a specific text.
y	Yank or copy text.
yy	Copy the line directly above the cursor.
c[range of lines]c	Begin a change in the specified range.
u	Undo the latest change.
U	Undo all changes in the current line.

 In case any editing was undone by mistake, you can press **Ctrl+R** to redo the latest undone changes.

Case Sensitivity

Most Vim options are case sensitive. For example, the p option pastes text you cut on the line directly below the cursor, whereas the P option pastes text you cut on the line directly above the cursor.

Counts

A *count* is a number that multiplies the effect of keystrokes in Vim. It can be used in combination with motions or operators or both. When used with a motion, cursor movement is multiplied according to the count specified. When used with editing operators, the action gets repeated the number of times specified.

Syntax

If count, motions, and operators are used together their syntax is `operator [count] {motion}`. This makes the cursor move and perform the action as many times as specified by the count.

The diff Command

The *diff command* is used to compare individual text files or contents of directories. The command displays the two files and the differences between them.

The `diff` command has various options that allow you to specify the nature of the output.

Option	Description
-b	Ignores spacing differences.
-i	Ignores case differences.
-t	Expands tab characters in output lines.
-w	Ignores spacing differences and tabs.
-c	Displays a list of differences with three lines of context. The output displays the identification of the files involved and their creation dates, and each change is separated by a line with a dozen * 's. The lines that are removed from file1 are marked with '–'; those that are added to file2 are marked with '+'. Lines that are shifted from one file to the other are marked in both the files with '!'.

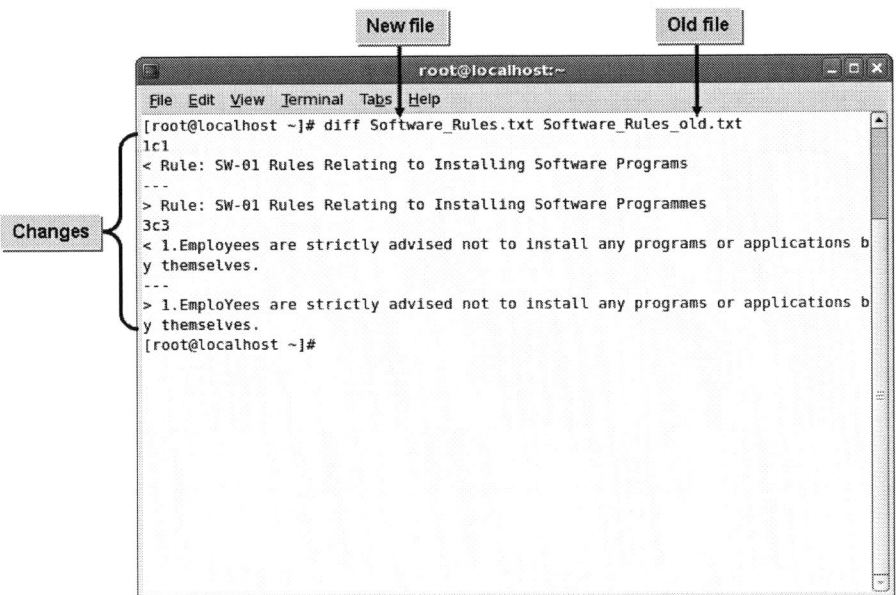

Figure 4-5: *Comparing two versions of the same document with the diff command to track changes.*

Syntax

The syntax of the `diff` command is `diff {file name 1} {file name 2}`.

The patch Command

The *patch command* updates text files with changes according to instructions contained in a patch file. This patch file contains listings produced by the `diff` command.

The wc Command

The *word count command (wc)* is used to count the number of lines, words, and characters of text files. If multiple files are specified, then the command displays the count for each file and the total count for all files.

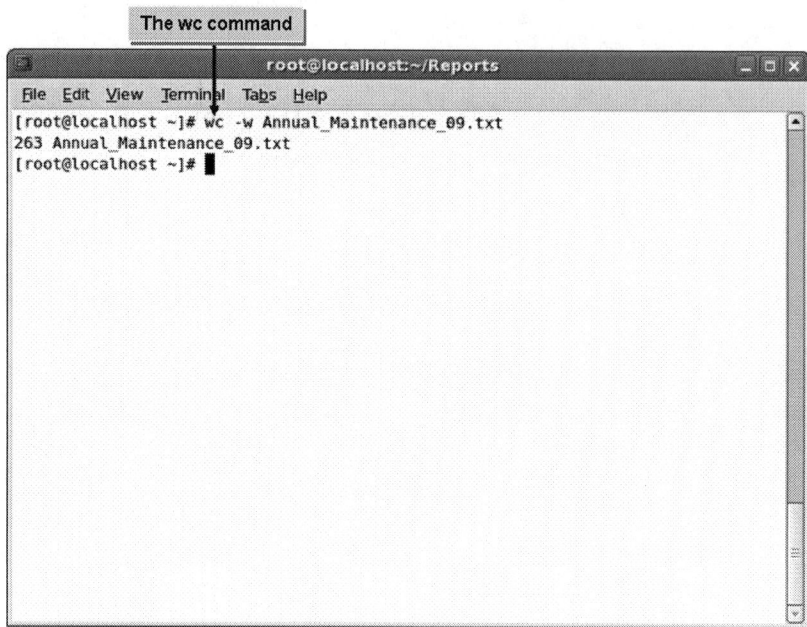

Figure 4-6: Counting words using the wc command.

The `wc` command provides various options that allow you to specify the nature of the output.

Option	Description
-c	Displays the byte count.
-m	Displays the character count.
-l	Displays the newline count.
-w	Displays the word count.

Syntax

The syntax of the `wc` command is `wc [command options] {file name}`.

Aspell

Aspell is a utility that functions as a spell checker in Linux. The syntax of the `aspell` command is `aspell [options]`. The `-c` option checks the file for incorrect spellings. The `-list` option produces a list of misspelled words from the standard input.

The tr Command

The *translate command (tr)* is used to translate strings from the standard input to the standard output. It is predominantly used to change the case of letters. This command acts only on a stream of characters and does not accept file names as arguments.

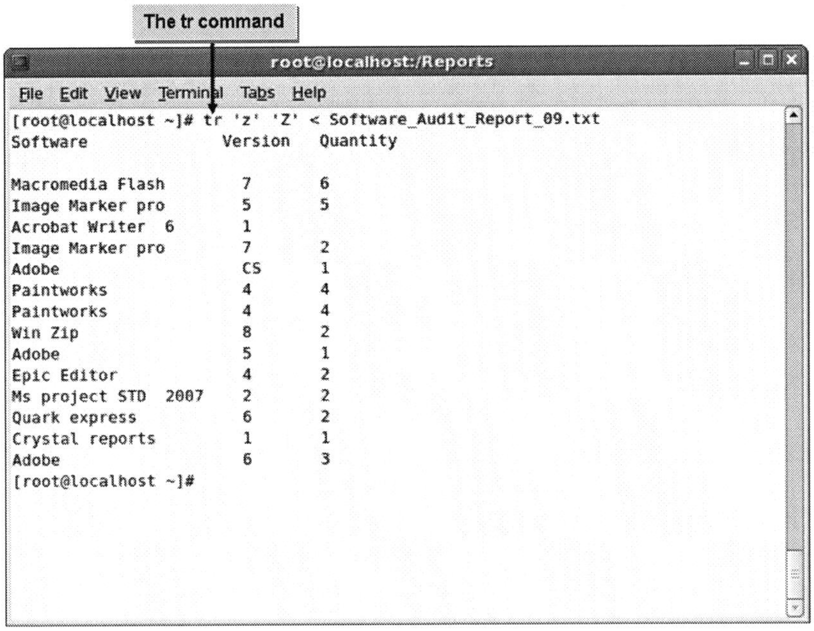

```
                    The tr command
                         |
          root@localhost:/Reports
File  Edit  View  Terminal  Tabs  Help
[root@localhost ~]# tr 'z' 'Z' < Software_Audit_Report_09.txt
Software              Version    Quantity

Macromedia Flash        7        6
Image Marker pro        5        5
Acrobat Writer  6       1
Image Marker pro        7        2
Adobe                   CS       1
Paintworks              4        4
Paintworks              4        4
Win Zip                 8        2
Adobe                   5        1
Epic Editor             4        2
Ms project STD  2007    2        2
Quark express           6        2
Crystal reports         1        1
Adobe                   6        3
[root@localhost ~]#
```

Figure 4-7: Editing text using the tr command.

Syntax

The syntax of the tr command is tr {'character 1'} {'character 2'} < {file name}, where character 1 is the character to be replaced.

The uniq Command

The *uniq command* is used to display duplicated lines in a sorted file. It compares only consecutive lines and therefore, the uniq command requires sorted output.

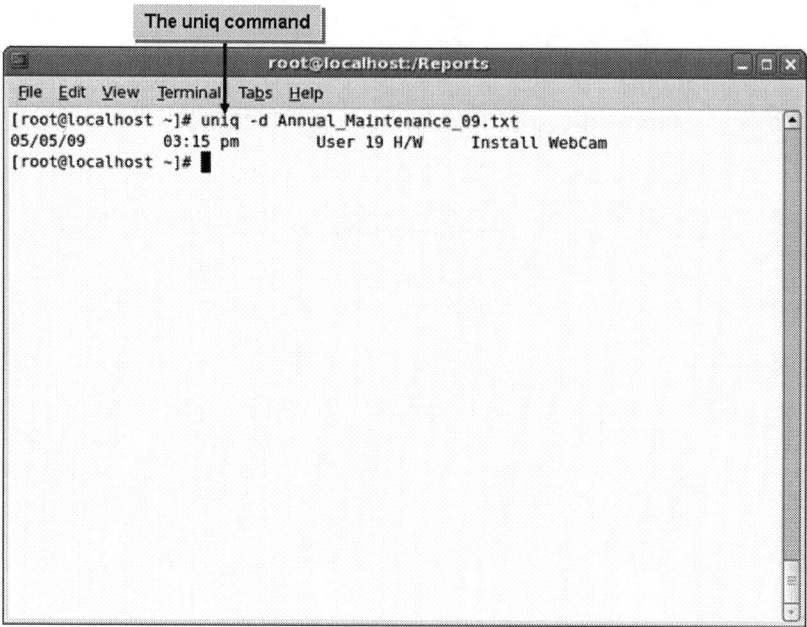

Figure 4-8: *Editing text using the uniq command.*

The `uniq` command provides various options that allow you to specify the nature of the output.

Option	Description
-u	Displays only unique lines.
-d	Displays only duplicated lines.
-c	Displays lines prefixed by the number of occurrences.

Syntax

The syntax of the `uniq` command is `uniq [command options] {file name}`.

Input and Output Redirection

When you want to redirect the contents of an existing file to another command for processing, the input and output redirection symbols can be used. The output redirection symbol > tells the shell to redefine standard output as a file. If the file does not exist, the shell creates it. The input redirection symbol < tells the shell to redefine standard input as something other than the keyboard input, usually a file.

For example, the `ls >list` command causes the shell to send the output of the `ls` command to a file named "list."

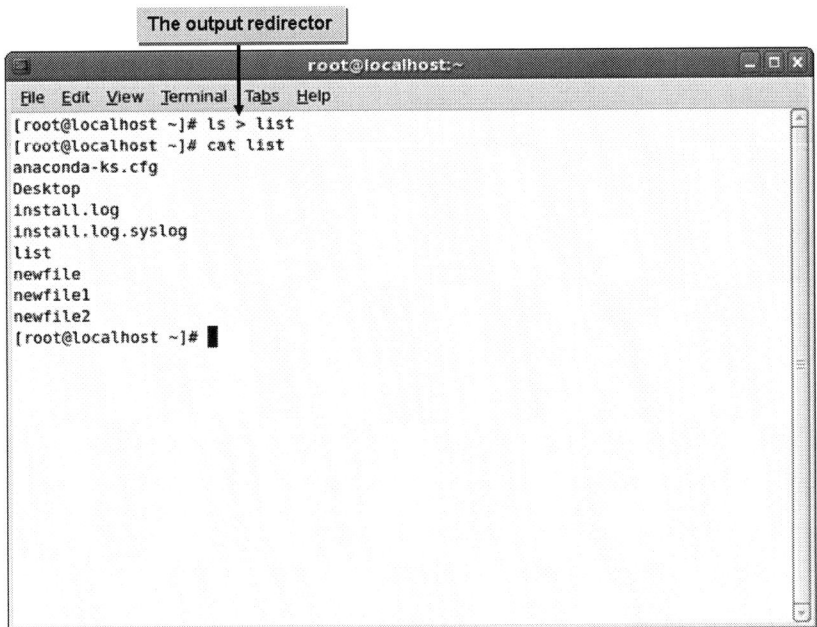

Figure 4-9: Redirecting the output of the ls command to the list file.

How to Create and Edit Files

Procedure Reference: Create a File and Enter Text Using the Vim Editor

To create a file and enter text using the Vim editor:

1. Log in as a user.
2. At the command prompt, enter vim *{file name}* to create a file.
3. Press **I** to switch to the insert mode.
4. Type the required content.
5. Press **Esc** to return to command mode.
6. Enter :wq to save and close the file.

Procedure Reference: Create a Text File from the Command Prompt

To create a text file from the command prompt:

1. Log in as a user in either the GUI or the CLI.
2. In the GUI terminal window, or in a CLI terminal, navigate to the directory where you want to create the file. If necessary, create a new directory at the desired location and make it the current directory.
3. At the command prompt, enter cat > *{file name}*.
4. Type the contents of the file and press **Enter** to move to a new line.
5. Press **Ctrl+D** to save the file and return to the command prompt.
6. If necessary, type cat *{file name}* to view the file contents.

Procedure Reference: Edit Text Files in the Command Mode

To edit text files in the command mode:

1. Log in as a user.

2. Enter `vim` *{file name}* to open a file.

3. Use the appropriate vim shortcuts to make necessary changes.

4. Enter `:wq` to save and close the file.

Procedure Reference: Open Multiple Windows Using the vim Command

To open multiple windows using the vim command:

1. Log in as a user.

2. Open multiple windows.

   - Enter `vim -o` *{file name 1}* *{file name 2}* `...` *{file name n}* to open different files in multiple windows.

   - Press **Ctrl+W+N** to open a new file in a new window.

   - Hold down **Ctrl+W** and use the arrow keys to navigate through the windows.

3. Use the appropriate Vim shortcuts to make necessary changes.

4. If necessary, press **Esc** to return to command mode.

5. Save and close the files.

   - Enter `:wq` to save and close the files one by one.

   - Or, enter `:qa` to close all files at the same time.

Procedure Reference: Count the Words in a File

To count the words in a file:

1. Log in as a user in the CLI.

2. Count the words in a file.

   - Enter `wc` *[command options]* *{file name}* to count the number of words, lines, bytes, and characters in the file.

   - Enter *{command}* `|` `wc` *[command options]* to count the number of words, lines, bytes, and characters in the output of the command.

Procedure Reference: Remove Duplicate and Adjacent Lines in a File

To remove duplicate and adjacent lines in a file:

1. Log in as a user in the CLI.

2. Remove duplicate and adjacent lines in a file.

   - Enter `uniq` *[command options]* *{file name}* to remove the duplicate and adjacent lines from the file.

   - Enter *{command}* `|` `uniq` *[command options]* to remove the duplicate and adjacent lines from the output of the command.

Procedure Reference: Compare Files in CLI

To compare files in CLI:

1. Log in as a user in the CLI.

2. Enter `diff` *{file name 1}* *{file name 2}* to compare files for differences in their content.

Procedure Reference: Compare Files in the GUI

To compare files in the GUI:

1. Press **Ctrl+Alt+F7** to switch to the GUI.

2. From the menu bar, choose **Application→Accessories→Terminal.**

3. Enter gvimdiff *{file name 1} {file name 2}* to compare files for differences in content.

4. Enter :q two times to return to the terminal.

Procedure Reference: Replace Characters

To replace characters:

1. Log in as a user in the CLI.

2. Replace characters.

   ● Enter tr *{'character 1'} {'character 2'} < {file name}* to replace one character with another one in the given file.

   ● Enter *{command}* | tr *{'condition 1'} {'condition 2'}* to replace one character with another one from the output of the command.

Working with Multiple Windows

You can choose to tile your windows horizontally or vertically. Press **Ctrl+W+V** to create a vertical split, or press **Ctrl+W+S** to split the screen horizontally.

ACTIVITY 4-1
Creating Text Files Using Vim

Before You Begin:
1. You have logged in as root in the CLI.
2. The first terminal is displayed.

Scenario:
As a junior system administrator who recently joined OGC, you have several tasks to be completed in a day. Because you are just getting used to your routine tasks, you decide to record the tasks by creating a file named Checklist.txt.

What You Do	How You Do It
1. Create a text file named Checklist.txt.	a. Enter **vim Checklist.txt** to create a file named Checklist.txt.
	b. Press **I** to switch to the insert mode.
	c. Observe that the text "INSERT" is displayed at the bottom-left of the screen.
2. Enter data into the file.	a. Enter **Update Antivirus** as the first entry in the file.
	b. Enter **Install New Printer** as the second entry.
	c. Enter **Fix keyboard issues** as the third entry.
	d. Type **Install New Monitor** as the fourth and last entry.
3. Save the file in execute mode and exit.	a. Press **Esc** to return to command mode.
	b. Enter **:wq** to save the file and quit the text editor.
	c. Enter **clear** to clear the terminal screen.

ACTIVITY 4-2
Editing Text Files in the Command Mode

Data Files:

Softwarelist.txt

Before You Begin:

1. You have logged in as root in the CLI.

2. The first terminal is displayed.

3. At the command line, enter `cp /085039Data/Managing_Files/* /root.`

4. Enter `clear`.

Scenario:

Your manager asks you to list the software used in your organization. You list the software in the Softwarelist.txt file. However, before submitting it, you want to ensure that the document is free from errors. You notice the following errors in the document:

● Image Maker appears as Image Marker.

● Photoshop has been entered as photoshop.

● Details about Paintworks have been duplicated.

By resolving these issues, you want to ensure that the document is ready for submission.

What You Do	How You Do It
1. Change the spelling of the text "Image Marker" to "Image Maker."	a. Enter `vim Softwarelist.txt` to open the Softwarelist.txt file.
	b. Move the cursor down to the first occurrence of the text "Image Marker Pro."
	c. To move the cursor to the next word, press **W.**
	d. Delete the first occurrence of the letter "r" in the word "Marker."

 A warning message may appear at the bottom of the screen stating that the file is read-only. This message can be ignored because the file will ultimately get saved with the changes made to it.

2.	Fix multiple occurrences of the error.	a.	Type **/Marker** and press **Enter** to search for the next occurrence of the word "Marker".
		b.	Change the text "Marker" to "Maker."
3.	Change the casing of the first letter in "photoshop."	a.	Press **J** to move to the next line.
		b.	Press **H** to place the cursor below the first occurrence of the letter "h" in the word "Photoshop."
		c.	Press **C** followed by **B** to delete the first letter.
		d.	In insert mode, type **P** to change the word to "Photoshop."
		e.	Press **Esc** to return to the command mode.
4.	Remove the duplicate entry of "Paintworks."	a.	To navigate to the second occurrence of the word "Paintworks," press the **Down Arrow** key two times.
		b.	To delete the duplicated line, press **D** two times.
		c.	Enter **:wq** to save and close the file.
		d.	Clear the terminal screen.

TOPIC B
Locate Files

You created and edited files. As a user or administrator, you will have to frequently locate files within the Linux filesystem. In this topic, you will locate files within the Linux system.

Learning how to locate files within Linux will reduce the amount of time you spend searching for files. There are different techniques available for locating files within Linux. These will save you time and effort as you manage larger filesystems.

The locate Command

The *locate command* performs a quick search for any specified string in file names and paths stored in the mlocate database. This database must be updated regularly for the search to be effective. The results displayed may be restricted to files users have permissions to access or execute.

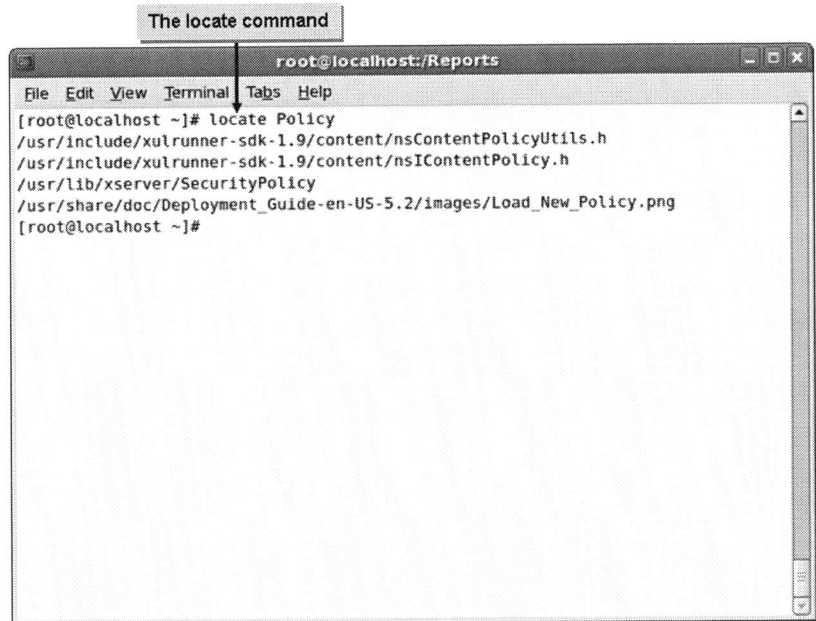

Figure 4-10: Searching files using the locate command.

Syntax
The syntax of the `locate` command is `locate [options] {string}`.

The locate Command Options
The `locate` command supports different options that enable you to make your search more effective. Some of the options are described in the table.

Option	Description
-r	Uses regular expressions in searching for file names.

Option	Description
-c	Displays only the number of matching entries found, rather than the file names.
-e	Returns only files that exist at the time of search.
-i	Ignores the casing in file names or paths.
-n number of entries	Returns only the first few matches up to the specified number.

Updating the mlocate Database

The updatedb command is used to update the /var/lib/mlocate/mlocate.db database. Though this is the default database searched by the locate command, there may be more databases containing file paths. If the database is not updated before performing a search, all files created after the last update will be excluded from the search.

The slocate Command

The slocate command, or secure locate command, searches a specific database that is built using the slocate -u command. The difference between the locate and slocate commands is that when a user types slocate *file name*, the slocate command searches the database and returns the location of the file only if the user has access permission to those files; whereas, the locate command returns the location of files whether or not the user has access permission to them.

Using grep

In its simplest form, grep is a search tool. It allows you to perform search actions, such as finding any instance you are searching for, in a file. For example, entering grep foo test returns all the lines that have a string matching "foo" in the file "test." The grep command can also be used to search a directory for a certain file. The ls -l | grep audit command returns a long listing of any files in the current directory whose name contains "audit."

 The term grep is derived from "Globally matching a Regular Expression and Printing the lines."

The whereis Command

The *whereis command* is used to view various details associated with a command. It locates the binary, source, and manual page files for the command. The whereis command has various options. Some of the frequently used options are listed in the following table.

Option	Used To
-b	Search only for binaries.
-m	Search only for manual sections.
-s	Search only for sources.
-u	Search for unusual entries.

Figure 4-11: The path to the ls command.

Syntax

The syntax of the whereis command is whereis *[-bmsu] [-BMS directory... -f] file name ....*

An Example of Using the whereis Command

On entering whereis ls, the following output is displayed:

```
ls: /bin/ls /usr/share/man/man1/ls.1.gz /usr/share/man/man1p/ls.1p.gz
```

Where /bin/ls indicates the location of the ls command and /usr/share/man/man1/ls.1.gz /usr/share/man/man1p/ls.1p.gz indicates the location of the man pages for the ls command.

The GNOME Search Tool

The *GNOME search tool* is a graphical utility used for searching files based on specific criteria. You can search for a file by its name, size, ownership, access time, or contents. This powerful GUI tool supports features such as case-insensitive search, search within a specific location, and wildcard searches. This tool uses a combination of search commands such as locate, find, and grep.

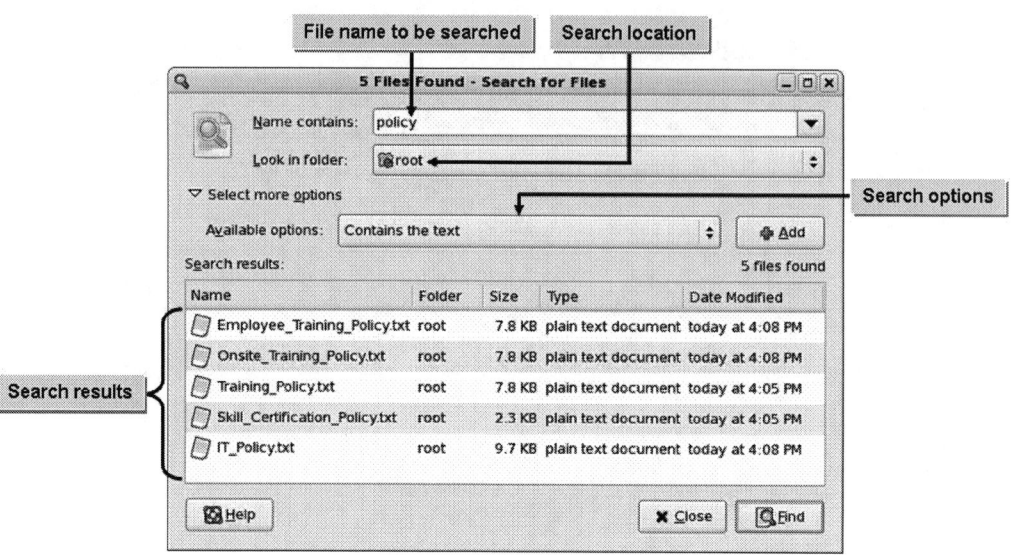

Figure 4-12: Searching files using the GNOME search tool.

kat

Kat is an application for KDE that is used to search for files with the help of meta information, full text, and thumbnails that are extracted and indexed from various types of files. It serves as a catalog and helps retrieve files quickly.

Beagle

Beagle is a GNOME desktop search application, which can also be used in KDE by installing Kerry. It is used to search for files, folders, documents, notes, images, videos, email messages, instant messaging content, web browser history, and RSS feeds. Beagle indexes files, which enables it to retrieve search results quickly. It also allows users to sort search results based on date modified, name, or relevance.

The find Command

The *find command* enables you to search a specific location for files and directories that adhere to some search criteria. It recursively searches the directory structure, including any subdirectories and their contents, beginning with the search location you enter. You can perform one or more actions on the files found.

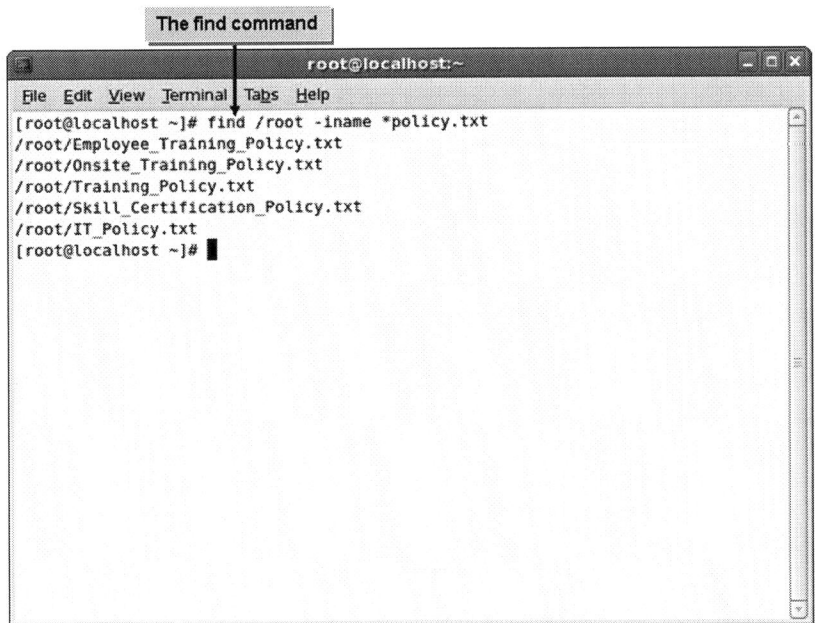

Figure 4-13: Searching files using the find command.

Syntax

The syntax of the `find` command is `find [options] {search locations} {search criteria} [actions]`.

find vs. locate commands

The `locate` command searches a database and retrieves information on files present on your system. However, failure to keep this database updated may produce outdated results. The `find` command, on the other hand, performs a live search of the filesystem and may concentrate on a specific location. The `find` command may take more time to complete a search than the `locate` command.

Working of the find Command

You can use the `find` command to search the entire directory structure for a file even if you remember a portion of the file name. One or more search paths can be designated and directory notations can be used as the search path. If no directory is specified, the `find` command uses the current working directory as the location to start the search. One or more criteria can be used to specify the conditions of a file or directory. In case of more than one search criterion, the file or directory must meet all the conditions specified before the results are displayed. The results displayed may be restricted to files users have permissions to access or execute. You can check the manual pages of the `find` command for more options.

Options for Files Found

When the system finds a listing that meets your criteria, there are several actions that can be performed on the results. These options are outlined in the following table.

Option	Action Performed
-print	Displays the location of the files found.

Option	Action Performed
-exec	Executes the command that follows.
-ok	Executes the command that follows interactively.
-delete	Deletes files found.
-fprint	Stores results in the target file.

The find Command Conditions

The find command can be used with one or more conditions. These conditions accept strings or numbers as arguments. Some of the frequently used conditions are listed in the following table.

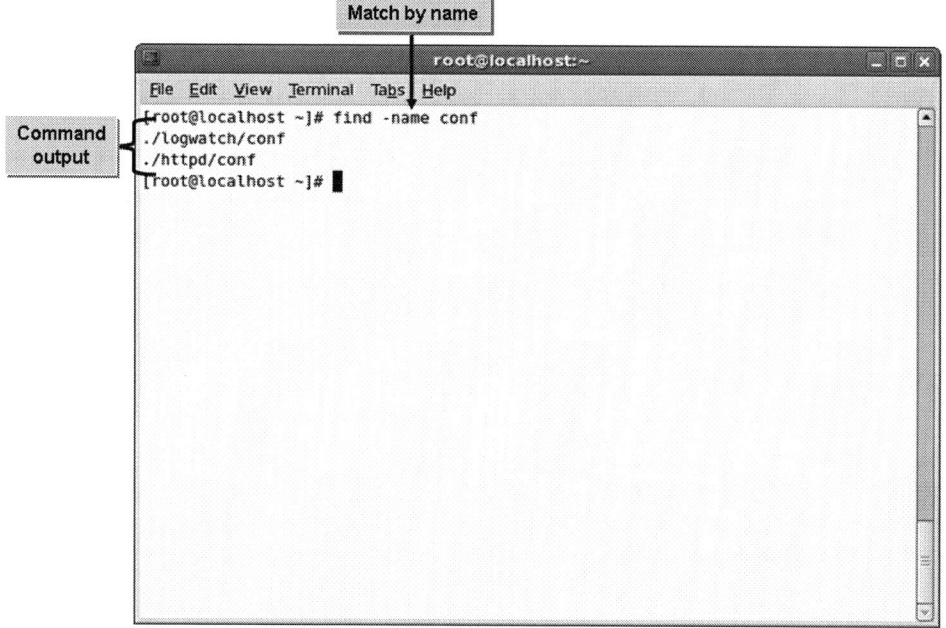

Figure 4-14: Using the –name condition in the find command.

Condition	Description
-name	Matches by name. Regular expressions may be used as arguments.
-iname	Matches by name, ignoring the case.
-user	Matches by user name or UID of the owner.
-group	Matches by group or GID of the owner group.
-size	Matches by size.
-perm	Matches by symbolic or octal permissions.
-type	Matches by file type.
-newer	Matches by comparing the modification time. Returns files modified later than reference files.

Condition	Description
-atime	Matches by access time in days.
-mtime	Matches by modification time in days.
-ctime	Matches by time of latest changes in a file. Arguments are counted in days.

Logical Operators for Conditions

You can combine conditions using logical operators. When more than one criterion is specified, by default, only those files that satisfy all conditions are returned. However, the logical operator OR can be applied to these conditions by using -o between conditions. Also, the NOT operator could be applied to conditions by using -not to negate a condition.

Numeric Arguments

Numeric arguments are used to specify a numeric value. The following table lists the numeric arguments for size and their description.

Use This Argument	If You Need To
n	List files that are equal to n units (default option).
+n	List files that are greater than n units.
-n	List files that are less than n units.

The following table lists the numeric arguments for time and their description.

Use This Argument	If You Need To
n	List files that were accessed n days ago (default option).
+n	List files that were accessed more than n days ago.
-n	List files that were accessed less than n days ago.

How to Locate Files

Procedure Reference: Search for Files from the Database

To search for files from the database:

1. Log in as root.

2. Enter `updatedb` to update the mlocate database with the file name and path information.

3. Enter `locate {string}` to search the updated database for the specified string.

Procedure Reference: Search for Files Using the GNOME Search Tool

To search for files using the GNOME search tool:

1. Log in as a user in the GUI.

2. Choose **Places→Search for Files** to open the search tool.

3. In the **Search for Files** window, in the **Name contains** text box, type the string to be searched.

4. If necessary, from the **Look in folder** drop-down menu, choose the location to perform the search.

5. If necessary, click the toggle button beside the text "Select more options" to specify additional search criteria such as **Date modified less than, Date modified more than, Size at least, Size at most, File is empty, Owned by user, Owned by group, Owner is unrecognized, Name does not contain, Name matches regular expression, Show hidden and backup files, Follow symbolic links,** and **Include other filesystems.** Click **Add** to add the selected option.

6. If necessary, click **Help** to view the manual on "Search for Files."

7. Click **Find** to search for the specified string.

ACTIVITY 4-3
Searching for Files from the Database

Before You Begin:

1. You have logged in as root in the CLI.

2. Enter `mv /085039Data/Managing_Packages/rhelsource /rhelsource` to move the `/rhelsource` directory.

3. On the terminal, enter `cd \rhelsource\Server` to navigate to the Server directory.

4. If necessary, enter `rpm -ivh kernel-headers*` to install the kernel-headers package.

5. Enter `clear` to clear the terminal screen.

Scenario:

You are required to make a report of all peripherals purchased in the past few years, to calculate further requirements. You want the details of all software licenses purchased by the organization. To locate the files and directories containing this information, you decide to perform a local search for the term "software."

What You Do	How You Do It
1. Search the database for filenames containing the word "software."	a. Enter **updatedb** to update the mlocate database.

This may take a few minutes. Please wait until the update is complete and the shell prompt reappears.

b. Enter **locate -i *software*** to search for all files containing "software" in their name.

c. Observe that all files, including system files, that contain "software" in their names are listed.

2. Ensure that all directory names containing the word "software" are listed.

a. Enter `cd /` to switch to the root directory.

b. Enter `ls -lR | grep -i "software" | more` to search all path names containing the term "software."

c. Press the **Spacebar** till you reach the end of the list, to check for any directories containing the term "software" in their name.

d. Observe that the software directory under /usr/src/kernels/2.6.18–128.el5–i686/include/config is displayed in the result.

e. Enter `clear` to clear the terminal screen.

ACTIVITY 4-4
Searching for Files in the GUI

Before You Begin:

1. You have logged in as root in the CLI.

2. On the terminal, enter `chown -R jsmith /085039Data/Locating_Files/*` to change the ownership.

3. Enter `mkdir /work_files` to create work_files directory.

4. Enter `cp -pR /085039Data/Locating_Files/* /work_files` to copy the files.

5. Enter `clear` to clear the terminal screen.

Scenario:

As a system administrator, it is your responsibility to perform a regular system cleanup. You want to clear all the unnecessary empty files. You decide to search for empty files on the Linux filesystem to mark them for deletion.

What You Do	How You Do It
1. Open the GNOME search tool.	a. Switch to the GUI.
	b. Log in as **root.**
	c. Choose **Places→Search for Files** to open the GNOME search tool.
2. Specify the search location as the /work_files directory.	a. In the **Search for Files** window, in the **Name contains** text box, type ***** to include all files for the search.
	b. From the **Look in folder** drop-down menu, select **Other** to open the **Browse** window.
	c. In the **Places** list box, double-click **File System** to display more destination directories in the right pane.
	d. In the **Browse** window, in the **Name** list box, scroll down to view more directories.
	e. In the **Name** list box, select **work_files** and click **Open** to select the /work_files directory and exit the window.

3. Search for empty files.

a. Click the toggle button beside the text "Select more options" to display more search options.

b. From the **Available options** drop-down list, select **File is empty** and click **Add** to restrict the search results to empty files.

c. Click **Find** to search for empty files within the /work_files directory.

d. Maximize the window and scroll down to observe all the empty files listed.

e. Click **Close** to close the **Search for Files** window.

TOPIC C
Link Files

Now that you know how to locate files within the Linux system, creating a link or shortcut to those files will enable you to locate them easily. In this topic, you will link files in Linux.

Linking files within Linux will help you keep track of frequently used files without having to navigate through the file structure to search for them each time. You can help users who are not familiar with Linux to access related files by linking the files.

Inodes

An *index node (inode)* is a computer's reference for a file. The *index node table,* or inode table, is a data structure that contains information about individual files in a filesystem. Inode is an entry in the table that contains information about the device where the inode resides, the file type, the mode of file, and the UID and GID of the owner. It also contains information about the number of links to the file, the number of bytes in the file, the time of access and modifications, the time when the inode itself was last modified, and the addresses of the file's blocks on the hard disk. The `ls -i` command is used to locate the inode number of a file.

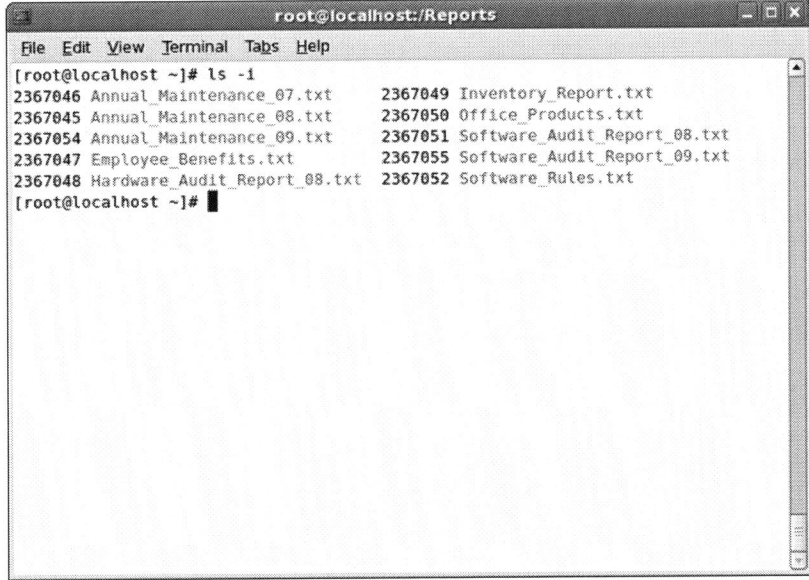

Figure 4-15: Files listed with the inode numbers.

The ln Command

The *ln command* is used to create a link to a file. A link allows a file name in one directory to point to a file in another directory. A link contains no data of its own, only a reference to another file. Any changes to the link will reflect in the original file.

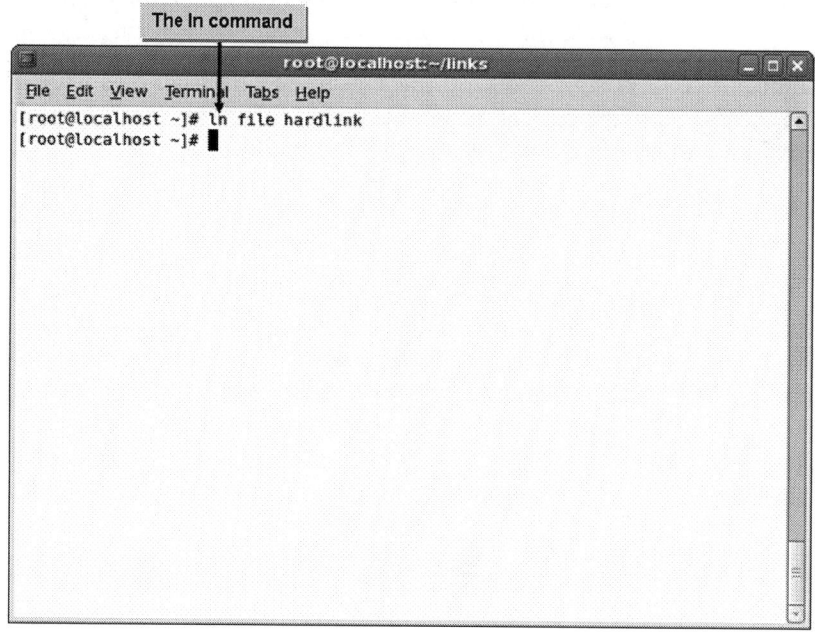

Figure 4-16: A link created using the ln command.

Syntax

The syntax of the `ln` command is `ln [option] Target {link name}`.

The ln Command Options

The `ln` command has various options. Some of the frequently used options are given in the following table.

Option	Used To
--backup	Back up existing destination files.
-f	Remove existing destination files.
-s	Make symbolic links instead of hard links.
-i	Prompt to remove destinations.
-v	Print the name of a file before linking.

Types of Links

Using the `ln` command, you can create two types of links: hard and symbolic.

Link	Description
Symbolic	A symbolic link is a reference to a file or directory that allows you to access mounted filesystems from a different directory. A symbolic link can be created between two filesystems. If the original file is deleted after a symbolic link is created, then the original content is lost. A symbolic link is also known as a soft link.
Hard	A hard link is a reference to another file; it allows the file's data to have more than one name in different locations in the same filesystem. Applications treat a hard link as a real file. If the original file is deleted after a hard link is created, all its contents will still be available in the linked file. Hard links cannot be created between two directories and also between two files in different filesystems.

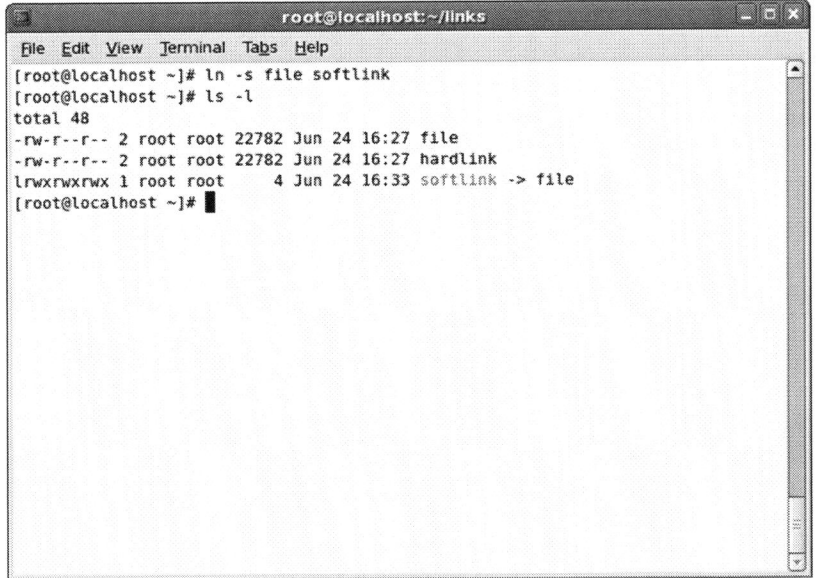

Figure 4-17: A hard link and soft link created for the same file.

 Symbolic and hard links are a feature of the ext2 filesystem and are common in filesystems of most Unix and Unix-like operating systems like Linux.

How to Link Files

Procedure Reference: View the Inode Number of a File or Directory

To view the inode number of a file or directory:

1. Log in as a user in the CLI.

2. Enter `ls -i` *{file or directory name}* to view the inode details.

Procedure Reference: Link Files

To link files:

1. Log in as a user in the CLI.

2. Create file links.

   - Enter `ln` *{source file} {destination file}* to create a hard link.

   - Enter `ln -s` *{source file} {destination file}* to create a soft link.

3. Enter `ls -i` *{source file} {destination file}* to view the inodes of the file.

ACTIVITY 4-5
Linking files

Data Files:

Audit_File_09, Software_List.txt, New_Policies.txt

Before You Begin:
1. You have logged in as root in the GUI.
2. Switch to the CLI.

Scenario:
You have been assigned the task of reviewing an updated employee policy document for casing errors, making a word count of the document, and creating links of the document as a backup in your local system. You also want to clean up your system by removing unused files from your current working directory and back up the policy document.

What You Do	How You Do It
1. List the files in the current working directory.	a. Enter **cd /root** to change the directory.
	b. Enter **ls -l** to list the files in the directory.
	c. Observe that all files in the current working directory are listed.
2. Move the Audit_File_09 file to the /jsmith directory and remove the Software_List.txt file.	a. Enter **mv -v Audit_File_09 /home/jsmith** to move the audit file to the /jsmith directory.
	b. Enter **ls -l /home/jsmith** to verify that the file transfer is complete.
	c. Enter **rm Software_List.txt** to remove the software file from the /root directory.
	d. Type **y** to confirm the deletion and press **Enter.**
	e. Enter **ls** to check whether the file is deleted.
	f. Observe that the Software_List.txt file has been deleted.

3. Edit the New_Policies.txt file for casing errors and generate the word count.

    a. Enter **cat New_Policies.txt** to view the contents of the file.

    b. Observe that casing of the letter "Y" in the word "EmploYees" is incorrect.

    c. Enter **tr 'Y' 'y' < New_Policies.txt** to change the casing of the letter "Y" in the word "EmploYees."

    d. Observe that the casing of "Y" has changed.

    e. Enter **wc -w New_Policies.txt** to count the words in the file.

    f. Observe that the word count of the file is displayed.

4. Create a hard link for the file.

    a. Enter **ln New_Policies.txt New_Policies_09.txt** to create a hard link for the file.

    b. Enter **ls New*** to view whether the hard link has been created.

    c. Observe that the hard link is created.

    d. Clear the terminal screen.

TOPIC D
Back Up and Restore Files

You know how to create, edit, locate, and link files. It is essential that you also know how to back up and restore these files when the need arises. In this topic, you will back up and restore files.

Learning how to back up and restore files will save you countless hours of repairing your system after a system failure. Backing up and restoring files allow you to keep an additional copy of files on your system as they existed at a specific point in time. If you ever have a system failure, these files can be used to restore your system.

Archiving

Definition:

Archiving is a method of storing data by copying data from a system disk drive onto a backup device. This is done to preserve a record of the data for future reference or to create data dumps. In the event of a network disruption resulting in data loss, the data can be retrieved from archives.

Example:

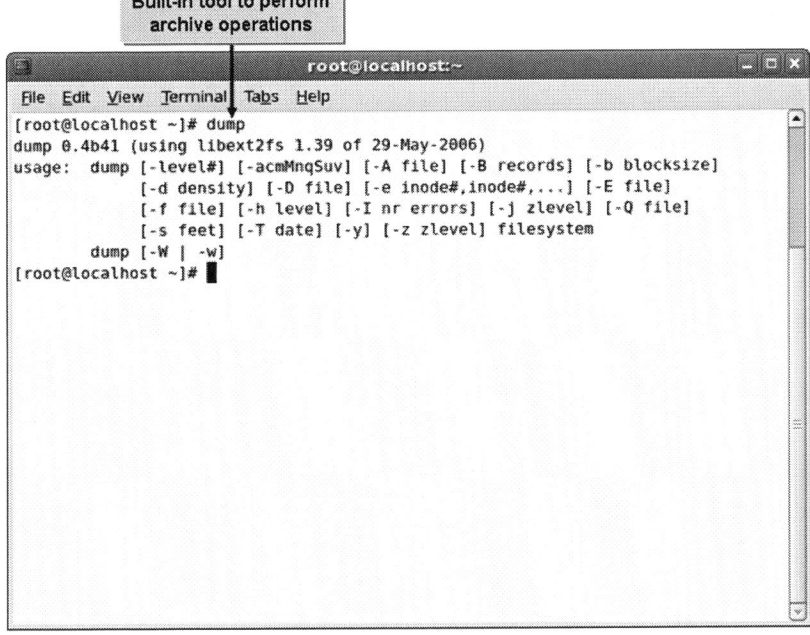

Figure 4-18: *Archiving files using the dump command.*

The cpio Command

The *cpio command* copies files to and from archives. It is included in standard Linux distributions. The cpio command has three operating modes.

Operating Mode	Description
Copy-out cpio -o	In this mode, the command copies files onto an archive. It reads the standard input to obtain a list of file names and then copies those files to the standard output.
Copy-in cpio -i	In this mode, the command copies files from an archive. It extracts files from the standard input.
Copy-pass cpio -p	In this mode, the command copies files from one directory tree to another. It reads the standard input to obtain the list of file names that are created and copied onto the destination directory.

The dd Command

The *dd command* copies and converts files to enable them to be transferred from one type of media to another. A selected input file is copied to a selected output file. If no files are selected, the standard input and the standard output are used.

Some of the common dd command options are provided in the following table.

Option	Used To
if=file name	Specify the file from which data will be read.
of=file name	Specify the file to which data will be written.
bs=Number of bytes per block	Specify the number of bytes at which data is read from an input file and written to an output file.
count=Number of blocks	Specify the number of blocks to be written to the output file from the input file.

Syntax

The syntax of the dd command is dd [operand]... or dd [option].

The dump Command

The *dump command* dumps all files in a filesystem on to a tape or another file. It can also be used to dump files modified after a specified date. The dump command has various options.

Some of the common dump command options are provided in the following table.

Option	Used To
0	Take a full backup.
-1 to 9	Take incremental or partial backups.
-b Maximum block size	Specify the number of kilobytes per dump record.
-f Location of the target file	Specify the target location.
-z Compression level 1-9	Specify the compression level.

Syntax

The syntax of the dump command is dump *{-level #} {dump file} {filesystem/file/directory}*.

The tar Command

The *tar command* allows you to create archives of data. You can use the command on previously created archives to extract files, store additional files, update files, and list files that were already stored. The tar command can also direct its output to available devices, files, or other programs using pipes.

 tar is derived from Tape ARchive.

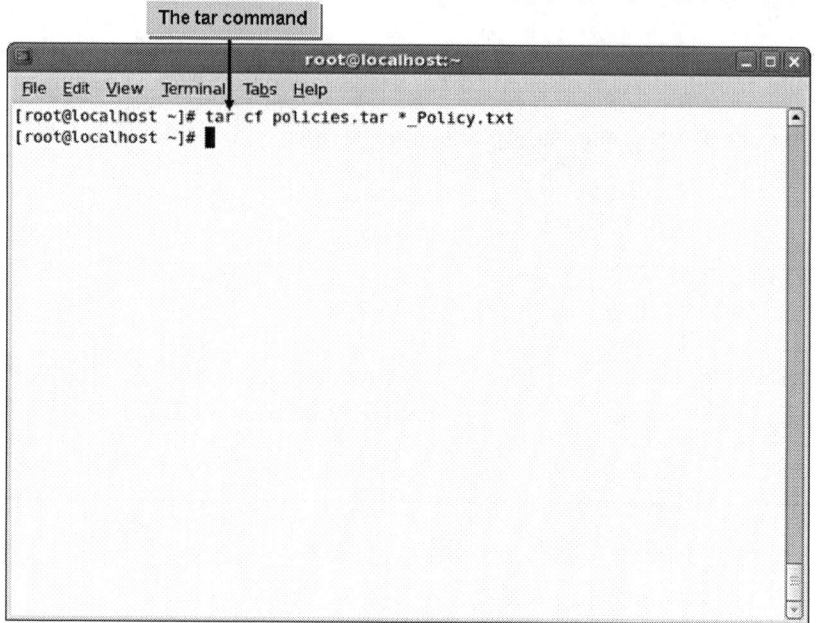

Figure 4-19: *Archiving files using the tar command.*

Syntax

The syntax of the `tar` command is `tar [archiving command options] {destination file}.tar {source directory}`.

The gzip Command

GNU zip (gzip) is a compressing utility that reduces the size of selected files. The `gzip` command has several options.

These command options are described in the following table.

Option	Description
-d	Decompresses the file.
-f	Forces compression or decompression of a file even if it has multiple links or if the file exists.
-h	Displays a help screen.
-L	Displays the `gzip` license.
-n	Omits to save the original file name and time stamp.
-N	Saves the original file name and time stamp.
-q	Suppresses all warnings.
-r	Descends into the directory and compresses files.
-v	Displays the name and percentage reduction of the compressed or decompressed file.
-t	Checks the compressed file for integrity.

Syntax

The syntax of the gzip command is gzip *[command options] {file name}.*

File Compression Utilities

File compression utilities, such as gzip, attempt to compress only regular files and ignore symbolic links. Compressed files can be restored to their original form using gzip -d, gunzip, or zcat. If the original file name saved in the compressed file is not suitable for its filesystem, a new name is provided from the original one.

File Archiving Utilities

There are various file archiving utilities that enable you to compress, decompress, and run other text-processing utilities on files. Some of the utilities are described in the following table.

Utility	*Description*
bzip2	Compresses files at a faster rate than the gzip command. The syntax of this command is bzip2 *{file name}.*
bunzip2	Decompresses files that are compressed using the bzip2 command. The syntax of this command is bunzip2 *{file name}.*
bzcat	Decompresses files that are compressed using the bzip2 command to the standard output. The syntax of this command is bzcat *{file name}.*
bzdiff	Runs the diff command on compressed files. The syntax of this command is bzdiff *{file name}.*
bzip2recover	Recovers data from damaged bzip2 files. The syntax of this command is bzip2recover *{file name}.*
bzless	Runs the less command on compressed files. The syntax of this command is bzless *{file name}.*
bzmore	Runs the more command on compressed files. The syntax of this command is bzmore *{file name}.*

 bzip is a compression utility currently replaced by bzip2.

The unzip Command

The unzip command is used to list, test, and extract compressed files in a ZIP archive. The unzip command comprises various options. A few of these options are described in the following table.

Option	Description
-c	Extracts files to the standard output.
-t	Tests files before extraction.
-f	Extracts new files and freshens existing files.
-z	Displays the archive comment.
-v	Extracts and lists files in a verbose manner.

 The unzip command extracts all files from the specified ZIP archive into the current working directory.

Syntax

The syntax of the unzip command is unzip [command options] {file name}.

Guidelines to Determine a Backup Strategy

An effective backup strategy provides a quick and painless recovery, minimizing the loss of data in the event of an unexpected crisis.

Guidelines

To choose an effective backup strategy, follow these guidelines:

- Determine the scope of the backup operation to be performed:
    - Do you need to back up data on a single computer?
    - Do you need to back up data on multiple computers?
    - Are the computers situated in a single location?
    - Are the computers spread across different locations?
- Make sure that you have all the necessary information about the data to be backed up:
    - Identify the amount of data that needs to be backed up.
    - Does the data reside on a single system?
    - Is the data distributed among several servers?
    - Can the data be easily replaced?
- Determine the most suitable time for performing backup operations so that users can continue working.
- Ensure that users are informed well in advance about scheduled backups.

- Review the storage space:
  - Do you have an adequate number of storage tapes?
  - Determine the reliability of the backup media.
  - Determine whether the previous backup versions can be erased or not. It is advisable to retain previous backup versions.
- Depending on the scope of the backup operation to be performed, determine if you have the required number of human resources to perform the backup operation.
- Test the backup operations performed and verify the integrity of the backed up files.

Example: A Good Backup Strategy

A major corporation, Our Global Company, recently suffered a catastrophic loss of data during a power outage caused by a snowstorm. As a preventive measure, Larry, the system administrator decides to update the organization's backup strategy. To begin with, he notices that team members regularly save work-in-progress files on their local hard drives. He also determines where the other mission critical files are stored. Based on these findings, Larry creates a backup plan that includes all computers on the network. He reviews the storage capacity of the current backup media, and finds it to be inadequate. After some research, he recommends to the management that a new storage system be purchased and installed. Finally, Larry consults various managers and team leads to determine the teams' work schedules. He schedules the backups from 10:00 P.M.–4:30 A.M. during which time there will be minimal disruption.

motd

The *message of the day (motd)* file is displayed to all users on a daily basis and can be used to inform users about scheduled backups. It requires less disk space than email messages. The contents of the /etc/motd file are displayed after a user successfully logs in.

The Hanoi Sequence

While performing incremental or partial backups, the Hanoi sequence helps minimize the number of tapes used. Backup procedures have several levels ranging from 0–9. Level 0 indicates a complete backup and ensures that the entire filesystem is copied. A level number greater than 0 indicates that all new files and files modified since the last backup of the same or lower level will be copied. This is known as an incremental backup.

It is practical to always start with a level 0 backup. A level 0 backup should be performed at regular intervals, preferably once a month or once every two months. Data should be stored in a set of fresh tapes each time a level 0 backup is performed. These tapes should be stored forever. After performing a level 0 backup, dumps of active filesystems need to be made on a daily basis. A modified "Tower of Hanoi" algorithm is used for this purpose. The sequence of dump levels followed in this method is 3 2 5 4 7 6 9 8 9 9.

Every week, a level 1 dump needs to be taken and the daily Hanoi sequence repeats beginning with a dump level of 3.

The /etc/issue and the /etc/issue.net Files

The */etc/issue.net* file is the login banner that users see when they make a network connection with the system. For example, when you use a command line tool to connect with a system, the content in the /etc/issue.net file is displayed. It includes all the welcome information text displayed whenever a new session is opened. The */etc/issue* and the /etc/issue.net files constitute the login banner that is displayed to local users. The /etc/issue file can be customized.

The restore Command

The *restore command* enables you to restore files or filesystems from backups made using the dump command. This command can be used across networks to restore data. Specific data can also be restored using the options of the restore command.

The following table describes common restore command options.

Option	Enables You To
-C	Compare the backup file with the source file.
-i	Run the restore command in restore mode to restore backups partially.
-r	Perform a complete recovery of the backed up files.
-f /Location of the backup file	Specify the location of the backup file.

Volume Number

While making backups of large files on removable storage devices, such as tape drives, the total size of the files will be split into smaller volumes and stored in multiple tape drives with each tape drive identified with a specific volume number. When you want to restore the backup made on multiple volumes, specify the volume number starting from the last volume number to the first volume number. The hard disk, because it is a single volume, will always have the volume number 1.

Restoring Files with the tar Command

The command tar -xvf will restore the entire contents of the source file or directory structure. To restore a portion of a tar file, use the path and name of the file you wish to extract. You must use the exact path and name that was used when you created the tar file. You can also make restores interactive by using the command tar -wxvf [destination] [source].

Restoring Files with the cpio Command

The main reason you need to back up data is so that you can retrieve the data if the file gets corrupted or deleted. If you use the cpio command to move files to another location, you will need to get the files out of the archive file so that you can use them. The format of the copy-in option is cpio -icdv < [archive_file name].

How to Back Up and Restore Files

Procedure Reference: Archive Using the dump Command

To archive using the `dump` command:

1. Log in as root in the CLI.
2. Enter `dump -0 -f {target file} {source file}` to make a complete backup.
3. Enter `dump -{Hanoi Sequence} -f {target file} {source file}` to add updates to the existing backup file.

Procedure Reference: Back Up Files Using the tar and gzip Commands

To back up files using the `tar` and `gzip` commands:

1. Determine the files you want to back up and put them in a directory.
2. Group all the files using the `tar` command.
3. Compress the tar file using the `gzip` command.
4. Save the file in another location (FTP site, CD, DVD, tape, floppy disk, and so on).

Procedure Reference: Restore Backups Using the restore Command

To fully restore the backups:

1. Log in as root in the CLI.
2. Navigate to the directory where you want to restore backed up files.
3. Restore backups.
   - Enter `restore -rf /{Location of the backup file}` to restore a backup taken using the `dump` command.

Procedure Reference: Restore Files from a Backup Using the gzip and tar Commands

To restore files from a backup using the `tar` and `gzip` commands:

1. Copy the files from your backup location (FTP site, CD, DVD, tape, floppy disk, and so on).
2. Unzip the files using the `gzip` command.
3. Untar the files using the `tar` command.
4. If needed, move the individual saved files back to their respective locations.

ACTIVITY 4-6

Performing Backups

Before You Begin:

1. You have logged in as root in the CLI.

2. Enter `mkdir Reports` to create the Reports directory in the root directory.

3. Enter `cd Reports` to navigate to the /root/Reports directory.

4. Enter `vi project` to create the project file to store the project data.

5. Save and close the file.

6. Enter `clear`.

Scenario:

Your colleague, Chris, is working on a very important project, and he wants to make a daily backup of his system. He also wants a reminder to be set to create backups whenever he logs in to his system.

All project-related files are in the /root directory and they need to be saved as project_backup in the /tmp directory.

Account information:

● Login name for the root user: root

● Password for the root user: p@ssw0rd

What You Do	How You Do It
1. Make a backup of /root files in the /tmp directory.	a. Enter `dump -0 -f /tmp/project_backup /root` to make a complete backup. b. Observe that the message "DUMP : DUMP IS DONE" is displayed in the last line indicating that the backup was successful. c. Enter **clear** to clear the terminal screen. d. Enter `bzip2 /tmp/project_backup` to compress the backup file.

2.	Set a reminder during system login to perform backups.	a.	Enter `vi /etc/issue`
		b.	Press **Shift+G** to navigate to the end of the file.
		c.	Press **O** to shift to a new line.
		d.	Type *Welcome to Linux! Remember to Backup Your Project Data*
		e.	Press **Esc.**
		f.	Save and close the file.
3.	Verify that the remainder is displayed when the user logs in the next time.	a.	Enter `logout` to verify that the reminder is displayed.
		b.	Observe that the message "Welcome to Linux! Remember to Backup Your Project Data" is displayed.
		c.	Log in as the **root** user.

ACTIVITY 4-7
Restoring Backup Data

Before You Begin:

1. You are logged in as root in the CLI.

2. Open the /etc/issue file in the text editor and remove the last line that reminds the user to backup project data. Save the file and close the editor.

3. Log out of the CLI. Log in as root in the CLI.

4. Enter `rm -rf /root/Reports`.

5. Enter `clear` to clear the terminal screen.

Scenario:

You observe that some of your project files are missing from the Reports directory. Because you make a daily backup of your work, you decide to restore the missing files from the backup. The backup file is available in the /tmp/project_backup.bz2 location.

What You Do	How You Do It
1. Identify the missing directory and files.	a. Enter `bunzip2 /tmp/project_backup.bz2` to decompress the file.
 Step 1a may take a few minutes.	b. Enter `restore -C -f /tmp/project_backup` to view the missing directory and files.
	c. Enter **clear** to clear the terminal screen.

2.	Switch to the restore mode.	a.	Enter `cd /`
		b.	Enter `restore -i -f /tmp/project_backup` to switch to the restore mode.
		c.	At the restore prompt, enter `cd root`

3.	Extract missing files.	a.	Enter `add Reports/` to add the directory that needs to be restored.
		b.	Enter `extract` to extract the directory from the backup file.
		c.	Enter *1* to specify the volume number.
		d.	Enter *y* to accept the default owner or mode of the files to be extracted.
		e.	Enter `quit` to quit the restore mode.
		f.	Enter `ls /root/Reports` to check if the Reports directory has been restored.
		g.	Observe that the project file has been restored.
		h.	Enter `clear` to clear the terminal screen.
		i.	Enter `logout`

TOPIC E
Manage Databases Using MySQL

You worked with files in a Linux filesystem. You may need to store data in a format that will allow you to easily retrieve it when required; a database will serve this purpose. In this topic, you will work with MySQL.

A text file can store volumes of data, but retrieving it will be a problem because you may have to manually locate the information you are looking for. Databases, such as MySQL, allow you to store data in an organized manner, which enables efficient retrieval of specific data. This will save you time and effort.

Databases

Definition:

A *database* is an organized collection of information. It is used to facilitate easy storage and retrieval of data. In a database, data may be grouped into a series of records, which can be further organized into smaller segments of data called *fields*. A table is the basic storage unit of a database and it consists of rows and columns. The model of a database decides the way the data is organized in it.

Example:

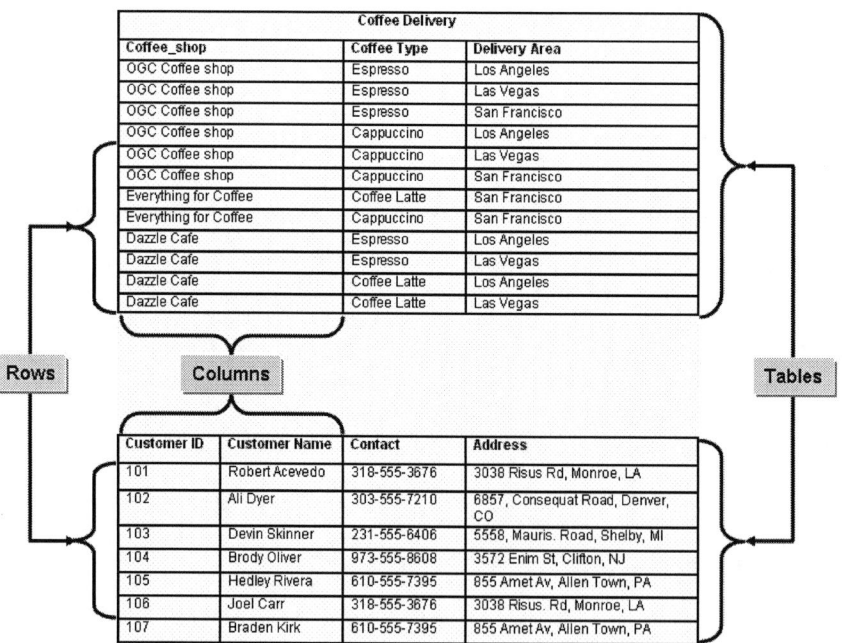

Figure 4-20: *A database consisting of two tables.*

Relational Databases

A *relational database* stores logically related data consistently in the form of related tables. These tables are linked through common fields or columns. The data stored is independent of files and is managed by a central database engine that processes queries and manipulates data. Every row of data contains an identification key that identifies data uniquely and helps in reducing redundancy.

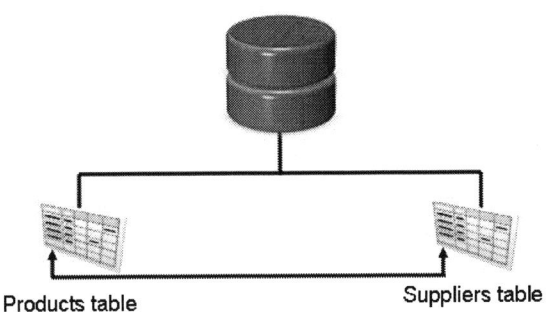

Products table   Suppliers table

Figure 4-21: An example of a relational database.

Flat File Database

A flat file database stores data as flat files, which are static plain text documents. Flat files contain data that is structurally unrelated. The data in flat file databases cannot be retrieved or modified easily.

MySQL

MySQL is an open source *Relational Database Management System (RDBMS)* used for managing data. It is developed and distributed by Sun Microsystems. It enables you to store, retrieve, manage, organize, and share your data optimally. Using MySQL, you can store data in one form and view it in various forms by analyzing and extracting only the relevant data from the database. MySQL also enables a group of networked computers to work together to enhance flexibility, efficiency, performance, scalability, and availability of the database, by eliminating time-consuming, error-prone tasks.

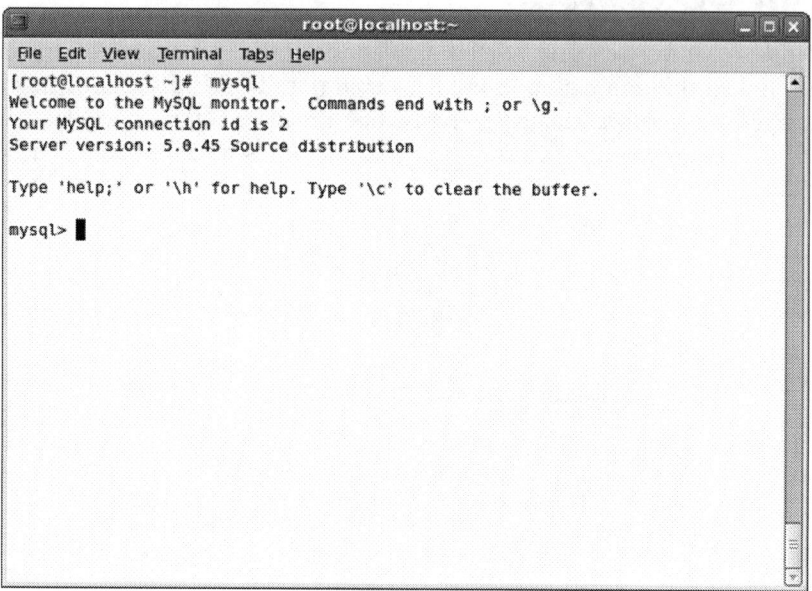

Figure 4-22: *The welcome screen of the MySQL client interface.*

The MySQL Configuration File

The main configuration file of MySQL, my.cnf, is located in the /etc/ directory. You can set the global options for the MySQL application in this file. The default options are usually sufficient; however, if you need to integrate MySQL with other applications, you may need to modify this file. This file allows you to set different options ranging from simple options, such as path to data directory; user name; and log file directory, to advanced options, such as table_cache and key_buffer, that can be set for the MySQL daemon.

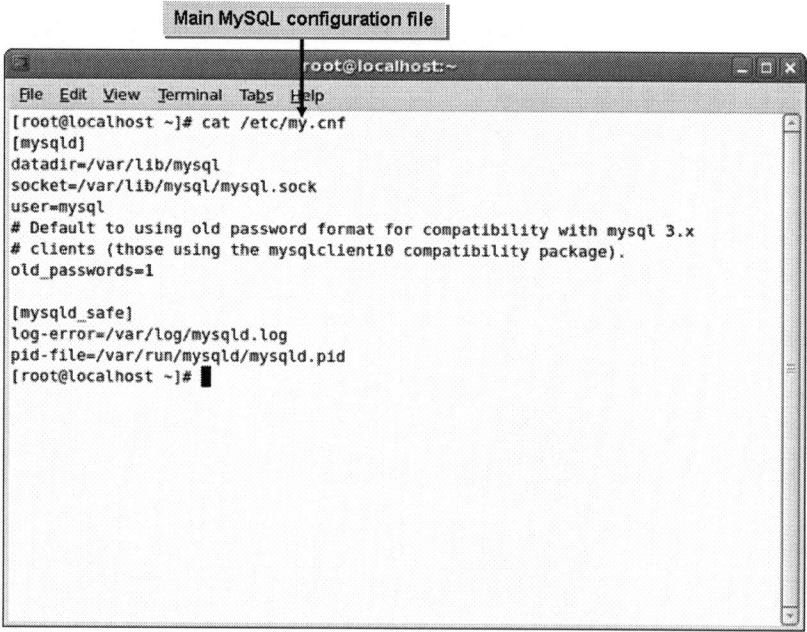

Figure 4-23: *The contents of the mysql configuration file.*

mysqld

The *mysqld* or MySQL daemon is also the MySQL server. It allows you to manage the MySQL server service. After installing MySQL, you need to manually start this daemon. You can start, stop, restart, or view the status of the MySQL server. This service needs to be running for clients to connect to and use MySQL.

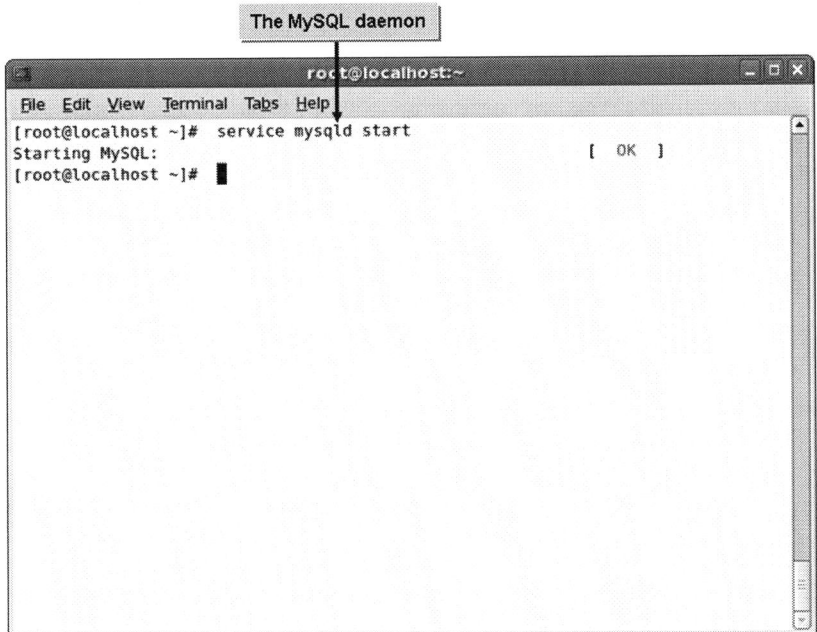

Figure 4-24: *Starting the mysqld service.*

MySQL Commands

Clients use MySQL commands to interact with the MySQL server.

MySQL Command	Allows You To
select	Retrieve all records or records that match a specific criteria.
create	Create objects, such as a database, a table, or indexes, inside an RDBMS.
alter	Modify the existing table or database.
update	Update the values in a table.
use	Make a particular database as the current database so that you can modify the objects of that database.
show	Display the tables that are available in the current database.
insert	Enter values into a row or record of the table.
describe	Display the structure of the table.

How to Manage Database Using MySQL

Procedure Reference: Install MySQL

To install MySQL:

1. Log in as root in the GUI.
2. Insert the required CD in the drive.
3. In the **File Browser** window, select the MySQL files and click install.
4. If necessary, select the additional files and restart the installation.
5. Verify that the installation was successful by viewing the message displayed.

Procedure Reference: Start the MySQL daemon service and set it to run automatically

To start the MySQL daemon service and set it to run automatically:

1. On the terminal, enter `service mysqld start` to start the mysqld service.
2. Enter `chkconfig mysqld` to automatically start the mysqld service at the system startup.
3. If necessary, enter `service mysqld status` to view the status of the mysqld service. You can use the `service mysqld stop` and `service mysqld restart` to stop the MySQL server or restart the server, respectively.

Procedure Reference: Locate the MySQL Configuration File

To locate the MySQL configuration file:

1. If necessary, enter the `update` command to update the locate database.
2. Change to the / directory.
3. Enter `locate my.cnf` to locate the path of the MySQL configuration file.
4. If necessary, open the my.cnf file in any text editor and modify the settings in the my.cnf file. Restart the server to apply the changes.

Procedure Reference: Use MySQL Commands

To use MySQL commands:

1. Type `mysql` to connect to the MySQL server.
2. At the **mysql** prompt, enter the required commands in the format `{commands}`; to use the MySQL commands.
3. Type `quit` to exit from the **mysql** prompt.

Procedure Reference: Execute an Existing sql Script

To execute an existing sql script:

1. Log in as root.
2. Copy the {filename.sql} file to the /var/lib/mysql directory.
3. Type `mysql` to connect to the MySQL server.
4. At the **mysql** prompt, type `use {database name}` to make it the current database.
5. Type `source {filename.sql};` to execute the sql commands.
6. If necessary, type the suitable sql commands to verify that the script was successfully executed.

ACTIVITY 4-8
Working with MySQL

Before You Begin:
1. Switch to the GUI.
2. Navigate to the /rhelsource/Server folder.

Scenario:
A junior database administrator joined your organization. As a Linux administrator, you are required to help the junior administrator install a web-based database on the Linux system. In addition, you need to ensure that clients are able to connect to the database.

What You Do	How You Do It
1. Select MySQL files.	a. In the **Server - File Browser** window, type **m** to navigate to MySQL packages.
	b. Observe that a text box is displayed at the bottom-left of the window.
	c. In the text box, type **y**
	d. Observe that the **mysql-5.0.45–7.el5.i386.rpm** file is automatically selected.
	e. Press **Page Down** to view the other files.
	f. Press **Ctrl** and click **mysql-server-5.0.45-7.el5.i386.rpm** to select it.
2. Select the other files.	a. Scroll down till you locate the perl-DBD package.
	b. Press **Ctrl** and click **perl-DBD-MySQL-3.0007-2.el5.i386.rpm** to select it.
	c. Press **Ctrl** and click **perl-DBI-1.52-2.el5.i386.rpm** to select it.
	d. Verify that the status bar displays the message "4 items selected (14.6 MB)."

3.	Install MySQL packages.	a.	Right-click any of the selected packages and choose the **Open with "Software Installer"** option.
		b.	In the **Installing packages** window, observe that four packages are listed.
		c.	Click **Apply.**
		d.	In the **Unable to verify perl-DBD-MySQL-3.0007-2.el5.i386** dialog box, click **Install anyway** to install the package.
		e.	Click **Install anyway** three times to install the remaining three packages.
		f.	In the **Software installed successfully** message box, click **OK.**
4.	Start the MySQL daemon and verify that the installation was successful.	a.	Choose **Applications→Accessories→Terminal** to display the terminal window.
		b.	Enter *service mysqld start* to start the MySQL daemon.
		c.	Observe that the **OK** status message is displayed after the "Starting MySQL" message, indicating that MySQL daemon was successfully started.
		d.	Enter *chkconfig mysqld on* to automatically start the MySQL daemon service.
		e.	Enter *mysql* to verify that you can connect to the MySQL server.
		f.	Observe that the **mysql** prompt is displayed indicating that MySQL is functional and you can use it to create databases.
		g.	Enter *quit* to exit the **mysql** prompt.
		h.	Enter `clear` to clear the terminal window.
		i.	Close the **Server - File Browser** window.

ACTIVITY 4-9

Executing Commands from Existing sql Script

Data Files:

users.sql

Before You Begin:

1. Switch to the CLI.

2. Log in as root.

3. Enter `cd /085039Data/Managing_Files` to change to the Managing_Files directory.

4. Enter `clear` to clear the terminal screen.

Scenario:

The database administrator has some sql scripts that need to be reused in Linux. You need to help the database administrator execute a sample script in Linux to populate a new database.

What You Do	How You Do It
1. Copy the users.sql file in the correct location and connect to MySQL.	a. On the terminal, enter **cp users.sql /var/lib/mysql** to copy the script file to the mysql directory.
	b. Enter **cd /var/lib/mysql** to change to the mysql directory.
	c. Enter **mysql** to connect to the MySQL server.
2. Create a new userinfo database and make it the current database.	a. At the **mysql** prompt, enter **create database userinfo;** to create the new database.
	b. Enter **use userinfo;** to make it the current database.
	c. Observe that the message "Database changed" is displayed.

3. Execute the `users` script and verify the values.

a. Enter **source users.sql;** to execute the script.

b. Observe that the message "Query OK" is displayed because the script is executed.

c. Enter **show tables;** to view the existing tables.

d. Enter **select * from users;** to view all the records in the users table.

e. Enter *quit* to exit the **mysql** prompt.

f. Enter **clear** to clear the terminal screen.

Lesson 4 Follow-up

In this lesson, you located files, linked related files, created and edited files using a text editor, backed up and restored files, and explored MySQL. This will help you customize the Linux system to your needs.

1. **How can you perform a comprehensive search on your system?**

2. **Which text editor in Linux will you prefer? Why?**

5 Working with Linux Permissions and Ownership

Lesson Time: 1 hour(s), 15 minutes

Lesson Objectives:

In this lesson, you will work with Linux permissions and ownership.

You will:

- Modify permissions on files and directories.
- Modify default permissions applied to files and directories.
- Change ownership of files and directories.
- Set advanced permissions.

Introduction

While working with Linux files, you may need to modify the permissions and ownership of these files. In this lesson, you will work with Linux permissions and ownership.

In Linux, changing permissions and ownership of files will enable you to restrict or assign those files to certain users. This will increase the overall security of your system. Novice users with high privileges can cause serious damage to a Linux system.

This lesson covers all or part of the following CompTIA Linux+ (2009) certification objectives:

- Topic A
  - Objective 5.2
- Topic B
  - Objective 5.2
- Topic C
  - Objective 5.2
- Topic D
  - Objective 5.2

TOPIC A
Modify File and Directory Permissions

Now that you can work with Linux files, you can begin to alter their permissions. In this topic, you will modify file and directory permissions.

Systems in your workplace may hold files and other data that should not be made accessible to all users. To prevent accidental modification or deletion of important information certain files should be accessible only to the root user or to the owner of the file. As a system administrator, it is your responsibility to modify file and directory permissions that will enable you to restrict or allow user access to system critical and generic files.

Permissions

Definition:

Permissions are access rights assigned to users, which enable them to access or modify files and directories. Permissions can be set at different levels and for different access categories. The `ls -l` command can be used to view the permissions of a file.

Example:

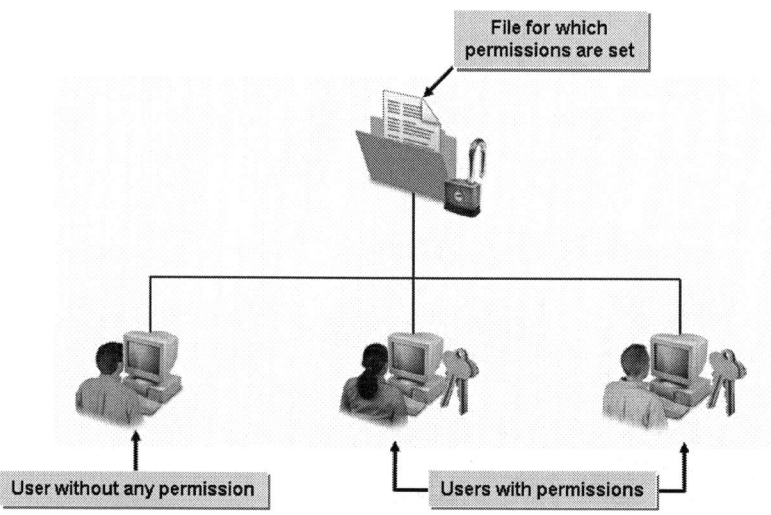

Figure 5-1: Permissions set for a few users.

The `ls -l` command gives you a long list of the files and directories in your current working directory. Each item in the list consists of 15 columns. The contents of the columns are described in the following table.

Column Number	Description
0	The first column (known as column 0) indicates whether it is a file (-) or a directory (d).

Column Number	Description
1-3	User (owner) permissions. The user for whom these permissions are valid is listed in column 11.
4-6	Group permissions. The group for whom these permissions are valid is listed in column 12.
7-9	Other users' permissions. Any other user besides the specified user and group receive these permissions.
10	Number of links. Files generally have a link count of 1. For directories, the link count is the number of directories under it plus two; one for the directory itself and one for the parent. (Links are similar to Windows 95/98 shortcuts; they point to the location where the file exists, and allow you to access and view the file.)
11	Displays the owner of the file or directory.
12	Displays the group to which the owner of the file belongs. All members of this group have the permission listed in columns 4-6. (The administrator adds users to a group so that permissions can be assigned to the group rather than to each individual user.)
13	Lists the size (in bytes) of the file or directory.
14	Displays the date and time the file was created or last modified.
15	Displays the file or directory name.

 Use the `ls -ld [directory name]` command to list entries of the specified directory. The contents of the directory will not be displayed.

Access Categories

Access categories in Linux permissions decide how Linux interprets the permissions of a file. If a user's UID matches the permissions of the file, the user level permissions are applied. If the GID of the user matches the permissions, group permissions are granted. If neither of the permissions match, the general permissions for others are applied. The symbols for the access categories are listed in the following table.

Access Category	Description
u	Modifies permissions at user level.
g	Modifies permissions at group level.
o	Modifies permissions for other users.
a	Modifies permissions for all users globally.

Permission String

The output of the `ls -l` command shows the permission string for a file or directory. The permission string contains ten characters. The first character indicates the type of file; *d* for directory and - for file. Characters at the second, third, and fourth positions denote permissions of the owner or user of the file or directory. Characters at the fifth, sixth, and seventh positions denote the group permissions, and the characters at the eight, ninth, and tenth positions denote the permissions for others.

Permission Levels

Permissions are granted or denied by the owner of the file. The following table lists the levels of various permissions and their description.

Level of Permission	Description
User level r/w/x permission	Only the owner can read, write, and execute the file.
Group level r/w/x permission	Only the members of groups to which the owner belongs to can read, write, and execute the file.
Other level r/w/x permission	All users can read, write, and execute the file.

File Owner

A *file owner* is the user who creates a file or directory. The file owner can set permissions to specify whether other users or groups have rights to read, write, or execute the file.

The chmod Command

The `chmod` command enables you to modify default permissions of a file or directory. Only the owner of the file or the system administrator can change the permissions for a file or directory.

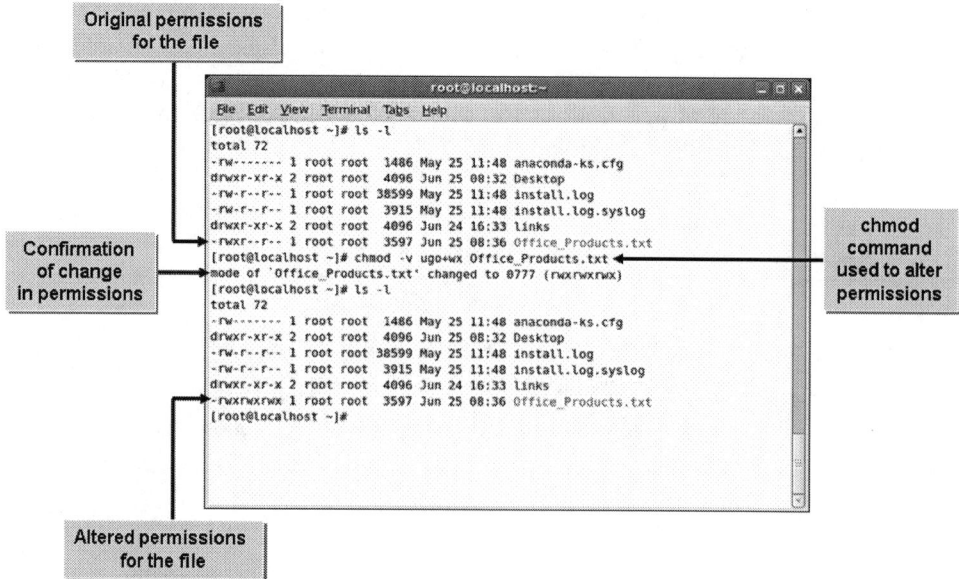

Figure 5-2: Modifying permissions using the chmod command.

Syntax

The syntax of the `chmod` command is `chmod [option] {mode} {file name}`.

The chmod Command Options

The `chmod` command supports different options to modify permissions. One or more of these options may be used at a time.

Option	Description
-c	Reports changes that are made in permissions.
-f	Hides most error messages.
-v	Displays a diagnostic entry for every file processed.
-R	Modifies permissions of files and directories recursively.

The chmod Modes

The `chmod` command supports two modes: the character mode and the numeric mode. The character mode allows you to set permissions using three components, namely, access categories such as `u/g/o/a`; operators such as `+/-/=`; and permission attributes such as `r/w/x`. The numerical mode is represented by three-digit numbers.

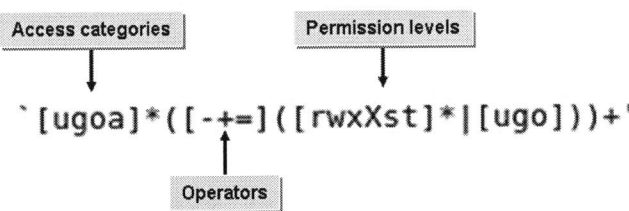

Figure 5-3: Components of the character mode.

Operators Associated with Permissions

Operators decide whether a permission is to be granted or removed. The common operators associated with Linux permissions are listed in the table below.

Operator	Description
+	Grants permissions.
–	Denies permissions.
=	Causes the permissions assigned to overwrite other existing permissions. Assigns permissions similar to those of the reference file.

Permission Attributes

Permission attributes define exactly what a user is allowed to do with a particular file. The three permission attributes are listed in the table.

Permission Attribute	Allows You To
r (read)	View file content.
w (write)	Modify file content.
x (execute)	Run a file (if it is an executable program and is combined with the read attribute).

Changing Permissions Using the Character Method

The permissions of a file or directory can be changed using the character method. The syntax of the chmod command when using this method is chmod *[options] {access categories}{operator}{permission levels} {file name or directory name}*.

Changing Permissions Using Octal Permission Numbers

Linux systems use octal (base-8) numbers to specify permissions. Each permission (r, w, and x) has an associated number.

Octal Number	Attribute	Letter
4	read	r
2	write	w
1	execute	x

By adding the octal numbers for the permissions you want to grant, you get the overall permission number to assign to a directory or file. Full permissions (read, write, and execute) are equivalent to 4 + 2 + 1, or 7. Read and write permissions are 4 + 2, or 6. The complete permissions are expressed as a three-digit number, where each digit corresponds to user, group, and other permissions, respectively.

The syntax of the number method to change permissions is chmod *{number} {file name}*.

How to Modify File and Directory Permissions

Procedure Reference: View File or Directory Permissions

To view file or directory permissions:

1. Log in as a user.
2. View the permissions of a file or directory.
   - View the permissions of a file or directory, as necessary, from the command line.
     - Enter `ls -l` *{file name}* to view the permissions of a file.
     - Enter `ls -ld` *{directory name}* to view the permissions of a directory.
   - View the permissions of a file or folder using the Nautilus browser.
     1. Right-click the file or folder and choose **Properties.**
     2. Select the **Permissions** tab to view the permissions of the file or folder.

Procedure Reference: Modify File or Directory Permissions

To modify file or directory permissions:

1. Log in as root.
2. Change the permissions of a file or directory in the CLI or the GUI.
   - Enter `chmod` *[command options]* *{file or directory name}* to modify permissions in the CLI.
   - Or, modify permissions in the GUI.
     1. Right-click the file or directory and choose **Properties.**
     2. Select the **Permissions** tab.
     3. From the **File Access** or **Folder Access** drop-down list, choose the desired permission for owner, owner groups, and other groups.

ACTIVITY 5-1

Modifying File and Directory Permissions Using the Command Line

Data Files:

Training_Policy.txt

Before You Begin:

1. You have logged in as root in the CLI.

2. Enter `cd /root` to change to the root directory.

3. Enter `cp -p /085039Data/Linux_Permissions/* /root` to copy the files.

4. Enter `chmod 700 Training_Policy.txt` to change the file permissions.

5. Enter `clear` to clear the terminal screen.

Scenario:

A new employee training policy is to be implemented in your organization and your human resources manager wants all employees to be able to read the newly created Training_policy.txt policy document. You have been assigned the task of allotting permissions to all users so that they can read the file.

What You Do	How You Do It
1. View the permissions of the Training_Policy.txt document.	a. Enter `ls -l` to view the permissions of the Training_Policy.txt file.
	b. Observe that the root user has read, write, and execute permissions on the Training_Policy.txt file, while the group and others do not have any permissions.

2. Modify the permissions using the character method and verify the change.

a. Enter `chmod -v go=r Training_Policy.txt` to modify the permissions using character mode.

b. Observe that the message "mode of Training_Policy.txt changed to 0744 (rwxr--r--)" is displayed, indicating that the group and others have now been granted read permission to the file.

c. Enter `ls -l` to view the new permissions of the Training_Policy.txt file.

d. Observe that the permissions of the file have been modified to allow all users to read the file.

e. Enter `clear` to clear the terminal screen.

ACTIVITY 5-2

Modifying File and Directory Permissions Using the Nautilus Browser

Data Files:

Skill_Certification_Policy.txt

Before You Begin:

1. You have logged in as root in both the CLI and the GUI.

2. Switch to the GUI.

3. On the terminal window, enter `cd /root` to change to the root directory.

4. Enter `chown jsmith Skill_Certification_Policy.txt` to change the file ownership.

5. Close the terminal window.

Scenario:

The human resources manager, Rachel, updated the company policy document Skill_Certification_Policy.txt on skill certification and wants you to make this policy document accessible to all employees. You want to show her how to modify the permissions of files and directories using the Nautilus browser because she is familiar only with the GUI.

What You Do	How You Do It
1. View the permissions of the Skill_Certification_Policy.txt file.	a. On the desktop, double-click **root's Home** to view the files and folders.
	b. In the **root – File Browser** window, right-click the **Skill_Certification_Policy.txt** file and choose **Properties.**
	c. In the **Skill_Certification_Policy.txt Properties** dialog box, select the **Permissions** tab to view the permissions of the file.
	d. On the **Permissions** tab, observe that **jsmith** is the owner of the file and has read and write access to the file. In addition, the group **Human_Resources** does not have any access to the file.

2. Modify the permissions of the Skill_ Certification_Policy.txt file using the **Properties** dialog box.

a. From the **Access** drop-down list, which is below the **Group** drop-down list, select **Read-only.**

b. From the **Access** drop-down list, which is below the **Others** drop-down list, select **Read-only.**

c. Click **Close** to save the modifications and exit the **Skill_Certification_Policy.txt Properties** dialog box.

d. Close the **root – File Browser** window.

TOPIC B
Modify Default Permissions

You can modify file and directory permissions. Now, you need to know how to alter default permissions of files. In this topic, you will modify default permissions in Linux.

Modifying default file permissions will allow you to set higher or lower security levels for files created by users. This will allow high-level users to create files that are completely secure from other users.

Default File and Directory Permissions

In Linux, default permissions are assigned to newly created files and directories based on user privileges. For files created by the root user, the default permission is 644, which means the root user has read (4) and write (2) permissions, while group users and others will have only read (4) permission. For directories created by the root user, the default permission is 755, which means the root user has read (4), write (2), and execute (1) permissions, while group users and others will have only read (4) and execute (1) permissions. In the case of users with more limited access rights, Linux assigns a permission of 664 for newly created files and 775 for newly created directories. These default permissions are determined by the user file creation mask or umask. However, the default permissions may be altered by the root user.

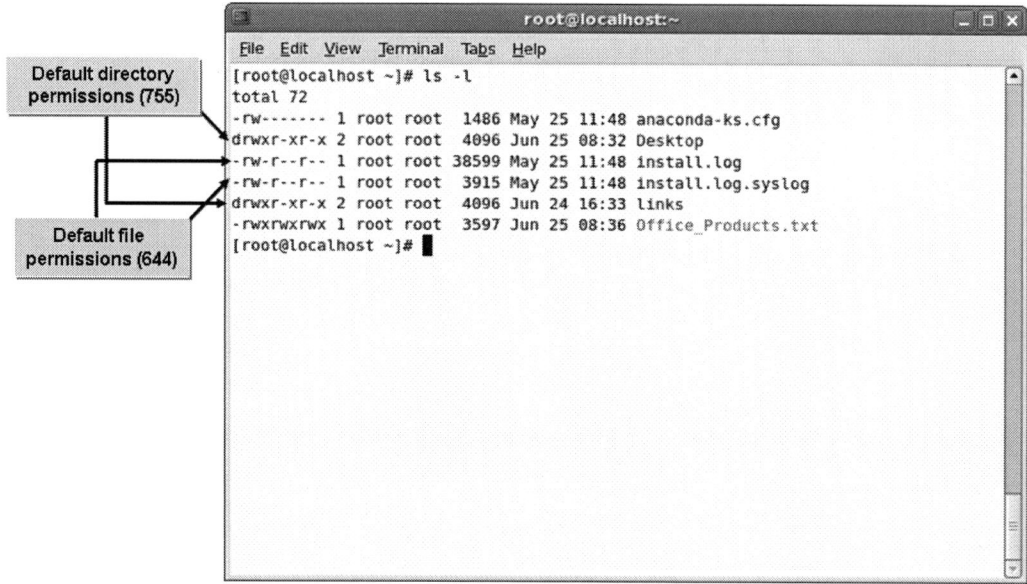

Figure 5-4: The ls command displaying the default file and directory permissions.

The umask Command

The *umask command* automatically alters the default permissions on newly created files and directories. The default permissions on newly created files and directories can be changed for security reasons.

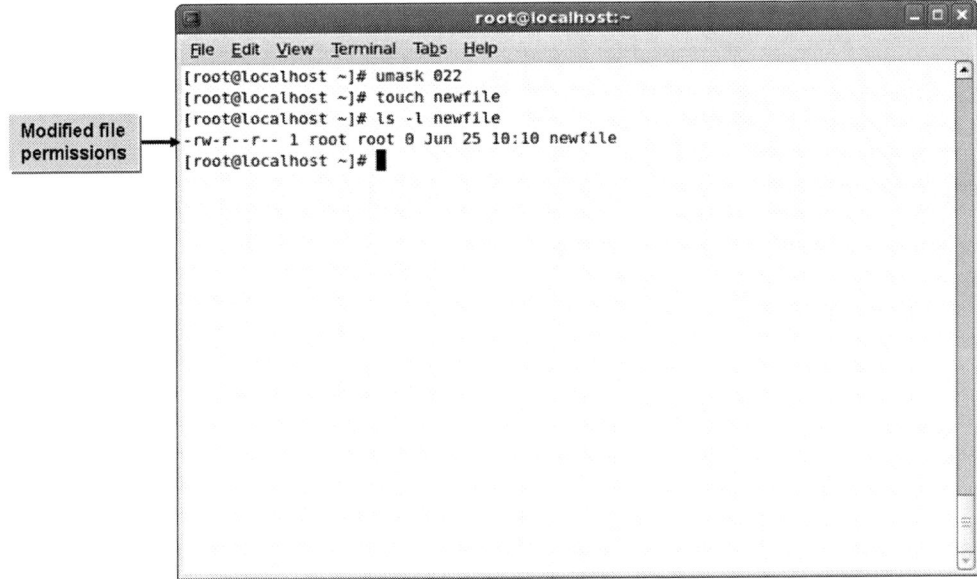

Modified file permissions

Figure 5-5: Default file permissions modified using the umask command.

Syntax

The syntax of the *umask* command is `umask` `number`.

The Effect of umask on Files

By default, the base permissions for nonexecutable files in Linux are `rw-rw-rw-` or 666. By entering `umask 022`, the permissions assigned to all files, created from that moment until the system is restarted, will be `rw-r--r--` (644). The numbers given with the `umask` command specify the permissions that need to be cleared from the default settings.

Number	Clears
0	Nothing from the users' default permissions, leaving `rw-`.
2	Write permission from the group, leaving just `r--`.
2	Write permission from others, leaving just `r--`.

These settings correspond to the default umask of the root user.

The Effect of umask on Directories

By default, the base permissions for directories in Linux are `rwxrwxrwx` or 777. By entering `umask 022`, the permissions assigned to all directories, created from that moment until the system is restarted, will be `rwxr-xr-x` (755). The numbers given with the `umask` command specify the permissions that need to be cleared from the default settings.

Number	Clears
0	Nothing from the users' default permissions, leaving rwx.
2	Write permission from the group, leaving just r-x.
2	Write permission from others, leaving just r-x.

These settings correspond to the default umask of the root user.

How to Modify Default Permissions

Procedure Reference: Modify Default Permissions

To modify default permissions:

1. Log in as root.

2. Enter umask *{umask number}* to change the default umask value.

3. Create a new file to verify that files created from now on have different default permissions.

ACTIVITY 5-3
Modifying Default Permissions

Before You Begin:

1. You have logged as root in the GUI.
2. The user account for chris already exists on the system.

Scenario:

Your colleague, Chris, creates large number of documentation files that are used by other users on the system. Your manager would like all files created by her, from now on, to be readable and modifiable by all users.

Account details of the user:

- User name: chris
- Password: myp@$$w0rd

What You Do	How You Do It
1. Change the umask value on Chris's system to 0000.	a. Switch to the fourth terminal. b. Log in as **chris** on Chris' system. c. Enter **umask** to view the current umask value. d. Observe that the umask value is displayed as **0002**. e. Enter **touch newfile1** to create a test file with existing permissions. f. Enter **umask 0000** to alter the umask value.
2. Check whether the umask value has been changed.	a. Enter **umask** to view the new umask value. b. Observe that the umask value is now displayed as **0000**.

3. Create a file and compare its permissions to an existing file.

   a. Enter **touch newfile2** to create a file.

   b. Enter **ls -l new*** to view the permissions of the files.

   c. Observe the difference in file permissions of **newfile1** and **newfile2.**

   d. Log out of the terminal.

TOPIC C
Modify File and Directory Ownership

With an understanding of default permissions, you can modify the owners of files and directories. A user or group may not want other users to access the files created by them. Also, users may require access to files created by other users. In this topic, you will modify file and directory ownership.

Imagine that you have been working on a project that is to be taken over by one of your colleagues. You will need to transfer the ownership of all the files you created for this project to your colleague. Modifying file and directory ownership will enable you to further customize your files and directories as well as your system security. This allows users to manage files associated with their profiles.

The chown Command

The `chown` command can be used to change the owner, group, or both for a file or directory. The following table describes how to use this command.

Command Syntax	Description
`chown {user name} {file name}`	Changes the owner but not the group.
`chown {user name.group name} {file name}`	Changes the owner and the group.
`chown {user name.} {file name}`	Changes the owner and the group. The group will be changed to the specified user's login group.
`chown {.group name} {file name}`	Changes the group but not the owner. This is the same as using the `chgrp` command.

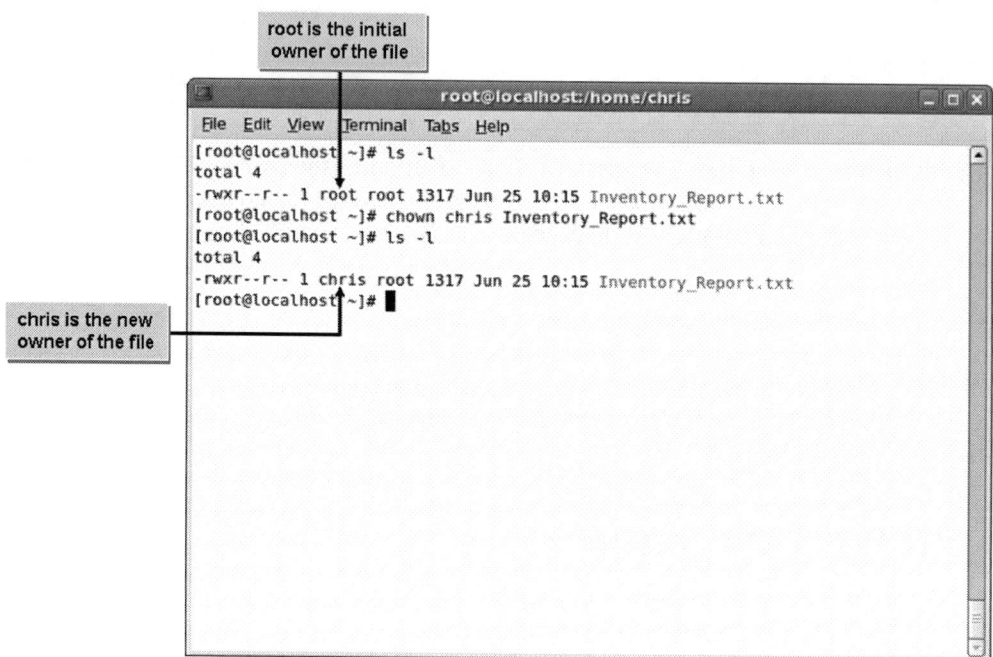

Figure 5-6: File ownership changed using the chown command.

Recursively Changing Ownership

You can combine the chown command with the -R option to recursively change ownership through a directory structure. You can also use metacharacters to change ownership of groups of files at the same time.

Changing Group Ownership

The chgrp command is used to change the group ownership of a file or directory. The syntax of the command is chgrp {group} {file name}.

How to Modify File and Directory Ownership

Procedure Reference: View File or Directory Ownership

To view file or directory ownership:

1. Log in as a user.
2. View the ownership of a file or directory in the desired mode.
    - View the ownership of a file or directory at the command prompt.
        - Enter ls -l {file name} to view the ownership of a file.
        - Enter ls -ld {directory name} to view the ownership of a directory.
    - View the ownership of a file or directory using the Nautilus browser.
        1. Right-click the file or directory and choose **Properties.**
        2. Select the **Permissions** tab to view the ownership of the file or directory.

Procedure Reference: Modify File or Directory Ownership

To modify file or directory ownership:

1. Log in as root.

2. Change the ownership of a file or directory.

● Modify file or directory ownership at the command prompt.

■ Enter chown *[command options] {file or directory name}* to change the user ownership of the file or directory.

■ Enter chgrp *[command options] {file or directory name}* to change the group ownership of the file or directory.

● Modify file or directory ownership using the Nautilus browser.

1. Right-click the file or directory and choose **Properties.**

2. Select the **Permissions** tab.

3. Make changes to the ownership as necessary.

■ From the **Owner** drop-down list, select the owner of the file or directory at user level.

■ From the **Group** drop-down list, select the owner of the file or directory at group level.

ACTIVITY 5-4

Modifying File and Directory Ownership Using the Command Line

Before You Begin:
Press **Ctrl+Alt+F1** to switch back to the first terminal.

Scenario:
Your colleague, Patrick, created a large number of files. He wants a centralized location to store them. As a system administrator, you decide to create a directory /work_files/pat_files, which Pat will have ownership of.

What You Do	How You Do It
1. Create the /work_files/pat_files directory and verify that it was created.	a. Enter **cd /work_files** to switch to the /work_files directory.
	b. Enter **mkdir pat_files** to create a work directory.
	c. Enter **ls -l** to view the contents of the /work_files directory with ownership details.
	d. Observe that the root is the owner of the pat_files directory.
2. Change the ownership of the pat_files directory to the user, patrick.	a. Enter **chown pat pat_files** to change the ownership of the work directory.
	b. Enter **ls -l** to view the directory contents with ownership details.
	c. Observe that the owner of the pat_files directory is Patrick.
	d. Clear the terminal screen.

TOPIC D
Set Advanced Permissions

Now that you have modified file and directory ownership, you can set advanced permissions for users. There may be instances when you have to use special permissions to enable users to access files or directories. In this topic, you will set advanced permissions.

While it is desirable to allow only users with root or administrative permissions to execute certain commands, sometimes other users need to be able to issue them. Setting advanced permissions will allow other users to execute and maintain system utilities so that the Linux+ administrator does not have to. This will save the administrator time and effort.

Special Permissions

Special permissions are used when normal permissions become inadequate, usually in the case of processes. Through special permissions, less privileged users are allowed to execute a file that can usually be run only by the root user. Set User ID (SUID), or setuid, is the permission that allows a user who executes a file to have similar permissions as the owner of the file. Set Group ID (SGID), or setgid, is the permission that allows a user who executes a file to have similar permissions as the group owner of the file.

The SUID and SGID Permissions

The SUID and SGID commands are powerful tools that enable users to perform tasks without problems that could arise with users having the actual permissions of that group or user. However, these can be dangerous tools too.

While changing the permissions of a file to be either SUID or SGID, the following points should be considered:

- Use the lowest permissions needed to accomplish a task. It is recommended not to give a file the same SUID or SGID as the root user. A user with fewer privileges often can be configured to perform the task.
- Watch for back doors. If the user runs a program with the SUID set to root, then the user retains root as the effective UID when the user goes through the back door. The following can be used as back doors:
  - Programs that enable you to shell out.
  - Programs with multiple entrances and exits.

The chattr Command

The `chattr` command is used to change the attributes of a file on a Linux filesystem.

The following table lists the description for the options used in the syntax of the `chattr` command.

Command Option	Used To
-R	Recursively change the attributes of directories and their contents.

Command Option	Used To
-V	Display the output of the chattr command and print the program version.
-v version	Set the version number of a file.

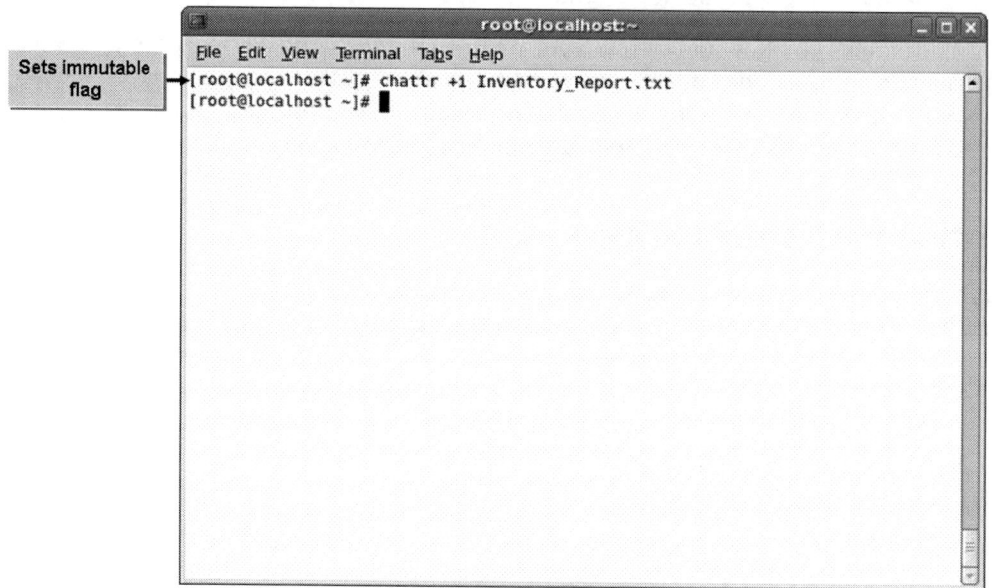

Figure 5-7: Attribute of the file set using the chattr command.

Syntax

The syntax of the chattr command is chattr [-RV] [-v *version*] { *mode* } *files*.

The lsattr Command

The lsattr command is used to list the file attributes of a file on a Linux filesystem.

The following table describes the options used in the syntax of the lsattr command.

Option	Used To
-R	Recursively list the attributes of directories and their contents.
-V	Display the program version.
-a	List all files in directories.
-d	List directories like files, instead of listing their contents.
-v	List the version number of the file.

Syntax

The syntax of the lsattr command is lsattr [-RVadv] [*files...*].

Sticky Bits

A *sticky bit* is a permission bit that provides protection for files in a directory. It ensures that only the owner of a file can delete the file or directory. A sticky bit also forces a program or file to remain in memory so that it need not be reloaded when it is invoked again. The sticky bit on the file indicates to the operating system that the file will be executed frequently. Files with sticky bits are kept in the swap space, or in the disk space, that is set aside for virtual memory.

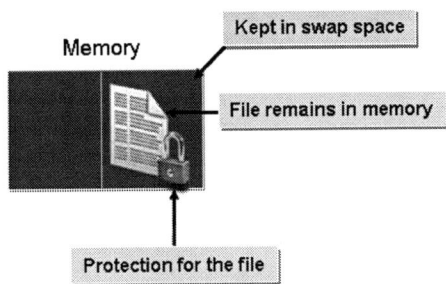

Figure 5-8: A file in the memory protected by a sticky bit.

The Immutable Flag

Definition:

The *immutable flag* is an extended attribute of a file or directory that prevents it from being modified. The immutable flag is not set on all files. It is set only on those files, such as configuration files, that should not be modified. A single directory can have a mix of mutable and immutable files and subdirectories. Also, an immutable subdirectory can have mutable files.

Example:

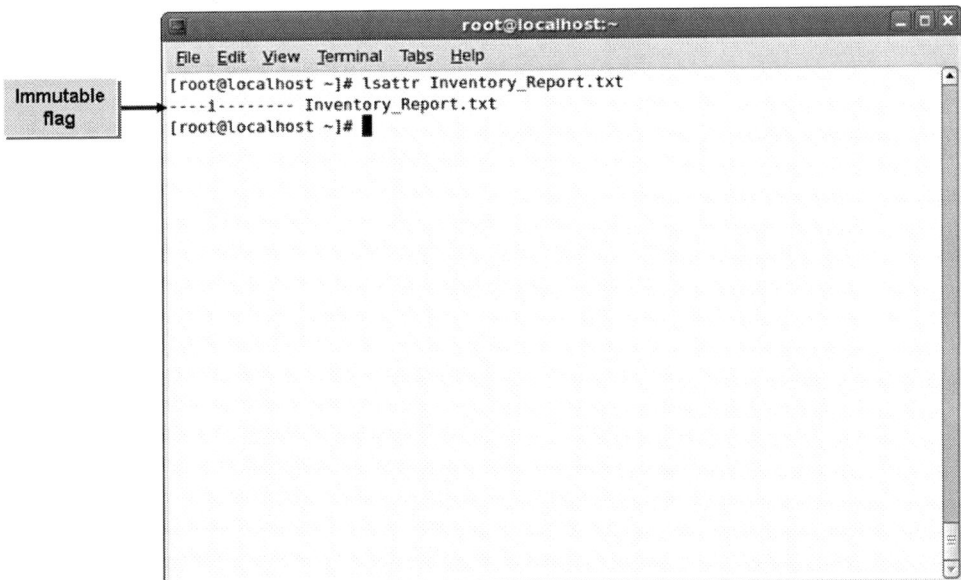

Figure 5-9: The immutable flag prevents modification of the file.

The Access Control List

The *Access Control List (ACL)* is a list of permissions attached to an object. Usually, a file object in Linux is associated with three sets of permissions—read (r), write (w), and execute (x), for the three user groups—file owner, group, and other. ACLs can be used for situations where the traditional file permission concept does not suffice. They allow the assignment of permissions to individual users or groups even if these do not correspond to the owner or the owning group.

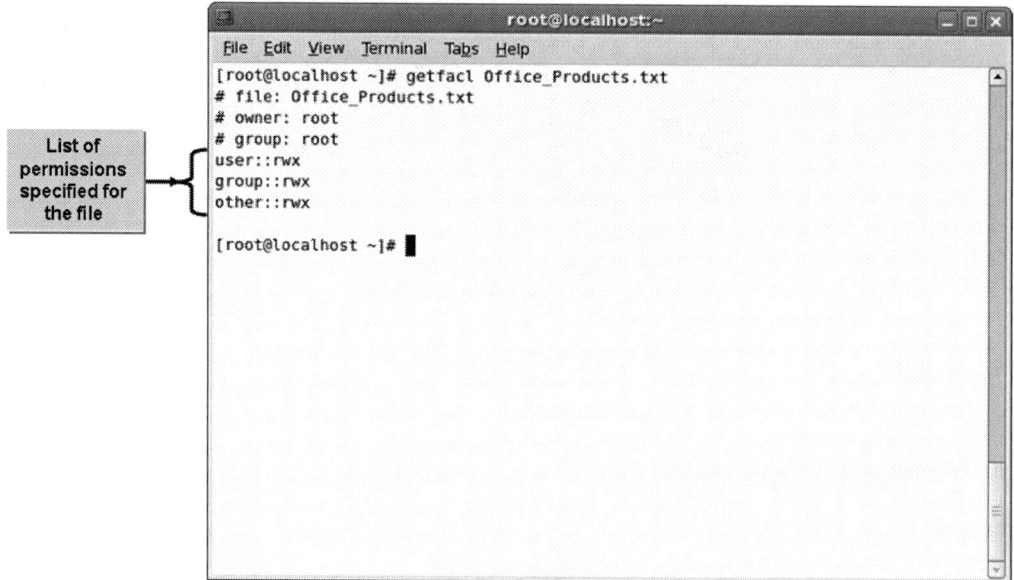

Figure 5-10: *The ACL of a file displayed using the getfacl command.*

Commands Associated with the ACL

ACLs can be managed at filesystem level, or at the file and directory level. To find out the ACL specifications of a file, you can use the `getfacl` command. To set the access control specifications for files and directories, you can use the `setfacl` command with its different options.

Advanced Permission Commands

Advanced permission commands can be used effectively to set special file or directory access rights for users. Some of the common commands to set these permissions are listed in the following table along with their syntax.

Command Syntax	Used To
chmod u{operator}s {file name}	Set SUID for a file.
chmod g{operator}s {Directory name}	Set SGID for a directory.
chmod o{operator}t {file name}	Set the sticky bit for a file.
umask Value	Set the default file creation mode.
chattr Operatori File/Directory name	Set the immutable flag for a file or directory.

How to Set Process Permissions

Procedure Reference: Set Special Permissions for Files and Directories

To set special permissions for files and directories:

1. Log in as a user.
2. Set special permissions for files and directories.
   - Enter `chmod u+s` *{file name}* to add the SUID permission for the file.
   - Enter `chmod g+s` *{directory name}* to add the SGID permission for the directory.
   - Enter `chmod +t` *{directory name}* to add the sticky bit permission for the directory.
3. If necessary, enter `ls -l` to verify the changes.

Procedure Reference: Manage ACLs for Files and Directories

To manage ACLs for files and directories:

1. Log in as root.
2. Manage ACLs for files and directories:
   - Enter `getfacl` *{file or directory name}* to view the ACL for the specified file or directory.
   - Enter `setfacl -m {g | u | o}:[user or group name]:[r,w & x combination]` *{file or directory name}* to set the ACL for the specified file or directory.
   - Enter `setfacl -m d:{g | u}:[user or group name]:[r,w & x combination]` *{directory name}* to inherit all the permissions for the newly created content in the specified directory name.
   - Enter `setfacl -x {g | u}:[user name]` *{file or directory name}* to set the ACL for the specified file or directory.

ACTIVITY 5-5
Setting User Access to Files

Data Files:

Salaryaccount.txt

Before You Begin:

1. You have logged in as root in the CLI.

2. Enter `useradd tax` to add a new user, tax. Enter `passwd tax` to change the password for the user, tax.

3. Type *myp@$$w0rd* and press **Enter.**

4. Type *myp@$$w0rd* and press **Enter** to confirm the password.

5. Create two other users by following step 2 to step 4 based on the details given below:

    User name: income, Password: myp@$$w0rd

    User name: expenditure, Password: myp@$$w0rd

6. Enter `usermod -G tax income` to add the income user to the tax group. Enter `usermod -G tax expenditure` to add the expenditure user to the tax group.

7. Enter `logout` to log out the root user.

8. Log in as tax. Type *myp@$$w0rd* and press **Enter.**

9. Enter `mkdir Finance` to create a new directory. Enter `logout` to log out the tax user.

10. Log in as root. Type *p@ssw0rd* and press **Enter.**

11. Enter `cp /085039Data/Linux_Permissions/* /home/tax/Finance` to copy the data files to the Finance directory. Enter `logout` to log out the root user.

Scenario:

You are working as a junior system administrator in an organization. The finance department consists of three user groups: Income, Expenditure, and Tax. Income and Expenditure are members of the Tax group. The finance manager does not want the Tax group to be able to change the Salaryaccount.txt document located in the /home/tax/Finance directory.

User account details:

- Login name for tax user: tax
- Password for tax user: myp@$$w0rd
- Login name for income user: income
- Password for income user: myp@$$w0rd
- Login name for expenditure user: expenditure
- Password for expenditure user: myp@$$w0rd

What You Do	How You Do It
1. Set the group read and execute permissions for the tax home directory.	a. Log in as **tax** in the CLI. b. Enter `cd ..` to switch to the home directory. c. Enter `ls -l` to view the access rights of the tax directory. d. Enter `chmod g+rx tax` to set the group read and execute permission for the tax home directory. e. Clear the terminal screen. f. Enter `ls -l` to view the changed access rights of the home directory of the **tax** user.
2. Remove the group write access for the Finance directory.	a. Enter `cd tax` to switch to the tax directory. b. Enter `ls -l` to view the access permissions of the Finance directory. c. Enter `chmod g-w Finance` to remove the group write permission of the Finance directory. d. Enter `ls -l` to view the changed access rights of the Finance directory. e. Log out of the account.
3. Set the read-only permission for the Finance directory.	a. Log in as **root**. b. Enter `chattr +i /home/tax/Finance` to set the immutable flag for the Finance directory. c. Log out of the terminal.

4.   Check whether the members of the **Tax** group are able to remove the Salaryaccount.txt file.

a.   Log in as the **income** user.

b.   Enter `cd /home/tax/Finance` to switch to the Finance directory.

c.   Enter `ls` to view the contents of the directory.

d.   Enter `rm Salaryaccount.txt` to verify if the Salaryaccount.txt file can be deleted.

e.   Observe that a prompt with a message to confirm the removal of a rights protected regular file is displayed.

f.   Enter `y` to confirm the removal of the file.

g.   Observe that a message is displayed to indicate that permission is denied because the immutable flag for the directory is set.

h.   Log out of the terminal.

Lesson 5 Follow-up

In this lesson, you modified permissions and ownership of files and directories in a Linux system. You also set process permissions to allow other users to execute a process generally run by an administrator, saving them both time and effort. You will now be able to efficiently control the security of your Linux system.

1. **How can you preserve confidentiality of information on Linux systems?**

2. **When should default permissions be modified?**

6 | Printing Files

Lesson Time: 1 hour(s), 30 minutes

Lesson Objectives:

In this lesson, you will print files.

You will:

- Configure a local printer.
- Format text in a file and print it.
- Manage print jobs and queues.
- Configure remote printing.

Introduction

You worked with files in Linux. Now, you may want to print files containing essential information. In this lesson, you will work with printer hardware and software.

Like all standard operating systems, Linux allows its users to print files. You may have trouble viewing lengthy files continuously on a monitor and may consider printing them on paper. Linux includes effective printing utilities that allow you to print configuration files and any other text documents you create.

This lesson covers all or part of the following CompTIA Linux+ (2009) certification objectives:

- Topic A
  - Objective 3.9
- Topic B
  - Objective 3.9
- Topic C
  - Objective 3.9
- Topic D
  - Objective 3.2

TOPIC A
Configure a Local Printer

You worked with various files in Linux and may want to print some of them. Before you can print a file, you must configure a printer to work with the Linux operating system. In this topic, you will configure a local printer to work with your system.

Computers at homes and offices are regularly used for printing. Like other operating systems, Linux also supports printing. However, not all printers are compatible with the Linux operating system. You must check for compatibility before selecting a printer to be used with a Linux system. Even compatible printers need to be configured with a system before they can be used for printing.

Printer Software

Definition:

Printer software is a program that enables a printing device to print text or graphics on a page. The printer software provided with a printer includes a driver and utilities. The printer driver allows users to choose settings for the printer. The printer utilities ensure that the printers are in operating condition.

Example:

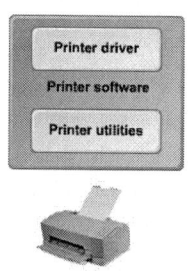

Figure 6-1: *Printer software comprises drivers and utilities.*

PostScript®

PostScript® is a *Page Description Language (PDL)* that tells a printer how to display text or graphics on a page. Laser printers primarily use PostScript for printing documents. The print quality is high because it resizes fonts and images without distortion. PostScript can work on different platforms and printers and therefore, can be used to share documents on the Internet.

Figure 6-2: *PostScript helps a system communicate with a printer.*

Linux Compatible Printers

PostScript is the standard PDL supported by Linux. PostScript printers support printing in Linux because PostScript Printer Definitions (PPDs) describe and provide access to printer-specific features. PPDs function as drivers for PostScript printers and they provide a unified interface for the printer's capabilities.

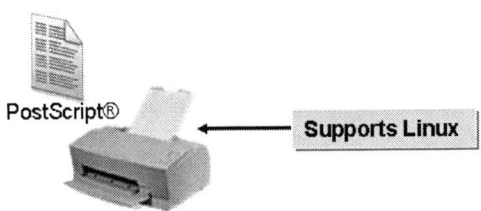

Figure 6-3: A PostScript printer.

 For information about specific distributions of Linux and installation of printer drivers, visit the website of the specific distribution.

Configuring a Local Printer

When Linux is installed, you can configure a printer to work with the operating system. Using the print system manager, you can add printers to the system. A local printer is attached directly to the Linux workstation via a parallel, serial, or USB port. A remote *Line Printer Daemon (LPD)* printer is attached to a Unix or Linux machine elsewhere on the network.

 LPD is a Linux system service for network printing.

CUPS

Common UNIX Printing System (CUPS) is a systematic print management system for Linux; this printing system allows a computer to function as a print server. A system running CUPS is a host that can initiate print jobs from client systems. These jobs are then processed and sent to the appropriate printer. The main advantage of CUPS is that it can process different data formats on the same print server. CUPS is designed for scheduling print jobs, processing administrative commands, and providing printer status information to local and remote programs. The CUPS configuration is accessed by using a browser window. By making changes through the browser interface, you can edit the cupsd.conf file, which is located in the /etc/cups directory.

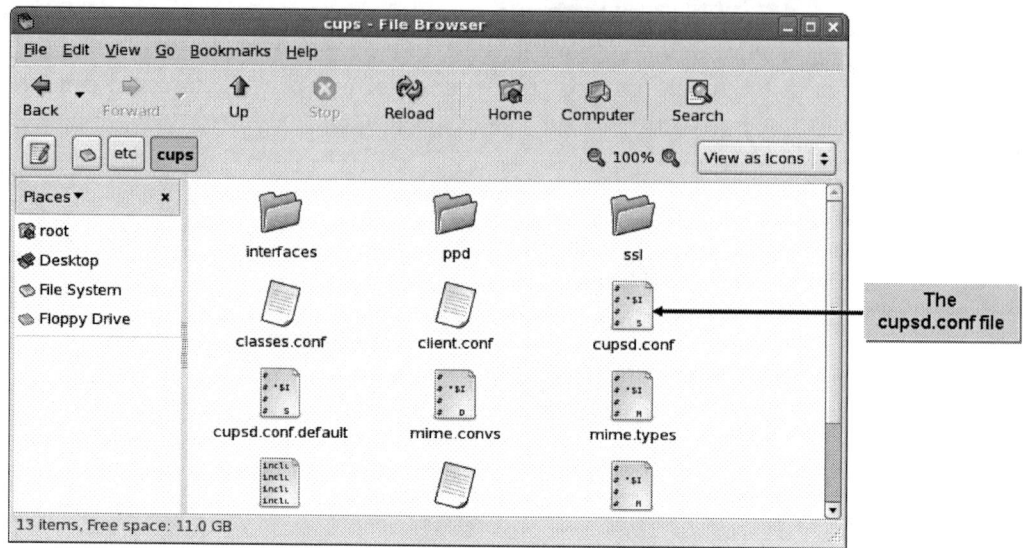

Figure 6-4: Accessing the cupsd.conf file located in /etc/cups directory.

The Print Process

The print process enables you to print a document. There are various steps involved in this process. When a user issues a command to print a document in an application, the following steps take place:

1. The application invokes the printing client software.

2. The file passes from the printing client to the printer *spooler*.

3. The file then passes through a number of filters that convert the document from one format to another, before being finally sent to the printer.

4. The printer then prints the file.

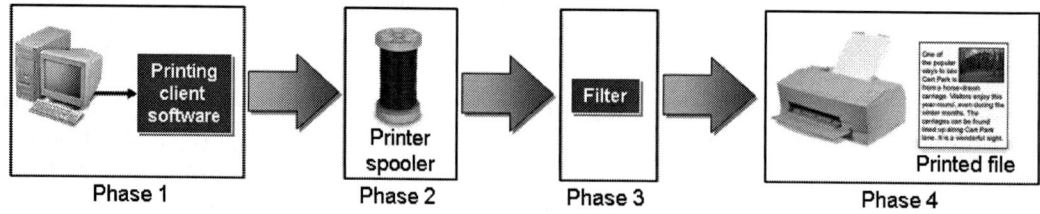

Figure 6-5: Process involved in printing a document.

Spooling

Spooling is the procedure by which print jobs are temporarily stored. If the printer is busy, each job is placed in a waiting line or print queue. These jobs are stored in a temporary storage space called *spool*. Files in the queue are printed when the printer becomes free. This prevents programs from having to wait during a slow printing process.

Print Queues

Definition:

A *print queue* is a temporary storage area that sorts incoming print jobs. Print queues are used by the print daemon, so that applications that need to use the printer do not have to wait to issue the command for printing until the current print job is completed. A list of print jobs contains details of the file being printed currently and the files yet to be printed. Print queues allow multiple users to share a printer.

Example:

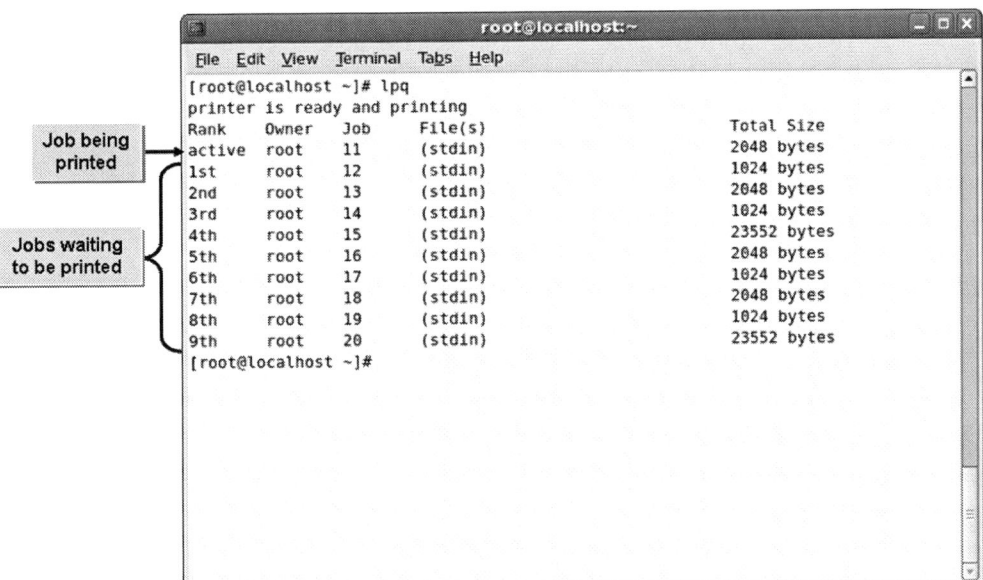

Figure 6-6: Print jobs in a queue.

How to Configure a Local Printer

Procedure Reference: Add a Printer Using the Printer Configuration Dialog Box

To add a printer using the **Printer Configuration** dialog box:

1. Connect the printer to the LPT1 port. Switch on the printer and load paper.

2. Log in as root in the GUI.

3. Open the **Printer configuration** window.

   ● On the terminal, enter `system-config-printer`.

   ● From the **Panel**, choose **System→Administration→Printing.**

4. In the **Printer configuration - localhost** window, on the tool bar, click **New Printer.**

5. In the **New Printer** dialog box, in the **Printer Name** text box, enter the name of the printer.

6. If necessary, in the **Description** text box, enter the description of the printer.

7. If necessary, in the **Location** text box, enter the location details of the printer.

8. Click **Forward** to continue with the printer installation.

9. In the **Select Connection** list box, in the **Devices** list box, select the printer device and click **Forward** to install the printer.

10. In the **Makes** list box, select the printer make and click **Forward.**

11. In the **Models** list box, select the corresponding model, and in the **Drivers** list box, select the corresponding driver and click **Forward.**

12. On the confirmation page, click **Apply** to add the new printer.

13. From the menu, choose **File→Quit** to close the **Printer configuration** dialog box.

Procedure Reference: Add a Printer Using the CUPS Browser Interface

To add a printer using the CUPS browser interface:

1. If necessary, press **Ctrl+Alt+F7** to shift to the GUI.

2. In the **GNOME Panel,** click the Web Browser icon to launch the web browser.

3. In the address bar, double-click the existing address to select it.

4. Enter `localhost:631` to launch the CUPS browser interface.

5. On the **Home** tab, in the **Welcome** section, click **Add Printer.**

6. On the **Add Printer** web page, in the **Add New Printer** section, in the **Name, Location,** and **Description** text boxes, type the name, location, and description of the printer, respectively. Click **Continue.**

7. On the **Administration** tab, in the **Device for {printer name}** section, from the **Device** list, select **LPT #1** to configure a local printer. Click **Continue.**

8. In the **Make/Manufacturer for {printer name}** section, in the **Make** list box, select the manufacturer of the printer. Click **Continue.**

9. In the **Model/Driver for {printer name}** section, in the **Model** list box, select the model number of your printer and click **Add Printer.**

10. In the **Authentication Required** dialog box, enter the root user name and password. Click **OK.**

11. If necessary, on the **Set Printer Options** web page, modify the settings as required and close the CUPS web browser interface.

ACTIVITY 6-1

Configuring a Generic Printer

Before You Begin:

1. Switch to the GUI.

2. The printer is connected to the parallel port (LPT1) of the system and is switched on.

3. Paper is loaded in the printer.

Scenario:

You want to print important files in Linux. However, you have not configured any printer on the Linux system and therefore, you decide to configure one.

What You Do	How You Do It
1. Add a printer to the Linux system.	a. Choose **System→Administration→ Printing.**
	b. In the **Printer configuration - localhost** dialog box, click **New Printer** to add a printer.
	c. In the **New Printer** dialog box, in the **Printer Name** text box, type *printer1* and press the **Tab** key.
	d. In the **Description** text box, type *Test* and press the **Tab** key.
	e. In the **Location** text box, type *Lab* and click **Forward.**

2. Select the make and model of the printer to be configured.

    a. In the **Devices** list box, ensure that **LPT #1** is selected and click **Forward.**

    b. In the **Makes** list box, ensure that **Generic** is selected and click **Forward.**

    c. In the **Models** list box, scroll down and select **PostScript Printer.**

    d. In the **Drivers** list box, select the **foomatic: Generic - Postscript.ppd (recommended)** option and click **Forward.**

    e. On the confirmation page, observe that a message "Going to create a new printer printer1 at parallel:/dev/lp0." is displayed.

    f. Click **Apply** to add the printer.

3. Check whether **printer1** has been added to the **Local Printers** list and make it the default printer of your system.

    a. Observe that **printer1** has been added to the **Local Printers** list.

    b. In the **Server Settings** section, click **printer1.**

    c. On the **Settings** tab, in the **Default Printer** section, click **Make Default Printer** to make **printer1** the default printer of your system.

    d. Close the **Printer configuration - localhost** dialog box.

ACTIVITY 6-2

Configuring a USB Printer in Linux

Before You Begin:

1. You have logged in as root in the GUI.

2. The USB printer is connected to the USB port of the system and is switched on.

3. Paper is loaded in the printer.

Scenario:

As a system administrator, you are asked to set up a printer in the Linux environment for the HR department. You identified that a USB printer is to be used for this purpose.

What You Do	How You Do It
1. Check the printer configuration.	a. Choose **System→Administration→Printing.**
	b. In the **Printer configuration - localhost** window, observe that in the **Local Printers** section, the USB printer is listed as it is automatically added.
	c. Select *{printer name}*.
	d. On the **Settings** tab, in the **Default Printer** section, click **Make Default Printer** to make it the default printer.
	e. Observe that the message "This is the default printer" is displayed.
2. Print the test page.	a. Click **Print Test Page** to print a test page.
	b. Observe that a message box is displayed with the text "Test page submitted as job *{job number}*."
	c. Click **OK** to print the test page.
	d. Collect the hardcopy of the test page and file it.
	e. Click **Cancel Tests** to cancel other tests.
	f. Close the **Printer configuration - localhost** window.

TOPIC B
Print Files

You configured a compatible printer to work with a Linux system. With the printer installed, you are ready to print files. In this topic, you will print files in the Linux system.

Printing a file is a routine task. Learning to print in Linux will save you time when documenting system information and changes. While you can print from the GUI, learning to print from the command line will give you greater freedom when printing from another location.

Printer Commands

Linux comprises various commands that facilitate the printing process. Some of the commands are described in the following table.

Command	Description
lp	Submits files for printing or alters a pending print job. The syntax of this command is lp *[command options] {file name}*.
lpr	Submits files for printing. Files entered on the command line are sent to the specified printer or to the print queue if the printer is busy. If no files are entered on the command line, the lpr command reads the print file from the standard input. The syntax of this command is lpr *[command options] {file name}*.
lpq	Displays the current print queue status. The syntax of this command is lpq *[command options] {Print queue name}*.
lprm	Cancels print jobs in the queue. The syntax of this command is lprm *{print job id}*.
lpc	Allows you to start or stop a printer, enable or disable queues, manage jobs in the queue, and obtain a status report on the printers and queues. The syntax of this command is lpc *[parameter]*.
lpstat	Displays CUPS status information. The syntax of this command is lpstat *[command options]*.
cancel	Deletes a print job from the print queue. The syntax of this command is cancel *[command options]*.

The lpr Command

The *lpr command* comprises various options that allow you to specify the nature of print output.

The `lpr` command options are described in the following table.

Option	Used To
-E	Force encryption when connecting to the server.
-P destination	Print files with the destination printer specified.
-# copies	Set the number of copies to print from 1 to 100.
-C name	Set the job name.
-l	Specify that the print file is already formatted and sent without being filtered to the destination.
-o option	Set a job option.
-p	Specify that the print file needs to be formatted with a shaded header that includes the date, time, job name, and page number of the file.
-r	Specify that the print files should be deleted after being printed.

The lpc Command

The *lpc command* comprises various options that allow you to manage print jobs.

The following table lists the frequently used `lpc` command options to control a print job.

Option	Used To
lpc defaultq	View the default queue for the printer.
lpc hold [Print queue name] [Job ID]	Hold the specified printer job in the queue.
lpc holdall [Print queue name]	Hold all new jobs given to the specified queue.
lpc release [Print queue name] [Job ID]	Release the print job that has been put on hold.
lpc noholdall [Print queue name]	Turn off the holdall option and allow all new print jobs to be executed (the jobs that were put on hold after running the holdall option should be activated using the release option).
lpc lpd	Determine if the lpd daemon is running.
lpc move [Print queue name] [Job ID] [Destination queue name]	Move the specified job to a different print queue.
lpc topq [Print queue name] [Job ID]	Place the specified job at the top of the print queue.
lpc lpq	View print jobs in the queue.

Option	Used To
lpc lprm [Print queue name] [Job ID]	Remove print jobs from the queue.

The pr Command

The pr command formats files before they are printed. By default, the pr command sends its output to the terminal screen, but is also used in combination with commands that send output to a printer. The pr command formats the files' header containing the page number, file name, date, and time.

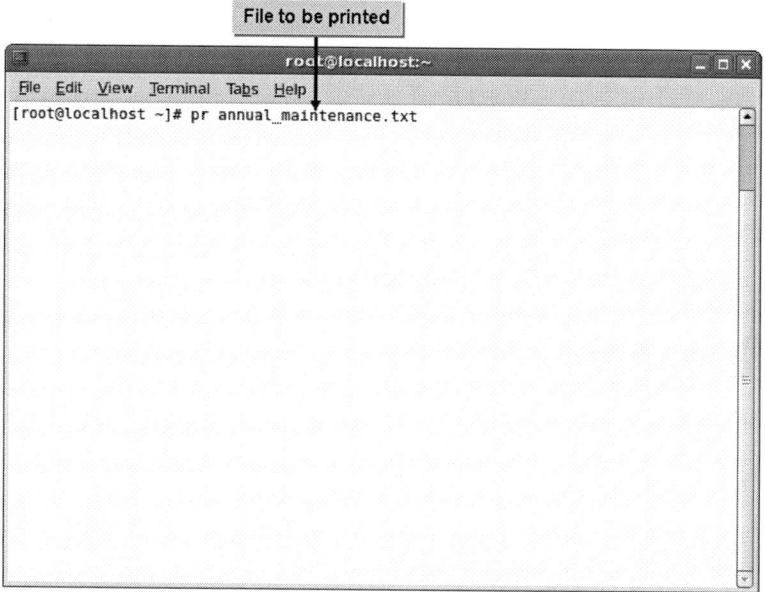

Figure 6-7: Printing a document using the pr command.

Syntax

The syntax of the pr command is pr [command options] {file name}.

The pr Command Options

There are many formatting options available for use with the pr command.

Option	Description
-column	Produces a multi-column output with the data arranged in columns.
-d	Produces a double-spaced output.
-m	Merges files.
-F	Wraps the lines of the input files to fit the column width.

Option	Description
-1[#]	Changes the page length of the output, where # is the number of lines per page.
-h [new header text]	Allows you to change what is included in the header at the top of each page, where [new header text] replaces the file name in the default header contents.

Using pr with Piping

When you format your output with the pr command, you can send the formatted output to a file to be printed using the redirection operators (>) and pipe. For example, pr -145 sales > sales.out creates the sales.out file, which is formatted and ready for printing. In addition, you can send the formatted file directly to the printer using the lpr command. For example, the pr -145 sales | lpr command sends the formatted sales file directly to the default printer.

How to Print Files
Procedure Reference: Print a File Without Text Formatting

To print a file without text formatting:
1. Change to the directory that contains the file you want to print.
2. Print the file using cat [file name] | lpr

Procedure Reference: Print a File With Text Formatting

To print a file with text formatting:
1. Change to the directory that contains the file you want to print.
2. Enter pr [options] {file name}| more to view the file with text formatting.
3. Enter pr [options] {file name}| lpr to print the file with text formatting.

ACTIVITY 6-3
Formatting Text for Printing

Before You Begin:
1. You have logged in as root in the GUI.
2. Display the terminal window.

Scenario:
Due to recent changes in the boot process and a hard disk upgrade, your manager asked you to print copies of system files for record keeping. Any further changes to these files should be documented and a new version should be printed. You decide to use text formatting features to fix any alignment issue before printing the files.

What You Do	How You Do It
1. Display the contents of the /etc/fstab and /etc/inittab files using the `more` command.	a. Enter **`more /etc/fstab`** to view the contents of the /etc/fstab file.
	b. Observe the contents of the /etc/fstab file displayed on the screen.
	c. Enter **`more /etc/inittab`** to view the contents of the first page of the /etc/inittab file.
	d. Press the **Spacebar** to view the next page of the /etc/inittab file.
	e. Observe the contents of the /etc/inittab file displayed on the screen.
	f. Press the **Spacebar** to view the remaining part of the file.
2. Display the /etc/inittab file using the `pr` command.	a. Enter **`pr /etc/inittab	more`**
	b. Observe that the date, title, and page number are displayed.
	c. Press the **Spacebar** to view the next page of the /etc/inittab file.
	d. Press the **Spacebar** to view the remaining part of the file. Observe the contents of the /etc/inittab file as displayed on the screen.

3. Preview the /etc/fstab file with double line spacing and the heading "The fstab entries."

   a. Enter **pr -d -h "The fstab entries" /etc/fstab | more** to preview the formatting applied to the file.

   b. Observe that "The fstab entries" is displayed as the heading and the file has double spacing between the lines.

   c. Press **Q** to close the preview and return to the command prompt.

4. Preview the /etc/inittab file contents, 30 lines at a time using the `pr` command.

   a. Enter **pr -130 /etc/inittab | more**

   b. Press the **Spacebar** to view the next page of the /etc/inittab file.

   c. Press the **Spacebar** to view the remaining parts of the file. Observe the contents of the /etc/inittab file as displayed on the screen.

   d. Enter **clear** to clear the terminal.

5. Print the /etc/inittab file with text formatting and the /etc/fstab file with and without text formatting.

   a. Enter **pr -130 /etc/inittab | lpr** to print the /etc/inittab file, 30 lines per page.

   b. Enter **pr -d -h "The fstab entries" /etc/fstab | lpr** to print the /etc/fstab file with "The fstab entries" as the heading and with double line spacing.

   c. Enter **cat /etc/fstab > lpr** to print the file without formatting.

TOPIC C
Manage Print Jobs and Queues

Now that you can print files, you will need to learn to control the information sent to a printer. In this topic, you will manage print jobs and print queues.

In the earlier versions of Linux operating systems, you were only able to send files directly to a printer. With the advent of updated drivers and printers with more memory, you can send files directly to a printer and manage the print jobs with the help of a print queue. You can view, edit, and cancel print jobs in the print queue. You will also be able to send high priority jobs for printing ahead of low priority jobs.

The printtool and printconf Commands

The `printtool` and `printconf` commands provide a graphical interface for setting up a printer queue.

Command	Description
printtool	Used in Red Hat Linux, versions 7.1 and earlier, to set up and configure both local and remote printers. It also allows you to configure Windows SMB printers.
printconf	Used to accomplish the same tasks as `printtool` in Red Hat Linux versions 7.2 and later.

How to Manage Print Jobs and Queues

Procedure Reference: Manage Print Jobs in the Print Queue in the CLI

To manage print jobs in the print queue in the CLI:

1. Log in as a user in the CLI.
2. Manage jobs in a queue.
   - Enter `lpr {file name}` to add a job to the print queue.
   - Enter `lpr -P {print queue name} {file name}` to add a job to a specific print queue.
   - Enter `lpq` to view all print jobs in the queue.
   - Enter `lpq -P {Print queue name}` to view the print jobs in a specific print queue.
   - Enter `lprm {print job id}` to remove the desired print job.

ACTIVITY 6-4

Managing Print Jobs and Queues

Data Files:

Software_List.txt

Before You Begin

1. You have logged in as root in the GUI.

2. The terminal window is displayed.

3. Enter `cp /085039Data/Printing_Files/* /root`.

4. Enter `clear` to clear the terminal window.

5. Enter `rpm -qai | lp &` to print the list of installed packages.

6. Enter `ls -l /rhelsource/Server/* | lp &` to print the list of available packages.

7. Enter `clear` to clear the terminal window.

Scenario:

You want to print the list of software applications required for your organization. You decide to connect to the local printer and print the file. You also decide to view the print queue to check the status of your file. Because the printout is needed immediately, it has to be printed first.

What You Do	How You Do It
1. Cancel the jobs in the print queue.	a. Enter **lpq** to view the jobs in the print queue.
	b. Observe that the files with job ids {job id 1} and {job id 2} are in the print queue.
	c. Enter **lprm {job id 1}** to cancel the job with id **{job id 1}.**
	d. Enter **lprm {job id 2}** to cancel the job with id **{job id 2}.**
	e. Enter **lpq** to view the jobs in the print queue.
	f. Observe that there are no jobs in the queue.
	g. Minimize the **root@srvA** window.
	h. Observe that two message boxes are displayed with the message "Printing of (stdin) on printer {printer name} was cancelled" for each of the canceled jobs.
	i. Click **Close** two times to close both the message boxes.
	j. Maximize the **root@srvA** window.
2. Add the new job to the print queue.	a. Enter **lpr Software_List.txt** to add the new job to the print queue.
	b. Observe that the first job was only partially printed. The Software_List.txt file is printed.
	c. Close the terminal window.

TOPIC D
Configure Remote Printing

With the understanding of managing your local printer jobs and queues, you will now be able to apply those techniques to print over a network. In this topic, you will connect and use remote printers.

Businesses and home users set up networks to transfer files. With this infrastructure in place, printing across networks is feasible. Being able to print with a remote printer allows you to minimize the number of printers required in your environment. You can have one printer for a larger number of users to share.

Print Servers

Definition:

A *print server* is a computer that enables a network of users to access the central printer. The print server acts as a buffer, storing information to be printed, until the printer is free. Print servers can be programmed to print jobs in the order in which they are received or in the order of priority.

Example:

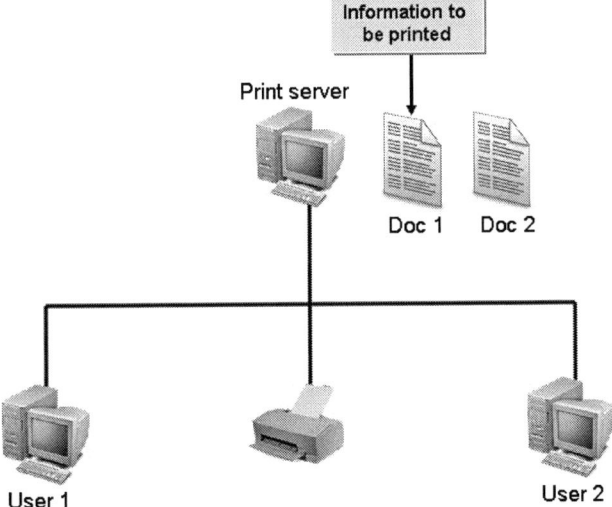

Figure 6-8: A print server manages print jobs over a network.

Remote Printing

In a network environment, users of a Linux system can print with remote printers via the Linux print system. When you enter the `lpr` command, the file you specify is copied into the remote spool directory, where it waits until the remote print server can print it. The remote print process is identical to the local print process.

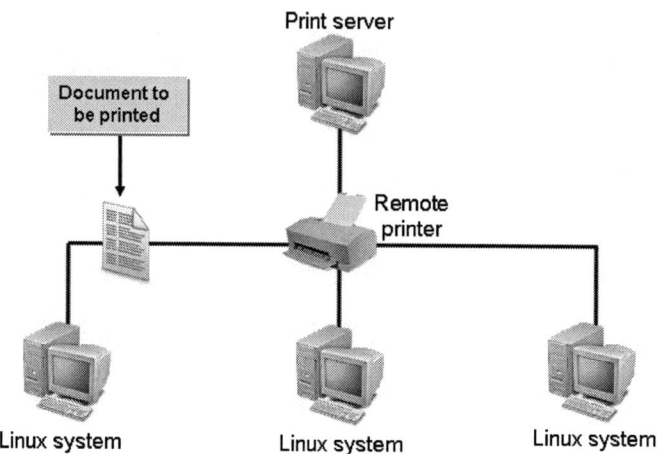

Figure 6-9: Printing on a network via the Linux print system.

Syntax

The syntax to print a document remotely is `lpr -P [printer name] [file name]`, where `[printer name]` is the name of the remote printer and `[file name]` is the name of the file you want to print.

Remote Printer Permissions

If you are setting up a remote printer, ensure that your machine has the correct permissions to access the remote printer. The permissions are specified in either the `/etc/hosts.lpd` file or the `/etc/hosts.equiv` file, on the machine to which the printer is attached. These files list the names of the remote computers that can use the local printer and can be modified to add or remove access to the printer.

Managing Remote Print Jobs

Just as you can manage local print jobs, such as removing jobs from a queue, holding jobs, or reordering jobs, you can also manage remote print jobs. You may not be able to do this as a regular user and may require someone with administrative access to the remote printer to do this for you. However, you should be able to hold or delete your own jobs.

Samba

Samba is a suite of network sharing tools that help in the sharing of files and printers on a heterogeneous network, which consists of computers running on different operating systems. Samba is an open source software application that provides enhanced interoperability with better performance and minimal maintenance. Using the Server Message Block (SMB) protocol, Samba enables Linux systems to communicate with computers running on other operating systems and share network resources like printers.

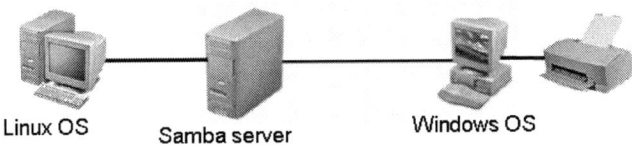

Linux OS   Samba server   Windows OS

Figure 6-10: Samba allows a Linux system to access a printer connected to a Windows operating system.

Samba Server

Samba allows Linux to emulate some services that a Windows server provides. It allows a user to share resources between Linux and Windows machines. Samba also provides enhanced network security by allowing Active Directory (AD) support. AD helps provide authenticated user access and restricted access permissions. By using shared network resources, you can make printing in AD easy and secure.

SMB Protocol

SMB is a client-server protocol that is used to share and transfer files on a network. It allows the client on the network to send, print, or scan requests to the server. The server in turn, makes the device available to the client. SMB is mostly used in computers that have Windows operating systems.

Configuring Samba

To configure Samba, you must edit the `/etc/samba/smb.conf` file. The following configuration options must be set in the file:

```
load printers = yes
printing = cups
printcap name = cups
```

In the [printers] section, you should have something similar to the following:

```
[printers]
comment = All Printers
path = /var/spool/samba
browseable = no
public = yes
guest ok = yes
writeable = no
printable = yes
printer admin = root, @ntadmins
```

After modifying the file, the Samba service must be restarted for the changes to take effect.

The printers.conf File

The printers.conf file, which is stored in the /etc/cups directory, defines the set of local printers on a network as shared resources. The list of printers gets generated automatically using the cupsd daemon. It can be configured in such a way that it allows only the explicitly publicized printers. The file contains a set of directives that define the features of the printer being shared.

How to Configure Remote Printing

Procedure Reference: Install Samba

To install Samba:

1. Log in as root in the GUI.
2. Mount the Linux installation CD-ROM that contains the latest version of samba packages.
3. Navigate to the /media/[name of the media]/Server folder.
4. Select the samba {package version}.rpm and perl - Convert -ASN1 - {package version}.rpm files.
5. Right-click and choose **Open with Software Installer.**
6. In the **Installing packages** window, verify that the two packages are listed and click **Apply** to start installing the packages.
7. If necessary, in the **Unable to verify {package name}** message box, click **Install anyway** to install the two packages.
8. In the **Software installed successfully** message box, click **OK** to complete the installation.

Procedure Reference: Share a Printer Using Samba

To share a printer using Samba:

1. Open the /etc/samba/smb.conf file.
2. Define a share for a printer.
    *   Specify the share name within brackets.

        [share name]
    *   Define the path to the spool file.

        `path = {path to the spool file}`
    *   Specify the printer name.

        `printer = {printer name}`
    *   Specify if the guest users are allowed to print. `public = {yes | no}`
    *   Specify the printing access for users. `printable = {yes |no}`
    *   If necessary, include a comment describing the shared printer. `comment = {Printer Description}`
3. Save and close the file.
4. Enter `testparm /etc/samba/smb.conf` to verify that the smb.conf file is formed.
5. Enter `chkconfig smb on` to start the service when the system boots.
6. Enter `service smb restart` to restart the Samba service.
7. Enter `ifconfig` to view the IP address of the system to which the printer is connected.
8. Verify that the printer shares you created are accessible from other Linux systems.

ACTIVITY 6-5
Configuring Remote Printers

Before You Begin:

1. On srvA, you have logged in as root in the GUI.

2. Double-click the **Computer** icon on the desktop.

3. Navigate to the /rhelsource/Server folder.

4. In the **Server** window, navigate and select the perl - Convert - ASN1 - 0.20 - 1.1.noarch.rpm and samba - 3.0.33 - 3.7.el5.i386.rpm files.

5. Right-click and choose **Open with "Software Installer."**

6. In the **Installing packages** window, verify that the two packages are listed and click **Apply** to start installing the packages.

7. In the **Unable to verify samba - 3.0.33 - 3.7.el5.i386** message box, click **Install anyway** to install the **samba - 3.0.33 - 3.7.el5.i386** package.

8. In the **Unable to verify perl - Convert - ASN1 - 0.20 - 1.1.noarch** message box, click **Install anyway** to install the **perl - Convert - ASN1 - 0.20 - 1.1.noarch** package.

9. In the **Software installed successfully** message box, click **OK** to complete the installation process.

10. Close the **Server - File Browser** window.

11. Choose **System→Administration→Printing** to display the **Printer configuration - localhost** window.

12. In the left pane, select **Server Settings.**

13. In the right pane, in the **Basic Server Settings** section, check the **Share published printers connected to this system** check box.

14. Click **Apply.**

15. Close the **Printer configuration - localhost** window.

16. Choose **Applications→Accessories→Terminal** to launch the terminal window in the GUI.

Scenario:

You configured a local printer on your Linux system. Because you have number of documents that need to be printed from other Linux systems, you decide to make the printer a shared printer and enable remote access to it with permission granted to the jsmith user account.

What You Do	How You Do It
1. Modify the smb.conf file to share the printer.	a. On the terminal window, enter `vi /etc/samba/smb.conf` to open the smb.conf file in the text editor.
	b. Navigate to the **Share Definitions** section.
	c. Navigate to the beginning of the line containing the *browseable* variable in the **printers** section.
	d. Press **I** to change to insert mode. Press **Enter** to insert a new line before the current line and press the **Tab** key.
	e. Press the **Up Arrow** key and press the **Tab** key to move to the previous line.
	f. Type `printer name = printer`
	g. Press the **Down Arrow** key and press **Backspace** two times.
	h. Type *yes* to make it browseable and press the **Down Arrow** key. Press **Backspace** two times.
	i. Type *yes* to allow the guest account to access the printer share.
	j. Press **Esc** to return to the command mode. Save the file and quit the editor.
2. Add a new smb user and restart the smb service.	a. Enter `smbpasswd -a jsmith` to add jsmith to the list of smb users.
	b. Press **Enter** two times to set a blank password.
	c. Enter `ifconfig` to view the IP address of the Linux system.
	d. Note down the IP address of the system.
	e. Enter `service smb restart` to restart the samba server.

3. Access the remote printer.

a. On srvB, log in as **root** in the GUI.

b. Choose **System→Administration→ Printing.**

c. In the **Printer configuration - localhost** dialog box, click **New Printer** to add a printer.

d. In the **New Printer** dialog box, in the **Printer Name** text box, type *printer1* and press the **Tab** key.

e. In the **Description** text box, type *Remote Printer* and press the **Tab** key.

f. In the **Location** text box, type *Printer on srvA* and click **Forward.**

g. In the **Devices** list box, observe that **LPT #1** is selected.

h. Select the **Windows Printer via SAMBA** option and click **Forward.**

i. In the right pane, observe that the MYGROUP share is displayed.

j. Double-click the **MYGROUP** share.

k. In the right pane, observe that SRVA is displayed.

l. Double-click the **SRVA** share.

m. In the right pane, observe that the printer is displayed.

n. Select the printer.

o. Observe that in the smb section, the printer path is filled in the text box. Click **Forward.**

4. Select the printer driver and set the remote printer as the default printer.

a. In the **Makes** list box, ensure that **Generic** is selected and click **Forward.**

b. In the **Models** list box, scroll down and select **PostScript Printer.**

c. In the **Drivers** list box, select the **foomatic: Generic - Postscript.ppd (recommended)** option and click **Forward.**

d. On the confirmation page, observe that a message "Going to create a new printer printer at smb://MYGROUP/SRVA/printer." is displayed.

e. Click **Apply** to add the printer.

f. Observe that in the **Remote Printers** section, a new printer, printer@srvA, is added.

g. In the right pane, click **Make Default Printer** to make the printer as the default printer.

h. Close the **Printer configuration - localhost** window.

5. Print install.log file on the remote printer.

a. On the desktop, double-click the **root's Home** folder.

b. In the **root - File Browser** window, double-click the install.log file.

c. Choose **File→Print** to print the file.

d. In the **Printer** dialog box, observe that the remote printer, printer@srvA, is selected. Click **Print.**

e. Switch to srvA.

f. On the task bar, click the **Web Browser** icon to launch the Firefox web browser.

g. In the address bar, select the existing address and enter **http://localhost:631/ jobs** to view the jobs in the print queue.

h. Click **Show Completed Jobs.**

i. Observe that the install.log file is displayed in the print queue.

j. Close the **Jobs CUPS 1.3.7 - Mozilla Firefox** window and the terminal window.

k. Switch to srvB.

l. Close the **gedit** window and the **File Browser** window.

Lesson 6 Follow-up

In this lesson, you worked with Linux printing services. You configured both local and remote printers, printed files using various printer commands, and managed print jobs and queues. You will now be able to set up printer connections and print backup records of files.

1. **What is the benefit of managing print queues?**

2. **What are the differences between a local printer and a network printer?**

7 | Managing Packages

Lesson Time: 2 hour(s)

Lesson Objectives:

In this lesson, you will manage packages.

You will:

- Manage packages using the RPM package manager.
- Verify packages.
- Upgrade and refresh packages.
- Configure repositories.
- Install packages using the YUM package manager.
- Manage packages using the Debian package manager.
- Work with source files.

Introduction

You explored the basic Linux environment, worked with files, and printed them. Now, you are ready to install software on your system. Packages facilitate the functioning of software. In this lesson, you will manage packages.

You will need to install software on your system to perform required tasks effectively. To do this, you need to learn about packages and package managers and how to install them on your system. Unless the packages are fully installed, the software will not function.

This lesson covers all or part of the following CompTIA Linux+ (2009) certification objectives:

- Topic A
  - Objective 1.8
- Topic B
  - Objective 1.8
- Topic C
  - Objective 1.8
- Topic D
  - Objective 1.8
- Topic E

- ■ Objective 1.8
- ● Topic F
  - ■ Objective 1.8
- ● Topic G
  - ■ Objective 1.8

TOPIC A
Manage Packages Using RPM

Installing software on your system will increase the capabilities of your computer and enable you to accomplish tasks faster. You need to know how to manage packages before you install software. In this topic, you will manage packages using the RPM package manager.

As a Linux+ professional, you will need to install software on systems. Software is a collection of packages. You can install the software only if you know how to add these packages on your system. Even if one package is not installed correctly, the software will not work. Installation of these packages is facilitated by package managers. Therefore, it is necessary to know about packages and package managers.

Packages

Definition:

A *package* is a collection of classes, functions, or procedures that can be imported as a single unit. Packages include all files required to run an application. Each package is compiled specifically for each Linux distribution and type of system. There are many types of packages, depending on the applications where they are used.

Example:

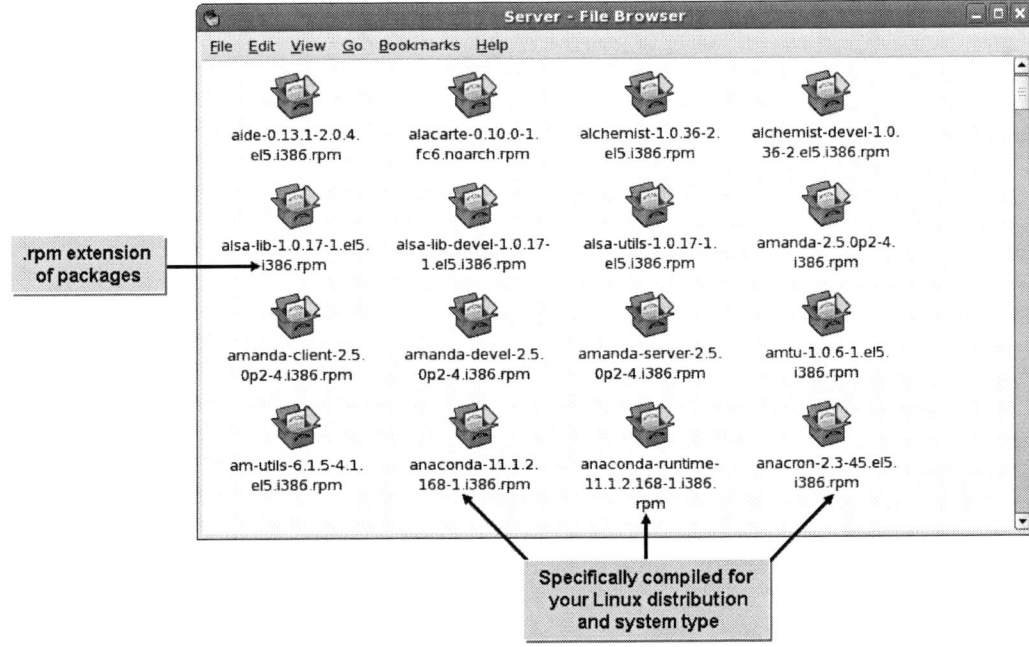

Figure 7-1: Packages in a Linux system.

Package Managers

Definition:

A *package manager* is a tool that enables you to search for packages and upgrade or remove them. It tracks the files that are provided with each package. Querying options are also provided by a package manager to list the installed packages and their characteristics. The naming convention followed by package managers for package files is name-version-release.architecture.rpm. The RPM package manager and the YUM (Yellow dog Updater, Modified) package manager are examples of package managers.

Example:

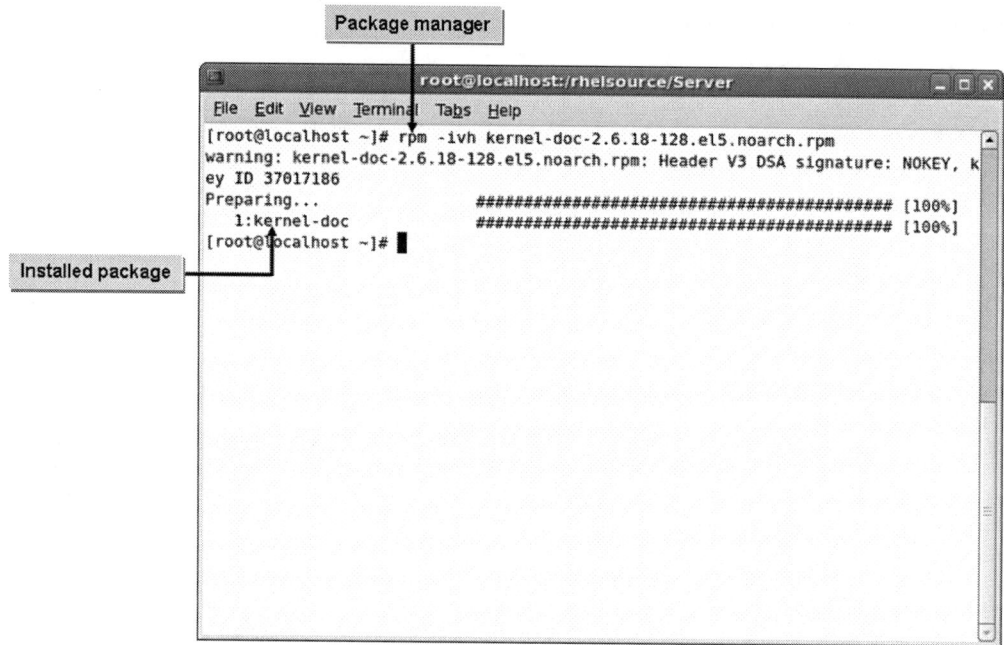

Figure 7-2: Installing a package using the RPM package manager.

Documenting Changes to Installed Packages

It is recommended that you document any changes you make to installed packages. This will help you troubleshoot issues and track the versions that have been previously installed.

Dependencies

Dependencies are the packages upon which a target package depends for its functionality. Dependency chains can run on for many levels. For example, package A will be installed only after package B is installed. Similarly, package B will be installed only after package C is installed. Installing five packages, each having their own dependencies, can be a cumbersome task. Package managers can fetch the required packages in an automated manner saving time and effort. RPM has several complementary utilities, such as up2date and yum, to manage dependencies. Dependency management is a major function of package managers.

Failed package installation →

Figure 7-3: Package installation fails due to unavailability of dependency packages.

The RPM Package Manager

The *RPM Package Manager (RPM)*, developed by Red Hat, is a tool for maintaining packages.

By providing a standard software packaging format, RPM enables easy administration and maintenance of Linux systems and servers. RPM provides a standard installation mechanism, information about installed packages, and a method for uninstalling and upgrading existing packages.

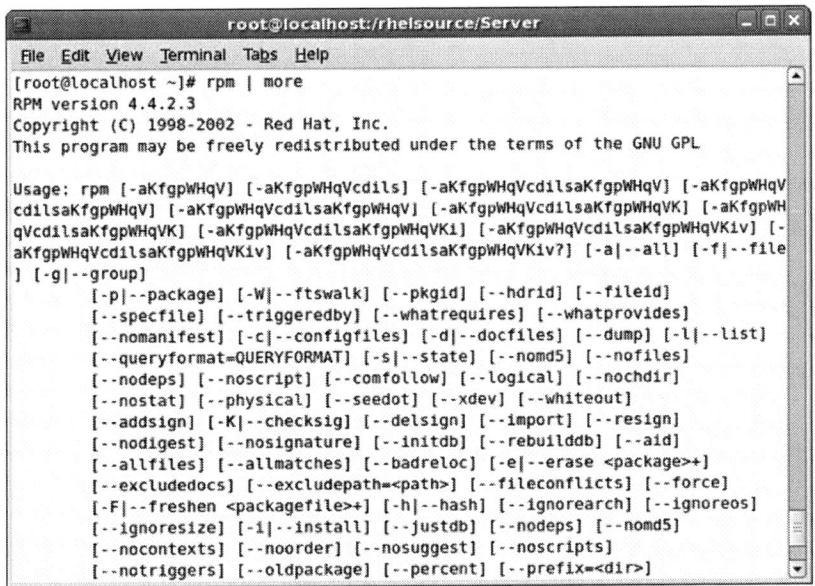

Figure 7-4: Various options of the rpm tool are displayed.

RPM is distributed under the GNU General Public License (GPL) and can be used with many distributions of Linux and even with other UNIX implementations.

The RPMS Directory

The Red Hat distribution includes the RPMS directory containing packages. You can also find packages on the Internet and FTP sites. One website where you can find packages is **http:// rpmfind.net**.

Installing Packages

When you install Linux, you may install all the packages it comes with. However, it is better to install only the packages you need. Later, when you need to install additional packages, you can use your CD (or whatever source you used) to obtain additional packages. You can check if updated versions of the package have been released and install the recent version.

The /usr/lib/rpm/* Directory

The /usr/lib/rpm/* directory contains the RPM tools required to manage the RPM packages. The /var/lib/rpm/* directory contains the RPM database of the installed packages. By default, the rpmrc file, which is the global RPM configuration file, is located in the /usr/lib/rpm directory. The rpmrc file contains information of the RPM architecture compatibility. If you want the RPM settings to be applicable for a system-wide configuration, place the rpmrc file in the /etc directory. If the rpmrc file is placed as .rpmrc in the home directory of any user, then the rpm settings will be applicable only for that specific user.

RPM Commands

Common RPM package management commands enable you to perform package management tasks.

Frequently used RPM package management commands are given in the following table.

Command	Enables You To
rpm -i {RPM package_file}	Install a package.
rpm -F {RPM package_file}	Reinstall the package.
rpm -U {RPM package_file}	Upgrade the package.
rpm -e {RPM package_name}	Remove the package.

RPM Components

The RPM package manager contains a number of components. Using these components, you can maintain a list of packages that are installed on the system.

Component	Description
The RPM local database	Tracks packages that are installed on the system.
The RPM package	Contains many executables and scripts required to install packages.
YUM	Acts as the front-end package installer for RPM.
RPM package files	Contains the source codes for the package.

RPM Queries

An RPM query is a function that is used to query RPM for information on both installed and uninstalled packages. There are various options, which give distinct outputs, for the `rpm -q` command.

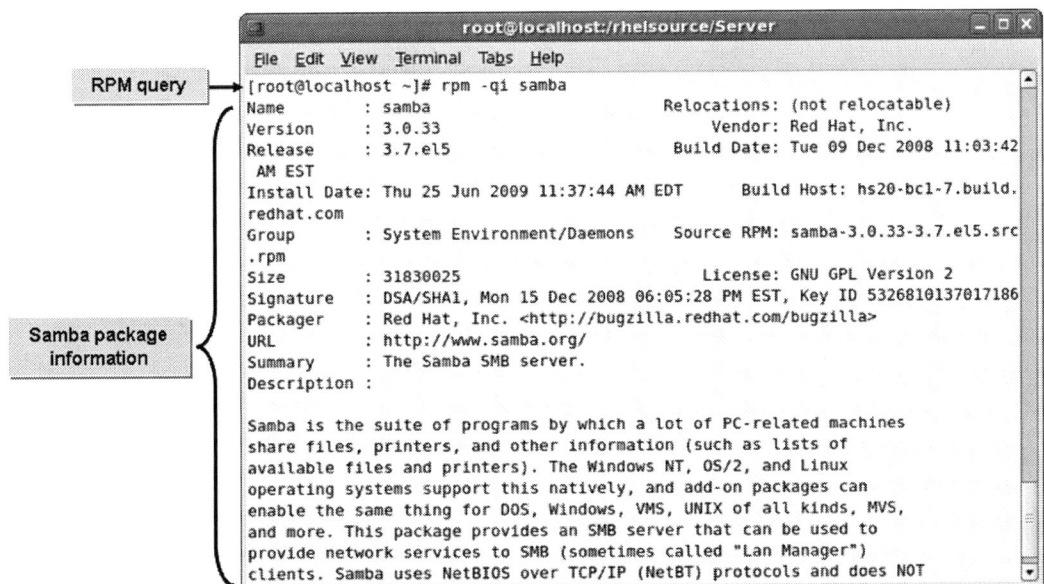

Figure 7-5: Basic details of the samba package obtained using an rpm query.

The options for the RPM query command are listed below.

Option	Enables You To
`rpm -qa`	List all packages that are installed on your system.
`rpm -qc` *package_name*	List the configuration files of the specified package.
`rpm -qi` *package_name*	Give the basic details of the package such as installed date, size, and summary.

Option	Enables You To
`rpm -ql package_name`	List the files in the package.
`rpm -qR package_name`	List the package dependencies.
`rpm -qa | grep package_name`	Send the results of the rpm query command to the grep command to search the results for a specific package.

Syntax

The syntax of an RPM query is `rpm -q {what_packages} {what_information}`.

How to Manage Packages Using RPM

Procedure Reference: Install Packages

To install packages:

1. Download the rpm file you would like to install.
2. Install the package using the `rpm -ivh [file name.rpm]` command.
3. If necessary, download the dependency packages.

Procedure Reference: Uninstall Packages

To uninstall packages:

1. Search for the rpm package you would like to uninstall using the `rpm -qi [package name]` command.
2. Uninstall the rpm package using the `rpm -e [package name]` command.

ACTIVITY 7-1
Managing Packages Using RPM

Data Files:

AdobeReader_enu-8.1.4-1.i486.rpm

Before You Begin:

1. On srvA, you have logged in as root in the GUI.

2. On the terminal, create a directory named rpms in the / directory.

3. Navigate to the /085039Data/Managing_Packages directory. Copy AdobeReader_enu-8.1.4-1.i486.rpm to the /rpms directory.

4. Change to the /rpms directory.

5. Enter clear to clear the terminal.

Scenario:

You have a lot of documentation in Linux that is available in the form of ebooks. You need to install the Adobe Reader application to enable users to view the ebooks in Linux.

What You Do	How You Do It

1. Install and check the version of the AdobeReader package.	a. Enter
	
	```rpm -ivh AdobeReader_enu-8.1.4-1.i486.rpm```
	to install the AdobeReader package.
	
	b. Observe that the progress bar is at **100%** indicating that the package was successfully installed.
	
	c. Enter
	
	```rpm -qi AdobeReader_enu``` to view the version number of the package.
	
	d. Observe that the **Version** is **8.1.4** and the **Release** is **1.**

2.   List the files in the AdobeReader package.

    a.   Enter

        `rpm -ql AdobeReader_enu` to view the list of files in the package.

    b.   Observe that the application files are installed in the /opt/Adobe/Reader8/bin directory.

    c.   Enter **clear** to clear the terminal window.

3.   Check the status of the files in the AdobeReader package.

    a.   Enter **rpm -qs AdobeReader_enu** to view the status of all files in the package.

    b.   Observe that the first column displays `normal` as the status for all files, indicating that the files are correctly installed.

    c.   Minimize the **root@srvA:/rpms** window.

    d.   On the desktop, double-click the **Adobe Reader 8** icon.

    e.   In the **Adobe Reader - License Agreement** dialog box, click **Accept** to accept the terms of the agreement.

    f.   Observe that the **Adobe Reader** window is displayed, indicating that the application was successfully installed.

    g.   Close the **Adobe Reader** window.

    h.   Restore the **root@srvA:/rpms** window.

    i.   In the **root@srvA:/rpms** window, enter **clear** to clear the screen.

TOPIC B
Verify Packages

In the previous topic, you managed packages using the RPM package manager. As a Linux+ system administrator you may have to verify and repair corrupt packages. In this topic, you will verify packages.

You will save time troubleshooting package installation and software problems if you know how to verify packages. You should also be able to verify the integrity of packages installed on your system.

RPM Verification

RPM verification compares the existing packages with the RPM package database and returns missing or corrupt packages. Various options allow you to verify specific information in the package.

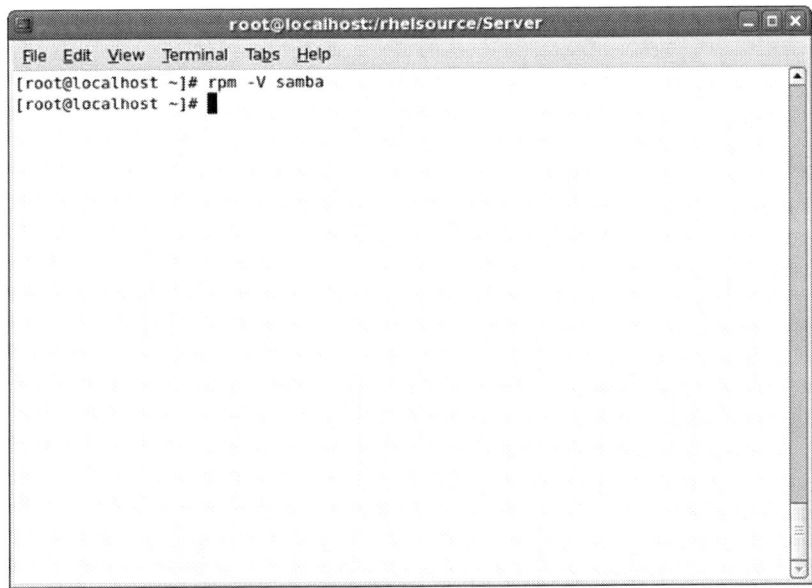

Figure 7-6: RPM is used to verify the state of the Samba package.

RPM verification options are listed below.

Option	Enables You To
rpm -Va	Verify all installed packages.
rpm -V package name	Verify a specific package.
rpm -V {file name}{package_name}	Verify a specific file in the package.

Syntax

The syntax for RPM verification is `rpm -V package_name`.

Importance of Verifying Packages

The integrity of a package can also be verified via the RPM system. This verification process can be used to ensure that package files are present in the correct directories without modifications and have the proper permissions. More specifically, RPM checks the size, MD5 checksum, permissions, type, owner, and group of each file in the package.

 MD5 checksum is like a file's finger print, it can be used to uniquely identify the file and verify its integrity.

Verification Error Codes

If all is fine with the package, no messages are displayed and you return to the command prompt. If a problem is detected, an eight-character string is displayed to alert you of the change. Based on this output, you can determine if the package needs to be reinstalled. The verification error codes are listed in the following table.

Error Code	Description
c	Configuration file error.
5	MD5 checksum test failed.
S	Change in file size since installation.
L	Symbolic link errors.
T	Current file modification time does not match the original file modification time.
D	Device attribute error.
U	Different user setting from the original.
G	Different group setting from the original.
M	Different permission or file type mode.

How to Verify Packages

Procedure Reference: Verify Packages

To verify packages:

1. Login as root.
2. Verify installed packages.
   - Verify all the rpm packages by using the `rpm -Va` command.
   - Verify an individual rpm package by using the `rpm -Vv [package name]` command.
   - Verify a specific file in the package by using the `rpm -V {file name}{package_name}` command.

ACTIVITY 7-2
Verifying Packages

Before You Begin:
1. You have logged in as root in the GUI.
2. The terminal window is displayed.

Scenario:
Your manager requested you to convert the previously used DOS and Mac files to UNIX format and ensure that the clients are able to access the Samba man pages. After ensuring that the applications are installed, you decide to verify that the packages are ready for use.

What You Do	How You Do It
1. Check whether the dos2unix and samba-client packages are installed.	a. Enter **rpm -q dos2unix** to check whether the dos2unix package is installed.
	b. Observe that the dos2unix - 3.1 - 27.1 package is installed.
	c. Enter **rpm -q samba-client** to check whether the samba-client package is installed.
	d. Observe that the **samba - client - 3.0.33 - 3.7.el5** package is installed.
2. Verify the dos2unix package.	a. Enter **rpm -Vv dos2unix**
	b. Observe that there are no errors and six lines are displayed.
3. Verify the samba-client package.	a. Enter **rpm -Vv samba-client**
	b. Observe that there are no errors and the files are listed followed by the directories.
	c. Enter **rpm -Vv samba-client	wc -1** to count the number of lines.
	d. Observe that the command displays a total of 26 lines.
	e. Enter **clear** to clear the terminal screen.

TOPIC C
Upgrade Packages

Now that you understand the methods for verifying packages, you can learn to upgrade packages. In this topic, you will upgrade packages by updating and refreshing installed packages.

One of the aspects of system administration is keeping the system's software up-to-date. Many applications are in active development and new releases are made available on a regular basis. These new releases may add functionality, fix bugs in older versions, or provide important security updates. RPM has the ability to quickly and easily upgrade software packages. This will save you from having to uninstall and reinstall a package, to have the newest version. Upgrading packages allows you to have the newest features of an application in the shortest amount of time.

Update/Freshen Packages

Packages can be easily upgraded by using the update or freshen option.

Option	Description
Update	Checks package versions against the package versions installed already. If the package is found, the package will be updated. If the package is not found, the package will be installed. The syntax that is used to update packages is `rpm -U [file name].rpm`.
Freshen	Checks package versions against the package versions installed already. If the package is found, the package will be updated. If the package is not found, the package will not be installed. The syntax that is used to freshen packages is `rpm -F [file name].rpm`.

Freshen Packages

Entering `rpm -Fvh *.rpm` automatically upgrades only those packages that have already been installed.

How to Update and Refresh Packages

Procedure Reference: Update Packages

To update packages:

1. Download the updated package.
2. Update the existing package using the `rpm -Uvh` *[file name.rpm]* command.
3. To verify that the package was updated, use `rpm -qi` *[package name]*.

ACTIVITY 7-3

Upgrading Packages

Data Files:

AdbeRdr9.1.0 - 1_i486linux_enu.rpm

Before You Begin:

1. You have logged as root in the GUI.

2. Navigate to the /085039Data/Managing_Packages directory. Copy AdbeRdr9.1.0-1_ i486linux_enu.rpm to the /rpms directory.

3. Enter clear to clear the terminal window.

Scenario:

You installed the PDF software on a Linux system to enable users to view e-books. Some users encounter errors when they try to open the latest e-books. After checking the errors, you decide to upgrade the PDF software to the latest version.

What You Do	How You Do It
1. Install the newer version of the Adobe Reader package.	a. Enter **rpm -Uvh AdbeRdr9.1.0-1_i486linux_enu.rpm** to upgrade the Acrobat Reader package.
	b. Observe that the progress bar is at **100%** for **AbodeReader_enu,** indicating that the package was successfully installed.

2. Verify that the Adobe Reader package is upgraded.

a. Enter **rpm -qi AdobeReader_enu** to view information about the package.

b. Observe that the **Version** is **9.1.0** and the **Release** is **1.**

c. Enter **cd /opt/Adobe/Reader9/bin** to change to the bin directory.

d. Enter **./acroread** to launch the application.

e. In the **Adobe Reader - License Agreement** dialog box, click **Accept** to accept the terms of the agreement.

f. Observe that the **Acrobat Reader** window is displayed.

g. Close the **Acrobat Reader** window.

h. Enter **clear** to clear the terminal window.

TOPIC D
Configure Repositories

You upgraded and refreshed installed packages. When managing a network, you may have to update the systems with the latest packages. You need to know where to obtain these packages. In this topic, you will examine repositories and how to use them to update systems.

Updating systems with the latest packages is one of the most important roles of a system administrator. To do this, you must know where the packages are available and how they can be downloaded.

Repositories

Definition:

A *repository* is a database that holds source code and compilations. There are two types of repositories, local and online. Software can be installed on a system only when repositories for the software are present on the system. The packages for the software are found in their respective repositories and are directly installed from them.

Example:

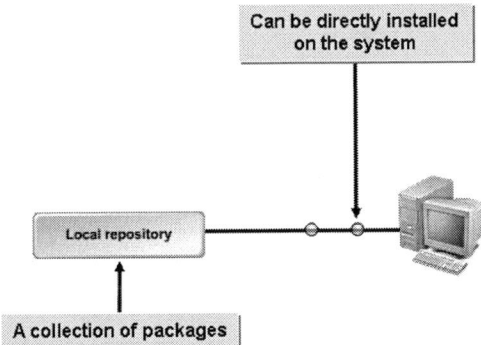

Figure 7-7: *A local repository.*

Types of Repositories

There are two types of repositories, *online repositories* and *local or private repositories*. Online repositories are found on the Internet. Packages can be directly downloaded from the Internet and installed on a system. Local or private repositories are stored on your system. The process of updating systems is greatly facilitated by repositories because the source files are readily available. Repositories make it easier for system administrators to update multiple systems simultaneously.

The createrepo Command

The *createrepo command* is used to create yum repositories. It generates XML metadata called *repomd* and creates a repository from existing rpm packages. The `createrepo` command has a number of options that facilitate the repository creation process.

Various options for the `createrepo` command are listed below.

Option	Enables You To
-p	Generate the output in the xml format.
-s	Select the checksum to be used to create the repository.
-c	Compare the repository with the checksum and check package integrity. Creates a cache directory for the package checksum.
-x	Exclude the specified files from the repository.
-h	Show the help menu.
-v	Run the command verbosely.

Syntax

The syntax of the `createrepo` command is `createrepo [Options] <Directory>`.

How to Configure Repositories

Procedure Reference: Creating a Private Repository

To create a private repository:

1. Log in as root.
2. Enter `mkdir /{directory name}` to create a directory.
3. Populate the directory with packages.
4. Enter `createrepo -v /{directory name}` to create a private repository.
5. If you add or remove any packages from the directory, run the `createrepo` command again.

Procedure Reference: Configuring Additional Repositories

To configure additional repositories:

1. Log in as root.
2. Enter `cd /etc/yum.repos.d` to navigate to the /etc/yum.repos.d directory.
3. Enter `vi {file name}` to create a file.
4. Switch to the insert mode.
5. Type the required information.
   - Enter *name = repository name* to set the repository name.
   - Enter *description of the repository* to give a description of the repository.
   - Enter *baseurl = {URL of the repository}* to set the repository's baseurl.
   - Enter *enabled = { 0 | 1 }* to control the status of the repository.
   - Enter *gpgcheck = { 0 | 1 }* to control the GPG signature verification.

6. Save and close the file.

GPG

GnuPG (GPG) is free software used for encrypting and signing packages or files. The encryption or signature is used to verify the authenticity of any file shared on the network.

ACTIVITY 7-4

Configuring Repositories

Before You Begin:

1. You have logged in as root in the GUI.
2. The terminal window is displayed.
3. Enter `cd /rhelsource/Server` to change to the Server directory.
4. Enter `clear` to clear the terminal window.

Scenario:

You have been assigned the task of updating a few systems on the network with the kickstart application. While installing, you find that there are hundreds of packages in the installation folder, and you have to search for the kickstart packages every time. So, you decide to make your job easier by creating a kickstart repository with specific packages, so that you can call the repository instead of searching for the packages.

What You Do	How You Do It
1. Install the createrepo package.	a. Enter **rpm -ivh createrepo-0.4.11-3.el5.noarch.rpm** to install the createrepo package.
	b. Observe that the progress bar is at **100%** indicating that the package was successfully installed.
	c. Enter **rpm -q createrepo** to verify that the package is installed.
	d. Observe that the **createrepo-0.4.11–3.el5** package is displayed.
	e. Enter **rpm -qi createrepo** to view information about the package.
	f. Observe that the **Version** is **0.4.11** and the **Release** is **3.el5.**

2. Create a private repository.

    a. Enter **cd /** to navigate to the **/** directory.

    b. Enter **createrepo -v /rhelsource** to create a private repository.

    c. Observe that the 2255 packages from /rhelsource/Server directory are entered into the repository.

 It will take some time to process all packages.

3. Configure the new repository.

    a. Enter **cd /etc/yum.repos.d** to navigate to the /etc/yum.repos.d directory.

    b. Enter **vi rhelsource** to create the rhelsource file.

    c. Switch to the insert mode.

    d. Enter ***name = rhelsource*** to specify the repository name.

    e. Enter ***My Local Repository*** to specify the repository description.

    f. Enter ***baseurl=file:///rhelsource/Server/*** to specify the base url.

    g. Enter ***enabled = 1*** to enable the repository.

    h. Type ***gpgcheck = 0*** to disable gpgcheck.

    i. Press **Esc** to exit to the command mode.

    j. Save and close the file.

4. Disable the gpgcheck in the yum configuration file.

   a. Enter `vi /etc/yum.conf` to navigate to the yum.conf file.

   b. Enter */gpg* to navigate to the gpgcheck=1 line.

   c. Switch to the insert mode.

   d. Change **gpgcheck=1** to *gpgcheck=0* to disable gpgcheck.

   e. Press **Esc** to exit to the command mode.

   f. Save and close the file.

   g. Enter `clear` to clear the terminal window.

TOPIC E

Manage Packages Using YUM

You managed package installation on a single computer using RPM. As a system administrator, your task involves installing software on multiple systems simultaneously within a short period of time. In this topic, you will manage package installation using YUM.

As a system administrator, you will be dealing with multiple systems at the same time. It is necessary that you install packages on all systems simultaneously and in the shortest possible time. Knowledge about the YUM package manager will help you install and manage packages on multiple systems simultaneously.

The YUM Package Manager

Yellow dog Updater, Modified (YUM) is a package manager that is used to update, install, and manage packages. YUM automatically detects and configures the dependencies for software packages and maintains a database of the installed software. YUM is widely used by system administrators because it is easy to work with. It supports both local and online repositories.

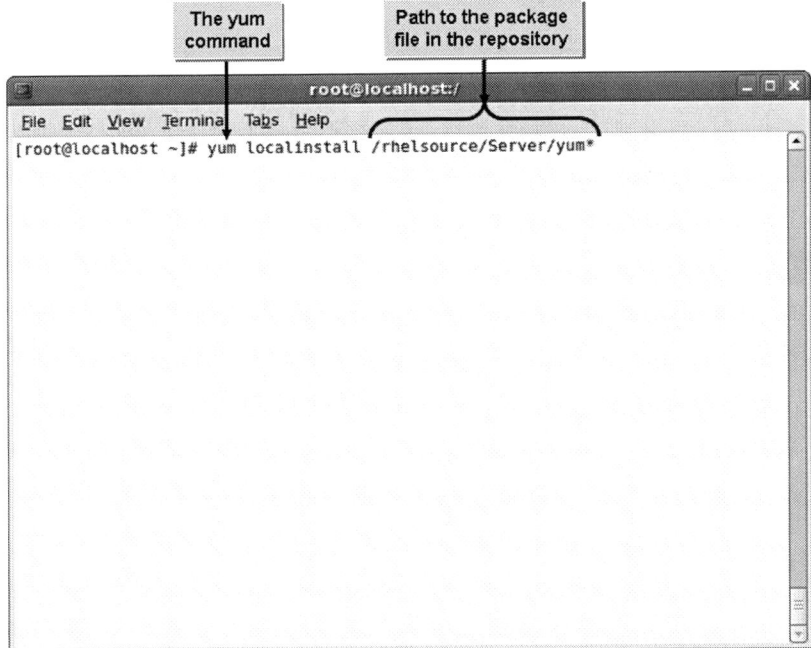

Figure 7-8: Installing a package from a local repository using the YUM package manager.

YUM Commands

YUM has various commands that can be used to maintain packages.

Command	Enables You To
install	Install a package.
update	Update packages. The command will update all packages when a package is not specified.
check-update	Check for available updates.
remove	Remove the specified packages.
list	Display the details of the specified package. When a package is not specified, it lists the status of all the packages on the system.
info	Display a brief description of the specified package.
localinstall	Install packages from a local repository.

Syntax

The syntax of the YUM command is yum *[options] {command} {package name}*.

How to Manage Packages Using YUM

Procedure Reference: Manage Packages Using YUM

To manage packages using yum:

1. Log in as root.
2. Manage packages using yum.
   - Enter yum install *{package name}* to install packages using YUM.
   - Enter yum remove *{package name}* to remove packages using YUM.
   - Enter yum info *{package name}* to display package description.
   - Enter yum update *{package name}* to update the system with the specified package.

ACTIVITY 7-5

Managing Packages Using YUM

Before You Begin:

1. You have logged in as root in the GUI

2. The terminal window is displayed.

3. Enter `cd /root` to change to the root directory.

4. Enter `clear` to clear the terminal window.

Scenario:

A meeting is scheduled at your company. You are required to install the ypbind service on the systems in the conference room, to enable network communication. You are also asked to brief users on the installed ypbind packages. You decide to install the packages and generate a description using the details displayed in the YUM output.

What You Do	How You Do It
1. Install the ypbind package using yum.	a. Enter `yum localinstall /rhelsource/Server/yp*` to install the package. b. At the **Is this ok [y/N]:** prompt, enter **y** to confirm download. c. Observe that the dependencies are updated and the **Complete!** message is displayed. d. Enter `clear` to clear the terminal window.
2. Check the status of the package.	a. Enter **`yum list ypbind`** to view the status of the ypbind package. b. Observe that **ypbind.i386** is listed under **Installed Packages.** c. Enter **`yum info ypbind`** to view the description of the ypbind package. d. Observe that the package version is **1.19** and the release is **11.el5.** e. Enter **`clear`** to clear the terminal window.

TOPIC F

Manage Packages Using the Debian Package Manager

In the previous topic, you managed packages using the YUM package manager. You may also need to manage packages in other distributions of Linux. In this topic, you will manage packages using the Debian package manager.

As a Linux+ administrator, you may need to remove obsolete packages to free hard disk space. It will be easier to delete unwanted packages if you know where they are installed. You will need to track all the files that were added during the installation of the packages. This can be done with a Debian package manager.

The Debian Archive Package Installation Process

The Debian Archive Package Installation process consists of three stages: check for dependency, unpack, and configure.

● In the *check for dependency* stage, the package manager checks the specified Debian archive package for the numerous dependencies required.

● In the *unpack* stage, the Debian archive package and its dependant packages are unpacked into the filesystem of the hard disk.

● In the final *configure* stage, the unpacked files can be configured with the default values or customized to suit your requirements. Apart from this, you can also choose to reconfigure the package and its dependencies later.

Figure 7-9: Stages in the Debian Archive Package Installation process.

DEB Tools

DEB tools are a suite of tools for package management of Debian-based Linux distributions. DEB tools are used to install, list, and remove packages conforming to the DEB packaging standard. Advanced Package Tool (APT) is a front end for the DEB suite of tools, designed to make it more user-friendly.

The tools included in the DEB suite are listed in the following table.

Tool	Description
dpkg	It is the main package management program. Its main purpose is to install and remove DEB packages.
dpkg-deb	It is the archive manipulation tool of the Debian package. It is used to extract the DEB package contents from a directory and display package information. It is also used to collect and remove information about Debian archives.
dpkg-split	It splits packages into smaller parts. It is useful for splitting packages into sizes of 1.44 MB, so that they can fit into a series of floppy disks.
dselect	It is a menu-driven, front-end interface of the dpkg package. Through this utility, you can install and remove packages.

Debian Archive Package Management Commands

Debian package management commands can be used to get information about the Debian archive packages.

Some Debian archive package management command options are described in the following table.

Option	Used To
dpkg -p [Debian package name]	View the version, dependencies, and integrity of the package.
dpkg -L [Debian package name]	List contents of the package.
dpkg -l [Debian package name]	View installation status.
dpkg --yet-to-unpack	Find packages that are yet to be installed.
dpkg -S [File or package name]	Find packages containing specific files or software.

The apt-get Command

The `apt-get` command is used to install or upgrade packages through the Internet or from the distribution CD. While installing or upgrading packages, the `apt-get` command accesses the website or the CD-ROM listed in the /etc/apt/sources.list file.

The `apt-get` command has various options.

Option	Used To
`apt-get install` *[Debian package name]*	Install packages
`apt-get remove` *[Debian package name]*	Uninstall packages
`apt-get upgrade` *[Debian package name]*	Upgrade packages

Syntax

The syntax of the `apt-get` command is `apt-get` *[options]* *{command}*.

The apt.conf File

The apt.conf file is the configuration file for the `apt-get` command. This file stores additional information such as the number of attempts to be made while downloading the packages and the available cache memory.

The /var/lib/dpkg/* Directory

The /var/lib/dpkg/* directory contains the Debian database of the installed packages. By default, the dpkg.cfg file, which is the dpkg configuration file, is located in the /etc/dpkg directory. The dpkg configuration file may contain all the dpkg command line options.

Alien

Alien is a program in Debian that converts packages in other Linux distribution file formats to Debian. It supports conversion among packages such as Linux Standard Base, RPM, deb, Stampede, and Slackware.

Example of Conversion

The `alien --to-deb /path/to/file.rpm` command will convert a `.rpm` package into a `.deb` package.

How to Manage Packages Using the Debian Package Manager

Procedure Reference: Install Packages Using the Debian Package Manager

To perform a command line installation of Debian archive packages using the Debian package manager:

1. Ensure that Debian Linux is installed on the system.
2. Log in as root in the CLI or in the GUI.
3. Enter `dpkg -i` *[Debian package file]* to install the Debian package.

Procedure Reference: Upgrade Packages Using the Debian Package Manager

To perform a command line upgrade of Debian archive packages using the Debian package manager:

1. Log in as root in the CLI or in the GUI.
2. Upgrade a Debian package.
   - Enter `dpkg --update-avail` *{Debian package file}*
   - Or, enter `dpkg-reconfigure` *{Debian package name}*

Procedure Reference: Uninstall Packages Using the Debian Package Manager

To perform a command line removal of Debian archive packages using the Debian package manager:

1. Log in as root in the CLI or in the GUI.
2. Enter `dpkg -r` *{Debian package name}* to uninstall packages.

Procedure Reference: Manage Packages Using the apt-get command

To manage packages using the apt-get command:

1. Login as root
2. Enter `apt-cache search {pattern}|{package name}` to search for files that match a specific pattern or a specific package.
3. Manage packages using suitable commands.
   - Enter `apt-get install {Debian package name}` to install a Debian package.
   - Enter `apt-get upgrade {Debian package name}` to upgrade a Debian package.
   - Enter `apt-get remove {Debian package name}` to uninstall a Debian package.

Procedure Reference: Install Alien Packages Using the alien Command

To install Alien packages using the `alien` command:

1. Log in as root in the CLI.
2. Type `alien -i` *{Package file name}* to install packages belonging to other distributions.

ACTIVITY 7-6

Managing Packages Using the Debian Package Manager

Data Files:

Training_Policy.txt

Before You Begin:

1. Reboot srvA and start Debian Linux on the system.

2. Login as root in the GUI.

3. Insert the **Debian 5.0.0 i386 Bin-1** disc in the CD drive.

4. Launch the terminal window.

5. On the terminal window, enter `cd /media/cdrom/debian/pool/main/l/less` to navigate to the less directory.

6. Enter `cp less_418-1_i386.deb /root` to copy the less package to the /root directory.

7. Enter `clear` to clear the terminal window.

Scenario:

A user, Mike, is trying to view the Training_Policy.txt file on the Debian Linux system. Because the text in the file is several pages long and the content scrolls on the screen, he is having trouble viewing the content of the file. You decide to install the less_418-1_i386.deb package on his system. After installation, you decide to make a note of the version number of the program for documentation purposes.

What You Do	How You Do It
1. Install the less package and view the package version number.	a. Enter **cd /root** to change to the root directory.
	b. Enter **dpkg -i less_418-1_i386.deb** to install the less package.
	c. Observe that the package is selected, unpacked, and set up, and the man db is processed.

2. View the Training_Policy.txt file using the `less` command.

a. Enter **dpkg -l less** to view the version number of the package.

b. Observe that the version of the less package installed is **418–1.**

c. Enter **less Training_Policy.txt** to view the first page of the file.

d. Press the **Spacebar** to view the next page of the file.

e. Observe that the next page is displayed. Enter *q* to close the file.

f. Enter **clear** to clear the terminal window.

TOPIC G
Work with Source Files

You managed packages using package managers that are specific to a Linux distribution. You may come across situations where you need to build packages from their source code. In this topic, you will work with source files.

Your ability to work with source files will give you the skill and flexibility to troubleshoot and manage packages in any Linux distribution. You will be in a position to install applications, irrespective of the availability of specific package managers.

makefile

makefile is a description file that contains the details of files, dependencies, and rules with which an executable application is built. It is used to configure, compile, and install the application or driver. System built-in rules for maintaining, updating, and regenerating groups of programs are overridden by the contents of makefile.

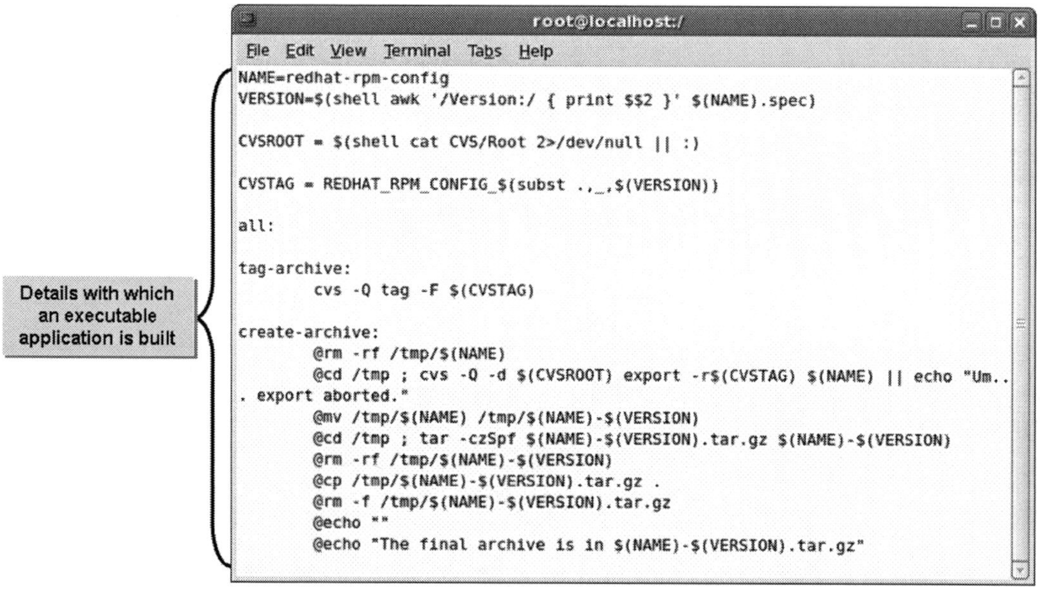

Figure 7-10: makefile is used to configure, compile, and install the application or driver.

makefile Commands
Some frequently used makefile commands are provided in the following table.

Command	Used To
./configure	Gather system information to compile the application.
make	Compile the application.
make install	Install the newly compiled program.
make uninstall	Uninstall a program.
make clean	Clean up after successfully compiling the application.

Command	Used To
make test	Install a perl module. It is an optional command in the package management function.

Autoconf

You can use autoconf to create shell scripts that automatically configure packages. The shell scripts created by autoconf can run independently.

Compiling from makefile

To compile an application, you need to be at the command line or work through a GUI. First, change to the directory that has been made by the package. Here, you should find an INSTALL file. Read the contents of the INSTALL file. Most tarballs include one or more of the following files: INSTALL, COPYING, README, or CHANGES. The INSTALL file usually includes a generic process for installing tarballs. If a program needs to be compiled in a certain way, you can find the necessary information in either the INSTALL or README file. This is how it works in theory, but it does not always work, usually due to dependencies on other programs.

makefile and Configure Script

Generally application vendors provide either makefile or a configure script to build an executable program. Both files come with default settings, and you can customize these files to suit your individual preferences. For example, you can specify the location where you need the files to be installed.

When you build a program using makefile, you need to make the necessary changes to the file, and you also need to update the necessary header files; otherwise, the installation will be incomplete. When a vendor has provided you with a configure script, you can make the desired changes to the script and then run the script. This will generate the necessary files along with makefile. Because it is not necessary to make any changes to makefile, you can proceed with the installation.

Drivers

A *driver* is a program that controls a device attached to a computer. Linux has a modular kernel, which allows hardware devices to be added to a system without recompiling the kernel as long as the modules for the devices are already compiled. Each driver will have specific instructions on how to create the module and install it. These driver instruction files will also list any dependencies that need to be installed.

How to Work with Source Files

Procedure Reference: Compile Applications or Drivers

To compile an application or driver:

1. Download the source code from the vendor.

2. Untar and unzip the files into a directory.

3. In the directory containing the files, issue the `./configure` command.

4. Next, issue the `make` command to compile the application.

5. To install the application, use the `make install` command.

6. To clean up the temporary files used during the compile process, use the `make clean` command.

ACTIVITY 7-7
Working with Source Files

Data Files:

httpd-2.2.11.tar.gz

Before You Begin:

1. Reboot srvA and start Red Hat Linux on the system.

2. Log in as root in the GUI.

3. Display the terminal window.

4. Enter `cd /085039Data/Managing_Packages` to change to the Managing_Packages directory.

5. Copy the httpd-2.2.11.tar.gz file to the /usr directory.

6. Enter cd /usr to make it the current directory.

7. Enter `clear` to clear the terminal window.

Scenario:

A colleague wants to install the latest version of the web server on a system running Linux. The necessary files have been downloaded, but your colleague needs help installing the web server from the downloaded source files.

What You Do	How You Do It
1. Extract the source files of the web server.	a. Enter **`gunzip httpd-2.2.11.tar.gz`** to unzip and extract the file. b. Enter **`tar xvf httpd-2.2.11.tar`** to extract the archived files. c. Enter **`clear`** to clear the terminal window.

2.	Configure the web source using the source code.	a.	Enter **cd httpd-2.2.11** to change the directory.
		b.	Enter **./configure --prefix=/etc/apache** to configure the httpd source file.
		c.	Enter **clear** to clear the terminal window.
		d.	Enter **make** to build the executable program.
		e.	Enter **clear** to clear the terminal window.
		f.	Enter **make install** to install the packages.
		g.	Enter **clear** to clear the terminal window.
3.	Start the web server service and verify that the home page is displayed.	a.	Enter **./httpd -d /etc/apache/ -k start** to start the httpd service.
		b.	Observe that the httpd service has started successfully.
		c.	Enter **firefox http://localhost** to launch the web browser from the terminal.
		d.	In the **Test Page for Apache Installation - Mozilla Firefox** window, observe that the message "It works" is displayed.
		e.	Close the **Test Page for Apache Installation - Mozilla Firefox** window.
		f.	On the terminal window, enter **clear** to clear the screen.

Lesson 7 Follow-up

In this lesson, you managed packages using package managers and explored the various repositories from where you can download the packages. This will enable you to easily install software packages on Linux systems.

1. **What are the pre-installation steps to be carried out before installing a package?**

2. **Why do you think it is important to create your own repositories?**

8 | Managing Kernel Services

Lesson Time: 1 hour(s), 45 minutes

Lesson Objectives:

In this lesson, you will manage kernel services.

You will:

- Identify the role and functions of the Linux kernel.

- Customize kernel modules.

- Create the initrd image.

- Manage device drivers.

- Monitor the hardware devices available in the computer system.

- Manage processes and resources.

Introduction

You managed packages. The kernel, being the core of the Linux operating system, handles various crucial functions such as system initialization, process scheduling, and memory and hardware management. In this lesson, you will explore the role of kernel services and kernel service configuration.

As a Linux system administrator, you may need to configure, modify, and customize the kernel to meet user requirements. Even a minor misconfiguration may cause kernel malfunction, rendering the system ineffective. Therefore, an in-depth knowledge of the kernel services is required to manage the kernel efficiently.

This lesson covers all or part of the following CompTIA Linux+ (2009) certification objectives:

- Topic A

  - Objective 2.1

- Topic B

  - Objective 1.6

  - Objective 1.10

  - Objective 1.11

  - Objective 2.1

- Topic D
    - Objective 1.11
    - Objective 2.1
- Topic E
    - Objective 1.11
- Topic F
    - Objective 2.1
    - Objective 2.9

TOPIC A
Explore the Linux Kernel

The first component that initializes in the Linux boot process is the kernel. It provides all the essential services that are required for running the computer, and controls the rest of the processes that happen on the computer. In this topic, you will identify the role of the Linux kernel and its functions.

If a system crashes or stops performing, it actually means that the kernel or an operation critical to the working of the kernel has crashed. As a Linux+ administrator, you need to understand the functionality of the kernel to be able to troubleshoot and provide solutions.

The Kernel

Definition:

The kernel is the core of an operating system on which all other components rely. It is loaded first and remains in the main memory. It contains the system-level commands and other functions that are hidden from users. The kernel manages filesystem access, memory, processes, devices, and resource allocation in a system. The kernel also controls all the hardware devices plugged into the system.

Example:

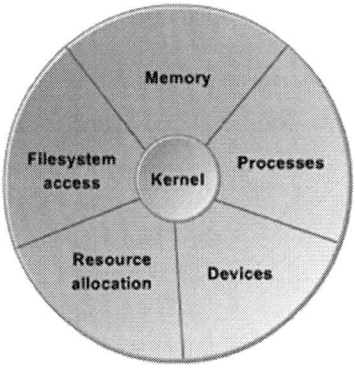

Functions of the kernel

Figure 8-1: *The kernel's role in an operating system.*

The Linux Kernel

The *Linux kernel,* which is the core constituent of the Linux operating system, manages all other resources on the system. It performs functions such as sharing resources and allocating of memory, input and output operations, security settings, and user access. It controls the interaction between software applications and underlying system resources. The kernel initializes itself during the boot process and then starts running the other processes. By default, the kernel loads with a minimal set of functions required to run a system. The kernel's functionality can be expanded by installing kernel modules. The kernel is required to synchronize the operations of multiple processes and govern resources.

Kernel Versions and Modules

Linux kernel versions refer to the different editions of the Linux kernel. Kernel versions are identified by their kernel number, which consists of four parts. The format of the version number is

`major_version_number.major_revision_number.minor_revision_number.fix_number`

The version number can be viewed using the `uname -r` command. Common kernel modules include input, ext3, CD-ROM, lp, udf, and jbd.

Kernel Layers

The kernel performs various functions to control and manage the operations of a system. It is composed of various layers.

Kernel Layer	Function
System Call Interface (SCI)	A layer that handles function calls sent from user applications to the kernel. A function call is basically a service request sent to the operating system's kernel for invoking system-level functions such as requests for processing time and memory allocation.
	This layer enables the kernel to schedule and process function calls and manage multiple function calls simultaneously.
Process management	A layer in the kernel that handles different processes by allocating separate execution space on the processor and ensuring that the running of one process does not interfere with the other processes.
	The kernel implements sharing of the processor time for executing multiple processes through process scheduling.
Memory management	A layer in the kernel that manages the computer's memory, which is one of the complex tasks performed by the kernel. Like processor sharing, the system's memory also needs to be shared among different application services and resources.
	The kernel maps or allocates the available memory to applications or programs on request and frees the memory automatically when the execution of the programs are complete, so that it can be allocated to other programs.
Filesystem management	A layer in the kernel that manages the filesystem, which involves storing, organizing, and tracking files and data on a computer.
	The kernel also supports a virtual filesystem that provides an abstract view of the underlying data that is organized under complex structures, so that it appears to be a single structure.

Kernel Layer	Function
Device management	A layer in the kernel that manages devices by controlling device access and interfacing between user applications and hardware devices of the computer.
	When the user application sends a system call, the kernel reads the request and passes it on to the drivers that manage the activities of that particular device. For this purpose, the kernel maintains a list of devices in the /dev directory.

Types of Kernels

Kernels can be classified as monolithic and modular, based on their organization.

Kernel Type	Description
Monolithic	In a monolithic kernel, all modules, such as device drivers or filesystems, are built-in.
	Monolithic kernels can interact faster with devices. But the major disadvantage is its huge size, which leads to higher usage of RAM.
Modular	In a modular kernel, only a minimal set of essential modules are built-in. The rest of the modules can be installed and the kernel can be rebuilt whenever necessary. A modular kernel is also known as a micro kernel or a dynamic kernel.
	Modular kernels are flexible and save memory usage because the kernel modules, which are loaded as required, are removed from the memory when the related devices are unmounted.

ACTIVITY 8-1
Exploring the Role and Functions of the Linux Kernel

Scenario:
As a system administrator, you may need to troubleshoot issues related to the kernel. So, you will like to explore the kernel concepts to refresh your knowledge.

1. **Which function is associated with the SCI layer of the kernel?**

   a) Passing requests to device drivers

   b) Sending service requests to the kernel

   c) Processor time allocation for functions

   d) Process scheduling functions

   e) File organization

2. **What are the major functions performed by the kernel? Select all that apply.**

   a) Kernel initialization

   b) Process management

   c) Memory management

   d) Module installation

   e) Dependency management

3. **True or False? The kernel maintains a list of all devices in the /boot directory.**

   ___ True

   ___ False

TOPIC B
Customize Kernel Modules

You familiarized yourself with the basic concepts of the Linux kernel. Kernel modules are functions that extend the capability of the kernel to support additional functionalities. In this topic, you will customize kernel modules.

The Linux kernel, by default, loads with a minimum set of kernel modules. When you want the kernel to support some additional functionalities, you have to install or load the necessary modules manually. Customizing the modules to suit user requirements will enable you to manage the kernel efficiently.

Kernel Modules

Definition:

A *kernel module* is a system-level function that extends the functionality of the kernel. It can be dynamically loaded into the kernel or unloaded from the kernel when required. It enables the kernel to update or recompile itself without requiring the system to reboot. The kernel module file consists of a .ko extension. The modules built for a specific kernel version may not be compatible with another version of the kernel.

Example:

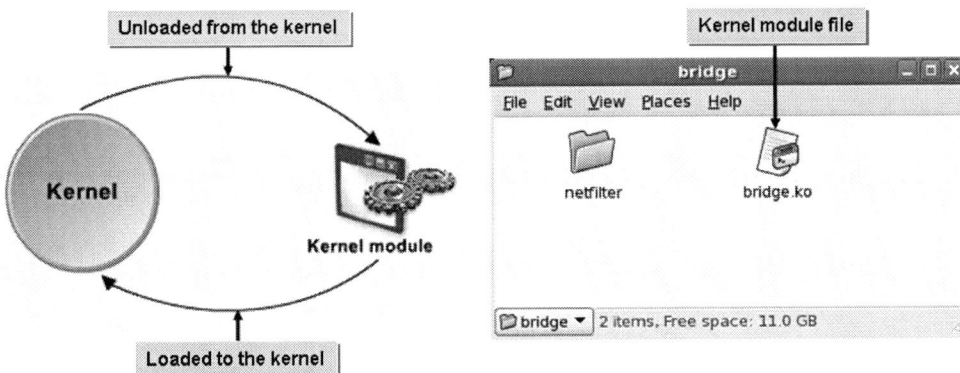

Figure 8-2: bridge.ko is the kernel module for network support.

Advantages of Kernel Modules

The advantages of kernel modules are:
- Kernel modules reduce the burden on the kernel. If kernel modules were not present, their functionalities have to be added directly to the kernel image, which can make the kernels larger.
- Kernel modules avoid rebuilding and rebooting of the system when a new functionality is required.
- Dynamic loading of kernel modules facilitate lower memory consumption.

Directories Containing Kernel Modules

The /lib/modules directory contains the modules of different kernel versions that are installed. It contains a directory named after the kernel's version number. A list of currently loaded modules is found in the /proc/modules file. Modules are stored across various directories based on the categories they belong to. The following table lists the directories containing modules.

Directories	Description
pcmcia	Contains modules for PCMCIA (PC card).
net	Contains modules for network-related products such as firewalls and protocols.
drivers	Contains modules for various types of hardware.
fs	Contains modules for various types of filesystems.
arch	Contains modules for architecture specific support.

Kernel Module Managing Utilities

A kernel module managing utility enables you to view, load, unload, or modify kernel modules.

Kernel Module Utility	Enables You To
lsmod	Display the currently loaded kernel modules, their size, usage details, and their dependent modules.
modinfo	Display information about a particular kernel module such as file name of the module, license, description, author's name, module version number, dependent modules, and other parameters or attributes. The syntax of this command is `modinfo {module options}`.
insmod	Install a module into the currently running kernel. This utility inserts only the specified module and does not insert any dependant modules. The syntax of this command is `insmod {file name} {module options}`.
modprobe	Add or remove modules from a kernel. This utility is capable of loading all dependant modules before inserting a specified module. • The syntax for adding a module is: `modprobe {module name}`. • The syntax for removing a module is: `modprobe -r {module name}`.

Command Options for modinfo

The command options for the `modinfo` command are listed in the table below.

Command Option	Enables You To
-V	Display the version number of the `modinfo` utility.
-n	Display the file name of the module.
-a	Display the author of the module.
-d	Display the description about the module.
-p	Display the parameters supported by the module.
-F	Print the field values, such as parameters, author, and description.

Command Options for insmod

The command options for the `insmod` command are listed in the table below.

Command Option	Enables You To
-e	Add persistent parameters for the module.
-f	Force the loading of a module even when there is a difference between the module's kernel version and the current kernel version.
-L	Prevent simultaneous loading of the same module.
-o {module name}	Specify a module name while installing the module.

Command Options for modprobe

The command options for the `modprobe` command are listed in the table below.

Command Option	Enables You To
-a	Add all modules specified in the command line.
-r	Remove all modules specified in the command line.
-v	Display the verbose of all commands when they are executed.
-l	List all modules that match the given wildcard information.
-t {directory name}	List all modules present in a specified directory.

The modprobe.conf File

The modprobe.conf file is a configuration file, which contains settings that apply persistently to all modules loaded on the system. It is used to configure modules and their dependencies and also specify module aliases.

 The /etc/modules.conf file was used to manage kernel modules in older versions of Linux.

The modprobe.conf file, which is located in the /etc/modprobe.d directory, has a number of options for configuring kernel modules.

Option	Used To
alias wildcard *module name*	Specify an alternate name for a module with a long name.
include *file name*	Add configuration files to the module.
options *module name option*	Specify the options to be added to each module before insertion into the kernel.
install *module name command*	Run the command specified without inserting the module into the kernel.

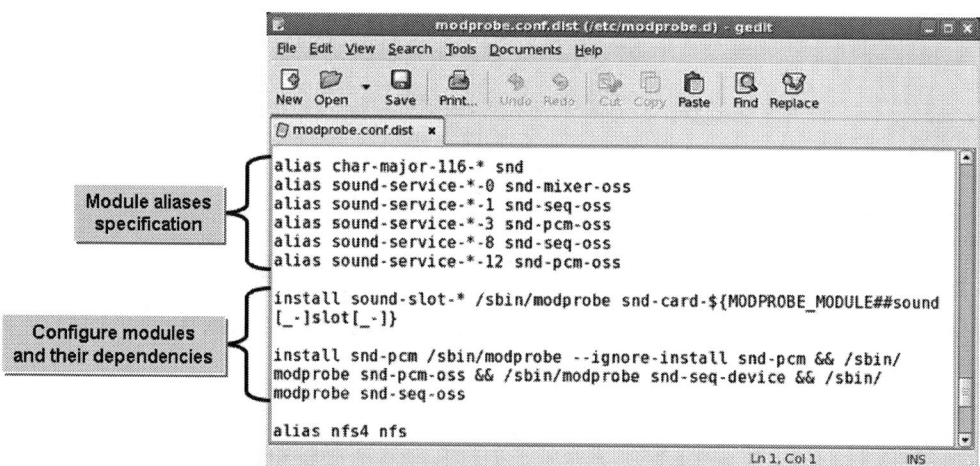

Figure 8-3: *The modprobe.conf file is used to configure the kernel modules.*

Kernel Options

Kernel options enable you to set the runlevel of the kernel. Some of the common kernel options are listed in the following table.

Kernel Option	If You Need To
1 or s	Switch to runlevel 1.
2	Switch to runlevel 2.
3	Switch to runlevel 3.
4	Switch to runlevel 4.
5	Switch to runlevel 5.

Types of Kernel Configuration

Linux kernels can be configured in two different ways. One form of configuration is persistent and the other is transactional.

Kernel Configuration Type	Description
Persistent	A persistent kernel configuration refers to the configuration of kernel settings that do not change even after the system is rebooted. The changes made to the kernel are permanent.
	The kernel configuration with the sysctl.conf file is persistent and does not get effaced when the kernel is initialized again.
Transactional	A transactional configuration refers to updating the kernel settings for a required service. These settings are not permanent and are reverted when the system is rebooted. The settings hold good only for a particular transaction of the kernel.
	The kernel configuration with the /proc file is transactional and the changes are reflected immediately.
	This type of configuration can be used for network services modification and features related to memory subsystems.

The /proc/version File

The /proc/version file specifies the version of the Linux kernel, the *GNU Compiler Collection (GCC)*, and the Linux distribution installed on the system.

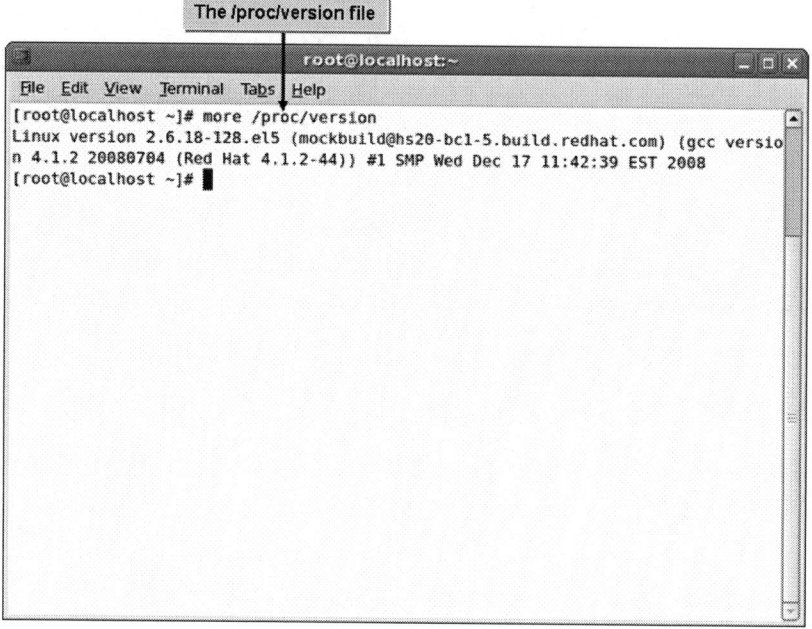

Figure 8-4: Details displayed by the /proc/version file.

 GCC originally stood for GNU C Compiler because it was produced by the GNU project

The /proc Directory

The /proc is a directory in the Linux virtual filesystem, which provides elaborate information about the kernel's running process. Some of the files in the /proc directory are listed in the table below.

File	Description
/proc/cmdline	Contains the command line passed to the kernel by the bootloader at boot time. This file contains no information.
/proc/cpuinfo	Stores the CPU information and system architecture dependent items.
/proc/devices	Contains the list of device drivers configured into the currently running kernel.
/proc/filesystems	Contains the list of filesystems that are configured into the kernel.
/proc/partitions	Contains partition information including the major and minor number of each partition, partition name, and number of blocks.
/proc/ip_forward	Permits interfaces on the system to forward packets to one other.

File	Description
/proc/meminfo	Contains memory information such as the used and unused memory on the system and the shared memory and buffers used by the kernel.

The sysctl Command

The `sysctl` command is used to view or set the kernel parameters at runtime. It has various options. Persistent kernel settings are added in the sysctl.conf file.

Command Option	Used To
`-w variable={value}`	Set a parameter value or to change the `sysctl` setting.
`variable={value}`	Set a key parameter value.
`-n`	Disable the printing of the key name while displaying the kernel parameters.
`-e`	Ignore errors about unknown keys.
`-a`	Display all parameter values that are currently available.
`-A`	Display all parameter values that are currently available in a table format.

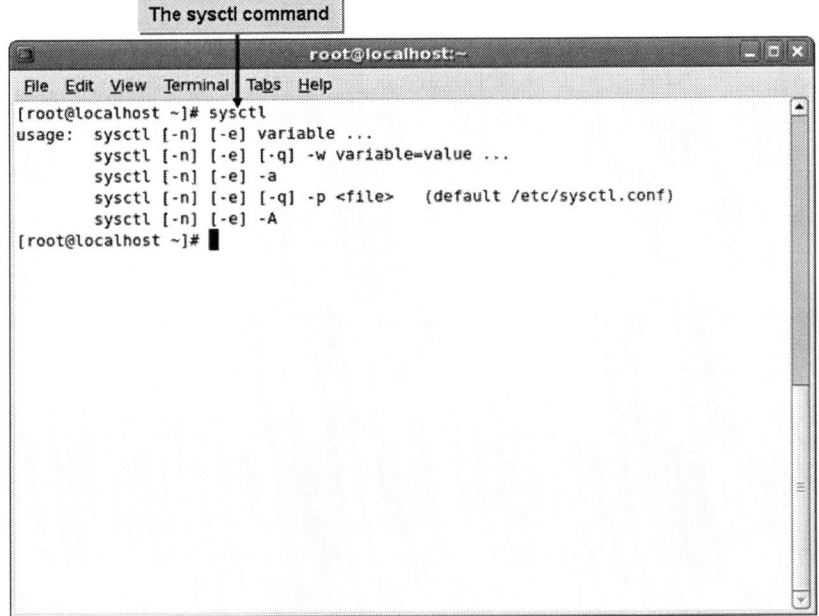

Figure 8-5: *The different options of the sysctl command.*

Syntax

The syntax of the `sysctl` command is `sysctl [command options] {kernel parameter}={value}`.

How to Customize Kernel Modules

Procedure Reference: Load Modules Using the insmod Command

To load modules using the `insmod` command:

1. Log in as root in the CLI.

2. Enter `insmod {module name}` to insert a specified module into the kernel.

3. Enter `modinfo [command options] {module name}` to view detailed information about the inserted module.

Procedure Reference: View Information About the Running Kernel Modules

To view information about the running kernel modules:

1. Log in as root in the CLI.

2. Enter `lsmod` to view the status of all loaded modules.

3. Enter `clear` to clear the terminal screen.

Procedure Reference: Add or Remove Modules Using the modprobe Utility

To load modules using the `modprobe` utility:

1. Log in as root in the CLI.

2. Enter `modprobe {module name}` to add the specified module and all its dependant modules into the kernel.

3. Enter `lsmod` to view the status of the loaded modules.

4. If necessary, enter `modprobe -r {module name}` to remove a loaded module.

Procedure Reference: Configure Modules Using the modprobe.conf File

To configure modules using the modprobe.conf file:

1. Log in as root in the CLI.

2. Enter `cd /etc` to remove a loaded module.

3. Enter `vi modprobe.conf` to open the modprobe.conf file.

    ● Specify the parameter to pass through when the module is loaded.

    ● Set the aliases for a module name.

4. Save and close the file.

Procedure Reference: Manage the Kernel Using the /etc/sysctl.conf File

To manage the kernel using the /etc/sysctl.conf file:

1. Log in as root in the CLI.

2. Open the /etc/sysctl.conf file.

3. Make the necessary modifications to the kernel settings.

4. Save and close the file.

5. Reboot the system.

Procedure Reference: Configure the Kernel Using the /proc Directory

To configure the kernel using /proc:

1. Log in as root in the CLI.

2. Enter `echo {value} > /proc/{file location whose value in the kernel needs to be changed}` to configure the kernel parameters.

3. Save and close the file.

Procedure Reference: Configure the Kernel Using the sysctl Command

To configure the kernel using the `sysctl` command:

1. Log in as root in the CLI.

2. Enter `sysctl [command options] {kernel parameter}={value}` to configure the kernel parameters.

ACTIVITY 8-2
Inserting and Configuring a Kernel Module

Before You Begin:
1. You have logged in as root in the GUI and the terminal window is displayed.
2. Enter cd / to change to the / directory.
3. On the terminal window, enter modprobe -r bcm203x to unload the kernel module for Bluetooth devices.
4. Enter clear to clear the terminal screen.
5. Switch to the first terminal in the CLI.

Scenario:
Your colleague, Mark, tried to transfer some documents from his Linux system to his mobile device. However, he was not able to do so. After examining the system, you find that the kernel module required for the Bluetooth support is not available.

What You Do	How You Do It
1. Insert the bluetooth kernel module.	a. Log in as **root** in the CLI.
	b. Enter **insmod /lib/modules/2.6.18-53.el5/⇒ kernel/drivers/bluetooth/bcm203x.kc** to insert the bluetooth module.
2. View information about the inserted bluetooth module.	a. Enter **modinfo ⇒ /lib/modules/2.6.18-53.el5/⇒ kernel/drivers/bluetooth/bcm203x.kc** to view information about the bluetooth module.
	b. Observe the displayed information about the loaded bluetooth module.

3. Configure the bluetooth kernel module.

a. At the command prompt, enter **cd /etc** to navigate to the /etc directory.

b. Enter **vi modprobe.conf** to open the modprobe.conf file for modification.

c. Press **Shift+G** to go to the last line.

d. Press **O** to switch to the insert mode and move to a new line.

e. On a new line, enter **alias blue bcm203x** to specify an alias name for the bluetooth module.

f. Press **Esc** to switch to the command mode.

g. Save and close the file.

h. Enter **logout** to log out.

TOPIC C
Create an initrd Image

You configured and customized kernel modules. The initrd image, or the initial ramdisk image, consists of all the kernel modules that were loaded during the boot process. Additional modules that are installed also need to be added to the initrd image to load them automatically at boot time. In this topic, you will create the initrd image to update the kernel.

The existing kernel in your system may have all the necessary modules, but at a later stage, you may need to update the modules when a new set of devices have to be supported. Knowing how to update the existing modules by creating the initrd image will enable you to provide support for new devices.

initrd

initrd refers to the initial ramdisk that is temporarily mounted as the root filesystem for loading startup programs and modules. The ramdisk loads along with the kernel, and its functionality is controlled by the kernel. initrd enables the system to be started in two phases. In the first phase, the system is booted with the minimum set of modules required to load the main or the permanent root filesystem. In the second phase, when the main root filesystem is mounted, the previously mounted initrd filesystem is removed and the ramdisk is released for installing additional modules on demand.

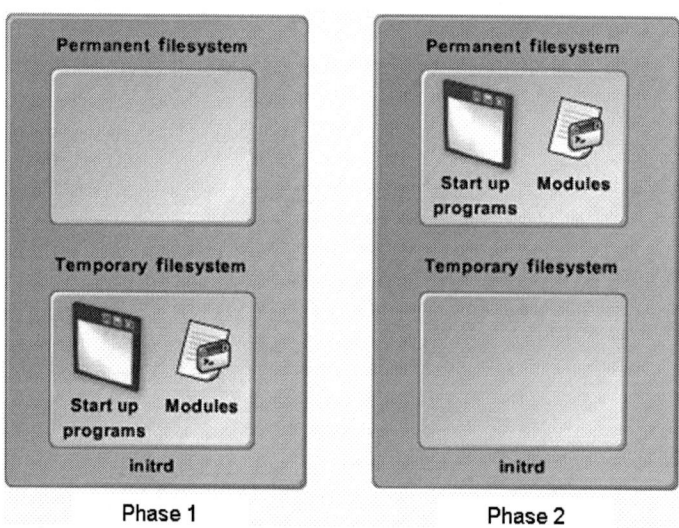

Figure 8-6: The initrd starts the system in two phases.

The initrd Image

The *initrd image* is an archived file containing all the essential files that are required for booting the operating system. It can be built or customized to include additional modules, remove unnecessary modules, or update existing modules.

The mkinitrd Command

The *mkinitrd command* is used to create the initial ramdisk image for pre-loading the kernel modules.

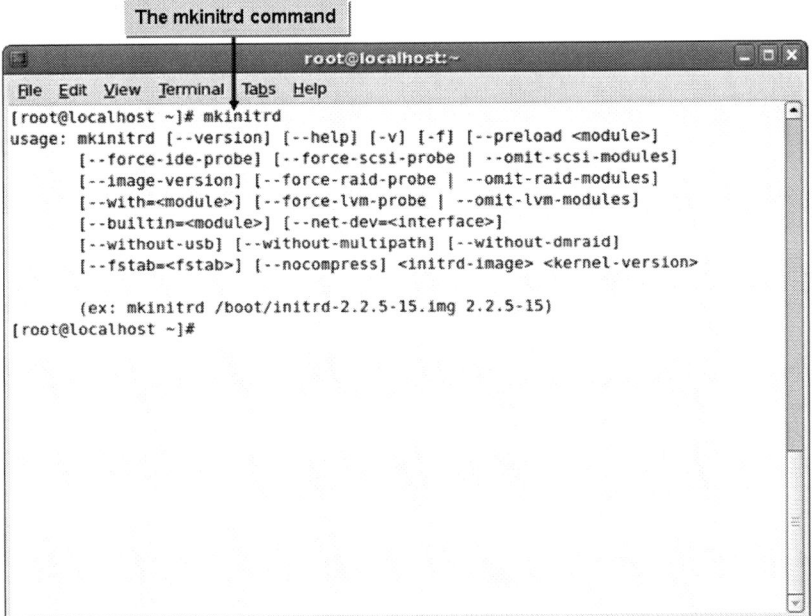

Figure 8-7: The options of the mkinitrd command.

Various options of the `mkinitrd` command are given in the following table.

Command Option	Used To
`--preload={module name}`	Load a module in the initrd image before the loading of SCSI modules.
`--with={module name}`	Load a module in the initrd image after the loading of SCSI modules.
`--builtin={module name}`	Specify that the module is already built into the currently loaded kernel, so that the `mkinitrd` command will omit it while creating the initrd image.
`--fstab={fstab}`	Automatically determine the type of filesystem that the root device is found on.

`--omit-lvm-modules`
`--omit-raid-modules`
`--omit-scsi-modules`
	Avoid loading the LVM, RAID, and SCSI modules, respectively, while creating the initrd image.

Command Option	Used To
-f	Overwrite an existing initrd image file.

How to Create an initrd Image

Procedure Reference: Create an initrd Image with Updated Information

To create an initrd image with updated information:

1. Log in as root in the CLI.
2. Enter mkinitrd *[command options]* /boot/initrd-*{kernel version number}*.img *{kernel version number}* to create an initrd image.
3. Update the /boot/grub/grub.conf file with the updated initrd information.

ACTIVITY 8-3

Creating an initrd Image to Update the Kernel

Before You Begin:

1. Reboot srvB and start Red Hat Linux on the system.

2. Switch to the CLI.

Scenario:

You have to troubleshoot a Linux system that has a booting issue. The system consists of a SCSI disk containing the Linux installation files. However, the kernel does not have an in-built SCSI module. Though the kernel can load and execute other modules, it will not be able to mount its root filesystem without loading the SCSI module first. Because the module resides in the root filesystem in /lib/modules/, you cannot pre-enable the SCSI support. You have updated the kernel and need to boot the new kernel.

What You Do	How You Do It
1. Create a new initrd image.	a. Log in as **root** in the CLI.
	b. Enter **mkinitrd /boot/new-initrd-image.img 'uname -r'** to create a new initrd image.

 In the `'uname -r'` section of the `mkinitrd /boot/new-initrd-image.img 'uname -r'` command, use the back quote (') key on the keyboard.

2. Update the GRUB configuration with the new initrd image.

   a. Enter **cd /boot/grub** to access the directory where GRUB is located.

   b. Enter **vi grub.conf** to edit the GRUB configuration file.

   c. Enter **:17** to navigate to the seventeenth line in the file.

   d. Press **I** to switch to the insert mode.

   e. Verify that the cursor is near the text that starts with "initrd /initrd-2.6.****.img" or "module /initrd-2.6.****.img."

   f. Type **#** to display the line as a comment.

   g. On a new line, type **module /new-initrd-image.img**

   h. Press **Esc** to switch to the command mode.

   i. Save and close the file.

   j. Enter **reboot** to load the new initrd image.

3. View the new initrd image and boot the system using it.

   a. When the system reboots and the GRUB splash screen displays the message **Booting Red Hat Enterprise Linux (2.6.****) in 3 seconds,** press **A** to enter the bootloader menu.

   b. If prompted for password, press **P** to view the **Password** prompt. At the prompt, enter your password.

   c. On the bootloader menu, verify that your currently installed Linux version is selected and press **E** to view its components.

   d. Observe that the newly created initrd image **module /new-initrd-image.img** is displayed in the boot sequence list.

   e. Press **B** to boot from the new initrd image.

TOPIC D
Manage Device Drivers

Throughout this lesson you have been performing various kernel service management tasks. Device management is another important service provided by the kernel. In this topic, you will manage Linux' kernel-based device drivers.

A system administrator has to read and write details to the driver files frequently when additional hardware is required or existing hardware is upgraded. Knowing how to access drives through /dev will enable you to handle this task effectively.

udev

udev is a device manager that manages the automatic detection and configuration of hardware devices. udev is an integral part of the kernel, which is initialized during boot time. The udev utility handles module loading for both cold- and hot-plug devices. It loads the modules for cold-plug devices, such as a monitor or a sound card, when the system is booted, and it loads the required modules for hot-plug devices, such as a USB drive or a camcorder, dynamically during system run time.

The /dev Directory

The /dev directory includes hardware and software device drivers.

Cold Plug vs. Hot Plug

Hot plug is the ability of a system to add or remove hardware without rebooting the system, while cold plug is the inability to do so. Hot-plug devices are detected by the system as they are plugged in, whereas cold-plug devices, such as conventional hard disks, are not sensed when connected to a running system; they need a complete reboot of the system to function. Some cold plug devices, such as hard disk, PCI, and RAM, can be connected only when the system is not running.

The /sys Directory

In Kernel 2.6 or above, the /sys directory contains information about hot-plug hardware devices and displays them in a hierarchical format. It is similar to the /proc filesystem because it contains information related to files loaded in the kernel memory.

Device Drivers

Definition:

A *device driver* is a software program that enables a computer's operating system to identify the characteristics and functions of a hardware device, communicate with it, and control its operations. It acts as an interface between the operating system and hardware devices such as hard drives, CD/DVD drives, printers, scanners, monitors, and keyboards. Device drivers can be part of the operating system or installed on demand.

Example:

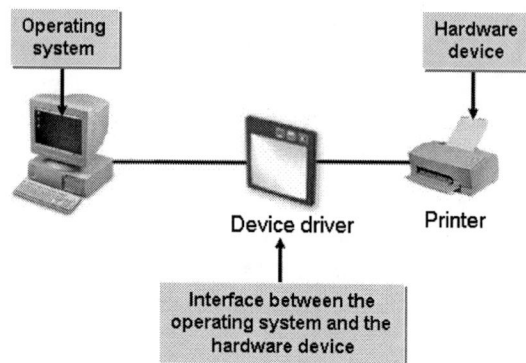

Figure 8-8: A printer driver is used by the operating system to communicate with your printer to print files or documents.

Device Tree

A *device tree* is a structure that lists all hardware devices installed on a system and assigns device nodes to them. It is auto generated by the computer's RAM when the computer is started, when a new device is installed, or when a device or system configuration is modified.

Device Nodes

A *device node* is an access point for device drivers; it is used while mapping service requests with device access. It represents a particular hardware resource in a device tree. It is also known as a device file or a device special file. This node contains vital information such as the device type, the major number, and the minor number. A *minor number* identifies a particular device and the *major number* identifies the device driver that controls this particular device. Device nodes are located in the /dev directory.

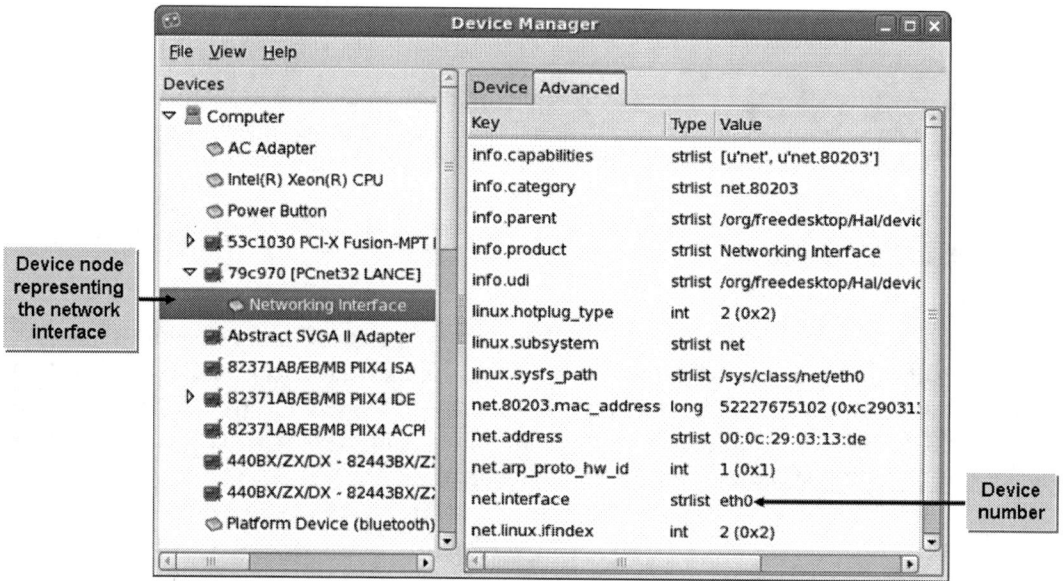

Figure 8-9: A device node representing the disk volume.

Types of Hardware Devices

Hardware devices can be divided into two types based on their usage or function.

Device Type	Description
Block devices	These are typically used for data storage. They buffer all the service requests received to choose the order in which the requests have to be responded. Block devices accept input and provide output in the form of blocks, which are of larger byte sizes. Examples are: ● Hard disks—/dev/hda and /dev/sda ● Software RAID—/dev/md[0–5]
Character devices	These are typically used for data streaming and do not use buffering to handle service requests. They accept input and provide output in smaller byte sizes. Examples are: ● Software devices—/dev/null and /dev/zero ● Virtual consoles—/dev/tty[0–6]

Special Devices

Linux provides a few special character devices that are useful occasionally.

Special Device	Description
/dev/zero	This special device provides unlimited null characters (0 bytes) for writing into any program or file. It is used for generating an empty file of certain size.
/dev/null	This special device does not provide any data to a program or file. It discards all data written to it. It is used as an output file when the output is not required by the user.
/dev/random	This special device functions as a random number generator. It gathers random input from device drivers and other sources on the system and saves it as bits in an *entropy* pool. It provides randomly generated output as bytes to applications within the number of bits in the pool. When the pool is exhausted, the /dev/random device will block the reading application until more random input is collected.
/dev/urandom	This special device functions similarly to /dev/random except that it does not block the reading application if the entropy pool is exhausted. It uses a software algorithm to generate alternate random input that may be less secure than the input generated by the system.

The mknod Command

The *mknod command* allows you to create device files that are not present using the major and minor node numbers of a device.

Syntax

The syntax of the mknod command is mknod `[OPTION]... NAME TYPE [MAJOR MINOR]`.

How to Manage Device Drivers

Procedure Reference: Access Drivers Through /dev

To access device driver files through /dev:

1. Log in as root in the CLI.

2. Enter who to check which terminal is being used and the users who are logged in.

3. Enter cat `/dev/{device node}` to view the device driver file.

4. Enter echo `{messages} > /dev/{device node}` to send messages using the specific device node.

Procedure Reference: Add Files Under /dev

To add files under /dev:

1. Log in as root in the CLI.

2. Add files under the /dev directory.

   - Create files in the /etc/udev/rules.d directory.

      a. Enter cd `/etc/udev/rules.d` to open the rules.d directory.

      b. Enter touch `{file name}` to view the timestamps of the device file.

      c. Switch to the insert mode.

      d. Enter vi `{file name}` to open the device file.

      e. Type the text as indicated below to add details to the file.KERNEL==`"{device}"`, NAME=`"{device node}"`

      f. Save and close the file.

   - Create files using the mknod command.

      a. Enter mknod `/dev/{device node} {device type} {major number} {minor number}` to create the device node.

ACTIVITY 8-4

Accessing Drivers Through /dev

Before You Begin:
On srvA, the GUI login screen is displayed.

Scenario:
Your company has a server to which many users log in with their user account to carry out their day-to-day operations. Due to the unscheduled emergency maintenance on the server, you may need to reboot the system if necessary. You now need to send a message to all the logged in users using the device node, so that they can save their data, complete their tasks, and log out of their systems.

What You Do	How You Do It
1. View information about users who have currently logged in.	a. Log in as **root** in the GUI.
	b. Choose **Applications→Accessories→ Terminal** to open the terminal.
	c. Enter **who** to check who is logged in to which terminal.
	d. Observe the list of current users displayed as the output.
2. Send messages using the device node in the /dev directory.	a. Enter **echo "Please save your work, the system will be down for⇒** **maintenance in 30 minutes" > /dev/tty1** to alert all current users using the specified device node.
	b. Enter **clear** to clear the terminal window.
	c. Switch to the CLI.
	d. Observe that the echoed message is displayed on the screen. Press **Enter** to return to the login prompt.
	e. Enter **clear** to clear the terminal screen.

TOPIC E
Monitor Hardware Devices

You accessed driver files and modified their parameters. Drivers are associated directly with the devices that are installed on your computer. In this topic, you will monitor various hardware devices.

A system administrator needs to keep track of all devices that are connected to a computer and monitor them continuously. Gaining knowledge about utilities that are used to track these hardware devices is essential for proper management of the Linux system.

Hardware Communication Channels

The kernel and the hardware devices communicate using major channels such as Interrupt Requests, Input/Output (I/O) addresses, and Direct Memory Address (DMA).

Hardware Communication Channel	Description
Interrupt ReQuests (IRQ)	An interrupt request is a signal sent by a hardware device to the kernel to request processing time in order to perform an operation. This enables the kernel to prioritize system events and allocate the CPU's processing time for devices.
Input/Output (I/O) Address	Every hardware device communicates with the operating system through a unique I/O address. The kernel uses this address to identify the requests sent to or from the device. It is also used to map the device with user applications requesting the device services.
Direct Memory Address (DMA)	A method by which hardware devices directly communicate with the memory to obtain memory allocation without going through the processor.

The Hardware Abstraction Layer

The *Hardware Abstraction Layer (HAL)* is a logical interface that enables software applications to interact with hardware devices at an abstract level through system calls. This layer converts generic system calls sent by software applications to detailed device-specific instructions. It enables an operating system to adapt to different kinds of hardware platforms without requiring any modifications in the kernel.

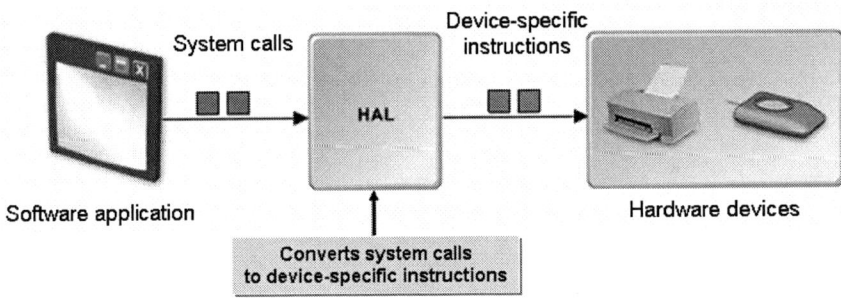

Figure 8-10: *HAL serves as an interface between software and hardware.*

The HAL Utilities

The HAL utilities enable you to view or monitor the hardware device connected to the computer.

HAL Utility	Used To
lspci	Display all peripheral components connected to a computer.
lsusb	Display all USB components connected to a computer.
hal-device	Display the list of all connected devices in text mode.
hal-device-manager	Display all connected devices in a graphical window. This utility is dependent on the udev command for device node information.

How to Monitor Hardware Devices

Procedure Reference: Monitor Hardware Devices

To monitor the hardware devices currently connected to a system:

1. Log in as root.

2. Monitor hardware devices.

    ● Enter lspci to list the status of all PCI devices.

    ● Enter lsusb to list the status all USB devices.

    ● Enter hal-device to list all devices.

    ● Enter hal-device-manager or choose **System→Administration→Hardware** to display the **Device Manager** window and view the list of all hardware devices and their related information.

ACTIVITY 8-5

Monitoring Hardware Devices on a Computer

Before You Begin:

1. Switch to the GUI.

2. You have logged in as root in the GUI.

3. The terminal window is displayed.

4. On the terminal window, enter `cd /rhelsource/Server` to navigate to the /rhelsource/Server directory.

5. Enter `rpm -ivh hal-gnome-0.5.8.1-38.el5.i386.rpm` to install the HAL device manager package.

6. Enter `clear` to clear the terminal window.

Scenario:

As part of your system administration task, you have to keep track of the devices used on all computers in the network and maintain a list of hardware resources that are in use.

What You Do	How You Do It
1. View all peripheral devices that are connected to the system.	a. On the terminal window, enter **lspci -v** to view the list of peripheral components and their related information.
	b. Observe the list of hardware devices being displayed along with the related information.
	c. Enter **clear** to clear the terminal window.

2. View all hardware devices that are connected to the system using the HAL device manager.

a. Enter **hal-device-manager** to view the list of all hardware devices and their related information.

b. Observe that the **Device Manager** window lists all hardware devices connected to the system in the left pane.

c. In the right pane, select the **Advanced** tab to view more information.

d. Observe that the details are listed under the **Key** column. Also observe that the active status of the horizontal scroll bar indicates that there are more columns on the right side.

e. Scroll to the right to view the **Type** and **Value** columns.

f. Close the **Device Manager** window.

g. Enter **clear** to clear the terminal window.

TOPIC F

Monitor Processes and Resources

You monitored hardware devices on your computer. Along with the hardware devices, software applications and programs work in conjunction to make the entire system work. Software programs are handled by the processor. In this topic, you will monitor processes to view how system resources are utilized and how the processor manages them.

As a system administrator, you may need to handle a number of running processes simultaneously. Based on the need, one program may require a higher priority than another. While the execution of one process is in progress, you may decide to pause or stop the process to start another important process. Performing process monitoring will help you manage multiple programs and their resource allocation.

Load Average

Load average is the average number of processes waiting to run on a system for the last 1 minute, 5 minutes, and 15 minutes. Ideally, the number should be less than one. This information can be used to check whether the system is busy. The load average information is specific to the operating system and the hardware.

Kernel State Monitoring Utilities

Kernel state monitoring utilities are used to gather information about the operating system, its running events, and processes.

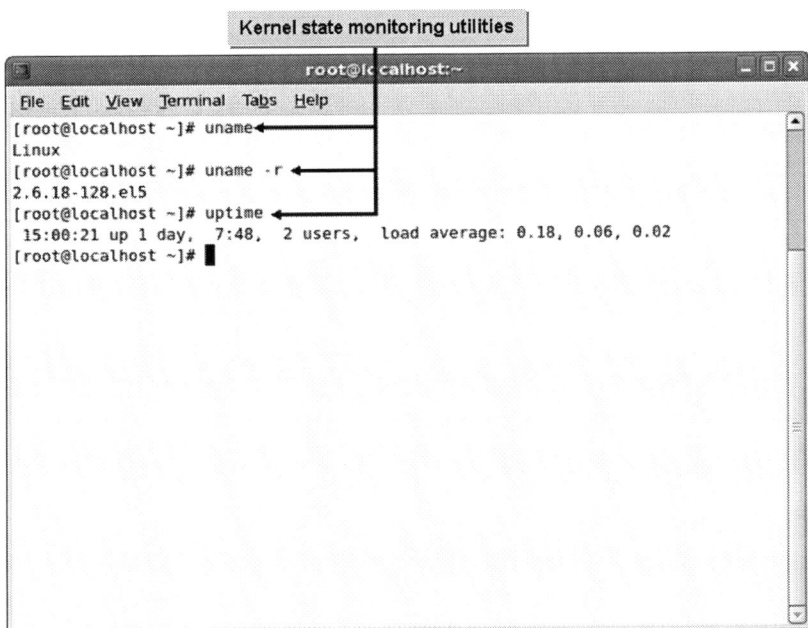

Figure 8-11: Output of various kernel state monitoring tools.

Kernel State Monitoring Utility	Enables You To
uname	Display the name of the operating system, its version, license, processor, and hardware details.
uptime	Display the duration for which the system has been running, the load average of the system, and how many users have logged on currently.
tload	Provide a graphical representation of the system and the load average for the past 1 minute, 5 minutes, and 15 minutes.

System Load

System load is a measurement of the amount of work done by a computer over a given period of time. It is represented in the form of three numbers. The first number indicates the system load during the last one minute, the second number indicates the system load during the last five minutes, and the last number indicates the system load during the last fifteen minutes.

Memory Monitoring Utilities

Memory monitoring utilities are used to view the usage of memory and other related statistics.

Memory Monitoring Utility	Enables You To
free	Display the total memory available on the system and the amount of memory that is free, used, shared, buffered, and cached.
vmstat	Display the statistics about virtual memory usage. It lists the details about currently running processes such as memory usage, interrupts or I/O address information, and processor allocation information.
pmap	Display the mapping of processes with memory resources.
iostat	Generate reports on CPU and device utilization. It provides input and output statistics for storage devices and partitions.

Command Options for the free Utility

The command options for the free utility are listed in the table below.

Command Option	Used To
-b	Display the amount of memory in bytes, kilobytes, megabytes, and gigabytes, respectively.
-k	
-m	
-g	

Command Option	Used To
-s {delay in seconds}	Update the memory statistics at a delay of the specified seconds.
-o	Disable the display of the buffer or cache information line.
-t	Display the total RAM and swap space.

Command Options for the vmstat Utility

The command options for the vmstat utility are listed in the table below.

Command Option	Used To
-a	Display the active or inactive memory.
-s	Display memory statistics in a list format.
-m	Display statistics in the form of slabs.
-d	Display disk statistics.
-p {disk partition}	Display statistics for the specified partition.

Command Options for the pmap Utility

The command options for the pmap utility are listed in the table below.

Command Option	Used To
-x {PID}	Report the memory map of processes in an extended format.
-d {PID}	Report the memory map of processes in a device format.
-q {PID}	Report the minimal required information of memory mapping.
-V	Display the version of the pmap utility.

Process Monitoring

Process monitoring is a mode of tracking the processes running on a system to determine its performance and reliability. Some processes that run continuously on a system, such as those initiated by databases and web servers, have to be monitored constantly, whereas others can be monitored occasionally. Process monitoring enables a user to identify the causes of low performance in processes and detect the processes run by unauthorized users.

Process monitoring can be performed with the help of utilities.

Utility	Enables You To
`top`	Display the list of processes in the descending order of CPU memory usage. It also displays details about the consumption of power, memory, and system resources at a given time. It helps track processes that consume high memory and system resources. The output of the command can also be redirected to a text file. In the KDE desktop environment, the `kpm` utility is used in place of the `top` command.
`GNOME system monitor`	Monitor system performance. It has three tabs, which list the performance history and status of various processes, resources, and filesystems on the system.
`sar`	Display the system utilization reports that are generated based on the system utilization data. These reports consist of various sections each of which consists of the type of data and the time at which the data was collected. By default, the `sar` reports list the data collected every 10 minutes. On an average, the report consists of 17 sections. The `sar` command is run automatically by a script called sa2 at specified time intervals.

Useful Keys to Manage Processes

The `top` command provides an interactive tool to manage processes by using some simple shortcuts. Some of the frequently used shortcuts are listed here.

Key	Function
Enter	Refreshes the status of all processes.
Shift+N	Sorts tasks in the decreasing order of their *Process ID (PID)*.
U	Displays processes belonging to the user specified at the prompt.
K	Terminates the process for which the PID is specified.
R	Renices the process for which the PID is specified.
H	Displays a help screen.
Q	Exits the task list.

sar Options

The `sar` command can be used to retrieve specific data by specifying the following options. Some of the frequently used options are listed in the table.

Option	Enables You To
`-A`	Display all reports generated on the current date.
`-b`	Display I/O statistics.

Option	Enables You To
-B	Display the number of bytes exchanged between the system and the disk.
-c	Display the number of processes spawned per second by the system.
-d	Display system activity for each block device.

The GNOME System Monitor

The *GNOME system monitor* is a GUI utility that is used to monitor system processes, resources, and filesystems. The **Processes** tab displays details about the currently running processes such as the name, status, ID, and CPU and memory usage. The **Resources** tab displays the CPU, memory, and swap usage history and network operations history. The **File Systems** tab displays information about currently mounted filesystems, related directories, type, and usage status.

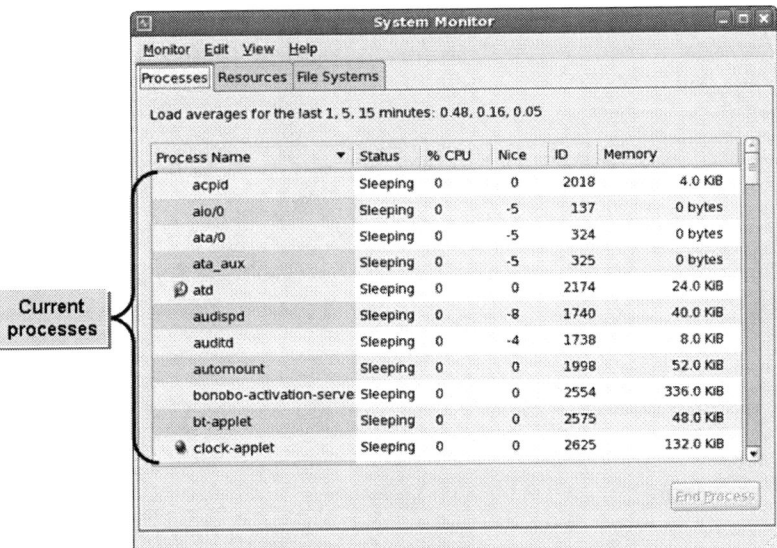

Figure 8-12: The GNOME system monitor displaying the system status.

How to Monitor Processes and Resources

Procedure Reference: Monitor the Kernel State

To monitor the kernel state:

1. Log in as root.
2. On the terminal, enter `uname [command options]` to view the information regarding the running kernel.
3. Enter `uptime` to view the running time of the system.
4. Enter `tload` to view the graphical representation of the systems load average.

Procedure Reference: Monitor the Memory Usage

To monitor the memory usage:

1. Log in as root.
2. On the terminal, enter `free [command options]` to view the free and used memory of the system.
3. Enter `vmstat [command options]` to report the virtual memory statistics.

Procedure Reference: Monitor the Processes Mapping

To monitor the processes mapping:

1. Log in as root.
2. Enter `ps [command options]` to view the running processes on the system.
3. Enter `pmap [command options] {pid}` to view the memory map of a process.

Procedure Reference: Manage Processes Using the GNOME System Monitor

To manage processes using the GNOME system monitor:

1. Log in as root in the GUI.
2. Choose **System→Administration→System Monitor** to open the GNOME system monitor.
3. On the **Processes** tab, scroll to locate the process.
4. Right-click on a running process to start, stop, kill, or change priority.
5. Choose **Monitor→Quit** to close the window.

ACTIVITY 8-6

Monitoring Processes and Resources

Before You Begin:
1. You have logged in as root in the GUI.
2. The terminal window is displayed.

Scenario:
Your company has expanded and a large number of users joined your network. Therefore, there are many services running on the main server. To reduce the load on the server, the company wants to add separate servers. As a system administrator, you are asked to submit data on the usage of the existing server to decide on the number of servers to be added and the applications that are to be moved to the additional servers.

What You Do	How You Do It
1. Monitor the kernel state.	a. Enter **uname -r** to monitor the kernel state.
	b. Observe that the kernel version **2.6.18–128.el5** is displayed.
	c. Enter **uptime** to view the running time of the system.
	d. Observe that information about the system start time, the duration, the number of currently logged in users, and the load average is displayed.
2. Monitor memory usage.	a. Enter **vmstat** to view the virtual memory statistics.
	b. Observe that the details are displayed for the memory, processes, swap, input/output, and system and CPU.
	c. Enter **free -m** to view the unused memory available on the system.
	d. Observe that details about **Memory** and **Swap** usage are displayed in the output.

3. Monitor processes.

a. Enter **ps aux | more** to view the processes that are currently running on the system.

b. Observe that a list of all processes with details regarding users who are running the processes, the process IDs, CPU and memory usage, virtual and resident set size, the terminal type, time, and the command is displayed.

c. Press **Q** to return to the prompt.

 VSZ and RSS are the virtual set size and resident set size attributes of a process that display how much memory has been occupied by a process.

d. Enter **clear** to clear the terminal window.

Lesson 8 Follow-up

In this lesson, you explored the purpose and organization of the kernel and managed its services. This will enable you to understand the kernel structure, monitor the kernel components, and configure the kernel services. As a Linux system administrator, customizing the kernel to suit your requirements will enable you to manage the kernel efficiently.

1. **How do you think modules affect the way kernels are loaded?**

2. **Why is process management important for operating systems?**

9 Working with the Bash Shell and Shell Scripts

Lesson Time: 2 hour(s)

Lesson Objectives:

In this lesson, you will work with the Bash shell.

You will:

- Perform basic Bash shell operations.
- Write a basic shell script.
- Use shell variables.
- Redirect standard input and output.
- Use control statements.

Introduction

In the previous lesson, you managed Linux kernel services. The Linux shell is an important constituent of the operating system, and it is essential to familiarize yourself with the Bash shell and perform basic operations in it. In this lesson, you will work with the Bash shell and write shell scripts.

The Bash shell functions as an intermediary layer between the user and the operating system. You can use shell scripts within a Bash shell to automate routine tasks. Although Bash is not the only shell available, it is one of the most common ones, and so familiarizing yourself with the Bash shell and its functions enables you to interact and work efficiently with the Linux operating system. Also, tedious and time-consuming administrative tasks can be simplified by automation, using scripts.

This lesson covers all or part of the following CompTIA Linux+ (2009) certification objectives:

- Topic A
  - Objective 2.2
- Topic B
  - Objective 2.1
  - Objective 2.2
- Topic C
  - Objective 1.9

- Topic D
  - Objective 2.1
- Topic E
  - Objective 2.2

TOPIC A
Perform Basic Bash Shell Operations

You are familiar with the shell application and its various types. You are now ready to run commands in the shell to perform basic file navigation in the operating system. In this topic, you will perform basic Bash shell operations.

The Bash shell is the most frequently used shell in Linux. It allows you to effectively perform tasks, such as file management, user and group administration, process management, text editing, and so on, using the command line. Basic Bash shell options allow you to perform simple tasks such as using strings to search for files on your system, reviewing commands that have been previously executed, and many more.

The Bash Shell

The *Bourne-Again SHell (Bash shell)* is the default shell in Linux. It is a superset of the Bourne shell and includes features from the Korn and C shells. The Bash shell facilitates command line editing, command history, command line completion, and shell scripting.

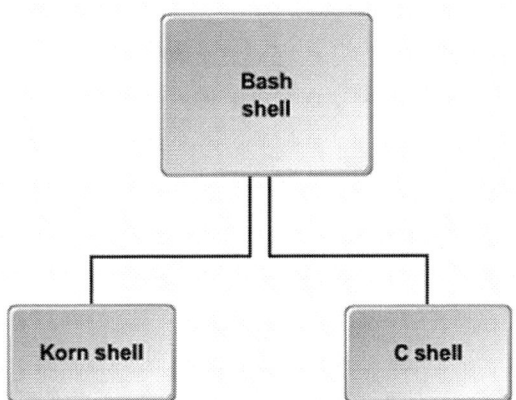

Figure 9-1: The Bash shell includes features from the Korn and C shells.

Bash Shell Functions

The shell is the basic component that provides the CLI in Linux. Some of the functions performed by the shell include:

- Prompting a user for input and waiting for a command to be entered.
- Verifying the correctness of the command and processing the command.
- Expanding wildcards by replacing special characters with portions of the string.
- Determining the source of input and the location of output.
- And, returning to the prompt after the completion of a command and restarting the cycle.

Wildcards

Wildcards are special characters that are used to substitute portions of a string. By using wildcards with appropriate arguments, you can search and locate files on your system. Wildcards are used to narrow down search criteria and obtain accurate search results.

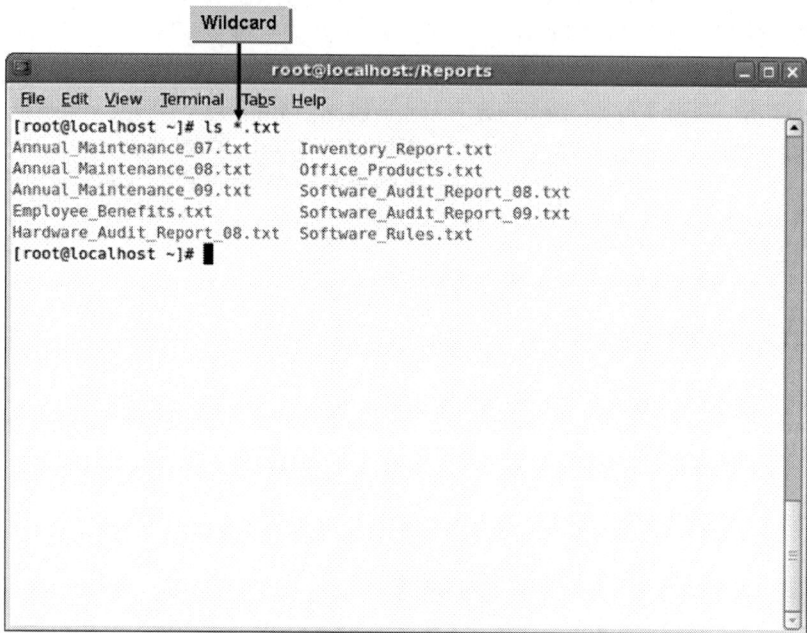

Figure 9-2: Using wildcards in a command.

The following table lists some of the frequently used wildcards.

Wildcard	Used To
*	Match zero or more characters in the file name.
?	Match a single character in the file name.
[abcde]	Match any of the listed characters.
[a-e]	Match any character in the range.
[!abcde]	Match any character that is not listed.
[!a-e]	Match any character that is not included in the range.
{linux, shell}	Match any word in the given options.
$	List file names that end with the character preceding the $ symbol.

Complex Wildcards

A complex wildcard is a combination of individual wildcards. For example, enter [a-z]?[1-9] to search for three characters—the first character is a letter, the last character a number, and the middle character can be a letter, a number, or a special character.

Globbing

Globbing is a function that expands file names (wildcards) using a pattern-matching behavior. The wildcards that globbing interprets are the * symbol, the ? symbol, sets of characters that are included within brackets, and special characters such as the ^ symbol.

Tab Completion

Tab completion facilitates auto completion of commands and file names. Pressing the **Tab** key completes the names of commands, files, directories, users, and hosts.

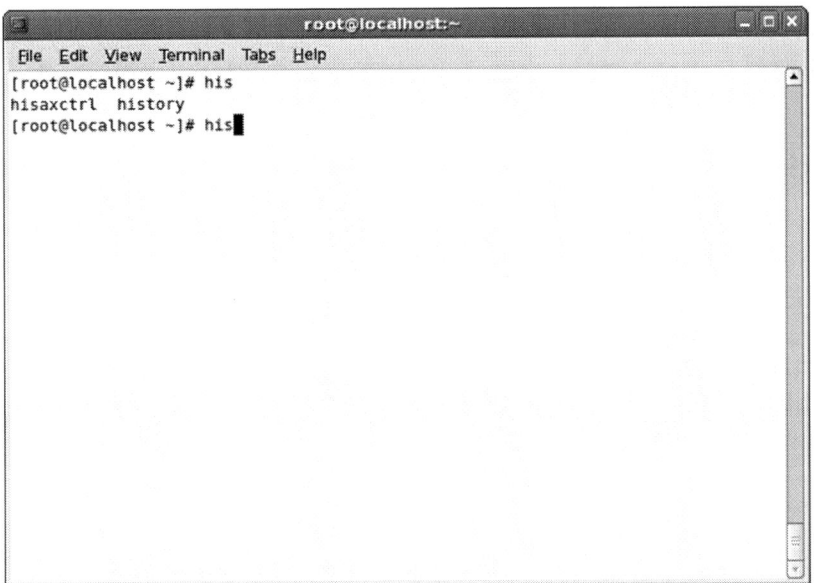

Figure 9-3: Tab completion entries for the text "his".

 Pressing the **Tab** key two times displays all files and directories that begin with the string you typed.

The history Command

The *history command* is used to view previously typed commands. It retrieves the specified number of commands from the ~/.bash_history file. You can use the **Up Arrow** or **Down Arrow** key to select the desired command. By simultaneously pressing **Alt and Plus Sign** (+), you can recall arguments that have been used with previously executed commands.

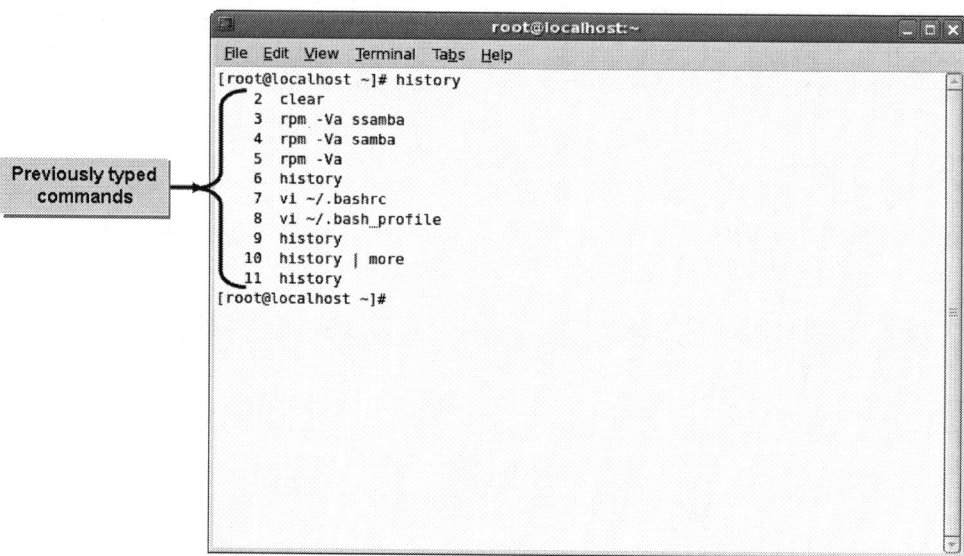

Figure 9-4: *Output of the history command.*

Recall Commands and Arguments

Pressing the **Up Arrow** key allows you to recall commands that have been run on the terminal. Pressing **Esc** followed by **Period** (**.**) is an alternate way of recalling arguments.

How to Perform Basic Bash Shell Operations

Procedure Reference: Perform a Search Using Wildcards

To perform a search using wildcards:

1. Log in as a user in the CLI.
2. Perform basic operations.

   * Enter `ls [wildcard]{string}[wildcard]` to list all the content that match the given pattern.

   * Enter `rm [wildcard]{string}[wildcard]` to remove all the content that matches the given pattern.

   * Enter `echo [wildcard]{string}[wildcard]` to print all the content that match the given pattern.

Procedure Reference: Detect a File name Using Tab Completion

To detect a file name using tab completion:

1. Log in as a user in the CLI.
2. Enter a unique character of the command and press the **Tab** key to complete the command.
3. Enter `{unique character of the file name}` and press the **Tab** key to complete the file name.

Procedure Reference: View the Recently Used Commands Using the history Command

To view the recently used commands using the `history` command:

1. Log in as a user in the CLI.

2. View the history of commands executed.

   ● Enter `history` to list all the previously used commands.

   ● Enter `!{history number}` to execute a particular command from the command history.

   ● Enter `!!` to repeat the previously executed command.

Procedure Reference: Perform Basic Command Line Expansion

To perform basic command line expansion:

1. Log in as a user in the CLI.

2. Perform basic command line expansion.

   ● Enter `{command} {common string}{{unique part of file 1, unique part of file 2}` when a file or directory name has a common string in it.

   ● Enter `{command} "{string}"` to print a string.

   ● Enter `{command 2} '{command 1}'` to send the output of one command as the input to another command.

ACTIVITY 9-1
Using Wildcards to Search for Files

Data Files:

Audit_File_2000.txt, Audit_File_2001.txt, Audit_File_2002.txt, Audit_File_2003.txt, Audit_File_2004.txt, Audit_File_2005.txt, Audit_File_2006.txt, Audit_File_2007.txt, Audit_File_2008.txt, Audit_File_2009.txt

Before You Begin:

1. You have logged in as root in the GUI and CLI.

2. The terminal window is displayed.

3. On the terminal window, enter
   `cp /085039Data/Working_with_Bash_and_Shell_scripts/* /root.`

4. Enter `y` to continue.

5. Enter `cd /root`.

6. Enter `clear` to clear the terminal window.

7. Switch to the CLI.

8. Log in to the system as root.

Scenario:

You have to create a report on audit file maintenance in your department. You want to generate a list of all the audit files created since the inception of the company, along with the date and time of creation, ownership details, and file access permissions. Therefore, you decide to use wildcards to search for the audit files in your Linux system.

What You Do	How You Do It
1. Search for the audit files using wildcards.	a. Enter `ls -l Audit*` to list all files that match the search pattern.
	b. Observe that the resultant files are displayed along with the date and time of creation, ownership details, and file permissions.
2. Display all file names using wildcards.	a. Enter `echo Audit*` to display all file names that match the search pattern.
	b. Observe the file names that are displayed.
	c. Clear the terminal screen.

ACTIVITY 9-2
Viewing the Command History

Before You Begin:
1. You have logged in as root in the first terminal of the CLI.
2. Enter `logout` to log out of the root user account.

Scenario:
While you were on vacation, your colleague, Joyce Smith, had been performing some of your tasks using your system and login name. Now that you are back, you want to view the commands she had executed, to create a log of the tasks executed on your system.

What You Do	How You Do It
1. View the command history.	a. Log in as **jsmith.**
	b. Type *hist* and press the **Tab** key to complete the command.
	c. Observe that the `history` command has been completed.
	d. Press **Enter** to view the command history.
	e. Observe the last few commands that have been executed on your system.
	f. Log out of the **jsmith** user account.
2. View the command history of the root user.	a. Log in as **root** in the CLI.
	b. At the command line, type *hist* and press the **Tab** key to view the command history.
	c. Observe that the `history` command has been completed.
	d. Press **Enter** to view the command history.
	e. Observe the last few commands executed by the **root** user.
	f. Clear the terminal screen.

ACTIVITY 9-3
Organizing Files Using Wildcards

Data Files:

Software_Audit_Report_2007.txt, Software_Audit_Report_2008.txt, Hardware_Audit_Report_2007.txt, Hardware_Audit_Report_2008.txt, Annual_Maintenance_Report_2008.txt, Annual_Maintenance_Report_2007.txt, New_Policies_2008.txt, Audit_File_2008.txt, Audit_File_2009.txt

Before You Begin:
1. You have logged in as root in the CLI.
2. The first terminal is displayed.

Scenario:

Your organization adopted a new system audit policy that requires you to organize your files in a proper directory structure and make a backup of the directory. You have been asked to create the necessary directory structure and relocate the files to ensure that the structure complies with your organization's standards.

The files that need to be organized are located in the /root directory.

What You Do	How You Do It
1. Create a directory structure with Audit_Reports as the root directory, containing three subdirectories named 2007, 2008, and 2009.	a. Enter **mkdir Audit_Reports** to create a directory.
	b. Enter **cd Audit_Reports** to switch to the newly created directory.
	c. Enter **mkdir 2007 2008 2009** to create multiple directories.
	d. Enter **ls** to list the directories.
	e. Observe that the newly created directories are listed.

2. Move the files related to the years 2007, 2008, and 2009 to their respective directories.

a. Enter **cd ..** to switch to the parent directory.

b. Enter **mv *2007.txt Audit_Reports/2007** to move the files with names that end with "2007" to the Reports/2007 directory.

c. Enter **ls Audit_Reports/2007** to verify that the files have been moved.

d. Observe that the files are listed, indicating that they have been moved.

e. Enter **mv *2008.txt Audit_Reports/2008** to move the files with names that end with "2008" to the Reports/2008 directory.

f. Enter **ls Audit_Reports/2008** to verify that the files have been moved.

g. Observe that the files are listed, indicating that they have been moved.

h. Enter **mv *2009.txt Audit_Reports/2009** to move the files with names that end with "2009" to the Reports/2009 directory.

i. Enter **ls Audit_Reports/2009** to verify that the files have been moved.

j. Observe that the files are listed indicating that they have been moved.

k. Clear the terminal screen.

3. Create a backup for the Audit_Reports directory in a different location.

a. Enter

```
cp -R Audit_Reports
/Reports_Backup
```
to recursively copy all files from the Audit_Reports directory to the /Reports_Backup directory.

b. Enter **ls /** to verify that the backup directory has been created.

c. Observe that the backup has been created.

4. Rename the Reports_Backup directory as Audit_Backup.

a. Enter **cd ..** to switch to the parent directory.

b. Enter **mv Reports_Backup Audit_Backup** to rename the Reports_Backup directory as Audit_Backup.

c. Enter **ls** to verify that the directory has been renamed.

d. Observe that the backup directory has been renamed.

e. Clear the terminal screen.

TOPIC B
Introduction to Shell Scripting

You worked with the basic Bash shell options to perform various tasks. To execute complex tasks using the operating system, it is essential to script a program for the respective task. In this topic, you will write a basic Bash shell script.

An in-depth knowledge of shell scripts is required to understand the working of the Linux system. As a Linux+ administrator, it is essential for you to work with shell scripts because it enables you to automate routine tasks, saving time and effort.

Shell Scripts

A shell script is a file that contains a list of commands to be read and executed by the shell. Frequently used commands can be stored in a shell script for repeated use. Every shell script starts with a line that designates the interpreter. This line instructs the operating system to execute the script.

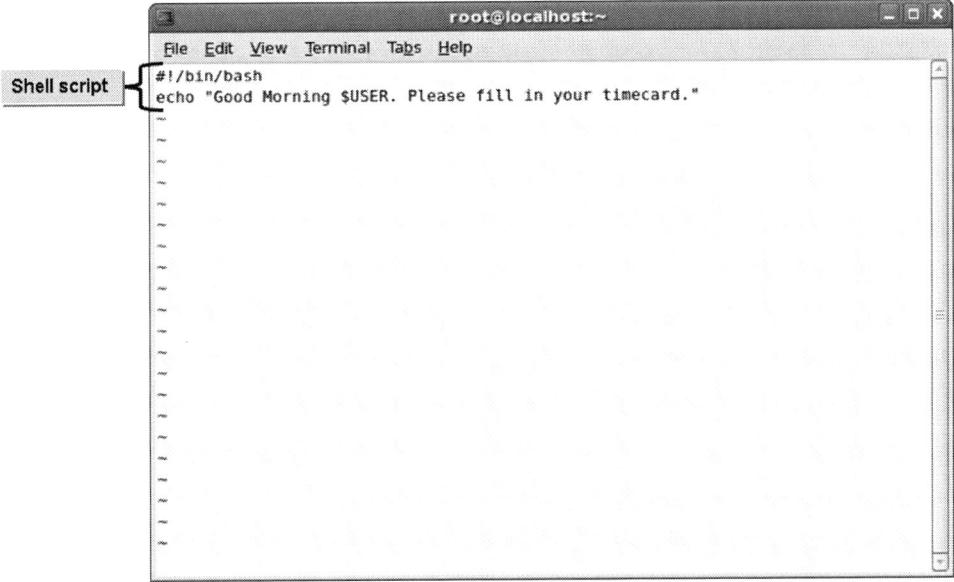

Figure 9-5: Creating a shell script.

Benefits of Scripts

Shell scripts allow you to perform various functions. These functions are listed below.

● Automation of commands and tasks of system administration and troubleshooting

● Creation of simple applications

● Manipulation of text or files

Command Line Operators

The Bash shell facilitates command line expansion, inhibition, and substitution with specific symbols called command line operators. These operators are described in the following table.

Operator	Description
$	Expands variables
'	Substitutes commands
\	Inhibits a single character
!	Substitutes history

#!/bin/bash

Bash scripts contain shell specific instructions that may not be compatible with other Linux shells. This will result in a Bash script running on certain shells while failing on the other Linux shells. To enable Bash scripts to run on all Linux shells, you need to add a line #!/bin/bash at the beginning of each script. This line will instruct the operating system to use the Bash shell when executing the script on an incompatible Linux shell.

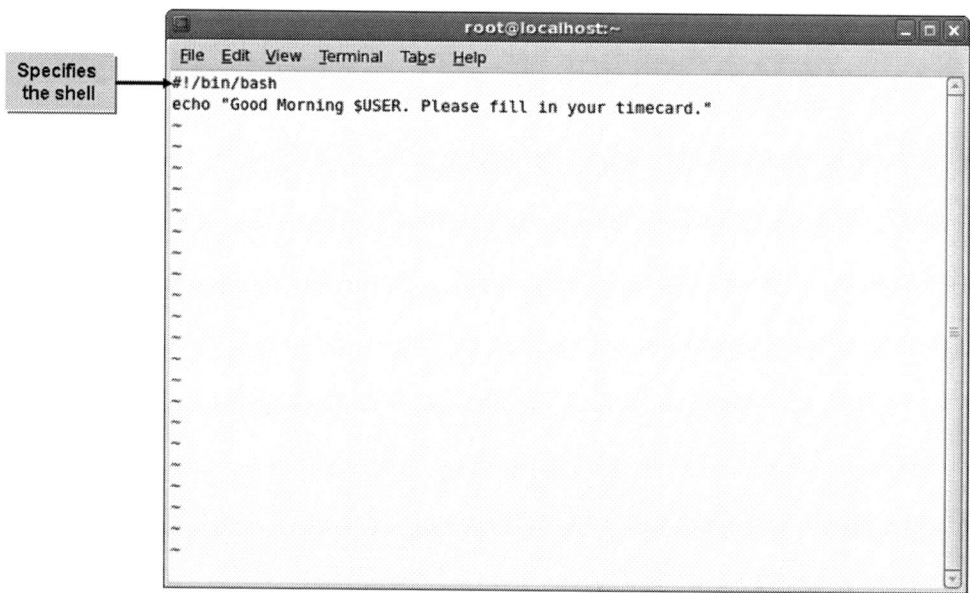

Figure 9-6: #!/bin/bash will enable bash scripts to run on all Linux shells.

The test Command

The test command is used to check file types and compare values. You can use the test command in your shell scripts to validate the status of files and perform relevant tasks. It evaluates the conditional expression EXPR and displays an exit status. The exit status is 0 if the expression is true, 1 if the expression is false, and 2 if an error occurs.

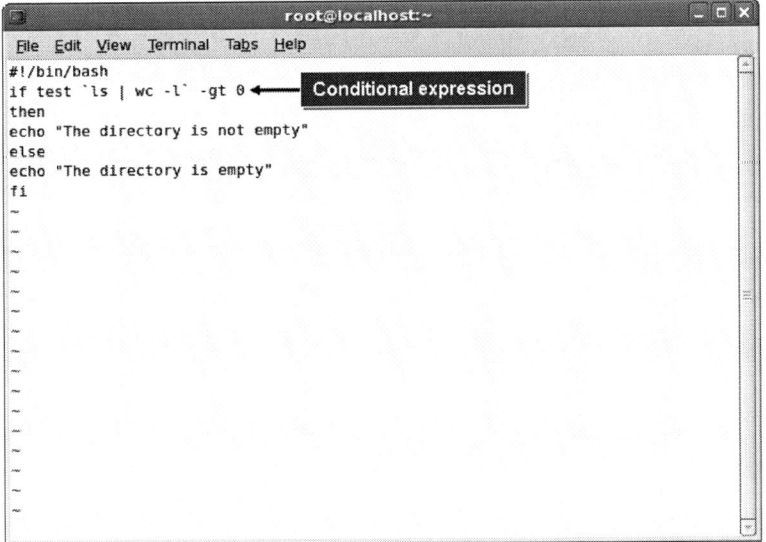

Figure 9-7: The test command is used to determine whether a directory is empty or not.

How to Write a Shell Script

Procedure Reference: Write a Bash Script

To write a Bash script:

1. Log in as a user in the CLI.
2. Enter vi *{name of the script file}* to write a Bash shell script.
3. Press **I** to switch to the insert mode.
4. Type #!/bin/bash to specify the shell.
5. Type the required command.
6. Press **Esc** to return to the command mode.
7. Enter :wq to save the file and exit the text editor.

Procedure Reference: Convert Script File to an Executable Script

To convert a file to an executable script:

1. Log in as a user in the CLI.
2. Write a Bash shell script.
3. Enter chmod a+x *{name of the script file}* to convert the file to an executable script.

Procedure Reference: Execute Scripts Using the Relative Path

To execute scripts using the relative path:

1. Log in as a user in the CLI.
2. Navigate to the directory where the script file is located.
3. Enter ls -l to verify that the script file has execute permissions.
4. If necessary, convert the script to an executable script.

5. Enter `./{name of the script file}` to execute the script.

Procedure Reference: Execute Scripts Using the Absolute Path

To execute scripts using the absolute path:

1. Log in as a user in the CLI.
2. Enter `/{Absolute path of the script file}/{name of the script file}` to execute scripts using the absolute path.

ACTIVITY 9-4
Displaying Directory Content and Time Using Scripts

Before You Begin:

1. You have logged in as root in the CLI.
2. The first terminal is displayed.

Scenario:

You want to remove the unused files on your system. Before proceeding with the cleanup, you want to list the contents of the current working directory. Therefore, you decide to write a script to list directory contents and display the current time simultaneously, to maintain a record of the time of listing.

What You Do	How You Do It
1. Write a simple Bash shell script.	a. Enter **vi helloworld** to open the script file in the vi editor.
	b. Press **I** to switch to the insert mode.
	c. Enter **#!/bin/bash** to specify the shell.
	d. Enter **echo "Hello World"**
	e. Enter **echo "The current date and time is : 'date'"**

 Ensure that you use back quotes (´) while typing the date command.

	f. Type **echo "The files in the current directory are $(ls 'pwd')"**
	g. Press **Esc** to switch to the command mode.
	h. Enter **:wq** to save the script.
	i. Clear the terminal screen.

2. Execute the Bash script.

a. Enter **chmod a+x helloworld** to convert the text file into an executable script.

b. Enter **./helloworld | less** to execute the script.

c. Navigate through the displayed content and observe that the files in the current working directory are listed below with the current date and time.

d. Press **Q** to exit the display.

e. Clear the terminal screen.

TOPIC C
Customize the Bash Shell

You wrote basic scripts. Now, it's time to configure the Bash shell. Because Linux features multiuser support, you may want to customize the behavior of the Bash shell to suit the requirements of each user and display the user's personal details. In this topic, you will work with shell variables and environment variables to customize the shell environment.

In a network environment there may be multiple users accessing the same system. You may want to personalize users' systems by customizing the shell environment to display individual user names. It may be tedious to write several scripts to perform this task for every user accessing the system. By using variables in a script file, you can customize the shell environment to display the name of the user logging in. Linux shell variables allow you to automate repetitive functions. Creating automated tasks that take the place of repetitive functions will save valuable time.

Variables

Variables refer to entities whose values change from time to time. Most shell variables are set either by the operating system when you log in, or by the shell when it is initially invoked. When you define a variable in a shell script, it is called a local variable of that particular script. The variable cannot be used directly on the command line or by other scripts. When you export the local variable using the `export` command, it becomes an environment variable, which can be used on the command line or by other scripts.

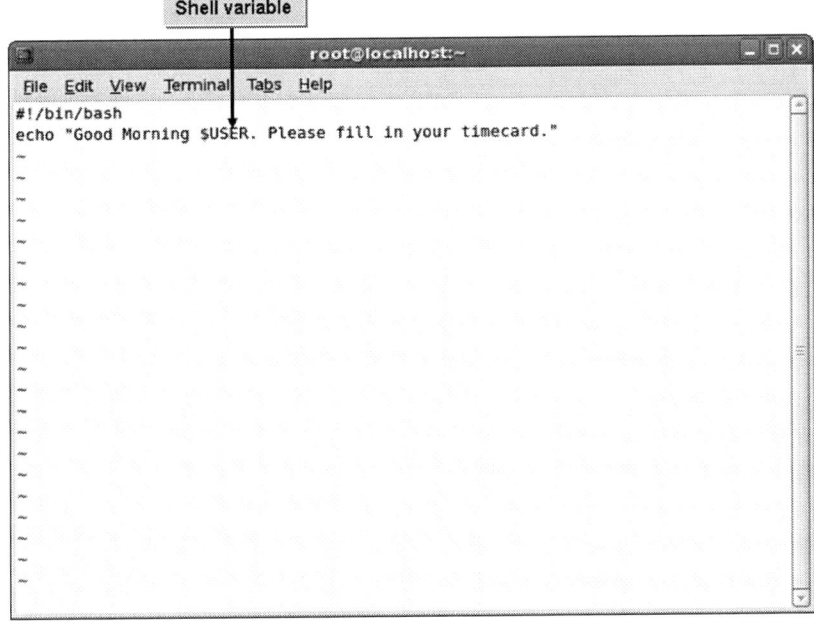

Figure 9-8: Using shell variables in scripts.

Syntax
The syntax of the `export` command is `export variable`.

Viewing Variable Values

Variables that are set by the operating system when you log in to a system are automatically exported. Variables created by the shell remain local in scope unless you manually export them. To display the value of a variable, use the echo command followed by a dollar sign ($) and the variable name (with no space between the $ and the variable name). For example, to view your default shell, enter echo $SHELL. The value of the variable is displayed on the screen. Like Linux commands, the shell variables are also case sensitive.

Declaring Variables

In addition to using and modifying predefined variables, you can also create variables. To create variable names, apply the following rules:

- A variable name must begin with an upper or lowercase letter or an underscore.
- The initial letter or underscore can be followed by any number of additional upper or lowercase letters, numbers ranging from 0 to 9, or an underscore.
- The following character combinations have special meanings and should not be used as variable names or to end a variable name: $@, $#, $$, $*, $-, $_, $?, and $0 to $9.

To assign a value to a variable, type the variable name followed by an equal sign and the value (with no spaces). To export a variable, making it accessible to commands and other shells, type export followed by the variable you want to export.

Special Shell Parameters

Shell treats some characters specially. Such characters cannot be assigned to variables because they convey special meaning. The following table contains the list of special characters and their description.

Character	Description
*	Signifies the positional parameters, starting from one.
@	Signifies the positional parameters, starting from one. When the expansion occurs within double quotes, each parameter expands to a separate word. For example, "$@" is equivalent to "$1" "$2". When there are no positional parameters, "$@" and $@ are removed and do not expand to anything.
#	Signifies the number of positional parameters in decimal.
?	Signifies the exit status of the most recently executed foreground pipeline.
-	Signifies the current option flags as specified upon invocation, by the set built-in command, or those set by the shell itself using the -i option.
$	Signifies the PID of the shell. In a subshell, it expands to the PID of the invoking shell, not the subshell.
!	Signifies the PID of the most recently executed background command.

Character	Description
0	Signifies the name of the shell or shell script. This is set at shell initialization. If Bash is invoked in a shell script file, $0 is set as the name of that file.
–	Signifies the absolute path name that is used to invoke the shell or shell script being executed as passed in the environment or argument list.

Working with the CDPATH Variable

In your directory structure, there may be directories that you will want to frequently switch between. By defining the required directory path in the CDPATH variable, you can easily switch to that path.

Environment Variables

An *environment variable* is a storage location in the operating system's command shell. It is accessible by all programs. An environment variable consists of a name, usually written in uppercase letters, and a value, such as a path name. Environment variables can be directly viewed from the shell.

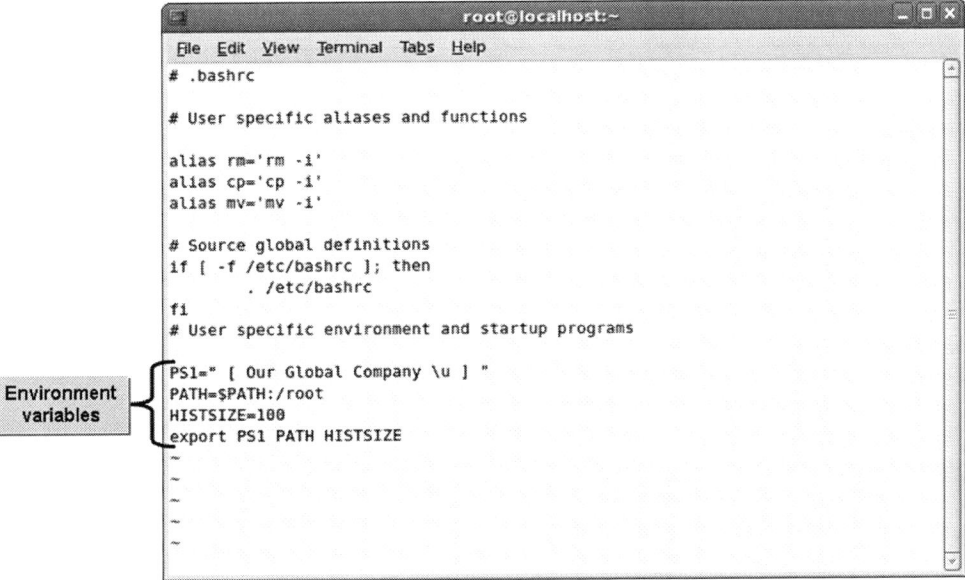

Figure 9-9: Assigning values to environment variables.

Referencing Environment Variables

You can use the existing environment variable in a new or existing shell by referring to it as $Environment variable.

Default Environment Variables

Some of the default environment variables and their functions are provided in the following table.

Environment Variable	Description
HOSTNAME=Hostname	Used to specify the hostname of the system.
SHELL=Shell path	Used to specify the shell path for the system.
MAIL=Mail path	Used to specify the path where the mail will be stored.
HOME=Home directory	Used to specify the home directory of the user.
PATH=User path	Used to specify the path in which the user needs to operate.
HISTSIZE=Number	Used to specify the number of entries to be stored in the command history.
USER=User name	Used to specify the name of the user.
EDITOR=Text editor name	Used to specify the preferred text editor for the environment.
TERM=Terminal name	Used to specify the name of the terminal used.
PRINTER=Printer name	Used to specify the default printer of the system.
PAGER=Command	Used to specify the command through which the content of long files need to be listed.
PS1= [Prompt]	Used to specify the primary prompt—the prompt that is displayed on login.
PS2= [Prompt]	Used to specify the secondary prompt.

The alias Command

The *alias command* is used to generate command line aliases. Aliases are shorthand for longer expressions. Using aliases, you can substitute a word in a command with a string. The shell maintains a list of aliases that are created and listed using the `alias` command. It also maintains a list of aliases that are removed using the `unalias` command.

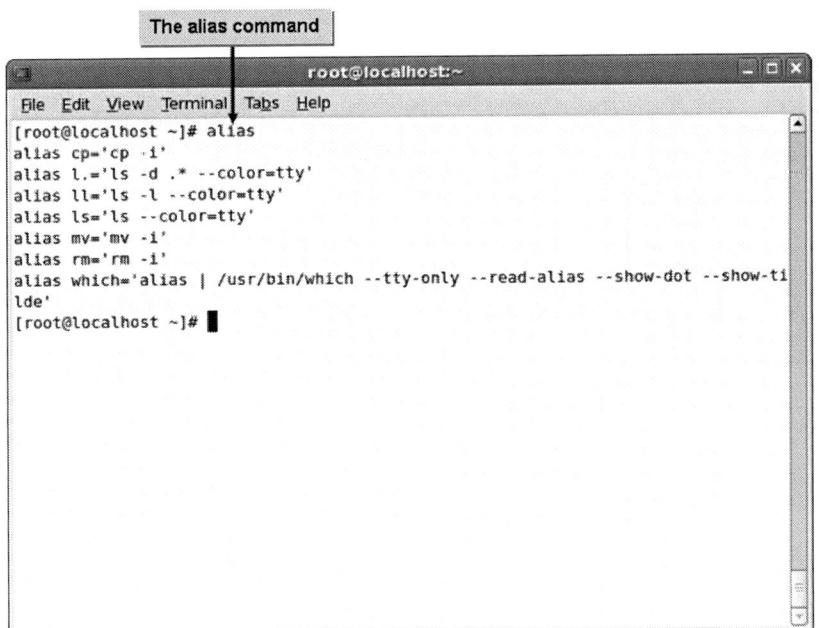

Figure 9-10: Viewing command line aliases.

Syntax

The syntax of the `alias` command is `alias {command}='{command} [options]'`.

$HISTFILESIZE

The $HISTFILESIZE environment variable allows you to set the maximum number of lines contained in the history file. It also allows you to specify the number of lines to be displayed on running the history command. For example, on assigning a value of 20 to this variable, the history file gets truncated to contain just 20 lines. The default value to this variable is 1000.

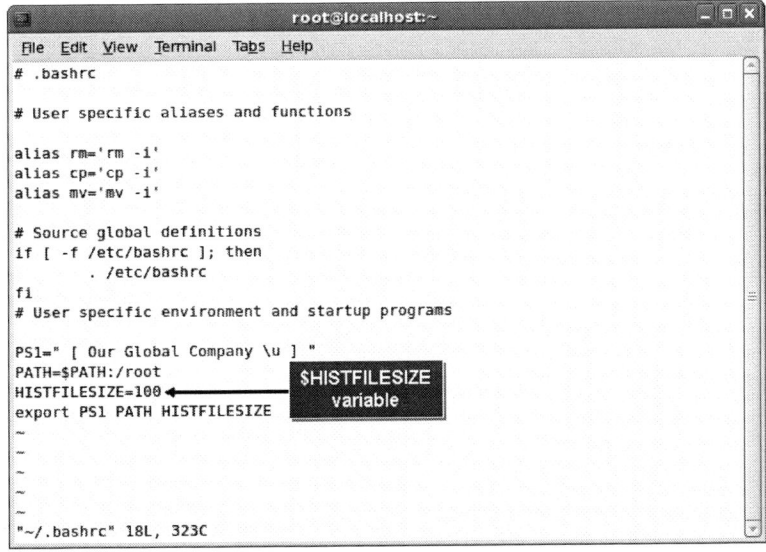

Figure 9-11: Assigning a value to the $HISTSIZE variable.

Search Paths

Definition:

A *search path* is a sequence of various directory paths that is used by the shell to locate files. Paths can be assigned to the *PATH* environment variable. The PATH variable comprises a list of directory names separated by colons. You can add a new path to an existing group of path names, modify a path, or delete a path. Usually directories that contain executable files are assigned to the PATH variable.

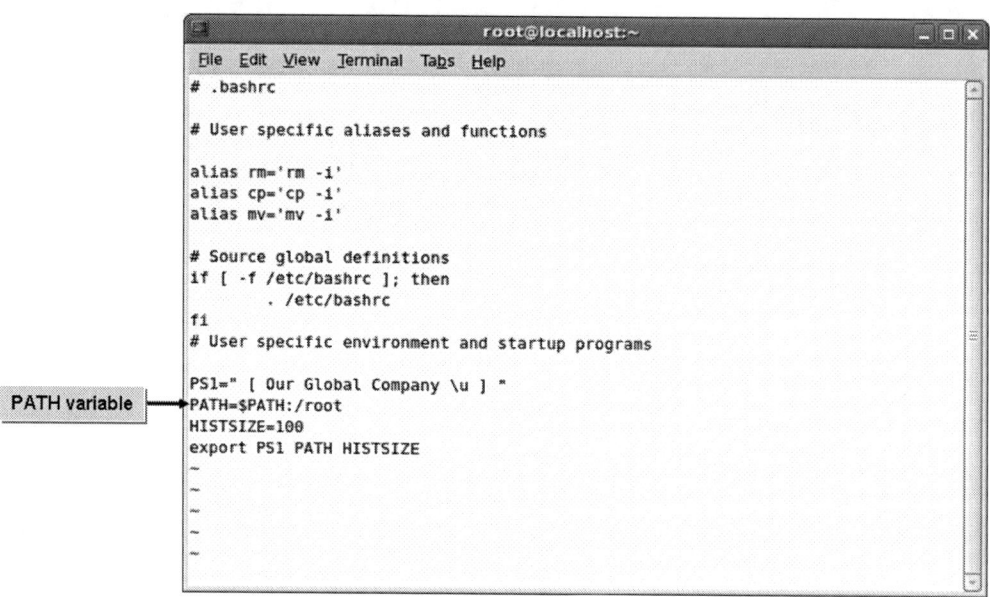

Figure 9-12: A search path defined in the .bashrc file.

Example:

The following is an example of a search path where the path names are separated by colons:

```
/home/user/bin:/usr/local/bin:/usr/bin:/bin
```

Non-Example:

The following is not a search path because the path names are not separated by colons:

```
/usr/bin /usr/local/bin
```

How to Use Shell Variables

Procedure Reference: Define Variables

To define variables:

1. Log in as a user in the CLI.

2. Enter *{VARIABLE}={Value}* to define a variable.

3. Enter echo *${VARIABLE}* to display the value associated with the variable.

Procedure Reference: Set Alias for a Frequently Used Command

To set alias for a frequently used command:

1. Log in as a user in the CLI.

2. Enter alias to view the default aliases.

3. Enter alias *{user defined name}*="*{command}*" to set alias for a frequently used command.

4. Enter alias to view the updated alias on the system.

Procedure Reference: Set Configuration Variables

To set configuration variables:

1. Log in as root in the CLI.

2. Enter vim ~/.bashrc to open a script file.

3. Make the necessary changes such as changing **PS1, HISTSIZE, PATH,** or **alias.**

4. Log out and log in as root for the changes to apply.

ACTIVITY 9-5

Using Shell Variables in Scripts

Before You Begin:

1. You have logged in as root in the CLI.

2. The first terminal is displayed.

3. Log out of root.

Scenario:

You have been assigned the task of creating a script to remind employees of your organization to fill in their timecards at the end of each day. You decide to use variables to define the names of the employees.

What You Do	How You Do It
1. Create the Filltimecard file.	a. Log in as **jsmith.**
	b. Enter **vim Filltimecard** to create a file.
	c. Switch to the insert mode.
	d. Enter **#!/bin/bash** to specify the shell.
	e. Enter **USER='whoami'** to specify the variable.
	f. Type **echo "Good Evening $USER. Please fill in your timecard."** to set the reminder.
2. Save and convert the file into an executable script.	a. Switch to the command mode.
	b. Save and close the file.
	c. Enter **chmod a+x Filltimecard** to convert the file into an executable script.

3. Test the script.

    a. Enter **cat Filltimecard** to view the contents of the file.

    b. Enter **./Filltimecard** to run the script.

    c. Compare the results with that of the **cat** command. Observe that your user name appears in place of the USER variable.

    d. Clear the terminal screen.

    e. Log out of the **jsmith** user account.

ACTIVITY 9-6

Customizing Systems Using Variables

Before You Begin:

The login screen of the first CLI terminal is displayed.

Scenario:

As an administrator, you need to set up Linux systems for new employees. Before the completion of the setup process, you have to customize the systems with the following details:

- The command prompt should reflect the company name.
- The Filltimecard script should be assigned a local path on the system.
- The command history should display the last 100 entries.

What You Do	How You Do It
1. Set the command prompt to reflect your company name.	a. Log in as **root**.
	b. Enter **vim ~/.bashrc** to open the ~/.bashrc file.
	c. On a new line, enter **PS1=" [Our Global Company \u] "** to change the primary prompt.
2. Set the file path and the history file size.	a. Enter **PATH=$PATH:/root** to assign the path, where the Filltimecard script is located, to the **PATH** variable.
	b. Enter **HISTSIZE=100** to assign a value of 100 to the history file content.
3. Export the variables and save the changes made to the file.	a. Type **export PS1 PATH HISTSIZE** to export the three variables.
	b. Switch to the command mode.
	c. Save and close the file.

4. Check the changes.

a. Log out of the **root** user account.

b. Log in as **root** to verify the change.

c. Observe that the prompt now displays the company name.

d. Enter **history | less** to view the command history.

e. Navigate through the history display. Observe that only the last 100 entries are displayed.

f. Quit the history page.

g. Clear the terminal screen.

TOPIC D
Redirect Standard Input and Output

You performed shell scripting using variables. As part of automating tasks using scripts, you may now want to manipulate the input and output of Linux commands and files. In this topic, you will redirect standard input and output.

Imagine that you need to create a troubleshooting report, which contains a command and the respective errors it generates after execution. In this situation, instead of keying the output or errors in the report, you can redirect the output of the command into the report. Redirection techniques help you accomplish certain tasks with speed and ease.

Standard Input

Standard input, or *STDIN,* is a *text stream* that acts as the source for command input. Usually standard input for the Linux command line is from the keyboard. In the case of GUI, the standard input can also be from the mouse. The standard input stream is buffered and lends itself to be redirected.

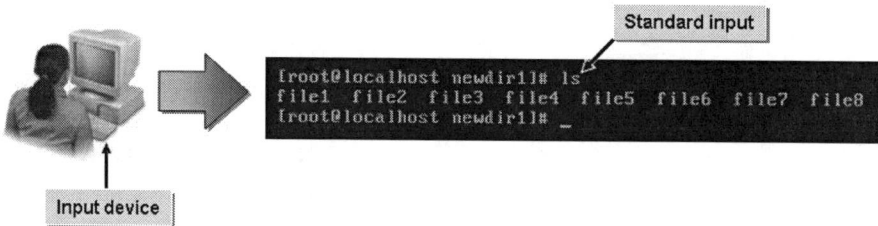

Figure 9-13: *Standard input entered using the keyboard.*

Standard Output

Standard output, or *STDOUT,* is a text stream that acts as the destination for command output. By default, standard output from the Linux command line is directed to the terminal screen. The standard output stream is buffered and lends itself to be redirected.

Figure 9-14: *Standard output displayed on the terminal.*

Standard Error

Standard error, or *STDERR,* is a text stream that is used as the destination for error messages. The STDERR stream is not buffered. By default, the standard error stream prints error messages on the terminal screen, but this can be changed by redirecting it to the desired location.

Figure 9-15: Standard error message displayed on the monitor.

Redirectors

A *redirector* is an operator that accepts input data from a source other than the keyboard, or sends data to a destination other than the monitor. It generally uses files as input or output. A redirector can redirect the output of a command to become the input for another command. It can also send output data to both the screen and a file.

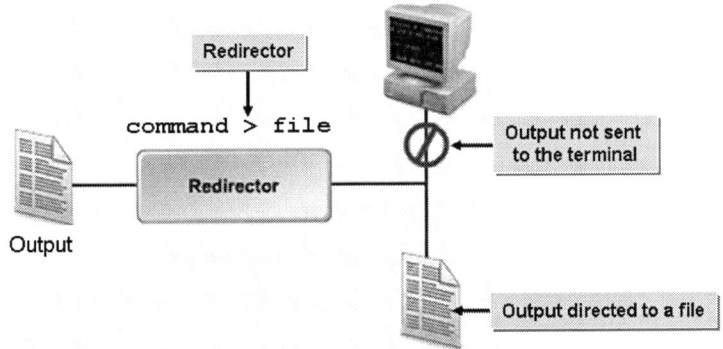

Figure 9-16: Output from a command redirected to a file.

There are some operators that are used to redirect input or output. The functions of frequently used operators are described in the following table.

Operator	Enables You To
>	Redirect the standard output to another file.
>>	Append the standard output to the end of the destination file.
2>	Redirect the standard error message to a file.
2>>	Append the standard error message to the end of the destination file.
&>	Direct all output of a command to a file.

Operator	Enables You To
<	Read the input from a file rather than from the keyboard or mouse.
<<string	Provide input data from the keyboard, indicating the end with the specified string.
=	Assign values to variables.
= =	Check if two values are equal to each other.

 The semicolon (;) is used to separate variables, commands, or values.

Examples of Redirection

`mail < myletter.txt`–The myletter.txt file will be taken as the input.

`ls > file1.txt`–The output of the `ls` command will be redirected to a file named file1.txt.

`ls file3.txt 2> errorfile.txt`–Assuming that file3.txt does not exist, the resulting errors will not be displayed on the screen, but they will be redirected to a file named errorfile.txt.

Pipes

Definition:

A *pipe,* denoted by the ¦ symbol, is an operator that combines commands. It uses the standard output of one command as the standard input for another command. The output format of the first command should be compatible with the format that the second command works with. Pipes can be used with most commands in Linux.

Example:

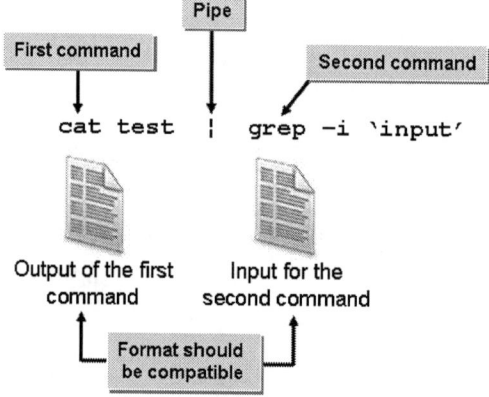

Figure 9-17: A pipe is used to combine two Linux commands.

Example of Commands Using the Pipe Character

ls | more–The output of the ls command is the input for the more command.

The xargs Command

The xargs command constructs and executes command lines. It adds arguments from the standard input to complete the command and then executes it. This process is repeated for the remaining input. Pipes are used to make the output of the first command, the input for the second command. The xargs command is used to make the output of the first command, the command line option for the second command.

The xargs command has various options.

Option	Used To
-I	Consider each line in the standard input as a single argument.
-L	Read a specified number of lines from the standard input and concatenate them into one long string.
-p	Prompt the user before each command.
-n	Read the maximum number of arguments from the standard input and insert them at the end of the command template.
-E	Represent the end of the standard input.
-t	Write each command to the standard error output before executing the command.
-s	Set the maximum allowable size of an argument list to a specified number of characters.
-x	Terminate the xargs command if it creates a command that is longer than the size given by the -s option.

The tee Command

The tee command reads the standard input, sends the output to the standard output device, and also copies the output to each specified file. This command enables users to log the output of a command in a file before sending it as the input to the next command; therefore, it serves as a helpful tool in troubleshooting. When used with the -a option, it appends the output to each output file instead of overwriting it. When used with the -i option, it ignores interrupt signals.

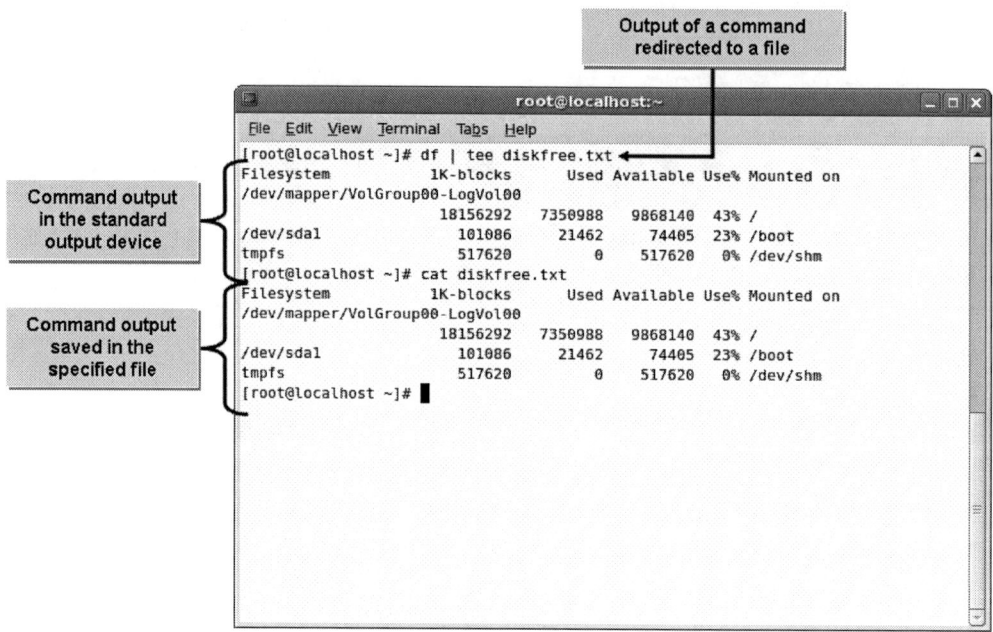

Figure 9-18: Output of the df command redirected to a file.

Command Substitution

Command substitution is the ability to reassign the output of a command as an argument to another command. The command line that needs to be reassigned is placed within back quotes (' '). The shell first executes the commands enclosed within the back quotes. It then replaces the entire expression, including the back quotes, with the output of the command.

Single and Double Quotation Marks

Single quotation marks (') are used in a shell command to disable any kind of transformation or modification. The shell considers whatever is enclosed within the single quotation marks as a single entity or parameter. If single quotation marks are used, substitution will not take place.

By employing double quotation marks (" "), the expansion of the file name is suppressed by the shell. Even if a wildcard, such as the asterisk (*) symbol, is enclosed within quotation marks, the standard feature of the wildcard (matching all characters) will be lost.

How to Redirect Input and Output

Procedure Reference: Redirect the Standard Output to a File

To redirect the standard output to a file:

1. Log in as a user.
2. Redirect the standard output to a file.
   - At the command prompt, enter *{command}* > *{file name}* to direct the standard output of the command to the specified file.
   - Enter *{command}* >> *{file name}* to append the standard output of the command to the end of the specified file.

Procedure Reference: Redirect the Standard Error to a File

To redirect the standard error as output to a file:

1. Log in as a user.
2. Redirect the standard error to a file.
   - Enter *{command}* 2> *{file name}* to direct the error message from the command to the specified file.
   - Enter *{command}* 2>> *{file name}* to append the error message from the command to the end of the specified file.

Procedure Reference: Redirect the Standard Output to a Command

To redirect the standard output to a command:

1. Log in as a user.
2. Enter *{command 1}* | *{command 2}* | *{command 3}* to redirect the output of one command as input to another command.

Procedure Reference: Redirect the Standard Output to a File and Command

To redirect the standard output to a file and command:

1. Log in as a user.
2. Enter *{command 1}* | tee *{file name 1}* | *{command 2}* | tee *{file name 2}* | *{command 3}* to save the output at various stages in files and direct the output to other commands.

Procedure Reference: Redirect the Standard Output and the Standard Error to a File and Command

To redirect the standard output and the standard error to a file and command:

1. Log in as user.
2. Redirect the standard output and the standard error.
   - Enter *{command}* > *{file name 1}* 2> *{file name 2}* to direct the standard output of the command to a file and the standard error message to another file.
   - Enter *{command}* &> *{file name}* to direct all the output of the command to a file.
   - Enter *{command 1}* 2>&1 | *{command 2}* to direct all the output of the command to another command.

Procedure Reference: Redirect the Standard Input

To redirect the standard input:

1. Log in as a user.

2. Redirect the standard input.

    - Enter *{command}* < *{file name}* to send a file as the input to a command.

    - Enter *{command}* <<*{string}* to accept input from the keyboard until a specified string is provided as input.

ACTIVITY 9-7

Redirecting Content

Data Files:

Hardwareinventory.txt, Softwareinventory.txt

Before You Begin:

1. You have logged in as root in the first terminal of the CLI.

2. Enter `vim ~/.bashrc` to open the ~/.bashrc file.

3. Remove the line starting with "PS1=."

4. Remove `PS1` from the line starting with "export."

5. Save and close the file.

6. Log out and log in as root

7. Clear the terminal screen.

Scenario:

On the main server, the data related to software inventory and hardware inventory are stored as separate files. You have been assigned the task of consolidating these files into a new file named Inventory.txt so that it can be viewed online.

What You Do	How You Do It
1. Redirect the contents of the Softwareinventory.txt and Hardwareinventory.txt files to the Inventory.txt file.	a. Enter **touch Inventory.txt** to create an empty file named Inventory.txt.
	b. Enter **cat Softwareinventory.txt > Inventory.txt** to redirect the contents of the Softwareinventory.txt file to the Inventory.txt file.
	c. Enter **cat Inventory.txt** to view the contents of the file.
	d. Clear the terminal screen.
	e. Enter **cat Hardwareinventory.txt >> Inventory.txt** to append the contents of the Hardwareinventory.txt file to the Inventory.txt file.

2. View the Inventory.txt file.

a. Enter `cat Inventory.txt | less` to view the contents of the file.

b. Press the **Spacebar** two times to navigate through the remaining pages in the file.

c. Press **Q** to exit and return to the shell prompt.

d. Clear the terminal screen.

TOPIC E
Use Control Statements in Shell Scripts

You redirected the standard input and output between commands and files. Now, you may want to write a simple shell script to automate repetitive tasks. In this topic, you will use control statements in shell scripts.

Consider a scenario where you want to greet users, by displaying either "Good Morning," "Good Afternoon," or "Good Evening," according to their login time. Using control statements, you can specify the time span for each message and display the relevant message depending on the time the user logs in.

Control Statements

A *control statement* is an instruction that determines the direction a program takes depending on a test condition. The direction can be different from the sequential order in which the instructions are listed. Control statements are associated with one or more action statements that will be executed only when a specified condition is satisfied.

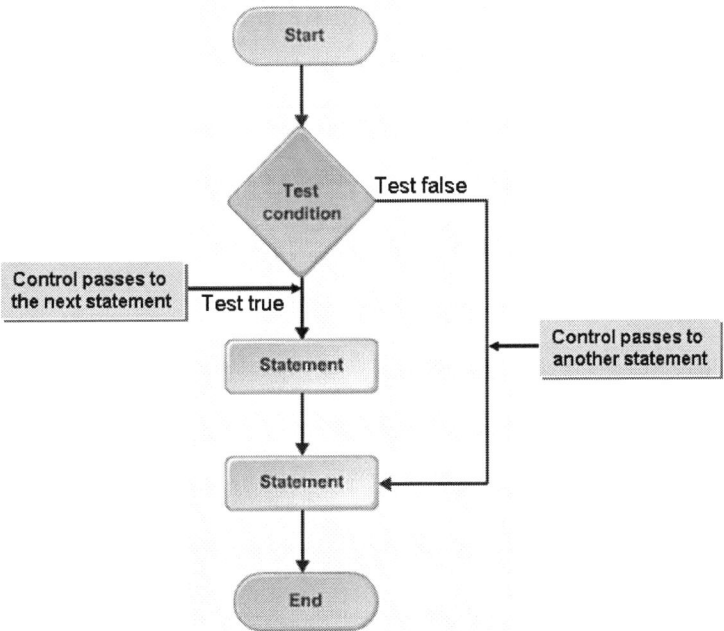

Figure 9-19: Control statements are used to change control flow.

Expressions

Expressions are a group of characters that are generally used to specify conditions. They are formed by combining variables and constants with operators. They are used in the `if` and `while` statements. Performing arithmetic comparisons and string comparisons and testing files are the main functions of expressions. If an expression contains the <, >, &, or | symbol, parentheses are required.

The if Statement

The most frequently used control statement is the `if` statement. An `if` statement contains a condition to be evaluated and one or more actions to be performed, if the condition is satisfied. If the condition is not satisfied, the actions are skipped and the next statement in the script is executed. The end of the set of instructions is indicated by the `fi` statement.

The if...else Statement

The `if...else` statement allows a choice between two actions based on the evaluation of a condition. If the condition is satisfied, the first action is performed; otherwise, the action following the `else` segment is performed. The end of the set of instructions is indicated by the `fi` statement. If there are more than two sets of instructions, one or more `elif` statements may be used to specify alternative sequences of action.

Looping Statements

Looping statements, also referred to as iteration statements, are a type of control statements that help you execute a part of the script repeatedly till a specific condition is met. The condition is tested based on the value of a variable. There are two types of loops supported by the Bash shell: the `for` loop and the `while` loop. In shell scripts, the commands to be iterated are enclosed within the `do` and `done` statements.

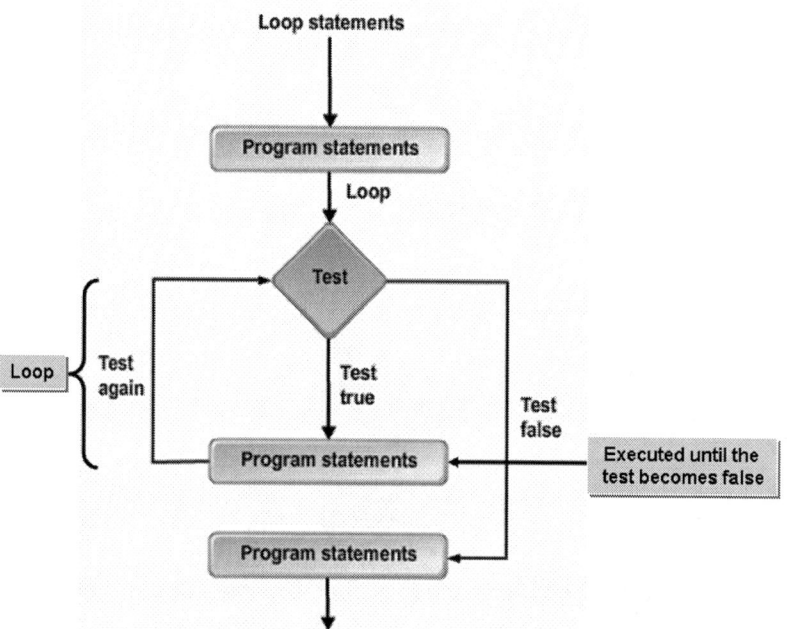

***Figure 9-20:** Loop statements are used to repeat a set of instructions.*

The for Loop

The *for loop* executes a part of the script as many times as specified by a numerical variable that is within the conditional part of the statement. The `for` loop is unique because the conditional part of the statement contains the initial value of the variable, the test condition, and the increment or decrement of the variable value.

The while Loop

The *while loop* enables you to repeat a set of instructions for a fixed number of times, till a specific condition is met. The condition is left open ended in a `while` loop. The first expression is evaluated, and if the expression is true, the actions in the loop are performed. The execution returns to the beginning of the loop and the expression is evaluated again. If the expression is false, execution passes to the next statement.

How to Use Control Statements

Procedure Reference: Use Control Statements

To use control statements in scripting:

1. Log in as a user.
2. On a terminal, enter `vi {name of the script file}` to write a Bash shell script.
3. Press **I** to switch to the insert mode.
4. Type `#!/bin/bash` to specify the shell.
5. Enter the commands you want to execute.
6. Use control statements or loops, as necessary.
   - Type

     ```
     if ( {Condition that needs to be satisfied} )
     then
     {Commands to be executed}
     fi
     ```
     to use the `if` statement.
   - Type

     ```
      if ( {Condition that needs to be satisfied} )
     then
     {Commands to be executed}
     else
     {Commands to be executed}
     fi
     ```
     to use the `if...else` statement.
   - Type

     ```
     for (( {Condition that needs to be satisfied} ; ⇒
     {Condition that needs to be satisfied} ))
     do
     {Commands to be executed}
     done
     ```
     to use the `for` loop.
   - Type

     ```
      while
     [{Condition that needs to be satisfied}]
     do
     {Commands to be executed}
     done
     ```
     to use the `while` loop.

7. Press **Esc** to return to the command mode.

8. Enter **:wq** to save the file and exit the text editor.

9. Enter `chmod a+x` *{name of the script file}* to convert the file to an executable script.

ACTIVITY 9-8

Writing a Script to Create Multiple Directories

Before You Begin:
You have logged in as root in the first terminal of the CLI.

Scenario:
You want to create individual work directories for all employees. Because the task of creating directories individually is time consuming, you decide to write a shell script to automate the process.

Following are the details for writing the Bash script:

- Name of the script: **createdir**
- Prompt text to remind the users to enter the number of directories required: Enter the Number of Directories Required
- Name of the variable to get the total number of directories: Numberofdir
- Name of the variable to be used in the `for` loop to store the number of directories: d

What You Do	How You Do It
1. Set the total number of directories.	a. Enter **vim createdir** to open a new file for the script.
	b. Switch to the insert mode.
	c. Enter **#!/bin/bash** to begin the shell.
	d. Enter **echo " Specify the number of directories to be created:"** to prompt the users.
	e. Enter **read Numberofdir** to read input from users.

2. Write the loop for creating directories.

   a. Enter **for ((d = $Numberofdir ; d > 0 ; d--))** to specify the loop condition.

   b. Enter **do** to indicate the beginning of iterated steps.

   c. Enter **mkdir Directory-$d** to create a directory.

   d. Type **done** to indicate the end of the iterated steps.

   e. Switch to the command mode.

   f. Save and close the file.

   g. Clear the terminal screen.

3. Execute the createdir script.

   a. Enter **chmod a+x createdir** to convert the file to an executable script.

   b. Enter **./createdir** to execute the script.

   c. Enter **10** to create ten directories.

   d. Clear the terminal screen.

4. Check whether the directories are created.

   a. Enter **ls** to view the directories that have been created.

   b. Observe that ten new directories have been listed on the screen.

   c. Clear the terminal screen.

Lesson 9 Follow-up

In this lesson, you customized the Bash shell and performed various operations in it. You also worked with shell scripts, redirected input and output in shells, and used control statements in scripts to automate repetitive tasks. This will enable you to efficiently perform your job as a system administrator.

1. Why do you use variables in scripts?

2. What is the most prominent feature of the Bash shell? Explain.

3. What are the various tasks you can perform by running a shell script?

10 | Managing Jobs and Processes

Lesson Time: 1 hour(s), 30 minutes

Lesson Objectives:

In this lesson, you will manage jobs and processes.

You will:

- Manage jobs and background processes.
- Prioritize processes.
- Work with delayed and detached jobs.
- Schedule jobs.
- Maintain the system time.

Introduction

You worked with shells and shell scripts in the Linux environment. There may be instances when various utilities need to be run simultaneously on a system. In this lesson, you will manage jobs and processes.

The multitasking capability of Linux enables you to perform many tasks, such as compiling a program, sorting a database, and creating a document, at the same time. When system resources are utilized simultaneously, system performance reduces. A system administrator should be able to manage system resources effectively by allocating the right amount of resources to every task run by users.

This lesson covers all or part of the following CompTIA Linux+ (2009) certification objectives:

- Topic A
  - Objective 2.1
- Topic B
  - Objective 2.1
- Topic D
  - Objective 2.8
- Topic E
  - Objective 3.12

TOPIC A

Manage Jobs and Background Processes

You set up Linux variables and executed shell scripts. You may need to manage many processes that can run simultaneously in a Linux environment. In this topic, you will manage multiple jobs and background processes.

Most systems can handle one user running multiple processes, but what happens when hundreds of users run applications simultaneously? As an administrator in such an environment, you need tools and options that allow you to manage system resources efficiently. Using Linux's multitasking capabilities, you can manage jobs and processes in the background.

Processes

Definition:

A *process* is an instance of a running program that performs a data processing task. A process consists of a sequence of steps stored in a system; these steps convert the input data to output data. Processes can be subdivided into threads. Every process is assigned a unique PID and includes time limits, shared memory, or child processes. Processes may run in the foreground or in the background of the system.

Example:

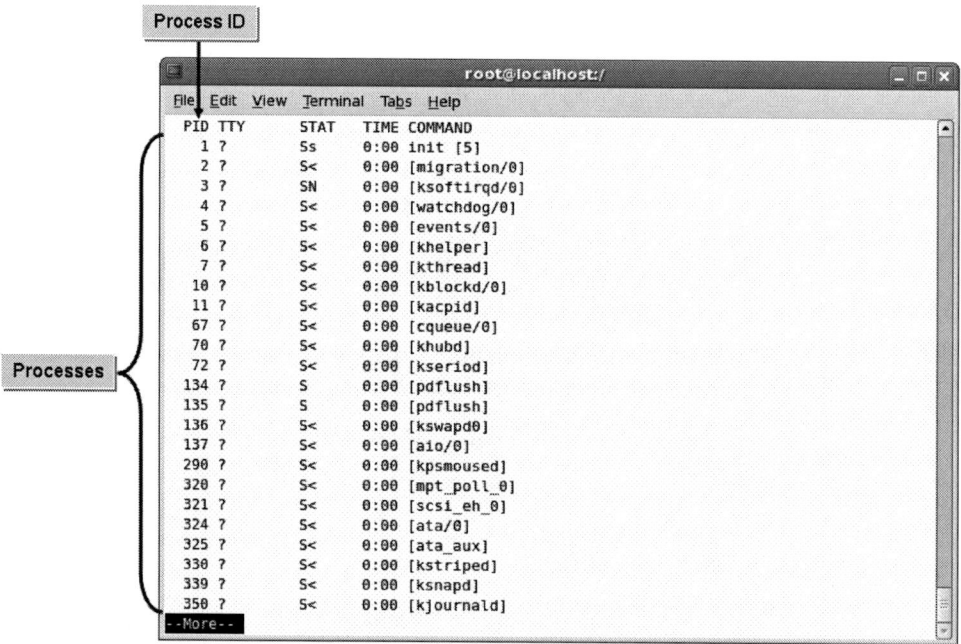

Figure 10-1: PIDs of processes running on a system.

The Process ID

Whenever a process is started, the system allocates a unique ID to identify the process. This ID is called the PID. Also, every process inherits the UID and GID of the user who starts the process. This is similar to the ownership of files and directories on the Linux filesystem.

The init Process

The first process, called `init` in Linux, is started by the kernel at boot time and never terminates. The PID of the `init` process is always 1.

Foreground Processes

A *foreground process* is a program with which a user is interacting at a particular time. Only one foreground process can be run at a time. As the user switches between programs, different programs become the foreground process at different times. A foreground process is initiated by entering a command at the prompt or by clicking a shortcut in the GUI.

Background Processes

A *background process* is a program that allows the Linux shell to execute a command that runs a job in the background, enabling processes to run simultaneously. While the user is interacting with the foreground process, a number of programs can run as background processes. The shell does not have to wait for one process to end before it can run more. A process can be run in the background by suffixing the invoking command with an ampersand (&) separated by a space.

Figure 10-2: A process initiated to run in the background.

Daemons

Daemons always run as background processes that never require user input. Other processes remain in the background temporarily, while the user is busy with the current foreground process.

The Program and Process Relationship

A *program* is a set of instructions describing how to carry out a task. A command that resides on your system is a program. When you enter a command at the prompt, a set of instructions perform a task.

A process is a program that executes instructions. The operating system creates a process to carry out that task. Processes have unique identities and exist until their tasks are completed. When the task is completed, the process is terminated. Each program running on a system is assigned a PID.

Multitasking

Definition:

Multitasking is a method of allowing the operating system to run concurrent programs simultaneously without degrading system performance. Multitasking enables several programs to share the same system resources. Processes spawned by multitasking are all active at the same time. They are not in a sequence or a suspended state, waiting to be run. Processes placed in a multitasking state remain active until completed, unless terminated or suspended by the user. One or more users may run multiple tasks on a system.

Example:

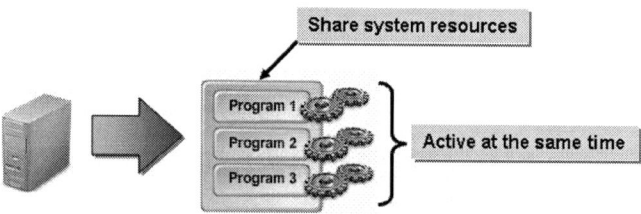

Figure 10-3: *Multitasking in a Linux system.*

The Jobs Table

The *jobs table,* invoked by the `jobs` command, is a table containing information about jobs running in the background. It contains entries only for those jobs that are running in the current shell. The jobs table contains a numeric label for each job indicating the order in which the jobs were started. In addition, the jobs table includes a plus sign (+) to designate the current or most recently started job, and a minus sign (-) to designate the job that was started just prior to the most recent job. It also includes the status and name of each job.

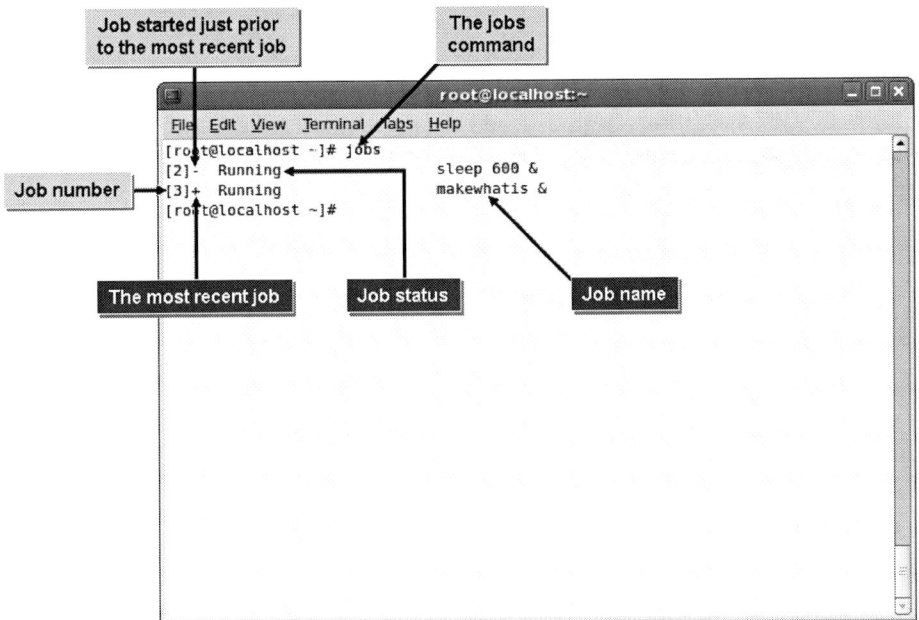

Figure 10-4: The jobs table listing jobs running in the current shell.

 The job name listed in the jobs table is actually the command that initiated the job.

 The plus (+) and minus (-) signs indicate only the order in which jobs are started. All jobs, however, are actually being run simultaneously.

Job Status

There are four possibilities for the status of a job.

Status	Description
Running	An active job.
Stopped	A job that has been suspended.
Terminated	A job that has been killed.
Done	A completed job.

Jobs in a New Shell

Any job that a user placed in the background will appear in that user's jobs table, but other users' jobs will not appear. If you were to start a new shell, the jobs table for the new shell will be empty. However, the jobs started in the previous shell will continue to run.

Suspend vs. Terminate a Process

The **Ctrl+Z** key combination suspends a job, while the **Ctrl+C** key combination terminates or kills the job. If you display the jobs table after you press **Ctrl+Z** to suspend a job, you will see that the current job is in a suspended state (labeled in the jobs table as "Stopped"). Although the jobs table lists jobs running in the background, a foreground job that gets suspended appears in the jobs table to remind the user that there is a suspended job waiting to be restarted or terminated. Refer to the following table for a summary of job control commands.

Action	Foreground	Background
Suspend a job	**Ctrl+Z**	Bring to foreground, then press **Ctrl+Z**
Terminate a job	**Ctrl+C**	`Kill %#`

Restarting a Suspended Job

The `bg` command, with the syntax `bg {%#}`, can be used to restart a specified background job that has been suspended. You can specify the number of the suspended job you want to restart after the percent sign. If there is only one job running in the background, then you don't have to specify the number. You can type `bg %` to restart it.

Bringing a Job to the Foreground

If you need to bring a job from the background to the foreground, use the `fg` command, with the syntax `fg {%#}`. This command brings the specified job to the foreground. You don't have to enter a number after the percent sign if there is only one job running in the background.

Job Control Tools

Job control tools enable you to manipulate the jobs appearing on the jobs table.

Tool	Enables You To
jobs	View the status of the jobs running in the background.
Ctrl+Z	Temporarily halt a running process.
fg {%job number}	Bring the specified process to the foreground.
bg {%job number}	Send the specified process to the background.
kill {%job number}	Terminate the specified process.

How to Manage Jobs and Background Processes

Procedure Reference: Manage Jobs

To manage jobs:

1. Type the command with an ampersand (&) after it to put a job in the background.
2. If necessary, execute additional commands.
   - Execute another command in the background using the ampersand.
   - Or, execute another command without putting it in the background.
3. Enter `jobs` at the command line to see the list of processes that are running in the background.
4. Manage the jobs that are running in the background.
   - Enter `kill %[job number]` to kill a process in the background.
   - Enter `fg %[job number]` to switch a background process to the foreground. Suspend and restart the job.
     a. Press **Ctrl+Z** to suspend a foreground job.
     b. Enter `bg %[job number]` to restart a suspended job.

ACTIVITY 10-1
Managing Jobs

Before You Begin:
1. You have logged in as root in the CLI.
2. The first terminal is displayed.

Scenario:
As a system administrator, you are asked to conserve the amount of time it takes to run jobs on the Linux system. You need to manage multiple jobs instead of running one job at a time. You can accomplish this by moving jobs to be processed in the background.

What You Do	How You Do It
1. Issue three commands and put them in the background.	a. Enter **sleep 300 &** to pause for 300 seconds.
	b. Enter **updatedb &** to update the mlocate database.
	c. Enter **sleep 200 &** to pause for 200 seconds.
	d. Enter **jobs** to view the list of processes running in the background.
	e. Verify that the three jobs are listed.
2. Terminate the last job.	a. Enter **kill %3** to kill the process that is executing the sleep 200 & command.
	b. Enter **jobs** to view the list of processes running in the background.
	c. Verify that the status of the third job displays "Terminated," to indicate that the job has been terminated.

3. Bring the second job to the foreground and suspend it.

a. Enter **fg %2** to move the job to update the mlocate database to the foreground.

b. Press **Ctrl+Z** to suspend the foreground job.

c. Verify that the status of the job is displayed as "Stopped," to indicate that the job has been stopped.

d. Enter **bg %2** to restart the suspended job.

e. Enter **jobs** to view the list of processes running in the background.

f. Verify that the job to update the mlocate database is running.

g. Enter **clear** to clear the terminal screen.

TOPIC B
Manage Processes Using the Process Table

While the jobs table is unique to each user's specific shell, the process table is for the entire system. In this topic, you will manage processes using the process table.

Monitoring system processes enables system administrators to track the usage of system resources. Tracking the processes running on a system helps you manage your resource allocation better. As a Linux+ administrator, you will find the process table useful because it contains entries for all the processes that are started by all the users on the system. With the process table, you can manage processes on the system in a Linux environment.

The Process Table

The *process table* is a record that summarizes the current running processes on a system. It enables the administrator to keep track of all processes run by different users. Some of the details displayed in a process table include the PID, the size of the program in memory, the name of the user who owns the process, and time tracking.

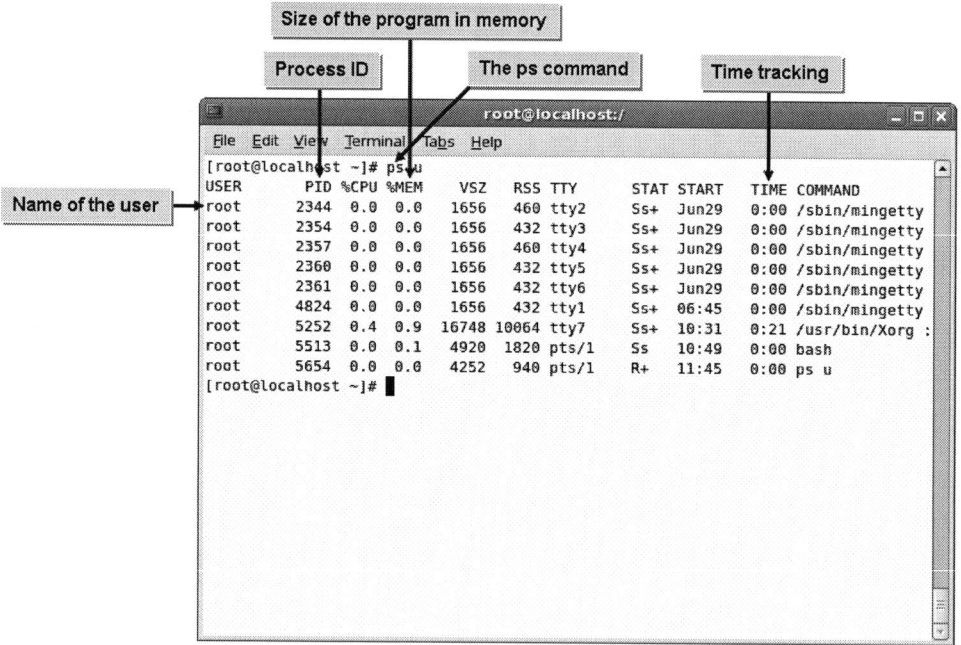

Figure 10-5: The process table listing processes running on the system.

The Process Table vs. the Jobs Table

The process table has options than are different from the jobs table. The process table can display all processes running on the system irrespective of which user started it, including system processes started automatically at boot time. However, the jobs table shows only the processes started in a user's current shell. Also, the unique PID of processes are displayed in the process table, while the jobs table shows only their job number according to the order in which they were started. In the jobs table, only the original process is displayed as an entry. In the process table, the original process and all subsequent processes that were started are displayed. So, a single entry in the jobs table may have more than one corresponding entry in the process table. Certain job control commands can be applied only by referring to processes by their job number.

The ps Command

The ps command invokes the process table. When the command is run without any options, it displays the processes run by the current shell with details such as the PID, the terminal associated with the process, the cumulated CPU time, and the command that started the process. However, different options may be used along with the command to filter the fields or the processes displayed.

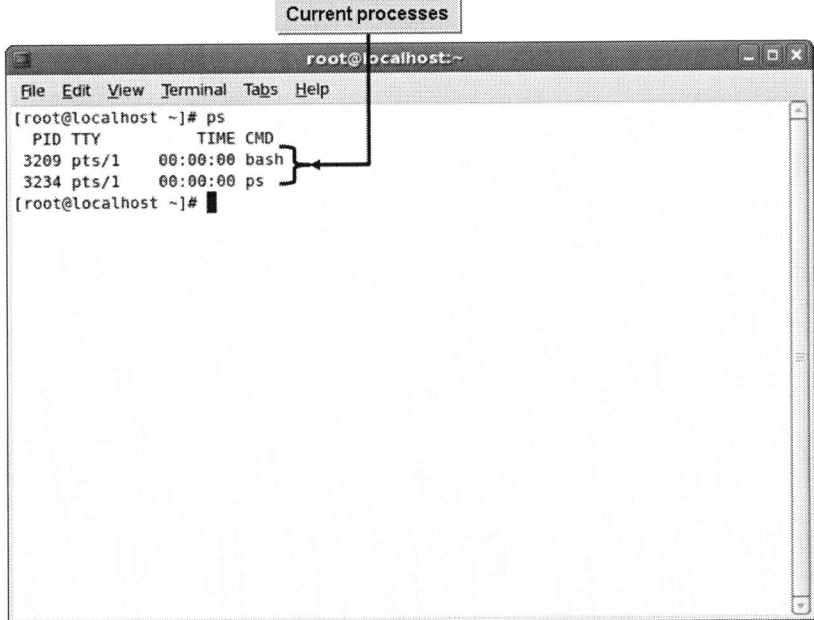

Figure 10-6: The ps command displaying the processes run by the current shell.

Syntax

The syntax of the ps command is ps *[options]*.

The ps Command Options

The ps command supports several options. Some of the important options are listed here.

Option	Description
a	Lists all user-triggered processes.
-e	Lists all processes.
-l	Lists processes using a long listing format.
u	Lists processes along with the user name and start time.
r	Excludes processes that are not running currently.

Option	Description
x	Includes processes without a terminal.
T	Excludes processes that were started by any terminal other than the current one.

 Unlike many commands in Linux, the ps command supports options with and without a hyphen before them. However, the function of the same options with or without a hyphen may differ greatly.

Command Options for Selective Display

Some common ps command options that can be used to select a specific set of processes are given in the following table.

Option	Used To
-U *User name*	Display the processes based on the specified user.
-p *PID*	Display only the specified process associated with the PID.
-C *Command*	Display all processes by command name.
--tty *Terminal number*	Display all processes running on the specified terminal.

Fields Displayed by the ps Command

Various options display different fields. The following table lists some of the fields that can be displayed using the ps command.

Field	Description
PRI	Process scheduling priority. Processes with low priority have higher numbers.
NI	Process nice value. Processes using less CPU time have higher numbers.
SIZE	Virtual image size.
RSS	Physical memory in KB.
WCHAN	Kernel function in which the process resides.
STAT	Status. Values include R (running), T (stopped), D (asleep and uninterruptible), S (asleep), Z (zombie), and N (positive nice value).
TT	The TTY or terminal associated with the process.
PAGEIN	The number of major page faults.
TRS	Resident text size.
SWAP	Number of KB of swap used.
SHARE	Amount of shared memory.

Child Processes

A process created by a running process is called a *child process*. The process table contains *parent processes* and any child processes that may have been started. There may be several levels of processes. The parent process can spawn a child process, the child process can spawn another child process, and so on. The parent process must be running for the child processes to run. Parent processes are assigned a unique *Parent Process ID (PPID)*.

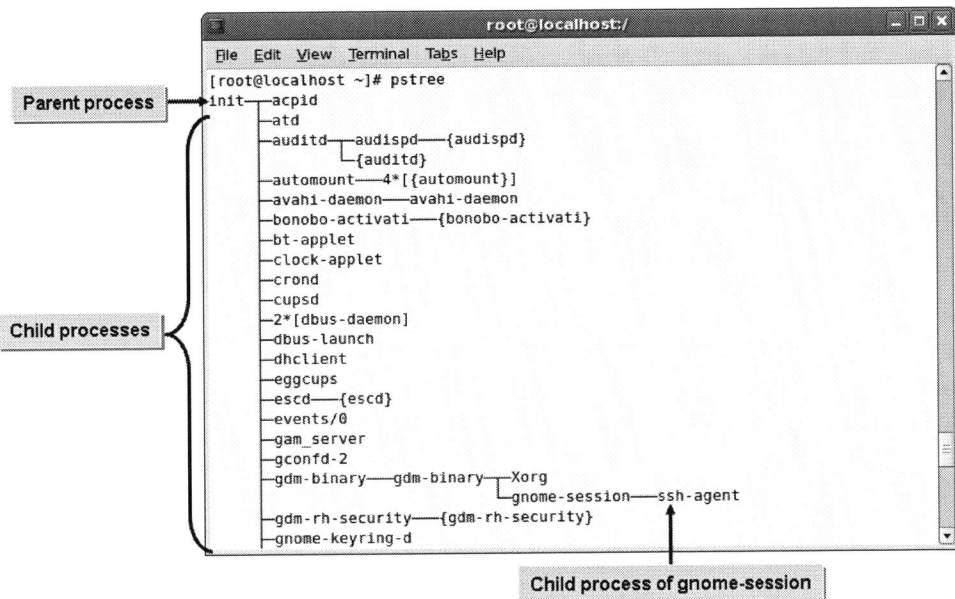

Figure 10-7: Process tree showing parent and child processes.

Identifying Child Processes

Identifying child processes is not an easy task, especially if there are multiple processes and child processes running at the same time. By examining the order of the PIDs, you may be able to determine the order in which the processes were created and infer which processes are related.

The pstree Command

The `pstree` command enables you to list the processes running in a Linux system in a tree-like format. This helps track parent and child processes. All processes are listed as child processes to `init` and this is represented by the initial branching. The processes started within a shell will branch out of the shell's parent process.

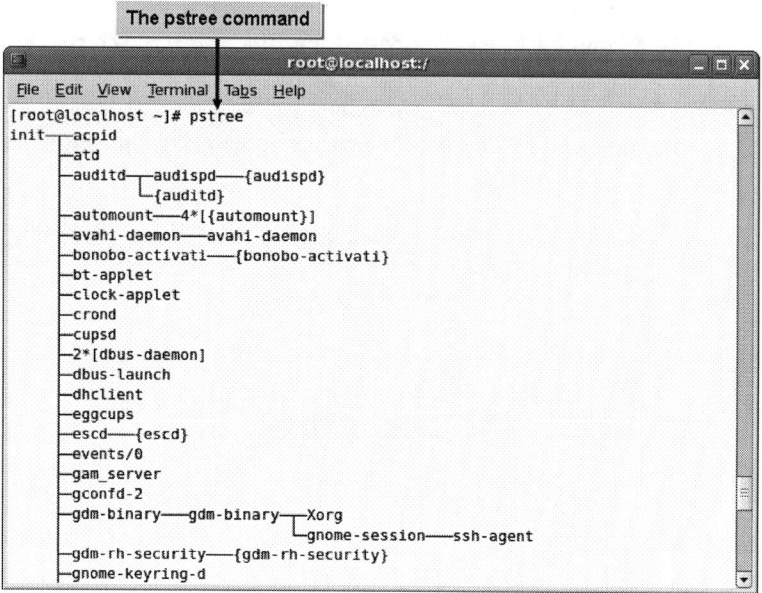

Figure 10-8: *The pstree command displaying parent and child processes.*

Process Identification Commands

Process identification commands enable you to extract information about processes using the name of the process or some other attribute associated with it.

Command	Description
pidof	Displays the PID of the process whose name is specified. Can be used only when the name of the process is known. However, it is recommended that a full path name of the process be given because more than one process could run with the same name. The syntax of this command is pidof *[command options] {string}.*
pgrep	Displays the PID of processes that match any given criteria such as the name or UID of the user who invoked it, the start time, the parent PID, and so on. The syntax of this command is pgrep *[command options] {process name}.*

The pidof Command Options

The pidof command supports only two options.

Option	Used To
-s	Instruct the program to display only one PID.
-c	Instruct the program to display the PIDs that are running from the same root directory.

The pgrep Command Options

The `pgrep` command supports different options by which one or more conditions for search may be specified.

Option	Used To
`-f`	Specify the full path name of the process.
`-l`	Print the name of the process along with its PID.
`-u`	Specify the UID of the user who started it.
`-G`	Specify the GID related to the process.
`-n`	Specify the most recent process.
`-o`	Specify the oldest process.

Signals

Definition:

Signals are messages sent to a process to perform a certain action. They are used to suspend or terminate processes. Signals may affect only the process specified and its child processes. Signals may be executed, caught, blocked, or ignored by processes.

Example:

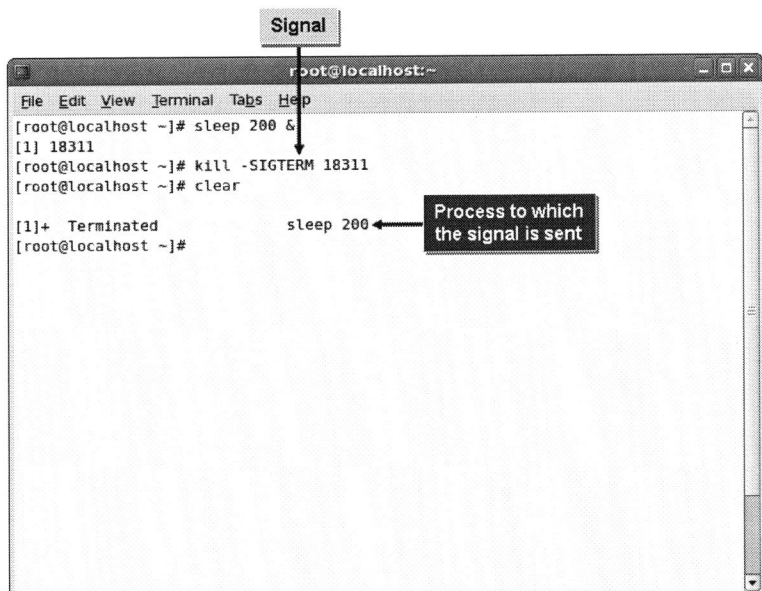

Figure 10-9: A signal sent to a process.

The kill Commands

Different commands are used to send signals to processes to end or "kill" them.

Command	Description
kill	Sends any specified signal, or by default the termination signal, to one or more processes. The PID must be specified as the argument. The syntax of this command is kill *[signal option] {PID}.*
pkill	Signals processes based on the name and other identifiers as in the pgrep command. The syntax of this command is pkill *[signal option] {command}.*
killall	Kills all processes by the name specified. The syntax of this command is killall *[signal option] {command}.*

 The kill command accepts either the PID or the job number as an argument. So, this command can also be used as a job control tool.

Kill Signal Options

You can either use the kill signal option or its corresponding numerical value to send a signal to terminate a process. The following table lists the most frequently used kill signal options and their description.

Option	Used To
SIGKILL or 9	Send the kill signal to a process.
SIGTERM or 15	Send the termination signal to a process.
SIGSTOP or 19	Stop a process.

 Sometimes even after closing an X session, some of the X applications may not get terminated properly. In such cases, you need to use the ps command to identify the PID of that application and then kill the process.

Using the PID Number to Terminate Processes

You can use the kill command with the process table to end processes. By entering kill followed by the PID, you can terminate specific processes.

When you use the kill command with the jobs table, you are working only with jobs that you started. However, the process table may display processes that do not belong to you. As a user, you can use the kill command only with processes that you own. As root, you can kill anyone's processes.

There are many options available with the `kill` command. These options are referred to as kill signals. Some processes cannot be eliminated by the `kill` command. To terminate these processes, use the `kill` command with the `-9` signal. This terminates the processes immediately.

Process States

Process states enable you to identify the stage that a process is in currently. They are indicated by a single letter notation in the process table.

The various process states are given in the table below.

State	*Description*
Uninterruptible sleep (D)	The process is permanently inactive.
Running (R)	The process may be running or ready to be run.
Interruptible sleep (S)	The process is waiting to be run after some specific trigger.
Stopped (T)	The process may be temporarily stopped by a job control tool or because it is being traced.
Dead (X)	The process has been killed. This state is never displayed.
Defunct (Z)	The process has ended, but only after its parent process. This implies that it has not been killed properly and it will remain as a "zombie."

The top Command

The `top` command lists all tasks running on a Linux system. It acts as a process management tool by allowing users to prioritize, sort, or terminate processes interactively. It displays a dynamic process status, reflecting real-time changes. Different keystrokes within this tool execute process management actions.

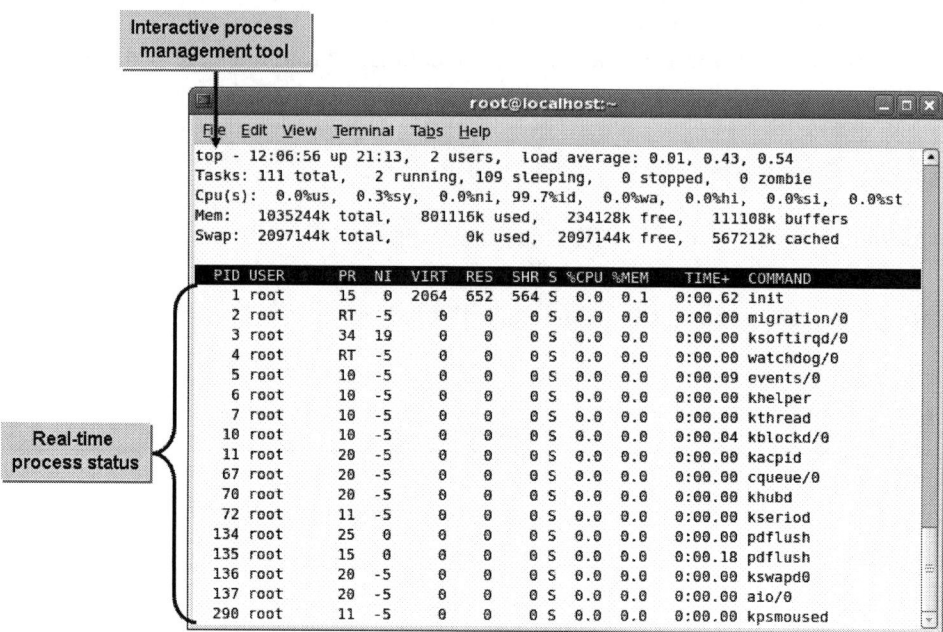

Figure 10-10: Managing processes using the top command.

Useful Keys to Manage Processes

The `top` command provides an interactive tool to manage processes by using some simple shortcuts. Some of the frequently used shortcuts are listed here.

Key	Function
Enter	Refreshes the status of all processes.
Shift+N	Sorts tasks in the decreasing order of their PID.
U	Displays processes belonging to the user specified at the prompt.
K	Terminates the process for which you specify the PID.
R	Renices the process for which you specify the PID.
H	Displays a help screen.
Q	Exits the task list.

The nice Command

The *nice command* allows you to assign a priority level to a process. The nice value of a process indicates how "nice" the process is to others in sharing system resources. You can run a command at a priority higher or lower than the command's normal priority. You must have root user authority to run a command at a higher priority. The priority of a process is often called its *nice value*.

The niceness of a process may range from -20 to 19, where -20 indicates the highest priority and 19 the lowest. In the absence of an increment value, the `nice` command assumes an increment of 10 by default. The priority once lowered for any process cannot be increased by normal users, even if they own the process. By default, all processes in Linux have a nice value of zero.

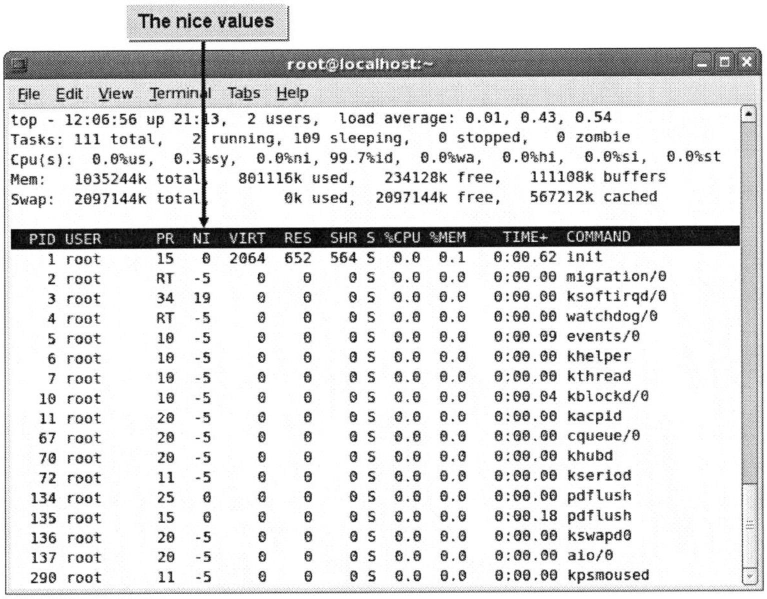

```
The nice values

                                    root@localhost:~                        _ □ ✕

File  Edit  View  Terminal  Tabs  Help

top - 12:06:56 up 21:13,  2 users,  load average: 0.01, 0.43, 0.54
Tasks: 111 total,   2 running, 109 sleeping,   0 stopped,   0 zombie
Cpu(s):  0.0%us,  0.3%sy,  0.0%ni, 99.7%id,  0.0%wa,  0.0%hi,  0.0%si,  0.0%st
Mem:   1035244k total,    801116k used,   234128k free,    111108k buffers
Swap:  2097144k total,         0k used,  2097144k free,   567212k cached

  PID USER      PR  NI  VIRT  RES  SHR S %CPU %MEM    TIME+  COMMAND
    1 root      15   0  2064  652  564 S  0.0  0.1  0:00.62 init
    2 root      RT  -5     0    0    0 S  0.0  0.0  0:00.00 migration/0
    3 root      34  19     0    0    0 S  0.0  0.0  0:00.00 ksoftirqd/0
    4 root      RT  -5     0    0    0 S  0.0  0.0  0:00.00 watchdog/0
    5 root      10  -5     0    0    0 S  0.0  0.0  0:00.09 events/0
    6 root      10  -5     0    0    0 S  0.0  0.0  0:00.00 khelper
    7 root      10  -5     0    0    0 S  0.0  0.0  0:00.00 kthread
   10 root      10  -5     0    0    0 S  0.0  0.0  0:00.04 kblockd/0
   11 root      20  -5     0    0    0 S  0.0  0.0  0:00.00 kacpid
   67 root      20  -5     0    0    0 S  0.0  0.0  0:00.00 cqueue/0
   70 root      20  -5     0    0    0 S  0.0  0.0  0:00.00 khubd
   72 root      11  -5     0    0    0 S  0.0  0.0  0:00.00 kseriod
  134 root      25   0     0    0    0 S  0.0  0.0  0:00.00 pdflush
  135 root      15   0     0    0    0 S  0.0  0.0  0:00.18 pdflush
  136 root      20  -5     0    0    0 S  0.0  0.0  0:00.00 kswapd0
  137 root      20  -5     0    0    0 S  0.0  0.0  0:00.00 aio/0
  290 root      11  -5     0    0    0 S  0.0  0.0  0:00.00 kpsmoused
```

Figure 10-11: The nice values of processes running on a system.

Syntax

The syntax of the command is `nice -n {priority} {command}`, where the priority is specified by a number.

The renice Command

The *renice command* enables you to alter the scheduling priority of a running process. When you renice a process group, it causes all processes in the process group to have their scheduling priority altered. When you renice a user, it alters the scheduling priority of all processes owned by the user. By default, the processes affected are specified by their PIDs.

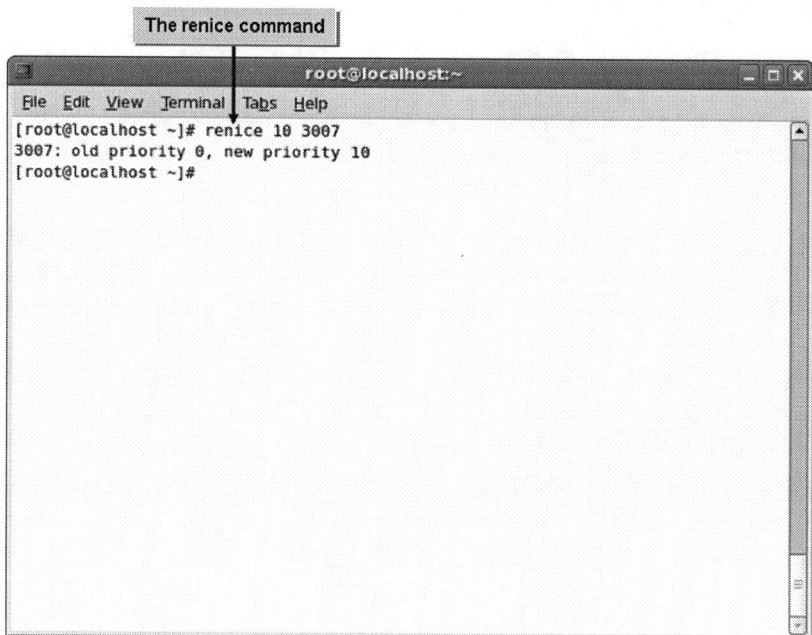

Figure 10-12: *Changing the priority of a process using the renice command.*

The Process Management Tool

The GNOME system monitor is an effective process management tool in the GUI. It provides a real-time display of all processes running on your system, and allows you to halt, resume, terminate, or renice any process. In addition to managing processes, the application also allows you to track system resources such as CPU usage and memory usage. It also displays details on filesystem allocation and the disk space used.

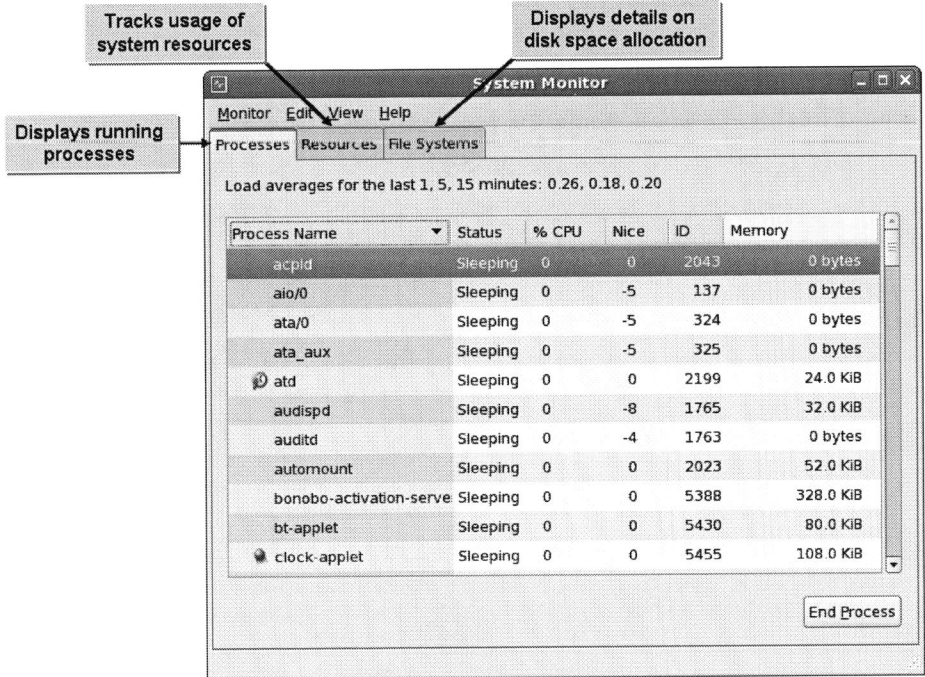

Figure 10-13: Managing processes using the GNOME system monitor.

How to Manage Processes Using the Process Table

Procedure Reference: Manage Processes

To manage processes:

1. Log in as root
2. Mange the processes on the system.
   - Enter `ps` to view the processes running from the current table.
   - Enter `ps -e` to view all processes running on the system.
   - Enter `kill [PID number]` to terminate a process.
   - Enter `kill -9 [PID number]` to terminate a process unconditionally.

Procedure Reference: Change the Priority of a Process

To change the priority of a process:

1. Log in as root.
2. Change the priority of a process as necessary.
   - At the command prompt, enter `nice -n {priority} {command}` to start the process with the specified priority.
   - Enter `renice {priority} [command options]` to change the priority of a running process with a specified priority.

Procedure Reference: Change the Priority of a Process Using the top Command

To change the priority of a process using the `top` command:

1. Log in as root.
2. Enter `top` to display processes sorted according to their CPU usage.
3. Press **R** to alter the priority of a particular process.
4. Enter the PID of the process for which you want to change the priority.
5. Enter the priority number.
6. Press **Q** to quit the display.

Procedure Reference: Manage Processes using the GNOME System Monitor

To manage processes using the GNOME system monitor:

1. Log in as root in the GUI.
2. Open the **System Monitor** window.
    - On the terminal window, enter `gnome-system-monitor`
    - Or, In the **GNOME Panel,** choose **System→Administration→System Monitor.**
3. On the **Processes** tab, scroll down or up to locate the process.
4. Right-click a running process to start, stop, kill, or change the priority.
5. Choose **Monitor→Quit** to close the window.

ACTIVITY 10-2
Managing Processes

Before You Begin:
1. You have logged in as root in the CLI.
2. The first terminal is displayed.

Scenario:
Some users complained of processes taking longer than normal to complete on the Linux server. You discover several processes running that are not needed and were never terminated. You need to manage the system processes and the processes issued by other users.

What You Do	How You Do It
1. View your current running processes and all other running processes.	a. Enter **ps** to list only the processes running on the current terminal.
	b. Observe that only some processes are listed.
	c. Enter **ps -e** to list all the processes running on the system.
	d. Observe that more processes are listed as compared to the output of the ps command.
2. Issue a command.	a. Enter **sleep 300 &** to pause for 300 seconds.
	b. Observe the PID of the sleep 300 & command.
	c. Enter **ps** to list only the processes running on the current terminal.
	d. Observe that the **sleep** command is in the list of running processes.

3. Terminate the command.

a. Enter the PID noted earlier in the format **kill** *[PID]* to terminate the process.

b. Enter **ps** to list only the processes running on the current terminal.

c. Observe that the `sleep` command is not in the list of running processes.

d. Enter **clear** to clear the terminal screen.

ACTIVITY 10-3

Prioritizing Processes

Before You Begin:
1. You have logged in as root in the CLI.
2. The first terminal is displayed.

Scenario:
You want to back up the local copy of your installation CDs. You expect the copying process to be time consuming and to continue after you log out of your system. You decide to increase the priority of the process to ensure that it is completed on time and to assign the process to continue even after you log out.

What You Do	How You Do It
1. View the processes on your system.	a. Enter `ps xl	less` to view all processes run by users.
	b. Examine the processes that have the highest nice value. Press **Page Down** to view the next page of the list.
	c. Press **Page Down** until you reach the end of the entire list.
	d. Press **Q** to exit the list.
	e. Clear the terminal screen.
2. Issue the command to copy the installation files as a background process.	a. Enter `cp -r /rhelsource/Server /opt/. &` to begin the copy process.
	The period (.) is also part of the code. Ensure that you include it while performing this step.
	b. Observe that the PID and the job number appear as a prompt.

3. Renice the copy process by using the `top` command.

a. Enter **top** to open the process management tool.

b. Press **R** to renice the process.

c. Enter **{PID}** to specify a process to renice.

d. Enter **-15** to specify the nice value.

e. Press **Q** to exit the process list.

f. Enter **ls /opt/Server** to view the files in the directory.

g. Observe that the files from the source CD are listed, which indicates that the copy process was successful.

h. Clear the terminal screen.

TOPIC C
Examine Delayed and Detached Jobs

You have a basic understanding of managing jobs and processes. In times of high CPU usage, you may have to delay or stop some jobs in order to complete jobs of higher priority at a faster pace. In this topic, you will delay and detach jobs.

Some jobs can take up a lot of system resources, and you may want to run these jobs when the system is less busy—for instance, during evening hours. Linux allows you to delay and even detach jobs, facilitating efficient utilization of system resources.

Delayed and Detached Jobs

Delayed and detached jobs are job processes that enable users to put off the start of a job.

Process	Definition
Delay a job	A *delayed job* is one that can run at some specified time after you issue the command. For example, a CPU-intensive job that could slow the system is one that you may want to delay for off-peak work hours.
Detach a job	A *detached job* is a job that can be set to run after you log out of the system. For example, a task that will not be completed until after you leave, can be set to continue running after you log out of the system.

Delaying the Start of a Process

To delay the start of a job, use the `sleep` command followed by the delay in seconds and the command name. The `sleep` command suspends any action upon the specified command for the specified number of seconds, and then the command specified is executed. The delay can be up to 2,147,483,647 seconds. This is roughly 596,523 hours; 24,855 days; or 68 years so the amount of time can easily be customized.

The nohup Command

The `nohup` (no hangup) command tells the program to ignore the hangup signal that was sent while disconnecting. The nohup.out file stores the output of the `nohup` command, which will normally be displayed on the terminal. The `nohup` command has various options.

Option	Used To
-a	Change the signal disposition of target processes.
-F	Forcefully grab the target process even if another process has control.
-g	Operate on a list of process groups.
-p	Operate on a list of processes.

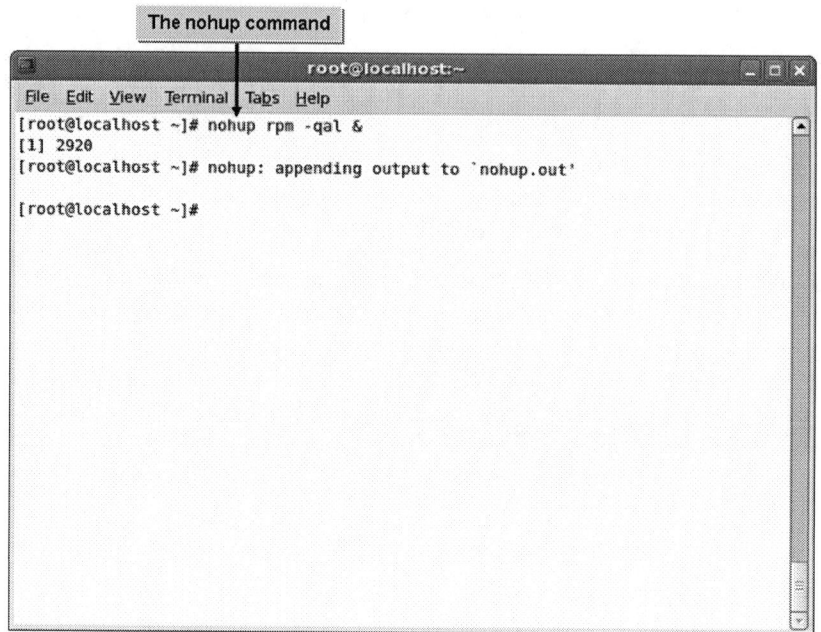

Figure 10-14: Enabling a background process to run after logging out of the system using the nohup command.

Running a Process After You Leave the System

If you have a task that cannot be completed until after you leave work, or if you have a task that is CPU intensive and may slow the system, you can start the task before you leave and specify that it continues even after you log out of the system. You can do this by using the nohup (no hangup) command. The nohup command should run in the background so that it does not tie up your terminal. To enable a command to run in the background after you have logged out, use the syntax nohup *[command]* &.

How to Work with Delayed and Detached Jobs

Procedure Reference: Delay a Job

To delay a job:

1. Login as root.
2. Determine which job you will like to schedule at a later time. Enter sleep *[number of seconds to delay]; [command to issue]* to schedule the job at a later time.

Procedure Reference: Detach a Job

To detach a job:

1. Login as root.
2. Determine which job you will like to run after you log out of the system. Enter nohup *[command to issue]* & to schedule the job to continue running even after you log out.

ACTIVITY 10-4
Detaching a Job

Before You Begin:

1. You have logged in as root in the CLI.

2. The first terminal is displayed.

3. On the terminal, enter `ps` to view the running processes.

4. In the **CMD** column, note the PID of the `cp` process.

5. Enter `kill {PID}` to kill the process.

6. Enter `clear` to clear the terminal screen.

Scenario:

You discovered that a large number of CPU-intensive jobs are being run during the normal business hours. Your manager gave you a list of jobs that are not time critical. You decide that the best time to run CPU-intensive applications is after you log out of the system.

What You Do	How You Do It
1. Issue a command to run in the background and log out.	a. On the terminal, enter **find /etc** to view the files that are available in the /etc directory.
	b. Observe that the /etc/sysctl.conf file is the last entry in the /etc directory.
	c. Enter **nohup find /etc -print &** to process the command in the background. Press **Enter** to continue.
	d. Observe that a message is displayed indicating that the output of the command is added to the nohup.out file.
	e. Enter **logout**

2. Log in as root and verify that the job is complete.

a. At the **login** prompt, enter *root*

b. At the **Password** prompt, enter *p@ssw0rd*

c. Enter `vim nohup.out` to open the nohup.out file.

d. Observe that the file contains a listing of files and directories in the /etc directory, which indicates that the job is complete.

e. Press **Shift+G** to move to the end of the file.

f. Observe that the /etc/sysctl.conf file is the last entry listed.

g. Press **:** to switch to the command mode.

h. Enter `q` to close the file.

i. Enter `clear` to clear the terminal.

TOPIC D
Schedule Jobs

You delayed and detached jobs to overcome high CPU usage. You may also need to designate jobs that are to be executed at a specific time. In this topic, you will schedule jobs.

As a system administrator, you may need to schedule repetitive tasks to run at a specific time. For example, you may schedule a backup process every night so that it does not affect the work schedule of the users. Scheduling jobs is an important part of a system administrator's daily tasks.

Cron

Definition:

A *cron* is a daemon that runs in the background on a Linux system and executes specified tasks at a designated time or date. A cron is normally used to schedule periodically executed tasks defined in the *crontab* file.

Example:

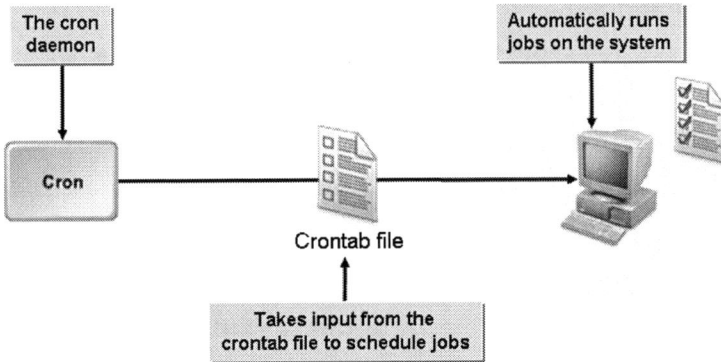

Figure 10-15: Cron executes specified tasks on the system.

Syntax

The syntax of the cron daemon is `cron [option] {mail command}`.

Cron Jobs

A task scheduled via cron is called a *cron job*. These jobs will run either at system level or at user level. The cron jobs that you create for users are stored in the /var/spool/cron/[User name] file. System default cron jobs are stored in the /etc/crontab file. Only a root user can add system level jobs.

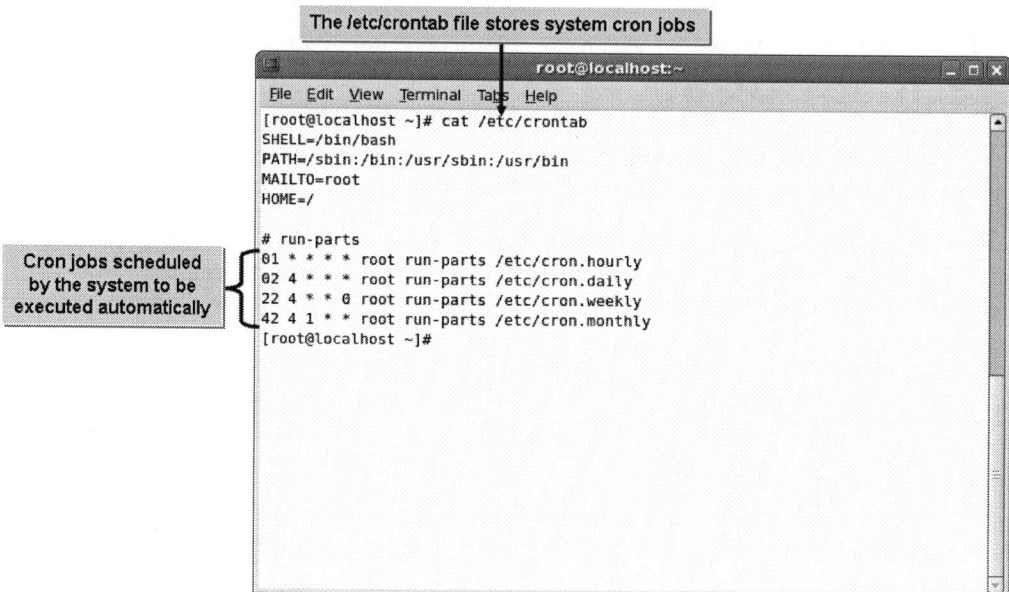

Figure 10-16: Cron jobs listed in the crontab file.

Setting Up Scheduled Jobs Using cron

Scheduling a cron job is accomplished by adding the job to the system-wide /etc/crontab file. The crontab file may also contain environment variables that will be passed to the commands at the time of execution. Jobs in the crontab file are called entries, and they include a time description, the user name to run the command, and the command. The format of a `crontab` entry is: `{Minute} {Hour} {Day of Month} {Month} {Day of Week} {user command}`. The time fields in the `crontab` entry are described in the following table.

Field	Allowed Values
Minute	0-59
Hour	0-23
Day of the month	1-31
Month	1-12 or Jan-Dec
Day of the week	0-7 (0 or 7 is Sunday) or Sun-Sat

In addition to specifying a particular time and day, a pattern can also be described by using asterisks (*) to specify all of a particular field. For example, an asterisk in the minute field indicates that the command should be carried out every minute. In addition to asterisks, time ranges are also permitted by separating values with a dash (-), and lists of values are specified by separating values with a comma (,).

The tmpwatch Command

The *tmpwatch command* is run as a daily cron job that is used to delete files, such as the files in the /tmp directory, which have not been accessed for some time and are utilizing disk space. There are a number of options for the `tmpwatch` command.

Option	Enables You To
-u	Delete files according to the time they were accessed.
-m	Delete files according to the time they were modified.
-a	Remove all file types, including directories.
-d	Restrict the `tmpwatch` command from removing directories, even if they are empty or marked for deletion.
-f	Remove files forcefully, overriding all access regulations.

Even if one error is encountered during the cleanup process, the `tmpwatch` utility will exit.

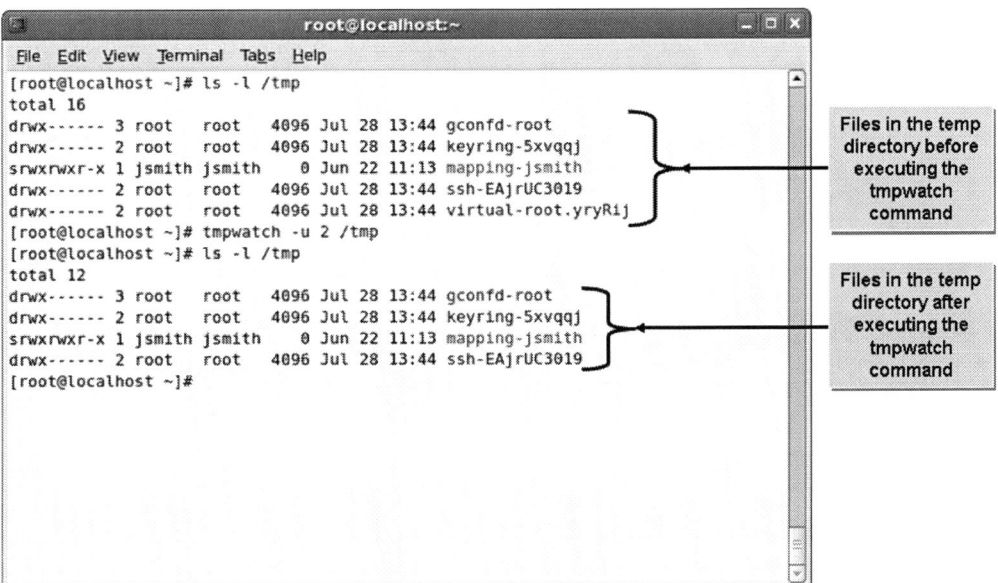

Figure 10-17: Deleting files in the /tmp directory using the tmpwatch command.

Syntax

The syntax of the `tmpwatch` command is `tmpwatch [options] {hours}`.

The logrotate Command

The *logrotate command* is run as a daily cron job that is used to compress, delete, or mail log files. It may be configured to run weekly or monthly depending on the log size. The configuration file for logrotate is /etc/logrotate.conf. The logrotate command has various options.

Option	Enables You To
-d	Turn on the debug mode to disable any changes from being made to the logs.
-f	Force log rotation by deleting old files irrespective of their importance and create new ones.
-m {subject} {recipient}	Mail the logs to the recipient. The default syntax is /bin/mail -s.

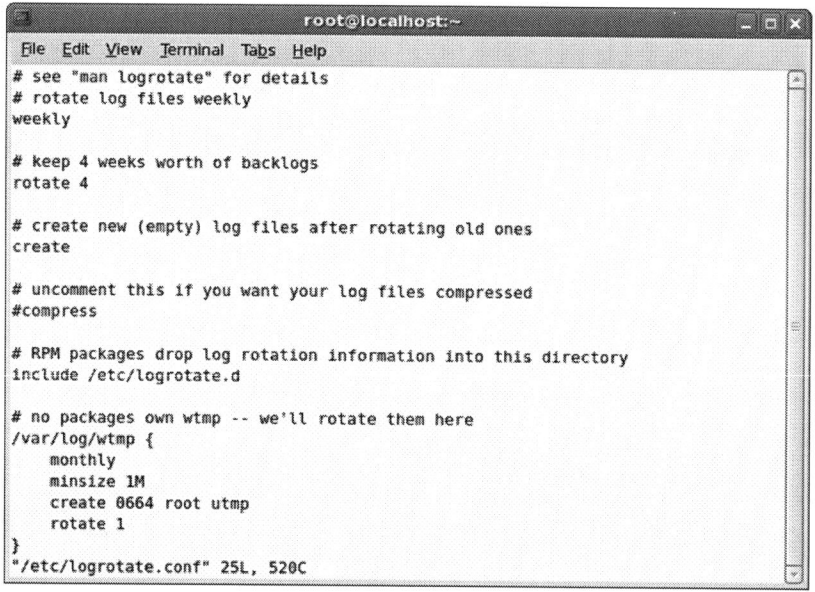

Figure 10-18: *The /etc/logrotate.conf file allows you to control the rotation of logs.*

The logwatch Utility

The *logwatch utility* is run as a daily cron job that is used to monitor logs. It is fully customizable via the /etc/logwatch/conf/logwatch.conf file. The utility searches logs and reports suspicious messages. It enables you to set detail levels for reports, such as 10, 5, and 0, which correspond to high, medium, and low detail levels, respectively.

The logwatch utility has various options.

Option	Enables You To
--detail level	Set the detail level of the log report.

Option	Enables You To
--print	Print the report generated by the command.
--range *range*	Set the range for analysis. It can accept any value among Yesterday, Today, and All.
--mailto *address*	Mail the results to the recipient's mail id.
save *file name*	Save the output to a file instead of displaying it.

System crontab Files

System crontab files are the configuration files for the cron utility. They are stored in the /etc/crontab file. The name of the user running the command is indicated in the sixth field of the file. When you create a crontab entry for a specific user, the sixth field contains the command that needs to be run at the specified time. System crontab files can be edited by the root user.

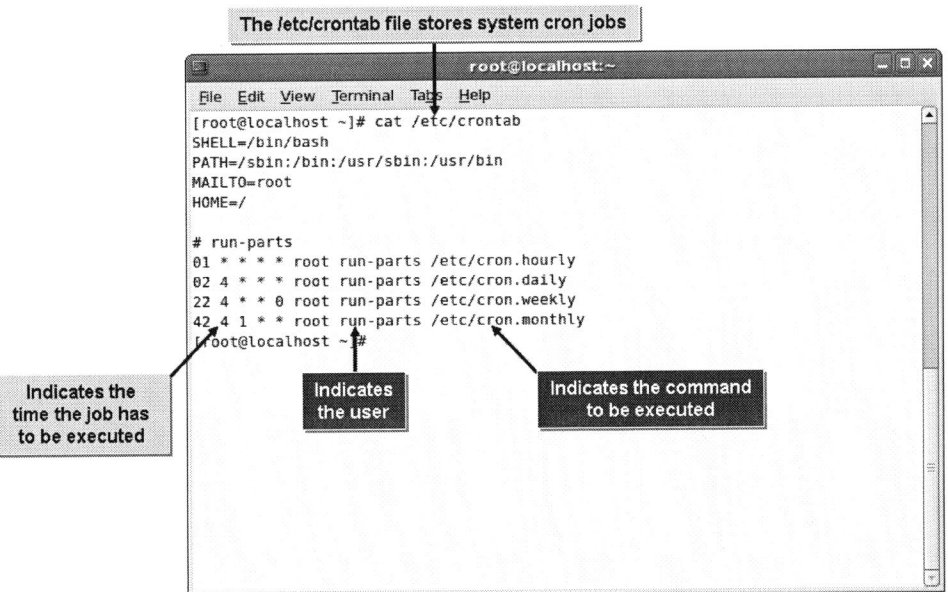

Figure 10-19: The /etc/crontab file with system-level cron jobs.

User crontab Files

In addition to system-level cron jobs, individual users can also schedule cron jobs. Unlike the system-level crontab, users have their own crontab file. The format of entries in this file is the same as that of the system-level crontab, with the exception of the user field. Because the entire crontab file is dedicated to a single user, the user field is not included. While the /etc/crontab file can be edited directly, user crontab files are best edited via the crontab utility.

The at Command

The *at command* executes a given set of commands at a specified time. This command is useful for executing a command set only once. Using either the -f option or input redirection, defined by the < symbol, the at command reads the list of commands from a file. This file needs to be an executable shell script.

The following table lists some frequently used at command options and their descriptions.

Option	Enables You To
atq	Display the job queue of all users except the superuser.
atq -V	Display the version number.
at -q [a-z]	Display the jobs in the specified queue.
at -m	Send mail to the user when the job is complete.
at -f file name	Read the job from the file rather than the standard input.
at -l	Print all jobs queued for the user.
at -v	Display the time that the job will be executed before reading the job.

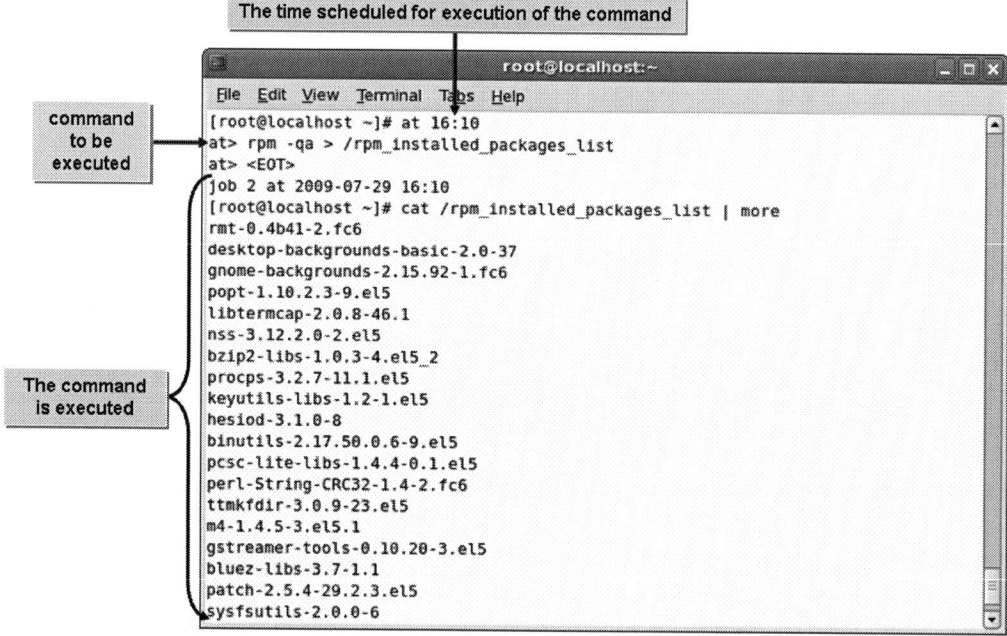

Figure 10-20: Executing a command at a specific time using the at command.

Syntax

The syntax of the at command is at *[options]* *{time}*.

Specifying Time Using the at Command

Some of the common time formats in which you can schedule a job are given in the following table.

Time Format	Description
HH:MM A.M. or HH:MM P.M.	Specifies the hour and minute.
MMDDYY or MM/DD/YY or DD.MM.YY	Specifies the day, month, and year.
JAN or FEB or MAR	Specifies the month.
SUN or MON or TUE	Specifies the day of the week.

Anacron

Definition:
Anacron is a daemon that executes jobs at intervals, which are specified in days, without requiring the system to be running continuously. Anacron is used to control the execution of daily, weekly, or monthly jobs.

Example:

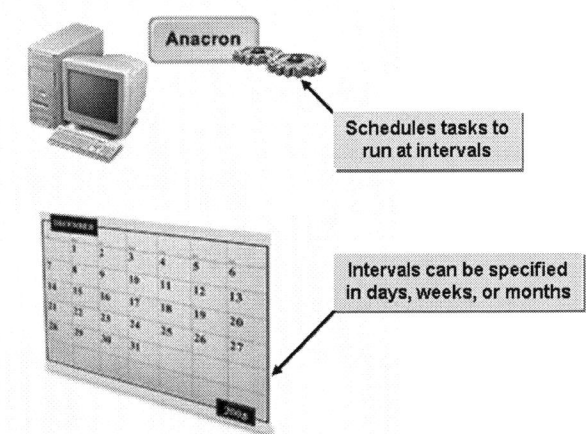

Figure 10-21: *The anacron daemon executing scheduled jobs.*

The /etc/anacrontab File
The /etc/anacrontab file is the configuration file for the anacron utility. This file has four fields. The first field displays the number of days the job has not been run, the second field displays the time after which the job has to be run (after reboot), the third field displays the job identifier, and the fourth field displays the job to be run by the anacron utility.

How to Schedule Jobs

Procedure Reference: Delegate Tasks Using the cron Command

To delegate tasks using the `cron` command:

1. Log in as root in the CLI.
2. Enter `crontab -e` to create a cron job for the root user.
3. Press **I** to switch to the input mode.
4. Type `{Minute} {Hour} {Day of Month} {Month} {Day of Week} {Command that has to be run}` to specify a schedule for the job.
5. Save and close the file to install the new cron job.
6. To verify that the new cron job has been executed, check if you have received a mail message regarding the job that has been scheduled.
7. Enter `crontab -l` to list the cron jobs.
8. Enter `crontab -r` to remove the job from the queue.

Configure Access to cron Services

To configure user access to cron services, you need to perform the following actions in the corresponding files listed in the table.

If You Need To	You Should
Allow cron services to users	Add users in the /etc/cron.allow file.
Deny cron services to users	Add users in the /etc/cron.deny file.

Procedure Reference: Schedule Jobs to Run at a Specific Time

To schedule jobs to run at a specific time:

1. Log in as root in the CLI.
2. Enter `at {Specific time format}` to specify an `at` job.
3. Enter `{Job that has to be run}` and press **Enter.**
4. Press **Ctrl+D** to exit the process.
5. To verify that the `at` job has been executed, check if you have received an email message for the job that has been executed.

Procedure Reference: Manage Jobs Using the at Command

To manage jobs using the `at` command:

1. Log in as root in the CLI.
2. Enter `atq` to view the queue of pending `at` jobs.
3. Enter `atrm {Job number}` to delete the job from the queue.

ACTIVITY 10-5

Scheduling Jobs Using crontab

Before You Begin:

1. You have logged in as root in the CLI.

2. The first terminal is displayed.

Scenario:

Your organization adopted a new policy that requires all users to fill in their time sheets every day. The senior system administrator asked you to create a reminder for all user systems.

Account information:

- Login name for whom the reminder needs to be scheduled: user1

- Password for user1: myp@$$w0rd

What You Do	How You Do It
1. Schedule a cron job to email a reminder everyday at a specified time.	a. Enter **useradd user1** to create the **user1** user account.
	b. Enter **passwd user1** to set the password for **user1.**
	c. At the **New UNIX password** prompt, enter *myp@$$w0rd*
	d. At the **Retype new UNIX password** prompt, enter *myp@$$w0rd*
	e. Enter **date** to view the system time.
	f. Enter **crontab -u user1 -e** to specify a cron job for **user1.**
	g. Observe that the text editor opens a temporary file automatically.
	h. Press **I** to switch to the insert mode.
	i. Type *## ## * * * /bin/echo⇒ "Please fill out your time sheet"* to schedule the cron job.
	j. Press **Esc** to switch to the command mode.
	k. Save and close the file.
	l. Enter **logout**
2. Check whether user1 received the reminder for the scheduled job.	a. After the specified time, log in as **user1** in the CLI.
	b. Enter **mail** to open the mailbox.
	c. Enter *1* to read the contents of the first email message.
	d. Observe that the mail contains a remainder to fill in the timecard.
	e. Enter **d** to delete the email message.
	f. Enter **q** to quit the mail service.
	g. Enter **logout** to log out of the **user1** account.

TOPIC E
Maintain the System Time

In the previous topic, you scheduled jobs to run at a specific time. You need to monitor system clocks so that all systems show the same time. In this topic, you will maintain the system time.

Suppose you work in a company with clients in various cities around the world. You may need to synchronize your system time with that of your client's time zone to enable easier business transactions.

Network Time Protocol

Network Time Protocol (NTP) is a standard Internet protocol for synchronizing the internal system clock with the *true time* or the *average time* on a number of high accuracy clocks around the world. NTP is used for transmitting and receiving time on TCP/IP networks. NTP is also used to set the clock of one computer to match that of another and synchronize it with the network clock.

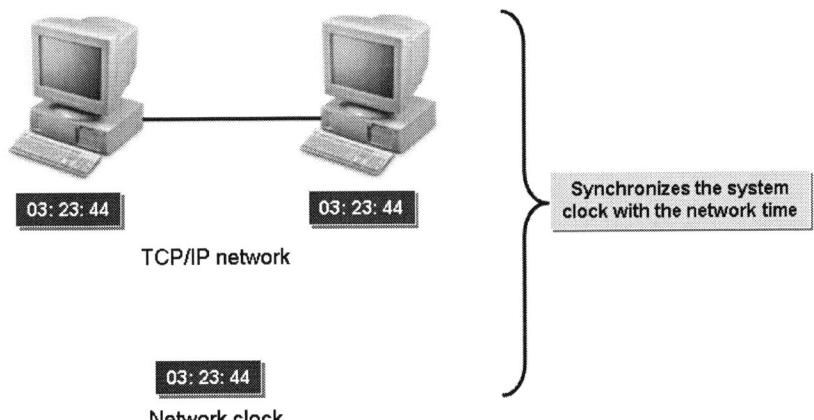

Figure 10-22: Synchronization of system clocks with network time using NTP.

Drift Files
The drift file is a file found in the /etc/ntp directory. The NTP drift file is used by the ntpd daemon to reset the time when the system is restarted. The drift file synchronizes the system clock and the clock drift to display the time from the NTP server.

The ntp.conf File

The *ntp.conf* file found in the /etc directory contains configuration options for the NTP server. The file contains settings for all hosts on local and public servers. The `ntpd` daemon reads the ntp.conf file for synchronization settings and then connects to the NTP server.

Universal Time Coordinated

Definition:

Universal Time Coordinated (UTC) is a time scale that forms the official measure of time in the world. UTC is independent of time zones. It was previously referred to as the *Greenwich Mean Time (GMT)*. It is the time at the prime meridian at Greenwich, England. Unlike GMT, leap seconds are also included in UTC.

Example:

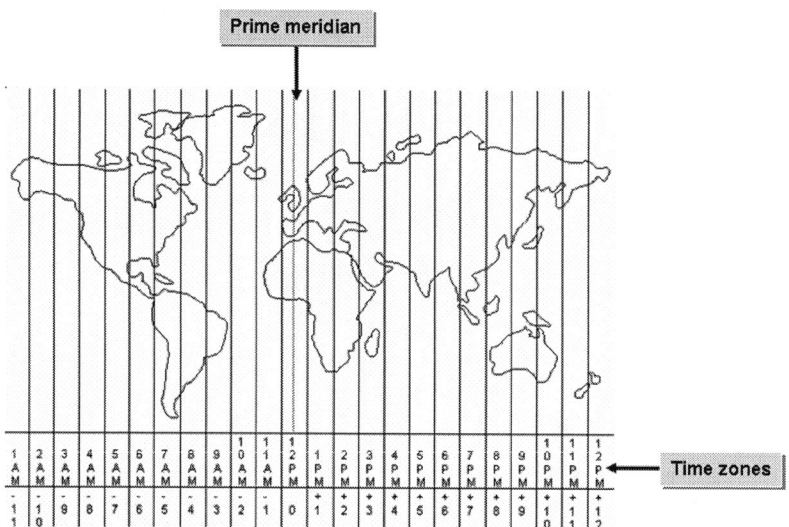

Figure 10-23: World time zone.

Leap Seconds

Leap second is the adjustment made to UTC, to account for the irregularity in the earth's rotation. The standard second is stable, while the motion of the earth is not. Therefore, occasionally, the standard minute is adjusted by adding a leap second. As a result, some minutes have 61 seconds. Standard hours are always 60 minutes, though one of the minutes may be a second longer than usual. Standard days are always 24 hours.

Clock Drift

Clock drift is the gradual variation in time that sets between the hardware clock and the system clock. The hardware clock is also known as the *Real Time Clock (RTC)*. It keeps track of the time when the system is turned off and not when the system is on. The system clock, however, functions only when the system is running and needs to be initialized at boot time. The hardware and system clocks will drift at different rates, apart from each other and also away from the real time. To synchronize both clocks, their drift rates need to be measured and corrected.

System Time

Definition:

System time is the time maintained by a computer's internal clock. It is a coordinated universal time with a resolution in milliseconds. The internal clock circuitry is backed up by a battery that keeps the clock running even when the computer is switched off. System time is used to date-stamp files with the time of their creation or revision. It can also be changed with difference in time zones.

Example:

Figure 10-24: *System time on the GNOME desktop.*

The system-config-date Command

The `system-config-date` command allows you to open the **Date/Time Properties** dialog box that facilitates changing the system date and time and configuring the time zone.

The Date/Time Format

The International Standardization Organization (ISO) specifies numeric representation of date and time. The standard format for date is YYYY-MM-DD, where YYYY represents the year in the Gregorian calendar, MM represents the month in the year, and DD represents the day in the month. The American format of date is MM-DD-YYYY. However, Europeans write the day before the month. The separators used with numbers also vary among countries. The common format for time is HH-MM-SS, where HH represents hours, MM represents minutes, and SS represents seconds.

How to Maintain the System Time

Procedure Reference: Synchronize the System Clock with the Remote Time Server Using the system-config-date Command

To synchronize the system clock with the remote time server using the system-config-date command:

1. Log in as root in the GUI.

2. Open the **Date/Time Properties** window.

    *   In the **GNOME Panel,** choose **System→Administration →Date & Time.**

    *   Or, on the terminal, enter system-config-date

3. Select the **Network Time Protocol** tab.

4. Synchronize the system clock with the remote time server using NTP.

    a. Check the **Enable Network Time Protocol** check box.

    b. Add a new NTP server.

        1. Click **Add** to add the NTP server.

        2. In the **New NTP Server** text box, enter the domain name of the NTP server to add it to the **NTP Servers** list.

        3. If necessary, in the message box with **"Host {ntp server} is not reachable or doesn't act as an NTP server,"** click **No** to discard the NTP server entry.

    c. Manage the existing NTP server list.

        *   Select the entry and click **Edit** to edit the existing entry.

        *   Select the entry and click **Delete** to delete the existing entry.

    d. If necessary, click the **Show advanced options** section to use the hidden advanced options.

        *   Check or uncheck the **Synchronize system clock before starting service** check box.

        *   Check or uncheck the **Use Local Time Source** check box.

5. Click **OK** to apply the settings and close the window.

Procedure Reference: Synchronize the System Clock with the Remote Time Server Using the /etc/ntp.conf File

To synchronize the system clock with the remote time server using the /etc/ntp.conf file:

1. Log in as root.

2. Enter cd /etc to navigate to the /etc directory.

3. Enter vi ntp.conf to open the ntp.conf file.

4. Specify the time server details.

   ● Enter `server { ip-address | FQDN of the time server }` to set the server details.

   ● Enter `drift file { drift file location }` to set the drift file location.

5. Save and close the file.

6. Enter `ntpdate` to manually reset the clock.

7. Enter `ntpq -p` to display a list and summary of the NTP servers known to the server.

 `ntpq` is a utility that is used to monitor the `ntpd` service and determine its performance.

ACTIVITY 10-6

Synchronizing System Clocks

Before You Begin:

1. The login screen of the first terminal in the CLI is displayed.
2. Switch to the GUI.
3. You have logged in as root in the GUI.
4. The terminal window is displayed.

Scenario:

In the company where you work as a system administrator, all employees are required to fill in their time cards, to keep track of their daily duties. You are assigned the task of standardizing the time displayed on all systems, to ensure that all users enter the correct time in their time cards. As part of the auditing task, you want to ensure that all systems on the network have their time synchronized to the time server. To ensure uniformity in the time cards, you decide to configure NTP.

What You Do	How You Do It
1. Open the ntp.conf file.	a. Enter **cd /etc** to navigate to the /etc directory.
	b. Enter **vi ntp.conf** to open the ntp.conf file.
2. Synchronize the system time with the server.	a. Press **Shift+G** to go to the last line of the file.
	b. Press **O** to switch to the insert mode and move to a new line.
	c. On the new line, type *server {IP address of server}*
	d. Press **Esc** to switch to the command mode.
	e. Save and close the file.

3. Enable NTP.

a. Enter `system-config-date` to open the **Date/Time Properties** window.

b. Select the **Network Time Protocol** tab.

c. Check the **Enable Network Time Protocol** check box to synchronize the system clock with the remote time server using NTP.

d. Verify that the NTP servers are displayed.

e. Click **OK** to apply the settings and close the window.

f. Observe that a message **"contacting ntp server"** is displayed.

g. Clear the terminal window.

Lesson 10 Follow-up

In this lesson, you managed essential jobs and processes in a Linux system. This will enable you to effectively track the usage of system resources and manage resource allocation efficiently.

1. **How can a system's performance be improved by managing processes?**

2. **Do you think automating system processes affect a system's performance? Why?**

11 Managing System Services

Lesson Time: 1 hour(s), 30 minutes

Lesson Objectives:

In this lesson, you will manage system services.

You will:

● Configure services to improve system performance.

● Monitor system logs.

● Configure SELinux.

Introduction

Now that you examined the way processes operate in a Linux environment, you can manage the services that run on a Linux system. These include basic services and other services that are required by the kernel to process requests.

With system services, you can make system resources available to different users. At times, you may need to start, stop, or restart services to keep a system running efficiently. By managing system services, you can ensure that the system is working at the optimum level and users are able to derive maximum benefits.

This lesson covers all or part of the following CompTIA Linux+ (2009) certification objectives:

● Topic A
  ■ Objective 3.1
● Topic B
  ■ Objective 1.6
  ■ Objective 2.3
● Topic C
  ■ Objective 5.3

TOPIC A

Configure System Services

In a Linux system, there are numerous services that will be running simultaneously. These services need to be secured and managed properly in an efficient manner to avoid clogging of system resources. In this topic, you will configure system services.

As a Linux+ administrator, you will often face problems, such as slow processing and improper system response, with your system. Often, these problems are a result of improperly managed services that utilize more system resources, causing other processes to run on minimal resources. By managing system services properly, you will be able to increase the efficiency of your system.

System Initialization

System initialization begins when a system is booted. It involves the loading of the operating system and its various components, including the boot process. System initialization is carried out by the init program in Linux. The init program refers to the configuration file and initiates the processes listed in it. This prepares the system to run the required software. Programs on the system will not run without system initialization.

The inittab File

The *inittab* file found in the /etc directory stores details of various processes related to system initialization. It also stores details of the runlevels in use.

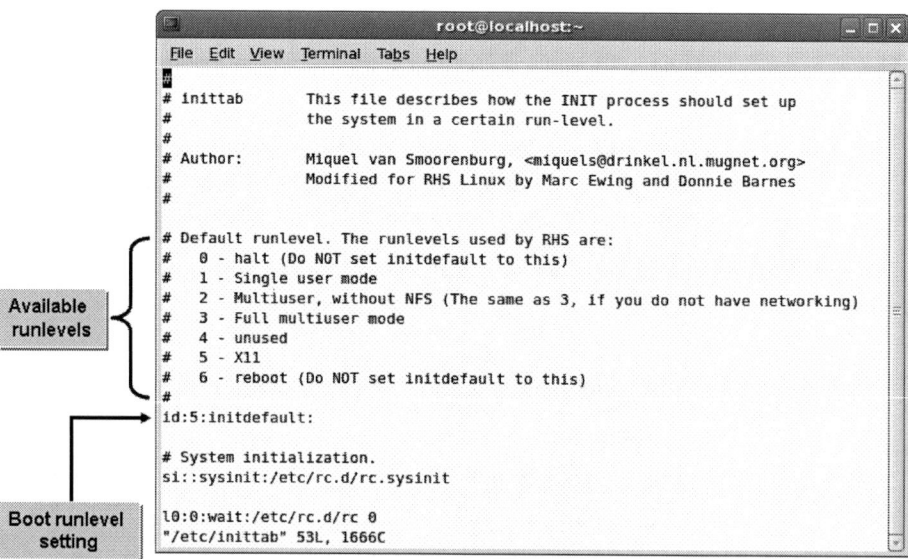

Figure 11-1: The inittab file showing runlevel details.

Data Storage Format

The inittab file stores data in the *id:runlevels:action:process* format.

The /etc/init.d Directory

The init.d directory found in the /etc directory stores initialization scripts for services. These scripts, called system V scripts, control the initiation of services in a particular runlevel. These runlevels are called system V runlevels. The scripts are invoked from the /etc/inittab file when system initialization begins, using the symbolic links found in the file. System V scripts are highly flexible and can be configured according to the needs of a user. Some of the services listed in the init.d directory are anacron, cups, and bluetooth.

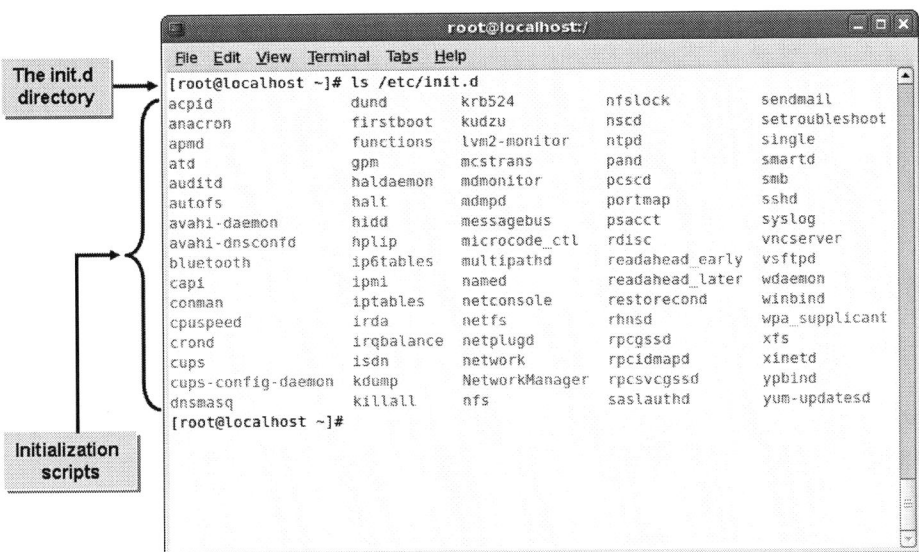

Figure 11-2: System and service initialization scripts are found in the init.d directory.

Syntax

The syntax for running scripts of the services in the /etc/init.d directory is / {service name} {start|stop|status|restart}.

The chkconfig Command

The chkconfig command can be used to control services in each runlevel. It controls services through the symbolic links found in the initialization scripts of services. It can also be used to start or stop services during system startup.

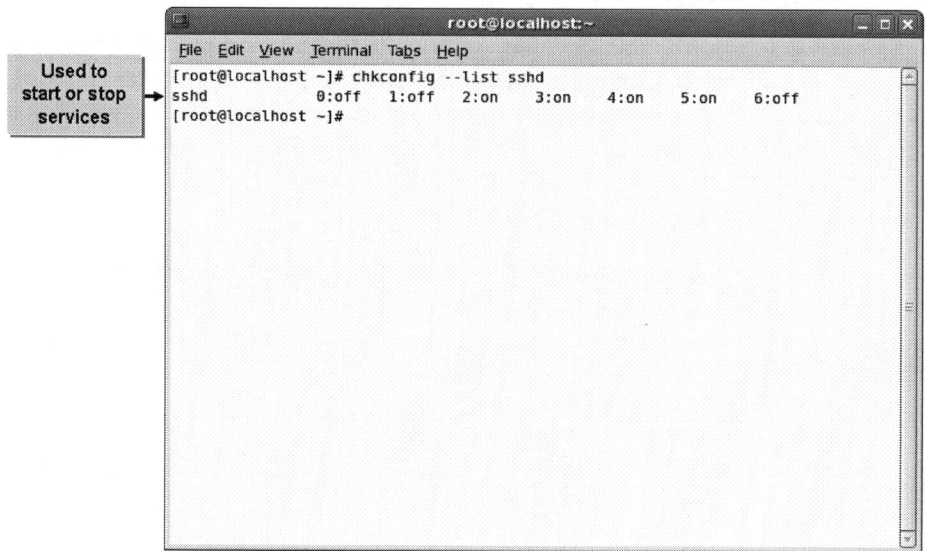

Figure 11-3: The chkconfig command and its functions.

The chkconfig command has various options. Some of the frequently used options are listed in the table.

Option	Enables You To
--level	Specify the runlevel in which the service has to be enabled or disabled.
--add	Add a service to the list of services managed by the chkconfig command.
--del	Delete a service from the list of services managed by the chkconfig command.
--list	List the services managed by the chkconfig command in all runlevels.
on	Start a service at system startup.
off	Stop a service at system startup.
reset	Reset the status of a service.

Syntax

The syntax of the chkconfig command is chkconfig *[option]* *{service name}* *{on|off|reset}*.

The /etc/sysconfig Directory

The /etc/sysconfig directory contains configuration files for services that should be started at system startup. These files contain the settings that describe how these services must be initialized when the system boots. Some of the services listed in the /etc/sysconfig directory include bluetooth, cups, irda, and kdump.

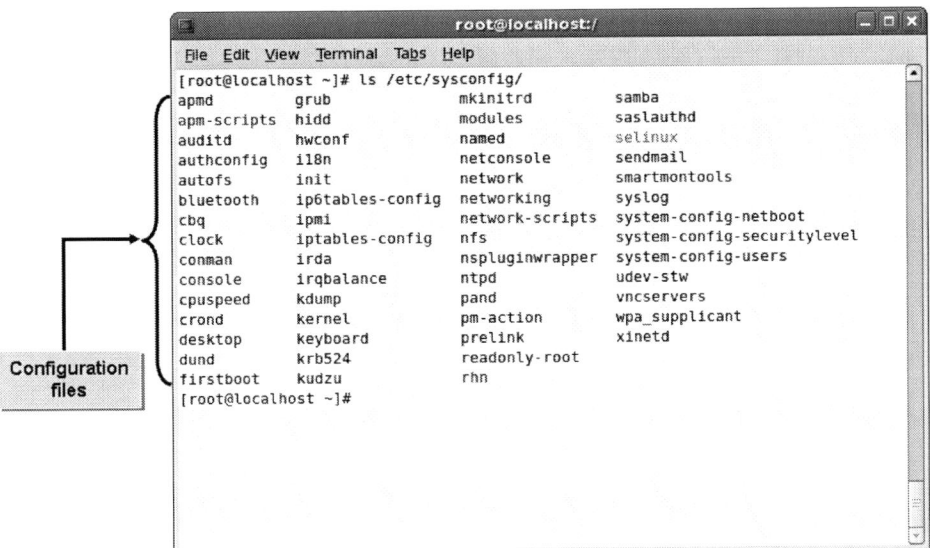

Figure 11-4: The sysconfig directory with various configuration files invoked during system startup.

The system-config-services Command

The `system-config-services` command enables you to start and stop system services in the current runlevel. It is an X-based graphical utility and should be run on the GUI terminal. The command opens the **Service Configuration** window, which displays two main tabs; the **Background Services** tab, which is used to control background services and daemons; and the **On Demand Services** tab, which is used to control the services managed by the `xinetd` command.

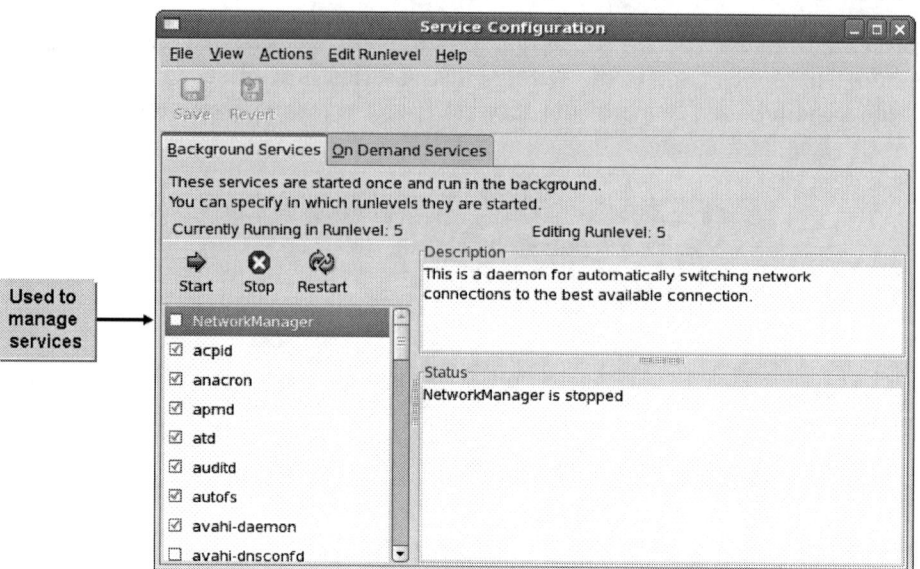

Figure 11-5: *The output of the system-config-services command.*

The inetd Command

The *inetd command,* also called the Internet "super-server", is a system service daemon that allows you to start programs needed for accessing different Internet services. When you request for a specific Internet service, inetd will start all the related services. It reduces the system load by running one daemon to support several related services without actually running all the daemons at the same time. The inetd command uses the file /etc/inetd.conf to configure services. inetd is no longer used in most of the latest versions of Linux distributions and is replaced by the *xinetd* command.

How to Configure Services

Procedure Reference: Configure Services Using the chkconfig Command

To configure services in different runlevels using the chkconfig command:

1. Log in as root.
2. Configure services in different runlevels.

    - Enter chkconfig --list *{Service Name}* to display whether the service name should be stopped or started in each runlevel.

    - Enter chkconfig --add *{Service Name}* to add a service to the chkconfig management.

    - Enter chkconfig --del *{Service Name}* to remove a service from the chkconfig management.

    - Enter chkconfig --level *{levels} {Service Name}* {on|off} to stop or start a service for the mentioned runlevel.

ACTIVITY 11-1

Enabling a Specific Service

Before You Begin:

1. You have logged in as root in the GUI.

2. The terminal window is displayed.

3. Enter cd / to change to the / directory.

4. Enter service bluetooth stop to stop the bluetooth service.

5. Enter chkconfig --level 2345 bluetooth off to turn off the bluetooth service at all runlevels.

6. Close the terminal window.

7. Switch to the CLI.

8. Log in as root.

Scenario:

As a system administrator, you enabled Bluetooth support in one of the systems to enable users to use their Bluetooth devices. The users are now complaining that the Bluetooth device is not recognized by the system. You realize that the problem occurred once the system was restarted. You need to prevent the problem from occurring again.

What You Do	How You Do It
1. Change the status of the bluetooth service at different runlevels.	a. Enter **chkconfig --list bluetooth** to check the status of the bluetooth service for different runlevels.
	b. Observe that the bluetooth service is disabled for all runlevels.
	c. Enter **chkconfig --level 2345 bluetooth on** to enable the bluetooth service to run in runlevels 2 to 5.
	d. Enter **chkconfig --list bluetooth** to check whether the status of the service is updated.
	e. Observe that the bluetooth service is now enabled for runlevels 2 to 5.

2. Start the bluetooth service.

a. Enter **service bluetooth status** to check the current status of the service.

b. Observe that the output shows that both **hcid** and **sdpd** are stopped.

 The Host Control Interface Daemon (hcid) manages all Bluetooth devices connected to the system.

 The Bluetooth Service Discovery Protocol Daemon (sdpd) in Linux keeps track of all bluetooth services registered on the system and responds to inquiries from remote Bluetooth devices.

c. Enter **service bluetooth start** to start the bluetooth service.

d. Observe that the "OK" status is displayed next to "Starting Bluetooth services," which indicates that the bluetooth service is started.

e. Enter **service bluetooth status** to check the status of the bluetooth service.

f. Observe that the messages **"hcid (pid {process id}) is running"** and **"sdpd (pid {process id}) is running"** are displayed, which indicates that the service has started.

g. Clear the terminal screen.

TOPIC B
Monitor System Logs

You configured system services to improve your system's efficiency. To ensure that the changes made to the system services are applied correctly, you need to track the status of each change you make. In this topic, you will monitor system logs.

As a system administrator, you will need to check whether all changes made to a system are applied, to ensure that the system is working fine. When managing system services, it will be practically impossible to manually track each change made to different services. You can track these changes using the system log files.

System Logs

Definition:
System logs are records of system activities that are tracked and maintained by the syslogd utility. The syslogd utility runs as a daemon. System logs are usually started at boot time. System log messages include the date, the process that delivered the message, and the actual message.

Example:

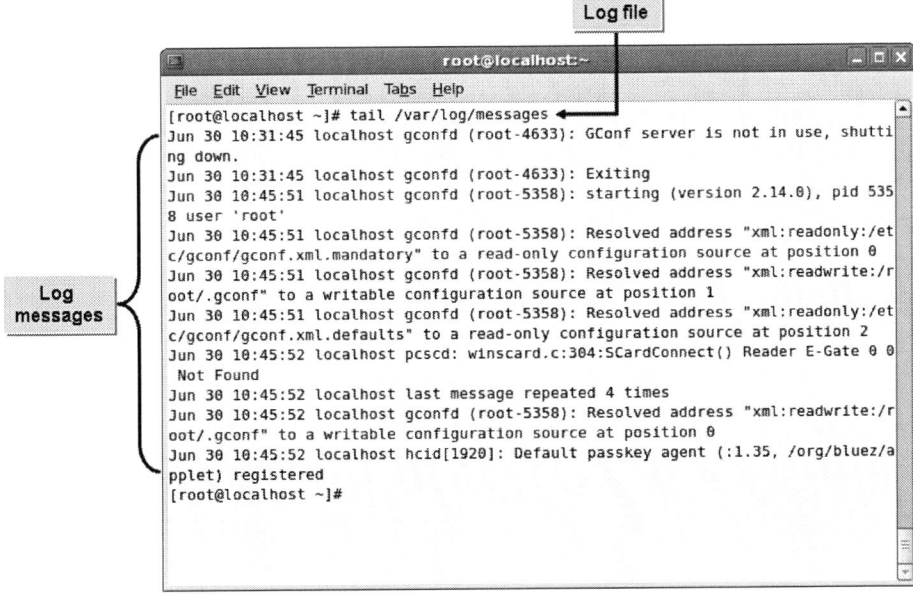

Figure 11-6: System logs and their messages.

Logging Services

A *logging service* is a daemon that is used to track logs or errors that are generated in a system. Log messages are stored in a separate file called *log file*, which is stored in the /var/log directory. The main log file is /var/log/messages. In addition to this log file, some services also create their own log files.

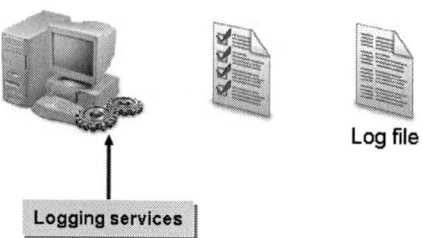

Figure 11-7: Tracking log files using logging services.

The Central Network Log Server

Definition:

The *central network log server* is a server that is used to implement centralized logging services. This server receives all syslog messages from the Linux or Windows servers and from network devices, such as routers, switches, firewalls, and workstations, across a network. The server logs data mining and online alerts, performs log analysis, and generates reports.

Example:

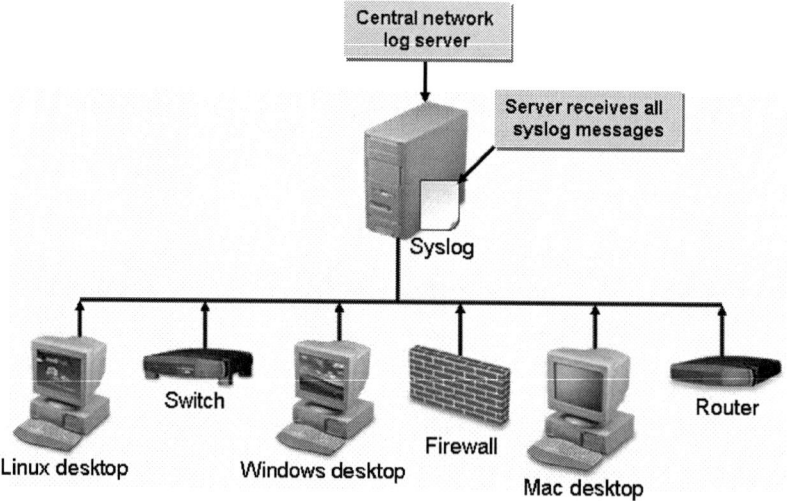

Figure 11-8: The central network log server receiving syslog messages from other servers and network devices.

Automating Log Analysis

During maintenance sessions, instead of manually parsing large log files, you can automate the log analysis by writing Perl or Bash scripts. For example, you can write a Perl script to automatically parse a mail log file and inform you about rejected email messages. Ensure that you make a `crontab` entry for the script.

Perl

Practical Extraction and Reporting Language (Perl) is a programming language that is used to write scripts. Perl has a powerful feature that is used for manipulating strings; this is why it is extensively used by web servers to process data received from client browsers.

Textutils

In your Perl scripts, you can use grep and other textutils to extract specific text from log files. Some textutils have been listed in the following table.

Use This Textutil Command	If You Need To
expand *file name*	Convert tabs in a file to appropriate number of spaces.
fmt *file name*	Format text to a specified width by filling empty lines for the specified file name.
head *file name*	Display the first ten lines of a file.
nl *file name*	Count the number of lines in a file.
od *file name*	Dump the specified files in octal format.
paste *one or more file names*	Merge lines of one or more files.
pr *file name*	Convert a text file to print.
split *file name*	Split a file into equal-sized files.
tac *file name*	Display files in reverse to standard output.
tail *file name*	Display the last ten lines of a file.
tr *{One format} {Another Format}*	Translate characters from one format to another and to the standard output.
unexpand *file name*	Convert white spaces to appropriate number of tabs for the specified file name.
uniq *file name*	Delete duplicate adjacent lines from a sorted file.
wc *file name*	Print the byte, word, and line counts of the specified file name.

Automatic Rotation

Automatic rotation is a system of regular rotation of logs to maintain a minimum log file size. The `logrotate` utility is used to perform automatic rotation. When executed, `logrotate` adds a .1 to the end of the file name of the current version of the log files. Previously rotated files are suffixed with .2, .3, and so on. Older logs have larger numbers at the end of their file names. Using automatic rotation, all copies of a file, with dates from when they were first created, will be stored. Log files can be rotated on a daily, weekly, or monthly basis. Automatic rotation saves disk space because older log files are pushed out when a size limit is reached.

The syslogd Utility

The *syslogd utility* tracks remote and local system logs. Logs are characterized by their host name and program field. The settings for `syslogd` are configured using the /etc/syslog.conf file.

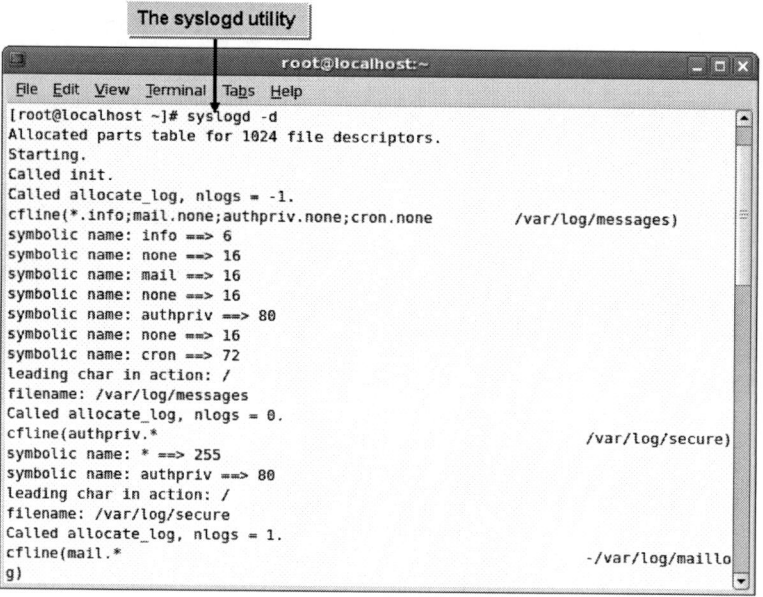

Figure 11-9: *Turning on the debug mode in the syslogd utility.*

The `syslogd` utility provides a number of options to manage specific functions. Some of the frequently used options are listed in the table.

Option	Used To
-d	Turn on the debug mode.
-f *file name*	Specify a new configuration file instead of /etc/syslog.conf.
-m *interval*	Specify a time interval between two lines.
-r	Enable the `syslogd` utility to receive messages from a network.

Syntax

The syntax of the `syslogd` utility is `syslogd [options]`.

The klogd Utility

The *kernel logging daemon (klogd)* tracks kernel messages by prioritizing them. It listens to the source for kernel messaging and intercepts the messages. `klogd` runs as a client of `syslogd`, where the kernel messages are sent through the `syslogd` daemon. `klogd` also acts as a standalone program.

The `klogd` command provides a number of options to manage specific functions. Some of the frequently used options are listed in the table.

Option	Enables You To
`-c` *n*	Set the default log level to n for messages. Where n ranges from 0 to 7.
	● 0–Emergency
	● 1–Alert
	● 2–Critical
	● 3–Error
	● 4–Warning
	● 5–Notice
	● 6–Information
	● 7–Debug
`-p`	Load the kernel module symbol information.
`-k` *file*	Use the specified file as the source to store the kernel module symbol information.
`-o`	Read and log all kernel messages in the buffer in a single read.
`-d`	Switch to a debugging mode.
`-f` *file*	Log messages to the file that is specified.
`-s`	Use the system call interface for buffering the kernel messages.

Syntax

The syntax of the `klogd` command is `klogd [options]`.

The /etc/syslog.conf File

The */etc/syslog.conf* file controls the location where the `syslogd` information is recorded. This file consists of two columns. The first column lists the facilities and severities of the messages. The second column lists the files the messages should be logged to. By default, most messages are stored in the /var/log/messages file.

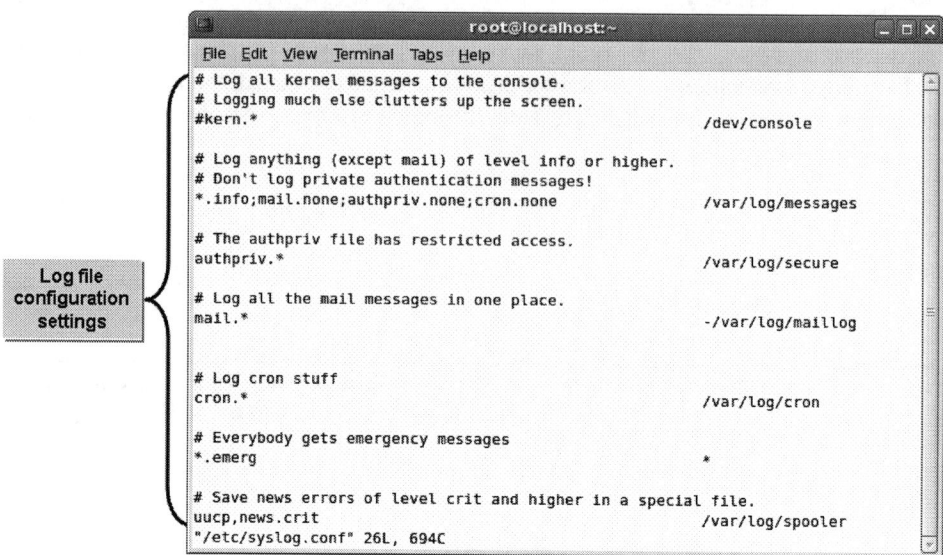

Figure 11-10: The syslog.conf file with the logging configuration settings.

Some applications maintain their own log files and directories independent of the syslog.conf file. Each service has its own log storage file. Some of the frequently used log files are listed in the table.

Log File	Description
/var/log/syslog	Stores the system log file, which contains information about the system.
/var/log/maillog	Stores mail messages.
/var/log/samba	Stores Samba messages.
/var/log/mrtg	Stores Multi Router Traffic Grapher (MRTG) messages.
/var/log/httpd	Stores Apache web server messages.

MRTG

MRTG is free software, licensed under GPL, that is used to monitor and measure the traffic load on network links. The traffic load on a network is represented in graphical form.

The Log File Analysis

The process of examining messages generated by logging daemons in log files is referred to as *log file analysis*. Log messages are created in a format that is specific to an application or a vendor, and are arranged in chronological order. During analysis, the format of log messages from different logging sources, such as operating systems, networks, and databases, is compared with a preset format. Also, log messages are categorized for each user with respect to the application, system, or system configuration accessed, to ensure user authentication.

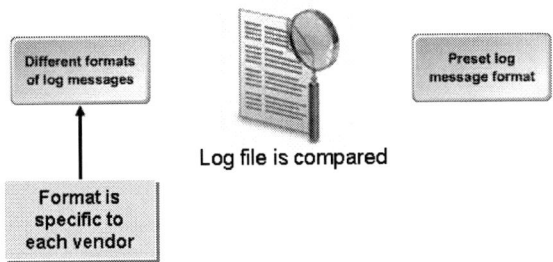

Figure 11-11: *Various steps involved in log file analysis.*

The lastlog Command

The *lastlog command* utilizes data from the /var/log/lastlog file to display the latest login details of all users. In addition to the login name, date, and time, it displays the terminal from where the user last logged in. The `lastlog` command is used by administrators to view user accounts that have never been used.

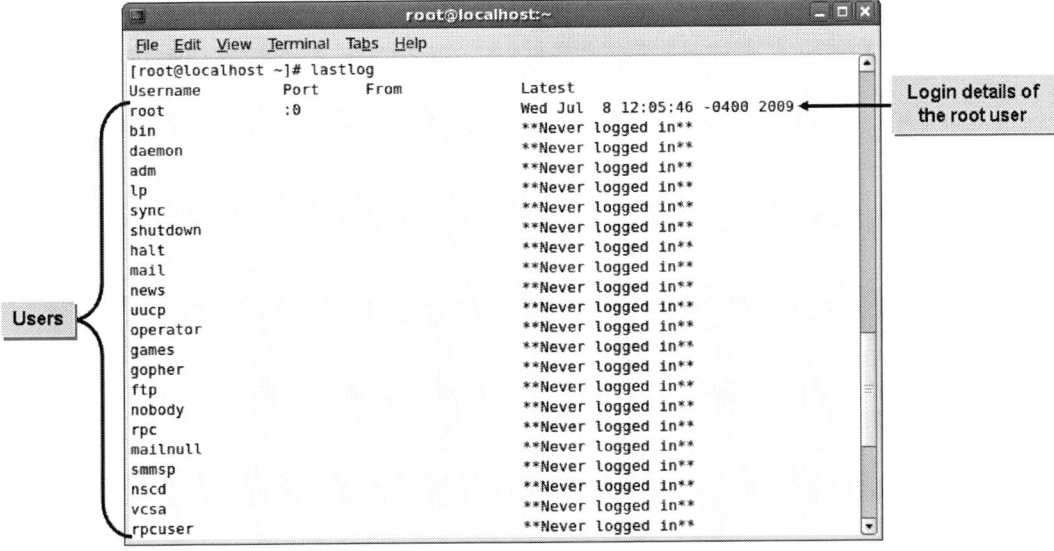

Figure 11-12: *The output of the lastlog command.*

The grep Command

The `grep` command searches a file or list of files for a string and prints the lines that match the search string. For example, you could search the file hardware.txt for all instances of the word "motherboard." The `grep` command has various options that allow you to specify search criteria.

The following table lists the options of the `grep` command.

Option	Used To
-h	Print matching lines without file names.
-w	Restrict the search to whole words only.
-c	Display a count of the number of matching lines and not the lines themselves.
-i	Ignore case while searching.
-l	List the file names that contain matching lines.
-n	Precede each line with the line number where it was found.
-s	Suppress the display of any error messages.
-e	Specify one or more patterns for searching.

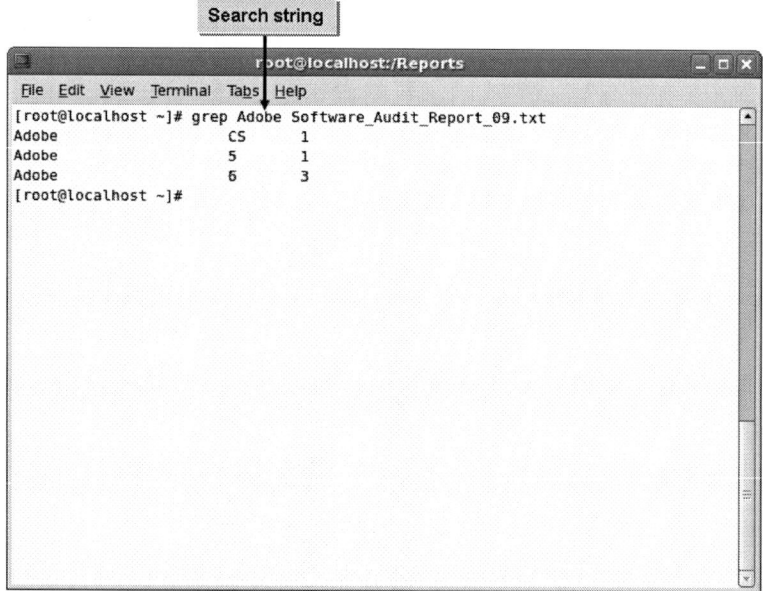

Figure 11-13: The grep command used to search for a string in a file.

Syntax

The syntax of the `grep` command is grep *[command options] {keyword} {file name}*.

The tail Command

The `tail` command is used to retrieve data from a file. By default, it displays the last ten lines of the file. The `tail` command has various options. Some of the frequently used options are listed in the table.

Option	Enables You To
`--retry`	Force the `tail` command to open a file that cannot be opened.
`-c {Total no. of bytes}`	Print the specified number of bytes from the end of a file.
`-f`	Update the output of the `tail` command if any changes are made to a file.

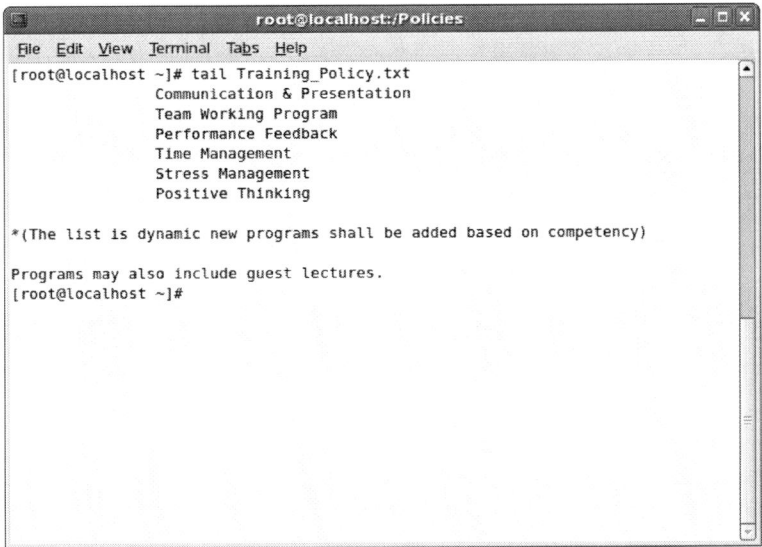

Figure 11-14: *The output of the tail command.*

Syntax

The syntax of the `tail` command is `tail [options] {file name}`.

The awk Command

The *awk command* is a command that performs pattern matching. The GNU's version of `awk` is called `gawk`. The `awk` keyword is followed by the pattern, the action to be performed, and the file name. The action to be performed is given within curly braces. The pattern and the action to be performed should be specified within single quotes. If the pattern is not specified, the action is performed on all input data; however, if the action is not specified, the entire line is printed. The `awk` command can be executed from the command line or from within an `awk` script file.

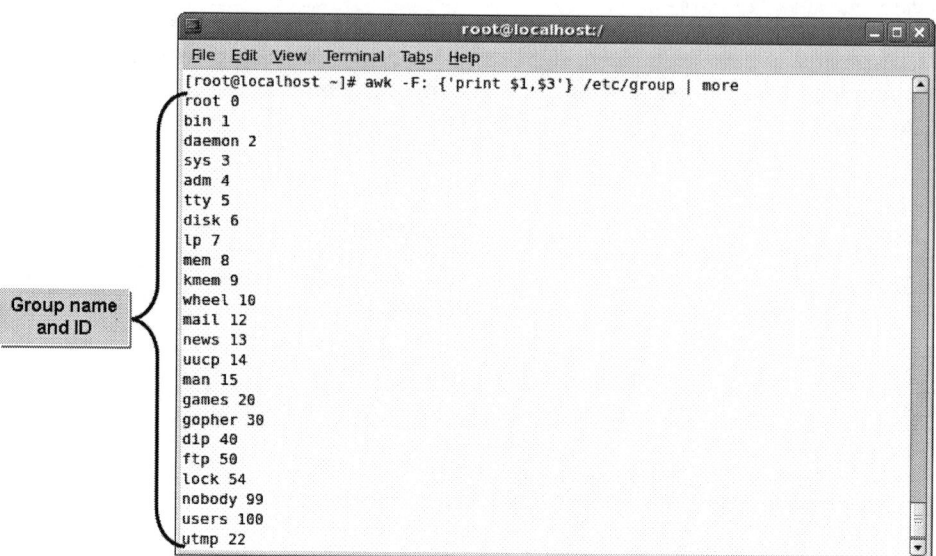

Figure 11-15: *Using the awk command to display only the group name and ID from the /etc/ group file.*

Syntax

The syntax of the `awk` command is `awk` *[options] {file}.*

Patterns

In awk scripts, you can provide patterns along with blocks of code. If a pattern matches any line in the input file, the code blocks in the script will be executed. The following table lists the types of patterns used.

Pattern	Description
/regular_expression/	Retrieves all records beginning with "a," "b," or "c."
	Example: /[abc]/
relational_expression	Retrieves all records whose first field contains the value "abc."
	Example: $1 == "abc"
pattern_1 && pattern_2	Retrieves all records whose first field contains the value "abc" and the second field contains the value "01."
	Example: ($1 == "abc") && ($2 == "01")
pattern_1 ‖ pattern_2	Retrieves records whose first field contains the value "abc" and the records whose second field contains the value "01."
	Example: ($1 == "abc") ‖ ($2 == "01")

Pattern	Description
pattern_1 ? pattern_2 : pattern_3	If the first field in a record contains the value "10," the fifth field is tested for its value. If the fifth record contains the value "20," then the record is printed. If the first field of a record does not contain the value "10," then the ninth field of the record is evaluated. If the ninth record contains the value "30," then the record is printed. Example: $1 == "10" ? $5 == "20" : $9 == "30"
pattern_1, pattern_2	Prints a range of records, starting from the record whose first field contains the value "01." The records will be printed until the awk command finds a record whose first field contains the value "02." Example: $1 == "01", $1 == "02"

The sed Command

The *sed command* is a command line program that can be used to modify log files or text files according to command line parameters. The sed command can be used for global search and replace actions. It has various options. Some of the common sed command options and their uses are given in the following table.

Option	Used To
d	Delete the specified lines.
-n,p	Print only the modified lines.
s	Substitute for first occurrence in the line.
s,g	Substitute globally for each occurrence in the line.

Syntax

The general syntax of the sed command is sed `'address/pattern/action' file name`. If there is an address, it follows the command name. The pattern formed by the user comes next, followed by the action to be performed when a match is found. The last argument is the name of the input file. The address, pattern, and action parameters are enclosed within single quotes.

How to Monitor System Logs

Procedure Reference: Configure System Logs

To configure system logs:

1. Log in as root.
2. Enter `gedit /etc/syslog.conf` to open the configuration file.
3. Type `Facility.Level of severity    /{Location of the file that stores the log messages}` to set the type and level of severity to be logged in the specified file.
4. Save and close the file.
5. Enter `service syslog restart` to restart the system log service and apply the changes.

Procedure Reference: Configure syslogd to Act as a Central Network Log Server

To configure `syslogd` to act as a central network log server:

1. Log in as root in the CLI.
2. Enter `gedit /etc/sysconfig/syslog` to open the syslog file.
3. Add the **-r** option to the **SYSLOGD_OPTIONS** parameter, **SYSLOGD_OPTIONS="-r -m 0."**
4. Save and close the file.
5. Enter `service syslog restart` to restart the `syslog` service.

Procedure Reference: Configure syslogd to Send Log Output to a Central Log Server

To configure `syslogd` to send the log output to a central log server:

1. Log in as root.
2. Enter `gedit /etc/syslog.conf` to open the system log configuration file.
3. Type `{Facility} {Level of severity} @{IP or FQDN of the log server}` to send the log output to a remote log server.
4. Save and close the file.
5. Enter `service syslog restart` to restart the system log service and apply the changes.

Procedure Reference: Search and Replace Strings

To search and replace strings:

1. Log in as a user in the CLI.
2. Search and replace strings.
   - Enter `sed 's/{old string}/{replacement string}/g' {file name}` to replace the old string with the replacement string even if multiple occurrences of the old string are found in a single line.
   - Enter `sed 's/Old string/Replacement string' file name` to replace only the first occurrence of the old string with the replacement string even if multiple occurrences of the old string are found in a single line.

Procedure Reference: Manually Extract Information from Log Files

To manually extract information from log files:

1. Enter `ls /var/log` to view the current list of system log files.

2. Use suitable commands to extract information from log files.

    ●   Enter `awk '{print ${column name} ${column name}}' file name}` to print the output of specific columns from the selected file.

    ●   Enter `grep -r "{d}"` to manually scan the log files and extract values that match the specific activity.

ACTIVITY 11-2
Configuring System Log Settings

Before You Begin:
1. You have logged in as root in the CLI.
2. Switch to the GUI.

Scenario:
As the system administrator, you are performing routine maintenance checks on network systems. You find that the logs show a couple of errors because they were not entered properly. You want only the warnings and alerts to be shown in the logs. So, you decide to configure the settings for syslog.

What You Do	How You Do It
1. Open the /etc/syslog.conf file.	a. Choose **Applications→Accessories→ Terminal** to open the terminal window.
	b. Enter **gedit /etc/syslog.conf** to open the syslog.conf file in the gedit program.
	c. Press **Ctrl+End** to move to the last line of the file.
2. Configure the syslog settings.	a. Type **mail 4 /var/log/test.log** to set the severity of the error to be logged for mail messages.
	b. Choose **File→Save** to save the file.
	c. Choose **File→Quit** to close the file and exit the **gedit** editor.
	d. On the terminal window, enter **service syslog restart** to restart the syslog service.
	e. Enter **clear** to clear the terminal window.

ACTIVITY 11-3
Configuring Syslogd

Before You Begin:
1. You have logged in as root in the GUI.
2. The terminal window is displayed.

Scenario:
As a system administrator, you want your system to act as the central server to store all system logs to easily track activities. To implement this, you connect additional users to your system. However, you want the messages to be automatically sent to your system and do not want to monitor each system individually. So, you decide to configure the system logs to accomplish your task.

What You Do	How You Do It
1. Configure syslogd to act as a central network log server.	a. Enter **gedit /etc/sysconfig/syslog** to open the syslog file in the gedit program.
	b. Choose **Search→Go to Line** to specify the line number to navigate to.
	c. In the text box, enter **6** to navigate to the sixth line containing SYSLOGD_ OPTIONS="-m 0"
2. Modify the settings in the /etc/ sysconfig/syslog file.	a. Position the cursor between " and **-m** in SYSLOGD_OPTIONS="-m 0".
	b. Add the **-r** option to the SYSLOGD_ OPTIONS parameter, to set it as **SYSLOGD_OPTIONS="-r -m 0"**.
	c. Choose **File→Save** to save the file.
	d. Choose **File→Quit** to close the file and exit the **gedit** editor.
3. Restart the syslog service.	a. Enter **service syslog restart** to restart the syslog service.
	b. Enter **clear** to clear the terminal window.

ACTIVITY 11-4
Analyzing Log Files

Before You Begin:

1. You have logged in as root in the GUI.
2. The terminal window is displayed.
3. Switch to the CLI.

Scenario:

Your manager asked you to analyze the log files and document the results. To do this, you need to:

- Monitor the usage of the root login to prevent unauthorized usage.
- Prepare a list of users with their login name, GID, and home directory.
- Generate a report with the group name and GID.

What You Do	How You Do It
1. Locate the instances of root login usage.	a. Enter **cd /var/log** to change to the log directory.
	b. Enter **grep "ROOT LOGIN" secure** to display the results of the root login.
	c. Observe the login details displayed in the results.
	d. Enter **clear** to clear the terminal screen.
2. Generate a list of users with their login name and other details.	a. Enter **cd /etc** to change to the etc directory.
	b. Enter **awk -F: {'print $1,$3,$6'} passwd** to list the login name, GID, and home directory for all users.
	c. Observe the details displayed for the user accounts.
	d. Enter **clear** to clear the terminal screen.

3. Generate a list of groups with GID.

    a. Enter **awk -F: {'print $1,$3'} group** to list the group name and GID for all groups.

    b. Observe the details displayed for the group accounts.

    c. Enter **clear** to clear the terminal screen.

TOPIC C
Configure SELinux

You monitored system log files to ensure that the changes made to the services are applied correctly. Information on a system needs to be protected from misuse or damage by using appropriate security measures, such as SELinux. In this topic, you will configure SELinux.

Even when the server is configured and running correctly, it is possible that security attacks may occur, which could be aimed at both organizations and individuals. Imagine that your company's servers are damaged and all your critical data are erased. You can prevent this by setting up the required security checks using SELinux.

Types of Access Controls

Access control is a method of restricting access to system resources. Only authorized programs will be allowed to access system resources. In Linux, there are two types of access controls.

Access Control Method	Description
Discretionary Access Control (DAC)	In DAC, the system checks the resources over which a user has access rights. The rights of the user are identified using the authentication information such as user identity and password.
	Under DAC, there are two types of permissions: the administrator permissions and the non-administrator permissions. For application programs to run, administrator access has to be provided. Administrator access provides full discretion over the filesystem and exposes it to security threats.
	For example, a malicious program or process started by a user having administrator access can damage data in a filesystem.
	DAC is the standard security strategy in Linux.

Access Control Method	Description
Mandatory Access Control (MAC)	In MAC, the system checks the resources over which a user does not have access rights. MAC is applied through SELinux. The rights of the user are identified using authentication such as the SELinux user identity, role, and type of access.
	MAC is the opposite of DAC, where permissions have to be defined for all processes (known as subjects) as to how they access resources (known as objects) such as files, directories, devices, memory resources, and other processes. An action is an operation, such as append, write, read, create, execute, and rename, that a subject can perform on the object. This is implemented using security policies that control the interaction between the processes and the objects.
	For example, when a subject tries to access an object, the security policy is checked to verify whether the subject is authorized to access the object before granting the access.

Security-Enhanced Linux

Security-Enhanced Linux (SELinux) is the default security enhancement feature provided with Red Hat Enterprise Linux, and is available on other distributions. It was developed by the U.S. National Security Agency while implementing various security policies on Linux operating systems. It provides additional filesystem and network security so that unauthorized processes cannot access or tamper with data, bypass security mechanisms, violate security policies, or execute untrustworthy programs. It enforces MACs on processes and resources, and allows information to be classified and protected based on its confidentiality and integrity requirements. This confines the damage caused to information by malicious applications.

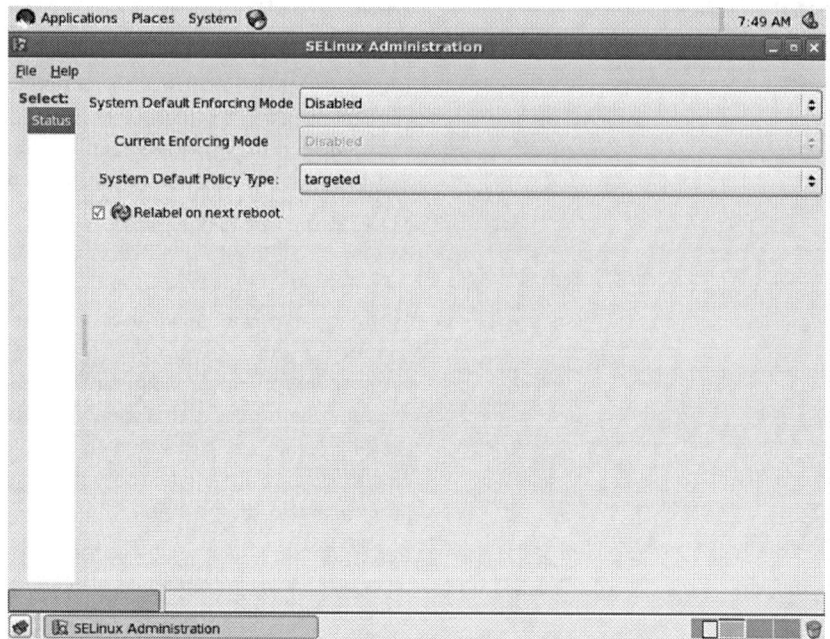

Figure 11-16: *The SELinux feature of Red Hat Enterprise Linux 5.*

 This feature comes as part of Red Hat Enterprise Linux (RHEL) 4 and the later versions.

SELinux Modes

SELinux has three different modes.

Mode	Description
Disabled	In this mode, SELinux is turned off. So, MAC will not be implemented and the default DAC method will be prevalent.
Enforcing	In this mode, all security policies are enforced. Therefore, processes cannot violate the security policies.
Permissive	In this mode, SELinux is enabled, but the security policies are not enforced. So, processes can bypass the security policies. However, when a security violation occurs, it is logged and a warning message is sent to the user.

Security Policies

A security policy defines access parameters for every process and resource on the system. Configuration files and policy source files located in the /etc/selinux directory can be configured by the root user.

Security Policy Type	Description
Targeted	According to the targeted policy, except the targeted subjects and objects, all other subjects and objects will run in an unconfined environment. The untargeted subjects and objects will operate on the DAC method and the targeted ones will operate on the MAC method. A targeted policy is enabled by default.
Strict	A strict policy is the opposite of a targeted policy, where every subject and object of the system is enforced to operate on the MAC method. However, a strict policy is not available in SELinux of the RHEL 5 version.

How to Configure SELinux

Procedure Reference: Control the SELinux State on the System

To control the SELinux state on the system:

1. Log in as root in the GUI.

2. Control the SELinux state on the system.

- To control the SELinux state using the /etc/sysconfig/selinux file:

    a. Enter vi /etc/sysconfig/selinux to open the selinux directory.

    b. Switch to the insert mode.

    c. Set SELINUX=*{enforcing | permissive | disabled}* to change the *SELINUX* variable to control the mode of the SELinux policy.

    d. Set SELINUXTYPE=*{targeted | strict}* to change the *SELINUXTYPE* variable to control the type of the SELinux policy.

    e. Save and close the file.

- Switch between the enforcing and permissive mode.

    a. Enter setenforce {1 | 0} to switch between the enforcing and the permissive mode, respectively.

    b. Enter getenforce to view the mode.

- To control the SELinux state using GUI tools:

    a. To open the **SELinux Administration** window:

    - Enter system-config-selinux to open the **SELinux Administration** utility.

    - In the **GNOME Panel,** choose **System→Administration→SELinux Management.**

b. Manage the SELinux settings.

- In the left pane, select **Status** to manage the mode and the policy type that are in the right pane.

- In the left pane, select **Boolean** to manage individual policies related to services that are in the right pane.

- If necessary, change other settings.

- On the menu bar, choose **File→Quit** to close the **SELinux Administration** window.

Procedure Reference: View the Security Context for Files and Processes

To view the security context for files and processes:

1. Log in as root in the CLI.

2. View the security context for files and processes.

- Enter `ls -Z [command option] {file or directory name}` to view the security context of the specified file or directory.

- Enter `ps -Z [command option] {process name}` to view the security context of the specified process.

Security Context

Security context is the collection of all security settings pertaining to processes, files, and directories. Security context consists of three elements: user, role, and type. Based on the security context attributes, SELinux decides how subjects access objects on the system.

Procedure Reference: Change the Security Context for Files

To change the security context for files:

1. Log in as root in the CLI.

2. Change the security context for files.

- Enter `chcon -[command option] {security context} {file or directory name}` to set the specified security context to the specified file or directory.

- Enter `restorecon {file or directory name}` to restore the default security context to the specified file or directory.

ACTIVITY 11-5
Configuring SELinux

Before You Begin:
On srvA, you have logged in as root in the CLI.

Scenario:
Your system contains confidential information that needs to be protected from any unauthorized access. You need to enable access control to prevent processes from reading or tampering data and programs, bypassing application security mechanisms, executing unauthorized programs, or interfering with other processes in violation of the system security policy.

What You Do	How You Do It
1. Configure the SELinux mode.	a. Enter `vi /etc/sysconfig/selinux` to configure the SELinux settings.
	b. Enter */SELINUX=disabled* to go to the SELinux mode configuration line.
	c. Press **I** to switch to the insert mode.
	d. Set **SELINUX=permissive** to configure access control.
2. Check the SELinux policy settings.	a. Verify that the security policy is set to **SELINUXTYPE=targeted.**
	b. Press **Esc** to switch to the command mode.
	c. Save and close the file.
	d. Enter `reboot` to apply the settings.

Lesson 11 Follow-up

In this lesson, you configured system services, monitored system logs, and configured SELinux. This will enable you to utilize your Linux system at its optimum level.

1.   How will you use system logs to troubleshoot system problems?

2.   Why is access control required?

12 Configuring Network Services

Lesson Time: 7 hour(s)

Lesson Objectives:

In this lesson, you will configure Linux services to provide users with network connectivity.

You will:

● Connect to a network.

● Configure routes.

● Configure DHCP services.

● Configure DNS servers.

● Implement network file sharing services.

● Configure NIS.

● Manage remote network systems.

Introduction

You configured basic Internet services on your computer. Sometimes, you may need to establish a connection with other computers to communicate with them. In this lesson, you will configure network services.

A network enables computers to communicate with each other and share data and software and hardware resources. Network services allow system administrators to disseminate information, administer systems remotely, enable communication through mail or chat systems, facilitate technology sharing, manage software licenses, and control unauthorized access.

This lesson covers all or part of the following CompTIA Linux+ (2009) certification objectives:

● Topic A

  ■ Objective 4.1

  ■ Objective 4.2

  ■ Objective 4.5

  ■ Objective 5.8

- Topic B
  - Objective 4.2
  - Objective 4.5
- Topic C
  - Objective 3.11
  - Objective 4.2
- Topic D
  - Objective 3.10
  - Objective 4.3
  - Objective 4.4
  - Objective 4.6
- Topic E
  - Objective 1.3
  - Objective 2.4
  - Objective 2.7
  - Objective 3.2
  - Objective 3.3
  - Objective 3.5
  - Objective 3.6
  - Objective 5.7
  - Objective 5.8
- Topic F
  - Objective 4.1
  - Objective 5.8
- Topic G
  - Objective 3.2
  - Objective 5.7

TOPIC A
Connect to a Network

You worked with data and other utilities solely on your computer. Sometimes, you may need to share data and devices with other computers on a network. In this topic, you will connect to a network.

As a network administrator, you will be managing and troubleshooting servers, network services, and workstations. To manage a network, you should understand the basic concepts of a network and its components. By connecting to a network, you will be able to implement network services required to efficiently manage a network with numerous systems.

Networks

Definition:

A *network* is a group of computers connected together, to communicate with each other and share resources. Each device on the network is referred to as a node. The components of a network are servers; clients; communication cables; resources, such as files or printers; network adapters; and network protocols.

Example:

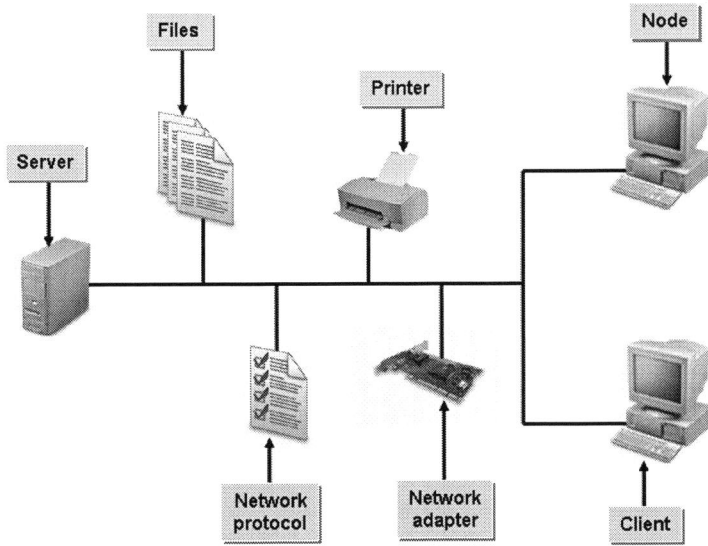

Figure 12-1: An example of a network.

Types of Networks

Networks can be broadly classified into two types based on their size.

Network Type	Description
Local Area Network (LAN)	A LAN is a network that connects computers in a small geographical area such as a floor or a building. Computers on a LAN are connected through Ethernet at speeds of 10 Mbps, 100 Mbps, or 1,000 Mbps. Compared to other types of networks, such as MAN and WAN, a LAN is a high-speed data network.
Wide Area Network (WAN)	A WAN is a network that connects computers in a wide geographical area. Computers on a WAN are connected through bridges, routers, hubs, and repeaters. This network can extend across a country or around the world. A WAN may connect LANs and MANs.

Metropolitan Area Network

A *Metropolitan Area Network (MAN)* is a network that connects computers in a broad geographical area such as a city and its suburbs. Computers on a MAN are connected through switches, access servers, and ISDN terminal adapters. This network is a medium-speed data network and can connect two or more LANs.

Network Protocols

Definition:

A *network protocol* is a set of rules that enable communication and data transfer among network devices. The rules specify how data should be shared among systems in the form of messages. The network protocol includes conventions that specify message acknowledgement or data compression. There are different types of protocols, including the Transmission Control Protocol/Internet Protocol (TCP/IP), Hyper Text Transfer Protocol (HTTP), and File Transfer Protocol (FTP).

Example: Data Transfer

TCP/IP contains rules that establish the method by which data is transmitted on virtually all networks today. It transmits data to the destination and acknowledges the source to ensure that the data is delivered.

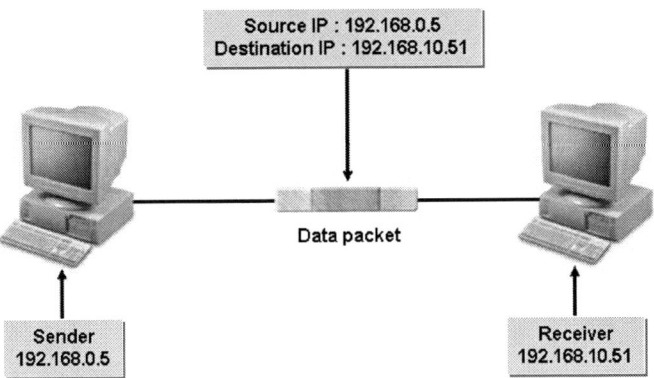

Figure 12-2: Data transmitted between two computers on a network.

Types of Network Protocols

A network protocol is chosen based on the network setup and network requirements. The protocols range from a high level to a low level, based on the network capacity.

Network Protocol	Description
Transmission Control Protocol/Internet Protocol (TCP/IP)	TCP/IP is used to transfer packets of data from one system to another on a network. TCP binds with IP and acts as a core layer for the Internet. TCP/IP guarantees that the packets are delivered in the same order in which they are sent.
HyperText Transfer Protocol (HTTP)	HTTP is used to transfer hypertext files across the World Wide Web. HTTP allows web browsers and web servers to communicate with each other to request a file and transfer contents. There are many versions of HTTP.
File Transfer Protocol (FTP)	FTP is used to send and receive files over the Internet. FTP is based on the client/server architecture. A user with an FTP client has to log on to a remote system, navigate to the filesystem, and upload and download files from that system.
Internet Control Message Protocol (ICMP)	ICMP is used to handle error and control messages. It does not transfer any application data but, transfers information about the status of the network. The *ping* utility uses ICMP for probe messages. It is useful in Internet protocol network management and administration.

IP Addresses

An *IP address* is a unique address that identifies a host on the Internet. It is a 32-bit binary number that is displayed as four decimal numbers, called octets, separated by periods (.). For example, 155.40.104.49 is an IP address.

The first two octets of the address identify the network on which a host resides, and the next two octets identify the host.

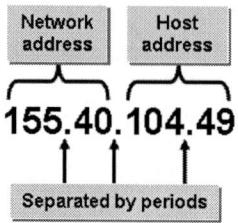

Figure 12-3: An IP address that identifies the network on which a host resides.

IP Versions

IP Version 4 (IPv4) and *IP Version 6 (IPv6)* are the two versions of the Internet protocol that are currently in use. With the number of hosts on the Internet growing at a fast pace, the earlier version, IPv4, which adopts a 32-bit addressing format, has limited unique IP addresses for public Internet access, apart from reserved and consumed addresses. There is a chance of running out of IP addresses and routing can become complicated. This can restrict future Internet access.

So, a new version of IP, called *IP Next Generation (IPng)* or IPv6, is being implemented on the Internet. The proposed Internet standard can increase the available pool of IP addresses by implementing a 128-bit binary address space. IPv6 also includes new efficiency features such as simplified address headers, hierarchical addressing, support for time-sensitive network traffic, and a new structure for unicast addressing.

IPv6 and IPv4 Compatibility

IPv6 is not compatible with IPv4; so at present, it is deployed on a limited number of test and production networks. Full adoption of the IPv6 standard will require a general conversion of IP routers to support interoperability.

Subnet Masks

Definition:

A *subnet mask* is a 32-bit number that is assigned to each system to divide the 32-bit binary IP address into network and node portions. This makes TCP/IP routable. A subnet mask uses a binary operation to remove the node ID from the IP address, leaving just the network portion. The network portion of an IP address can also be referred to as a net mask. Subnet masks use the value of eight 1s in binary, or 255 in decimal, to mask an entire octet of the IP address. A subnet mask acts as a filter that tells the server whether an IP address is on a local network or on a remote network. Subnet masks help routers identify whether a data packet needs to be retained on the local network or sent to another network.

Example:

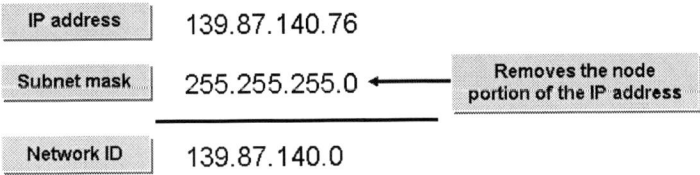

Figure 12-4: The subnet mask removes the node portion of the IP address.

IP Address Classes

The designers of the TCP/IP suite defined five ranges of addresses, called address classes, for specific network uses and sizes. Changes in the Internet, since the early 90s, have rendered classful addresses obsolete. One of the final remnants of classful addressing is the use of the terms Class A, Class B, and Class C to describe common subnet masks.

Class and Subnet Mask	Description
Class A 255.0.0.0	*Class A* subnet masks provide a small number of network addresses for networks with a large number of nodes per network. • Number of nodes per network: 16,777,214 • Network ID portion: First octet • Node ID portion: Last three octets Class A addresses are used only by extremely large networks. Large telephone companies and ISPs leased most Class A network addresses early in the development of the Internet.
Class B 255.255.0.0	*Class B* subnet masks offer a larger number of network addresses, each with fewer nodes per network. • Number of nodes per network: 65,534 • Network ID portion: First two octets • Node ID portion: Last two octets Most companies leased Class B addresses to use them on Internet-connected networks. In the beginning, there were plenty of Class B addresses to go around, but now there are few.
Class C 255.255.255.0	*Class C* addresses offer a large number of network addresses for networks with a small number of nodes per network. • Number of nodes per network: 254 • Network ID portion: First three octets • Node ID portion: Last octet Because there can be more Class C networks than any other type, they are the only addresses still available.

Classless Addressing

Because the traditional IP address classes have limitations on the number of available addresses in each class, there are now various implementations that utilize classless addressing. In these schemes, there is no strict dividing line between groups of addresses, and the network address or node address division is determined entirely by the number of 1 bits in the subnet mask.

Broadcast Addresses

Definition:

A *broadcast address* is a special IP address that is used to send messages to all hosts with the same network address. On IP networks, the general broadcast address is 255.255.255.255.

Example:

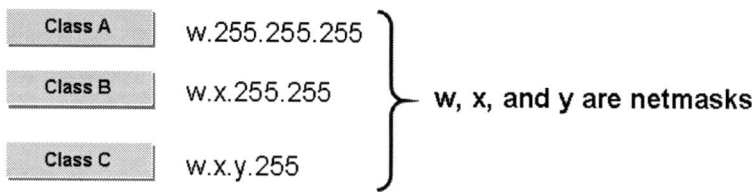

Figure 12-5: Broadcast address formats for the three classes.

Format of Broadcast Addresses

A broadcast address may vary depending on the class of the IP address. The following table lists the format of different broadcast addresses for different classes of octets w.x.y.z.

Class	Subnet Mask	Netmask/ Network Part	Host Part	Broadcast Address
A	255.0.0.0	w	x.y.z	w.255.255.255
B	255.255.0.0	w.x	y.z	w.x.255.255
C	255.255.255.0	w.x.y	z	w.x.y.255

Ports

Definition:

On a network, a *port* is an access point to a logical connection. It serves as a channel through which information can be exchanged directly among networked computers. Many ports can operate simultaneously on a computer to provide services to different applications. A unique port number identifies the type of application that is sending or receiving data. It also informs the computer as to which application program running on the computer should process the data that is being sent or received through a particular port. Ports are identified by numbers between 0 and 65,536.

Example:

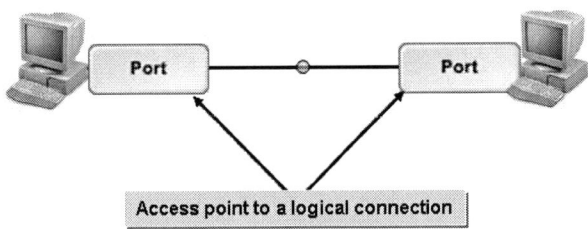

Figure 12-6: Transfer of data through ports on a network.

Allocation of Port Numbers

Just as several people live at the same address, such as in an apartment, multiple network applications may reside at the same IP address. In an apartment, suite numbers may be used in conjunction with the street address to identify which occupant should receive a mail. Similarly, the IP address along with a specific port number is allocated for different applications.

There is a scheme for identifying specific applications that share an IP address—and that is the addition of a port to the IP address. For example, a web server and an FTP server may both run on the same server, at 24.95.112.13. Web servers typically are set up to run on port 80, and FTP servers run on port 21. To identify the FTP server, you could use the address 24.95.112.13:21. The colon character separates the port address from the rest of the IP address.

Most servers enable the administrator to specify the port on which a service should run. The ability to specify the port number can be useful when multiple services, such as two web servers, are running on the same computer. One server may run on port 80 and the other on port 81.

Ports Allocated for Different Services

Ports can be allocated to different services based on the types of applications supported by a network.

Port Number	Description
1	TCP Port Service Multiplexer (TCPMUX)
5	Remote Job Entry (RJE)
7	ECHO
18	Message Send Protocol (MSP)
20	File Transfer [Default Data] (FTP–Data)
21	File Transfer [Control] (FTP–Control)
22	Secure Shell Login (SSH)
23	Telnet
25	Simple Mail Transfer Protocol (SMTP)
29	MSG ICP
37	Time
42	Host Name Server
43	WhoIs
49	Login Host Protocol

Port Number	Description
53	Domain Name System (DNS)
69	Trivial File Transfer Protocol (TFTP)
70	Gopher Services
79	Finger
80	HTTP
103	X.400 Standard
108	SNA Gateway Access Server
109	POP2
110	POP3
115	Simple File Transfer Protocol (SFTP)
118	SQL Services
119	Network News Transfer Protocol (NNTP)
123	Network Time Protocol
137	NetBIOS Name Service
139	NetBIOS Datagram Service
143	Interim Mail Access Protocol (IMAP)
150	NetBIOS Session Service
156	SQL Server
161	SNMP
179	Border Gateway Protocol (BGP)
190	Gateway Access Control Protocol (GACP)
194	Internet Relay Chat (IRC)
197	Directory Location Service (DLS)
389	Lightweight Directory Access Protocol (LDAP)
396	Novell Netware over IP
443	HTTPS
444	Simple Network Paging Protocol (SNPP)
546	DHCP Client
547	DHCP Server
631	Internet Printing Protocol (IPP)
1080	Socks
3306	MySQL

Port Ranges

The Internet Assigned Numbers Authority (IANA), an international agency, separates port numbers into three blocks: well-known ports, which are preassigned to system processes; registered ports, which are available to user processes and are listed as a convenience; and dynamic ports, which are assigned by a client operating system when there is a request for service.

Block	Description
Well-known ports	Port range: 0 to 1,023. Well-known ports are pre-assigned for use by common, or well-known, services. Often the services that run on these ports must be started by a privileged user. Services in this range include HTTP on TCP port 80, IMAP on TCP port 143, and DNS on UDP port 53.
Registered ports	Port range: 1,024 to 49,151. These ports are registered by software makers for use by specific applications and services that are not as well known as the services in the well-known range. Services in the registered port range include SOCKS proxy on TCP port 1080, Kazaa peer-to-peer file sharing on TCP port 1214, and Xbox Live on TCP and UDP port 3074.
Dynamic or private ports	Port range: 49,152 to 65,535. These ports are set aside for use by unregistered services and by services that need a temporary connection.

Network Interfaces

A *network interface* is a point of connection between two systems. It can be implemented using hardware or software. There are different types of network interfaces.

Network Interface Type	Description
Physical	A physical network interface is implemented using a hardware device.
	For example, an Ethernet interface (denoted by ethX, where X refers to the number of the interface) is set up using a Network Interface Card (NIC).
Virtual	A virtual network interface is implemented through software support.
	For example, a loopback interface (*lo*) simulates a network interface without the help of a physical device. It is used to test network connectivity and accuracy of data transmission by sending data back to the generating source address.

Network Interface Cards

Definition:

A *Network Interface Card (NIC)* is a small circuit board that enables a computer to connect to a network. A network interface is created between two or more computers using NIC. To connect to different networks—such as a wired or a wireless network—more than one NIC can also be installed on a computer. The different NICs connected to a system are numbered. The NIC can be built into the motherboard of the computer, connected through a USB port, or can be an internal or external adapter card that is installed into one of the computer's expansion slots. After the NIC is installed, it has to be configured to connect to a particular network using the required network addresses and settings.

Example:

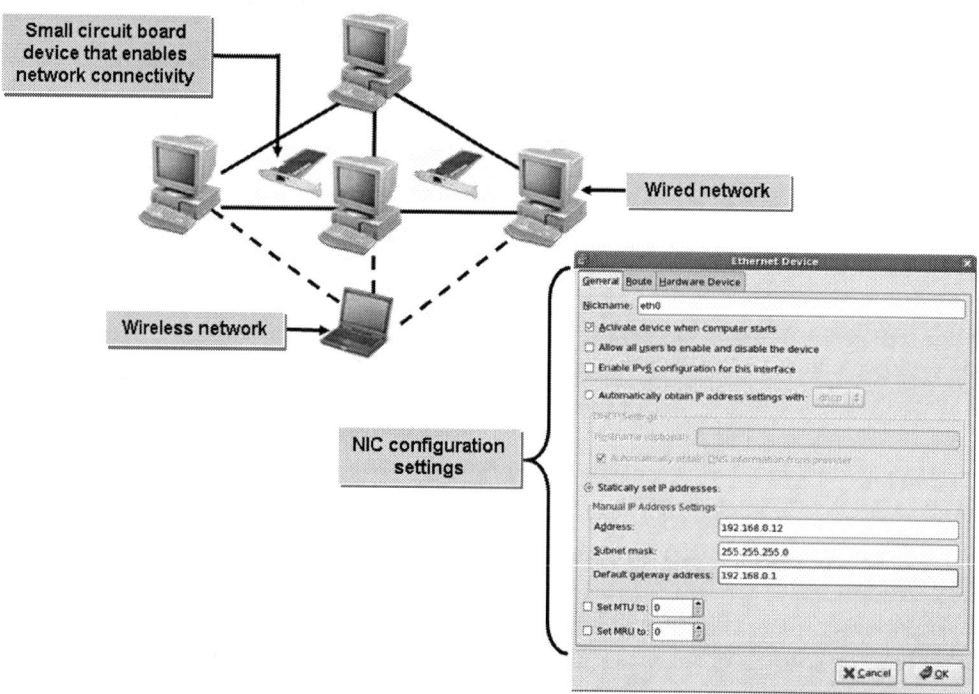

Figure 12-7: A NIC helps to connect computers and other devices on a network.

NIC Characteristics

NICs have some special characteristics that distinguish them from other types of adapter cards.

Characteristic	Description
Network connection port	Network adapter cards will have one or more ports that are configured to connect specifically to a given type of network cable. Some older cards had several types of ports so that they could connect to several different types of network cable. Network connections today are standardized and almost all use one port type.

Characteristic	Description
Physical network address	Each network adapter has a globally unique *physical address* burned onto the card by the card manufacturer. The physical address uniquely identifies every individual card that connects to the network cable or media. For this reason, the physical address is also called the *Media Access Control (MAC) address.* MAC addresses are six bytes long. A typical MAC address may appear as 00-00-86-47-F6-65, where the first three bytes are the vendor's unique ID and the next three uniquely identify that card's vendor.
Status indicator lights	Network adapters, including those built into most network devices, typically have one or more *Light Emitting Diodes (LEDs)* that can provide information on the state of the network connection.
	• Most adapters have a *link light* that indicates if there is a signal from the network. If the link light is not lit, there is a problem with the cable or the physical connection.
	• Most adapters also have an *activity light* that flickers when packets are received or sent. If the light flickers constantly, the network may be overused or there may be a device generating network noise.
	• Some multi-speed adapters have a *speed light* to show whether the adapter is operating at 10 Mbps (Ethernet), 100 Mbps (Fast Ethernet), or 1,000 Mbps (Gigabit Ethernet).
	• Some types of equipment combine the functions of more than one light into *dual-color* LEDs. For example, a green flickering light may indicate normal activity, while an orange flickering light indicates network traffic collisions.

The ifconfig Command

The *ifconfig command* is used for configuring network interfaces for Linux servers and workstations. It is also used to view the current TCP/IP configuration of a system, including the IP address and the netmask address.

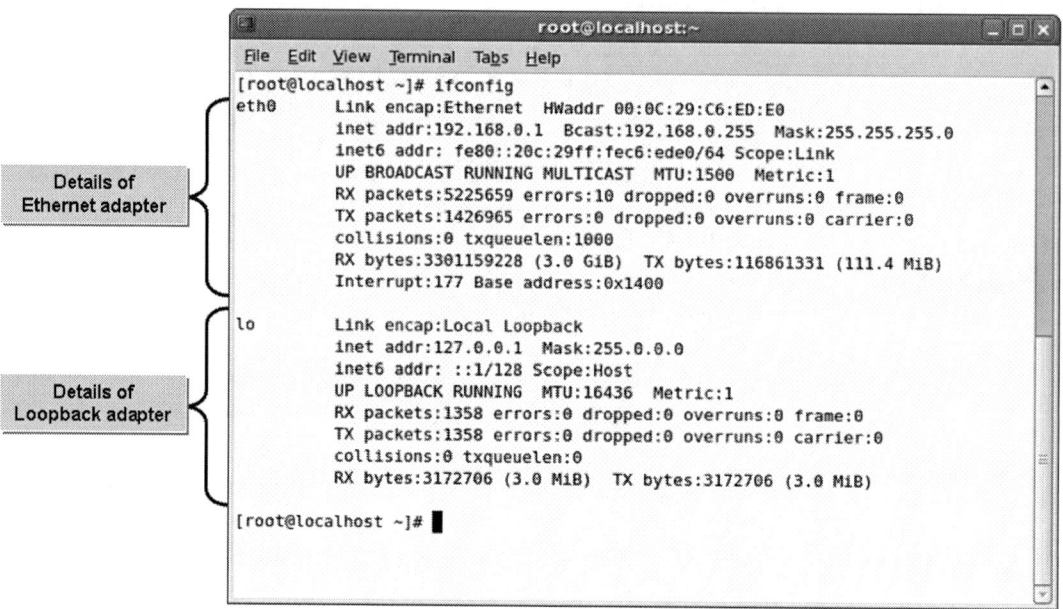

Figure 12-8: The output of the ifconfig command.

Syntax

The syntax of the *ifconfig* command is `ifconfig {interface name} {options or address}`.

The ifconfig Command Options

The `ifconfig` command has many options. The most frequently used options are provided in the following table.

Option	Function
up	Activates the interface.
down	Deactivates the interface.
address	Sets the IP address.
netmask addr	Sets the network mask for the interface.
dstaddr addr	Sets the remote IP address.

The ifconfig Command Interface

Linux provides an interface to the `ifconfig` command that makes configuration of a network device very simple. This interface is made up of the `ifup` and `ifdown` commands and two or more configuration files. The configuration files are the /etc/sysconfig/network file, which specifies the network configuration, and one or more files in the /etc/sysconfig/network-scripts directory, which contain device-specific networking information. For a system with a single Ethernet card, device-specific information is stored in the /etc/sysconfig/network-scripts/ifcfg-eth0 file.

The `ifup` and `ifdown` commands are used to start and stop specific network devices, respectively. The syntax of these commands is *[command] [device name]*, where *[command]* is either `ifup` or `ifdown` and *[device name]* is the name of the device such as eth0, eth1, and so on.

Because the `ifup` and `ifdown` commands control only a single network device, it is often easier to use the `/etc/init.d/network` command with the `start` or `stop` parameters. This command starts (or stops) all network devices simultaneously.

The iwconfig Command

The *iwconfig command* is used for configuring wireless network interfaces for Linux servers and workstations. It is similar to the `ifconfig` command, except that it is used to set and view the parameters of wireless network interfaces.

Syntax

The syntax of the *iwconfig* command is `iwconfig {interface name} {options or address}`.

The iwconfig Command Options

The `iwconfig` command has various options, which are provided in the following table.

Option	Function
essid	Sets the ESSID, also called network name or domain ID, which is used to identify cells that are part of the same virtual network.
nwid/domain	Sets the network ID, which differentiates the wireless network from other networks and identifies nodes belonging to the same cell.
nick	Sets the nickname or the station name that is used by some wireless tools.
mode	Sets the operating mode of the device.
freq/channel	Sets the operating frequency or channel of the device.
ap	Registers the access point given by the address.
rate/bit	Sets the bit-rate.
txpower	Sets the transmit power.
sens	Sets the sensitivity threshold.
retry	Sets the maximum number of retries.
rts	Sets the size of the smallest packet for which the node sends Request To Send (RTS).
frag	Sets the maximum size for fragments that can be transferred.
key/enc	Sets the encryption or scrambling keys and security mode.
power	Sets power management parameters.
commit	Applies all pending changes.

Cell

A cell is a network zone covered under a tower or access point.

RTS

RTS is a signal sent by a communication device to a receiving device, to verify if the receiving device is ready to accept the data that is to be sent to it. For example, a modem sends an RTS to a computer before it transmits data.

Subnets

Subnets are logical subsections of a single large network. Each segment requires its own network address and host identifiers, and it is treated as a subnet of the original network. Subnets are used in large organizations, such as universities and corporations, where it is necessary to divide the network into smaller, more manageable segments.

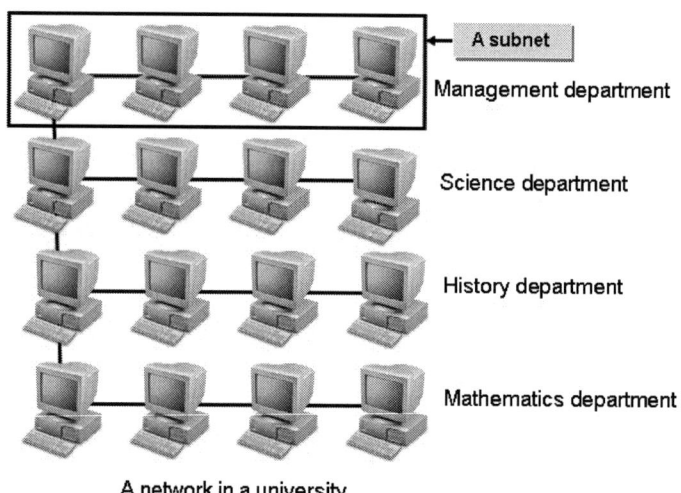

A network in a university

Figure 12-9: A subnet in a University network.

The Lightweight Directory Access Protocol

Definition:

The *Lightweight Directory Access Protocol (LDAP)* is a communication protocol that defines the transport and format of messages used by a client to access the *directory service*. LDAP stores information in a directory in the form of a hierarchical tree structure. It authenticates users before they are allowed to query or modify the information that resides in a directory. LDAP is run on TCP/IP networks.

Example:

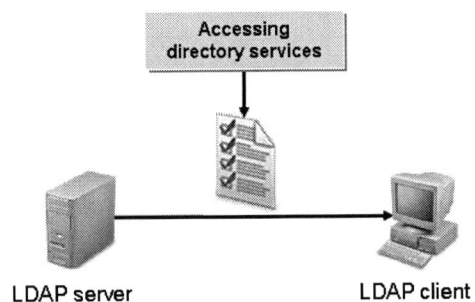

Figure 12-10: A client accessing directory service through LDAP.

LDAPv3

LDAPv3 provides strong authentication and data security to Internet protocols using the *Simple Authentication and Security Layer (SASL)*. LDAPv3 controls extended operations and is internationalized through the use of Unicode. It provides secure transmission of data through the *Secure Socket Layer (SSL)*.

The Stand-Alone LDAP Daemon

The *Stand-alone LDAP Daemon (slapd)* is an LDAP directory service. The slapd allows users to create and provide their own directory service that can be connected to the global LDAP directory service. It supports different platforms and provides a certification-based authentication. It can be configured dynamically using LDAP, and the configuration file slapd.conf is created in the /etc/openldap directory. The slapd directory service provides the features of data security, TCP wrappers, access control based on the LDAP authentication information, domain name and IP address, and high-performance database back-end. It also supports in configuring multiple databases simultaneously, multi-threading, creating shadow copies of directory service, and providing LDAP proxy service.

The LDAP Process

The LDAP directory service is a client-server model that enables network clients to use the directory service available on servers. The following stages are involved with the LDAP process.

1. The LDAP client sends a request to access the directory service.

2. The LDAP server accepts the request and authenticates the user. If the user is valid, it allows the user to access the directory service. Otherwise, it returns an error message.

3. The user sends a request to the server, to search for information.

4. The server processes the request. It sends either the result or a pointer where the information is available to the client.

5. The client uses the information sent by the server.

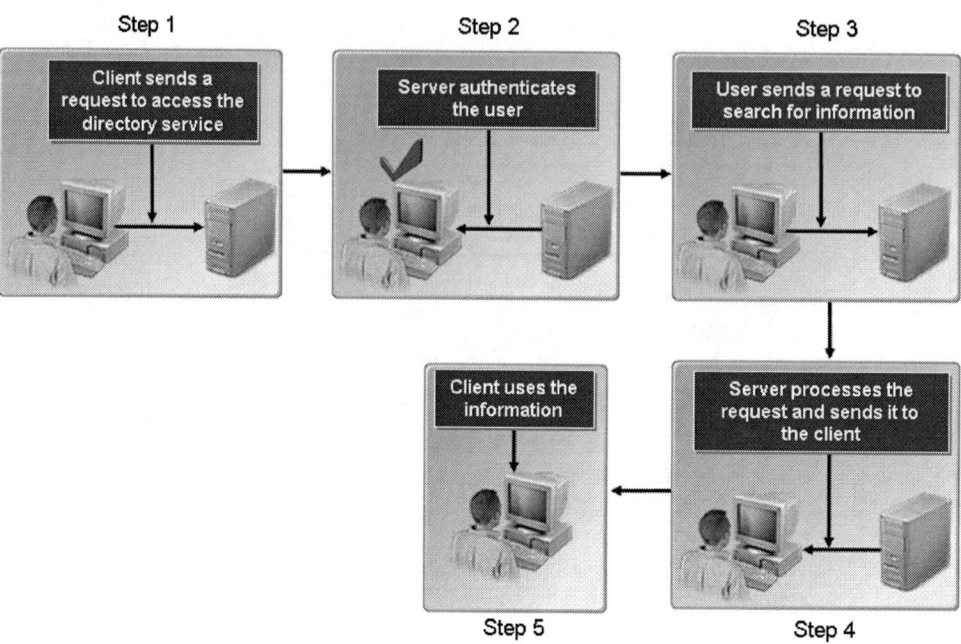

Figure 12-11: *The different stages in the LDAP process.*

How to Connect to a Network

Procedure Reference: Configure a NIC Manually

To manually configure a NIC:

1. Log in as root in the CLI.
2. Enter `service network stop` to stop the network service.
3. Enter `cd /etc/sysconfig/network-scripts`.

 The /etc/sysconfig/network-scripts/ directory contains various network scripts, such as ifcfg-eth0, that will be executed whenever the system starts up.

4. Enter `vi ifcfg-{Device name}`.
5. Make the necessary changes in the file.
   - Change **BOOTPROTO=dhcp** to **BOOTPROTO=static** and press **Enter** to change the booting protocol to static.
   - Type `IPADDR={IP Address}` and press **Enter** to specify the IP address of the NIC.
   - Type `NETMASK={Netmask}` to specify the netmask address.
6. Save and close the file.
7. Enter `service network start` to restart the network service.

BOOTPROTO

The *BOOTPROTO* is a variable that is used to specify the mode in which a NIC is configured. If **BOOTPROTO=static**, then the NIC will be configured manually. If **BOOTPROTO=dhcp**, then the NIC will contact the DHCP server to get the IP information.

Procedure Reference: Configure a NIC Automatically

To automatically configure a NIC:

1. Ensure that the DHCP server is configured and running. If necessary, check with your system administrator.

 A DHCP server automatically allocates IP addresses to a client.

2. Log in as root in the CLI on a client system.
3. Enter `cd /etc/sysconfig/network-scripts`.
4. Enter `vi ifcfg-{Device name}` to open the device file.
5. Modify **BOOTPROTO=static** to **BOOTPROTO=dhcp** to change the booting protocol to dhcp.
6. Save and close the file.
7. Enter `service network restart` to restart the network service.
8. If necessary, enter `ping -[options] [Destination IP address]` to check the network connectivity.

The pump and dhcpclient Commands

The `pump` and `dhcpclient` commands were used by older versions of Linux to get the IP address from the DHCP server. In the latest version, when you configure **BOOTPROTO=dhcp** in the /etc/sysconfig/network-scripts/ifcfg-{Device name} file and restart the network service, it automatically gets the IP address from the DHCP server.

The ping Command Options

The `ping` command is used to test network connectivity. A few frequently used `ping` command options are described in the following table.

If You Need To	Use This `ping` Option
Ping the destination IP address for a specified number of times.	`-c {Number}`
Ping the destination IP address at regular intervals.	`-i {Number}`
Broadcast the ICMP packages for a specified network.	`-b {Broadcast ID}`

The ping Command Restriction

Because the `ping` command generates ICMP traffic to the target hosts, a firewall can be set to block this traffic. Therefore, the `ping` command should be relied upon only when there are no known firewalls blocking the ICMP traffic.

Procedure Reference: Set a Temporary IP Address and Establish a Temporary Connection with Other Networks

To set a temporary IP address and establish a temporary connection with other networks:

1. Log in as root in the CLI.
2. Enter `service network status` to view the status of the active devices.
3. Enter `ifconfig` to view the details of all the configured devices.
4. Enter `ifconfig -a eth[Number] [New IP address]` to set a temporary IP address to the specified NIC device.
5. If necessary, enter `service network restart` to revert to the original IP address.

Procedure Reference: Add a New NIC

To add a new NIC:

1. Install the NIC.
   a. shutdown the system and disconnect it from the power source.
   b. Remove the cabinet.
   c. Insert the NIC card in the free PCI slot.
   d. Close the cabinet.
   e. Connect the network cable to the NIC.
   f. Connect to the power source and restart the system.
2. Log in as root in the CLI.
3. Enter `cd /etc/sysconfig/network-scripts` to navigate to the network-scripts directory.
4. Enter `touch ifcfg-eth{Device name}` to create a blank file.
5. Enter `vi ifcfg-eth{Device name}`.
6. Type `DEVICE=eth{Device name}` and press **Enter** to specify the device name.
7. Type `ONBOOT=yes` and press **Enter** to automatically activate the device when the system starts.
8. Type `BOOTPROTO=static` and press **Enter.**
9. Type `IPADDR={IP Address}` and press **Enter.**
10. Type `NETMASK={Netmask}`.
11. Save and close the file.
12. Enter `service network restart` to restart the network service.

Procedure Reference: Disable a NIC

To disable a NIC:

1. Log in as root in the CLI.

2. Disable the NIC.

- Enter `cd /etc/sysconfig/network-scripts` and delete the corresponding `ifcfg-eth{Number}` file in the directory.

- Or, enter `ifdown eth{Number}`.

To enable the NIC, the `ifup eth{Number}` command is given.

Delete a NIC

To delete any NIC devices, delete the corresponding `ifcfg-eth{Number}` file located in the /etc/sysconfig/network-scripts/ directory.

A NIC does not have to be physically removed from a system to delete it.

Procedure Reference: Configure a Wireless Network Interface Using the iwconfig Command

To configure a wireless network interface using the `iwconfig` command:

1. Log in as root in the CLI.

2. Specify the different parameters for the wireless interface.

- Enter `iwconfig {device number} essid {ess id | network name}` to set the network name for the wireless device.

- Enter `iwconfig {device number} nwid {network id | domain id}` to set the network id for the wireless device.

- Enter `iwconfig {device number} nickname {nickname}` to specify the nickname for the wireless device.

- Enter `iwconfig {device number} mode {Ad-Hoc|Managed|Master|Repeater|Secondary|Monitor|Auto}` to set the mode of the wireless device.

- Enter `iwconfig {device number} freq|channel {frequency value | channel number}` to set the frequency or channel for the wireless device.

- Enter `iwconfig {device number} ap {access point id}|any|off` to set the access point for the wireless device.

- Enter `iwconfig {device number} rate {bit rate}|auto` to set the bit-rate for the wireless device.

- Enter `iwconfig {device number} key {key value}` to set the encryption key for the wireless device.

3. View the details of the configured wireless devices.
    - Enter `iwconfig` to view the details of all the configured wireless devices.
    - Enter `iwconfig {device number}` to view the details of a specific wireless device.

4. Restart the network service to apply the changes.

Procedure Reference: Configure the LDAP Client

To configure the LDAP client:

1. Log in as root in the CLI.
2. Enter `authconfig-tui` to use the **Authentication Configuration** utility to configure the LDAP client.
3. In the **Authentication** section, select **Use LDAP Authentication.**
4. Press **F12** to go to the next screen.
5. If necessary, in the **LDAP Settings** screen, check the **Use TLS** option to transfer the encrypted password.
6. In the **Server** text box, type the LDAP server information.
7. In the **Base DN** text box, type the base distinguished name.
8. Press **F12** to finish and close the wizard.

ACTIVITY 12-1
Connecting to a Network Manually

Before You Begin:
1. The system, srvB, is rebooted and the GUI login screen is displayed.
2. Log in to the GUI as root.
3. Switch to the first terminal of the CLI.

Scenario:
You are working as a system administrator in a startup company. Your responsibilities include setting up and configuring network connectivity in your organization. An employee has joined your organization. You need to assign the employee a system and make it part of the existing network. The network configuration details of the system are as follows:

- IP address of the system: 192.168.0.248
- Netmask: 255.255.255.0

What You Do	How You Do It
1. Identify the IP address of the system.	a. Log in as **root** in the CLI.
	b. Enter **ifconfig** to view the inet addr: 192.168.0.*X*.

 inet addr or InetAddress is a class that identifies the IP address of a host on a network.

 *X* represents the different host octet values provided by the DHCP server to all students.

c. Observe that the results contain details about Ethernet and loopback devices. In addition, observe that the HWaddr is displayed along with the details about the received (RX) and transmitted (TX) packets.

d. Enter **clear** to clear the terminal screen.

2. Configure the IP address manually.

   a. Enter `cd /etc/sysconfig/network-scripts` to change to the network-scripts directory.

   b. Enter `vi ifcfg-eth0` to open the device file.

   c. Observe that the default configuration of the NIC is displayed.

   d. Change `BOOTPROTO=dhcp` to `BOOTPROTO=static` and press **Enter.**

   e. Enter `IPADDR=192.168.0.X` to set the IP address for the NIC device.

   f. Enter `NETMASK=255.255.255.0` to specify the netmask address.

   g. Press **Esc** to switch to the command mode.

   h. Save and close the file.

   i. Enter `service network restart` to restart the network service.

   j. Enter `clear` to clear the terminal screen.

3. Test the network connectivity.

   a. Enter `ping -c 5 192.168.0.2` to check network connectivity.

   b. Observe that the response from **192.168.0.2** is displayed five times with the **ttl** and **time,** which indicates that the network is functional. In addition, observe that the statistics section displays details about the number of packets transmitted and received, percentage of packet loss, and total time taken.

   c. Enter `clear` to clear the terminal screen.

TOPIC B
Configure Routes

You configured the IP settings for network interfaces. Routing allows you to manage data transmission traffic on networks. It enables data to be transmitted from a source to its destination through different routes. In this topic, you will configure routes.

Computers on a network interact with each other simultaneously at numerous instances. If one computer on a network communicates with many computers at the same time, and if the data transmission routes or communication paths are not configured, it may lead to a system crash due to flooding of information. Therefore, the routes for information transmission have to be configured to avoid collision in network traffic.

Routers

Definition:

A *router* is a networking device that connects multiple networks. Routers enable data to be exchanged among networks by examining and determining the best network path for data to travel. A router can be a dedicated device or can be implemented as a software application running on a network enabling device.

Example:

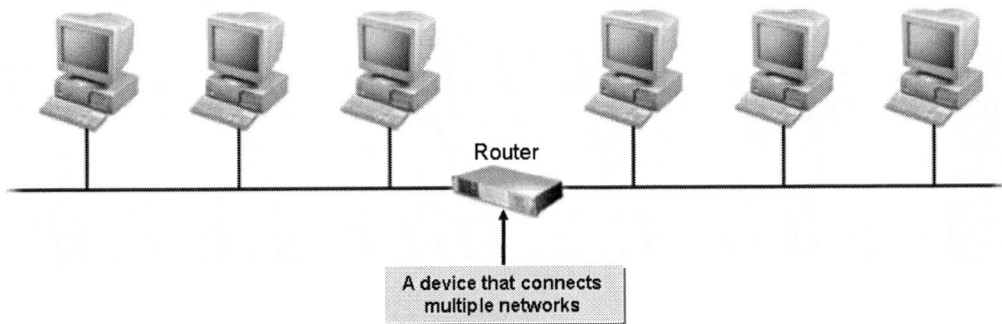

Figure 12-12: A router connecting two networks.

Routing

Definition:

Routing is the process of selecting the best route for moving data packets from a source to its destination on a network. To assist the process of routing, a router applies appropriate algorithms to generate and maintain an information base about network paths. It considers various metrics, such as the path bandwidth, path reliability, and communication costs, while evaluating the available network paths to determine the optimal route for forwarding a packet. Once the optimal route for a packet is assigned, packet switching is done to transfer the packet from the source host to the destination host.

Example:

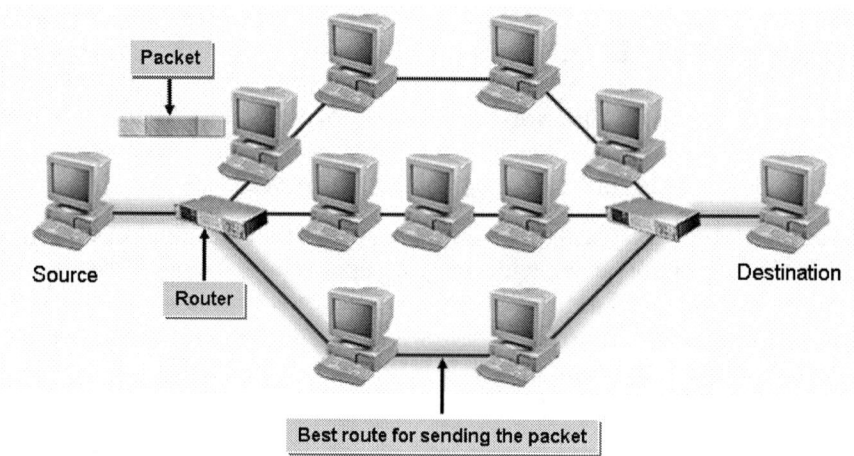

Figure 12-13: Example of routing on a network.

Packets

A *packet* is a formatted unit of data being sent across a network. In addition to the user data, it comprises control information, such as the source and destination addresses, which is required to deliver the user data. A packet is also known as a *datagram*.

Packet-Switching Technology

Packet-switching technology is used for transmitting data among computers on a network. In a packet-switched network, a message is broken into packets, which are transmitted individually or switched to their required destination. During the process, each packet may follow a different path, but at the destination, the packets are reassembled to form the original message sent from the main destination. This technology ensures greater routing and transporting efficiency on a network. The Internet is a packet-switched network.

Benefits of Packet-Switched Networking

The benefits of a packet-switched network lie in the underlying technology of dividing a message to be sent over the Internet into packets. When data is transported in packets rather than in one big stream of data, the packets do not all have to move through the same path. Because the data is broken up into small packets, the packets can be sent across the Internet over various paths, eventually (in a fraction of a second) reaching their destination, where the packets can be reassembled into the original data. This means that one or more of the smaller networks, which make up the Internet, can go out of service without preventing the packets from ultimately reaching their destination, because the packets can simply take a different path to get there. If a few packets never reach their destination, they can be resent over a different path.

If files were not broken up into smaller packets, the entire file will have to be resent if any part of it did not reach the destination intact. Having multiple paths and breaking up files into small packets increase the reliability of the network.

Routing Tables

Routers exchange information with each other by building a table of network addresses. This information base is called a *routing table*. Routers refer to this table to determine where to forward the packets. If a router that is attached to four networks receives a packet from one of these networks, it will determine which of the other three networks is the best route to send the packet so that it could reach its destination quickly.

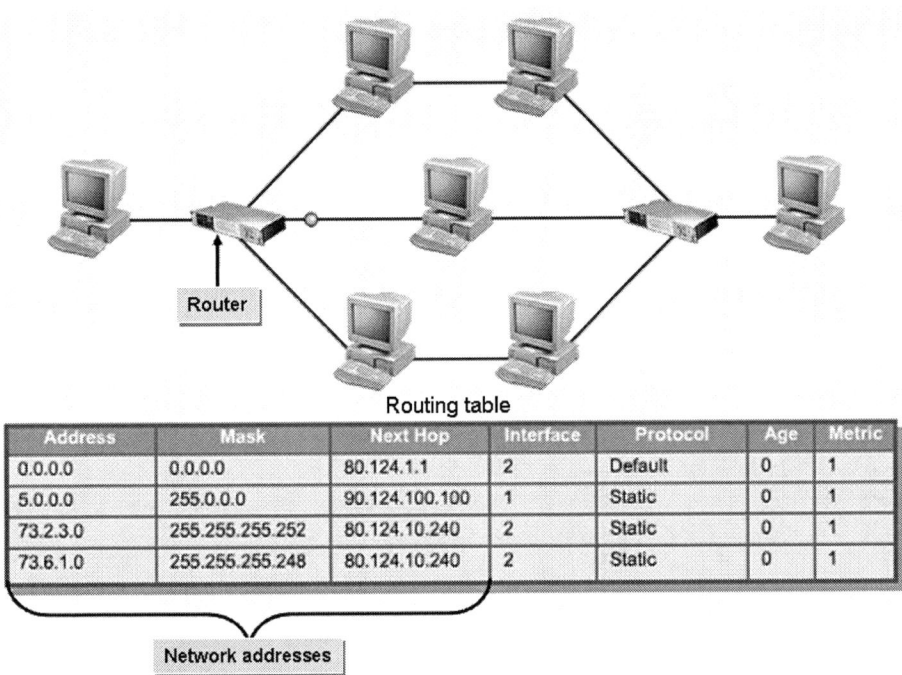

Routing table

Address	Mask	Next Hop	Interface	Protocol	Age	Metric
0.0.0.0	0.0.0.0	80.124.1.1	2	Default	0	1
5.0.0.0	255.0.0.0	90.124.100.100	1	Static	0	1
73.2.3.0	255.255.255.252	80.124.10.240	2	Static	0	1
73.6.1.0	255.255.255.248	80.124.10.240	2	Static	0	1

Network addresses

Figure 12-14: A routing table that comprises network addresses.

The route Command

The route command manipulates the kernel's IP routing tables. Its primary use is to set up static routes to specific hosts or networks. When the add or del option is used, the route command modifies the routing tables. Without these options, the route command displays the contents of the routing tables.

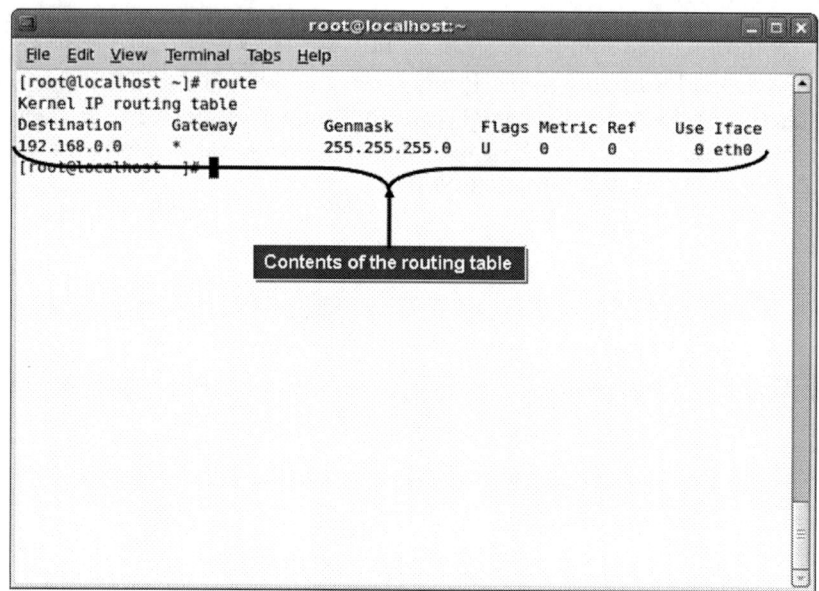

Figure 12-15: The output of the route command.

Routing Examples

The following table displays a few routing examples.

Command	Description
`route add -net 127.0.0.0`	Adds the normal loopback entry, using netmask 255.0.0.0 (class A net, determined from the destination address) and associated with the lo device, assuming this device was previously set up correctly with ifconfig(8).
`route add -net 192.56.76.0 netmask 255.255.255.0 dev eth0`	Adds a route to the network 192.56.76.x via eth0. The Class C netmask modifier is not really necessary here because 192.* is a Class C IP address. The word "dev" can be omitted here.
`route add default gw mango-gw`	Adds a default route, which will be used if no other route matches. All packets using this route will be gatewayed through mango-gw. The device that will actually be used for that route depends on how mango-gw can be reached—the static route to mango-gw will have to be set up before.
`route add -net 192.57.66.0 netmask 255.255.255.0 gw ipx4`	Adds the net 192.57.66.x to be gatewayed through the former route to the SLIP interface.
`route add -net 10.0.0.0 netmask 255.0.0.0 reject`	Installs a rejecting route for the private network 10.x.x.x.

Gateways

Definition:

A *gateway* is a device, software application, or system that converts data between incompatible systems. Gateways can translate data among different operating systems, email formats, or totally different networks. It can link two dissimilar networks, operating on varying protocols, enabling them to communicate with each other and exchange information.

Example:

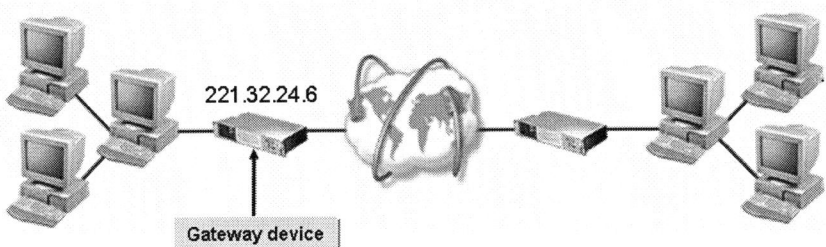

221.32.24.6

Gateway device

Figure 12-16: A gateway device linking dissimilar networks.

The Default Gateway

The *default gateway* is the gateway that acts as a network segment's access point to all other external networks and the Internet. The IP address assigned to the default gateway router is called the *default gateway address*. It is particularly important because this address is configured as the access point to all computers on that network segment. It provides an access path for packets in and out of the network segment.

The traceroute Command

The `traceroute` command is used to print the route that packets take to reach their destination, which is useful in troubleshooting some network or Internet connectivity problems. A few options for the `traceroute` command are listed in the following table.

Option	Description
-d	Sets the socket level debug option.
-n	Prints hop addresses numerically.
-i	Specifies the interface through which traceroute should send packets.
-g gateway	Specifies a source route gateway.
-r	Bypasses the normal routing tables and sends the packets directly to a host on an attached network.
-w waittime	Sets the time, in seconds, to wait for a response to a probe.

 Like traceroute, tcpdump is another network monitoring package that can be installed on a Linux system.

The netstat Command

The `netstat` command displays statistics about a network, including socket status, interfaces that have been auto-configured, memory statistics, and routing tables. With no arguments, the default `netstat` command displays open sockets. Some of the frequently used `netstat` command options are described in the following table.

Option	Displays
`-r` or `--route`	The kernel routing tables.
`-g` or `--groups`	The multicast group membership.
`-ir` or `--interface` or `--interface=iface`	A table of all network interfaces or the specified interface.
`-M` or `--masquerade`	A list of masqueraded connections.
`-s` or `--statistics`	A summary of statistics for each protocol.
`-e` or `--extend`	Additional details.

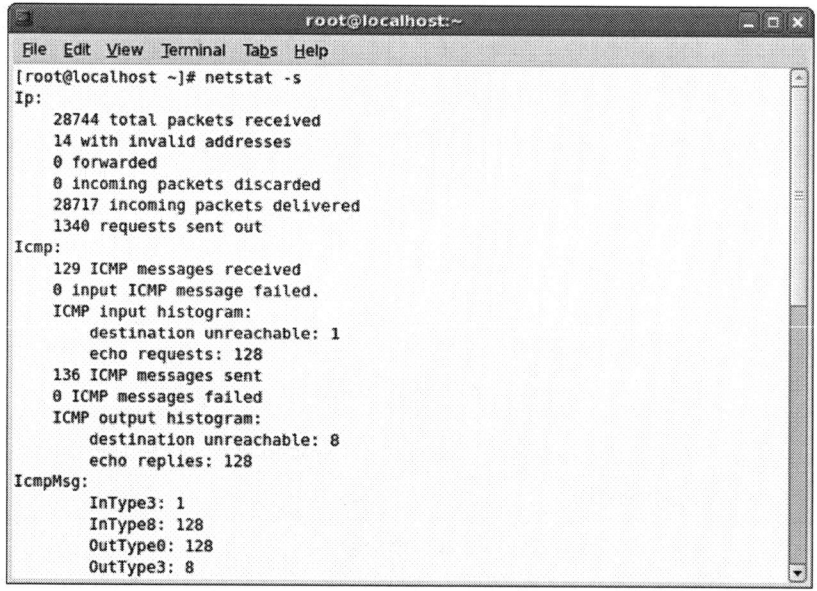

Figure 12-17: *The netstat command displaying a summary of statistics for each protocol.*

How to Configure Routes

Procedure Reference: Configure a Route for the IPv4 Address

To configure a route for the IPv4 address:

1. Log in as root in the CLI.

2. Enter `ip route add {network part of IPv4 address}/{length} via {gateway IPv4 address}` to add a static route.

3. To make the static route persistent:

    a. Enter `ifdown eth{device number}` to stop the network interface service.

    b. Enter `cd /etc/sysconfig/network-scripts` to open the network-scripts directory.

    c. Enter `vi route-eth{device number}` to open the NIC configuration file.

    d. Specify `{network part of IPv4 address}/{length} via {gateway IPv4 address}` to configure the route.

    e. Save and close the file.

    f. Enter `ifup eth{device number}` to start the network interface service.

4. To view the updated routing table:

    *   Enter `route`
    *   Enter `netstat -r`
    *   Or, enter `ip route`

The ip Command

The `ip` command is used to show or manipulate routing, policy routing, devices, and tunnels. The syntax of the `ip` command is `ip [Options] Object {Command ¦ help}`.

Procedure Reference: Check the IPv4 Connectivity

To check the IPv4 connectivity:

1. Log in as root in the CLI.

2. Check the IPv4 connectivity.

    *   Enter `ping [command options] {IPv4 or hostname of destination system}` to check the connectivity between the two systems.

    *   Enter `traceroute [command options] {IPv4 or hostname of destination system}` to view the network path to the destination system.

    *   Enter `mtr [command options] {IPv4 or hostname of destination system}` to check the connectivity of the network path to the destination system.

 mtr is a network diagnostic utility that combines the functionality of the `traceroute` and `ping` commands.

Procedure Reference: Configure the Default Gateway for the IPv4 Address

To configure the default gateway for the IPv4 address:

1. Log in as root in the CLI.

2. Configure the default gateway.

- To configure the default gateway globally:
    a. Enter `cd /etc/sysconfig` to open the sysconfig directory.
    b. Enter `vi network` to open the network settings file.
    c. Switch to the insert mode.
    d. Enter `GATEWAY={IPv4 address of the gateway system}` to specify the IP address of the gateway.
    e. Save and close the file.
    f. Enter `ifdown eth{device number}` to stop the device.
    g. Enter `ifup eth{device number}` to start the device.

- To configure the default gateway for each NIC:
    a. Enter `ifdown eth{device number}` to stop the network interface service.
    b. Enter `cd /etc/sysconfig/network-scripts` to open the network-scripts directory.
    c. Enter `vi ifcfg-eth{device number}` to open the NIC configuration file.
    d. Specify `GATEWAY={IPv4 address of the gateway system}` to set the IP address of the gateway.
    e. Save and close the file.
    f. Enter `ifup eth{device number}` to restart the network interface service.

Procedure Reference: Configure a Route for the IPv6 Address

To configure a route for the IPv6 address:

1. Log in as root in the CLI.
2. Enter `ip -6 route add {network part of IPv6 address}/{length} via {gateway IPv6 address}` to add a static route.
3. To make the static route persistent:
    a. Enter `ifdown eth{device number}` to stop the network interface service.
    b. Enter `cd /etc/sysconfig/network-scripts` to open the network-scripts directory.
    c. Enter `vi route6-eth{device number}` to open the file containing route settings.
    d. Specify `{network part of IPv6 address}/{length} via {gateway IPv6 address}` to configure the route.
    e. Save and close the file
    f. Enter `ifup eth{device number}` to start the network interface service.
4. Enter `ip -6 route` to view the updated routing table.

Procedure Reference: Check the IPv6 Connectivity

To check the IPv6 connectivity:

1. Log in as root in the CLI.

2. Check the IPv6 connectivity.

    ● Enter ping6 *[command options] {IPv6 or hostname of destination system}* to check the connectivity between the two systems.

    ● Enter traceroute6 *[command options] {IPv6 or hostname of destination system}* to view the network path to the destination system.

    ● Enter tracepath6 *[command options] {IPv6 or hostname of destination system}* to trace the network path and calculate the associated MTU to the destination system.

Procedure Reference: Configure the Default Gateway for the IPv6 Address

To configure the default gateway for the IPv6 address:

1. Log in as root in the CLI.

2. At the command prompt, enter cd /etc/sysconfig to open the sysconfig directory.

3. Enter vi network to open the network settings file.

4. Switch to the insert mode.

5. Specify IPV6_DEFAULTGW=*{IPv6 address of the gateway system}* to set the IP address of the gateway.

6. Save and close the file.

7. Enter ifdown eth*{device number}* to stop the device.

8. Enter ifup eth*{device number}* to start the device.

ACTIVITY 12-2
Configuring Routes

Before You Begin:
1. On srvB, you logged in as root in the CLI.
2. The first terminal is displayed.

Scenario:
You configured network connectivity and IP addresses on a new system. Now, you need to configure the router settings to connect to other computers on the network.

What You Do	How You Do It
1. Specify the router settings for automatic configuration of routes.	a. Enter **ifdown eth0** to stop the network interface service.
	b. Enter **cd /etc/sysconfig** to configure the default gateway.
	c. Enter **vi network** to open the file.
	d. Press **Shift+G** to go to the last line.
	e. Press **O** to switch to the insert mode and move to a new line.
	f. On the new line, type **GATEWAY= 192.168.0.2**
	g. Press **Esc** to switch to the command mode.
	h. Save and close the file.

2. Start the network interface and view the updated routing table.

a. Enter **ifup eth0** to start the network interface service.

b. Enter **ifconfig** to view the IP address.

c. Observe that the IP address of srvB is **192.168.0.X.**

d. Enter **route** to view the updated routing table.

e. Observe that the gateway address is displayed.

f. Enter **clear** to clear the terminal screen.

TOPIC C
Configure DHCP

You configured routers for transmission of data among computers on a network. Now, you will list the characteristics of DHCP in order to set up DHCP services so that network clients can obtain IP addresses automatically. In this topic, you will configure DHCP services.

In a large network, it can be very difficult for a network administrator to allocate IP addresses manually. You could accidentally assign the same IP address to more than one system. By configuring DHCP, you can automatically allocate unique IP addresses to systems on a network.

The Bootstrap Protocol

Definition:

The *Bootstrap Protocol (BOOTP)* is a network protocol that passes requests sent from a diskless workstation to a server node. It uses the *User Datagram Protocol (UDP)* as the transport protocol. The BOOTP server acts as an address server. As the BOOTP hosts are added to the network, they automatically request and receive IP addresses. The BOOTP protocol is used for booting diskless nodes, configuring a network system automatically , and booting the operating system without user support.

 BOOTP is the predecessor to DHCP.

Example:

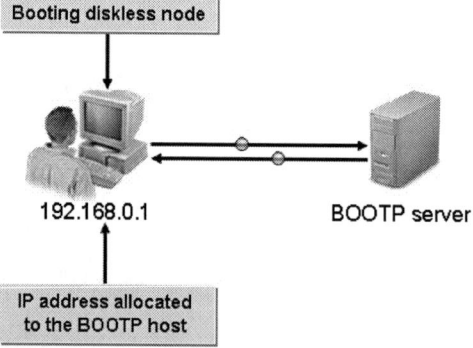

Figure 12-18: A BOOTP server allocating an IP address to a host.

DHCP

The *Dynamic Host Control Protocol (DHCP)* allocates IP addresses on an as-needed basis to a client. Instead of using static IP addressing, DHCP leases a temporary IP address to the client for a specified period of time.

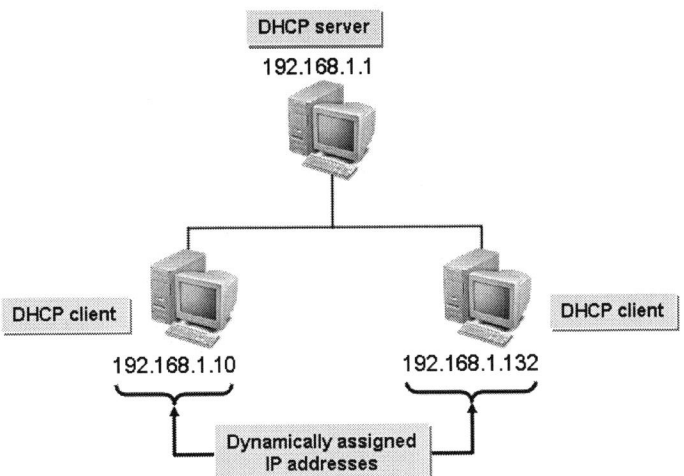

Figure 12-19: A DHCP server assigning IP addresses to clients.

DHCP Client

A DHCP client is a system that gets network connectivity information from the DHCP server.

DHCP Components

There are a variety of components in a DHCP implementation, but not all have to exist in every DHCP setup.

Component	Function
Options	Items, in addition to an IP address and subnet mask, that may be assigned to client systems such as default gateways and DNS server addresses.
Scope	The range, or pool, of addresses for a given subnet that a DHCP server will assign.
Reservation	An option whereby a client consistently gets the same configuration information after every initialization.
Lease	The process of assigning an IP address and its associated options to a client for a finite or infinite period of time.

Allocation of IP Addresses

IP addresses can be allocated in three different ways.

Type of Allocation	Description
Manual	To allocate IP addresses manually, the administrator has to visit each host. Hosts can be either workstations or servers. Smaller organizations that have plenty of IP addresses for workstations and servers often use this method. When IP address assignments need to change, this method requires higher maintenance by the administrator.
Automatic	By using automatic allocation, the DHCP server assigns a permanent IP address to the host. The administrator need not visit each system. While this method reduces the amount of administrative time, it does require an adequate supply of IP addresses.
Dynamic	By using dynamic allocation, the DHCP server assigns a temporary IP address to the host. The administrator need not assign the IP addresses, and a limited number of IP addresses serves a larger organization. When a workstation boots, it requests an IP address from the DHCP server along with other information, such as the DNS server IP address, the gateway IP address, and the subnet mask. The DHCP server takes an address from a pool of IP addresses and gives it to the workstation to use temporarily. The administrator can configure how long the address is leased.

The dhcpd.conf File

Definition:

The *dhcpd.conf* file is used to configure the DHCP server. To make changes on a Linux DHCP server, the dhcpd.conf file can be edited. By default, the file is located in the /etc directory, but the location of the file can be changed. Any changes made in the dhcpd.conf file will not take effect until the DHCP daemon is restarted. The dhcpd.conf file contains two types of statements: parameters and declarations. It also includes the `shared-network`, `subnet`, `host`, and `group` declarations.

 Usually, the dhcpd.conf file is created as an empty file when you install DHCP from the RPM package. However, you can copy the source content from a sample dhcpd.conf file, which is located in the /usr/share/doc/dhcp-<version-number>/etc directory. After copying the content, you can edit it according to your requirements.

Example:

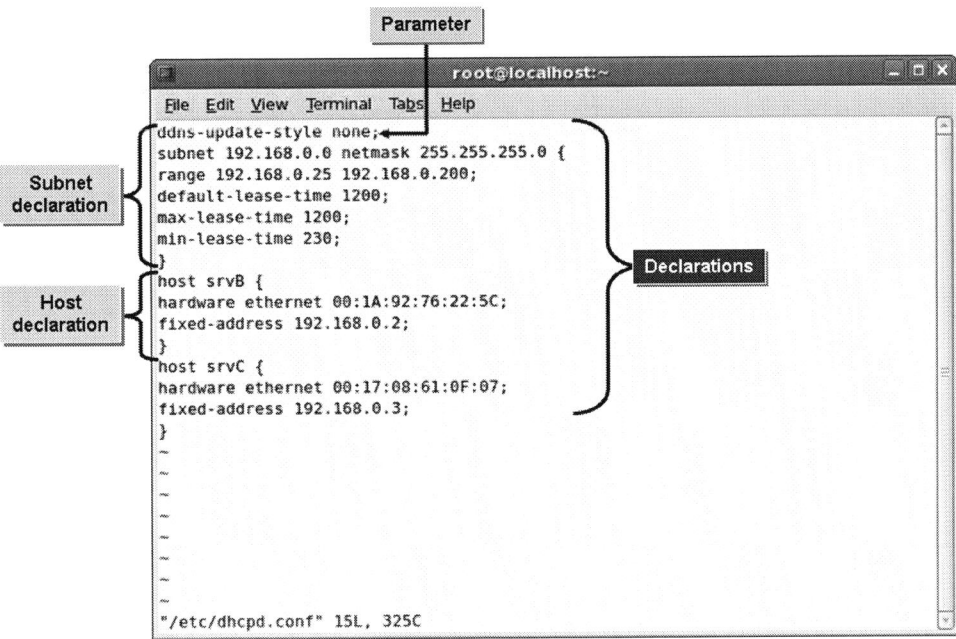

Figure 12-20: Configuring the DHCP server using the dhcpd.conf file.

Parameters

Parameters are commands that state how to perform a task and what network information has to be sent to the client. Parameters that start with the `option` keyword are referred to as options. The options are used to configure DHCP services. Parameters that do not start with the `option` keyword specify how the DHCP server should work. These parameters are not optional. Parameters that are enclosed within curly braces and declared before the sections are referred to as global parameters. Global parameters are applicable to all sections declared below them.

Declarations

The declarations in the dhcpd.conf file are described in the following table.

Declaration	Description
`shared-network`	The `shared-network` declaration is used on a network that contains multiple subnets sharing the same physical network. The syntax of the `shared-network` declaration is
	`shared-network shared network name {[ parameters... ] [ declarations... ]}.`
	Parameters that are common to all subnets on a network should be mentioned in the global parameters. Parameters that are specific to each subnet should be mentioned in the `subnet` declaration. It is recommended that you have several subnet declarations within the `shared-network` declaration.

Declaration	Description
subnet	The `subnet` declaration is used to define subnets on a network. The syntax of the `subnet` declaration is: `subnet subnet address netmask netmask address {[ parameters... ] [ declarations... ]}.` Global parameters should be specific to the subnet. The most important global parameter is the `range` statement, `range [ dynamic-bootp ] [ low_address ] [ high_address ];` that defines the IP address range. The server assigns IP addresses based on the specified range. The `dynamic-bootp` flag is used to assign IP addresses specified in the range dynamically to both the BOOTP and DHCP clients.
host	The `host` declaration is used to specify parameters to a specific host. The DHCP server identifies a host using the NIC address or dhcp-client identifier. If you want the DHCP server to provide a fixed IP address to the host, the `host` declaration is used. Such reserved IP addresses should be removed from the `range` parameters. The syntax for the `host` declaration is `host hostname {[ parameters... ]}.`
group	The `group` declaration is used to group parameters that are common to all declarations specified in a file. Therefore, the common properties will have to be specified only once, instead of specifying in each and every declaration. The group declaration is mostly used to group common host parameters. The syntax of the `group` declaration is `group {[ parameters... ] [ declarations... ]}.`

DHCP Parameters

Some frequently used DHCP parameters are listed in the following table.

Parameter	Description	Example
`option routers IP address of the router;`	Assigns the specified IP address to the router used on a network.	`option routers 192.168.2.13;`

Parameter	Description	Example
`range {first IP address of the range} {last IP address of the range};`	Specifies the range of IP addresses to be dynamically allocated to computers on a subnet.	`range 192.168.0.1 192.168.0.100;`
`max-lease-time time in seconds;`	Specifies the maximum time, in seconds, for which an IP address can be leased to a client.	`max-lease-time 1200;`
`default-lease time time in seconds;`	Specifies the default time, in seconds, for which an IP address will be leased if a client does not request a specific lease time.	`default-lease time 1200;`
`min-lease-time time in seconds;`	Specifies the minimum time, in seconds, for which an IP address can be leased to a computer.	`min-lease-time 1200;`
`hardware ethernet network interface address;`	Identifies a computer on a network.	`hardware ethernet 00:04:75:E9:3A:55;`
`fixed-address fixed IP address;`	Specifies the static IP address that is to be assigned to a client. This IP address should be excluded from the `range` parameters specified in the dhcpd.conf file.	`fixed-address 192.168.0.1;`
`option dhcp-client-identifier string or network interface address;`	Identifies a client on a network. It is usually specified within a `host` declaration.	`option dhcp-client-identifier "srvA";`

The DHCP Process

DHCP is a system-V service that handles client requests on a network and allocates IP addresses. The service gets activated on the system by installing the DHCP package. The DHCP process can be divided into a number of phases.

1. In the IP request phase, a client broadcasts the IP address request to the DHCP server.

2. In the IP release phase, the DHCP server receives the request and processes it. It responds to the request by sending the IP address, the subnet mask, the duration of lease, and the IP address of the DHCP server to the client.

3. In the client acceptance phase, the client accepts the information and broadcasts it to the network server so that the server ensures that the IP addresses used by the clients are unique.

4. In the server verification phase, the server sends a message to the client stating that it received the acceptance and the client is configured to use TCP/IP.

5. In the lease renewal phase, when half of the lease time has expired, the client sends a request to the server to extend the lease time or sends a request for a new IP address.

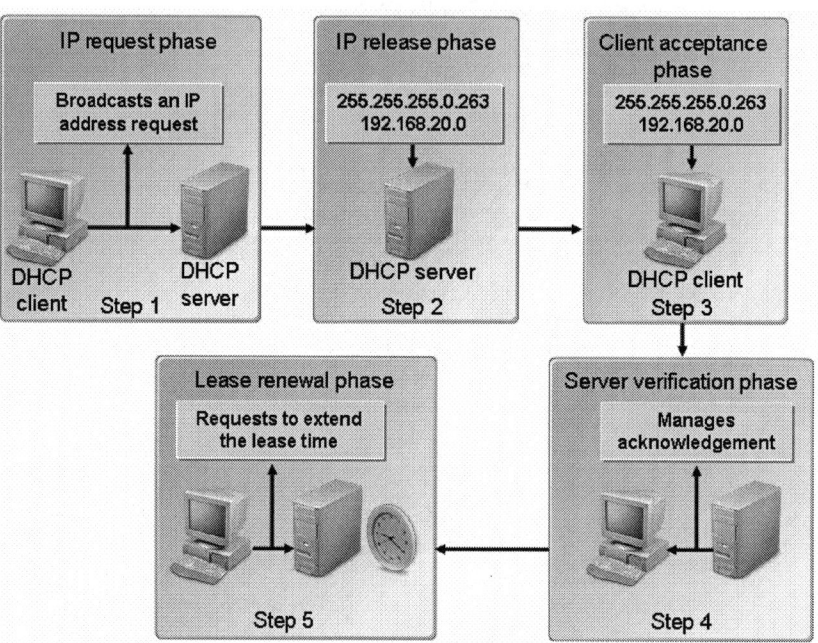

Figure 12-21: *Different phases of the DHCP process.*

The dhcpd Daemon

The dhcpd daemon controls the DHCP functions. It can be controlled by the `dhcpd` command. The `dhcpd` command supports many options that help maintain a DHCP server.

Option	Description
`-p port`	Allows dhcpd to listen on a port other than port 67. Also mentions the UDP port number on which dhcpd should listen.
`-f`	Runs dhcpd as a foreground process instead of a background process.
`-d`	Allows dhcpd to log all its activities in a standard error descriptor. This is used for debugging the activities of dhcpd.
`-q`	Avoids printing the entire copyright message that is displayed on startup.

Option	Description
-t	-T	Allows the server to test the configuration file for the correct syntax without performing any network operations. This helps in testing new configuration files before installing them. A similar feature can be applied to a lease database file using the -T option.
-cf config-file	Allows the use of an alternate configuration file.
-lf lease-file	Allows the use of an alternate lease file.

 DHCP client daemon (dhcpcd) is an implementation of the dhcp client. It runs on the client machine and configures it to work smoothly without additional configuration.

Syntax

The syntax of the dhcpd command is dhcpd [options].

General Guidelines to Maintain DHCP Servers

Some general guidelines that are required to maintain a DHCP server are:

- Ensure that the number of IP addresses are reserved and maintained with respect to the number of hosts on the network.

- Ensure that the lease period of hosts is changed according to the situation such as a scheduled maintenance.

- Ensure that free IP addresses are available after a major change of all lease periods.

Static Hosts

Definition:

A *static host* is a host that always receives the same IP address from the DHCP server. The server detects the static host using the dhcp-client-identifier or hardware ethernet option, which is sent by the host to the server. If the host does not send the dhcp-client-identifier information, the server identifies the static host using the NIC address of the host. Declaring static hosts on a network aids in the easy identification of systems because the IP address remains the same.

Example:

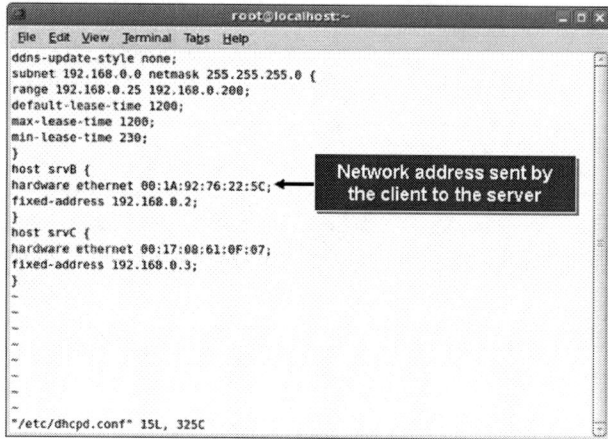

Figure 12-22: Static host declaration in the dhcpd.conf file.

Leases

Definition:

A *lease* is the amount of time, measured in seconds, given by the DHCP server to a client for using an IP address. The DHCP server specifies the lease time for an IP address using the `min-lease-time`, `default-lease-time`, and `max-lease-time` options. For static hosts, the lease time will not be specified.

Example:

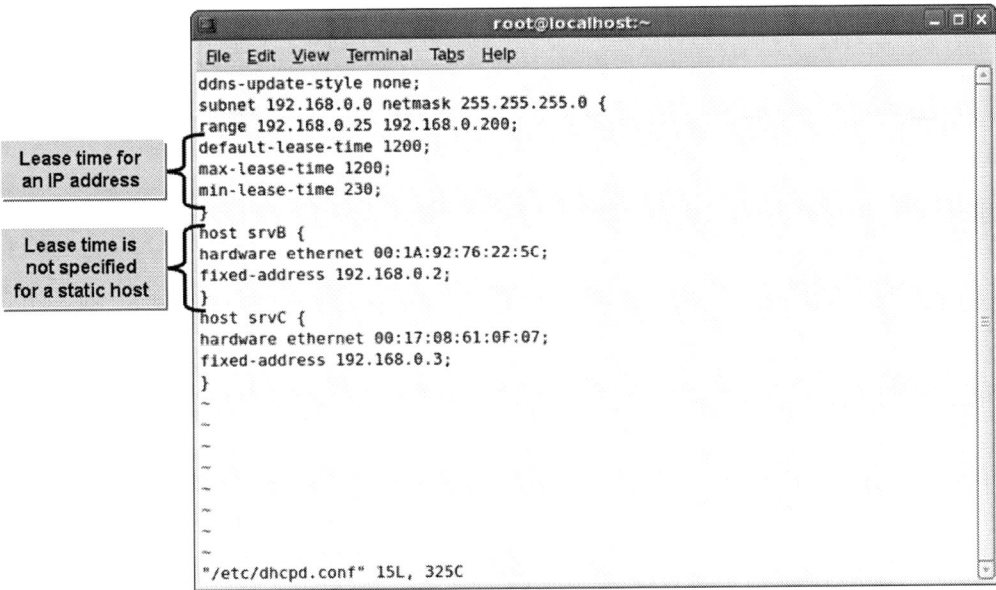

Figure 12-23: Lease time declaration in the dhcpd.conf file.

The Lease Database

Definition:

The *lease database* is a database that stores information about leases. The lease database is stored as a file named dhcpd.leases in the /var/lib/dhcpd directory. At the time of IP address allocation, the DHCP lease information is automatically stored in the database. The database contains information such as the lease time, the assigned IP address, the start and end dates of the lease, and the MAC address of the client's NIC.

 The lease database cannot be modified manually. The DHCP service will get corrupted if any manual changes are made to the database.

Example:

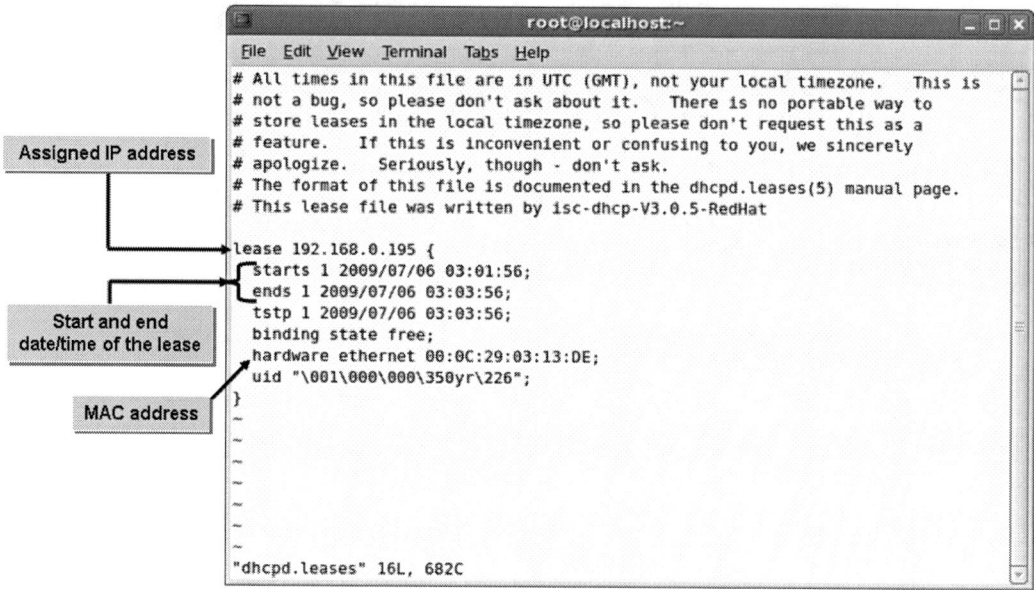

Figure 12-24: Lease time specification in the dhcpd.leases file.

How to Configure DHCP Services

Procedure Reference: Configure a DHCP Server

To configure a DHCP server:

1. Log in as root.

2. Navigate to the /etc directory.

3. Using an editor, open the dhcpd.conf file.

4. On a new line, enter `ddns-update-style none;` to indicate that DNS has not been implemented.

5. In the file, specify the global parameters that you want to set for the network. For example, if you have a common SMTP server for the entire network, enter `option smtp-server IP address 1 [, IP address 2...];` as the global parameter.

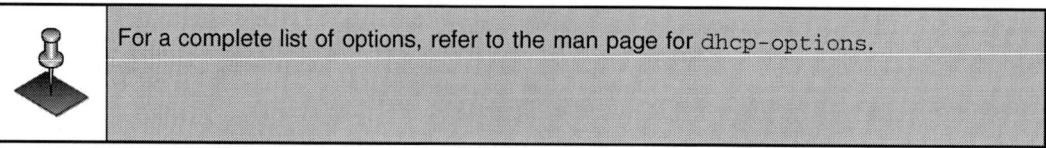

6. For each subnet on your network, create a `subnet` declaration and define the subnet-specific parameters.

```
subnet subnet IP address netmask netmask address {
   range first IP address of the range
last IP address of the range;
   default-lease-time time in seconds;
   max-lease-time time in seconds;
}
```

7. If necessary, include optional declarations.

- Declare static hosts and specify the parameters applicable to hosts.

```
host hostname {
    hardware ethernet ethernet address;
    fixed-address fixed IP address;
}
```

- Declare BOOTP hosts and specify the parameters applicable to BOOTP hosts.

```
host hostname {
    hardware ethernet ethernet address;
    fixed-address fixed IP address;
    file name "boot file name";
    server-name name of the server from which the host will boot;
}
```

- Declare shared networks and specify the parameters and declarations applicable to shared networks.

```
shared-network <shared network name> {
[parameters common for the entire shared network]
....
[declarations]
....
}
```

- Declare groups and specify the parameters and declarations applicable to groups.

```
group {
    [parameters common for the group]
....
    [declarations]
....
}
```

8. Save and close the file.

9. Enter `touch /var/lib/dhcpd/dhcpd.leases` to create the dhcpd lease file.

10. Start the DHCP server.

- Enter

    `service dhcpd start` to start the dhcpd daemon.

- Or, if the service is already running, use

    `service dhcpd restart` to restart the dhcpd daemon for the configuration changes to take effect.

11. If necessary, enter `chkconfig dhcpd on` to start the service on boot.

Procedure Reference: Configure the DHCP Client

To configure the DHCP client and get an IP address from a DHCP server:

1. Log in as root in the CLI.

2. Enter `vi /etc/sysconfig/network-scripts/ifcfg-ethDevice name` to open the device file.

3. Verify that `BOOTPROTO=dhcp`.

4. Save and exit.

5. Enter `service network restart` to apply the settings.

6. Enter `ifconfig` to verify that the system has received an IP address.

dhclient is a utility that allows you to configure one or more network services with the DHCP protocol. dhclient will assign a static address if the protocol fails.

ACTIVITY 12-3

Configuring the DHCP Server

Before You Begin:

1. srvA is rebooted and the GUI login screen is displayed.

2. Switch to the first terminal of the CLI.

3. Log in as root.

4. At the command line, enter `yum localinstall /rhelsource/Server/dhcp*` to install the DHCP packages.

5. Enter y to proceed with the installation.

6. Clear the terminal screen.

Scenario:

Your IT manager has defined the network layout planned for a new branch of your organization, OGC Systems. The network will include two Linux servers, (srvA and srvB), and 150 workstations. The DHCP service is installed on srvA for which the IP address 192.168.0.1 has been manually configured. You need to configure DHCP so that srvB and the workstations dynamically receive IP addresses from srvA. From the network policy documentation, you find that the IP addresses to be assigned can range from 192.168.0.25 to 192.168.0.200.

What You Do	How You Do It
1. Create a `subnet` declaration.	a. Navigate to the /etc directory.
	b. Using the vi editor, open the dhcpd.conf file.
	c. Navigate to the last line in the file.
	d. On a new line, enter **ddns-update-style none;** to specify that DNS has not been implemented.
	e. Enter **subnet 192.168.0.0 netmask 255.255.255.0 {** to begin the `subnet` declaration.
	f. Enter **range 192.168.0.25 192.168.0.200;** to specify the range of IP addresses for your network.
	g. Enter **default-lease-time 1200;** to specify the default lease time for the IP addresses assigned to the subnet.
	h. Enter **max-lease-time 1200;** to specify the maximum lease time for the IP addresses assigned to the subnet.
	i. Enter **}** to close the `subnet` declaration. *See Code Sample 1.*
	j. Press **Esc** to switch to the command mode.
	k. Save and close the file.
	l. Clear the terminal screen.

Code Sample 1

```
ddns-update-style none;
subnet 192.168.0.0 netmask 255.255.255.0 {
range 192.168.0.25 192.168.0.200;
default-lease-time 1200;
max-lease-time 1200;
}
```

2. Create a `host` declaration.

    a. Begin the `host` declaration for srvC and press **Enter.**

    b. Enter **hardware ethernet {network interface address of srvC};** to specify the network interface address.

    c. Enter **fixed-address 192.168.0.203;** to specify the fixed IP address of srvC.

    d. Type **}** to complete the `host` declaration.

       See Code Sample 2.

    e. Press **Esc** to switch to the command mode.

    f. Save and close the file.

    g. Clear the terminal screen.

Code Sample 2

```
host srvC {
hardware ethernet network interface address;
fixed-address 192.168.0.203;
}
```

---

3. Create the lease database.

    a. Enter **touch /var/lib/dhcpd/dhcpd.leases** to create the lease database.

    b. Clear the terminal screen.

---

4. Start the dhcpd service.

    a. Enter **service dhcpd start** to start the DHCP server.

    b. Enter **chkconfig dhcpd on** to start the DHCP server on boot.

    c. Clear the terminal screen.

---

5. Check whether the DHCP settings have taken effect.

a. Switch to the system labeled srvB.

b. Enter **system-config-network-tui** to open the network configuration utility.

c. Enable DHCP support for the NIC, eth0, by selecting the **Use DHCP** option.

d. Exit the network configuration utility.

e. Enter **service network restart** to request the DHCP server for an IP address.

f. Enter **ip addr** to verify that the IP address 192.168.0.X/24 has been assigned to srvB.

g. Clear the terminal screen.

TOPIC D
Configure DNS

You configured DHCP services to automatically assign IP address to network systems. To connect to a network computer and access its resources, you need to be aware of either its IP address or its name. The DNS translates and resolves IP address and their equivalent host or domain names on networks. In this topic, you will configure DNS.

Computers on a network identify each other through their IP addresses. However, it is difficult for network users to remember IP addresses. So, IP addresses of network computers and devices are replaced by descriptive names, for users to locate network resources and share information and services among them. The translation between the IP address and their descriptive names is handled by DNS, which needs to be configured by the network administrator.

The Domain Name System

The *Domain Name System (DNS)* is a distributed, hierarchical database system that maintains information about domain names and their equivalent IP addresses on a network. It uses this information to translate a fully qualified domain name into its numeric IP address or vice versa. IP addresses are used by networked computers to locate, connect, and communicate with each other. DNS translates IP addresses to their corresponding domain names. It works like a central system to ensure that there are no duplicate domain names and IP addresses on the network.

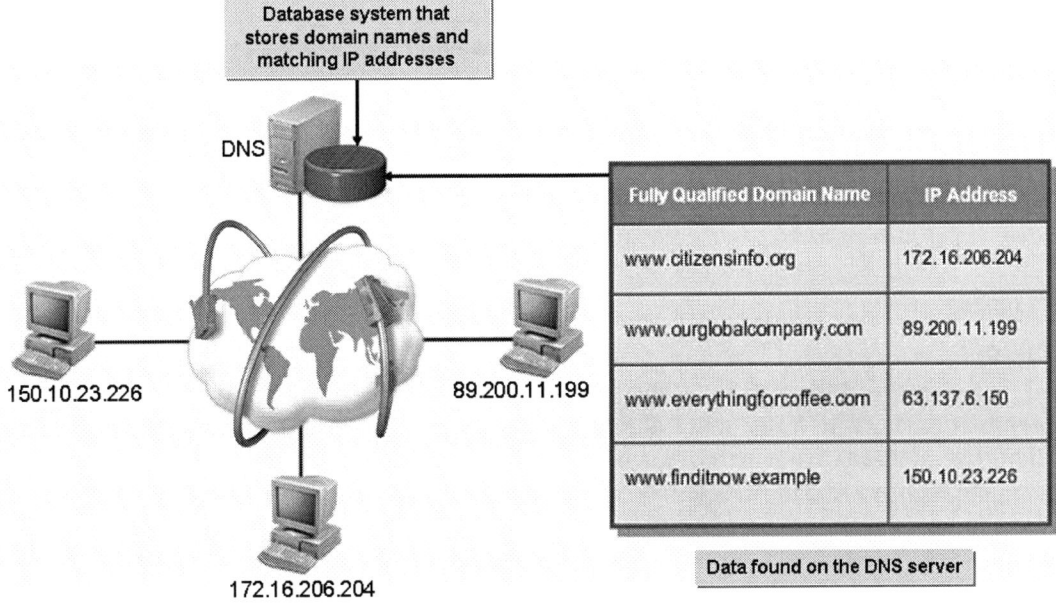

Figure 12-25: Allocation of domains using DNS.

DNS Utilities

Various utilities are used to resolve DNS hostnames. Some of the resolving utilities are dig, host, and nslookup.

Domain Names

Definition:

A *domain name* is a label given to a *domain,* which is a node in the hierarchical structure of data stored in DNS. It is the concatenation of all labels from the node to the root node. A domain name is represented by a string and each node is separated by a period (.). Each domain name is unique within its parent domain.

Example:

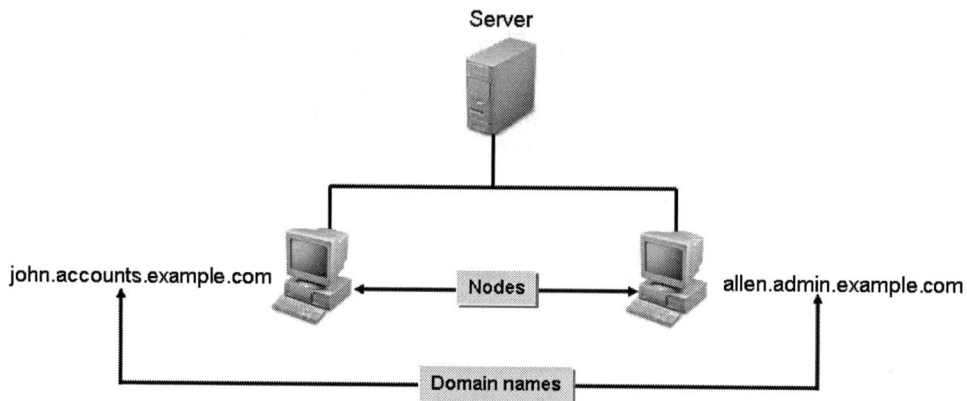

Figure 12-26: Assigning domain names to systems.

Subdomains

A subdomain is a part of a larger domain name. A DNS hierarchy comprises a root-level domain, followed by top-level domains, second-level domains, and subdomains. Each top-level domain contains subdomains, which are referred to as child domains.

Fully Qualified Domain Name (FQDN)

A *Fully Qualified Domain Name (FQDN)* is a method by which systems are uniquely identified in the worldwide network. A complete domain name consists of a hostname, second-level domains, and the top-level domain.

Zones

Definition:

A *zone* is a point of delegation in a DNS tree structure that maps to a domain. A zone can map to an entire domain with all its child domains or to a specific portion of a domain. Each zone will have one authoritative name server or one or more secondary name servers. There are two types of zones: forward and reverse.

Example:

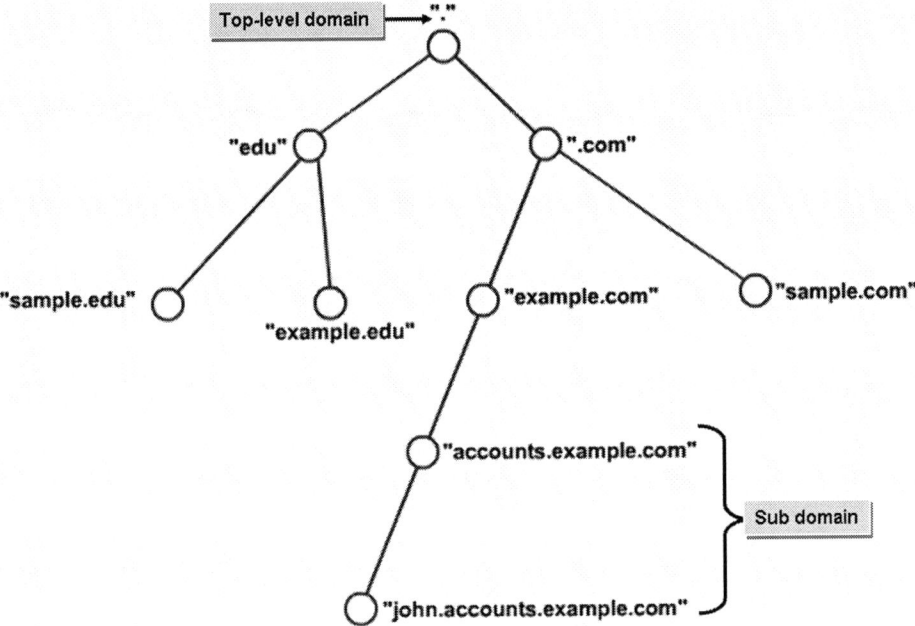

Figure 12-27: Delegation of domains using zones.

Forward and Reverse Zones

The two main DNS zones are forward and reverse zones.

Zone	Description
Forward zone	A zone that is used for mapping hostnames to IP addresses. It contains information on the time allocated for the DNS server to get updated.
Reverse zone	A zone that is used for mapping IP addresses to hostnames. A reverse zone can be used to resolve the IP address of a domain to trace unauthorized users.

Zone Files

A *zone file* contains information about a particular namespace that is necessary to resolve domain names to IP addresses. Each zone file contains resource records and, optionally, directives. Comments in the zone file are added after a semicolon. A zone file is named according to the value set to the `file` option of the zone statement in the named.conf file. By default, zone files are stored in the /var/named directory.

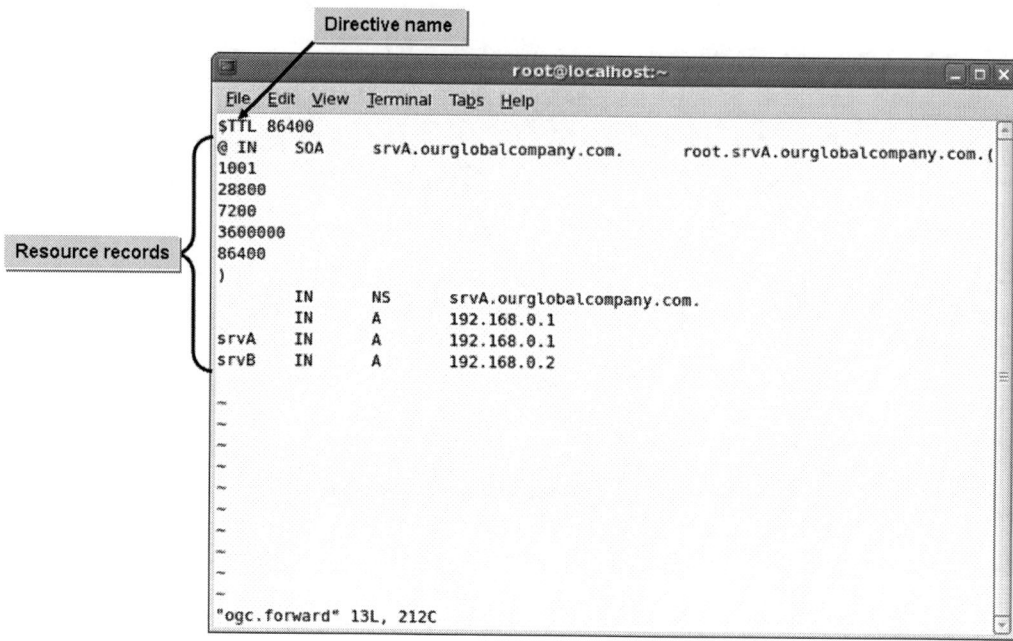

Figure 12-28: *A forward zone file.*

Root Hints

Root hints are files in DNS servers that contain host information including names and addresses of the root DNS servers. It is used to locate authoritative DNS servers and resolve names outside authoritative DNS domains.

Namespace

Namespace is the part of the name that must be unique for DNS to function. For any given domain, the subdomain must not contain two hosts or subdomains of the same name.

Syntax for Zone Files

The syntax for writing a zone file is:

```
$TTL time to live in seconds
$ORIGIN domain name
$INCLUDE file name
@ IN SOA master server name
email address of the domain administrator
(
serial number
time in seconds to refresh
time in seconds to retry
minimum TTL in seconds
)
 IN DNS Record
DNS server name
 IN DNS Record
preference value
mail server name
hostname IN A IP address
alias name IN CNAME real name of the host
```

Zone File Directives

A *zone file directive* specifies the task to be performed by the name server and the settings of a zone. The directive begins with a dollar ($) sign followed by the directive name. Directives are optional and are usually specified at the beginning of the zone file.

Frequently used directives are listed in the following table.

Directive	Description
$INCLUDE	Configures the named daemon to include another zone file in the current zone file, at the location where the directive appears. The additional zone setting can be stored in a separate zone file apart from the main zone file.
$ORIGIN	Appends the domain name to unqualified records that contain only the hostname. Any name specified in the resource record, which does not end with a trailing period (.), will have the $ORIGIN directive value appended to it.
$TTL	Sets a default Time to Live (TTL) value for the zone. The TTL value is the duration in seconds. A zone resource record is valid and each resource record contains its own TTL value that overrides the $TTL directive.

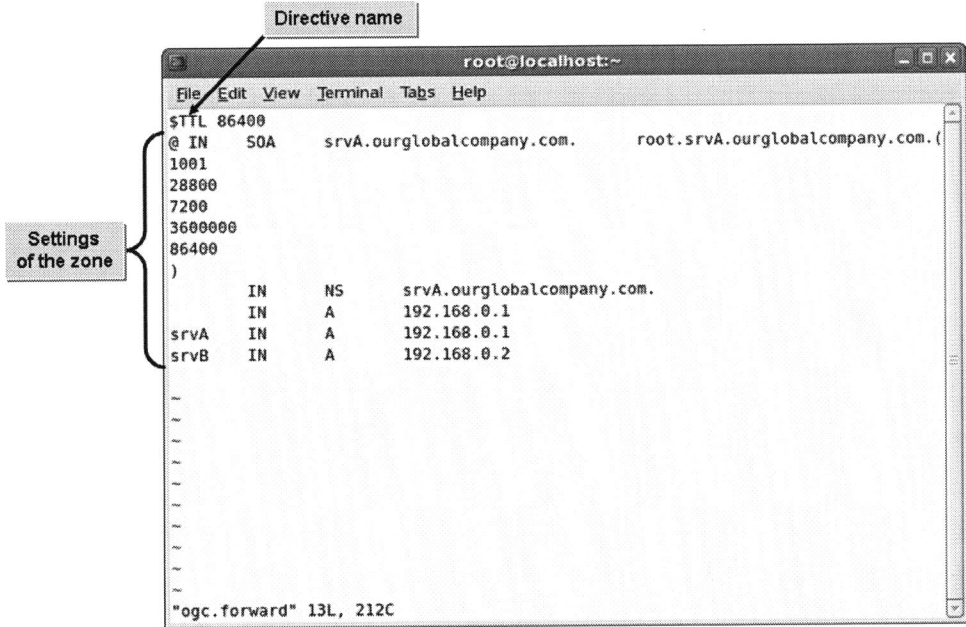

Figure 12-29: Assigning directives in the zone file.

DNS Components

DNS has three major components that are used for resolving domain names and IP addresses.

DNS Component	Function
Resolver	The *resolver* is a client-based software program that sends a request to DNS name servers for translating a domain name to its IP address or vice versa.
	Local and remote resolvers are the two types of resolvers. The local resolver is responsible for querying the local name server while the remote resolver is responsible for querying the preferred, secondary, and authoritative name servers.
	The /etc/hosts file maintains a database of the hostnames and the IP addresses to which they are connected. The file is referenced before starting DNS. The entries in the file help the resolver resolve the hostnames and the IP addresses.
	The resolv.conf file is used for configuring the domain name resolver. The file specifies the IP addresses of name servers to use while naming resolutions. You can specify up to three name servers, where priority is given to the first name server listed. If the resolv.conf file does not exist or if the file has no entries for name servers, the resolver attempts to configure the local host as the name server.
Name servers	A *name server* is a program or a server that implements the domain naming system on a network. It consists of a database of domain names and IP addresses. The name server that controls name resolution for a particular zone is said to be authoritative for that zone. name servers can be of different types.
Domain namespace	The *domain namespace* comprises information about the hierarchy of domains and the hosts under each domain; it is referred to by the name servers for mapping domains.

The Domain Name Resolution Process

The process of domain name resolution involves a number of phases:

1. The DNS query containing the domain name is sent by an application to the resolver, requesting an IP address.

2. The resolver searches its cache for matching domain names. If any entries are found, then the respective IP address is forwarded to the client application. In case the entries are not found, then the query is forwarded to the name server.

3. The name server, if authoritative for the zone, sends the reply to the resolver. If the name server is nonauthoritative, then the secondary name server forwards the query to the primary or authoritative name server, which sends the reply to the resolver.

4. The resolver then resolves the IP address and sends the reply to the client.

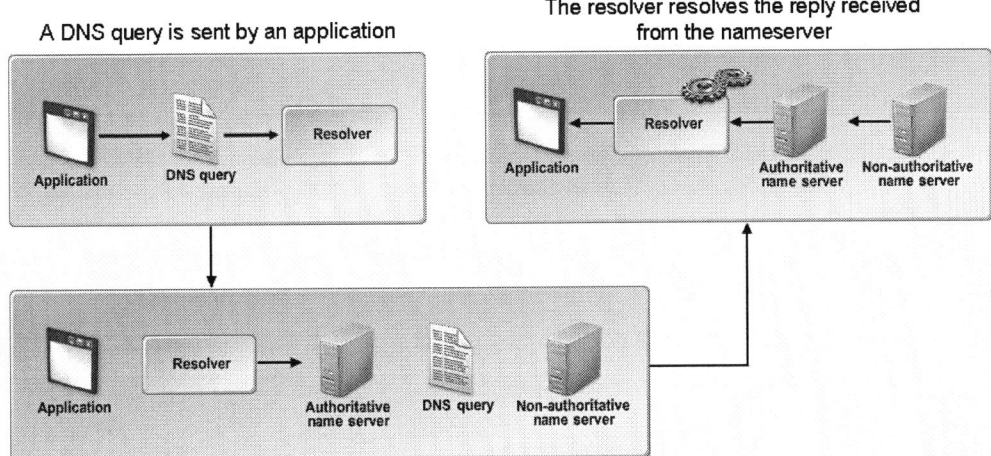

Figure 12-30: The various steps in the domain name resolution process.

Types of DNS Name Servers

A network can have more than one name server. The role of a name server varies according to its configuration.

DNS name server	Description
Master server or primary server	Maintains the original information about zones and zone records specific to a namespace. The zone data is stored in the form of files called zones or master files. Any changes in the zones are updated in the zone files by the master server.
Slave server or secondary server	Processes the requests sent by the other name servers to resolve the hostnames for which it acts as an authoritative server. Information about zones is transferred from the primary server to the slave server using the zone transfer replication process.

DNS name server	Description
Caching-only server	Provides names to IP resolution services. It is not an authoritative server to any zone. Answers for all resolutions are cached in the memory for a fixed period of time. The length of time for which a record may be retained in the caching name server is controlled by the TTL field associated with each resource record.
Forwarding server	Forwards the requests for name resolution to a specific list of name servers. If the name server is unable to resolve the request, then the request will fail. There can be more than one forwarding server, which can be queried in turn until the name is resolved or the list is exhausted. Forwarding servers must be configured when you do not want the name server in your site to directly interact with other Internet sites.

BIND

Berkeley Internet Name Domain (BIND) is a domain name service that resolves hostnames to IP addresses. BIND supports operating systems such as Windows, Linux, Unix, Solaris, and Novell. In Linux, BIND is implemented using the `named` daemon. The configuration information of BIND is stored in the /etc/named.conf file. Information about zones and cache files is stored in the /var/named directory.

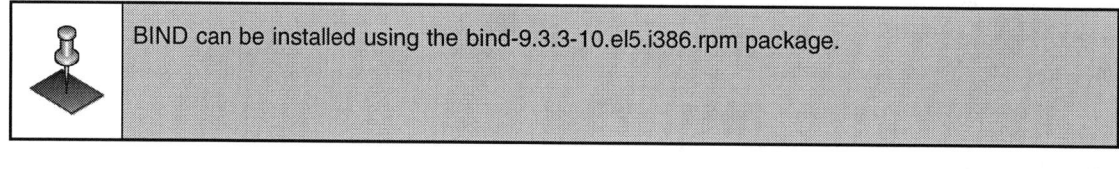

BIND can be installed using the bind-9.3.3-10.el5.i386.rpm package.

Figure 12-31: The BIND hostname translation process.

The stub Resolver

The *stub* resolver is a DNS resolver that increases resolution speed by accepting queries from a client and distributing them to multiple DNS servers. It supports all applications and services. The stub resolver references the /etc/nsswitch.conf file to obtain the order in which queries should be handled and to determine the services that must be used. Based on the settings in this file, the stub resolver retrieves information from the database. The default setting for name server resolution is `hosts: files dns`, which means that the resolver will first use the hostnames listed in the local files and then use DNS to resolve the query.

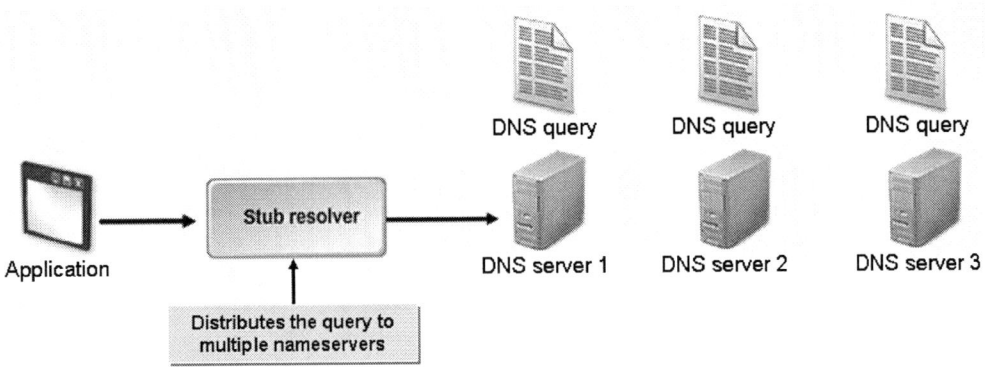

Figure 12-32: *Functions of the stub resolver.*

The dig Utility

The `dig` utility interacts with name servers and displays the results to users. It may be configured to query a single name server or multiple name servers in the form of batches. It references the /etc/resolv.conf file for the list of name servers to be queried.

Various options can be used to configure the `dig` utility based on user requirements. Some of the frequently used command options are listed in the table.

Command Option	Description
-b	Sets the source IP address of the query. The utility will query name servers using this IP address.
-f	Enables the utility to query name servers based on the processes listed in the specified file.
-p	Specifies the port to be used to send queries.
-4	Forces the utility to use only the IPv4 protocol for querying.
-6	Forces the utility to use only the IPv6 protocol for querying.
-t *query type*	Sets the query type. Some of the valid query types are `soa`, `axfr`, `ixfr`, and `mx`.

Various query options can be used to configure the `dig` utility based on user requirements. Some of the frequently used query options are listed in the table.

Query Option	Enables You To
+tcp	Set the resolver to use the TCP service to query the name server.
+domain=*somename*	Create a search list for desired domains.
+search	Configure the resolver to use the search list specified in the /etc/resolv.conf file or through the +domain option.
+nssearch	Configure the resolver to search for name servers based on the zones in which they are defined.
+identify	Display the IP address and port number of the name server that answers the query.
+trace	Trace the DNS query for root name server information from the /etc/resolv.conf file.

Syntax

The syntax of the dig utility is dig *[command options]* *{query options}* *{Fully Qualified Domain Name | IP address}*.

The host Utility

The host utility is a DNS lookup utility, similar to the dig utility. It is used to convert system names to IP addresses and vice versa. The host utility has various options.

Option	Enables You To
name	Set the domain name to be looked up by the host utility.
-t *{query type}*	Set the type of query to be sent to the name server.
-W *{seconds}*	Set the time the resolver must wait for a reply before quitting.
-s	Force the resolver to terminate the querying process once it fails without retrying.

Syntax

The syntax of the host utility is host *[Command Options]* *{FQDN | IP Address}*.

The nslookup Utility

The `nslookup` utility is used to query name servers over the Internet and verify whether the name-to-IP address mapping is correct in the DNS configuration files. It operates in two modes—interactive and noninteractive. The interactive mode allows a client to query the name server for specific information. The noninteractive mode displays only standard information on the host.

Syntax

The syntax of the `nslookup` command is `nslookup host name or FQDN`.

Resolver Files

Various files are used to configure resolvers for resolving domain names and hostnames.

File	Description
The hosts file	The /etc/hosts file contains the hostname to IP address mapping information for systems on a network. In older versions of Linux, the /etc/networks file was used for this purpose.
The host.conf file	The /etc/host.conf file contains information on how the hostname lookups are to be performed. For example, if the /etc/host.conf file contains the line "order hosts,bind," the hostname lookup will be performed first in the local /etc/hosts file and then in DNS. The default entry in the /etc/hosts file is "order hosts,bind."
The nsswitch.conf file	The /etc/nsswitch.conf file, or the name server switch configuration file, contains information about each and every database and the order in which they work. The first column contains information about the database and ends with a colon; the remaining columns specify the order in which the database should use the service. For example, in the file entry `hosts: files dns`, `hosts` refers to the hostsdatabase. This means that the host entries in the local files will have higher priority than the entries in the DNS server. In case the hostname entries are not found in the local files, the search will continue in DNS.
The resolv.conf file	The /etc/resolv.conf file, or the resolver configuration file, is a set of routines in the C library that provide access to the Internet DNS. The resolver configuration file contains a list of keywords with values that are read by the resolver routines, the first time they are invoked by a process. The three different configuration options are name server, domain, and search.

The named.conf File

Definition:

The *named.conf* file is a user-defined configuration file that is used to manage the BIND service. This file is invoked when the named service starts. It contains statements and comments. Statements define zone settings and comments contain messages or descriptions about the statements inside a file. Comments can either be single-line or multi-line text.

 Single-line comments start with // and multi-line comments start with /* and end with */.

Example:

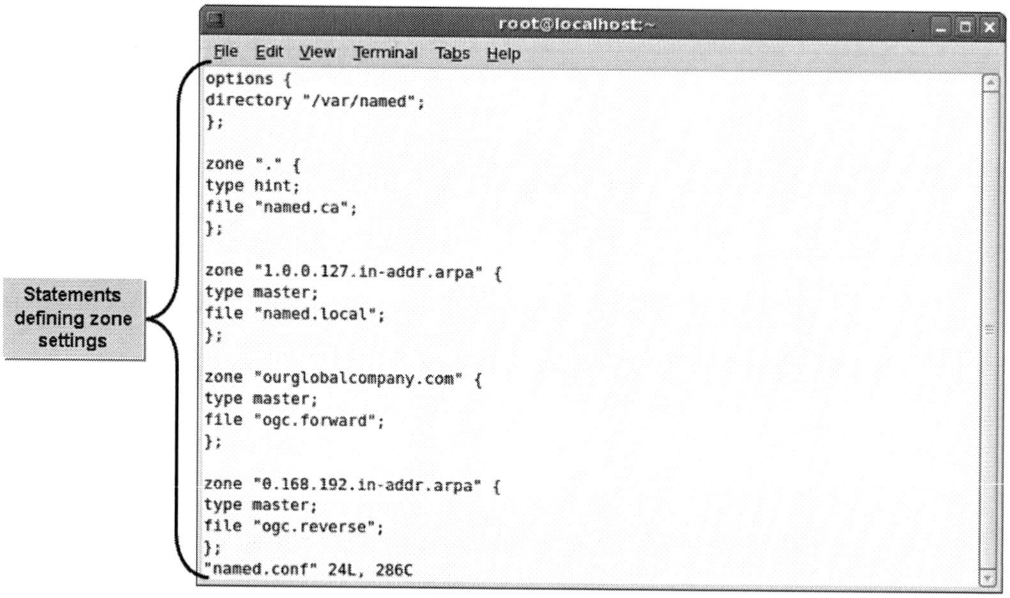

```
                              root@localhost:~                      _ □ X
File  Edit  View  Terminal  Tabs  Help
options {
directory "/var/named";
};

zone "." {
type hint;
file "named.ca";
};

zone "1.0.0.127.in-addr.arpa" {
type master;
file "named.local";
};

zone "ourglobalcompany.com" {
type master;
file "ogc.forward";
};

zone "0.168.192.in-addr.arpa" {
type master;
file "ogc.reverse";
};
"named.conf" 24L, 286C
```

Statements defining zone settings

Figure 12-33: Various declarations in the named.conf file.

DNS Resource Records

A *DNS resource record* defines parameters for a zone. It contains five components: the fully qualified domain name, the TTL, the record class, the record type, and the record data. The format of the resource record is defined by Request for Comments (RFC). The record data in the resource record depends on the record type.

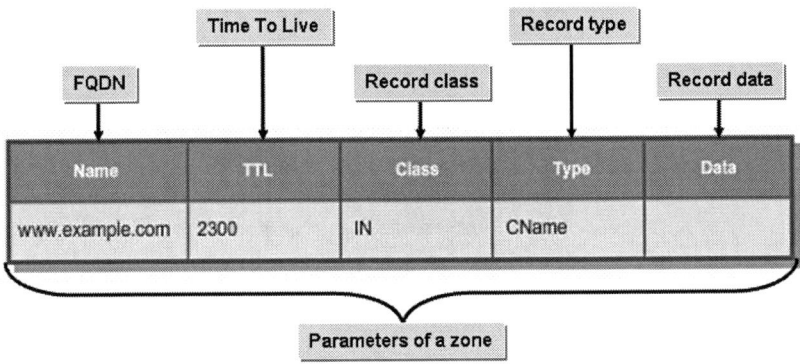

Figure 12-34: Interpretation of a DNS resource record.

Various DNS records and the format used for each are given in the table.

DNS Record	Description

SOA	The Start Of Authority (SOA) record is used to specify information about a zone in the string of fields format. The SOA record tells the server to be authoritative for the zone. Each zone will contain only one SOA record. The format of an SOA record is:
	
	`@ IN SOA primary nameserver`
	`hostmaster email(`
	`serial number`
	`time to refresh`
	`time to retry`
	`time to expire`
	`minimum TTL`
	`)`

NS	A Name Server (NS) record is used to define the authoritative name server for a specific zone. The format of the NS record is `IN NS nameserver`. The name server should be an FQDN. It can either be a primary server or a slave server.
A	An Address (A) record is used to assign an IP address to a name. The format of the A record is `hostname IN A IP address`. The IP address should not be terminated with a period (.). If the hostname is omitted, the A record will point to the default IP address at the top of the namespace.
PTR	The Pointer (PTR) record is used for reverse name resolution mapping. It is used in the reverse map zone files to map an IP address to a name. The format of the PTR record is `last IP digit IN PTR FQDN of system`. The `last IP digit` specifies the last number in an IP address, which should point to a particular system's domain name. The PTR record should always end with a period. For example, `253 IN PTR srvA.example.com`

DNS Record	Description
MX	A Mail eXchange (MX) record is used to specify the relative preference of mail servers for a zone. The MX record format is IN MX priority valuemail server name. The highest priority value is 0, which is assigned to a host where the mail is destined. Two hosts can have the same priority to distribute mail equally between them. Any number of MX records can be defined for a domain.
CNAME	A Canonical Name (CNAME) record is used to map an alias name to the real name. The CNAME record is also referred to as alias record. The format of the CNAME record is alias name IN CNAME real name. CNAME records are generally used to point to another domain.
TXT	A Text (TXT) record is used to map text with a host name. It is used to validate genuine email sources from a domain.

Statements

A *statement* is a collection of options that define the domain name settings. Statements contain a set of options enclosed within curly braces and are terminated by a semicolon (;). Statements can also contain blocks of sub statements.

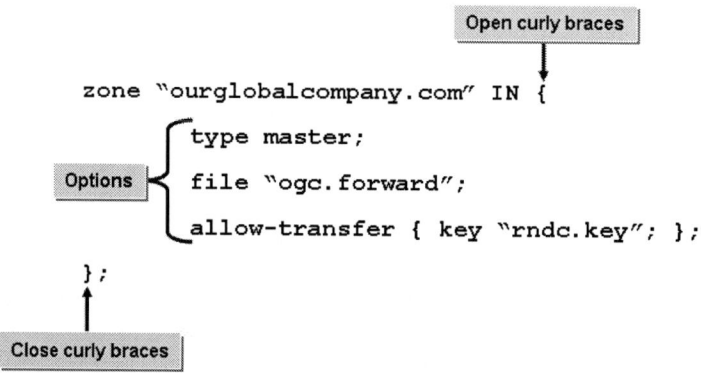

Figure 12-35: The use of a statement in a zone file.

The include Statement

The *include statement* is used to specify the file name that needs to be included in the named.conf file. The `include` keyword is followed by the file path. Any confidential information, such as a key's description, can be provided in a separate file instead of specifying it in the named.conf file.

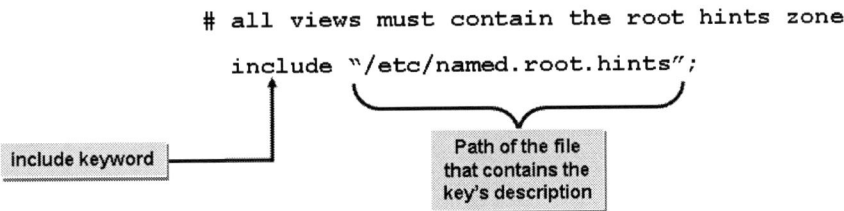

Figure 12-36: *Adding a file using the include statement.*

Syntax

The syntax of the `include` statement is `include "file name";`

The options Statement

The *options statement* is used to define the global server configuration, such as the location of the `named` utility, and the type of queries that can be allowed. This statement is also used to set default values for other statements. The `options` keyword is followed by a set of options enclosed within curly braces and should end with a semicolon (;).

```
options keyword ──▶ options {
                        directory "/var/named";
                        forwarders {
                            192.168.1.99;            Global server
                        };                           configuration
                    };
```

Figure 12-37: *The use of the options statement.*

There are many options that can be provided in the `options` statement. Some of the frequently used options are listed in the table.

Option	Description
`allow-query`	Specifies the hosts that are allowed to query the name server. By default, all hosts are permitted to query the name server. The `allow-query` option can have an ACL name or a collection of IP addresses.
`allow-recursion`	Specifies the hosts that are allowed to perform recursive queries on the name server. By default, all hosts are permitted to perform recursive queries on the name server.

Option	Description
blackhole	Specifies a list of hosts that should not be allowed to query the name server. The default value is none.
directory	Specifies the working directory of the server. By default, the working directory is set to /var/named, the directory from which the server was started. The specified directory should have an absolute path.
forwarders	Specifies a list of valid IP addresses of name servers that named will query if the local cache fails to resolve. Requests are forwarded to these name servers for resolution.
forward	Specifies the behavior of the forwarders directives, first or only. The first option specifies that named initially queries the name servers listed in the forwarders directive before resolving the hostname itself. The only option specifies that named will resolve only if the name servers specified in the forwarders directive fail to resolve queries.
listen-on	Specifies the interfaces and ports that the server will listen and answer queries to. The listen-on option accepts an optional port and a collection of IP addresses. An option statement can have multiple listen-on statements.
recursion	Specifies whether recursion should be disabled or not. If the name server is disabled, it will not send queries on behalf of the name servers or resolvers, and will not cache data as well.
notify	Specifies whether the named daemon should notify the slave servers when a zone is updated. The notify option can be set to yes, no, or explicit. By default, the notify option is set to yes, so the slave server will be notified about the changes. If the notify option is set to explicit, then the slave servers mentioned in the also-notify list of the zone statement will be notified.

Syntax

The syntax of the options statement is:

```
options {
    option;
    option;
};
```

The zone Statement

The *zone statement* is used to define the characteristics of a zone. Options specific to a zone and the path of the zone file can be specified in this statement. The *zone* keyword is followed by the zone name and its class type. You can specify the options related to the zone within curly braces.

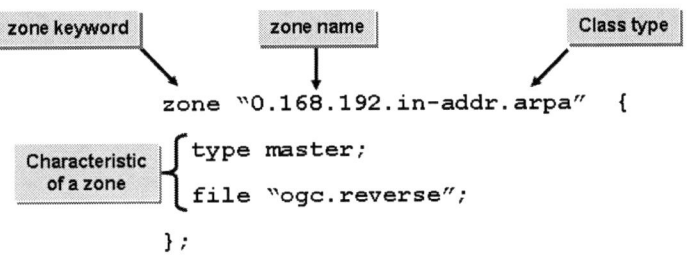

Figure 12-38: Declaring zones using the zone statement.

Syntax

The syntax of the `zone` statement is:

```
zone "zone name" zone class {
    zone option;
    zone option;
};
```

Zone Statement Options

Among the various options that can be specified in the `zone` statement, `type` is an important option. Using this option, you can specify the type of zone to be created and whether the zone is a `master` zone or a `slave` zone.

Some of the other zone options are `allow-query`, `allow-transfer`, `allow-update`, `masters`, `file`, and `notify`.

Types of Zone Classes

In the zone statement, the zone name is followed by the zone class where you can specify the type of the zone class to be created. There are three types of zone classes that can be specified in the zone statement.

Zone Class Type	Description
IN	Represents the Internet. It indicates that the zone is used for Internet services. IN is the default zone class type.
HS	Represents Hesiod, a name resolution protocol. It indicates that the zone uses Hesiod to share information such as users, groups, and printers. This information is stored in databases that may occasionally incur changes.
CH	Represents ChaosNet. It indicates that the zone uses the ChaosNet protocol, which is used specifically for LAN. The zone information for the protocol can be specified with the CHAOS class. Also, BIND uses ChaosNet to retrieve the version number of BIND.

Specifying the zone class is optional and it is assumed that the zone statement uses IN, if not specified.

The rndc Utility

The *rndc utility* is a BIND utility that allows command line administration of the named daemon from the local or remote host. This utility communicates through a TCP connection and sends commands authenticated with digital signatures. It also reads the /etc/rndc.conf configuration file to obtain the settings on how to contact the name server and to decide the algorithm and the key to be used.

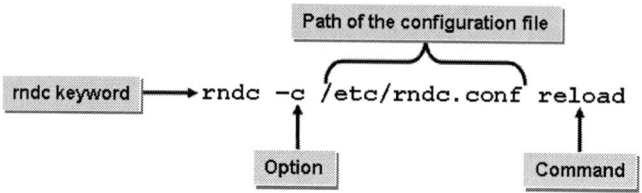

Figure 12-39: *Implementation of the rndc utility.*

The rndc utility can be used along with various commands.

Command	Description
reload	Reloads the configuration file and the zones.
reload zone [class]	Reloads the specified zone.
stats	Writes the server statistics onto the statistics file.
status	Displays the status of the server on the screen.
stop	Saves the pending updates of the zones to the master files and then stops the server.
halt	Stops the server without updating the changes.
flush	Flushes all server's caches.
restart	Restarts the server.

There are various options for the rndc utility. Some of the frequently used options are listed in the table.

Option	Enables You To
-b source address	Specify the source address for establishing connection to the server. By providing multiple instances, you can specify both IPv4 and IPv6 addresses.
-c config file	Specify the configuration file that rndc must use instead of reading the default /etc/rndc.conf file.

Option	Enables You To
`-k key file`	Specify the key file that `rndc` must use instead of the default /etc/rndc.key key. `rndc` uses the default key only if the configuration file is not available for authenticating commands sent to the server.
`-s server`	Specify the address of a server that will respond to queries other than the default server specified in the /etc/rndc.conf configuration file.
`-p port`	Specify the TCP port to which the commands must be sent.
`-V`	Specify that the log messages should be verbose.
`-y key id`	Specify the key ID to be used instead of the default key specified in the /etc/rndc.conf file. The key ID is used to validate control messages.

Syntax

The syntax of the `rndc` utility is `rndc [rndc options] {rndc command}`.

The controls Statement

The *controls statement* is used to configure various security requirements that are needed by the `rndc` command to administer the `named` service. The `controls` statements are also referred to as control channels. Control channels are used by the `rndc` utility to send commands and retrieve results from the name server. The *controls* keyword is followed by a set of options enclosed within curly braces.

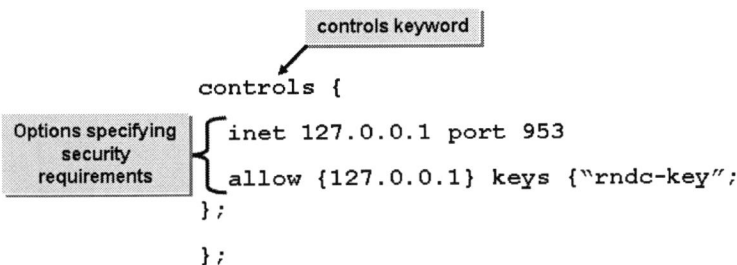

Figure 12-40: The rndc configuration using the controls statement.

Syntax

The syntax of the `controls` statement is:

```
controls {
    option 1;
    option 2;
};
```

The Default Control Channel

If the `controls` statement is not provided, then the `named` utility will set up a default control channel listening on the loopback address. If the `controls` statement does not have the key clause, then the `named` utility will load the command channel key from the /etc/rndc.key file.

How to Configure DNS Servers

Procedure Reference: Install DNS

To install DNS on your system:

1. Log in to the Linux server as root.
2. Enter `rpm -qi bind` to check whether the bind package is installed.
3. If bind and related packages are not installed, then install them from the installation media.

    a. Mount the Linux installation CD-ROM that contains the latest version of BIND.

    b. Enter `cd /media/cdrom/Server` to access the installation CD.

    c. Enter `rpm -ivh bind-{version}.{release}.rpm` to install BIND.

    d. Enter `rpm -ivh caching-nameserver{version}.{release}.rpm` to obtain an initial configuration.

    e. Enter `rpm -ivh bind-chroot-{version}.{release}.rpm` to run BIND in the chrooted environment.

    f. Enter `rpm -qi bind` to check whether the BIND package is properly installed.

Procedure Reference: Configure the DNS Service

To configure the DNS service on your system:

1. Log in as root.
2. Enter `cp /etc/named.caching-nameserver.conf /etc/named.conf` to use the named.cachingnameserver.conf file as a template.
3. Configure DNS.

    a. Specify the global configuration options.

    b. Add zone statements for the root, loopback domain, and forward and reverse zones.

    c. Create forward and reverse zone files.

4. Enter `named-checkconf -f /etc/named.conf` to check the named syntax.
5. Start the named service.

    a. Enter `service named start` to start the named daemon.

    b. Or, if the named service is already running, enter `service named reload` to reload the named daemon.

    c. Enter `rndc reload` to reload the zone files.

    d. Enter `chkconfig named on` to start the named service at system startup.

Procedure Reference: Configure DNS Hostname Lookup

To configure DNS hostname lookup:

1. Log in as root.

2. Configure the client.

   a. Enter `vi /etc/resolv.conf` to edit the resolver configuration file.

   b. Press **I** to enter the insert mode.

   c. Type `nameserver {DNS Server IP address}` to define the IP address of a name server that the resolver should query.

   d. Save and close the file.

3. Query the DNS server.

   a. Enter `dig [Command Options] [Query Options] {Fully Qualified Domain Name | IP Address}` to resolve hostnames and IP addresses.

   b. Or, enter `host [Command Options] {FQDN | IP Address}`

Procedure Reference: Configure a Master DNS Server

To configure a master DNS server:

1. Log in as root.

2. Using the vi editor, open the /etc/named.conf file.

3. Add an `include` statement. For example, you can add an `include` statement to include a file, such as rndc.conf, which contains sensitive configuration statements.

```
include "file name";
```

4. Add an options statement to include the location of the directory that will contain the zone and cache files.

```
options {
directory "/var/named";
};
```

5. If necessary, specify other global configuration options such as `notify` and `listen-on` in the `options` statement.

```
options {
    directory "/var/named";
    notify yes;
    listen-on port {port number} { network interface};
};
```

6. If necessary, using a `zone` statement, declare the zone for the root DNS servers. Within the `zone` statement, include the `type` clause to indicate that the zone points to root servers. Also, include the `file` clause to help the DNS server locate the root servers during startup.

```
zone "." IN {
   type hint;
   file "named.ca";
 };
```

7. If necessary, declare a zone for the loopback domain. Within the `zone` statement, include the `type` and `file` clauses, which indicate that the server is the master of its own loopback address and that the domain information can be obtained from the named.local file.

```
zone "0.0.127.in-addr.arpa" {
   type master;
   file "named.local";
};
```

8. Declare the zone for which the server will be authoritative. The `zone` statement should contain the `type` clause, which designates the server as the master of the zone. The statement should also contain a `file` clause, which specifies the forward zone file that will contain the resource records for this zone.

```
zone "domain name" IN {
    type master;
    file "zone file name";
};
```

9. Declare the reverse zone for resolving names from IP addresses. Like the other `zone` statements, the `zone` statement for the reverse zone should contain the `type` and `file` clauses.

```
zone "reverse domain name" {
    type master;
    file "reverse zone file name";
};
```

10. Enable the `rndc` utility to control the named service by adding a controls statement.

```
controls {
inet 127.0.0.1 allow {localhost;}
};
```

11. Save and close the file.

12. Enter `service named start` to start the named service.

 The named daemon may not start if semicolons and parentheses are not used properly in the configuration file.

Procedure Reference: Create a Forward Zone File

To create a forward zone file:

1. Log in as root.

2. Navigate to the zone directory that you specified in the `options` statement. The /var/ named directory is the default directory.

3. Enter `vi zone file name` to create a zone file.

4. Switch to the insert mode.

5. If necessary, add zone file directives to specify settings applicable to the zone. For example, you can add a `TTL`, `ORIGIN`, or `INCLUDE` directive.

```
$TTL {time to live in seconds}
$ORIGIN {domain name}
$INCLUDE {file name}
```

6. Add global parameters applicable to the zone by using an SOA record.

```
@ IN SOA master server name
email address of the domain administrator
(
    serial number
time in seconds to refresh
time in seconds to retry
minimum TTL in seconds
    )
```

7. Add NS records to announce the authoritative DNS servers for the zone.

    `IN NS DNS server name`

8. If necessary, type `IN MX {preference value} {mail server name}` to add MX records to indicate the email servers to be used by the domains controlled by the zone.

9. Type `hostname IN A IP address` to add hosts using A resource records.

10. If necessary, type `alias name IN CNAME real name of the host` to add alias names for specific hosts using the `CNAME` resource record.

11. Save and close the file.

Procedure Reference: Create a Reverse Zone File

To create a reverse zone file:

1. Navigate to the zone directory that you specified in the `options` statement. The /var/ named directory is the default directory.

2. Enter `touch zone file name` to create a zone file.

3. If necessary, add zone file directives to specify settings applicable to the zone. For example, you can add a `TTL`, `ORIGIN`, or `INCLUDE` directive.

    ```
    $TTL time to live in seconds
    $ORIGIN domain name
    $INCLUDE file name
    ```

4. Add global parameters applicable to the zone by using an SOA record.

    ```
    @ IN SOA master server name
    email address of the domain administrator
    (
        serial number
    time in seconds to refresh
    time in seconds to retry
    minimum TTL in seconds
        )
    ```

5. Type `IN NS DNS server name` to add NS records to announce the authoritative DNS servers for the zone.

6. Type `last octet of the IP address IN PTR FQDN of the host` to add PTR records to associate IP addresses to fully qualified domain names.

7. Save and close the file.

Procedure Reference: Configure a DNS Slave Server

To configure a DNS slave server:

1. Enter `vi /etc/named.conf` to create and edit the named.conf file.

2. Specify the global configuration options and the zone statements for the root, loopback domain, and forward and reverse zones in the zone statements.

    ```
    zone "." {
    type hint;
    file "named.ca";
    };
    zone "0.0.127.in.addr.arpa"{
    type master;
    file "zone file name";
    masters master server's IP address;
    };
    ```

3. Save and close the file.

4. Create forward and reverse zone files, similar to the ones you created for the master DNS server.

5. Enter `chown root.root {file name}` and `chown 700 {file name}` to make the file readable only by the root user.

6. Enter `service named start` to start the named service.

Procedure Reference: Configure a Cache-Only Server

To configure a cache-only server:

1. Using an editor, open the named.conf file.

2. In the named.conf file, specify the global configuration options and the `zone` statements for the root and loopback domain.

3. In the `zone` statement, for the forward and reverse zones, ensure that you change the zone type to caching-only.

4. Save and close the file.

5. Start the named service.

6. Verify that the DNS server resolves hostnames and IP addresses.

Procedure Reference: Configure a Forwarder

To configure a DNS server as a forwarder:

1. Open the named.conf file.

2. In the `options` statement, include the forward and forwarders clauses.

    ```
    forward first;
    forwarders {
        IP address of your ISP's DNS server;
    };
    ```

3. Press **Esc** to switch to the command mode. Save and close the file.

4. Verify that the DNS server resolves hostnames and IP addresses.

Procedure Reference: Configure Logging

To configure logging in to a DNS server:

1. Open the /etc/named.conf file.

2. Add a `logging` statement with a `channel` clause to define the log with a user-defined file name, size, version, and the level of security.

```
logging {
    channel channel name {
        file "log file name";
        [versions number of versions];
        [severity severity level];
    };
};
```

3. In the `logging` statement, add a `category` clause for each `channel` clause to define the category of messages.

```
logging {
    channel channel name {
        different channel options
    };

    category message category {
        channel name;
    };
};
```

4. Press **Esc** to switch to the command mode. Save and close the file.

5. Enter `service named restart` to restart the named service.

The Logging Statement

The `logging` statement is used to implement multiple types of logs. It contains the `channel` and `category` clauses. The `channel` clause is used to define how logging messages are handled. Messages are written to a customized log with a user-defined file name, size, version, and the level of security. The `category` clause defines the category of messages sent to the channel. A `logging` statement can contain more than one `channel` clause, and each clause should have a `category` option defined. The `logging` keyword is followed by the `channel` and `category` clauses enclosed within curly braces. The `channel` and `category` clauses are terminated by a semicolon (;).

By default, standard messages of the named service are notified in the `syslog` daemon; these messages are stored in the /var/log/messages directory. The default category, also called `default`, uses built-in channels to perform normal logging without any special configuration. Configuration file errors are logged in the system log location rather than the location specified in the configuration file, despite executing the `logging` statement. Logging takes effect only after the entire content of the named.conf file is read at server startup.

ACTIVITY 12-4
Configuring a DNS Server

Before You Begin:

Navigate to the C:\085039Data\Configuring_Network folder to view the activity setup for this activity.

Open the Lesson 12 Activity 4.htm file to view the steps.

Scenario:

You obtained a domain name, ourglobalcompany.com, for OGC Systems. You want the DNS server to resolve the IP addresses 192.168.0.2 and 192.168.0.3 to the hostnames srvA.ourglobalcompany.com and srvB.ourglobalcompany.com. The parameters for the forward and reverse zones are given in the table:

Parameters	Forward Zone	Reverse Zone
TTL value	86400 seconds	86400 seconds
Serial number	1001	1001
Length of the refresh cycle	28800 seconds	28800 seconds
Length of the retry cycle	7200 seconds	7200 seconds
Duration for the slave server to respond to queries	3600000 seconds	604800 seconds
The default TTL value for negative caching servers	86400 seconds	86400 seconds

What You Do	How You Do It
1. Create a zone file for the forward domain.	a. On the system labeled srvA, navigate to the /var/named directory.
	b. Using the vi editor, open the ogc.forward file.

2. Enter the TTL directive and the SOA record for the forward zone.

a. Enter **$TTL 86400** to specify it as the TTL value.

b. Type **@** and press **Tab.**

c. Type **IN** and press **Tab.**

d. Type **SOA** and press **Tab.**

e. Enter **srvA.ourglobalcompany.com. root.srvA.ourglobalcompany.com. (**

f. Enter **1001** as the serial number for the zone file.

g. Enter **28800** as the length of the refresh cycle.

h. Enter **7200** as the length of the retry cycle.

i. Enter **3600000** as the time for which slave server can respond to queries without updating its zone file.

j. Enter **86400** as the default TTL for negative caching servers.

k. Enter **)** to complete the SOA record.

See Code Sample 1.

Code Sample 1

```
$TTL 86400
@   IN   SOA    srvA.ourglobalcompany.com. root.srvA.ourglobalcompany.com. (
1001
28800
7200
3600000
86400
)
```

3. Enter NS and A records for the forward zone.

a. Press the **Tab** key and type **IN**

b. Press the **Tab** key and type **NS**

c. Press the **Tab** key and enter **srvA.ourglobalcompany.com.**

d. Press the **Tab** key and type **IN**

e. Press the **Tab** key and type **A**

f. Press the **Tab** key and enter **192.168.0.2**

g. Press the **Tab** key and type **srvA**

h. Press the **Tab** key and type **IN**

i. Press the **Tab** key and type **IN**

j. Press the **Tab** key and enter **192.168.0.2**

k. Press the **Tab** key and type **srvB**

l. Press the **Tab** key and type **IN**

m. Press the **Tab** key and type **IN**

n. Press the **Tab** key and enter **192.168.0.3**

o. Press **Esc** to switch to the command mode.

p. Save and close the file.

See Code Sample 2.

Code Sample 2

```
   IN   NS    srvA.ourglobalcompany.com.
   IN   A    192.168.0.2
srvA   IN   A    192.168.0.2
srvB   IN   A    192.168.0.3
```

4. Create a zone file for the reverse domain resolution.

    a. Using the vi editor, open the ogc.reverse file.

    b. Enter **$TTL 86400** as the TTL value.

    c. Create an SOA record with the following values:

- Serial number-1001
- Refresh rate-28800
- Retry rate-7200
- Expiry time-604800
- Minimum TTL-86400

       See Code Sample 3.

    d. Create an NS record for the DNS server that has the hostname srvA.ourglobalcompany.com.

    e. Enter **1 IN PTR srvA.ourglobalcompany.com.** to add a PTR record.

    f. Add a PTR record for **srvB.**

       See Code Sample 4.

    g. Press **Esc** to switch to the command mode.

    h. Save and close the file.

    i. Clear the terminal screen.

Code Sample 3

```
$TTL 86400
@  IN   SOA    srvA.ourglobalcompany.com. root.srvA.ourglobalcompany.com. (
1001
28800
7200
604800
86400
)
```

Code Sample 4

```
   IN   NS   srvA.ourglobalcompany.com.
1  IN   PTR   srvA.ourglobalcompany.com.
2  IN   PTR   srvB.ourglobalcompany.com.
```

5. Specify the global configuration options and the zone statements for the root and loopback domains in the named.conf file.

a. Navigate to the /etc directory.

b. Using the vi editor, open the named.conf file.

c. Enter **options {** to begin the options statement.

d. Enter **directory "/var/named";** to specify the location of zone configuration files

e. Enter **};** to complete the options statement.

See Code Sample 5.

f. Enter **zone "." {** to begin the zone statement for root servers.

g. Enter **type hint;** to indicate that the zone file contains pointers to the root servers.

h. Enter **file "named.ca";** to specify the zone file name.

i. Complete the zone statement.

See Code Sample 6.

j. Create a zone statement for the loopback zone, indicating that the zone is of type master and named.local is the zone file.

See Code Sample 7.

Code Sample 5

```
options {
directory "/var/named";
};
```

Code Sample 6

```
zone "." {
type hint;
file "named.ca";
};
```

Code Sample 7

```
zone "1.0.0.127.in-addr.arpa" {
type master;
file "named.local";
};
```

6. Add `zone` statements for the forward and reverse zones.

   a. Create a `zone` statement for the ourglobalcompany.com forward zone, and specify the ogc.forward file as the forward zone file.

     See Code Sample 8.

   b. Create a `zone` statement for the 0.168.192.in-addr.arpa reverse zone, and specify the ogc.reverse file as the reverse zone file.

     See Code Sample 9.

   c. Press **Esc** to switch to the command mode.

   d. Save and close the file.

   e. Clear the terminal screen.

 The ⇒ symbol indicates that the command is to be typed on the same line.

   f. Enter **yum localinstall /rhelsource/Server/**⇒ **caching-nameserver**⇒ **-9.3.4-10.P1.el5.i386.rpm** to install the caching-nameserver package.

   g. Observe that the package installation is complete.

   h. Enter **clear** to clear the terminal screen.

Code Sample 8
```
zone "ourglobalcompany.com" {
type master;
file "ogc.forward";
};
```

Code Sample 9
```
zone "0.168.192.in-addr.arpa" {
type master;
file "ogc.reverse";
};
```

7.	Start the named service.	a.	Enter **service named configtest** to check the named configuration.
		b.	Enter **service named start** to start the named service.
		c.	Enter **chkconfig named on** to start the DNS server every time the system boots.

 If any data exists in the resolv.conf file, the data must be deleted.

		d.	Using the vi editor, open the /etc/resolv.conf file.
		e.	Enter **nameserver 192.168.0.2** to specify the IP address of the DNS server.
		f.	Switch to the command mode.
		g.	Save and close the file.
		h.	Clear the terminal screen.

8.	Add the DNS name server data to the /etc/resolv.conf file on **srvB.**	a.	Using the vi editor, open the /etc/resolv.conf file.
		b.	Enter **nameserver 192.168.0.2** to specify the IP address of the DNS server.
		c.	Switch to the command mode.
		d.	Save and close the file.

9.	Check whether the DNS service resolves hostnames and IP addresses.	a.	Enter **host srvA.ourglobalcompany.com** to resolve the IP address of srvA.
		b.	Observe that the IP address of srvA is displayed.
		c.	Enter **host 192.168.0.3** to resolve the hostname of the IP address 192.168.0.3.
		d.	Clear the terminal screen.

TOPIC E

Implement Network File Sharing Services

You managed networks using DNS and DHCP services. Now, you will manage network services so that users can easily access and share resources on a network. In this topic, you will implement network file sharing services.

As a system administrator managing large networks, you are responsible for efficient resource management. There may be instances where users will need to access files and resources, such as printers, across a network. Therefore, you may want to ensure secure and fast sharing of files and directories across a network. By configuring network file sharing services, you will be able to do this with ease.

FTP

The File Transfer Protocol (FTP) is a protocol for transferring files over the Internet. FTP is based on client/server architecture. A user with an FTP client can log in to a remote FTP server, navigate the filesystem, and upload or download files from that system.

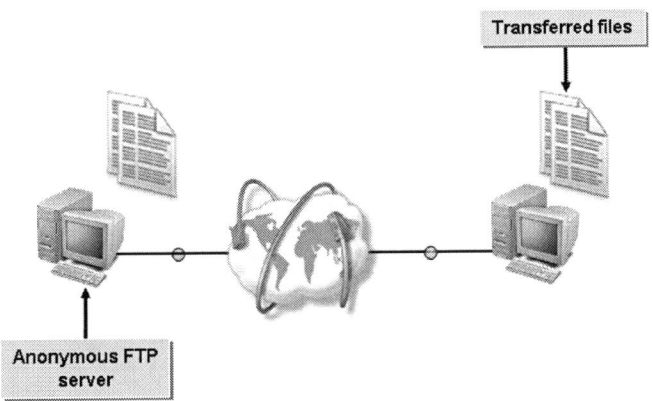

Figure 12-41: Files transferred from an FTP server to a client.

Any user can gain FTP access to the server and access his or her home directory after entering the user name and password. There are three files that can be configured to limit access to the FTP server.

File	Description
/etc/ftpaccess	The main configuration file for FTP, which includes the following options: • `loginfails`—This option specifies how many login attempts users are given before they are denied access. • `allow` or `deny tool access`—This option specifies whether or not utilities, such as `chmod`, can be used by the specified connection type (anonymous, guest, or all). • `email`—This option determines who the errors are emailed to. By default, this is set to root. • `message`—This option displays the default files.

File	Description
/etc/ftphosts	The /etc/ftphosts file is used to specify whether specific accounts are able to access the FTP server. Entries include allow or deny with the syntax, allow|deny user name host. For example, allow anonymous 192.167.100.* lets anyone on the 192.167.100 network to access the FTP server anonymously. Replacing allow with deny in this example will prevent anonymous access by users on the 192.167.100 network.
/etc/ftpusers	The text file ftpusers contains a list of users who may not log in to the FTP server using the FTP server daemon. This file is used for system administration. It also improves security within a TCP/IP environment. The file contains a list of users who may have no business using FTP, or those with too many privileges, blocking their log in through the FTP server. Such users can include root, daemon, bin, uucp, and news.

Authenticated vs. Anonymous FTP

There are two methods that are used to access a Linux server via FTP: authenticated and anonymous. Authenticated access requires that the user has a user name and password for the FTP server. To connect to the server, the user enters the user name and password and gains access to his or her home directory on the system. The user can download files from the server via the FTP get command and upload files via the FTP put command according to permissions set for that user or that user's group.

Anonymous FTP provides a public file directory where any user can download (and sometimes upload) files. An anonymous FTP server is simply an FTP server that accepts the user name anonymous with any password and allows that user to access a directory of public files. One common use for an anonymous FTP server is to provide a public repository for downloading updates for systems.

When determining whether or not to provide anonymous FTP access to a server, there are a number of security concerns to consider. The primary concern is that an anonymous user can upload files to your server for others to download without your knowledge. To avoid this, the default anonymous FTP installation restricts access to download files.

TFTP

The *Trivial File Transfer Protocol (TFTP)* is an unauthenticated version of FTP that runs over UDP. It is generally used for diskless workstations, where the system obtains its kernel from a TFTP server. To implement TFTP, you need to create a directory on your computer that will be the TFTP root. Sensitive information should not be stored in this directory. The TFTP daemon cannot go outside of this root directory, so it cannot access files such as password or user files.

Data Types

The client can specify the type of data to be transferred and stored. File types include:

- ASCII, which is the default file type. The ASCII file type is frequently used to transfer text files.

- EBCDIC, which is also used to transfer text files, but only when both the client and server systems are both EBCDIC systems.

- Binary, which is used for transferring image files.

- Local, which is used for transferring binary files with different byte sizes. Here, the sender may specify the number of bits per byte for the file transfer.

The Very Secure File Transfer Protocol Daemon

The *Very Secure File Transfer Protocol Daemon (VSFTPD)* is used for sending and receiving files from one computer to another through the Internet. It provides a secure way of transferring files in Linux-based operating systems. It provides greater security, better performance, and more stability than the previous versions of FTP. It allows anonymous or virtual user access. The vsftpd.conf file, which is stored in the /etc/vsftpd directory, is the main configuration file.

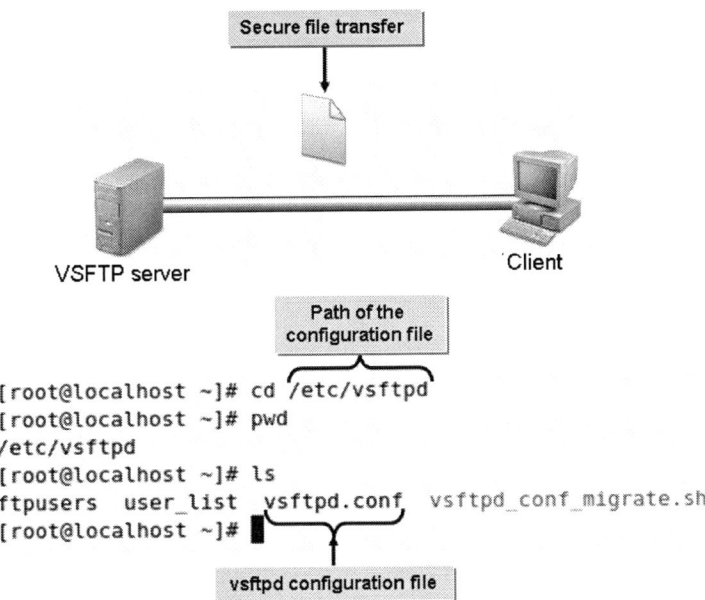

Figure 12-42: Transferring a file using an FTP server.

vsftpd Configuration Files

vsftpd RPM installs the vsftp daemon in the /usr/sbin/vsftpd directory and the daemon listens on ports 20 and 21. There are some default files that are installed while configuring VSFTPD.

File	Description
/etc/vsftpd/vsftpd.conf	Configures vsftpd.
/etc/init.d/vsftpd	Runs the initialization script for vsftpd.
/etc/vsftpd/user_list	Controls the user access for the FTP server using the `userlist_deny` directive specified in the vsftpd.conf file. Depending on whether the directive is set to `YES` or `NO`, the user access is decided.
/etc/pam.d/vsftpd	Defines the requirements for a user to access the FTP server. It is a PAM configuration file for vsftpd.

PAM

Pluggable Authentication Modules (PAM) is the interface layer of the authentication subsystem. PAM allows existing applications to use NIS for user authentication. It also provides a way to develop programs that are independent of authentication schemes. The PAM interface is supplemented by NIS client utilities, which can be found in the yp-tools and ypbind RPM packages. PAM works closely with NIS to resolve these commands.

The vsftpd.conf File Directives

The vsftpd.conf file configures vsftpd using a list of directives. Some of the directives are listed in the table.

Directive	Description
userlist_enable	Allows or denies access rights for the users listed in the user_list file. When this option is set to YES, then access to the FTP server is provided, based on the names listed in the user_list file.
userlist_deny	Controls user access based on the names listed in the user_list file. This option will be considered only when the userlist_enable option is set to YES. When the userlist_deny option is set to YES, then the users listed in the user_list file will be denied access to the FTP server and vice versa.
local_enable	Allows local users to log in to the system.
tcp_wrappers	Provides access to the FTP server using TCP wrappers.
xferlog_enable	Allows vsftpd to log connection to the log server and then log the file transfer information to the vsftpd.log file.
xferlog_file	Specifies the location of the vsftpd.log file, which stores all log messages. By default, the location is set to /var/log/vsftpd.log file.
xferlog_std_format	Allows vsftpd to log the file transfer information in the vsftpd.log file in a standard ftpd xferlog format.

FTP Servers

Various FTP servers provide different FTP services.

FTP Server	Description
Pure-FTPd	Provides an easy, quick, and secured way of transferring files among the UNIX-based operating systems such as Linux, OpenBSD, NetBSD, and Solaris. The pure-ftpd.conf file is used to configure Pure-FTPd and is stored in the /etc/pure-ftpd directory.
ProFTPd	Provides an easy way of transferring files among multiple virtual FTP servers. It runs as a standalone server and provides chroot capabilities depending on the filesystem. The proftpd.conf file is used to configure ProFTPd and is stored in the /etc directory. The proftpd.conf file is similar to Apache's configuration file.

FTP Configuration Files

The FTP configuration files are created and stored with respect to the FTP server that is configured. It contains directives and comments. Directives control the login behavior and access mechanism, anonymous user access to the server, and local user access. The directive name is followed by an equal operator and a value. There should be no space on either side of the equal operator. The comments begin with a # symbol. For example, `anonymous_enable= YES`
`# Allow anonymous FTP?`

FTP Connection Modes

An FTP connection between a client and a server can be established through two basic modes.

Mode	Description
Active	In the active FTP mode, the client sends a signal to the server, specifying the port through which the server should connect. The server in turn connects to the client through the specified port.
	This mode was developed when firewalls were not common. With the widespread implementation of firewalls, it was found that many problems arose because firewalls blocked the server from establishing a connection with the client.
Passive	In the passive FTP mode, the client confirms the port with the server and then initiates the connection with it. Because the connection is established by the client, it is not blocked by the firewall.

Data Transfer Modes

Data can be transferred through FTP using two common modes.

Mode	Description
ASCII	American Standard Code for Information Interchange (ASCII) mode transfers files only in text format. Some examples of ASCII files are .txt, .asp, and .html.
Binary	Binary mode transfers files in its original form and format. Some examples of binary files are .avi, .jpg, .png, and .mp3.

The ftp Command

The `ftp` command is used to transfer files to and from an FTP server. The `ftp` command has various options. The following table lists the basic `ftp` command options.

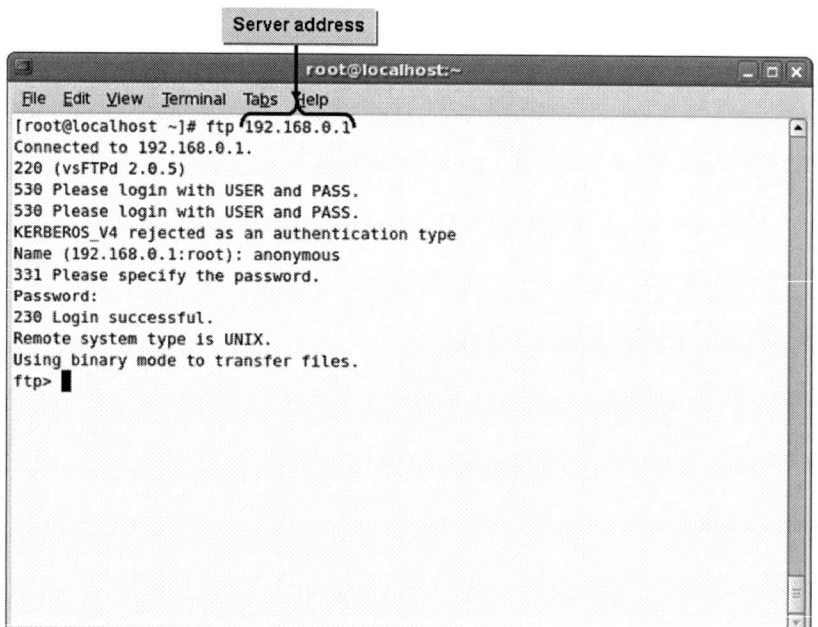

Figure 12-43: The ftp command is used to connect a client to a server using anonymous login.

Option	Used To
-p	Enable passive mode of file transfer.
-d	Enable debugging.
-g	Disable file name globbing.
-i	Disable interactive prompting.
-n	Disable auto-login while initially connecting.

Option	Used To
-v	Display all responses from the server.

Syntax

The syntax of the ftp command is ftp *[Command options] {hostname}*.

Network File System

Definition:

Network File System (NFS) is a networking protocol that allows a computer to access files stored on a network as though they are on a local disk. Using NFS, computers running on different operating systems can share files and disk storage space. NFS allows files stored on networked computers to be represented within a single directory tree. NFS uses the TCP/IP protocol. Filesystems that use the NFS protocol are called NFS filesystems. The NFS protocol has different versions, such as NFS version 2, NFS version 3, and NFS version 4.

Example:

Figure 12-44: Accessing files through NFS.

The Remote Procedure Call

Definition:

The *Remote Procedure Call (RPC)* is a package that contains a collection of tools and library functions, which enable a system to execute a program transparently which in turn enables other systems to communicate remotely. RPC is stored on an RPC server. When a client sends an RPC request to invoke a procedure, the server communicates with the client in the eXternal Data Representation (XDR) format. RPC uses UDP and TCP sockets to transport data to the remote host. Programs in RPC are uniquely identified by a program number. Details about a program and its corresponding program number are available in the /etc/rpc file.

Example:

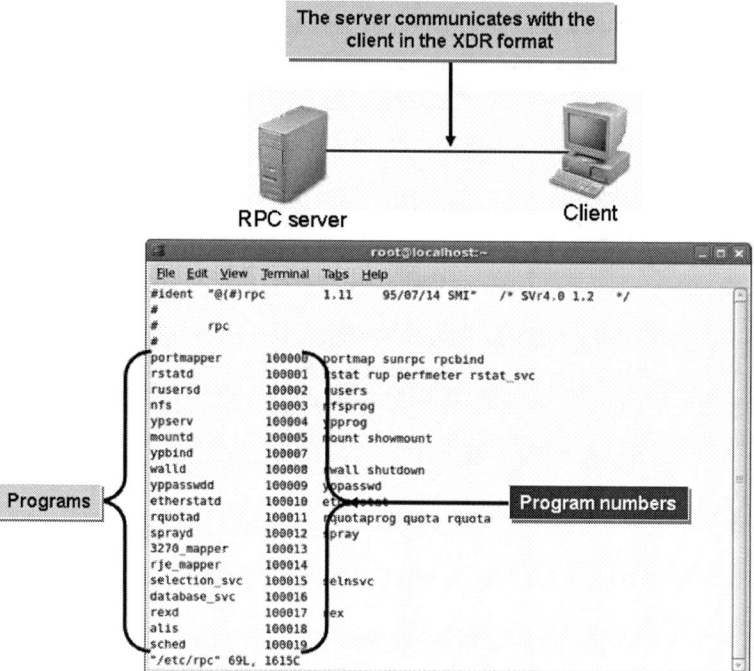

Figure 12-45: The output of the /etc/rpc file.

The XDR Format

The *eXternal Data Representation (XDR)* format is a standardized representation of data in the binary format. The XDR format allows systems to communicate across a network, especially across heterogeneous networks. It is developed using the C API programming language. XDR formats are defined in the rpc.h header file. It is primarily used in all Linux- and UNIX-based systems.

The Portmapper

Definition:

The *portmapper* is a program that an RPC application uses to register the port numbers used by the application. This program is stored in the /sbin directory or in the /usr/sbin directory. The portmapper acts as a service agent for all RPC servers running on a system. To access a service with the given program number, the client first queries the portmapper to get information about the port number where the service is available. The portmapper accepts the request, processes it, and returns the TCP and UDP port numbers of the service to the client.

When a system tries to access the portmapper, it reads the hosts.allow and hosts.deny files, which are stored in the /etc directory. These files list the IP addresses of systems to which access is allowed or denied using the `portmap` variable. The portmapper controls a set of daemons such as nfsd, mountd, ypbind/ypserv, rquotad, lockd, statd, ruptime, and rusers.

 In Linux, the portmapper is referred to as portmap or rpc.portmap.

Example:

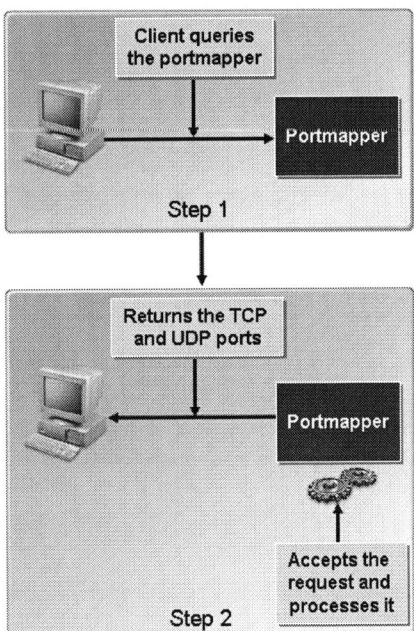

Figure 12-46: The working of the portmapper program.

The portmap Daemon

Definition:

The *portmap* service is a daemon that dynamically assigns ports to RPCs for communication between clients and servers. It maps a service name to the port number in which the service is running. It maintains a portmapper that contains a list of ports and the services that are available for access at each port. The portmap program is stored in the /sbin directory. The portmap service can be started only by a superuser.

Example:

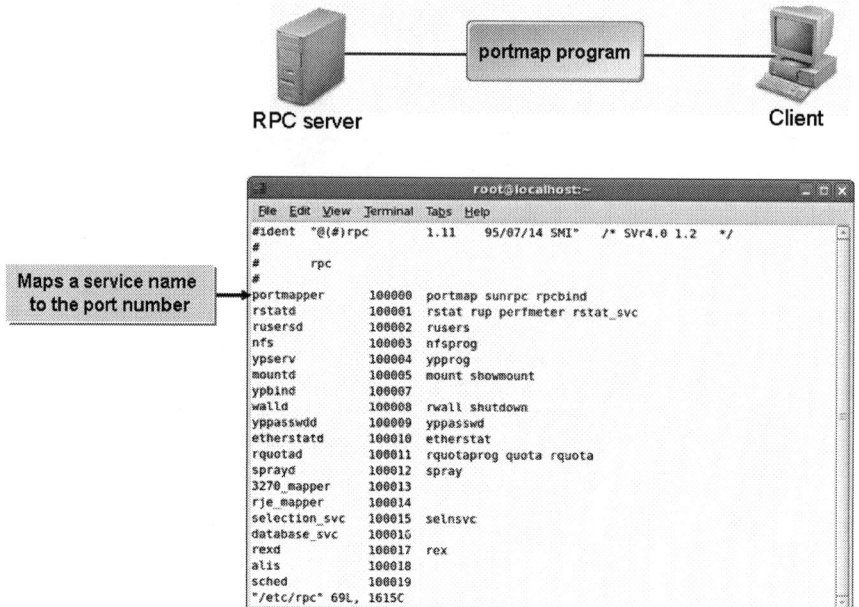

Figure 12-47: *The portmap program runs between a server and a client to dynamically assign ports to RPCs.*

NFS Daemons

NFS is implemented by four daemons:

- The `rpc.nfsd` daemon is the primary daemon that handles all NFS requests.

- The `rpc.mountd` daemon evaluates the permissions for an exported filesystem before it is mounted.

- The `rpc.lockd` daemon provides lock recovery on crashed systems.

- The `rpc.statd` daemon handles file locking issues.

NFS Firewall Options

The portmapper is used to assign ports dynamically to RPC services. This may lead to difficulty when setting up firewalls. Therefore, ports are controlled using the /etc/sysconfig/nfs file. By default, the portmapper is assigned to port 111 TCP and UDP, and nfsd is assigned to port 2049 TCP and UDP. The other daemons that are used are `mountd`, `statd`, `lockd`, and `rquotad`. Variables that are defined in the nfs file are listed in the table. These variables are assigned to a port value that is not being used by any service. While configuring firewalls, all these assigned ports and default ports are allowed to access NFS.

Variable	Description
MOUNTD_*PORT*	Specifies the TCP and UDP ports used by the mountd service.
STATD_*PORT*	Specifies the status of TCP and UDP ports used by the statd service.
LOCKD_*TCPPORT*	Specifies the TCP port used by the lockd service.

Variable	Description
LOCKD_*UDPPORT*	Specifies the UDP port used by the lockd service.

The Exports File

Definition:

The *exports file* is a configuration file that is used to export a filesystem. This file contains definitions, such as the directory to be exported and the clients who can access the directory. Clients are addressed by their hostnames, IP address ranges, IP address or subnet mask combinations, or NIS workgroups. The export options for the client are specified within parentheses, beside the client list. The exports file is stored in the /etc directory. By default, hosts will have read-only access to the filesystem. The exports file can be activated or deactivated using the exportfs command.

Example:

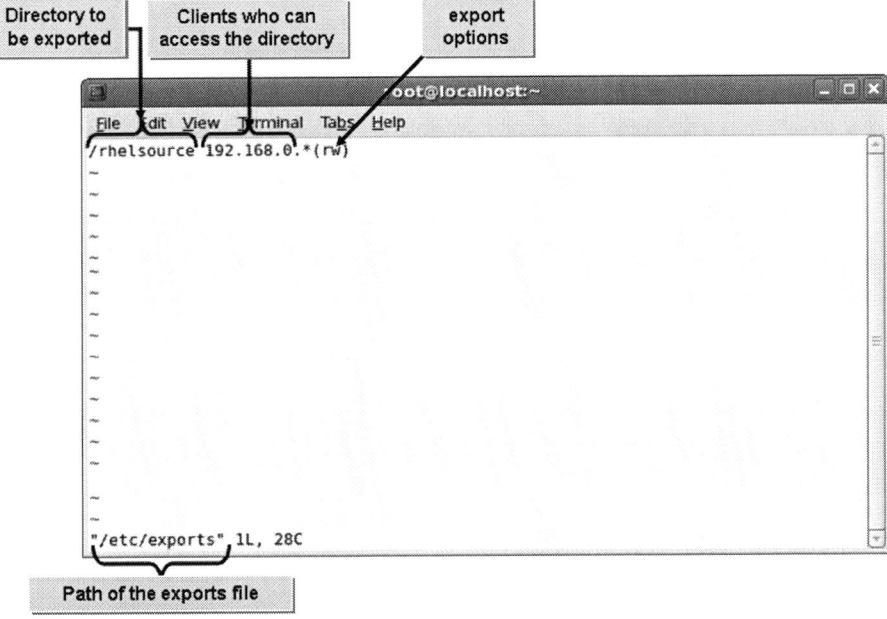

Figure 12-48: Defining the export options to export the filesystem.

NFS Shares on the Client-Side

On the client side, NFS shares are mounted using the mount command. The syntax of the mount command is: mount *nfs-type* -o *options* remote host:*remote directory local directory*, where *nfs-type* refers to the version of NFS used, *options* refer to the mount options, *remote directory* refers to the location from where the filesystem is to be mounted, and *local directory* refers to the local directory to which the filesystem is to be mounted. During system reboot, the filesystem has to be remounted manually using the mount command.

There are two ways in which the filesystem can be mounted automatically during system reboot.

Mount Type	Description
/etc/fstab	A line of code is added to the /etc/fstab file that is referenced by the netfs service. NFS shares are mounted when the initialization script runs from the /etc/init.d/netfs file. The syntax of the line that is added is: *{server IP address or host name}:{exported filesystem} {mount point} nfs {mount options} 0, 0*
autonfs	It is an automount utility that is used to mount and unmount filesystems automatically without the need for system resources. It comprises kernel modules that implement the filesystems and a user space daemon to control other functions. It uses the /etc/auto.master file as the main configuration file.

The rsync Utility

Definition:

The *rsync utility* is a utility that is used to synchronize files among systems. It compares two files and sends only the differences in the compressed form, instead of sending the entire file. The `rsync` daemon is managed using the rsyncd.conf file stored in the /etc directory. The `rsync` utility uses the rsync algorithm to determine differences between files.

Example:

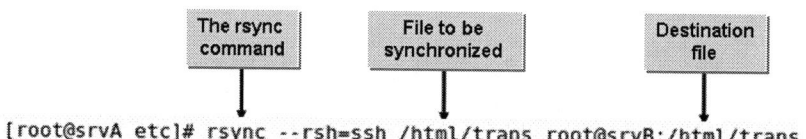

Figure 12-49: *An example of using the rsync command.*

Syntax

The syntax of the `rsync` utility is `rsync {source file or folder} {destination file or folder}`.

SMBFS and CIFS

The *Samba File System (SMBFS)* and the *Common Internet File System (CIFS)* are the standard filesystems that are used in Linux to mount and access shared resources available on a heterogeneous network. SMBFS is used exclusively for Linux systems. CIFS, which is a virtual filesystem, is widely used to share network files and resources. CIFS provides advanced features, such as authentication, Unicode, distributed caching, and other core kernel functions. SMBFS and CIFS can also be construed as client protocols that enable a Linux system, with Samba installed, to act as a server for a network.

Samba Daemons

Samba has three daemons: smbd, nmbd, and winbindd. The smbd and nmbd daemons are controlled by the SMB service and the winbindd daemon is controlled by the WINS service.

Daemon	Description
smbd	The Server Message Block Daemon (smbd) is used for sharing network resources. It is also used to provide user authentication, access control for network resources, and data sharing using the SMB protocol. By default, it listens to the SMB traffic in ports 139 and 445 and is invoked from the /usr/sbin/smbd directory.
nmbd	The *NetBIOS* Name Service Daemon (*nmbd*) is used to handle WINS requests and resolve NetBIOS names. By default, it listens to the NMB traffic in port 137 and is invoked from the /usr/sbin/nmbd directory.
winbindd	The winbindd is used to resolve the user and group information from a Windows NT server in such a way that it is understandable by a UNIX platform. It allows Windows users to access a Unix system using the RPC calls, PAM, and *Name Service Switch (NSS)*.

NSS

NSS is a protocol that enables services to access databases to check for user accounts from various sources. This is very useful in situations where one database has to be accessed by multiple services. For example, the hosts database can be accessed by various services, such as NIS and DNS, through NSS.

The WINS Service

The *Windows Internet Naming Service (WINS)* is a service that implements the Windows-specific method of name resolution. WINS consists of two main components: the WINS server and the WINS client. WINS translates the IP address on a Windows network to a NetBIOS name. It uses a distributed database that contains the IP addresses and names of the computers on the network. The database is periodically updated with the latest information.

The lmhosts File

Samba uses the lmhosts file to resolve NetBIOS names to IP addresses. The structure of this file is similar to the /etc/hosts file, but the hostnames follow NetBIOS naming conventions. The default location of the lmhosts file is same as that of the smb.conf file, that is /etc/samba.

The smbclient Command

The `smbclient` command is used to transfer files across a network and view the names of shared resources. The following table lists some options provided by the `smbclient` command.

Option	Used To
-N	Suppress password prompting.
-L *host name*	Specify that the shares from the specified host be displayed.
-s *path*	Specify the location of the smb.conf file.
-U *user name*	Specify the Samba user name.

It is also used as a tool for retrieving files. The syntax for retrieving the files is `smbclient //machine/service`.

The nmblookup Command

The `nmblookup` command is used to resolve the NETBIOS names to IP addresses. The following table lists some of the frequently used `nmblookup` command options.

Option	Used To
-T	Resolve IP addresses to hostnames.
-s *path*	Specify the location of the smb.conf file.
-M	Locate the master browser.
-S	Display the node status.

The Samba Configuration File

The smb.conf file, which is stored in the /etc/samba directory, is the main configuration file for a Samba service. The initialization script runs from the /etc/init.d/smb file. The smb.conf file is structured similar to the Windows.ini file. This file contains a share definition for every directory or device that needs to be shared. A typical share definition contains the share name, the path of the directory or device that is shared, and other options that allow or deny access to the share. Each share is defined as a section within brackets, with the share name specific to the resource being shared.

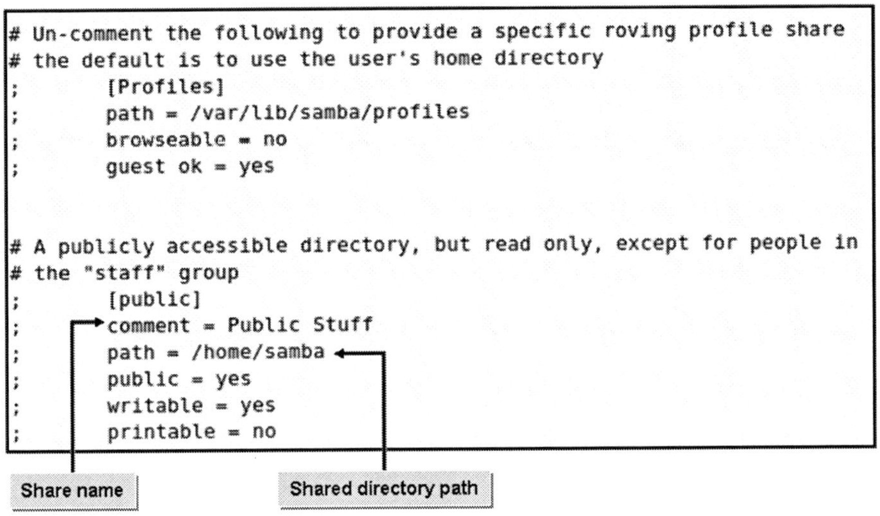

```
# Un-comment the following to provide a specific roving profile share
# the default is to use the user's home directory
;          [Profiles]
;          path = /var/lib/samba/profiles
;          browseable = no
;          guest ok = yes


# A publicly accessible directory, but read only, except for people in
# the "staff" group
;          [public]
;          comment = Public Stuff
;          path = /home/samba
;          public = yes
;          writable = yes
;          printable = no
```

Share name   Shared directory path

Figure 12-50: The Samba shares defined in the smb.conf file.

By default, the smb.conf file comprises three sections: global, homes, and printers. Each section consists of its own options specific to the share. The global section defines options such as the workgroup name, log size, and the security mode that are applicable to the server as a whole. It defines the default options that are common to all the other shares. The options given in the global section can be overridden by other sections. The homes section consists of options, such as `browseable` and `writable`, that define user access of files in home directories. The printers section consists of options, such as `path` and `guest ok`, that define the sharing of printers and their services.

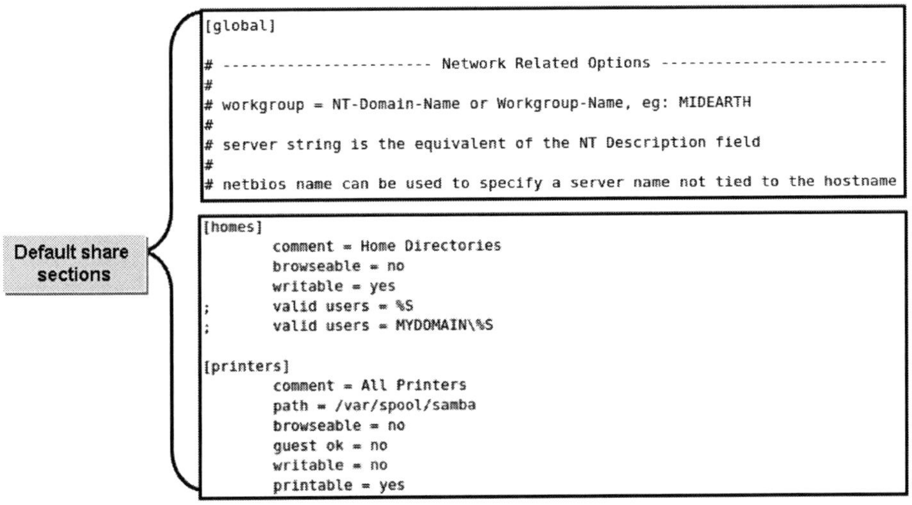

```
[global]

# --------------------- Network Related Options ----------------------
#
# workgroup = NT-Domain-Name or Workgroup-Name, eg: MIDEARTH
#
# server string is the equivalent of the NT Description field
#
# netbios name can be used to specify a server name not tied to the hostname
```

Default share sections

```
[homes]
          comment = Home Directories
          browseable = no
          writable = yes
;         valid users = %S
;         valid users = MYDOMAIN\%S

[printers]
          comment = All Printers
          path = /var/spool/samba
          browseable = no
          guest ok = no
          writable = no
          printable = yes
```

Figure 12-51: Default Samba shares defined in the smb.conf file.

Each section in the samba.conf file comprises its own options specific to the share. The syntax for defining an option is `option = value`. Some frequently used options are listed in the table.

Option	Description
public	Specifies whether the share is accessed by all users. It is set to either yes or no.
browseable	Specifies whether the share is part of the browse list. It is set to either yes or no.
writable	Specifies whether the shared file is only readable or both readable and writable. It is set to either yes or no.
printable	Specifies whether the share is allowed to access the printer. It is set to either yes or no.
group	Specifies the primary group that is used to connect to the share. It is set to the group name.

Configuration Tools for Samba

Various tools, such as system-config-samba and samba-swat, are available to configure Samba in the GUI. However, it is recommended to edit the smb.conf file manually in the CLI.

Tool	Description
system-config-samba	Used for creating, modifying, and managing Samba shares. It is activated by installing the system-config-samba package.
samba-swat	It is a Samba web administration tool. It includes a wizard that helps in configuring Samba quickly. Each section of the smb.conf file is specified as a separate swat screen. The samba-swat tool is activated by installing the samba-swat package.

Global Configuration Options in the smb.conf File

Some frequently used global configuration options in the smb.conf file are listed in the following table.

Option	Used To	Parameters To Be Specified
server string = Parameter	Specify a brief description of the server.	String
log file = Parameter	Indicate the location where a log file for each user will be stored.	Log file path
encrypt passwords = Parameter	Indicate if encrypted passwords should be used.	Boolean
password server = password server address	Specify the password server.	FQDN of the password server

Option	Used To	Parameters To Be Specified
smb passwd file = *Parameter*	Specify the location of the password file to be used if the security level is set to user.	Name of the password file with the full path
hosts allow = *Parameter*	Specify the hosts that can access Samba shares.	Hostnames or IP addresses separated by a space
idmap uid = *range of user ID*	Specify the range of the UID to be used to map Windows and Linux systems.	Range of the UID
idmap gid = *range of group ID*	Specify the range of the GID to be used to map Windows and Linux systems.	Range of the GID

Options for Defining a Share in the smb.conf File

Some frequently used options for a share definition are listed in the following table.

Option	Used To	Parameters To Be Specified
create mode	Specify the permissions to be set for any file that is created in a share.	Bits representing permissions
directory mode	Specify the permissions to be set for any directory that is created in a share.	Bits representing permissions
invalid users	Specify the user names that do not have access to a share.	User names or group names separated by a comma
write list	Specify a group that has write access to a share.	User names or group names separated by a comma
guest ok	Specify whether default guest users are allowed to log in to the system or not.	Boolean
max connections	Specify the maximum number of connections for a share.	A number

Samba Authentication Mechanism

Samba authenticates users based on the `security` option set in the smb.conf file. The `security` option can be set to various levels.

Security Level	Description
Share-level security	A share can be configured to have more than one password. Each password can limit access to the share. For example, a password may allow read-only access while another may permit read-write access. A user with a valid password can access the share.
User-level security	A share can be configured to permit access for specific users. Users can access the share by providing the user name and password. The Samba server authenticates the users and allows access to the share.
Server-level security	Server-level security is similar to the User-level security. In Server-level security, Samba authenticates users through another server that contains password details. The server that contains the password details can be a Samba server or a Windows NT Primary Domain Controller (PDC).
Domain-level security	Samba must be a member of a Windows domain to implement domain-level security. Samba uses the Windows PDC to authenticate a user based on the user name and password used to log in to the windows domain. Users will have access to several shares based on the rights granted to them. They will not be authenticated each and every time a user accesses the share.
ADS-level security	Active Directory Service-level (ADS) security is similar to the Domain-level security. However, ADS-level security uses NT4 style security that depends on RPCs. When using ADS, Samba allows users to join as native AD members, allowing them to access shares without authentication every time.

How to Implement Network File Sharing Services

Procedure Reference: Configure FTP Manually

To manually configure the FTP service:

1. Log in as root in the CLI.
2. If necessary, install the vsftpd-{version}.{release}.rpm package.
3. Enter `service vsftpd start` to start the FTP service.
4. If desired, enter `chkconfig vsftpd on` to set the service to start automatically on reboot.
5. If desired, enter `service vsftpd stop` to stop the FTP service.
6. If desired, enter `service vsftpd restart` to restart the FTP service.

Procedure Reference: Connect to a Remote Terminal Using FTP

To connect to a remote terminal using FTP:

1. Log in as root in the CLI.
2. Enter `ftp {IP address of the ftp server}` to connect to another system by FTP.
3. Enter the user name and password.
4. Perform the necessary tasks on the remote computer.
5. If necessary, enter `bye` to log out of the FTP service.

Procedure Reference: Install an FTP Server

To install an FTP server:

1. In the Linux server, log in as root.
2. At the command line, enter the command to install the FTP server.

   - Enter `rpm -ivh vsftpd-{version}.{release}.rpm` to install vsftpd.

    If you do not have the Linux installation CD-ROM, you can download the latest version of vsftpd from **www.vsftpd.beasts.org.**

   - Enter `rpm -ivh pure-ftpd-{version}.{release}.rpm` to install Pure-FTPd.

    If you do not have the Linux installation CD-ROM, you can download the latest version of Pure-Ftpd from **www.pureftpd.org.**

   - Enter `rpm -ivh proftpd-{version}.{release}.rpm` to install ProFTPd.

    If you do not have the Linux installation CD-ROM, you can download the latest version of ProFTPd from **www.proftpd.org.**

3. Verify that the FTP has been installed.

   - Enter `rpm -qi vsftpd` to verify that vsftpd has been installed.
   - Enter `rpm -qi pure-ftpd` to verify that Pure-FTPd has been installed.
   - Enter `rpm -qi proftpd` to verify that ProFTPd has been installed.

Procedure Reference: Configure a vsftpd FTP Server for Anonymous Uploads

To configure an FTP server for anonymous uploads:

1. Navigate to the /etc/vsftpd directory.
2. Open the vsftpd.conf file.
3. Locate the line that reads "anonymous_enable=YES" and uncomment it, to enable anonymous logins.
4. Locate the line that reads "write_enable=YES" and verify that it is not commented, to grant write permission to all users.
5. Enable anonymous uploads.

   - Locate the line that reads "anon_upload_enable=YES" and uncomment it.
   - Locate the line that reads "anon_mkdir_write_enable=YES" and uncomment it.

6. If necessary, change the ownership of the uploaded files.

   - Locate the line that reads "chown_uploads=YES" and uncomment it, to change the ownership.
   - Locate the line that reads "chown_username=whoever" and uncomment it. In the line "chown_username=whoever", replace `whoever` with the name of the user who will own the uploaded files.

7. Save and close the file.
8. Enter

   ```
   service vsftpd start
   ```

   to start the `vsftpd` daemon.

9. If necessary, enter `chkconfig vsftpd on` to start the service on boot.
10. If necessary, connect the FTP client to the FTP server to upload or download files.

Procedure Reference: Configure FTP to Run in chroot Mode

1. Navigate to the /etc/vsftpd directory.
2. Open the vsftpd.conf file.
3. Enable the chroot list file settings.

   - Locate the line that reads "chroot_list_enable=YES" and uncomment it, to enable the list.
   - Locate the line that reads "chroot_list_file=/etc/vsftpd/chroot_list" and uncomment it, to enable the list file.

4. Save and close the file.
5. Add the users who need to be added to the chrooted list in the /etc/vsftpd/vsftpd.chroot_list file.
6. Start the `vsftpd` daemon using the `service vsftpd start` command.

Procedure Reference: Mount Remote Filesystems

To mount remote filesystems using NFS:

 After you exported a directory or filesystem for a user, the user can now use the exported directory or filesystem by mounting the remote filesystem to the local directory using NFS.

1. Log in as root in the CLI.
2. Mount the remote filesystem.
   a. Enter `showmount -e` *{IP address of the NFS server}* to view the export list of the NFS server.
   b. Enter `mount -t nfs` *IP address of the NFS server:*`/Directory/Filesystem /`*{Local mount point}* to mount the remote filesystem on the specified mount point.
3. Enter `mount` to verify that the remote filesystem is mounted.
4. If desired, enter `umount /`*{Local mount point}* to unmount the filesystem.

Procedure Reference: Mount Remote Filesystems Automatically

To automatically mount remote filesystems using NFS:

1. Log in as root in the CLI.
2. Automatically mount the remote filesystem.
   a. Enter `showmount -e` {IP address of the NFS server} to view the export list of the NFS server.
   b. Enter `vi /etc/fstab`.
   c. Type *{IP address of the NFS server}:*`/Directory/Filesystem /`*{Local mountpoint}* `nfs defaults` *{filesystem frequency} {filesystem order}* to mount the remote filesystem on the specified mount point when booting the system.
   d. Save and close the file.
3. Verify that the remote filesystem is automatically mounted on booting the system.
   a. Reboot the system.
   b. Log in as root.
   c. Enter `mount` to verify that the remote filesystem is mounted.

The showmount Command Options

The `showmount` command displays the mount information of the NFS server. The following table gives some common `showmount` command options and their description.

Option	Description
-e	The NFS server's export list.
-d	The directories mounted by any client.

Option	Description
-a	The client's hostname and the mounted directory.

Managing the NFS Server

NFS server management includes tasks such as starting the server and activating the list of exported filesystems. The following table lists common commands that are used to manage the NFS server.

If You Need To	Enter
Start the NFS server	`service nfs start`
Stop the NFS server	`service nfs stop`
Restart the NFS server	`service nfs restart`
Activate the list of exported filesystems	`exportfs -r`
Deactivate the list of exported filesystems	`exportfs -ua`

Procedure Reference: Configure Samba Using the GUI

To configure Samba using the GUI:

1. Log in as root in the GUI.

2. Display the terminal and enter `system-config-samba`.

3. Specify the workgroup.

    a. In the **Samba Server Configuration** window, choose **Preferences→Server Settings.**

    b. In the **Server Settings** dialog box, in the **Workgroup** text box, specify the workgroup name.

    c. In the **Description** text box, specify the details about the workgroup.

4. Specify the authentication mode.

    a. Select the **Security** tab.

    b. From the **Authentication Mode** drop-down list, select the desired authentication mode and fill the necessary details.

    c. Click **OK.**

5. Share home directories.

    a. Choose **File→Add Share.**

    b. In the **Create Samba Share** dialog box, click **Browse.**

    c. In the **Select Directory** dialog box, in the **Folders** list, double-click to select the directory you want to share and then click **OK.**

    d. In the **Description** text box, specify the details of the shared directory.

    e. Set the desired permission for the share: **Writable, Visible,** or both.

    f. On the **Access** tab, select the desired permission and click **OK.**

6. Choose **File→Quit.**

 The Samba service will start as soon as you perform the above step.

7. Verify that the shared directory is accessible from a Windows system.

   a. Start the Windows system.

   b. Log in as administrator.

   c. Display the **Windows Explorer** window.

   d. In the **Windows Explorer** window, in the address bar, type `//{Name or IP address of the samba server}/{Share name}` and press **Enter** to access the shared directory. The display of the shared directory may take some time depending on the network speed.

Set Permission to Filesystems

If a conflict arises between the permission set for a directory and the permission set for that directory while sharing the directory, its effective permission will always be the minimal permission. Some of the possible file permission combinations that will be implemented during a conflict are given in the following table.

Directory Permission	Share Permission	Effective Permission
Read	Read	Read
Read	Write	Read
Write	Read	Read
Read/write	Read	Read
Read	Read/write	Read
Read/write	Read/write	Read/write

ACTIVITY 12-5

Configuring an Anonymous vsftpd Server

Before You Begin:

1. On srvA, you have logged in as root in the CLI.

2. At the command line, change directory to the root directory.

3. Enter `clear` to clear the terminal screen.

Scenario:

You are a network administrator for a software development company that has branches in many countries. The teams at various locations frequently exchange large files through email. However, sharing large files using email affects mail server performance. So, you want to create a common directory on a server where users can upload and download files.

What You Do	How You Do It
1. Install FTP.	a. On the server labeled **srvA,** navigate to the /rhelsource/Server directory.
	b. Enter `rpm -ivh` ⇒ `vsftpd-2.0.5-12.el5.i386.rpm` to install the `vsftpd` package.
	c. Enter `rpm -qi vsftpd` to display information about the installed FTP version.
	d. Clear the terminal screen.

2.   Configure FTP to allow anonymous access.

     a.   Using the `vi` editor, open the /etc/vsftpd/vsftpd.conf file.

     b.   Locate the line that reads "write_enable=YES" and verify that it is not commented.

     c.   Locate the line that reads "#anon_upload_enable=YES" and uncomment it.

     d.   Locate the line that reads "#anon_mkdir_write_enable=YES" and uncomment it.

     e.   Save and close the file.

     f.   Clear the terminal screen.

     g.   In the /var/ftp directory, create a directory named ***upload*** and grant full access to all.

     h.   Start the vsftpd service.

     i.   Enter **chkconfig ⇒ vsftpd on** to start the vsftpd service whenever the system boots.

     j.   Clear the terminal screen.

3.   Access the FTP server from another system on your network.

     a.   On the system labeled **srvB,** ensure that you are in the root folder. Enter **ftp 192.168.0.2** to connect to the FTP server.

     b.   Log in as ***anonymous*** without providing a password.

     c.   Navigate to the upload directory.

     d.   Enter **put /root/install.log mylogfile** to upload the install.log file.

     e.   Observe that the file is uploaded successfully.

     f.   Enter **bye** to quit FTP.

     g.   Clear the terminal screen.

ACTIVITY 12-6

Exporting a Filesystem using NFS

Before You Begin:

1. Switch to srvA.
2. On srvA, you have logged in as root in the CLI.
3. The first terminal is displayed.
4. Enter cd /root to change to the root directory.
5. Enter clear to clear the terminal screen.

Scenario:

You are going to install a software application on some new systems. You created a /rhelsource directory containing the software. You want to share this directory with the 192.168.0.0 network along with read or write permission to facilitate easy access.

What You Do	How You Do It
1. Export the /rhelsource directory.	a. Enter **vi /etc/exports**
	b. Press **I** to switch to the insert mode.
	c. Type **/rhelsource 192.168.0.*(rw)** to export the /rhelsource directory to the 192.168.0.0 network.
	d. Press **Esc.**
	e. Save and close the file.
	f. Enter **clear** to clear the terminal screen.
2. Activate the nfs service.	a. Enter **service nfs start** to start the nfs service.
	b. Enter **exportfs -r** to activate the exported filesystem.
	c. Enter **showmount -e** to view the export list.
	d. Observe that the exported /rhelsource directory is listed.
	e. Enter **clear** to clear the terminal screen.

ACTIVITY 12-7

Sharing a Filesystem Using Samba

Before You Begin:

1. On srvA, you have logged in as root in the CLI.

2. The first terminal is displayed.

3. Enter `service smb start` to start the Samba service.

4. Enter `chkconfig smb on` to automatically start the Samba service.

5. Enter `cd /rhelsource/Server` to change to the Server directory.

6. Enter `rpm -ivh system-config-samba-1.2.41-3.el5.noarch.rpm` to install the system-config-samba package.

7. Enter `clear` to clear the terminal screen.

8. Switch to the GUI. Log in as root and display the terminal window.

Scenario:

You shared a common directory, /rhelsource, consisting of all the software programs through NFS. Some of the network users in your company, who use Windows as their operating system, find that they are not able to access the common directory. The Windows users are in a workgroup named "mygroup."

What You Do	How You Do It
1. Specify the work group.	a. Enter **system-config-samba** to modify samba configuration.
	b. In the **Samba Server Configuration** window, choose **Preferences→Server Settings**.
	c. In the **Server Settings** dialog box, in the **Workgroup** text box, verify that the workgroup name is set as **mygroup.**
	d. In the **Description** text box, triple-click and type **swprograms**
2. Specify the authentication mode.	a. Select the **Security** tab.
	b. From the **Authentication Mode** drop-down list, select **Share** and click **OK.**

3.	Share the /rhelsource directory.	a.	Choose **File→Add Share** to display the **Create Samba Share** dialog box.
		b.	In the **Directory** text box, type */rhelsource*
		c.	In the **Description** text box, click and type *software programs*
		d.	Check the **Writable** and **Visible** check boxes to specify the permission level.
4.	Set permission for the /rhelsource directory.	a.	Select the **Access** tab.
		b.	Select **Allow access to everyone** and click **OK.**
		c.	Choose **File→Quit.**
		d.	Enter `chkconfig smb on` to start the Samba server on reboot.
		e.	Enter `reboot` to reboot the server.
5.	Verify that the user is able to access the /rhelsource directory from a Windows workstation.	a.	Reboot srvB and boot in Windows OS.
		b.	Log in to the system.
		c.	Close the **Welcome Center** window.
		d.	Choose **Start→Network.**
		e.	In the **Network** window, in the address bar, enter *//srvA/*
		f.	Double-click the **rhelsource** folder to view the contents.
		g.	Close the **rhelsource on srvA** window.

TOPIC F
Configure NIS

Now that you can configure cross-platform file sharing on a network, you can begin to perform domain management services. In this topic, you will configure the Network Information Service (NIS).

Organizations with global operations invariably have branch offices in the major cities of the world. In such instances, information must be shared among employees in various offices. Storing the login and contact information in a centralized system will enable users to access it no matter where they are located. Network Information Service (NIS) allows you to centralize the storage of user information in order to provide authentication to services across the enterprise. Additionally, you can configure NIS to store group account information in a database, for all users on the network.

Network Information Service

Definition:

Network Information Service (NIS) is a network service that manages information about all systems and users on a network. It is a centralized information administration system that enables network users to maintain data integrity. It allows the distribution of consistent data throughout the network. NIS distributes information from the database to all hosts, to maintain consistency of configuration information across systems on the network.

Example:

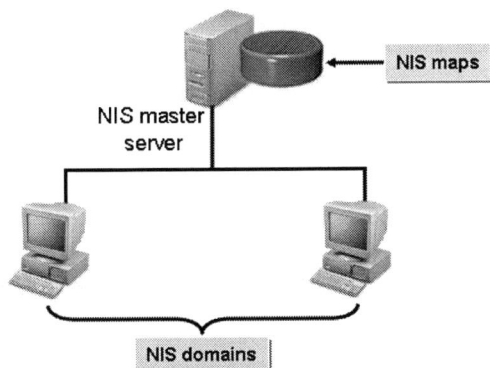

Figure 12-52: NIS managing information on a network.

NIS Components

NIS consists of four major components.

Component	Description
Maps	NIS stores information such as user name, password, and group name in database files; referred to as NIS maps. Each map consists of a pair of files. A map is made up of key-pair values and is stored in the database management library format. NIS maps can be created by running `make` in the /var/yp directory.
NIS Domain	An NIS domain is a group of hosts that share the same set of maps. The hosts within a domain share password, hosts, and group file information. Maps are stored in a subdirectory having the same name as the domain in the /var/yp directory. By default, the NIS domain name is specified in the /etc/sysconfig/network file. Each domain consists of a single master NIS server. A client can belong to only one domain.
NIS Master Server	NIS stores the database that contains network information in the master server. The master server also contains the source files for various maps. The `ypserv` process should be run on the server to manage the NIS server. The configuration settings of the master server are specified in the ypserv.conf file that is stored in the /etc directory.
NIS Slave Server	An NIS slave server is a secondary server that balances the load on the master server. The slave server contains a copy of the database and source files. Any update made on the maps or database will be updated to the slave server by the master server using the `ypush` command. When the master server is down, then the slave server will act as a master server and resolve the queries sent by the client. The information about the slave server is specified in the /var/yp/ypservers file.

NIS Maps

There are many standard maps supported by NIS.

File	Map	Description
/etc/hosts	hosts.byname, hosts.byaddr	Maps an IP address to the corresponding hostname.
/etc/networks	networks.byname, networks.byaddr	Maps an IP network address to the network name.

File	Map	Description
/etc/passwd	passwd.byname, passwd.byuid	Maps an encrypted password to the respective user login name.
/etc/group	group.byname, group.bygid	Maps GIDs to group names.
/etc/services	services.byname, services.bynumber	Maps service description to a service name.
/etc/rpc	rpc.byname, rpc.bynumber	Maps RPC service numbers to the corresponding RPC service names.
/etc/protocols	protocols.byname, protocols.bynumber	Maps protocol numbers to protocol names.
/usr/lib/aliases	mail.aliases	Maps mail aliases to mail alias names.

The securenets file

NIS will listen to all networks after the installation of the daemons: ypserv, and ypxfrd. Both the daemons restrict user access by using the /var/yp/securenets file. The securenets file contains only the range of IP addresses to which the daemons have to respond. By default, the NIS will listen to all networks after the installation of daemons where the securenets file remains empty. You can add the specific range of IP addresses to the file so that the daemons will respond only to those networks.

The netgroup File

The netgroup file contains a list of user groups on the network along with their permissions. This helps in checking the permissions while performing remote mounts and working in remote logins and remote shells. The user groups are defined in the format:

```
Groupname member1, [member 2....]
```

where member1 refers to another group name, which consists of three fields. They are hostname, user name, and domain name. For example, a group named systems is defined as systems (analytical, cwarden, ourglobalcompany), where analytical refers to the hostname, cwarden refers to the user name, and ourglobalcompany refers to the domain name. If any of the fields are left empty, then it is considered as the wildcard. For example, in a group defined as systems (analytical, -, ourglobalcompany), the host analytical belongs to the group systems in the domain ourglobalcompany but there are no users for this group.

Information About NIS Maps

Any NIS user can display information about NIS maps. The following table lists the commands that are used to display the maps.

Command	Enables You To
ypcat map name or its alias	List the values in a map.
ypmatch -x	List the aliases of maps.
ypwhich -m	List the available maps and the master server names.

Command	Enables You To
`yppoll map alias name`	Display the version and master server of a map.

NIS Servers

An NIS server provides centralized directory and authentication services for a network. Multiple NIS servers, in a master/slave(s) configuration, are often used in larger NIS installations. The NIS server can be explicitly configured, or the client can automatically find an NIS server via a network broadcast.

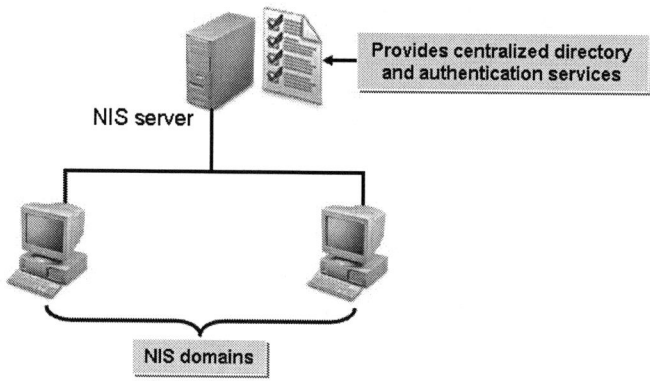

Figure 12-53: An NIS server on a network.

NIS Utilities

NIS clients query an NIS server to perform user authentication and obtain information about a user. The NIS service is supported by several utilities.

Utility	Description
makedbm	Creates a database file for an NIS map.
ypbind	Gathers and records NIS domain and server information.
ypcat	Prints all key values, for the specified NIS database. Lists data in a map.
ypinit	Builds and installs an NIS database and initializes NIS client's ypservers list.
ypmatch	Finds a specific entry in a map. Displays the NIS map's key values.
yppasswd	Changes your password in the NIS database.
yppoll	Displays the specified NIS map version and master server.
yppush	Propagates data from NIS master to NIS slave server.
ypset	Sets binding to a particular server.
ypwhich	Finds the NIS server name used by the client. Lists the name of the NIS server and the nickname translation table.
ypxfr	Transfers data from the NIS master to the NIS slave server.

How to Configure NIS

Procedure Reference: Install an NIS Server

To install an NIS server:

1. Log in as root.

2. Mount the Linux installation media that contains the RPMs for the NIS server.

 If you do not have the Linux installation media, you can download the NIS RPM from **www.rpmfind.net.**

3. Navigate to the /media/[name of the media]/Packages directory.

4. Install the `ypserv`, `yp-tools`, and `ypbind` packages using the commands.

   ```
   rpm -ivh ypserv*.rpm

   rpm -ivh yp-tools-*.rpm

   rpm -ivh ypbind*.rpm
   ```

5. Verify that the packages have been installed.

   ```
   rpm -qi package name
   ```

Procedure Reference: Configure an NIS Server

To configure an NIS server:

1. Add the NIS domain name to the network file.

   a. Open the /etc/sysconfig/network file.

   b. Add the `NISDOMAIN` statement, specifying the NIS domain name.

      ```
      NISDOMAIN=domain name
      ```

   c. Save and close the file.

2. Add NIS server information to the yp.conf file.

   a. Open the /etc/yp.conf file.

   b. Add the domain name in one of the three formats:

      - ```
        domain domain name server server's host name
        ```

      - ```
        ypserver server's host name
        ```

      - ```
        domain domain name broadcast
        ```

   c. Save and close the file.

3. Restart the `portmap` daemon to inform the NIS client about the ports on which the NIS server will be listening to requests.

   ```
   service portmap restart
   ```

4. Enter `service yppasswdd start` to start the `yppasswdd` daemon and service new password requests from NIS users.
   ```

5. Start the `ypserv` daemon to start the NIS server.

    ```
    service ypserv start
    ```

6. Initialize the NIS domain to create appropriate authentication files for the domain.

    a. At the command line, enter `/usr/lib/yp/ypinit -m`.

    b. The hostnames you added in the yp.conf file will be displayed. If required, enter other NIS server hostnames.

    c. Press **Ctrl+D.**

    d. When you are prompted to confirm the server name, type *y* and press **Enter.**

7. Start the `ypbind` and `ypxfrd` daemons.

8. Verify that the daemons are running on the localhost.

    ```
    rpcinfo localhost
    ```

9. Create NIS maps to update the NIS domain's authentication files with the user and system information. To do so, navigate to the /var/yp directory and then run the `make` utility.

    ```
    cd /var/yp
    make
    ```

10. Using the `ypmatch user name passwd` command verify that the NIS user information is updated.

Procedure Reference: Configure an NIS Slave Server

To configure an NIS slave server:

1. Verify that the master NIS server is up and running.

2. In the master NIS server, in the `/var/yp/Makefile` file, change the `NOPUSH` parameter to `false` so that the maps are updated in the slave servers.

    ```
    NOPUSH=false
    ```

3. In the master server, modify the ypservers file.

    a. Open the /var/yp/ypservers file.

    b. Add the slave server names on separate lines.

    c. Save and close the file.

4. In the slave server, log in as root.

5. Ensure that the `ypserv`, `yp-tools`, and `ypbind` packages are installed.

6. Enter `/usr/lib/yp/ypinit -s server host name` to configure the slave server.

7. Start the `portmap`, `ypserv`, `ypbind`, `yppasswdd`, and `ypxfrd` daemons.

8. Enter `rpcinfo localhost` to verify that the daemons are running on the localhost.

Procedure Reference: Update the NIS Files Manually

To manually update the NIS files on a slave server:

1. On the NIS master server, log in as root.

2. At the command line, use the `yppush` command with the `-h` option.

    ```
    yppush -h {host name of slave server} {map to be updated}
    ```

Procedure Reference: Install an NIS Client

To install an NIS client:

1. On the Linux server, log in as root.

2. Mount the Linux installation media that contains the RPMs for the NIS client.

3. Navigate to the /media/[name of the media]/Packages directory.

4. Enter `rpm -ivh yp-tools-{version}.{release}.rpm`
   `rpm -ivh ypbind-{version}.{release}.rpm` to install the `yp-tools` and
   `ypbind` packages.

5. Enter `rpm -qi package name` to verify that the packages have been installed.

Procedure Reference: Configure NIS Clients

To configure NIS clients:

1. Log in as root.

2. Use the `authconfig-tui` utility to configure the NIS files.

   a. At the command line, type `authconfig-tui` and press **Enter.**

   b. Select the **Use NIS** option.

   c. Press **F12** to navigate to the next page.

   d. In the **Domain** text box, type the NIS domain name.

   e. In the **Server** text box, type the NIS server name.

   f. Press **F12.**

3. Modify the nsswitch.conf file to specify that NIS should be used for login authentication. To do so, you can use the template provided by NIS.

   a. Open the /etc/nsswitch.conf file.

   b. Specify NIS as the preferred service for all databases.

   ```
   service name: nis dns files db
   ```

   c. Save and close the file.

 Instead of manually changing the nsswitch.conf file, you can overwrite it with the sample file located in the /usr/share/doc/yp-tools-{version}.{release} directory.

4. Add an empty field to the authentication files to restrict addition of users.

   a. At the end of the /etc/passwd file, add a plus sign followed by six colons.

   ```
   +::::::
   ```

   b. At the end of the /etc/group file, add a plus symbol followed by three colon symbols.

   ```
   +:::
   ```

   c. At the end of the /etc/shadow file, add a plus symbol followed by eight colon symbols.

   ```
   +::::::::
   ```

5. Start the `portmap`, `yppasswdd`, and `ypbind` daemons.

6. Verify that the daemons are running on the localhost.

```
rpcinfo localhost
```

Procedure Reference: Change Passwords of NIS Users

To change the password of NIS users:

1. At the command line, type yppasswd with the -p option and the NIS user name, and press **Enter.**

```
yppasswd -p NIS user name
```

2. Enter the root password and press **Enter.**
3. Enter the new password for the NIS user and press **Enter.**
4. When prompted, re-enter the password and press **Enter.**

ACTIVITY 12-8
Configuring an NIS Server

Before You Begin:

1. On srvA, switch to the CLI.

2. Log in as root in the CLI.

3. The first terminal is displayed.

4. At the command line, change to the /rhelsource/Server directory.

5. Enter `rpm -ivh ypserv-2.19-5.el5.i386.rpm` to install the ypserv-2.19-5.el5.i386.rpm package.

6. Enter `cd /root` to change to the root directory.

7. Clear the terminal screen.

Scenario:

You are responsible for managing a large network that has many servers to provide different network services. To manage the network easily, you want to maintain information about users and systems at a centralized location.

What You Do	How You Do It
1. Name the NIS domain you want to create.	a. On the server labeled **srvA,** open the /etc/sysconfig/network file.
	b. On a new line, type **NISDOMAIN=⇒ srvAdomain**
	c. Press **Esc** to switch to the command mode.
	d. Save and close the file.
	e. Clear the terminal screen.

2.	Add NIS server information to the yp.conf file.	a.	Using the `vi` editor, open the /etc/yp.conf file.
		b.	To specify the domain and server names, at the end of the file, type **domain** ⇒ **srvAdomain server** ⇒ **srvA.ourglobalcompany.com**
		c.	Press **Esc** to switch to the command mode.
		d.	Save and close the file.
		e.	Clear the terminal screen.
3.	Start all NIS daemons other than the ypbind daemon.	a.	Enter **service portmap restart** to restart the portmap daemon.
		b.	Enter **service yppasswdd start** to start the yppasswdd daemon.
		c.	Enter **service ypserv start** to start the ypserv daemon.
		d.	Enter **chkconfig yppasswdd on** to set the yppasswdd daemon to run when booting the system.
		e.	Enter **chkconfig ypserv on** to set the ypserv service to run when booting the system.
4.	Initialize the NIS domain.	a.	Enter **/usr/lib/yp/ypinit -m**
		b.	Press **Ctrl+D** to indicate that only one server is being set up.
		c.	Enter **y** to confirm the server name.
		d.	Clear the terminal screen.
		e.	Enter **service ypbind start** to start the ypbind daemon.
		f.	Enter **chkconfig ypbind on** to set the ypbind service to run when booting the system.
		g.	Enter **rpcinfo -p localhost** to verify that all NIS daemons are running.
		h.	Clear the terminal screen.

5. Create NIS maps.

    a. Navigate to the /var/yp directory.

    b. Enter **make** to create the maps.

    c. Enter **ypmatch jsmith passwd** to verify that the NIS user information is updated.

    d. Clear the terminal screen.

ACTIVITY 12-9

Configuring an NIS Client

Before You Begin:

1. Reboot srvB to start Red Hat Linux.
2. Switch to the first terminal of the CLI.
3. Log in as root
4. Enter `clear` to clear the terminal screen.

Scenario:

In your organization, employees in the marketing department work from different offices. Therefore, you decided to set up a central location where they can store their files. Now, you want to enable them to access the central location from any office. As the first step, you set up an NIS server to centrally store user authentication information.

What You Do	How You Do It
1. Configure NIS files.	a. Enter **authconfig-tui** to start the authconfig-tui utility.
	b. Select the **Use NIS** option.
	c. Press **F12** to navigate to the next page.
	d. In the **Domain** text box, type *srvAdomain*
	e. In the **Server** text box, type *srvA.ourglobalcompany.com*
	f. Press **F12** to accept the configuration changes.
	g. Clear the terminal screen.

2.	Enable Linux to check NIS for login authentication.	a.	Enter `mv /etc/nsswitch.conf /etc/nsswitch.conf.bak` to rename the existing nsswitch.conf file in the /etc directory.
		b.	Enter `cp /usr/share/doc/yp-tools-2.9 ⇒ /nsswitch.conf /etc/nsswitch.conf` to copy the nsswitch.conf file from the /usr/share/doc/ yp-tools-2.9 directory to the /etc directory.

 The ⇒ symbol is used in the step only to bring the step to the next line. It is not part of the code and there- fore, students need not type the symbol.

3.	Restrict new entries to the password file.	a.	Using the `vi` editor, open the /etc/passwd file.
		b.	At the end of the file, add a plus symbol followed by six colon symbols.
		c.	Press **Esc** to switch to the command mode.
		d.	Save and close the file.
		e.	Clear the terminal screen.
4.	Restrict new entries to the group and shadow files.	a.	At the end of the /etc/group file, add a plus sign followed by three colons.
		b.	Press **Esc** to switch to the command mode.
		c.	Save and close the file.
		d.	Clear the terminal screen.
		e.	At the end of the /etc/shadow file, add a plus symbol followed by eight colon sym- bols.
		f.	Press **Esc** to switch to the command mode.
		g.	Save and close the file to apply the changes to the read-only file.
		h.	Clear the screen.

5. Restart NIS daemons.

a. Restart the `portmap` and `ypbind` daemons.

b. Set the ypbind service to run when booting the system.

c. Enter **rpcinfo -p localhost** to verify that the NIS daemons are running.

d. Clear the terminal screen.

TOPIC G
Manage Remote Network Systems

You configured NIS services to manage a centralized network system. In situations such as adding new systems to a network, you will directly communicate with the server and modify the data on the server to connect your computer to the server. In this topic, you will explore SSH and VNC and examine their functions to communicate with remote systems.

As a system administrator, you will address the needs of users who are scattered across different locations. There may be some meetings or conferences that require you to connect to the server remotely. Your capability as a system administrator will increase if you knew how to connect to remote systems. You can access data remotely and troubleshoot all systems from one location.

Secure Shell

Definition:

Secure Shell (SSH) is a network protocol that controls the secure flow of data among computers on a network. SSH architecture contains the transport layer, the user authentication layer, and the connection layer. The client places a request, which is authenticated by the user authentication layer. This transfers the request to the server, which is authenticated by the transport layer, through the connection layer. By making use of public-key cryptography to encrypt data, this architecture makes SSH flexible and secure. There are many versions of SSH such as SSH1 and SSH2.

Example:

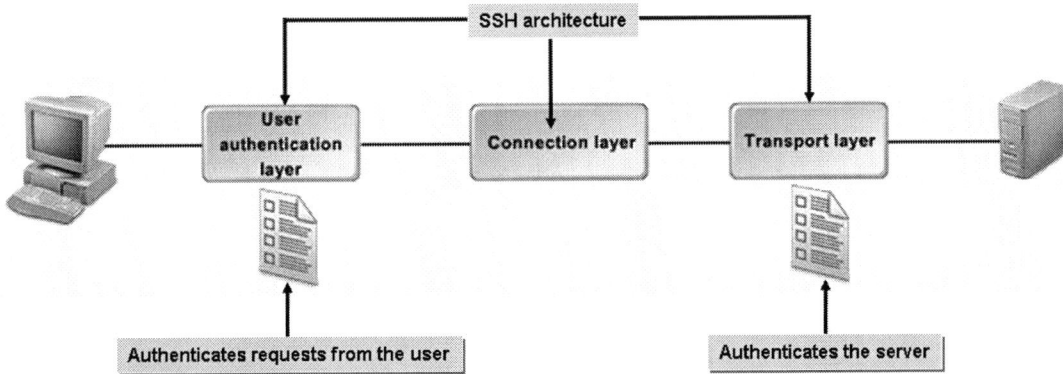

Figure 12-54: SSH controlling secure communication on a network.

OpenSSH

OpenSSH is a free version of the SSH protocol that is included with most Linux distributions. Data to be transmitted passes through a secure tunnel that is formed between two systems. Telnet transmits data, which includes passwords, that can be easily intercepted by any system on the network. OpenSSH provides a strong client-server authentication method for data transmitted by Telnet and similar applications.

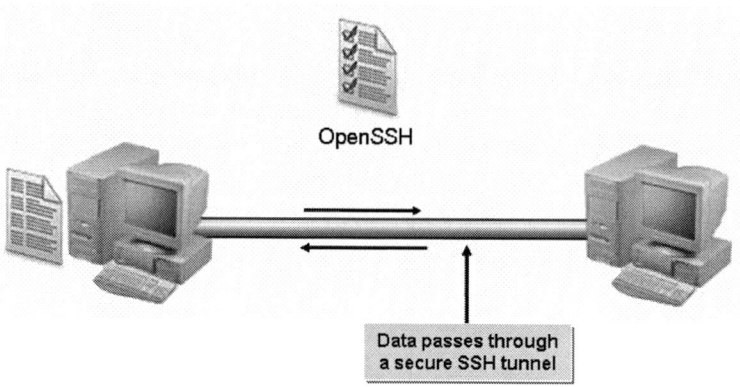

OpenSSH

Data passes through
a secure SSH tunnel

Figure 12-55: *Data transfer using the OpenSSH tunnel.*

The ssh-keygen Command

The *ssh-keygen command* generates, manages, and converts authentication keys. The following table lists some options of the `ssh-keygen` command.

Use This ssh-keygen Command Option	If You Need To
-b *bits*	Specify the number of bits to be created in the key.
-c	Change the comment in the public and private key files.
-f *file name*	Specify the file name of the key file.
-l	Show the fingerprint of the specified public key file.
-p	Change the passphrase of a private key file instead of creating a new private key.

Public and Private Keys

Both private keys and public keys are involved in the authentication process. Each key is a collection of alphanumeric and special characters that uniquely identify each system. A private key is involved in public key authentication that is retained on the local system. A public key is involved in public key authentication that is made known to remote systems. The private key is retained on the local system. The public key is made known to remote systems. The private key is never transmitted to the destination server. A meaningful message will result only when the destination's private key is combined with the public key of the original server. While logging in to a remote system, the private and public keys are combined by the remote server for verification. The keys need to match if a user has to log in to the system and transfer files. Authenticity is established by the remote server, which then grants the necessary permissions.

Key Files

The key pairs that you create using SSH are stored in different files depending on the algorithm you use.

Files Created	Algorithm
id_dsa, id_dsa.pub	DSA
id_rsa, id_rsa.pub	RSA with SSH protocol version 2
identity, identity.pub	RSA with SSH protocol version 1

The /etc/ssh/sshd_config File

The /etc/ssh/sshd_config file is the SSH server configuration file. Most lines in this configuration file are commented, indicating the default settings that have been applied. You can remove the comment and change the default settings. A few SSH server configuration file options are listed in the following table.

Use This sshd Option	If You Need To
X11Forwarding yes	Run or stop running a program on one system and display the X window output on another system.
X11Forwarding no	Stop running a program on one system and display the X window output on another system.
PermitRootLogin	Allow the root user to login via SSH.
MaxStartups *Number*	Specify the maximum number of connections that can be made to a host.
LoginGraceTime *Time in seconds*	Drop connections if the connection is not established within the login grace time.
AuthorizedKeysFile *file name*	Specify the location of the file that contains the authentication keys.
PermitEmptyPasswords *yes/no*	Specify whether a null password is allowed or denied.

The sftp Command

The `sftp` command is used to create a secure FTP tunnel through SSH. Thus, it provides the functionality of FTP with the security of SSH. Secure FTP is compatible with all normal FTP commands in the interactive mode.

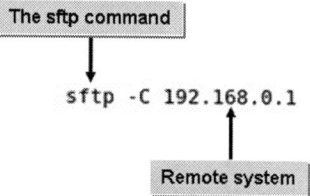

Figure 12-56: *Connecting to a remote system using sftp.*

Syntax

The syntax of the command is `sftp hostname` or `sftp user@hostname`. The command can also be used with the `-C` flag to allow file compression.

Tunneling

Tunneling is a layered protocol model in which one protocol is layered over another. The inner protocol called the payload protocol is encapsulated within another protocol called the delivery protocol. This provides security and flexibility to the connection. Some of the tunneling protocols are GRE, GTP, and MPLS.

An SSH tunnel is created when an SSH protocol connection is made. SSH tunneling enables users to access websites and bypass firewalls by setting up proxy servers. A protocol that is blocked by the firewall is encapsulated within a different protocol that is not blocked by the firewall, thus establishing the connection.

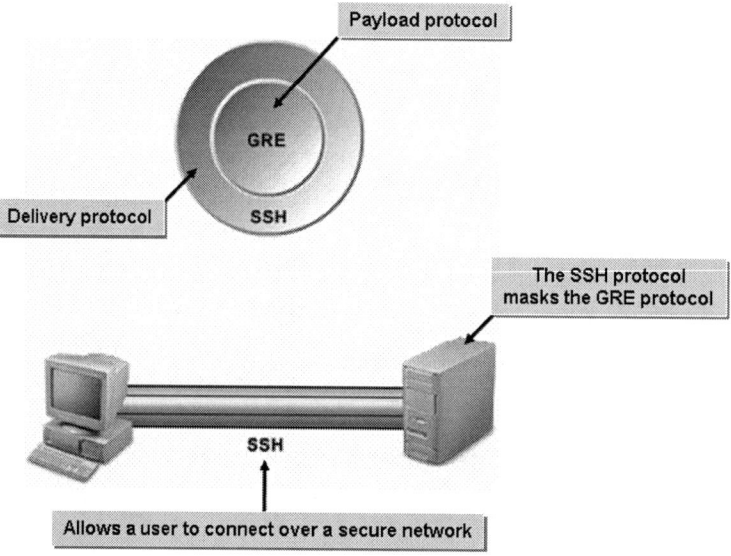

Figure 12-57: *The tunneling protocol and its architecture.*

Virtual Network Computing

Definition:

Virtual Network Computing (VNC) is a platform-independent system through which a user can control a remote system. The virtual network is made up of the VNC client, the VNC server, and the VNC protocol. The client views the output that is displayed by the server through the VNC protocol. The user can run multiple VNC sessions at a given time. However, the display for each VNC client may differ from the VNC server display.

Example:

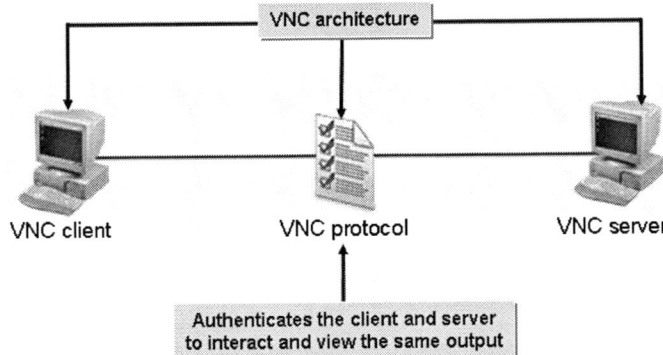

Figure 12-58: The VNC protocol enables the client to view the output displayed by the VNC server.

The vncserver Command

The `vncserver` command is used to start a system with VNC. The $HOME/.vnc/xstartup file allows a user to control applications running on the remote system. You can specify the display number that the VNC server will use when it is started.

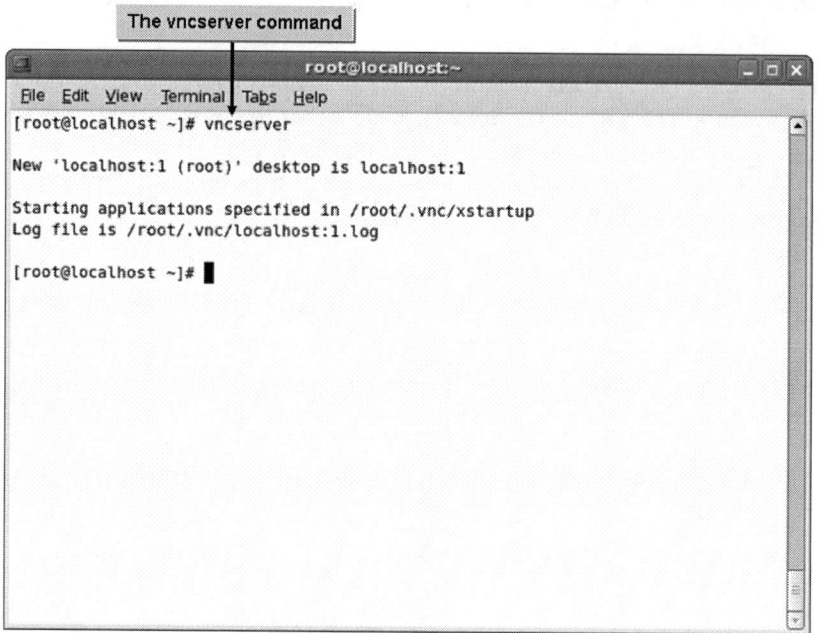

Figure 12-59: VNC enabled on a Linux system.

The vncserver command has various options.

Option	Enables You To
-name *desktop name*	Specify the desktop name.
-geometry *resolution*	Specify the screen resolution of the remote desktop.
-depth *depth*	Specify the pixel depth of the desktop. The accepted values are 8, 15, and 24.
-pixelformat *format*	Specify the pixel format such as RGB and BGR.

Syntax

The syntax of the vncserver command is vncserver *{:display number}* *{-option}*.

The vncviewer Command

The vncviewer command is used to view the VNC client. There are various options for specifying the vncviewer parameters.

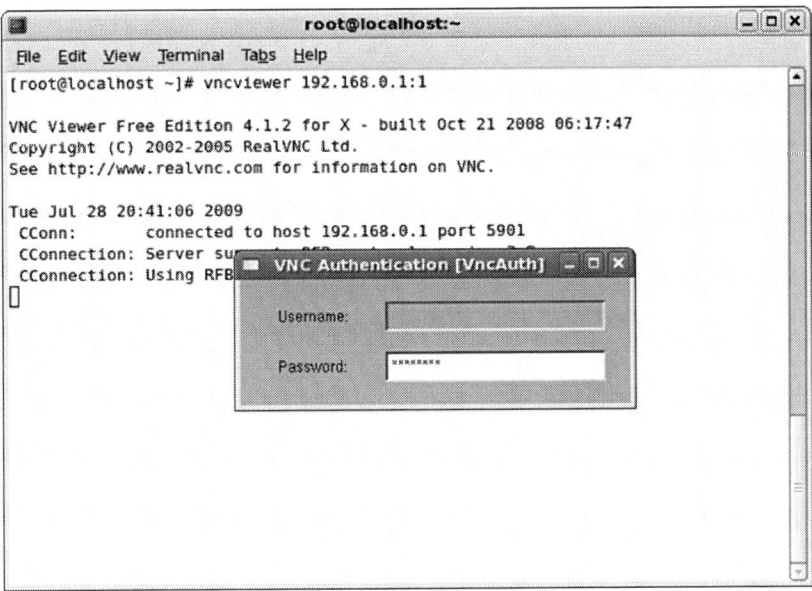

Figure 12-60: *The vncviewer command is used to connect to a VNC server.*

Option	Enables You To
-display *Xdisplay*	Specify the X display.
-listen *port*	Search for reverse connections from the VNC server.
-Shared	Keep multiple VNC connections open.
-FullScreen	Start the VNC client in the full-screen mode.
-via *gateway*	Create a tunnel to a gateway system and then connects the client to the host.

The rdesktop Utility

rdesktop is an open source utility, released under GPL. It enables a client system running Linux to log in to a system running Microsoft Windows, on a network. It supports Microsoft's Remote Desktop Protocol (RDP). The rdesktop command can be used to log in to a remote Windows system.

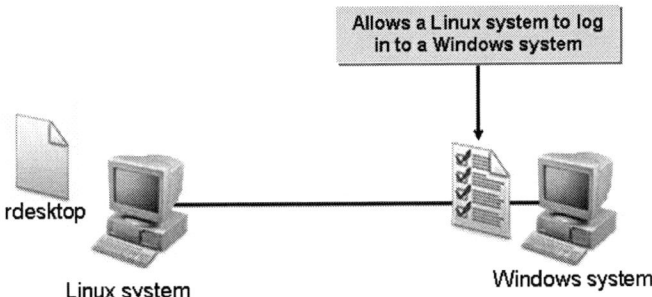

Figure 12-61: *A Linux system logging in to a Windows system with the help of rdesktop.*

Syntax

The syntax of the `rdesktop` command is `rdesktop [options] server[:port]`.

The rdesktop Command Options

Some frequently used `rdesktop` command options are listed in the following table.

Option	Used To
-u	Specify the user name for authentication on the server.
-d	Specify the domain for authentication.
-s	Start a specific application instead of Explorer.
-c	Specify the initial working directory for the user.
-p	Specify a password for authentication.

RDP

RDP is a multi-channel protocol that allows users running various other operating systems to connect to a system running Microsoft Windows and vice versa, on a network.

The Simple Network Management Protocol

The *Simple Network Management Protocol (SNMP)* enables you to remotely monitor and configure network components such as bridges, routers, network cards, and switches.

SNMP management requires two primary elements: a network manager and an SNMP agent.

Element	Description
Network manager	The software running on a workstation through which the network administrator monitors and controls the different hardware and software systems that comprise a network.
SNMP agent	A piece of software running on network equipment that implements the SNMP protocol. SNMP defines exactly how a network manager communicates with an SNMP agent.

Remote Monitoring

Remote Monitoring (RMON) is a network management protocol that allows network information to be gathered at a single workstation. For RMON to work, network devices, such as hubs and switches, must support it.

How to Manage Remote Network Systems

Procedure Reference: Communicate Using Secure Shell

To communicate using secure shell:

1. Log in as a user.

2. Connect securely to another computer.

   a. Enter `ssh {user name}@{hostname or IP of the destination}` to connect to the remote host.

   b. If prompted, add the host as a trusted host.

   c. Enter the password to log in to the system.

3. Execute commands securely in another computer.

   a. Enter `ssh {user name}@{hostname or IP of the destination}` to connect to the remote host.

   b. If prompted, add the host as a trusted host.

   c. Enter the password to log in to the system.

   d. Enter the command to execute the required action.

4. Create a tunnel using SSH.

   a. Enter `ssh -L {port number}:{remote server IP or FQDN}:{port number} {user name}@{remote server IP or FQDN}` to create a tunnel using SSH.

   b. If prompted, add the host as a trusted host.

   c. Enter the password to log in to the system.

5. Authenticate the tunnel with SSH keys.

   a. Enter `ssh-keygen -d` to generate a key.

   b. Press **Enter** three times to generate the keys **id_dsa** and **id_dsa.pub** in **/root/.ssh.**

   c. Log in as root in the second system with which you want to establish an SSH connection.

   d. Enter `ssh-keygen -d`.

   e. Press **Enter** three times to generate the keys **id_dsa** and **id_dsa.pub** in **/root/.ssh.**

   f. Enter `scp /root/.ssh/id_dsa.pub {user name}@{IP or FQDN of the first system}:/root/.ssh/authorized_keys` to copy the public key from the second system to the first system.

   g. If prompted add the host as a trusted host.

   h. Enter the password to log in to the system.

   i. Enter `scp /root/.ssh/id_dsa.pub {user name}@{IP or FQDN of the first system}:/root/.ssh/authorized_keys` to copy the public key from the first system to the second system.

   j. If prompted, add the host as a trusted host.

   k. Enter the password to log in to the system.

Procedure Reference: Transfer Files Securely to Another Computer

To transfer files securely to another computer:

1. Log in as a user in the CLI.

2. Enter scp *[command option]* *{source file or folder name}* *{user name}@{hostname or IP of the destination}:/{destination file or folder name}* to transfer files using the scp utility.

3. If prompted, add the host as a trusted host.

4. Enter the password to transfer the file.

Procedure Reference: Run the VNC Server

To run the VNC server:

1. Log in as root in the GUI.

2. On the terminal, enter vncserver to start the VNC server.

3. Enter the VNC server password, which will be used by clients when connecting to this server.

4. Confirm the password.

5. Write down the **{server name}:{screen number}** that is displayed.

Procedure Reference: Connect to the VNC Server using the VNC Viewer

To connect to the VNC server using the VNC viewer:

1. Log in as root in the GUI of the client system.

2. On the terminal, enter vncviewer *{server name}:{screen number}* to view the VNC server.

3. In the **VNC Authentication** window, in the **Password** text box, enter the password of the server to connect to the VNC server.

ACTIVITY 12-10
Communicating Using Secure Shell

Before You Begin:

1. On srvA, you have logged in as root in the CLI.

2. The first terminal is displayed.

3. At the command line, copy the meeting_report file from the /085039Data/Configuring_Network directory to the root directory of srvA.

4. Enter ssh-keygen -d to generate a key.

5. Press **Enter** three times to generate the keys **id_dsa** and **id_dsa.pub** in **/root/.ssh**.

6. Clear the terminal screen.

Scenario:

A lecture is scheduled to take place at your office. As a system administrator, you have been asked by users to establish a secure connection between the system in the lecture hall and their systems, so that they can access the meeting_report file on their systems remotely. You decide to configure SSH to establish the connection and secure it using authentication keys.

What You Do	How You Do It
1. Connect to another computer on the network.	a. At the command line, enter **ssh root@192.168.0.2** to connect to the server.
	b. Enter **yes** to continue.

 If you are prompted to continue connecting, enter **yes**.

	c. If prompted, at the **root@192.168.0.2's password:** prompt, enter **p@ssw0rd**
	d. Verify that the last login time is displayed.
	e. Enter **cat meeting_report** to view the contents of the meeting_report file.
	f. Enter **logout**

2. Create a tunnel using SSH.

   a. On srvB, enter `ssh -L 3128:192.168.0.2:3128 root@192.168.0.2` to create a tunnel using SSH.

   b. If prompted, to continue connecting, enter *yes*

   c. If prompted, at the **root@192.168.0.2's password:** prompt, enter *p@ssw0rd*

   d. Verify that the last login time is displayed.

   e. Enter `logout`

3. Authenticate the tunnel with SSH keys.

   a. Enter `ssh-keygen -d` to generate a key.

   b. Generate the keys **id_dsa** and **id_dsa.pub** in **/root/.ssh.**

 If prompted, to overwrite the file, enter **y.**

   c. Enter `scp /root/.ssh/id_dsa.pub root@192.168.0.2:/root/` ⇒`.ssh/authorized_keys` to copy the public keys to the server.

 The ⇒ symbol is used in the step only to bring the step to the next line. It is not part of the code and therefore, students need not type the symbol.

   d. If prompted, at the **root@192.168.0.2's password:** prompt, enter *p@ssw0rd*

   e. Observe that the file is copied to the server.

4. Copy the keys from the server to the client.

   a. Enter `ssh root@192.168.0.2` to connect to srvA.

 If you are prompted to continue connecting, enter *yes*.

b. If prompted, at the **root@192.168.0.2's password:** prompt, enter **p@ssw0rd**

c. Enter `scp /root/.ssh/id_dsa.pub root@192.168.0.X:/root/`⇒ `.ssh/authorized_keys` to copy the public keys to the client.

d. If prompted, at the **root@192.168.0.X's password:** prompt, enter **p@ssw0rd**

e. At the prompt, enter **yes** to continue.

f. Observe that the file is copied to the client.

g. Enter `logout` to log out of the server.

ACTIVITY 12-11

Implementing VNC

Before You Begin:

To be done on srvA:

1. You have logged as root in the CLI.

2. Switch to the GUI.

3. Log in as root.

4. Display the terminal window.

5. Ensure that the packages vnc-4.1.2-9.el5.i386.rpm and vnc-server-4.1.2-9.el5.i386.rpm are installed before commencing with this activity. Otherwise, you can install the packages using the `yum localinstall /rhelsource/Server/vnc*` command.

6. On the terminal window, enter `vncserver` to start the VNC server.

7. Enter the VNC server password that is used by the clients when connecting to this server.

8. Confirm the password.

9. Make a note of the server name and the screen number that is displayed.

 Instead of the server name, the IP address of the server can also be used.

10. Enter `mkdir /employee` to create the employee directory.

11. Enter `clear` to clear the terminal window.

Before You Begin:

To be done on srvB:

1. You have logged in as root in the CLI.

2. Switch to the GUI.

3. Log in as root.

4. If necessary, install the VNC viewer package.

Scenario:

As the system administrator, you want to maintain a list of users and their IP addresses to track network resources. You find that system details of the users have not been updated on the server.

What You Do	**How You Do It**
1. Connect to the VNC server using `vncviewer`.	a. On srvB, in the GUI, from the menu bar, choose **Applications→Accessories→ Terminal** to open the terminal.
	b. Enter **vncviewer 192.168.0.2:X** to view the VNC server.
	c. In the **VNC Authentication** window, in the **Password** text box, enter ***p@ssw0rd***
	d. Position the mouse pointer on the terminal.
	In the place of X, students should type their respective screen numbers provided by the instructor.
2. Create the employee file in the / employee directory.	a. Enter **cd /employee** to navigate to the employee directory.
	b. Enter **vi employee192.168.0.X** to create the employee file.
	 In the place of X in employee192.168.0.X, students should enter their respective system numbers.
	c. Press **I** to switch to the insert mode.
	d. Enter ***Name=XXXXX***
	 In the place of XXXXX, students should enter their name.
	e. Enter ***Employee IP=192.168.0.X***
	In the place of X, students should enter their respective system numbers.

f. Press **Esc** to exit the command mode.

g. Save and close the file.

h. Click the close button to exit the VNC server.

i. Enter **exit** to close the terminal window.

3. Verify that the file was successfully created.

a. Switch to srvA

b. On the terminal window, enter **cd /employee** to change to the employee directory.

c. Enter **cat employee192.168.0.X** to view the contents of the file.

 In the place of X, students should enter their respective system numbers.

d. Observe that the contents of the file are displayed, which indicates that the file was successfully created.

e. Enter **clear** to clear the terminal window.

Lesson 12 Follow-up

In this lesson, you configured and managed various network services and remote network systems. You will now be able to disseminate information, administer systems remotely, enable communication through mail or chat systems, facilitate technology sharing, manage software licenses, and control unauthorized access.

1. **What are the advantages of managing IP addresses centrally on a network?**

2. **Discuss the points that must be considered before you enable DNS on a network.**

13 | Configuring Basic Internet Services

Lesson Time: 2 hour(s)

Lesson Objectives:

In this lesson, you will configure basic Internet services.

You will:

- Configure a web server.

- Implement Apache access control.

- Configure a Squid proxy server.

- Configure email services.

- Control Internet services.

Introduction

In the previous lesson, you configured basic client services. Now, you want to implement a business-oriented service that allows you to share resources and communicate across various platforms on a network. In this lesson, you will implement web services.

The Internet offers various services such as email, file sharing and downloading, and web browsing. Employees of an organization will often need to access the Internet and communicate with clients across various platforms. As a system administrator, you want to implement a simplified service that provides interoperability among applications and involves cost-effective communication. Internet services facilitate the ability to share and transfer resources across various networks securely.

This lesson covers all or part of the following CompTIA Linux+ (2009) certification objectives:

- Topic A
  - Objective 3.3
  - Objective 3.4
  - Objective 3.5
- Topic B
  - Objective 3.3
- Topic C

- ■ Objective 3.4
- ● Topic D
  - ■ Objective 3.8
- ● Topic E
  - ■ Objective 3.1
  - ■ Objective 3.5

TOPIC A
Configure a Web Server

You managed remote network systems. Now, you need to share information through the Internet because this is the most simplified and standardized way of communication. To begin with, you want to host a website on a web server. In this topic, you will configure a web server.

Your company is growing with an increasing customer base. Management is determined to establish the company worldwide. As a Linux+ administrator, you may need to implement a service, such as a web server, that enables a simplified and efficient way of communication with low technology cost, thereby improving the business process. Your ability to configure web servers appropriately will enable you to meet this business need.

Web Servers

Definition:

A *web server* is a software application that is run on a system to provide world wide web services. It has a static IP address and a domain name, and is always connected to the Internet. The server provides web pages to client web browsers across the Internet. The web server can host web pages, scripts, multimedia files, and programs and serve them to clients using HTTP.

Example:

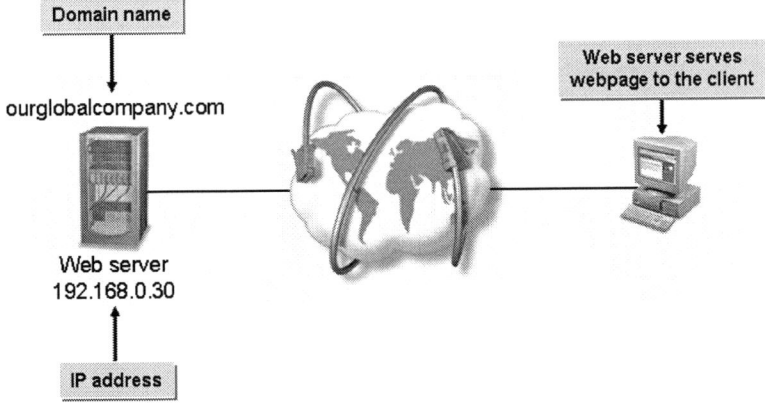

Figure 13-1: A web server provides web pages to a client computer.

The Apache Web Server

The *Apache* web server is an open source web server in which multiple user requests are processed by relocating them into separate modules known as Multiprocessing Modules (MPMs). An MPM combines all network ports on a machine, accepts requests, and reallocates these requests to separate handlers. After processing the requests, the Apache web server responds to them based on the MPM that is used. These modules are chosen during the configuration and then compiled on the server. Only one MPM can be chosen at a time.

Apache also allows you to choose between processes and threads. Threads are processes that consume fewer resources and improve the performance of the server. These processes can be executed as threads based on the MPM that is chosen. Apache supports a wide variety of operating systems each of which supports a default MPM. Apache also provides the functionality of dynamically loaded modules, where the modules are compiled separately and loaded on the server any time, using the `LoadModule` directive rather than initially building the modules on the server. This avoids the process of recompiling the server whenever the modules are added to or removed from the server.

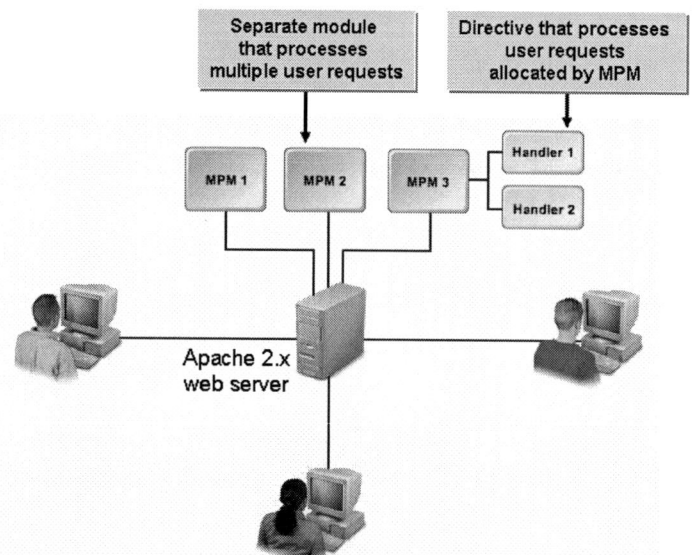

Figure 13-2: Processing a request on the Apache web server.

Enable and Disable Modules

The `LoadModule` directive allows you to enable a specific module on the web server. To disable a module, locate the line containing the module in the httpd.conf file and uncomment or remove the line. Save the file and restart the httpd service for the changes to apply.

Popularity

The Apache web server is the most frequently used web server on Linux networks. The original version of Apache was developed for UNIX. The later versions of Apache supports other operating systems including Windows, Solaris, and OS X.

Apache Modules

Apache has a set of compiled modules that extend its core functionality. The modules can be integrated with Apache as add-ons.

Module	Description
mod_access	Used for restricting access to clients, based on the client request that involves the characteristics such as the client hostname and IP address.
mod_ssl	Used for providing a secure support for the Apache server using the Securer Socket Layer (SSL) and Transport Layer Security (TLS) protocols.
mod_php	Used for recognizing PHP scripts.
mod_spelling	Used for correcting URLs written with any capitalization issues and misspelling issues.
mod_perl	Used for recognizing Perl scripts.
mod_cgi	Used for recognizing Common Gateway Interface (CGI) scripts.

Hypertext Preprocessor (PHP)

Hypertext Preprocessor (PHP) is an open source scripting language that is used to create dynamic web pages. PHP is a server-side scripting language, and so scripts written in PHP are executed on the server and the client will not be able to view the code. PHP is compatible with any type of database.

The php.ini configuration file controls the behavior of PHP in Linux. By default, PHP looks for the file in the current working directory, using the path specified by the environment variable PHPRC or the path specified while compiling. It has various functions, for example, it can be used to change the severity of errors that need to be logged.

Apache Configuration Directives

There are a set of directives defined in the Apache distribution. Each directive is set to specific values and defines specific formats. Some of the frequently used directives are listed in the table.

Directive	Description
ServerAdmin	Specifies the email address that is used in error messages sent to a client.
CustomLog	Specifies the log file name and the log format.
LogFormat	Describes the format of the access log files. It defines either of the two forms: the form that uses a single argument, which specifies the explicit format or the form that uses a nickname to define the explicit format.

Directive	Description
MinSpareServers	Specifies the minimum number of idle child server processes.
MaxSpareServers	Specifies the maximum number of idle child server processes.
DocumentRoot	Defines the path of the directory from which httpd will run the files to serve web hosting. When a user requests a path, it is appended to the URL path defined in the `DocumentRoot` directive.

The httpd.conf File

The httpd.conf file is the main configuration file that is used to configure the Apache web server. It is stored in the /etc/httpd/conf directory. The http service is enabled using the httpd package. By default, httpd is installed in the /usr/sbin directory and the initialization script runs from the /etc/init.d/httpd file. The httpd.conf file uses directives to control the operations of the Apache web server, define its parameters, and set virtual hosts.

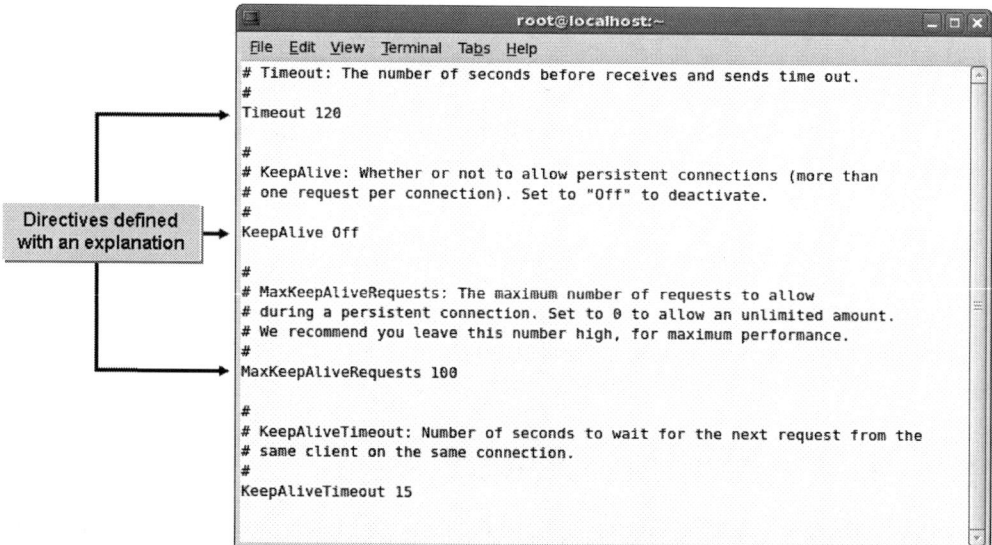

Figure 13-3: Various directives defined in the httpd.conf file.

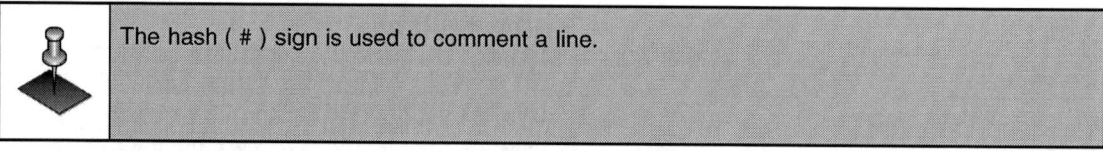

The hash (#) sign is used to comment a line.

By default, the httpd.conf file contains all possible directives. Some of the frequently used directives are explained in the table.

Directive	Description
ServerName	Used to set the hostname, port, and request scheme of a machine hosting the web server while redirecting URLs. The syntax of the ServerName directive is: ServerName *alias hostname with the port number.*
AllowOverride	Used to specify the list of directives that are used in .htaccess files. The directives in the .htaccess file override the earlier configuration directives. If the directive is set to None then the server does not refer to the .htaccess file. The syntax of the AllowOverride directive is: AllowOverride *[All	None	{Any combination of Options, FileInfo, AuthConfig, Limit}].*
Addtype	Used to map a MIME-type file name extension to a specified file type. The syntax of the Addtype directive is: Addtype *MIME-type File type.*
DirectoryIndex	Used to list a set of files that the server needs to look through, when a client requests an index of a directory. The syntax of the DirectoryIndex directive is: DirectoryIndex *file name.*
UserDir	Used to set the location from where the client receives the document as the user's home directory. The syntax of the UserDir directive is: UserDir *file name.*

The MIME Type Configuration

Multipurpose Internet Mail Extensions (MIME) is a standard Internet format that supports ASCII character sets, non-ASCII character sets, non-text attachments, and multiple parts in a message body. These formats are used in email messages and web pages. The SMTP and HTTP protocols support the MIME formats. The AddType directive is used to configure the MIME types in an Apache server. It supports the email messages sent through the Internet.

The .htaccess Files

The .htaccess files are used to implement configuration changes in individual directories. They are used to configure a directory that is to be set up for recognizing CGI scripts. The changes made to the directives of a file stored in the directory will be applied to the directory. The .htaccess files follow the same syntax used in the httpd.conf file. The directives to be used in the .htaccess file are determined by the AllowOverride directive, which specifies the value to permit the directive. Information whether the directive is available in the .htaccess file is specified in the respective documentation of the directive.

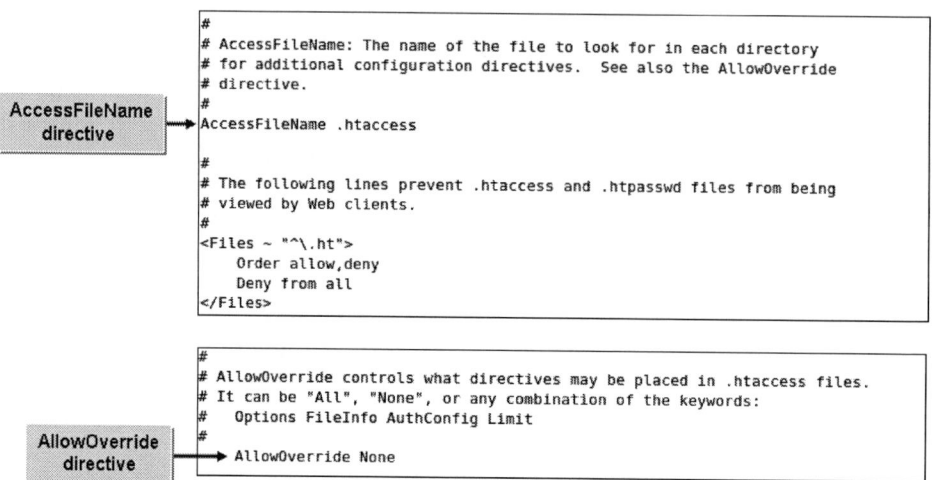

```
#
# AccessFileName: The name of the file to look for in each directory
# for additional configuration directives.  See also the AllowOverride
# directive.
#
AccessFileName .htaccess

#
# The following lines prevent .htaccess and .htpasswd files from being
# viewed by Web clients.
#
<Files ~ "^\.ht">
    Order allow,deny
    Deny from all
</Files>
```

```
#
# AllowOverride controls what directives may be placed in .htaccess files.
# It can be "All", "None", or any combination of the keywords:
#   Options FileInfo AuthConfig Limit
#
AllowOverride None
```

Figure 13-4: *Configuring a directory to recognize CGI scripts.*

Syntax for Renaming the .htaccess File

The .htaccess file can be renamed using the `AccessFileName` directive where the syntax is: `AccessFileName` *new file name.*

The order Statement

The `order` statement, which is included in the mod_access module, provides the access control for a system. It operates along with the `Allow` and `Deny` directives. It involves three passes. In the first pass, it processes all the `Allow` or `deny` directives based on their specification. In the second pass, it processes the directive other than the first pass directive. In the third pass, it processes the requests that do not match either the `Allow` or `Deny` directives. The syntax is:

`Order Ordering Allow from` *hostname* `|` *IP address or the IP address range*
`Deny from` *hostname* `|` *IP address or the IP address range,*

where the ordering value is set to either "`Allow, deny`" or "`Deny, allow`".

The apachectl Command

The Apache HTTP Server Control Interface (apachectl) is the interface that allows an administrator to control the functioning of the HTTP service using the `apachectl` command. The `apachectl` command supports various options.

Option	*Used To*
`start` or `apachectl -k start`	Start the apache daemon. If the daemon is already running, it displays an error message.
`stop` or `apachectl -k stop`	Stop the apache daemon.
`restart` or `apachectl -k restart`	Restart the apache daemon. If the daemon is not running, it starts the daemon.
`fullstatus`	Display the full status report of the services running and requested by clients. It requires the mod_status module to be enabled on the system.

Option	Used To
status	Display the status report of the services requested by clients. The report does not include the list of running services.
configtest or apachectl -t	Run the configuration file test that either reports the success state as "Syntax Ok" or displays an error message. It is also used to test the syntax of the ssl.conf file.
graceful or apachectl -k graceful	Restart the Apache httpd daemon. It starts the httpd daemon if it is not running.
graceful-stop or apachectl -k graceful-stop	Stop the Apache httpd daemon.

Figure 13-5: Running the configuration file test for apachectl.

Syntax

The syntax of the apachectl command is apachectl
start|stop|restart|status|configtest.

The httpd Daemon

The `httpd` daemon is a standalone daemon that runs the Apache service. There are many command line options that can be used with this daemon. Some of the options are listed in the table.

Option	Description
-h	Displays a list of command line options that are used.
-l	Displays a list of modules.
-L	Displays a list of directives along with arguments.
-S	Displays the settings that are parsed from the config file.
-t	Runs the syntax configuration test for the httpd.conf file. It is also used to check the syntax of the ssl.conf file.

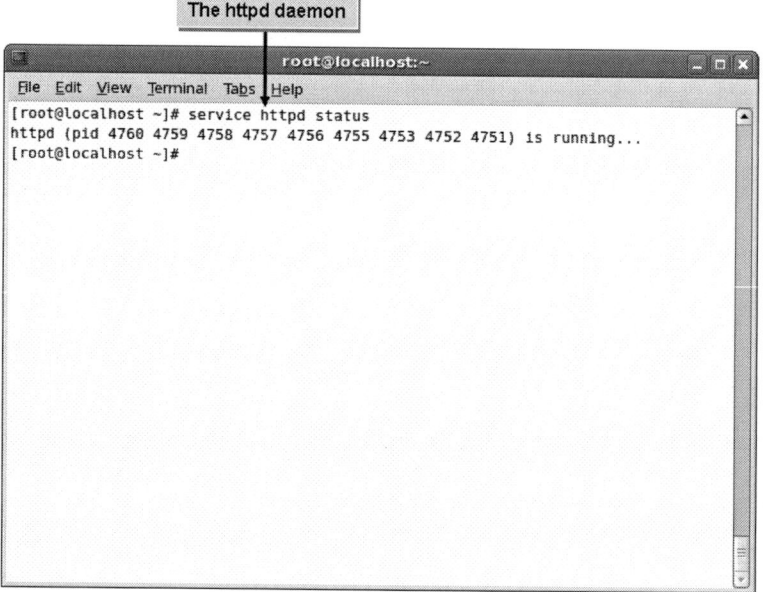

Figure 13-6: PIDs of the httpd daemons running on the system.

Text-Based Web Browsers

Definition:

A *text-based web browser* is an application that is used to access web pages in the CLI mode. It does not support graphics or images and can run either in color or mono mode. The browser requires the URL of a website to be displayed on the screen of a system. The web browser has menus and options that you can use to navigate through web pages.

Example:

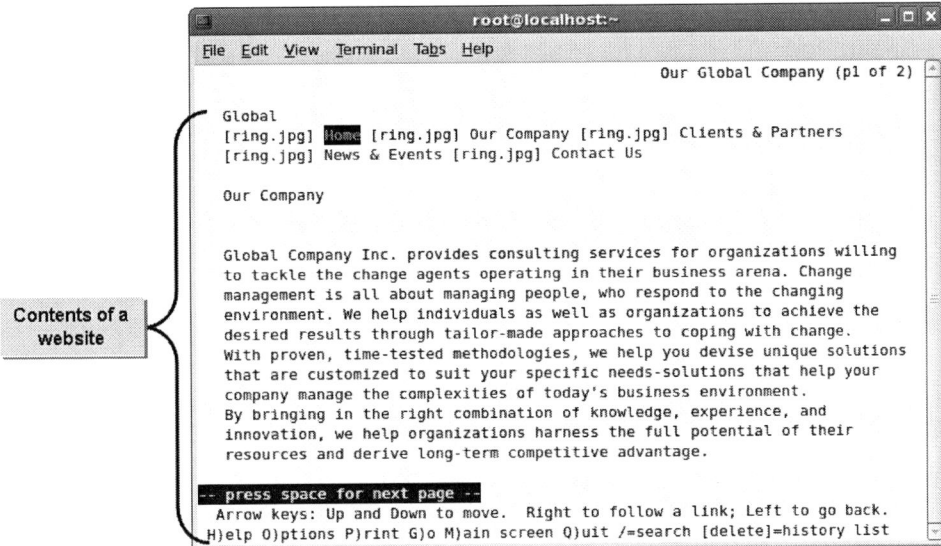

Figure 13-7: Accessing a website using a text-based web browser.

ELinks

Elinks is a non-GUI, text-based web browser. It supports color text display, table rendering, background downloading, menu-driven configuration interfaces, tabbed browsing, and slim code. It handles local files and works with remote URL protocols such as HTTP, HTTPS, and FTP. The `links` command allows you to open the text-based web browser.

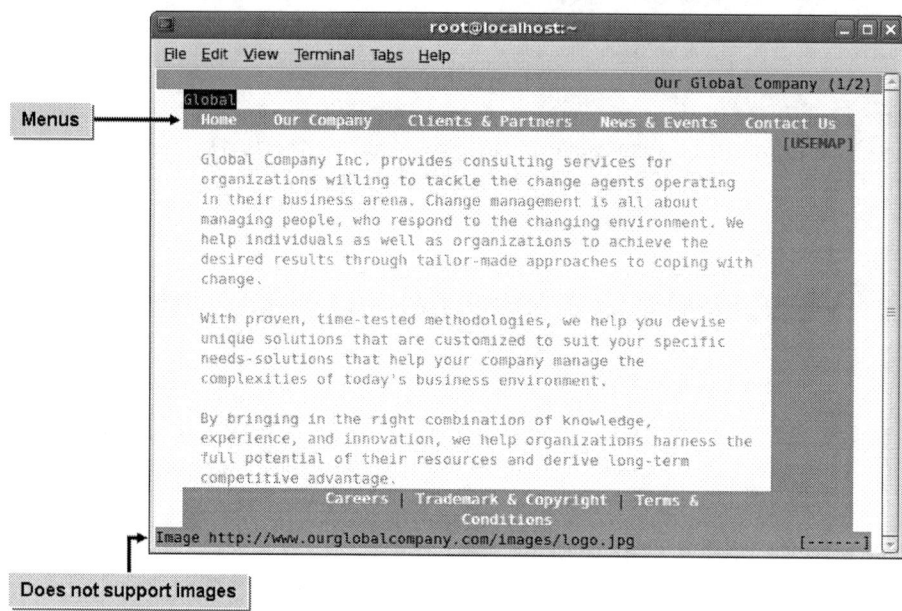

Figure 13-8: *The elinks web browser.*

Syntax

The syntax of the links command is links *[options]* *{URL}.*

The wget Command

The wget command facilitates content retrieval from websites. It supports deriving content via the HTTP-, HTTPS-, FTP- and TCP/IP-based protocols, recursive downloads, offline viewing of html pages, and proxies. This command is noninteractive and is effective over slow and unstable network connections. If a download does not complete due to a network problem, wget automatically continues the download from where it stopped, until the entire file is retrieved.

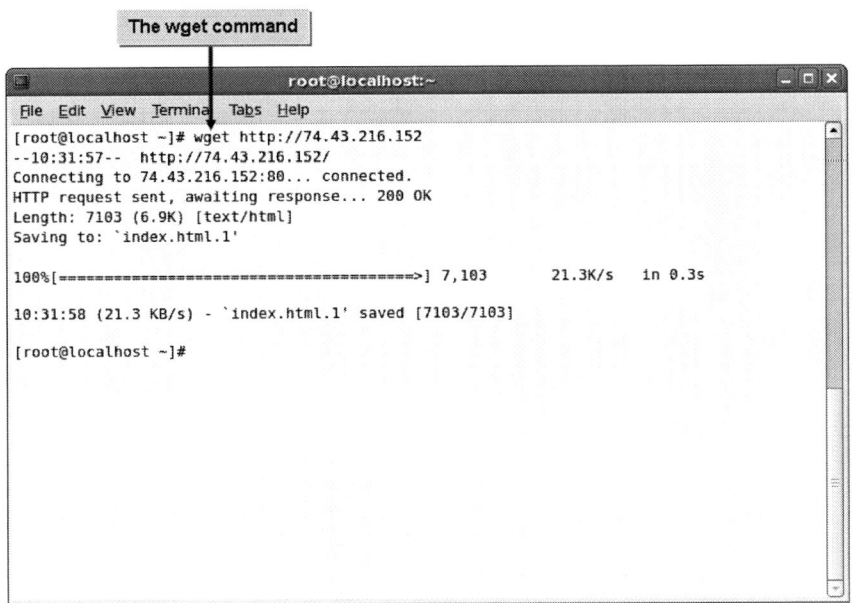

The wget command

```
                        root@localhost:~

File  Edit  View  Terminal  Tabs  Help
[root@localhost ~]# wget http://74.43.216.152
--10:31:57--  http://74.43.216.152/
Connecting to 74.43.216.152:80... connected.
HTTP request sent, awaiting response... 200 OK
Length: 7103 (6.9K) [text/html]
Saving to: `index.html.1'

100%[====================================>] 7,103      21.3K/s   in 0.3s

10:31:58 (21.3 KB/s) - `index.html.1' saved [7103/7103]

[root@localhost ~]#
```

Figure 13-9: *Retrieving web pages using the wget command.*

Syntax

The syntax of the wget command is wget *[command options]*
http://*{hostname or IP of the destination}*.

The curl Command

Curl is a command line tool that is used to transfer data to or from a server, using the URL
syntax. It is an open source software that runs on a variety of operating systems. It supports
protocols such as FTP, HTTP, FTPS, HTTPS, SCP, SFTP, TELNET, TFTP, LDAP, LDAPS,
TFTP, DICT, and FILE. Curl increases file transfer speed by attempting to reuse connections
for multiple file transfers to or from the same server.

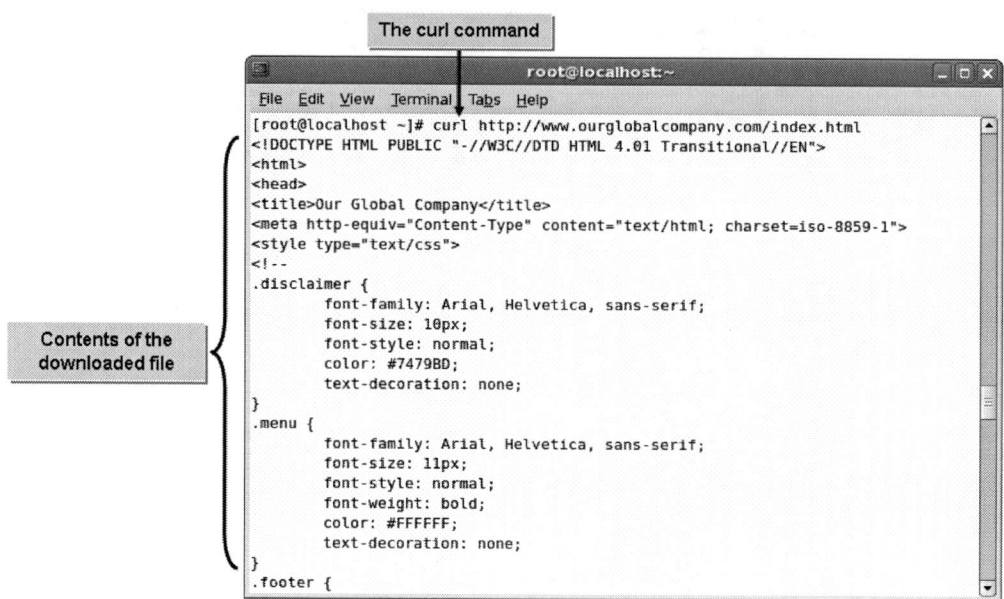

Figure 13-10: *Downloading a file using the curl command.*

Syntax

The syntax of the curl command is `curl [options] {URL...}`.

Application Servers

An *application server* is a server program running on a computer connected to a distributed network. It makes the most of an application program that is accessible across the network. An application server makes custom applications available to multiple concurrent users. It can also be used to develop, run, and manage applications. It consists of three tiers: the first-tier GUI, the middle-tier business logic, and the third-tier database and transaction server.

Tomcat

Tomcat is an open source application server that implements a *Java servlet* and renders JavaServer pages. It provides a Java HTTP web server environment for Java code to run on a Linux system. Tomcat can run programs in response to user requests and send the dynamic results to users. Tomcat possesses an internal web server, which is useful while running multiple applications. It can be used along with other web servers such as Apache, Sun Java System Web Server, and Microsoft Internet Information Server.

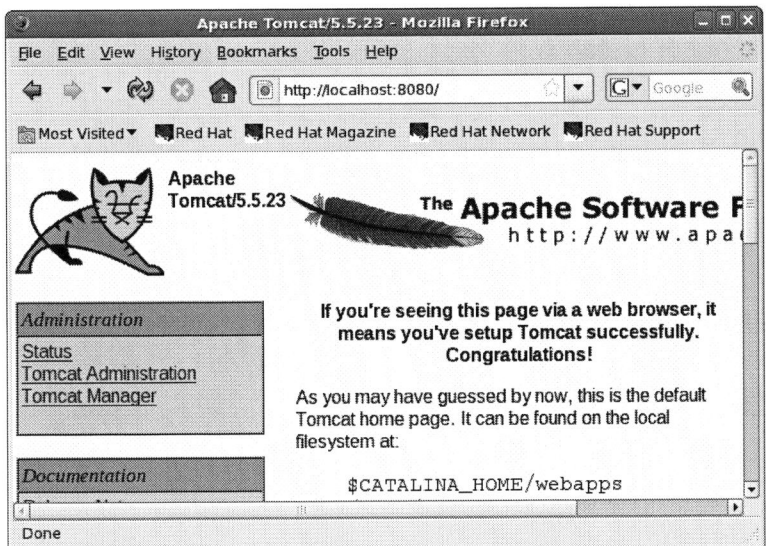

Figure 13-11: *The Tomcat application homepage on a Linux system.*

Java Servlets

A Java Servlet is a Java object file that is developed as a component and can be run on a server. Because a servlet is a Java program, it enables you to exploit the full power of Java within web applications. It allows you to access Java class library functions such as network connections and database access. The servlet is a component and can be invoked from HTML, Java Server Page, or by another servlet. Because the Java servlet can be invoked from an HTML document, it provides the HTML page with powerful server-side processing capability.

Containers

A container, also called web engine or web container, is a special web server that supports the execution of servlets. It combines the basic function of a web server with java-specific optimization and extensions. It translates specific URLs into servlet requests. A container contains information such as the functionality and URL of registered servlets. This information is used to uniquely identify servlets and deliver service requests to the appropriate servlets. Servlets can be added to and removed from the container without affecting the running servlets. Tomcat is a example of a servlet container.

How to Configure a Web Server

Procedure Reference: Install Apache

To install Apache:

1. Log in as root.

2. Mount the Linux installation media that contains Apache.

3. Navigate to the /media/[name of the media]/Server directory.

4. Install the dependency packages for Apache.

   a. Enter `rpm -ivh apr-{version}.{release}.rpm`.

   b. Enter `rpm -ivh postgresql-libs-{version}.{release}.rpm`.

   c. Enter `rpm -ivh apr-util-{version}.{release}.rpm`.

5. Enter `rpm -ivh httpd-{version}.{release}.rpm` to install Apache.

6. Enter `rpm -qi httpd` to verify that Apache has been installed.

7. If necessary, enter `umount /media/cdrom` to unmount the installation CD.

Procedure Reference: Configure the Apache Web Server

To configure the Apache web server:

1. Log in as root.

2. Using the vi editor, open the httpd.conf file.

   • Open the httpd.conf file from the /etc/httpd/conf directory when Apache is installed using RPM.

   • Open the httpd.conf file from the /[Installation Directory]/conf directory when Apache is installed from a user source.

 If you install Apache using RPM, then the httpd.conf file is created in the /etc/httpd/conf directory. The installation directory varies if you install Apache from a user agent.

3. Locate the `ServerAdmin` statement and enter the email address of the webmaster.

   `ServerAdmin {email address}`

4. Locate the `ServerName` option and then enter the IP address of the web server.

   `ServerName {IP address: Port}`

5. Locate the `DocumentRoot` option and enter the path of the directory that is used to serve web content.

   `DocumentRoot {Absolute path of the web content directory}`

6. Locate the `DirectoryIndex` option and enter the list of index files for the directory.

   `DirectoryIndex {List of index files}`

7. Save and close the file.

8. Enter `service httpd start` to start the httpd service for the configuration changes to take effect.

9. Enter `chkconfig httpd on` to enable the httpd service during system startup.

 Update the DNS zone file if you want to use hostnames for the web server.

Procedure Reference: Tune the Apache Server

To tune the Apache server:

1. Log in as root.
2. Using the vi editor, open the /etc/httpd/httpd.conf file.
3. Set the Apache configuration settings to tune the server.
   - Locate the `MaxKeepAliveRequests` directive and specify the maximum number of requests that are allowed.

     `MaxKeepAliveRequests = {Maximum number of requests}`
   - Locate the `StartServers` directive and set the initial number of server processes.

     `StartServers = {Number of processes}`
   - Locate the `MinSpareServers` directive and specify the minimum number of spare servers.

     `MinSpareServers = {Minimum number of spare servers}`
   - Locate the `MaxSpareServers` directive and specify the maximum number of spare servers.

     `MaxSpareServers = {Maximum number of spare servers}`
   - Locate the `MaxClients` directive and specify the maximum number of client connections that run in parallel.

     `MaxClients = {Maximum number of client connections}`
   - Locate the `KeepAlive` directive and set it to `On` or `Off` to allow or prevent more than one request per connection.

     `KeepAlive = On|Off`
   - Locate the `KeepAliveTimeout` directive and specify the time limit for a request with respect to the connection.

     `KeepAliveTimeout = {Number of seconds}`
4. Save and close the file.
5. Enter `service httpd configtest` to test the configuration file.
6. Enter `service httpd restart` to restart the httpd service for the configuration changes to take effect.

Procedure Reference: Configure the Apache Namespace

To configure the Apache namespace:

1. Log in as root.
2. Using the vi editor, open the /etc/httpd/conf/httpd.conf file.
3. Locate the `UserDir` option and uncomment the line to allow users to allocate a separate space for their web content.

   `UserDir enable {user name}`

4. Uncomment the directory section defined for the home directory to control access to `UserDir` directories.

```
<Directory /home/user name/public_html>
AllowOverride FileInfo AuthConfig Limit
Options MultiViews Indexes SymLinksIfOwnerMatch IncludesNoExec
<Limit GET POST Options>
Order allow,deny
Allow from all
</Limit>
<LimitExcept GET POST Options>
Order deny,allow
Deny from all
</LimitExcept>
</Directory>
```

5. Save and close the file.

6. Enter `mkdir /home/user name/public_html` to create a directory for the web content.

7. Copy the user's own web content into /home/{user name}/public_html.

8. Enter `chown -R user name:User group /home/user name` to change the ownership permission of the user's home directory.

9. Enter `chmod -R 755 /home/user name` to change the permissions of the user's home directory.

10. Enter `service httpd configtest` to test the configuration file.

11. Enter `service httpd restart` to restart the httpd service for the configuration changes to take effect.

12. Access the website and verify the configuration.

```
http://localhost/~user name
```

Procedure Reference: Configure the Apache Log

To configure the Apache log:

1. Log in as root.

2. Using the vi editor, open the /etc/httpd/conf/httpd.conf file.

3. Locate the `ErrorLog` statement and specify the location where error logs should be stored.

```
ErrorLog {location of error logs}
```

4. Locate and specify the `CustomLog` directive.

    a. Specify a log format by using the `LogFormat` directive.

    ```
    LogFormat "format" format name
    ```

    b. Define a `CustomLog` directive that uses the log format you created.

    ```
    CustomLog logs/access_log format name
    ```

 The naming convention for the access_log file can be changed according to user requirement. By default, it is named as access_log and generally it is renamed as access.log.

5. Enter `service httpd configtest` to check whether the httpd.conf file is configured correctly.

6. Enter `service httpd restart` to restart the httpd service for the configuration changes to take effect.

ACTIVITY 13-1
Configuring a Web Server

Before You Begin:
1. On srvA, you have logged in as root in the GUI.
2. The terminal window is displayed.
3. Enter `cd /root` to navigate to the root directory.
4. On the terminal window, copy the english.html file and the Our Global Company_files directory from the /085039Data/Web_Services directory to the /var/www/html directory.
5. Clear the terminal window.

Scenario:
Your company runs a chain of retail stores and wants to set up an online web store, which will provide information about the store and facilitate online shopping. Now, you want to configure the web server to facilitate web hosting. Also, you want to configure the web server in such a way that PHP pages are included in the website.

What You Do	How You Do It
1. Check whether httpd has been installed on the system.	a. Verify that the apr package has been installed on the system.
	b. Verify that the postgresql-libs package has been installed on the system.
	c. Verify that the apr-util package has been installed on the system.
	d. Verify that the httpd package has been installed on the system.
	e. Clear the terminal window.
2. Enable PHP support on the system.	a. Enter `yum localinstall /rhelsource/Server/⇒ php-common-5.1.6-23.el5.i386.rpm` to install the php-common package.

 The ⇒ symbol is used in the step only to bring the step to the next line. It is not part of the code and therefore, students need not type the symbol.

b. Enter **yum localinstall /rhelsource/Server/**⇒ **php-cli-5.1.6-23.el5.i386.rpm** to install the php-cli package.

 The ⇒ symbol is used in the step only to bring the step to the next line. It is not part of the code and therefore, students need not type the symbol.

c. Enter **yum localinstall /rhelsource/Server/**⇒ **php-5.1.6-23.el5.i386.rpm** to install the php package.

 The ⇒ symbol is used in the step only to bring the step to the next line. It is not part of the code and therefore, students need not type the symbol.

d. Clear the terminal window.

---

3. Specify alias names for the web server.

a. Navigate to the /var/named directory.

b. Using the `vi` editor, open the ogc.forward file.

c. At the end of the file, type **www   IN CNAME   srvA** to add a CNAME record.

d. Press **Esc** to switch to the command mode.

e. Save and close the file.

f. Restart the named service.

g. Clear the terminal window.

4.	Configure the web server to allow web hosting.	a.	Navigate to the /etc/httpd/conf directory.

4. Configure the web server to allow web hosting.

a. Navigate to the /etc/httpd/conf directory.

b. Using the vi editor, open the httpd.conf file.

c. Locate the line "#ServerName www.example.com:80" and change it to `ServerName www.ourglobalcompany.com:80`

d. Press **Esc** to switch to the command mode.

e. Locate the "<Directory "/var/www/html">" statement.

f. Locate the line `AllowOverride None` in the **<Directory "/var/www/html">** statement.

g. Change the `AllowOverride None` parameter to `AllowOverride AuthConfig`

h. Press **Esc** to switch to the command mode.

i. Locate the line "DirectoryIndex index.html index.html.var" and change it to `DirectoryIndex english.html english.html.var`

j. Press **Esc** to switch to the command mode.

k. Save and close the file.

l. Clear the terminal window.

5. Start the httpd service to apply configuration changes.

a. Enter `service httpd start` to start the httpd service.

b. Enter `chkconfig httpd on` to start the httpd service when the system boots.

c. Clear the terminal window.

6. Access the website that you have set up.

a. Enter `firefox http://ourglobalcompany.com` to open the website in the Firefox browser.

b. Observe that the homepage of Our Global Company is displayed in the Mozilla Firefox web browser.

c. Close the web browser window.

d. Clear the terminal window.

TOPIC B
Implement Apache Access Control

You configured a web server. You may need to host multiple websites on a single web server and secure it to restrict unauthorized access. In this topic, you will implement Apache access control.

Your organization may have intranet sites for employees. Because the number of users accessing the intranet sites will be fewer when compared to the Internet websites, you decide to host both websites on the same server. To do so, you will need to use security methods to segregate data for the two sites. As a system administrator, it is also essential to ensure the general security of data stored on the server. Therefore, you will need the skills to set up access control appropriately.

Virtual Hosts

Definition:

A *virtual host* is a system that enables management of more than one domain. It can have more than one domain or IP address. The virtual host can be name based or IP based. The `VirtualHost` directive is used to define a virtual machine. Details, such as the IP address, web page information, log format, and domain name, are specified in the httpd.conf file.

Example:

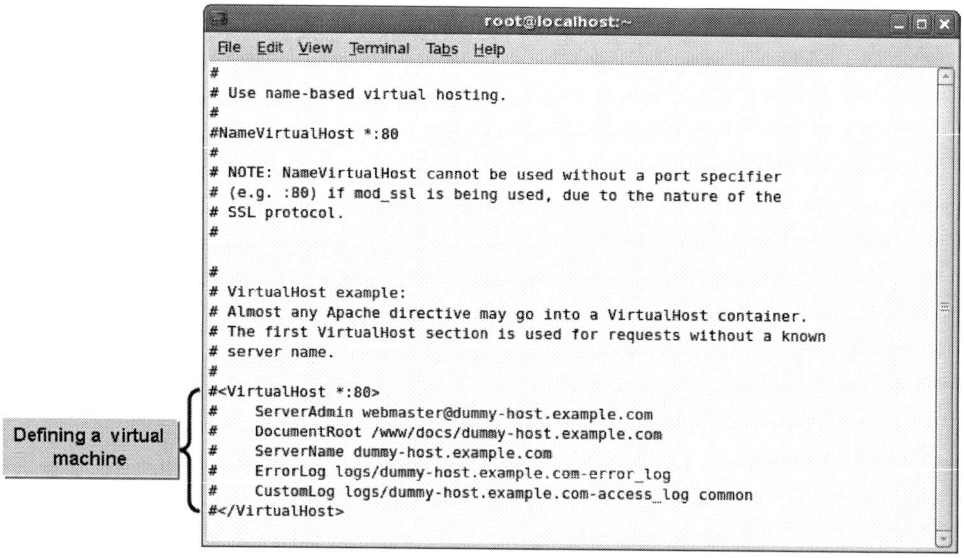

Figure 13-12: A list of domains managed by the vitualhost system.

IP-Based Virtual Hosting

IP-based virtual hosting enables multiple websites based on IP addresses to be hosted by a system. The server will be assigned to more than one IP address, and each IP address will point to a website. To define an IP-based virtual host, the IP address of the web server should be specified in the `VirtualHost` directive.

Name-Based Virtual Hosting

Name-based virtual hosting is a method by which a system can host more than one website based on the host name. In this method, many hosts can have the same IP address. This method is preferred to host multiple websites on the same web server. The server will be assigned to more than one host name and each host name will point to a website. A name-based virtual hosting can be configured using the `NameVirtualHost` directive. The IP addresses of the hosts that need to be served are specified in the `NameVirtualHost` directive, provided the IP addresses are associated with a network interface on the server. In addition, the server can be made to listen or restrict the IP address specified in the `NameVirtualHost` directive using the `Listen` or `BindAddress` directive, respectively. The `NameVirtualHost` directive is followed by the `VirtualHost` directive defined for each host that needs to be served.

The Transport Layer Security Protocol

Definition:

Transport Layer Security (TLS), the third version of Secure Sockets Layer (SSL), is a protocol that provides secure communication between servers and clients. TLS establishes a secure communication channel between a server and a client and then encrypts data that needs to be transmitted. TLS uses cryptography to provide authentication and securely transfer data. The mod_ssl is the Apache module that is used for enabling TLS and SSL on the Apache server. The ssl.conf configuration file is stored in the /etc/httpd/conf.d directory. It is used to provide TLS support to the Apache server.

Example:

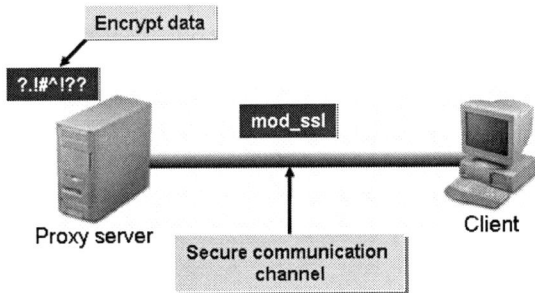

Figure 13-13: Secured communication between the server and the client.

Digital Certificates

A *digital certificate* is a digital document that authenticates a specific public key belonging to an individual or a company. It contains the individual's name or the company name, the serial number, the expiration dates, a copy of the certificate holder's public key, and the digital signature of the certificate issuing authority. Digital certificates can be self-signed or signed by a Certificate Authority (CA). They are required to set up a secure web server. The digital certificate is stored in the /etc/pki/tls/certs directory.

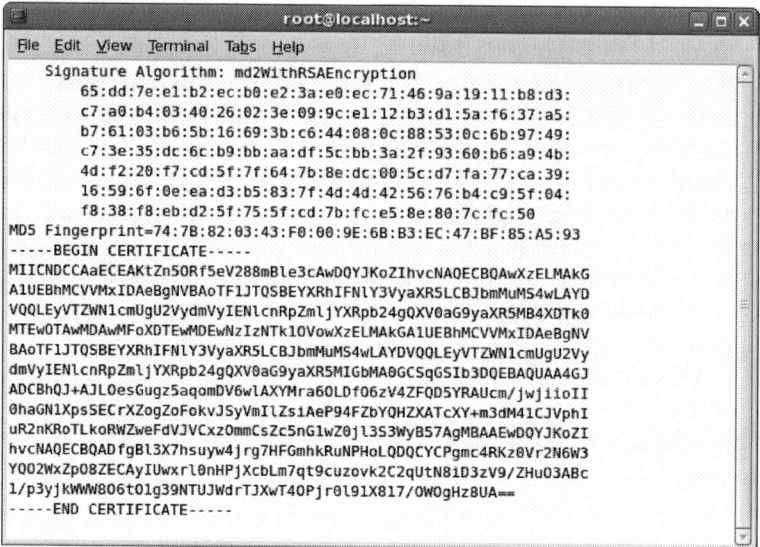

Figure 13-14: A digital certificate stored on a server.

The Common Gateway Interface

The *Common Gateway Interface (CGI)* is a protocol that provides a way for the web server to communicate with external dynamic content created using CGI scripts or programs. These CGI scripts are usually created using the Perl language. The Apache server recognizes the CGI scripts using the `ScriptAlias` directive. This directive is used to specify the directory that is set for CGI programs. The `mod_perl` module allows the Apache web server to speed up the process of recognizing CGI programs. It provides high-level authentication and authorization of users and also avoids repeated compilation of similar Perl programs. The .htaccess files are primarily used to configure a directory that is to be set up for recognizing CGI scripts.

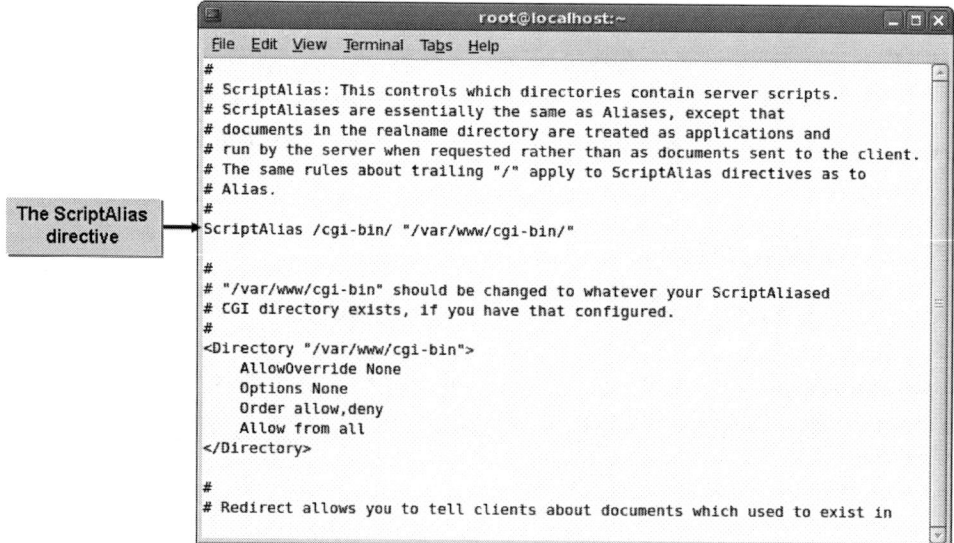

The ScriptAlias directive

Figure 13-15: The ScriptAlias directive in the Apache configuration file.

Syntax

The syntax of the `ScriptAlias` directive is: `ScriptAlias /cgi-bin/`
`/Directory path/cgi-bin/`, where the resource request beginning with `/cgi-bin/`
will be retrieved from the CGI directory.

Execute CGI From Non-ScriptAliased Directories

In the httpd.conf file specify the following settings:

1. Activate the `cgi-script` handler with the `AddHandler` directive.

2. In the `Directory` statement, specify `ExecCGI` in the `Options` directive.

How to Implement Apache Access Control

Procedure Reference: Configure Virtual Hosts

To configure virtual hosts:

1. Log in as root.

2. Using the vi editor, open the /etc/httpd/conf/httpd.conf file.

3. If necessary, enter `NameVirtualHost {IP address}:port number` to specify
    the IP address of the web server.

4. Add a `VirtualHost` directive for each virtual host you want to define.

    a. Begin the `VirtualHost` declaration with the IP address or the hostname. The
        lesser than (<) and greater than (>) symbols at the beginning and end of the
        `VirtualHost` keyword are mandatory.

    b. Specify the email address of the administrator in the `ServerAdmin` directive.

    c. Specify the IP address of the server in the `ServerName` parameter.

    d. Specify the directory where the HTML files will be stored using the
        `DocumentRoot` parameter.

    e. Specify the file name with its absolute or relative path where the errors will be
        logged using the `Errorlog` parameter.

    f. Specify the access log file name with its absolute or relative path using the
        `Customlog` parameter.

    g. Complete the `VirtualHost` declaration.

        ```
        <VirtualHost {IP address/hostname}:port number>
        ServerAdmin {User name}@{Domain name}
        DocumentRoot {DocumentRoot location}
        ServerName {IP address/FQDN}
        Errorlog {Path of the error log file}
        Customlog {Path of the access log file} {Log level}
        </VirtualHost>
        ```

5. Save and close the file.

6. Enter `service httpd configtest` to check whether the httpd.conf file is config-
    ured correctly.

7. Enter `service httpd restart` to restart the httpd service.

Procedure Reference: Restrict User Access

To restrict user access:

1. Log in as root.

2. Using the vi editor, open the /etc/httpd/conf/httpd.conf file.

3. Add a `Directory` statement to deny access from a specific domain.

```
<Directory "location of web pages">
Order deny,allow
Deny from {domain name} | {IP address}
</Directory>
```

 If a Directory statement exists, you can edit the statement according to your requirement.

4. Save and close the file.

5. Enter `service httpd configtest` to check whether the httpd.conf file is configured correctly.

6. Enter `service httpd restart` to restart the httpd service for the configuration changes to take effect.

7. Log in as a user from the denied domain.

8. Verify that you are denied access when you access the website hosted on your web server.

Procedure Reference: Authenticate Users to Access a Website

To authenticate users to access a website:

1. Log in as root.

2. Using the vi editor, open the /etc/httpd/conf/httpd.conf file.

3. Add a `Directory` statement to regulate access to the website.

```
<Directory "Location of the html page">
{
AllowOverride AuthConfig
}
</Directory>
```

 If you want to authenticate users when they access a virtual host, you need to place the directory declaration within the virtual host declaration.

4. Enter `htpasswd -mc {password file name} {user name}` to create users who can access the website.

5. When prompted, enter and reenter the password for the user you created.

6. Create a user group and add a list of HTTP users to the group.

   - Enter `vi Document Root/.htgroup` to open the .htgroup file and locate the `Document Root` directive.

   - Type `{Group Name} : {List of HTTP users}` to define a user group and add the list of HTTP users separated by space.

   - Save and close the file.

7. Enter `chgrp apache Document Root/{password file name} Document Root/{group file name}` to specify that Apache is the group owner of the password and group files.

8. Enter `chmod g+r Document Root/{password file name} Document Root/{group file name}` to provide group read permission for the password and group files.

9. Define the access control rights for the website.

   a. Enter `vi Document Root/.htaccess` to create and open the .htaccess using the vi editor.

   b. Enter `Authname "message"` to specify the message to be displayed in the authentication dialog box.

   c. Enter `Authtype basic` to specify the type of authentication.

   d. Enter `Authuserfile "Document Root/.htpass"` to specify the file that contains details about the users who have access to the website.

   e. Enter `AuthGroupFile "Document Root/.htgroup"` to specify a group file.

   f. Specify the users who can access the website.

   - Type `require valid-user` to specify that all valid users (created using the htpasswd command) can access the website.

   - Type `require user [user name 1] [user name 2]` to specify that only specific users can access the website.

   - Or, type `require group {Group Name}` to specify that only a specific group can access the website.

   g. Save and close the file.

10. Enter `service httpd configtest` to check the configuration of the httpd.conf file.

11. Enter `service httpd restart` to restart the httpd service to reload the configuration file.

12. If necessary, access the website to verify the authentication.

Procedure Reference: Enable SSL

To enable SSL:

1. Log in as root.

2. Install the packages required for SSL.

   - Enter `rpm -ivh distcache-{version}.{release}.rpm`.

   - Enter `rpm -ivh mod_ssl-{version}.{release}.rpm`.

3. Navigate to the /etc/pki/tls/certs directory.

4. Enter `make certreq` to request a Certificate Authority (CA) certificate.

5. When prompted, enter the password for the certificate and keys.

6. When prompted, enter information such as the country, state, locality, organization name, organization unit name, server's hostname, webmaster's email address, and password.

7. Create a public or private key pair.

   a. Enter make *Private key file*.crt to create the private key.

   b. When prompted, enter the password for the certificate and the keys.

   c. When prompted, enter the information such as the country, state, locality, organization name, organization unit name, server's hostname, webmaster's email address, and password.

8. Using the vi editor, open the /etc/httpd/conf.d/ssl.conf file.

9. Locate the *SSLCertificateFile* variable and specify the server's certificate path.

   SSLCertificateFile *Absolute directory path\certificate file*.crt

 By default, the directory path is set to the /etc/pki/tls/certs directory.

10. Locate the *SSLCertificateKeyFile* variable and specify the key file.

    SSLCertificateKeyFile *Absolute directory path\key file*.key

 By default, the directory path is set to the /etc/pki/tls/private directory.

11. Save and close the file.

12. Enter service httpd configtest to check whether the httpd.conf file is configured correctly.

13. Enter service httpd restart to restart the httpd service.

14. Access the website and verify that SSL is enabled.

ACTIVITY 13-2
Maintaining a Web Server

Before You Begin:
1. On srvA, you have logged in as root in the GUI.
2. The terminal window is displayed.
3. Create a directory named german in the /var/www directory.
4. Copy the german.html file from the /085039Data/Web_Services directory to the /var/www/german directory.
5. Clear the terminal window.

Scenario:
OGC Systems is planning to expand its operations globally. As part of its expansion strategy, the company devised various strategies to establish its presence in new markets. One of the plans is to host an official website in different languages for its widespread customer base, so that it can reach out to a wider audience. The web design team designed the German version of the customer website, and you want to use the existing web server to host the new website. You also want to ensure that the new website is accessible only to customers in that specified region.

What You Do	How You Do It
1. Specify alias names for the web server.	a. Navigate to the /var/named directory.
	b. Using the `vi` editor, open the ogc.forward file.
	c. At the end of the file, type `german    IN    CNAME    srvA` to add a CNAME record.
	d. Press **Esc** to switch to the command mode.
	e. Save and close the file.
	f. Restart the named service.
	g. Clear the terminal window.

2. Add `VirtualHost` directives to the English and German websites.

a. Using the vi editor, open the /etc/httpd/conf/httpd.conf file.

b. At the end of the file, enter **NameVirtualHost 192.168.0.2** to specify the IP address of the web server.

c. Enter **<VirtualHost www.ourglobalcompany.com>** to begin the first VirtualHost directive.

d. Enter

ServerName 192.168.0.2

to specify the IP address of the server.

e. Enter **DocumentRoot /var/www/html** to specify the directory where the HTML files will be stored.

f. Enter

DirectoryIndex english.html

to specify the file.

g. Enter **</VirtualHost>** to complete the VirtualHost directive.

See Code Sample 1.

h. Add a **VirtualHost** directive with the server name **german.ourglobalcompany.com** and Document Root location /var/www/german.

See Code Sample 2.

i. Press **Esc** to switch to the command mode.

j. Save and close the file.

k. Restart the httpd service.

l. Clear the terminal window.

Code Sample 1

```
NameVirtualHost 192.168.0.2
<VirtualHost www.ourglobalcompany.com>
ServerName 192.168.0.2
DocumentRoot /var/www/html
DirectoryIndex english.html
</VirtualHost>
```

Code Sample 2

```
<VirtualHost german.ourglobalcompany.com>
ServerName 192.168.0.2
DocumentRoot /var/www/german
DirectoryIndex german.html
</VirtualHost>
```

3.	Create users who can access your website.	a.	Navigate to the /var/www/html directory.
		b.	Enter

b. Enter

htpasswd -mc /var/www/html/.htpasswd webuser

to create the webuser user.

c. Enter **@webuser1** as the password.

d. When prompted, retype **@webuser1**

e. Observe that the password for webuser is added.

f. Enter **chgrp apache .htpasswd** to specify that apache is the group owner of the password file.

g. Enter **chmod g+r .htpasswd** to provide group read permission for the password file.

<table>
<tr>
<td>

4. Configure Apache to authenticate users.

</td>
<td>

a. Using the vi editor, open the .htaccess file.

b. Enter **Authname "This is a trusted website."** to specify the message to be displayed in the authentication dialog box.

c. Enter **Authuserfile "/var/www/html/.htpasswd"** to indicate the name of the file that contains details about users who have access to the website.

d. Enter **Authtype basic** to specify the type of authentication.

e. Type **require valid-user** to specify that all valid users can access the website.

   See Code Sample 3.

f. Press **Esc** to switch to the command mode.

g. Save and close the file.

h. Clear the terminal window.

</td>
</tr>
</table>

Code Sample 3

```
Authname "This is a trusted website."
Authuserfile "/var/www/html/.htpasswd"
Authtype basic
require valid-user
```

5. Check whether you are able to access the English and German versions of the website.

a. Enter `firefox http://ourglobalcompany.com` to open the website in the Firefox web browser.

b. In the **Authentication Required** dialog box, in the **User Name** text box, type *webuser* and press the **Tab** key.

c. In the **Password** text box, type *@webuser1* and then press the **Tab** key and **Enter.**

d. On the toolbar, click **Never for This Site** to prevent Firefox from prompting you to save the password.

e. Close the web browser window.

f. Enter `firefox http://german.ourglobalcompany.com` to open the German website in the web browser.

g. Observe that the home page of the German version of Our Global Company is displayed.

h. Close the web browser window.

i. Clear the terminal window.

TOPIC C

Implement Access Control in a Proxy Server

You implemented web services on your network. It is now critical to ensure that only authorized users are allowed to access websites through the server. In this topic, you will configure a proxy server.

According to the organization policy, you may have to provide the Internet access to all employees. However, inappropriate usage of the Internet can affect server performance. Therefore, you may want to restrict user access to certain websites and monitor the usage with the help of a proxy server.

Proxy Servers

Definition:

A *proxy server* is a server that acts as an intermediary between a web browser and a web server. It contains cache information of the web server and intercepts all requests sent to the web server. A proxy server comprises a main server utility, programs for performing authentication, and management tools. The proxy server supports data transmitted through HTTP, FTP, and Gopher protocols.

Example:

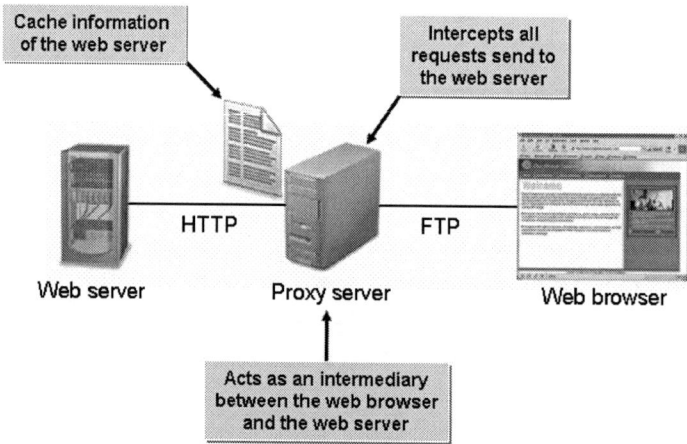

Figure 13-16: Data transmission occurring through a proxy server.

The Squid Server

Squid is a proxy server that is used for caching Internet data. When a client requests data, Squid accepts the request and forwards it to a remote server, which is the original server, or to another proxy server. Squid receives the data, stores a copy of it in the cache, and then sends it to the respective client machine. The copy of the data that is stored in the cache is used to serve client requests in the future. The caches can be arranged in a hierarchy using the lightweight *Internet Cache Protocol (ICP)*. Squid supports data transfer using FTP, HTTP, *Gopher*, and SSL protocols.

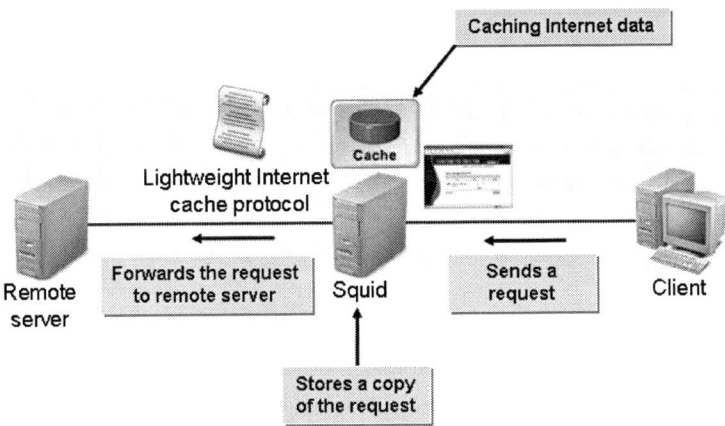

Figure 13-17: Functioning of a Squid proxy server.

The Squid web server is referred to as a web accelerator. In such instances, it serves one or more dynamic documents apart from serving some static documents and operates faster, thereby optimizing server and network performance. It protects the original web server from being attacked by external data and invalid URLs because it hides the original web server.

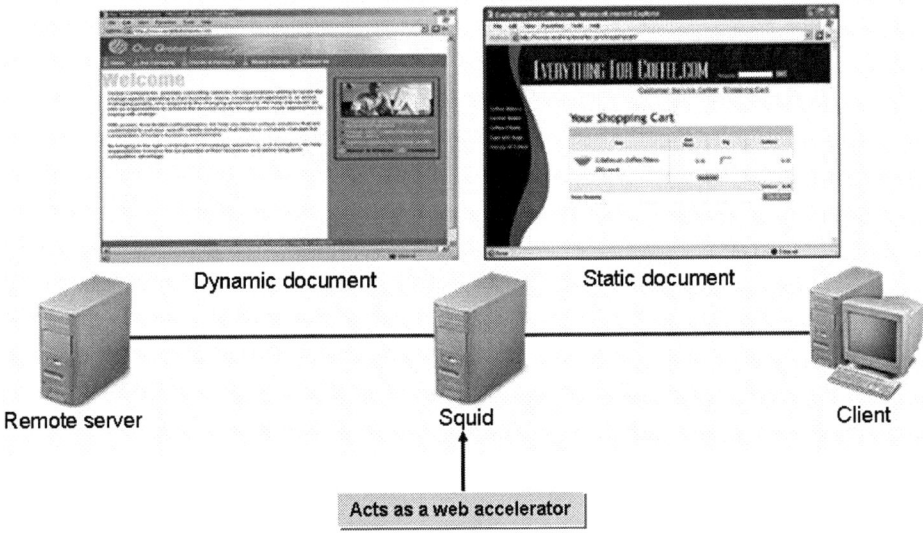

Figure 13-18: The Squid proxy server acting as a web accelerator.

ICP

ICP is a protocol that is used for coordinating and communicating among web caches. It queries proxy servers for caches.

Gopher

The Gopher protocol is a TCP/IP application layer protocol that is used to search and retrieve documents from the Internet.

The squid.conf File

The squid.conf file, stored in the /etc/squid directory, is the main configuration file used to configure Squid. The squid daemon runs from the /usr/sbin directory and listens on port 3128. The initialization script runs from the /etc/init.d/squid file. By default, the squid.conf file contains tags that are used to set parameters to the server.

There are various parameters defined in the squid.conf file. Each parameter is set to a value that defines the server functionality. Some parameters are described in the table below.

Parameter	Description
cache_mem	Specifies the amount of memory that Squid will use for caching popular requests. By default, it is set to 8 MB.
maximum_object_size	Specifies the maximum size of the cache.
minimum_object_size	Specifies the minimum size of the cache.
cache_dir	Specifies the type of storage system and the directory name where the cache files are stored.

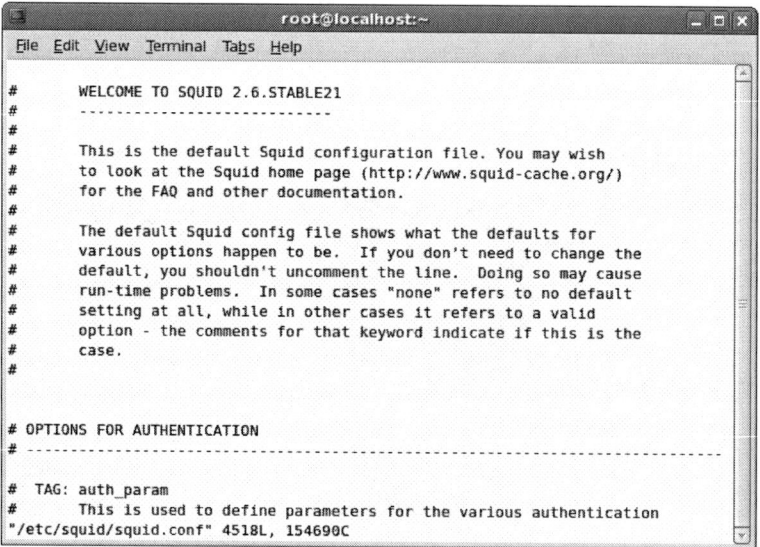

Figure 13-19: The main squid configuration file.

The Access Control List in Squid

The *Access Control List (ACL) in Squid* contains a set of entries that define the permissions to access a system and all the resources within it. ACL can be defined in the squid.conf file using the `acl` keyword followed by an ACL name and its type. ACLs can be filtered based on users, domains, file name extensions, source or destination IP addresses, regular expressions that match the pattern, destination ports, and protocols. The definitions given in the ACL may or may not gain access to the server.

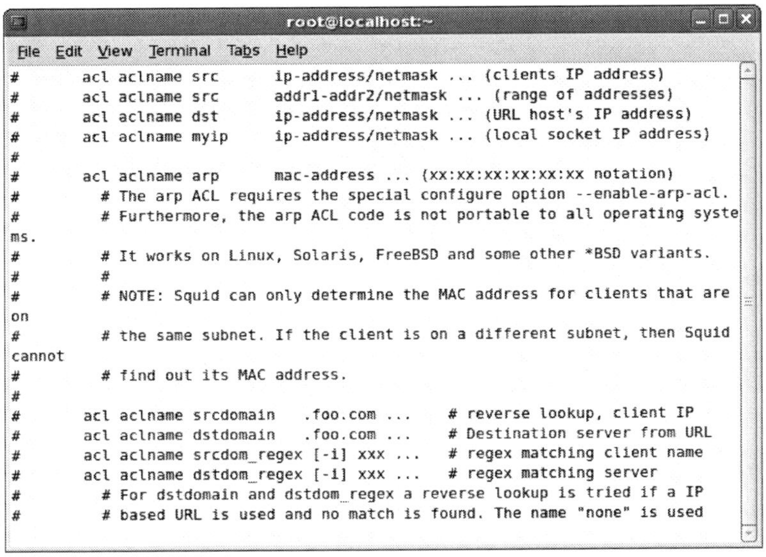

```
#        acl aclname src         ip-address/netmask ... (clients IP address)
#        acl aclname src         addr1-addr2/netmask ... (range of addresses)
#        acl aclname dst         ip-address/netmask ... (URL host's IP address)
#        acl aclname myip        ip-address/netmask ... (local socket IP address)
#
#        acl aclname arp         mac-address ... (xx:xx:xx:xx:xx:xx notation)
#          # The arp ACL requires the special configure option --enable-arp-acl.
#          # Furthermore, the arp ACL code is not portable to all operating syste
ms.
#          #
#          # It works on Linux, Solaris, FreeBSD and some other *BSD variants.
#          #
#          # NOTE: Squid can only determine the MAC address for clients that are
on
#          # the same subnet. If the client is on a different subnet, then Squid
cannot
#          # find out its MAC address.
#
#        acl aclname srcdomain    .foo.com ...      # reverse lookup, client IP
#        acl aclname dstdomain    .foo.com ...      # Destination server from URL
#        acl aclname srcdom_regex [-i] xxx ...      # regex matching client name
#        acl aclname dstdom_regex [-i] xxx ...      # regex matching server
#          # For dstdomain and dstdom_regex a reverse lookup is tried if a IP
#          # based URL is used and no match is found. The name "none" is used
```

Figure 13-20: Various ACLs defined in the squid.conf file.

Syntax

ACLs can be defined with respect to various parameters. Some of the ways to define an ACL are listed in the table.

Syntax	Description
`acl acl name src IP address/netmask`	Identifies clients based on the IP address and netmask.
`acl acl name dst IP address/netmask`	Identifies the URL host's IP address.
`acl acl name myip IP address/netmask`	Identifies the local socket's IP address.
`acl acl name time {day abbreviations} {start hr:minutes-end_hr:minutes}`	Specifies the days and time during which the proxy server can be accessed.
`acl acl name urlpath_regex words in the URL`	Specifies the URLs to be rejected based on the specified keywords.

Access Control Operators

An access control operator is a tag that is used to specify the type of access an ACL is permitted or denied. The access control operator is followed by the `allow` or `deny` keyword and then the ACL name. There are many types of operators provided in the squid.conf file. The most common access operators are listed in the table below.

Operator	Used To
http_access	Allow or deny access to HTTP ports. For example, `http_access allow	deny hostname	all` .
icp_access	Allow or deny access to send and receive ICP queries to and from caches.
no_cache	Remove matching patterns from the cache.

How to Implement Access Control in a Proxy Server

Procedure Reference: Install Squid

To install Squid:

1. Log in as root.
2. Mount the Linux installation media that contains Squid.
3. Navigate to the /media/[name of the media]/Server directory.
4. At the command line, enter `rpm -ivh squid-{version}.{release}.rpm` to install Squid.
5. Enter `rpm -qi squid` to verify that Squid has been installed.
6. Unmount the installation media.

Procedure Reference: Configure Squid

To configure Squid:

1. Log in as root.
2. Using an editor, open the /etc/squid/squid.conf file.
3. Locate the line the "http_port 3128" and uncomment it to specify that the squid daemon will listen on port 3128 for requests.
4. Enter `cache_dir Cache location path {Maximum cache size} {Maximum number of subdirectories in first tier} {Maximum number of subdirectories in second tier}` to specify the cache requirements.
5. Save and close the file.
6. Enter `service squid start` to start the Squid service.
7. Enter `chkconfig squid on` to enable the Squid service during system startup.
8. On the system that has access to the proxy server, modify the browser settings with respect to the proxy server hostname and port.

Procedure Reference: Implement Access Policies

To implement access policies:

1. Log in as root.

2. Using an editor, open the /etc/squid/squid.conf file.

3. Define an ACL for a range of IP addresses, domain, hour, days, URL, port, protocol, method, user name, or type of browser. For example, you will use the following syntax to define an ACL for an IP address.

    ```
    acl {acl name} {acl type} {MAC address | IP address/netmask}
    ```

4. Add an http_access statement to allow or deny access to specific ACLs.

    ```
    http_access allow acl name
    http_access deny acl name
    ```

5. Save and close the file.

6. Enter `service squid restart` to restart the Squid service.

Procedure Reference: Enable Proxy Authentication

To enable proxy authentication:

1. Log in as root.

2. Using the vi editor, open the /etc/squid/squid.conf file.

3. Add the `auth_param` statement to specify the authentication scheme that Squid should use.

    ```
    auth_param authentication scheme {authentication parameter} {setting}
    ```

4. Define an ACL to specify that the proxy authorization is required for accessing websites.

    ```
    acl acl name proxy_auth REQUIRED
    ```

5. Enter `http_access allow acl name` to specify that only proxy authenticated users can access websites.

6. Save and close the file.

7. Enter `service squid restart` to restart the Squid service.

ACTIVITY 13-3

Configuring the Proxy Server

Before You Begin:

1. On srvA, you have logged in as root in the GUI.

2. Switch to the CLI.

3. Enter `cd /root` to navigate to the root directory.

4. Enter `yum localinstall /rhelsource/Server/squid-2.6.STABLE21-3.el5.i386.rpm` to start installing the Squid package. Enter `y` to complete the package installation.

5. Clear the terminal window.

Scenario:

You are a network administrator in an organization that has different teams handling design, content development, online customer support, and office administration. You have just installed a proxy server. Now, you need to configure the proxy server so that the settings comply with the guidelines in the Internet access policy document provided by the IT manager. The guidelines are:

● The administrative staff need access to the Internet only during lunchtime on weekdays; other employees must be able to access the Internet all the time.

● No pornographic sites should be accessible.

The administration team is in the 192.168.1.0/255.255.255.0 subnet, and the other teams are in the 192.168.0.0/255.255.255.0 subnet.

What You Do	How You Do It
1. Provide rights to the administrative team to access the Internet only during the lunch hour; allow the other teams to access the Internet all the time.	a. On the system labeled **srvA**, using the vi editor, open the /etc/squid/squid.conf file.
	b. Locate the text "http_port 3128" and verify that the line is uncommented.
	c. Locate the line with content "#http_access allow our_networks."
	d. Press **O** to switch to the insert mode and move to a new line.
	e. Enter **acl myhosts src 192.168.0.0/255.255.255.0** to define the myhosts ACL.
	f. Enter **acl admin src 192.168.1.0/255.255.255.0** to define the admin ACL.
	g. Enter **acl lunch time MTWHF 12:00-13:00** to define an ACL for lunchtime.
	h. Enter **http_access allow myhosts** to grant access to the myhosts ACL.
	i. Enter **http_access allow lunch** to grant access to everyone during lunchtime on weekdays.
	j. Enter **http_access deny admin** to deny access to the admin ACL.
	k. Enter **visible_hostname srvA.ourglobalcompany.com** to declare srvA as a visible_hostname. *See Code Sample 1.*

Code Sample 1

```
acl myhosts src 192.168.0.0/255.255.255.0
```

```
acl admin src 192.168.1.0/255.255.255.0
acl lunch time MTWHF 12:00-13:00
http_access allow myhosts
http_access allow lunch
http_access deny admin
visible_hostname srvA.ourglobalcompany.com
```

2. Deny access to pornographic sites.

    a. Enter **acl restricted_site urlpath_regex -i porn** to create the restricted_site ACL.

    b. Enter **http_access deny restricted_site** to deny access to the restricted_site ACL.

        See Code Sample 2.

    c. Press **Esc** to switch to the command mode.

    d. Save and close the file.

    e. Enter **service squid start** to start the Squid service.

    f. Clear the terminal window.

Code Sample 2

```
http_access deny admin
acl restricted_site urlpath_regex -i porn
http_access deny restricted_site
```

TOPIC D
Configure Email Services

You have set up a proxy server for your users, and now you need to provide client and server email services by defining the email process. In this topic, you will configure email services.

It wasn't long ago that organizations conducted business communications using only the internal mail room and the postal service. Today, however, we communicate electronically with email and instant messaging. Understanding how mail clients operate is critical to implement an email service.

Mail Protocols

Definition:

A *mail protocol* is a set of rules that enable distribution of email messages from a mail server. Using a mail protocol, an email message may be stored on a server or transmitted to a client's computer when read. Mail protocols enable users to create and manage folders on a server, search for messages, or delete messages. POP, IMAP, and SMTP are the most frequently used mail protocols.

Example:

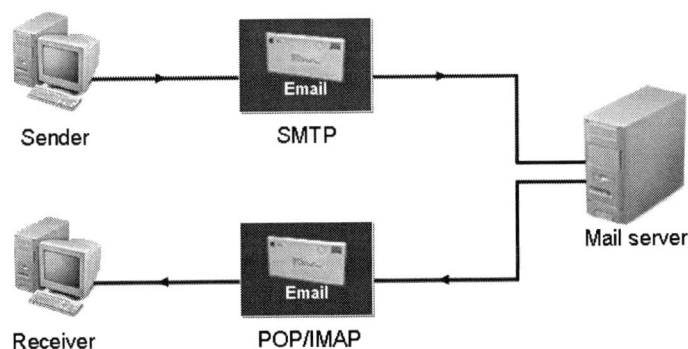

Figure 13-21: Email messages are distributed using the POP, IMAP, and SMTP protocols.

The Simple Mail Transfer Protocol

The *Simple Mail Transfer Protocol (SMTP)* is a protocol that defines a set of rules to enable interaction between a program sending an email message to a server and a program receiving an email message from a client. The Mail Transfer Agent (MTA) or the Mail User Agent (MUA) acts as an SMTP client. The SMTP server always listens to port 25 for client responses. SMTP uses TCP for transmitting messages and IP for routing purposes. It contains a number of status codes that are used to set specific conditions for communication between the server and the client. It also contains a set of commands that are used for communication between the server and the client.

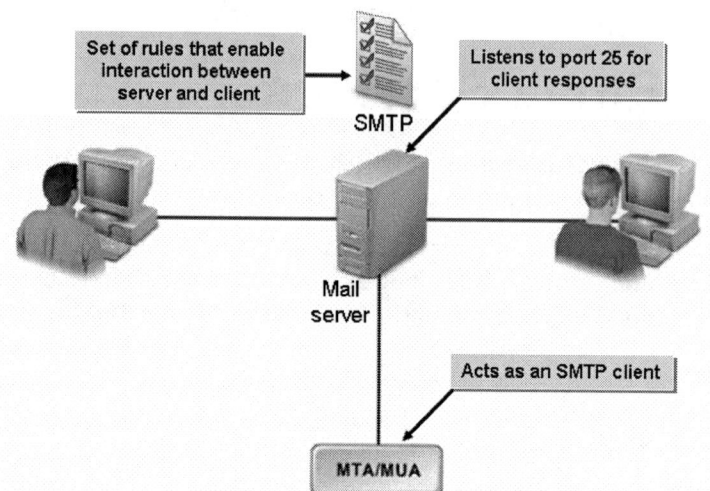

Figure 13-22: Communication between clients using SMTP.

In addition to text messages, graphics and attachments can also be transferred through email using Extended SMTP (ESMTP). The Extended HELLO (EHLO) command is used by ESMTP clients to communicate with the server and the server responds with one of the three status codes: success, failure, or error.

Mail Spooling

Spooling is a method of handling delays in delivering email messages. If there is an email delivery delay, SMTP at the originating computer spools the message. If there is no delay, SMTP at the originating computer sends the email message to the destination computer using the TCP connection. SMTP on the destination computer receives the email message and puts it in the user's mailbox. The same process occurs in reverse when a user at the destination computer sends a reply to a user at the originating computer.

POP3

Post Office Protocol version 3 (POP3) is used to retrieve email messages over the TCP connection on port 110. The POP client connects to the server and retrieves all messages. It then stores them on the client PC as new messages, deletes them from the server, and disconnects from the server. It supports MIME formatted email messages. In general, POP3 supports the transmission of messages and passwords in clear text format. It also provides authentication for the messages by encrypting the messages using the SSL protocol over TCP on port 995.

IMAP

The *Internet Message Access Protocol (IMAP)* is used to retrieve email messages over the TCP connection on port 143. The client retrieves all messages from the server, which retains the messages until the user deletes them. Although it transmits messages and passwords in cleartext format, it supports SSL encryption of messages over TCP on port 993. It supports MIME formatted email messages.

Mail Queues

Definition:

A *mail queue* is a waiting area for email messages that need to be processed by a computer. Mail queues are organized in such a way that the first item added to the queue is also the first item that is sent out of the queue.

Example:

Figure 13-23: The email messages are arranged in a queue.

Mail Transfer Agents

Definition:

A *Mail Transfer Agent (MTA)* is a mail transport program on the Internet that is used to send email through SMTP. It also handles the routing of email. MTA does not provide mailbox handling features. MTA uses SMTP to indicate the success or failure in the delivery of messages to a client and forms a separate queue for a set of failed messages. MTAs often use Local Mail Transport Protocol (LMTP), derived from SMTP, in instances where the storage of mail queues is not allowed at the server end. MTAs allow clients to handle the mail queues instead of allowing the server to handle the mail queues.

Example:

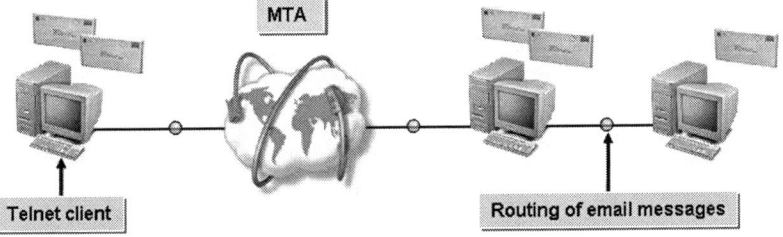

Figure 13-24: Routing of email messages through a MTA.

Types of MTAs

MTAs support features such as virtual hosting; automatic resending of messages in case of failed delivery; and spamassassin—a mail filter that is used to identify spam messages. Each MTA supports various features that provide a default access control feature on the server.

MTA	Description
Sendmail	A standard MTA that supports various Unix-based operating systems. It is designed to function in such a way that it runs as a single entity. It supports various MTAs and MDAs. It is an MTA that is still used from earlier days.
Postfix	A fast and secure MTA that can be administered easily. It is similar to Sendmail but varies in its internal functionality. Unlike Sendmail, Postfix supports a modular functionality. It is a free, open MTA and can be used as an alternative for Sendmail.
Exim	A flexible and a freely available MTA. Unlike other MTAs, it has extensive features that allow the administrator to control the mail transfer through the system. The latest version has been developed into an ACL-based system, which provides more detailed and flexible controls. This helps in the integration of antivirus and anti-spam measures in MTA.

Mail User Agents

Definition:

A *Mail User Agent (MUA)* is a program that is used to read and compose email messages. It is also referred to as an email client application. MUA acts as an interface between a user and an MTA and contains mailboxes for storing messages. MUAs can either have a graphical interface, such as Thunderbird and Evolution Mail, or a text-based interface such as mutt.

Example:

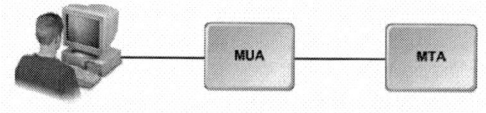

Figure 13-25: MUA acts as an interface between a user and an MTA.

Mail Delivery Agents

Definition:

A *Mail Delivery Agent (MDA)* is a program that delivers an incoming email messages to the intended recipient's mailbox. MDA uses SMTP to send new mail messages, and it uses POP3 or IMAP to retrieve messages. It also distributes and sorts messages on a local machine so that MUA can access them.

Example:

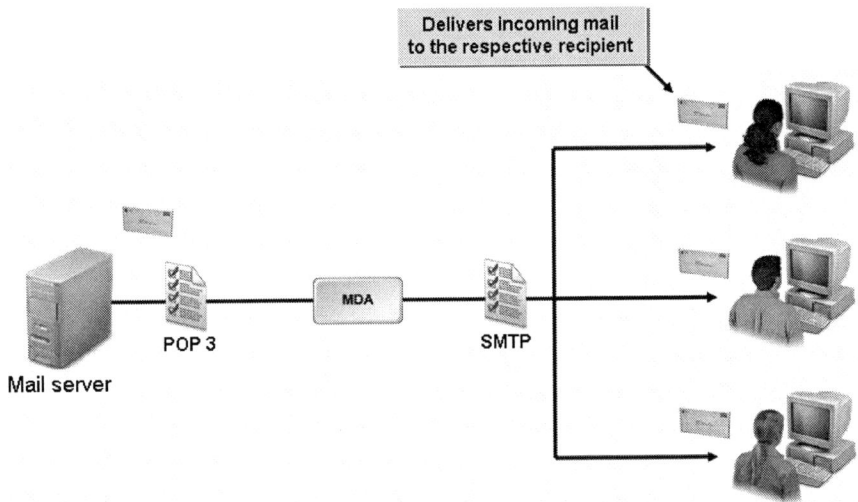

Figure 13-26: Email messages are delivered to clients using MDA.

Mail Forwarding

Mail forwarding is a feature that allows email messages sent to one address to be automatically forwarded to another address. Mail forwarding can also redirect mail going to a certain address to one or several other addresses.

The Electronic Mailing Process

The electronic mailing process describes the sequence of steps involved in creating, transmitting, and storing messages from a sender to a recipient. There are five stages involved in the electronic mailing process.

1. The sender composes the message to be sent. The sender's MUA formats the message in an email format. It uses SMTP to send the message to the sender's MTA.

2. The sender's MTA checks for the destination address that is provided by SMTP. Based on the destination address, it sends a request to the DNS server to look for the specific domain name in the DNS server using the UDP protocol. The DNS server sends a response with an MX record that lists the mail exchange servers supported by the domain.

3. Based on the response from the DNS server, the sender's MTA sends the message to the recipient's MTA using SMTP.

4. The recipient's MTA again sends the message to the recipient's MDA, which delivers the email to a spool where all the recipient's messages are stored.

5. The recipient's MUA retrieves the message from the spool through a retrieval agent known as the *Mail Retrieval Agent (MRA)* using protocols such as POP3 and IMAP. The recipient then opens the received message.

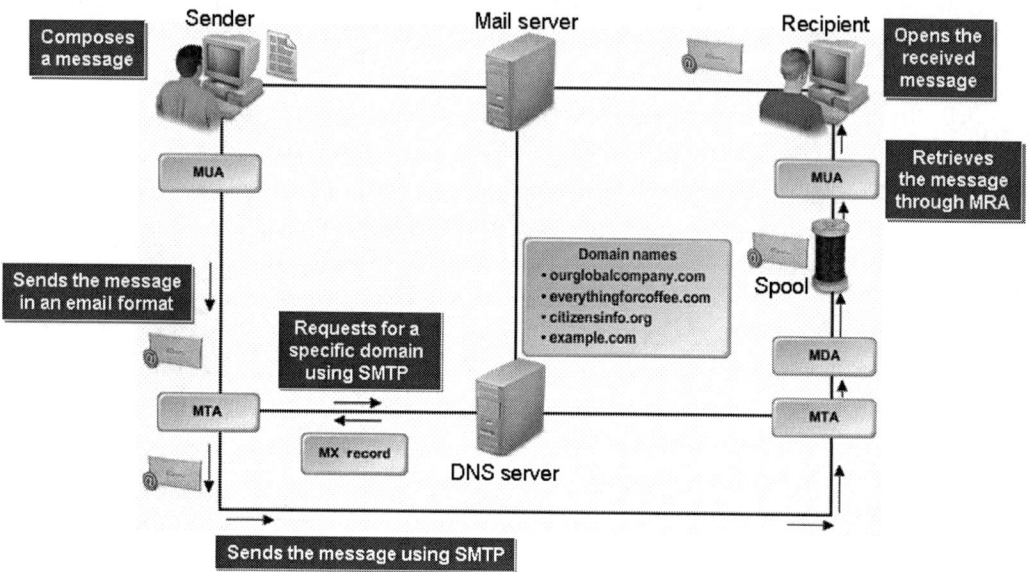

Figure 13-27: *The process of sending an email from one system to another.*

How to Configure Email Services

Procedure Reference: Install Postfix

To install Postfix:

1. Log in as root.
2. Mount the Red Hat Enterprise Linux installation media that contains Postfix.
3. Navigate to the /media/[name of the media]/Server directory.
4. At the command line, enter `rpm -ivh` `postfix-{version}.{release}.i386.rpm` to install Postfix.
5. Enter `rpm -qi postfix` to verify that Postfix has been installed.

Procedure Reference: Configure Postfix for Incoming Email Messages

To configure Postfix for incoming email messages:

1. Log in as root.
2. Set the Fully Qualified Domain Name.
    a. Enter `hostname {Fully Qualified Domain Name}`.
    b. Open the /etc/sysconfig/network file and ensure that the Fully Qualified Domain Name is updated.
3. Using the vi editor, open the /etc/postfix/main.cf file.
4. Set the system to receive mail messages from remote servers.
    a. Locate the "inet_interfaces = all" directive and uncomment the line.
    b. Locate the "inet_interfaces = localhost" directive and comment the line.

5. Locate the "mydestination" directive and uncomment the line to specify a list of domains that are controlled by the Postfix mail server.

    `mydestination = $myhostname, localhost.$mydomain, localhost, $mydomain, mail.$mydomain, www.$mydomain`

6. Save and close the file.

7. Enter `service postfix start` to start the postfix service.

8. Enter `netstat -plt | grep master` to verify that the Postfix server is listening to all interfaces.

9. Enter `chkconfig postfix on` to enable the postfix service during system startup.

Procedure Reference: Configure Postfix for Outgoing Email Messages

To configure Postfix for outgoing email messages:

1. Log in as root.

2. Navigate to the /etc/postfix directory.

3. Using the vi editor, open the main.cf file.

4. Masquerade the domain for outgoing email messages.

    a. Locate the "myorigin" directive and uncomment it.

    b. Type `masquerade_exceptions = root` to masquerade the root user.

5. Save and close the file.

6. Enter `service postfix restart` to restart the postfix service.

Procedure Reference: Configure Email Aliases Using Sendmail or Exim

To set an email alias using Sendmail or Exim:

1. Using the vi editor, open the /etc/aliases file.

2. Add email aliases. An alias can be a local user name or a file name, a command, an include file, or an external address.

    `user name:    alias1, [alias2, alias3...]`

    ● Add an alias for a user name that exists on the local system.

      `<user name>:<alias name for the user>`

    ● Add an alias for an external email address to which you want the message to be forwarded.

      `<user name>:<email address>`

    ● Add an alias for a list of users to whom you want the mail to be forwarded. The list of users is specified in a separate file.

      `<user name>    :include: <path to the file containing user names>/`
      `<file name>`

    ● Add a file name to which you want to append the messages received by a user.

      `<user name>:    <path to the file>/<file name>`

    ● Or, add an alias to enable Sendmail process commands that receive messages from the standard input.

      `<user name>:    <|command>`

3. Save and close the file.

4. Enter `newaliases` to update the aliases database file.

Procedure Reference: Configure Email Aliases Using Postfix

To configure email aliases using Postfix:

1. Using the vi editor, open the /etc/postfix/main.cf file.
2. Verify whether the `alias_maps` variable is defined with the location of the aliases file.

    ```
    alias_maps = hash:/etc/aliases
    ```

3. Save and close the file.
4. Using the vi editor, open the /etc/aliases file.
5. Add an alias for a user name that exists on the local system.

    ```
    user name:alias name for the user
    ```

6. Save and close the file.
7. Enter `newaliases` to update the aliases database file.
8. Enter

    ```
    service postfix restart
    ```

    to restart the postfix service.

Procedure Reference: Configure Local Aliases

To configure local aliases:

1. Log in as root.
2. Using the vi editor, open the /etc/postfix/main.cf file.
3. Locate the `alias_maps` directive and verify whether the directive is defined with the location of the aliases file.

    ```
    alias_maps = hash:/etc/postfix/aliases
    ```

4. Locate the `alias_database` directive and verify whether the directive is defined with the location of the aliases file.

    ```
    alias_database = hash:/etc/postfix/aliases
    ```

5. Save and close the file.
6. Using the vi editor, open the /etc/postfix/aliases file.
7. Add email aliases.

    ```
    user name:alias1, [alias2, alias3]
    ```

    *   Add an alias to a user name that exists on the local system.

        ```
        user name:alias name for the user
        ```

    *   Add an alias to an external email address to which the mail is to be forwarded.

        ```
        user name:email address
        ```

    *   Add an alias to a file that contains the list of users to whom the mail messages are to be forwarded.

        ```
        user name:include:path to the file containing user names|File names
        ```

    *   Add an alias to the Sendmail command that receives messages from the standard input.

        ```
        user name:|command
        ```

8. Save and close the file.
9. Enter `postalias /etc/postfix/alias` to update the alias database file.

10. Enter `service postfix restart` to restart the postfix service.

Procedure Reference: Configure Virtual Aliases

To configure virtual aliases:

1. Log in as root.
2. Configure the prerequisite settings for virtual alias.

   a. Using the vi editor, open the /etc/postfix/main.cf file.

   b. Locate the `mydestination` directive and define the domains that will be controlled by the mail server.

   ```
   mydestination = $myhostname, localhost.$mydomain, localhost,
   $mydomain, mail.$mydomain, www.$mydomain, /etc/postfix/mydestination
   ```

   c. Save and close the file.

   d. Using the vi editor, open the /etc/postfix/mydestination file.

   e. Type `List of domains` to specify the list of domains that are controlled by the Postfix. A sample mydestination file will be as given below.

   ```
   ourglobalcompany.com
   ourglobalcompany.org
   ourglobalcompany.net
   ```

   f. Save and close the file.

3. Using the vi editor, open the /etc/postfix/main.cf file.
4. Define the `virtual_alias_maps` variable below the `alias_maps` variable.

   ```
   virtual_alias_maps = hash:/etc/postfix/virtual_maps
   ```

5. Save and close the file.
6. Using the vi editor, open the /etc/postfix/virtual_maps file.
7. Map email addresses to user names.

   ```
   {user name@Domain name} user name
   ```

8. Map email messages destined to a domain to a specific user in another domain.

   ```
   @Domain name {user name@Domain name}
   ```

9. Map email messages destined to a domain to another domain.

   ```
   user name@Domain name1 {user name@Domain name2}
   ```

10. Save and close the file.
11. Enter `postmap virtual_maps < virtual_maps` to rehash the virtual alias file.
12. Enter `service postfix restart` to restart the postfix service.

Procedure Reference: Configure Outbound Address Rewriting

To configure outbound address rewriting:

1. Log in as root.
2. Navigate to the /etc/postfix directory.
3. Using the vi editor, open the main.cf file.
4. Below the definition of the `alias_maps` directive, type `smtp_generic_maps = hash:/etc/postfix/generic_map` to enable outbound address rewriting.
5. Save and close the file.

6. Using the vi editor, create a file, generic_map.

7. Type *{User name@DomainName1}* *{User name@DomainName1}*

8. Save and close the file.

9. Enter `postmap generic_map < generic_map` to rehash the file.

10. Enter `service postfix restart` to restart the postfix service.

Procedure Reference: Configure Postfix Restrictions

To configure postfix restrictions:

1. Log in as root.

2. Using the vi editor, open the /etc/postfix/main.cf file.

3. At the end of the file, enter `smtpd_sender_restrictions = check_sender_access hash:/etc/postfix/sender_access,` [comma separated list of zero or more mail sender restrictions] to define restrictions for the sender.

4. Enter `smtpd_client_restrictions = check_sender_access hash:/etc/postfix/client_access,` [comma separated list of zero or more mail client restrictions] to define restrictions for the client.

5. Enter `smtpd_recipient_restrictions = check_sender_access hash:/etc/postfix/recipient_access,` [comma separated list of zero or more mail client restrictions] to define restrictions for the recipient.

6. Save and close the file.

7. Navigate to the /etc/postfix directory.

8. Open the sender, recipient, or client access file.

9. Define the restrictions.

   - Type *DomainName* `RELAY` to allow relaying.

   - Type *DomainName* `OK` to accept mail messages from the domain specified.

   - Type *DomainName* `REJECT` to reject the mail messages sent from the domain specified.

   - Type *DomainName* `ERROR:` *{### message}* to reject the mail from the sender and display an arbitrary message.

   - Type *DomainName* `DISCARD` to discard messages after accepting them.

10. Save and close the file.

11. Enter `postmap` *sender or recipient or client access file* `< postmap` *sender or recipient or client access file* to build the respective access database.

12. Enter `service postfix restart` to restart the postfix service.

ACTIVITY 13-4
Configuring Postfix

Before You Begin:

1. On srvA, switch to the GUI. Choose **System→Administration→Network.** In the **Network Configuration** dialog box, select the **DNS** tab.

2. In the **Hostname** text box, type *srvA.ourglobalcompany.com* and press the **Tab** key. Enter *192.168.0.2* as the primary DNS and the DNS search path.

3. Select the **Hosts** tab. In the **Address** text box, type *192.168.0.2* as the IP address. In the **Hostname** text box, enter *srvA.ourglobalcompany.com* as the host name. In the **Aliases** text box, enter *srvA ourglobalcompany.com* as the aliases.

4. In the **Add / Edit Hosts entry** dialog box, click **OK.** Save the configuration and click **OK** to restart the network service.

5. On srvA, switch to the CLI. You have logged in as root in the CLI. The first terminal is displayed. At the command line, enter `service sendmail stop` to stop the sendmail service. Enter `chkconfig sendmail off` to stop enabling the sendmail service during system startup. Clear the terminal screen.

6. On srvB, switch to the GUI. Choose **System→Administration→Network.** In the **Network Configuration** dialog box, select the **DNS** tab. In the **Hostname** text box, type *srvB.ourglobalcompany.com* and press the **Tab** key. Enter *192.168.0.2* as the primary DNS and the DNS search path.

7. Select the **Hosts** tab. In the **Address** text box, type *192.168.0.3* as the IP address. In the **Hostname** text box, enter *srvB.ourglobalcompany.com* as the host name. In the **Aliases** text box, enter *srvB* as the aliases.

8. In the **Add / Edit Hosts entry** dialog box, click **OK.** Save the configuration and click **OK** to restart the network service. Switch to the CLI of srvA.

Scenario:

Your company has already implemented a mail server using Sendmail for the domain ourglobalcompany.com. Now, due to the organizational growth, the number of users accessing the mail server has increased, thus decreasing the performance of the server. As the system administrator, you decide to migrate the mail server from Sendmail to Postfix.

 In steps 2 and 7, change the IP address as *192.168.0.X* to match your DNS server address.

What You Do	How You Do It
1. Install Postfix.	a. On the system labeled srvA, install the **`postfix-2.3.3-2.1.el5_2.i386.rpm`** package.
	b. Enter `alternatives --set mta` `/usr/sbin/sendmail.postfix` to set Postfix as default MTA.
2. Configure incoming mail on the server labeled srvA.	a. Navigate to the /etc/postfix folder.
	b. Using the `vi` editor, open the main.cf file.
	c. Locate the line "inet_interfaces = all" and uncomment it.
	d. Locate the line "inet_interfaces = localhost" and comment it.
	e. Press **Esc** to switch to the command mode.
	f. Locate the "#mydestination = $myhostname" code.

	g. Uncomment the lines
	`#mydestination = $myhostname,`
	`localhost.$mydomain, localhost,`
	`$mydomain,` and `#mail.$mydomain,`
	`www.$mydomain, ftp.$mydomain`.

3. Configure email aliases on the server labeled srvA.

a. Locate the "alias_maps = hash:/etc/aliases" directive.

b. The cursor is placed after `alias_maps = hash:`. To change the alias file location to /postfix/aliases, move the cursor to end of /etc/. Enter **postfix/**

c. Press **Esc** to switch to the command mode.

d. Locate the "alias_database = hash:/etc/aliases" directive.

e. The cursor is placed after `alias_database = hash:`. To change the alias file location to /postfix/aliases, move the cursor to the end of /etc/. Enter **postfix/**

f. Press **Esc** to switch to the command mode.

g. Save and close the file.

h. Using the `vi` editor, open the aliases file.

i. Enter **hr: chris, pat,**

j. Type **root: jsmith**

k. Press **Esc** to switch to the command mode.

l. Save and close the file.

m. Enter **postalias /etc/postfix/aliases** to update the aliases database file.

n. Start the postfix service.

o. Set the postfix service to run on booting the system.

4. Check the mail configuration.

a. Switch from the system labeled srvA to the system labeled srvB. Switch to the CLI.

b. On the system labeled **srvB,** enter `mail hr@ourglobalcompany.com`

c. At the **Subject** prompt, enter `Test mail - Postfix`

d. Enter `This is a test mail for postfix.`

e. Type the period (.) and press **Enter.**

f. At the **cc** prompt, press **Enter.**

g. Switch from the system labeled srvB to the system labeled srvA.

h. On the system labeled srvA, enter `mail -u chris`

i. Observe that the mail with the subject "Test mail - Postfix" is displayed.

j. Quit the mailbox.

k. View the mail messages in pat's mailbox and quit the mailbox.

l. Enter `clear` to clear the terminal screen.

5. Configure the email restriction on the server labeled srvA.

a. Using the `vi` editor, open the main.cf file.

b. At the end of the file, enter

`smtpd_sender_restrictions = check_sender_access hash:/etc/postfix/sender_access` to define sender restrictions.

c. At the end of the file, enter

`smtpd_recipient_restrictions = check_recipient_access hash:⇒ /etc/postfix/recipient_access,⇒ reject_unauth_destination` to define recipient restrictions.

d. Press **Esc** to switch to the command mode.

e. Save and close the file.

f. Using the `vi` editor, open the sender_access file.

g. Enter **junk@junkmail.com ERROR: 550 MAIL DISCARDED** to discard the messages after accepting them.

h. Press **Esc** to switch to the command mode.

i. Save and close the file.

j. Enter **postmap sender_access < sender_access** to build the access database with respect to the sender.

k. Using the `vi` editor, open the recipient_access file.

l. To reject eric's mail, enter **eric@ourglobalcompany.com REJECT**

m. Press **Esc** to switch to the command mode.

n. Save and close the file.

o. Enter **postmap recipient_access < recipient_access** to build the access database with respect to the recipient.

p. Restart the postfix service.

q. Clear the screen.

6. Check whether the mail message from junkmail.com is rejected.

    a. Switch from the system labeled srvA to the system labeled srvB.

    b. On the system labeled srvB, enter **telnet ourglobalcompany.com 25**

    c. Enter **HELO ourglobalcompany.com**

    d. Enter **MAIL FROM: junk@junkmail.com**

    e. Enter **RCPT TO: chris@ourglobalcompany.com**

    f. Observe that the error message, "451 4.3.5 Server configuration error", is displayed indicating that the junk mail filter is working.

    g. Quit the Telnet connection.

7. Check whether the recipient eric is denied access to receive mail messages.

    a. On the system labeled **srvB,** enter **telnet ourglobalcompany.com 25**

    b. Enter **HELO ourglobalcompany.com**

    c. Enter **MAIL FROM: chris@ourglobalcompany.com**

    d. Enter **RCPT TO: eric@ourglobalcompany.com**

    e. Observe that the error message, "Recipient address rejected: Access denied," is displayed.

    f. Quit the Telnet connection.

    g. Clear the terminal screen.

TOPIC E
Control Internet Services

You configured email services. There are numerous services and benefits that the Internet offers. This has made the Internet a basic necessity in almost all organizations. In this topic, you will control Internet services.

Internet services are crucial for the effective functioning of businesses. Any disruption or problems in Internet services could paralyze regular work and cost organizations dearly. As a Linux+ system administrator, it is your primary responsibility to ensure that Internet services are running without any problems all the time.

The xinetd Daemon

The *xinetd* daemon controls the system services on a network and is based on the client-server architecture. Various services are listed in the configuration files of `xinetd`. When the daemon receives a request from a port for a particular service, it checks with the configuration files and then starts the appropriate server containing the service. This enables faster service management over the network because requests are handled immediately. Services that are managed by `xinetd` include file sharing services, Telnet, rsync, and time services. The settings for these services can be controlled using the /etc/xinetd.conf file or by using the service-specific files found in the /etc/xinetd.d directory.

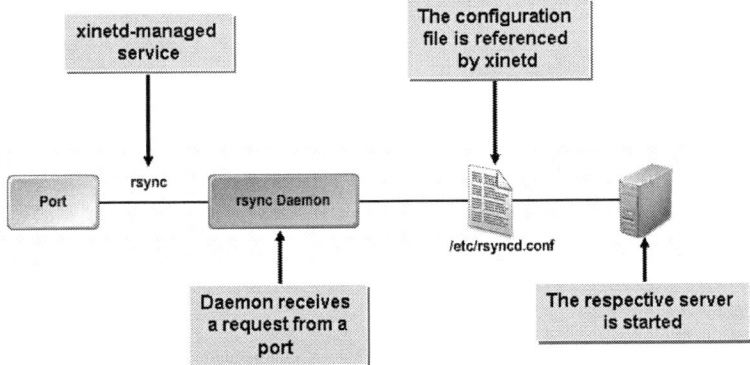

Figure 13-28: The xinetd daemon controls services on clients and servers.

Telnet

Definition:

Telnet is a terminal emulation protocol that enables a user on a site to simulate a session on a remote host. In other words, it allows a user to log in to another computer over the network. It does this by translating keystrokes from the user's terminal to instructions recognized by the remote host, and then carrying the output back to the user's terminal and displaying it in a format native to the remote host. This service is transparent; it gives users the impression that their terminals are directly attached to the remote host. The remote computer needs to have a Telnet server, and the user's computer needs to have a Telnet client. The remote computer accepts input directly from the user's computer. The output is directed to the screen of the user's computer.

Example:

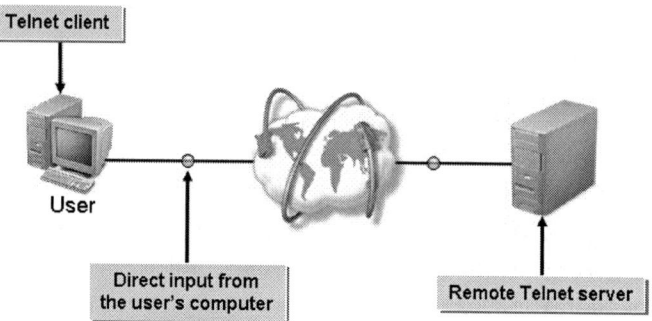

Figure 13-29: A Telnet client communicating with a remote Telnet server.

Disadvantages of Telnet

Telnet is not a very secure protocol because it transmits passwords as plain text. Telnet has largely been replaced by SSH because it offers better security.

The /etc/xinetd.conf File

The /etc/xinetd.conf file is the configuration file for the xinetd daemon. It contains a list of services that are managed by the xinetd daemon. It is referenced by the daemon each time a request is sent for a service to be started or stopped. The file is divided into parts, with one part for each service containing the service settings. Services can be single threaded or multithreaded.

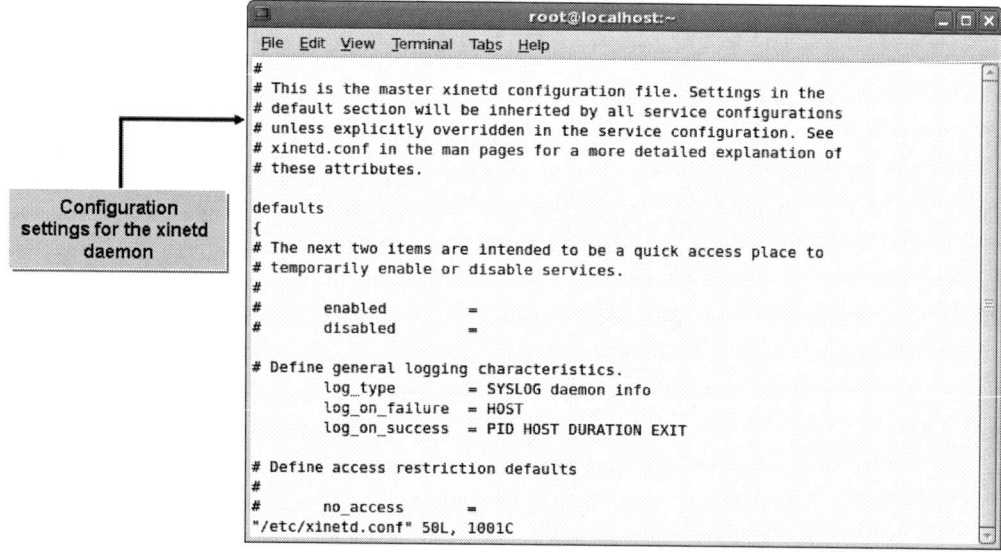

Figure 13-30: The xinetd.conf file with its various configuration settings.

The /etc/xinetd.conf file can be highly configured according to user requirements using a number of options. Some of the frequently used options are listed in the table.

Option	Enables You To
`service`	Specify the service name.
`wait`	Specify whether the service is single threaded or multithreaded.
`user`	Specify the UID for the process running on the server.
`server`	Specify the executable that is to be launched on the server when the service is invoked.
`disable`	Specify whether a service is enabled or disabled.

Syntax

The syntax for specifying services in the xinetd configuration files is *{Attribute} {Assignment Operator} {Value}*.

The libwrap.so Libraries

The libwrap.so files are libraries that are linked to services controlled by the `xinetd` daemon. There are three main library files: libwrap.so, libwrap.so.0, and libwrap.so.0.7.6. These files are found in the /usr/lib directory and they control the TCP services and additional network access settings, including the settings found in the network access configuration files.

The /etc/xinetd.d Directory

The /etc/xinetd.d directory contains configuration scripts for services managed by `xinetd`. Some of the services listed in this directory are ftp, kerberos, and rsync. Each service can be individually configured using its respective configuration file found in this directory. The options in the service configuration files are similar to those found in the /etc/xinetd.conf file.

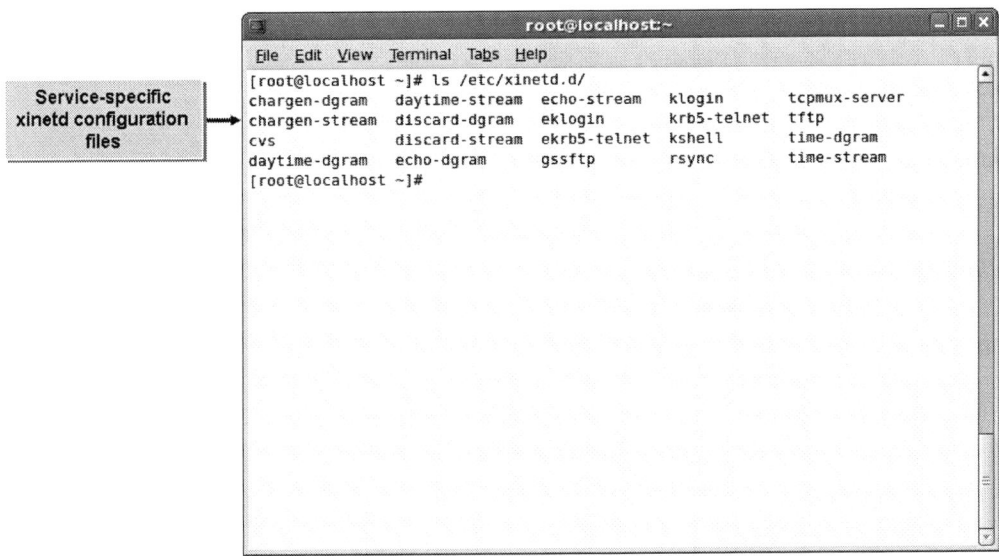

Figure 13-31: The xinetd.d directory contains configuration files for xinetd-managed services.

xinetd Access Controls

The `xinetd` daemon has a set of functions that are used to control access to services managed by it. These access controls are of two types: host based and time based. Together, these functions restrict the host access on a network.

Access Control Type	Description
Host-based	Host-based access controls are implemented by restricting hosts in the `xinetd` service configuration file through the `no_access` and `only_from` options. Host Pattern Access Controls are used to specify host patterns when host-based access controls are implemented. Hosts may be specified in the form of their IP addresses, netmask ranges, network names, or hostnames.
Time-based	Time-based access controls are implemented by adding the `access_times` option to the service configuration file.

Service and Application Access Controls

Service access controls and *application access controls* are essentially daemons that are used to restrict access to certain important services and applications, such as those that control network connections and security policies. Some examples of these daemons are `squid` and `httpd`. These daemons restrict access by referring to the hostnames or IP addresses of systems trying to access a service, with the list provided in the libwrap.so file or the `xinetd` configuration files. If the systems have the required permission, the daemons will permit them to access the protected services and applications.

How to Control Internet Services

Procedure Reference: Configure Services Managed by xinetd

To configure services managed by `xinetd`:

1. Log in as root.
2. Enter `ls -l /etc/xinetd.d/` to list the services managed by the xinetd daemon.
3. Manage the xinetd daemon at system startup.
   - Enter `chkconfig --list xinetd` to make sure that the `xinetd` daemon is configured to start in the desired runlevel.
   - Enter `chkconfig --level {levels} xinetd {on|off}` to update the runlevel configuration of the xinetd daemon.
   - Enter `service xinetd {start|stop|status|restart|reload}` to manage the status of the xinetd daemon.
4. Manage services controlled by the xinetd daemon.
   - Enter `chkconfig {Service Name} {on|off}` to enable or disable the specified service at system startup.
   - Or, manage the service using configuration files found in the /etc/xinetd.d directory.

a. Enter `vi /etc/xinetd.d/{Service Configuration File}` to edit the service-specific configuration file.

b. Edit the "disable = {yes|no}" line, to disable or enable the service.

c. Edit `<Attribute> <Assignment Operator> <Value> <Value>` to define the service-specific settings that override the global settings for all services managed by the `xinetd` daemon.

d. Save and close the file.

e. Enter `service xinetd reload` to reload the xinetd daemon with the applied changes.

Procedure Reference: Define the Global Settings in the /etc/xinetd.conf File

To define the global service settings in the /etc/xinetd.conf file:

1. Log in as root.
2. Enter `vi /etc/xinetd.conf` to edit the xinetd daemon configuration file.
3. Edit `{Attribute} {Assignment Operator} {Value} {Value}` to define the global settings for all services managed by xinetd daemon.
4. Save and close the file.
5. Enter `service xinetd restart` to apply the changes.

Procedure Reference: Configure Access Control for xinetd Managed Services

To configure access control for xinetd managed services:

1. Log in as root.
2. Define service-specific access control in the /etc/xinetd.conf file.

a. Enter `vi /etc/xinetd.d/{Service Configuration File}` to edit the service-specific configuration file.

b. Type `only_from = {List of IP Addresses}` to define the remote hosts for which the particular service is available.

c. Type `no_access = {List of IP Addresses}` to define the remote hosts for which the particular service is unavailable.

d. Type `access_times = hour:min-hour:min` to define the time intervals when the service can be accessed.

3. Save and close the file.
4. Enter `service xinetd restart` to apply the changes and restart the xinetd daemon.

ACTIVITY 13-5
Enabling Service Access Controls

Before You Begin:
1. On srvA, you have logged in as root in the CLI.
2. Switch to the first terminal of the CLI.
3. Enter `cd /root` to navigate to the root directory.
4. Enter `clear` to clear the terminal screen.

Scenario:
You are working as a system administrator at OGC Systems. Your organization has several branches, and you want to enable employees working in different branches to communicate with each other. You want to use the telnet protocol to ensure secure transfer of files and add tunneling capability. In addition, you have to configure the service to start automatically during system startup. Finally, you also have to ensure that the service is inaccessible from the system with IP address 192.168.0.205 because it will be accessed by unauthorized users.

What You Do	How You Do It
1. Install the Telnet service on the system.	a. Enter **yum localinstall /rhelsource/Server/telnet*** to install the Telnet service.
	b. Observe that the **Transaction summary** displays that one package is to be installed. Also, observe that the total download size is **35k.**
	c. Enter **y** to download and install the package.
	d. Observe that the message "Complete" is displayed indicating that the Telnet service is installed.

2.	Enable the Telnet server.	a.	Enter `vi /etc/xinetd.d/telnet` to open the telnet configuration file.
		b.	Observe that the default configuration entries are displayed. Also, observe that the service is disabled as indicated by **disable=yes.**
		c.	Enter */dis* to navigate to the "disable = yes" line.
		d.	Switch to the insert mode.
		e.	Change **disable = yes** to **disable = no**

3.	Enable access control for the Telnet service.	a.	On a new line, press the **Tab** key.
		b.	Enter *only_from* and press the **Tab** key. Enter *= 192.168.0.0/24* to allow the service to be accessed only from 192.168.0.0.
		c.	Press the **Tab** key and enter *no_access*. Press the **Tab** key and enter *= 192.168.0.205* to deny access to the service for all users from 192.168.0.205.
		d.	Switch to the command mode.
		e.	Save and close the file.

4.	Configure xinetd to start at system boot.	a.	Enter `service xinetd start` to start the xinetd service.
		b.	Enter `chkconfig xinetd on` to enable the xinetd service to start at system startup.
		c.	Clear the terminal screen.

Lesson 13 Follow-up

In this lesson, you configured an Apache web server, implemented access control for the Apache and a proxy server, configured email services, and controlled Internet services. Now, you will be able to implement a cost-effective solution for communication, sharing, and transfer of resources across a network.

1. **How will you secure your Apache server?**

2. **What are the benefits of implementing a proxy server on a network?**

14 Securing Linux

Lesson Time: 1 hour(s), 30 minutes

Lesson Objectives:

In this lesson, you will implement measures to secure Linux.

You will:

● Implement encryption services.

● Secure user accounts.

● Configure iptables.

● Implement auditing for security purposes.

● Detect intrusion.

Introduction

In the previous lesson, you configured basic Internet services. Poor security can lead to damage or loss from disgruntled employees, hackers, or competitors. In this lesson, you will secure a Linux system connected to a network.

To properly secure a Linux system, an administrator has to understand how different threats affect the system. Specific security measures that allow the administrator to control the transfer of sensitive data and restrict unauthorized users from accessing the network need to be implemented.

This lesson covers all or part of the following CompTIA Linux+ (2009) certification objectives:

● Topic A

■ Objective 3.2

■ Objective 5.6

● Topic B

■ Objective 2.3

■ Objective 5.4

● Topic C

■ Objective 4.3

● Topic E

■ Objective 5.5

TOPIC A
Examine the Basics of System Security

You worked with the Internet and email services. These services are prone to treats from hackers, which can cause serious problems. A security breach in an organization's network cannot be compromised because sabotage or data theft could affect business badly. These instances can be avoided by securing the systems and sending data in a secured format that can be comprehended only by the user to whom the data is directed. In this topic, you will examine the basics of system security.

Computer security is a critical part of business strategy, and organizations continually demand new levels of protection. On a network, there are various web and mail services that can be implemented. Though these facilitate data transfer, there is always the risk of data theft associated with these services. Without a proper security and encryption mechanism governing these services, transferring sensitive data securely is impossible.

Keys

A *key* is a block of information that authorizes users to access data. A key can be assigned beforehand to a user or can be randomly generated at runtime.

While logging in to a remote machine, the private and public keys are combined by the remote server for verification. The user can log in and transfer files only if the keys match. Authenticity is established by the remote server, which then grants the necessary permissions.

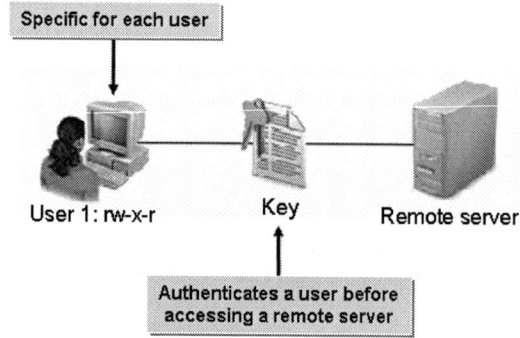

Figure 14-1: Securing data using a key.

Keys are of two types: public and private.

Key Type	Description
Public	A *public key* is the key that is transmitted to the destination server along with the request. This is compared with the private key of the destination. Only when these two are related, the user is authenticated.
Private	A *private key* is retained on the local system and is not transmitted to the destination server. Data is sent to the user along with the sender's public key. The user can access the data only when the private key of the user is authenticated by the public key of the sender.

Authentication

Authentication verifies that users are who they say they are. In data communication, authenticating a sender is necessary to verify that the data came from the right source. A receiver is authenticated as well, to verify that the data is going to the right destination.

There are several methods for ensuring authentication.

Method	Description
The known_hosts file	When you connect to a remote host, the host sends your public host and server keys for authentication. Your system looks up the known_hosts file to locate an entry for the host's keys, and if an entry is found, you will be granted access.
SSH server	An SSH server automatically generates public host and server keys for authentication purposes. Server keys are automatically regenerated every hour to ensure security.
Challenge Handshake Authentication Protocol (CHAP)	A security authentication protocol that encrypts the user name and password information using a key and transmits them over the network. CHAP is supported on lines using Point-to-Point Protocol (PPP) encapsulation.
Password Authentication Protocol (PAP)	A security authentication protocol for logging in to a network. With PAP, the unencrypted user name and password are transmitted over the network to the server. This information is checked against a table containing user name and password pairs of all the users on the network. PAP is supported only on PPP lines.
Kerberos	A network authentication service that is used by client/server applications. Kerberos creates a key, or ticket, for each user logging in to the network. The tickets are embedded along with the message to identify the sender.

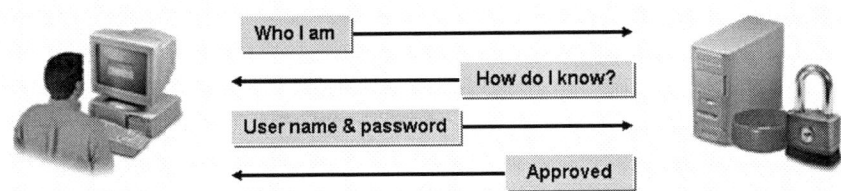

Figure 14-2: The authentication process.

Authentication Factors

The number of factors that are used to show the identity of a user through authentication determines how effective authentication can be. The three types are:

- One-factor authentication, which provides what you know, such as a password or PIN. It is based on recalling a piece of information from your memory or by writing the information down. This type of authentication is the least effective.

- Two-factor authentication, which combines what you have with what you know. For example, your ATM card combined with the PIN provides access to your bank account.

- Three-factor authentication, which also provides proof of the user's identity through biometrics. It uses physiological identification characteristics such as fingerprints, voice recognition, or signature recognition. This is the best type of authentication.

Biometric Authentication

To increase the level of reliability of systems and ease of use to users (beyond password authentication), biometric authentication can be introduced. When this type of system is added to an authentication scheme, it is considered to be a strong authentication. The designation of strong is given because a user is not only identified digitally, but by his or her physiological characteristics, through fingerprint scanning, iris scanning, or hand geometry.

The sshd_config File

The sshd_config file contains options to enable encrypted communication among hosts on an insecure network. SSH is implemented using the sshd daemon.

Encryption

Encryption is a method of controlling user access to information by configuring data to appear as codes that cannot be interpreted by unauthorized users. To authorized users, though, this data appears in its original form. Passwords can also be used to protect data along with encryption. There are various protocols, such as SSH, SSL, and SECURENET, that can be used to implement encryption on a network.

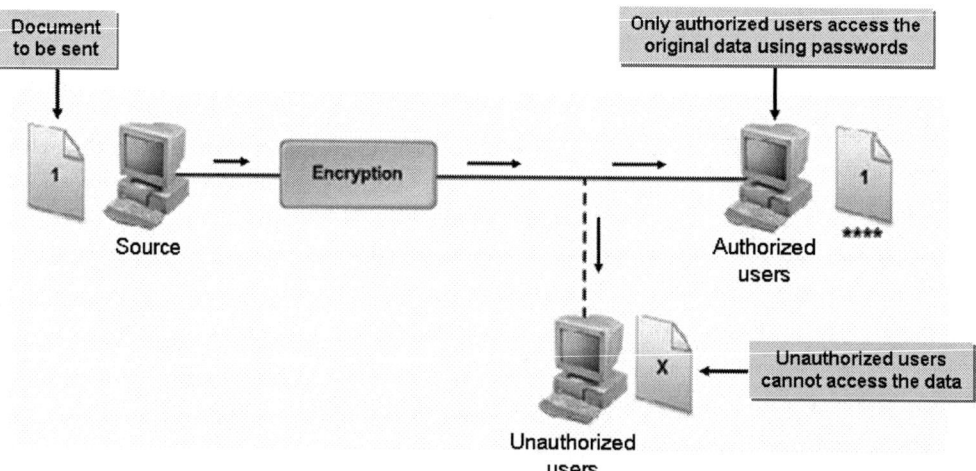

Figure 14-3: Securing data using encryption.

Encryption Solutions

Authorized users of encrypted computer data must have the key that was used to encrypt the data in order to decrypt it. There are different solutions for encrypting data using specific *algorithms*. Some of the algorithms are described in the following table.

Solution	Description
Blowfish	Blowfish is a symmetric block cipher that provides strong encryption and uses key sizes up to 56 bytes (a 448-bit key). Its features include: • Strong key support, handling, and cryptography. • Security to wipe files and clear empty disk space.
3DES	3DES (pronounced "triple dez") is a block cipher algorithm that can encrypt and decrypt data using a single secret key. 3DES uses three stages of *DES (Data Encryption Standard),* making it a very secure option. Anything encrypted by DES encryption has 72,000,000,000,000,000 (or 72 quadrillion) possible keys.
MD5	*Message-Digest algorithm 5 (MD5)* is a command-line utility that generates and verifies *message digests* (digital signatures) using the MD5 algorithm. The MD5 algorithm is intended for digital signature applications, where a large file must be compressed in a secure manner before being encrypted with a private (secret) key under a public-key cryptosystem. MD5 is also used to check the integrity of files.

Random Number Generation

Random number generation is an encryption method in which the kernel is used to generate random numbers that are assigned to files before transfer. Only when the numbers are matched by the recipient is the transfer completed. The algorithm that governs random number generation is the *Pseudo Random Number Generation (PRNG)* algorithm. In Red Hat Linux, the kernel files, /dev/random and /dev/urandom, act as the random number generators. Using the concept of permutations and combinations, these kernels are able to generate numbers with millions of digits from a single source number.

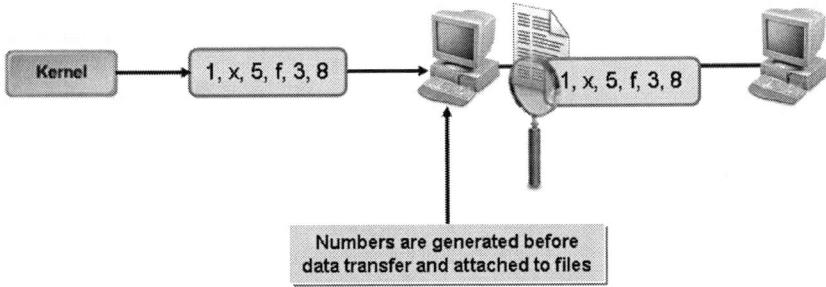

Figure 14-4: Securing data using the random number generation method.

Cryptographic Hashes

Cryptographic hashes are used in an encryption method in which arbitrary data is encapsulated within a fingerprint, which is attached to a file. A fingerprint is a fixed string called the hash value, checksum, or message digest. The data in the file can be checked for authenticity by verifying the hash value. When any modifications are made to a file, its hash value also changes. There are various algorithms, such as md2, md5, sha, and sha1, that implement cryptographic hash functions.

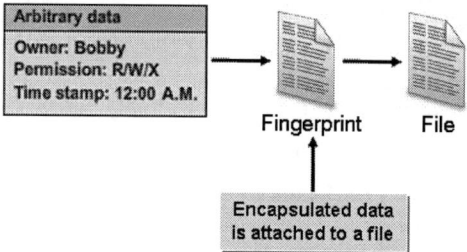

Figure 14-5: Securing data using the cryptographic hashing method.

Various utilities are used to check the hash values of files.

Utility	Enables You To
sha1sum	Check files for improper sha1 checksums. The syntax of this utility is sha1sum --check {file name}.
md5sum	Check files for improper md5 checksums. The syntax of this utility is md5sum --check {file name}.

Symmetric Encryption

Symmetric encryption is carried out using only a single key, which is used for both encryption and decryption. There are various utilities that perform symmetric encryption.

Utility	Function
passwd	Used to change the login password. Users who are currently logged in can change only their login password, and not that of other users. However, this does not apply to the root user. When you type the passwd command at the command prompt, you are asked to enter your current password and then the new password you want to set. The new password is effective the next time you log in to the system.
gpg	Used to encrypt messages using the GNU Privacy Guard (GnuPG) encryption system. The utility has various commands and options. The syntax of this utility is gpg [options] {command} {arguments}.

Utility	Function
`openssl`	Used to encrypt and decrypt messages using the SSL protocol through creation of keys, certificates, and signatures. The syntax of this utility is `openssl {command} [options] {arguments}`.
`make`	Used to generate digital certificates and key pairs. This command must be run from the /etc/pki/tls/certs/ directory. The syntax of the `make` utility is `make {key file|digital certificate}`.

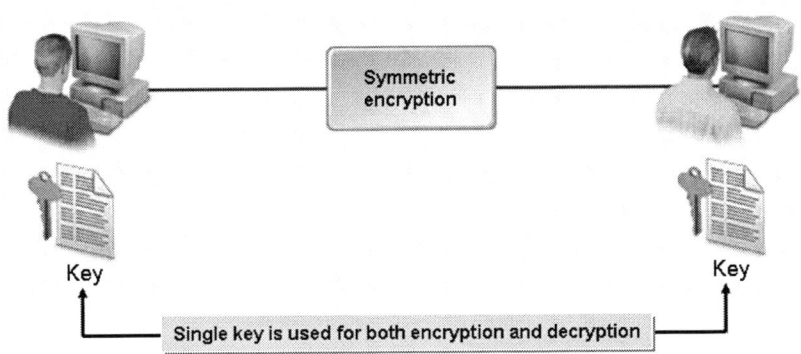

Figure 14-6: Key generation in symmetric encryption.

Asymmetric Encryption

Asymmetric encryption is carried out using two keys in the form of key pairs. While one key is used for encryption, another key is used for decryption.

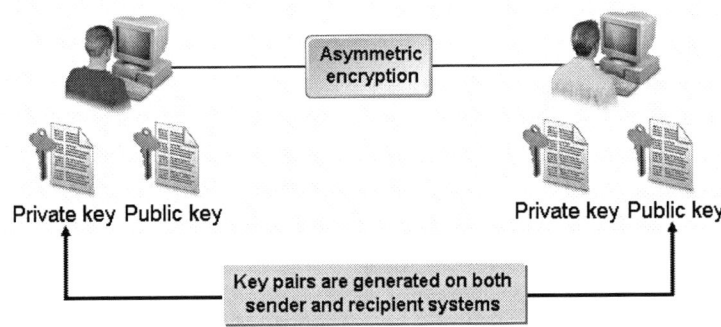

Figure 14-7: Key generation in asymmetric encryption.

There are two main protocols involved in asymmetric encryption: protocol 1 and protocol 2. Only one protocol can be implemented at a time.

Protocol	Description
Protocol 1	In protocol 1, only one key is exchanged between a sender and a recipient.
	1. The recipient first generates a key pair, which contains a public key and a private key.
	2. The request is then sent to the sender in an encrypted form along with the public key of the recipient. The private key is retained with the recipient.
	3. The sender receives the request, authenticates the public key sent by the recipient, and then returns the requested information in the encrypted form along with the public key of the recipient.
	4. The recipient receives the information along with its public key and decrypts it by authenticating the public key with its private key.
Protocol 2	In protocol 2, digital signatures are used along with key encryption. A digital signature is a unique ID created when a message digest of the sender is encrypted.
	1. The sender first generates a key pair, which contains a public key and a private key. Using the private key and the message digest, the sender generates a digital signature.
	2. The public key is transmitted to all systems on a network. The request is then sent by the recipient to the sender.
	3. The sender receives the request and returns the information in an encrypted form along with its digital signature.
	4. The recipient receives the information and decrypts it by authenticating the digital signature of the sender with its public key.

Rogue Public Keys

Rogue public keys are generated by unauthorized users to bypass public key cryptography. These are used to decrypt information that they are not supposed to access. Generation of rogue keys can be prevented by using public key fingerprints, forming trusted groups, and issuing digital certificates through trusted certificate authorities.

Digital Certificate Types

A digital certificate is a method of symmetric encryption. There are two main types of digital certificates.

Certificate Type	Description
Certificate Authority	*Certificate Authority certificates* are generated by a common and trusted Certificate Authority (CA) on receiving a certificate signature request (csr). The advantage of using this method is that generation of rogue digital certificates can be prevented.
Self-signed	*Self-signed certificates* are generated by the users themselves and contain the public key of the user as the signature. Therefore, any user can create a self-signed certificate. However, this certificate does not provide guarantee about the identity of the user or the organization.

 The X.509 format is a standard format for public key certificates.

Package Integrity

Each package in Linux is assigned a public key, which is installed along with the package. *Package integrity* is the method of checking packages for these public keys to ensure that the package is sourced from a trusted vendor. It is necessary to perform a package integrity test before installing a package because installing a package from an unreliable source may lead to improper installation and virus attacks. The yum command always installs packages along with their public keys from the Red Hat online repository.

The rpm command can be used to check file integrity.

Command	Enables You To
rpm --verify *package name*	Verify whether the package is installed or not.
gpg --import /etc/pki/rpm-gpg/RPM-GPG-KEY-redhat*	Import public keys to the rpm database.
rpm --checksig *package name*	Check whether the package has valid signatures.
rpm --addsig *package name*	Assign valid signatures to the package.

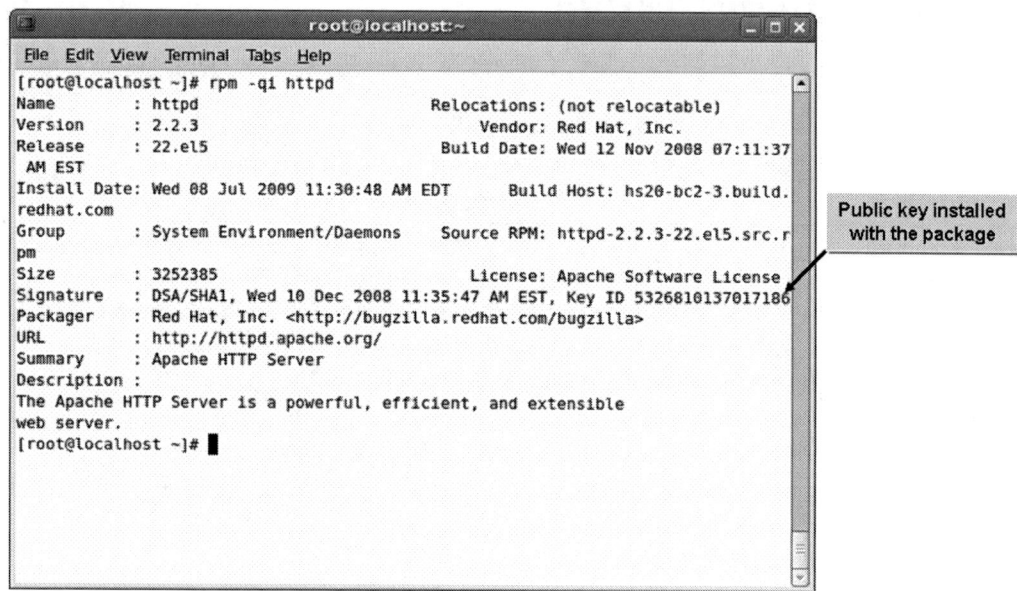

Figure 14-8: *Package information displaying the installed public key.*

RADIUS

Remote Authentication Dial In User Service (RADIUS) is a client/server protocol that facilitates centralized authentication, authorization, and accounting over a network. User information is stored in a central database, which is shared by all remote servers. When a user sends a request to access a service or resource, RADIUS enables remote access servers to communicate with a central server to verify the authenticity of the user. It usually utilizes the user's login and password stored in the /etc/passwd file on the server, to verify the user's credentials. It allows secure transmission of passwords by encrypting them with the MD5 algorithm. The RADIUS server is widely used by Internet Service Providers (ISPs).

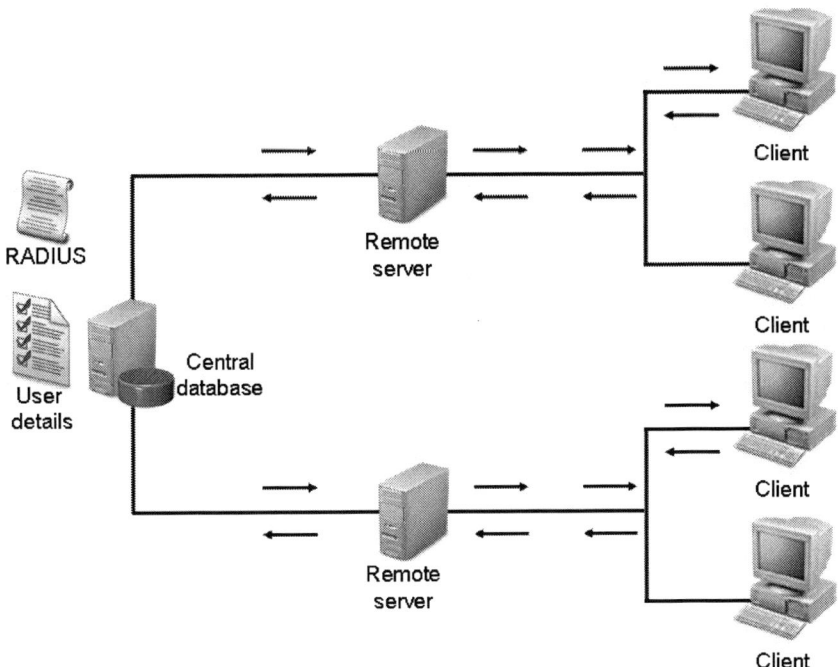

Figure 14-9: RADIUS protocol providing authentication services on a network.

The RADIUS Server as a Network Access Server

When a network contains several remote access servers, you can configure one of the servers as a RADIUS server and all other servers as RADIUS clients. The RADIUS clients will pass all authentication requests to the RADIUS server for verification. User configuration, remote access policies, and usage logging can be centralized on the RADIUS server. In this configuration, the remote access server is generically known as the Network Access Server (NAS).

How to Implement Encryption Services

Procedure Reference: Configure Encryption

To configure encryption:

1. Log in as root.
2. Enter vi /etc/{application}/{configuration file} to open the file.
3. Locate the line that contains the encryption details
4. If necessary, uncomment the line.
5. Modify the line to change the type of encryption.
6. Save the file and exit from the editor.
7. Restart the daemon service of the application or device for the changes to apply.

Procedure Reference: Implement Cryptographic Services

To implement cryptographic services:

1. Log in as root.

2. Implement cryptographic services.

- Enter `openssl rand` *Options Number of pseudo-random bytes* to generate a random number.

- Or, generate a message digest.

  ■ Enter `sha1sum` *[command options] {File Name}* to compute and check the SHA1 message digest.

  ■ Enter `md5sum` *[command options] {File Name}* to compute and check the MD5 message digest.

  ■ Enter `openssl dgst` *{Message digest options} {File Name}* to output the message digest of a supplied file.

- Implement symmetric encryption using the `gpg` command.

  ■ Enter `gpg --symmetric` *{File Name}* to encrypt a file with symmetric encryption.

  ■ Enter `gpg -d` *{File Name}* to decrypt an encrypted file using the `gpg` command.

- Implement encryption using the `openssl` command.

  a. Enter `openssl enc -e -salt -`*{bf|des3|cast5-cbc}* `-in` *{Absolute or relative path of file to be encrypted}* `-out` *{Absolute or relative path of encrypted file}* to encrypt the file and store the output in another file.

  b. Enter the symmetric encryption password when prompted.

  c. Enter `openssl enc -d -`*{bf|des3|cast5-cbc}* `-in` *{Absolute or relative path of encrypted file}* `-out` *{Absolute or relative path of decrypted file}* to decrypt the file and store the decrypted data in another file.

  d. Enter the encryption password when prompted.

Procedure Reference: Verify Package Integrity Using the rpm Command

To verify file integrity using the `rpm` command:

1. Log in as root.
2. Verify package integrity.

- Enter `rpm --verify` *{Package Name}* to report files that differ from the original rpm version.

- Enter `rpm --import /etc/pki/rpm-gpg/RPM-GPG-KEY-*` to import GPG keys to add them to packages.

- Enter `rpm --checksig` *{Package Name}* to verify whether the rpm package was packaged by Red Hat.

Procedure Reference: Generate Digital Certificates

To generate a digital certificate:

1. Log in as root.
2. Generate keys using the `openssl` command.

  A. Enter `openssl genrsa -out` *{Absolute or relative path of key file} {Key size}* to generate a public or private key pair.

  B. Enter `openssl req -new -key` *{Absolute or relative path of* *key file}* -out *{Absolute or relative path of certificate request file}* to generate a certificate signature request.

C. Enter required information such as the country name, state, city, organization name, organizational unit name, server name, email, and if necessary, a challenge password and the optional company name.

D. Enter openssl req -new -key *{Absolute or relative path of key file}* -out *{Absolute or relative path of certificate file}* -x509 to generate a self-signed certificate.

E. Enter required information such as the country name, state, city, organization name, organizational unit name, server name, email, and if necessary, a challenge password and the optional company name.

3. Generate digital certificates using the make command.

A. Enter make -C /etc/pki/tls/certs *{File Name}*.key to generate a public or private key pair.

B. Enter make -C /etc/pki/tls/certs *{File Name}*.csr to generate a certificate signature request.

C. Enter make -C /etc/pki/tls/certs *{File Name}*.crt to generate a certificate.

D. Enter make -C /etc/pki/tls/certs *{File Name}*.pem to generate a key and a certificate in one file.

ACTIVITY 14-1
Configuring Encryption

Before You Begin:
1. On srvA, you have logged in as root in the CLI.
2. The first terminal is displayed.

Scenario:
While analyzing log files, you detect failed attempts to access the SSH service. You decide to configure the Linux server so that it encrypts the information with Blowfish before transmitting data using SSH.

What You Do	How You Do It
1. Edit the /etc/ssh/ssh_config file.	a. Enter **vi /etc/ssh/ssh_config** to open the file.
	b. Locate the text "Cipher."
	c. Uncomment the line "# Cipher 3des."
	d. On the same line, delete "3des."
	e. Press **I** to switch to the insert mode.
	f. Press the **Spacebar** and type **blowfish**
	g. Press **Esc** and enter **:wq** to save and close the file.
2. Restart the sshd service.	a. Enter **service sshd restart**
	b. Enter **service sshd status** to check whether the service is started.
	c. Verify that the openssh-daemon is running.
	d. Enter **clear** to clear the terminal screen.

ACTIVITY 14-2

Implementing Encryption

Before You Begin:

1. On srvA, you have logged in as root in the CLI.

2. The first terminal is displayed.

Scenario:

OGC Systems hosted an English website and a German website for customers. To make the sites accessible and to meet the required security standards, you want to ensure that the websites are displayed as trusted sites.

What You Do	How You Do It
1. Generate a private key on the web host.	a. Enter `yum localinstall /rhelsource/Server/distcache-1*` to install the distcache packages.
	b. Enter `yum localinstall /rhelsource/Server/`⇒ `mod_ssl-2.2.3`⇒ `-22.el5.i386.rpm` to install the mod_ssl package.
	c. On the system labeled srvA, navigate to the /etc/pki/tls/certs directory.
	d. Enter `clear` to clear the terminal screen.
	e. Enter `make server.crt` to generate a key.
	f. At the **Enter pass phrase** prompt, enter *ourglobalcompany*
	g. Enter *ourglobalcompany* again to verify the pass phrase.
	h. At the **Enter pass phrase for server.key** prompt, enter *ourglobalcompany*
	i. At the **Country Name** prompt, enter *U.S.*
	j. At the **State or Province Name** prompt, enter *New York*
	k. At the **Locality Name** prompt, enter *ABC Avenue*
	l. At the **Organization Name** prompt, enter *OGC Systems*
	m. At the **Organizational Unit Name** prompt, enter *System Support*
	n. At the **Common Name** prompt, enter *srvA.ourglobalcompany.com*
	o. At the **Email Address** prompt, enter *root@srvA.ourglobalcompany.com*

2. Generate a digital certificate.

a. Enter `make certreq` to generate a certificate request.

b. At the **Enter pass phrase for /etc/pki/tls/ private/localhost.key:** prompt, enter *ourglobalcompany*

 This prompt may not appear at all times.

c. At the **Country Name** prompt, enter *U.S.*

d. At the **State or Province Name** prompt, enter *New York*

e. At the **Locality Name** prompt, enter *ABC Avenue*

f. At the **Organization Name** prompt, enter *OGC Systems*

g. At the **Organizational Unit Name** prompt, enter *System Support*

h. At the **Common Name** prompt, enter *srvA.ourglobalcompany.com*

i. At the **Email Address** prompt, enter *root@srvA.ourglobalcompany.com*

j. At the **A challenge password** prompt, enter *administrator*

k. At the **An optional company name** prompt, press **Enter.**

3.	Add the key and digital certificate to the web host.	a.	Enter `vi /etc/httpd/conf.d/ssl.conf` to open the SSL configuration file.
		b.	Locate the line "SSLCertificateFile /etc/pki/ tls/cert/localhost.crt."
		c.	Delete **localhost.crt**.
		d.	Switch to the insert mode.
		e.	Type ***server.crt*** to set the server.crt file as the default certificate file.
		f.	Press **Esc** to switch to the command mode.
		g.	Locate the line "SSLCeritificateKeyFile /etc/pki/tls/private/localhost.key."
		h.	Delete **private/localhost.key.**
		i.	Switch to the insert mode.
		j.	Type ***certs/server.key*** to set the certs/ server.key file as the key file.
		k.	Press **Esc** to switch to the command mode.
		l.	Save and close the file.
4.	Check whether the settings have been applied.	a.	Enter `clear` to clear the terminal screen.
		b.	Restart the web service.
		c.	At the **Enter pass phrase** prompt, enter ***ourglobalcompany*** indicating that the certificate and key has been applied.
		d.	Observe that the web service is restarted only when the correct pass phrase is entered.
		e.	Clear the terminal screen.

TOPIC B
Secure User Accounts

You are now familiar with encryption and basic system security. You need to provide users with a secure computing environment. In this topic, you will secure user accounts.

Given the reputation Linux has as a secure operating system, there may be an inherent tendency to take a casual approach to user security. However, as a Linux+ administrator, it is important to institute organizational policies that help establish best practices in your Linux user community. By doing so, you will limit the potential for disasters, especially as your company user base grows.

Environment Files

In Linux, there are several environment files that can be customized.

File	Description
/etc/hosts.allow	Allows access to certain services and hosts.
/etc/hosts.deny	Denies access to certain services and hosts.
/etc/limits	Limits users' resources when a system has shadow passwords installed.
/etc/login.defs	Sets user login features on systems with shadow passwords.
/etc/passwd	Displays the user name, real name, home directory, encrypted password, and other information of a user.
/etc/securetty	Identifies secure terminals from which the root user is allowed to log in to.
/var/log/secure	Tracks user logins. It is recommended to check this file periodically.

The /etc/login.defs File
The /etc/login.defs file is used with shadow passwords to set the initial path and other parameters, including how often a user must change passwords and what is acceptable as a password.

Login Levels

In Linux, you can provide root-level or user-level access to resources. By default, the root user has login privileges to all information on the system, but other users have limited login privileges.

Login Level	Description
Root login	The root user is considered a specific user account, with a UID of 0. It has privileges that no other user on the system has.
	Specifically, the root user can navigate anywhere on the system, change any file, and manipulate system controls, including user accounts, storage devices, and kernel parameters.
	The system administrator(s) will generally have his or her own user accounts with normal user privileges, and the root account. As a rule of thumb, you should do as much as possible under your own UID before working from the root user account.
User login	User accounts must be created with security in mind. The user name, or login ID, and the password are stored in two different files, /etc/passwd and /etc/shadow, and are set up with restricted access rights for added security.
	The user account file, /etc/passwd, is set up to be read-only by everybody except the root user.

Alias for the Root User

If you are using the Bash shell, you can create an alias for root as a precautionary measure. An alias, in this case, is an entry in the .bashrc file where you can define additional actions for specific default commands. For example, the rm command, which is used for removing or deleting files, can be given an alias that prompts you for additional information, based on the criteria you set.

The su Command

The *substitute or switch user command (su)* is used to change the ownership of a login session without logging out. It is generally used to switch ownership between an ordinary user and a root user, to change access permissions for administrative work.

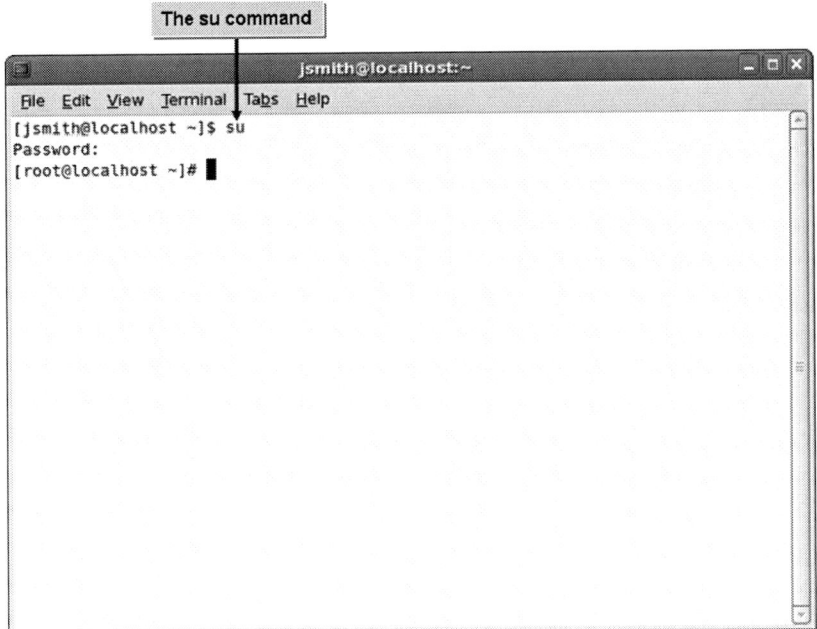

Figure 14-10: *Switching users using the su command.*

The Login Shell vs. the Non-Login Shell

A *login shell* is a shell that is created during a user login. On the other hand, a *non-login shell* is a shell that you can invoke from within a login shell. For example, running the su command from a login shell, invokes the non-login shell. However, the su – command can be used to run commands in the login shell. GNOME terminals and executed scripts are non-login shells. The logout command can be run only in login shells, whereas, the exit command that can be run in both the login and non-login shells.

The id Command

You can use the id command to view user identities. This allows you to identify the owner of the current login session.

The sudo Command

The *super user do (sudo) command* allows users to run programs with the security privileges of the root user. The sudo command accomplishes its task by allowing a user to run the specified command as the root user. The user must be configured to use the specified command (or all commands). It prompts you for your password and confirms your request to execute a command by checking a file, called sudoers. This file is configured by the system administrator. This allows system administrators to give certain users or groups access to some or all commands without users knowing the root password. It also creates a log of all commands and arguments used, to maintain a record.

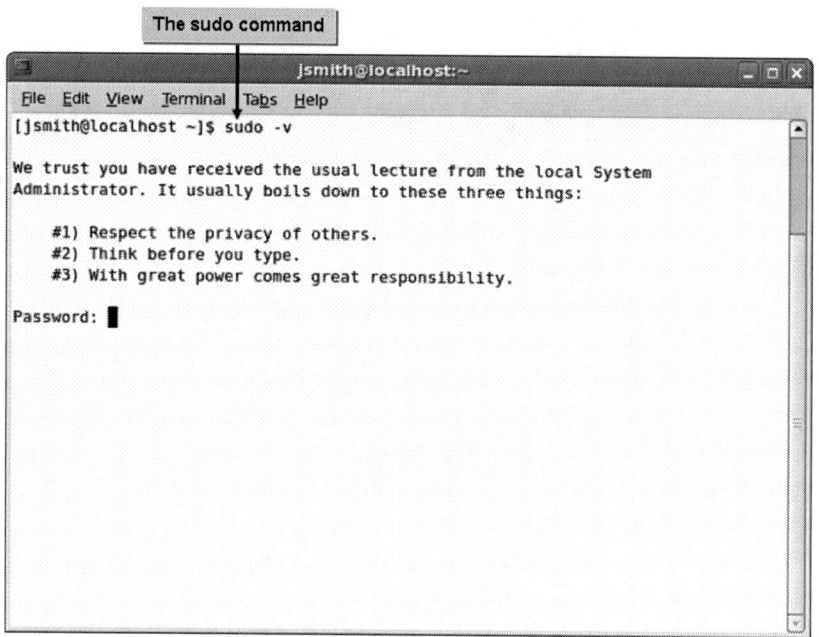

Figure 14-11: Using the sudo command to perform tasks with root privileges.

Syntax

The syntax of the sudo command is sudo `command-name command-options`. For example, sudo `shutdown -h now` will begin a system shutdown, if a user has permission to access the shutdown command via sudo.

After executing the sudo command, the user will be prompted for his or her password. This is an extra security measure to ensure that unauthorized users cannot access the sudo command from authorized users' login session without their knowledge.

Password Policies

A *password policy* is a set of guiding principles that help form effective passwords. A password policy divides users of a system into various categories with differing levels of access to resources.

Guidelines

A password policy may have the following rules:

- Passwords need to be at least seven characters long.
- Passwords must be made up of numbers, upper and lower case letters, and special characters such as punctuation.
- Passwords must not be a recognizable English word.
- Passwords must be changed every three months.
- Password policies encourage users to avoid writing down their passwords.
- Password policies may also be enforced by training.

Example: A Good Password Policy

Rudison Technologies Ltd. follows a strict password policy. Employees are instructed to choose passwords comprising a minimum of eight characters with a combination of numbers, upper and lower case letters, and special characters such as punctuation. Employees are prompted by the system to change their passwords every month. This has helped enhance the security of company data.

How to Secure User Accounts

Procedure Reference: Execute Commands as a Superuser

To execute commands as a superuser:

1. Log in as a user other than root.
2. Enter sudo *{command which needs root access}* to run the command as the superuser.
3. Enter the password of the superuser or the user.
4. Observe that the command has been executed.

Procedure Reference: Disable Root Access for Telnet and FTP Services

To disable root access for Telnet and FTP services:

1. Log in as root.
2. Disable root access for the Telnet service.
   a. Open the /etc/securetty file in any editor.
   b. Remove the entries tty0–tty9.
   c. Save the file.
   d. If necessary, restart the Telnet service.
3. Disable root access for the FTP service.
   a. Open the /etc/vsftpd/ftpusers file in any editor.
   b. Remove the root entry.
   c. Save the file.
   d. If necessary, restart the vsftp service.

ACTIVITY 14-3
Resetting a Password

Before You Begin:

1. On srvA, you have logged in as root in the CLI.
2. The first terminal is displayed.
3. Log out of the root user account.

Scenario:

You have administrative access to your Linux system. Your colleague, Eric, has forgotten the password to log in to his system.

What You Do	How You Do It
1. Switch to the root user account.	a. Log in as **jsmith.**
	b. Enter **su - root** to switch to the **root** user account.
	c. Enter *p@ssw0rd*
	d. Enter **whoami** to view your user name.
	e. Observe that you are logged in as the **root** user.
2. Change the password for the user, Eric.	a. Enter **passwd eric** to change the password of the user **Eric.**
	b. Enter *myp@$$w0rd1* to reset the password.
	c. Enter *myp@$$w0rd1* to confirm the password.
	d. Observe that the password is reset.
	e. Enter **exit** to exit the **root** user account.

3. Verify that the password is changed and log out of the system.

a. Enter **su eric** to switch to the **eric** user account.

b. At the password prompt, enter *myp@$$w0rd* to log in with the old password.

c. Observe that the login fails because the password is incorrect.

d. Enter **su eric** to switch to the **eric** user account.

e. At the password prompt, enter *myp@$$w0rd1* to log in with the new password.

f. Observe that the login is successful.

g. Enter **exit** to exit the current user account.

h. Observe that you have switched back to the **jsmith** user account.

i. Enter **logout** to log out of the **jsmith** user account.

ACTIVITY 14-4

Securing User Accounts

Before You Begin:

1. On srvA, the first terminal of the CLI is displayed.
2. Log in as root.
3. At the command line, change the password of eric to `myp@$$w0rd`.
4. Copy /etc/securetty to /etc/securetty.bak.
5. Copy /etc/vsftpd/ftpusers to /etc/vsftpd/ftpusers.bak.
6. Clear the terminal.

Scenario:

While researching ways to secure the Linux system, you come upon a few articles stating that the root user should not have access to certain remote services to protect the security of the system. Your manager would like you to secure the local user accounts on the Linux server. You decide to implement the necessary security features to prevent the root login from being used for Telnet and FTP services, to protect it from misuse.

What You Do	How You Do It
1. Disable root access for the Telnet service.	a. Enter **vi /etc/securetty** to open the file.
	b. Locate "tty1" and delete the line.
	c. Press **D** two times to delete the tty entries from tty2 to tty11.
	d. Enter **:wq** to save and close the file.

2.	Access the Telnet service as the root user.	a.	Switch to srvB.
		b.	Enter **telnet 192.168.0.2** to access the Telnet service.
		c.	Enter *root* as the user name.
		d.	Enter *p@ssword* as the password.
		e.	Observe the system displays "Login incorrect" because access is denied for the root user.
		f.	Press **Ctrl+]** to continue.
		g.	Enter **quit** to return to the command prompt.
		h.	Enter **clear** to clear the terminal screen.
3.	Delete root access for the vsftp service.	a.	Switch to srvA.
		b.	Enter **vi /etc/vsftpd/ftpusers** to open the file.
		c.	Locate "root" and delete the line.
		d.	Enter **:wq** to save and close the file.
4.	Access the ftp service as the root user.	a.	Switch to srvB.
		b.	Enter **ftp 192.168.0.2** to access the ftp service.
		c.	Enter *root* as the user name.
		d.	Observe that access is denied for the **root** user.
		e.	Enter **quit** to return to the command prompt.
		f.	Enter **clear** to clear the terminal screen.

TOPIC C
Enable Firewall Functionality

You secured user accounts as a level of security defense on your network. Now, you will look at packet filtering to provide firewall functionality to routers, gateways, and Linux servers and workstations. In this topic, you will implement iptables to provide firewall functionality by packet filtering.

When dealing with data navigating through your network, you will want to implement additional filtering. Understanding iptables will enable you to provide firewall functionality by packet filtering to secure the Linux system. As a Linux+ administrator, you will need to provide a secure network and continuity of services especially on large networks.

Firewalls

Definition:

A *firewall* is a software program or a hardware device that protects a system or a network from unauthorized access by blocking unsolicited traffic. A firewall allows incoming or outgoing traffic that has specifically been permitted by an administrator. It also allows incoming traffic that is sent in response to requests from internal hosts. Firewalls often provide logging features and alarms that track security problems and report them to the administrator. Firewalls use packet filtering and proxy servers to implement security on a network.

Example:

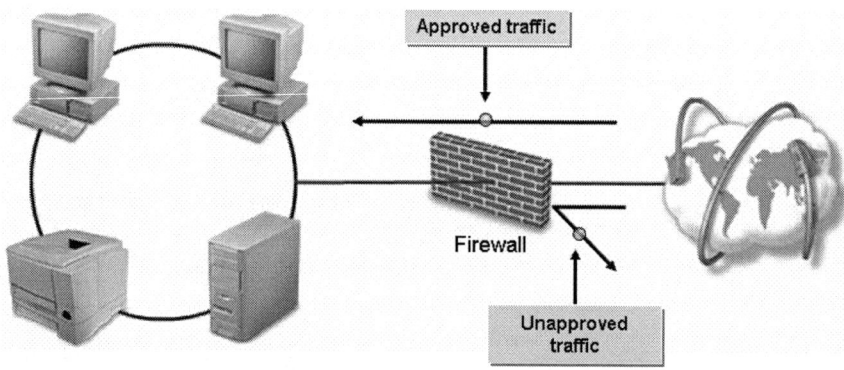

Figure 14-12: Firewall protects a network by filtering incoming and outgoing traffic.

Software Firewalls

The word "firewall" is generally used to refer to software-based firewalls. Software firewalls can be useful for small home offices and businesses. The firewall provides many features that can be configured to suit various computing needs. Some features include:

● Enabling or disabling port security on certain ports.

● Filtering inbound and outbound communication. A user can set up rules or exceptions in the firewall settings to limit access to the web.

● Reporting and logging activity.

● Protecting systems from malware and spyware.

- Blocking pop-up messages.
- Assigning, forwarding, and triggering ports.

Hardware Firewalls

A hardware firewall is a hardware device, either stand-alone or built into most routers, that protects computers on a private network from unauthorized traffic. They are placed between the private network and the public network to manage inbound and outbound traffic and network access.

Firewall Positioning

A firewall can be positioned logically between the internal network and the external world. In addition, it can be positioned between internal corporate networks and on individual servers. It is recommended to configure the firewall to either deny or grant access, based on the rules assigned by the security administrator.

Packet Filtering

Packet filtering is a process of passing or blocking incoming and outgoing packets after inspecting each packet for user-defined content, such as an IP address. It was the first type of firewall that was used to protect networks by reading packet headers. Packet filtering was limited by the fact that it was designed to look only at packet header information. *Netfilter* is a framework that implements packet filtering in Linux, to manage firewalls and secure data. It contains a number of modules that inspect packet headers and filter packets with improper headers. The packets pass through various stages before they are sent to their destination. The packets are filtered at specific points and the filtered packets are sent to the next stage. Based on user requirements, netfilter activities can be configured.

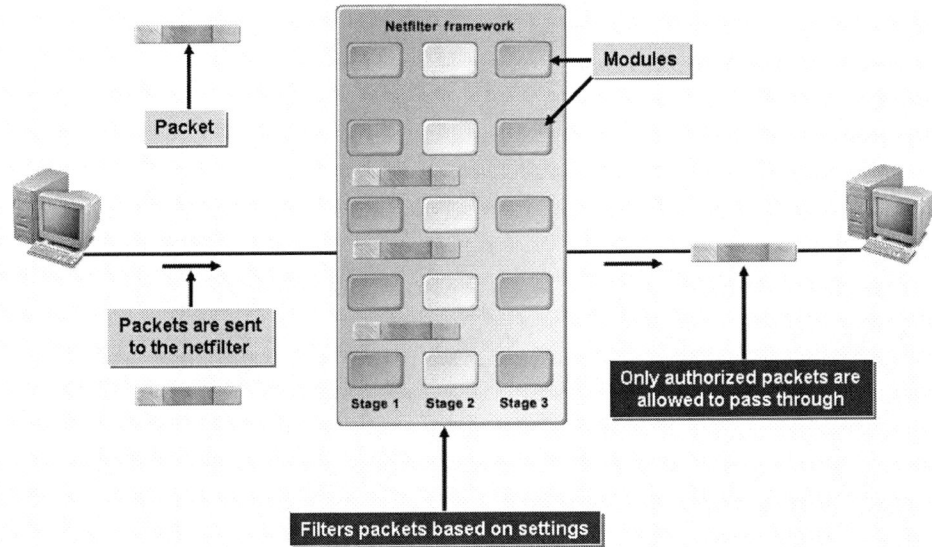

Figure 14-13: The working of the netfilter framework.

Proxy Server Implementation

A proxy server, also known as an application gateway, is a much more secure and flexible firewall solution than a pure packet filter. The proxy software can be configured to intercept network traffic. The proxy recognizes the request and sends the request to the server. In this way, the internal client never connects directly to the external server; thus, the proxy functions as the intermediary, communicating to both the client and the server. The major advantage is that the proxy software can permit or deny traffic based on the actual data in the packet, and not simply the header.

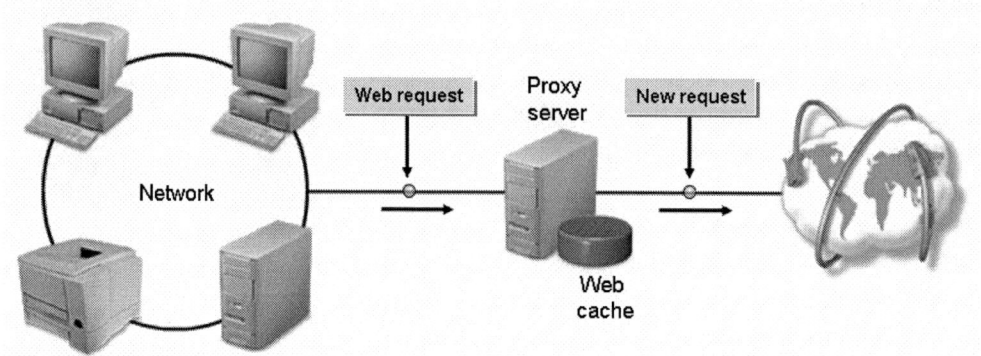

Figure 14-14: The functioning of a proxy server on a network.

The iptables Program

Definition:

The *iptables* program is a firewall program in Linux that provides protection to the internal network. The iptables program uses rule sets, called *chains*, to implement *IP filtering*. There are three iptables: filter, nat, and mangle.

Example:

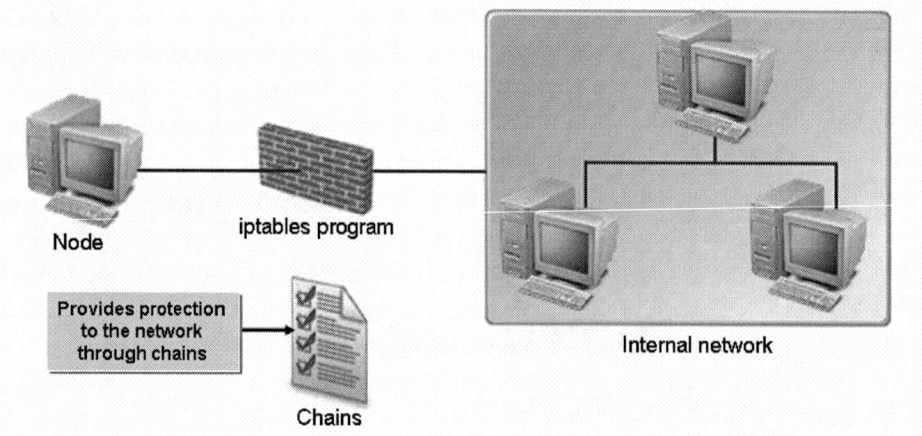

Figure 14-15: Protecting a network through chains defined using the iptables program.

Syntax

The syntax of the *iptables* program is `iptables [-t table] {commands} {chain/rule specification} [options/parameters]`.

The ipchains Program

The *ipchains* program is a Linux tool for managing packet filtering on a Linux server. Support for ipchains is compiled directly into the Linux kernel, where the ipchains tool inserts and deletes rules from iptables. These rules define whether packets are permitted or denied from being sent or received by a Linux system.

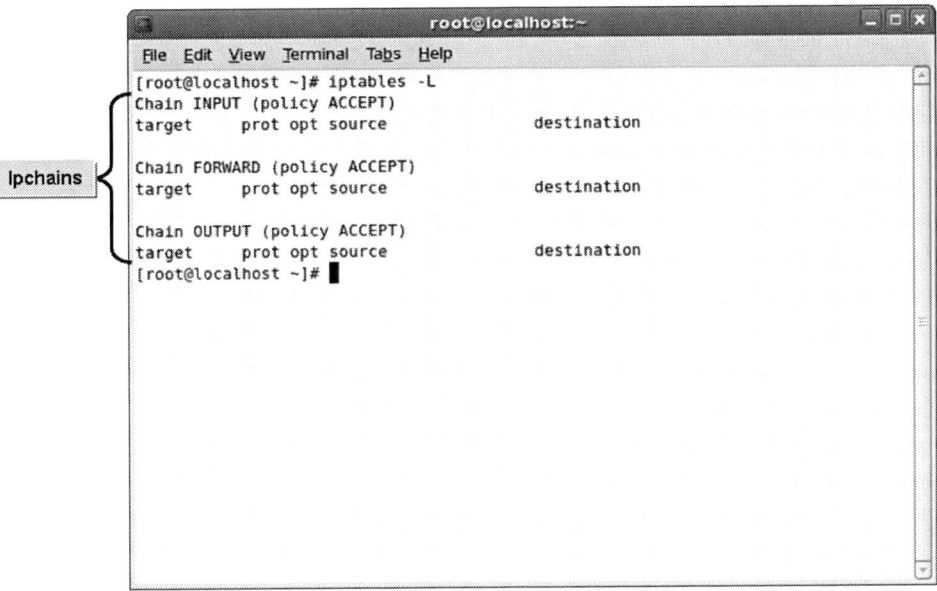

Figure 14-16: *A list of all the rules in the IP chains*

iptables and ipchains

One of the differences between ipchains and iptables is that iptables can be configured to be a stateful packet filter. With an iptable, the headers within a packet are examined against a known set of rules (the chain) in sequence. If the packet matches a rule, a decision is made for that packet based on what is specified (the target). If a match is not found, then the packet is examined against the next rule in the sequence. This continues until all the rules are exhausted. At this point, iptables look to ipchains to make the default policy decision.

Each iptable contains specific chains. The filter table contains the INPUT, OUTPUT, and FORWARD chains. The nat table contains the PREROUTING, POSTROUTING, and OUTPUT chains and is used on networks where only outgoing packets have to be filtered. The mangle table contains the INPUT, OUTPUT, FORWARD, PREROUTING, and POSTROUTING chains and is used on large networks where both incoming and outgoing packets have to be filtered.

Syntax

To check your installation for ipchains, use the command `rpm -q iptables`.

Use of ipchains

ipchains are used to block access to privileged ports of a Linux server. By blocking access to all incoming traffic, an administrator can prevent network access to a Linux workstation connected to a network.

How to Implement iptables

Procedure Reference: Configure iptables

To configure iptables:

1. Log in as root.

2. Enter `service iptables start` to start the `iptables` service.

3. Enter `chkconfig iptables on` to automatically start the `iptables` service at the system startup.

4. Manage the rules using `iptables`.

   - Enter the `iptables -A forward -p icmp -j ACCEPT` to add a rule.

   - Enter the `iptables -D forward -p icmp -j ACCEPT` to remove a rule.

ACTIVITY 14-5
Configuring iptables

Before You Begin:
1. Switch to srvA.
2. On srvA, you have logged in as root in the CLI.
3. At the command line, copy /etc/securetty.bak to /etc/securetty.
4. Overwrite the existing securetty file.
5. Copy /etc/vsftpd/ftpusers.bak to /etc/vsftpd/ftpusers.
6. Overwrite the existing ftpusers file.
7. Clear the terminal screen.
8. Enter `exit` two times to log out.
9. Log in as root.

Scenario:
Your need to implement a firewall on the Linux server. So, you decide to set up iptables on the Linux system. You need to check whether you are able to add and remove rules from the iptables.

What You Do	How You Do It
1. Start the iptables service.	a. Enter **`service iptables start`** to start the iptables service.
	b. Enter **`chkconfig iptables on`** to automatically start the iptables service at system startup.
	c. Enter **`ps ax	grep iptables`** to view the processes related to iptables.
	d. Verify that **iptables** is listed.
2. Add a rule to the iptable.	a. Enter **`iptables -A INPUT -s 0/0 -i eth0 -d 192.168.0.1 -p TCP -j ACCEPT`** to add a new rule to accept TCP packets during the INPUT phase.
	b. Enter **`iptables -L	more`** to view the permissions for **INPUT, FORWARD,** and **OUTPUT** chains.
	c. Verify that the new rule is added.

3. Drop a rule from the iptable.

    a. Enter `iptables -D INPUT -s 0/0 -i eth0 -d 192.168.0.1 -p TCP -j ACCEPT` to drop the rule related to TCP packets.

    b. Enter `iptables -L | more` to view the permissions for **INPUT, FORWARD,** and **OUTPUT** chains.

    c. Verify that the rule is removed.

    d. Clear the terminal screen.

TOPIC D
Implement Security Auditing

You implemented iptables to make the Linux working environment secure for users. You will need to set up auditing for files and authentication in order to identify and trace possible security breaches. In this topic, you will implement security auditing.

A network may contain confidential data to which only a select few people have access. This data may include financial reports, budgetary information, or personnel reviews. It's your responsibility to monitor the permissions and security levels on this data, so wouldn't you like to know if intruders are attempting to access the data for which they do not have proper permission? When you implement security auditing, you can attain instant access to detect and record security-related events on your network.

How to Implement Security Auditing

Procedure Reference: Implement Security Auditing

To implement security auditing:

1. Set iptables to send possible intrusions to the log files by using the `iptables` command.
2. Enter the `service iptables save` command to save the iptables rule.
3. Direct the output from the iptables output to the /var/log/iptables file.

ACTIVITY 14-6

Implementing Security Auditing

Before You Begin:

1. On srvA, you have logged in as root in the CLI.
2. The first CLI terminal is displayed.
3. Enter `cd /root` to navigate to the root directory.
4. Enter `clear` to clear the terminal screen.

Scenario:

Your need to implement security auditing on your network. You decide to output the dropped packets from the iptables firewall to a log file where it can be reviewed for possible intrusion attempts.

What You Do	How You Do It
1. Set iptables to send possible intrusions to a log file.	a. Enter **iptables -N LOG_DROP** to create a chain named LOG_DROP.
	b. Enter ```iptables -A LOG_DROP -j LOG ⇒ --log-tcp-options --log-level ⇒ 3 --log-ip-options ⇒ --log-prefix "[Dropped Packet] : "``` to append a new rule to the LOG_DROP chain.
	c. Enter **iptables -L** to view the rules.
	d. Observe that the LOG rule is listed in the rules of the **LOG_DROP** chain.
	e. Enter **iptables -A LOG_DROP -j DROP** to append a new rule to the LOG_DROP chain.
	f. Enter **iptables -L** to view the rules.
	g. Observe that the DROP rule is listed in the rules of the **LOG_DROP** chain.
	h. Enter **service iptables save** to save the iptables rules.

2. Direct the iptables' output to /var/log/iptables.

a. Enter **vi /etc/syslog.conf** to open the syslog.conf file.

b. Press **Shift+G** to go to the end of the file.

c. Press **O** to switch to the insert mode and move to a new line.

d. Enter **#Log iptables results to iptables log** to specify a description about directing iptable results to the log file.

e. Type **kern.3** and press the **Tab** key and then type **/var/log/iptables** to direct the results to the log file.

 kern is used to log all kernel messages to the console.

f. Press **Esc** and enter **:wq** to save and close the file.

g. Enter **touch /var/log/iptables** to create the /var/log/iptables file.

h. Enter **service syslog restart** to restart the syslog service.

TOPIC E
Detect Intrusion

You implemented security auditing. To secure files that contain confidential data, you need to constantly monitor the network. In this topic, you will implement an intrusion detection system.

If your network is connected to the public network, there are chances that intruders may trace packets on the network and misuse the services on the system. As a Linux+ administrator, you need to implement a service on your network that will monitor the incoming and outgoing packets, and send an alert if any of the files or services have been corrupted or manipulated.

Network Monitoring Utilities

Various utilities are available for monitoring network devices and the systems connected to them.

Utility	Used To
nmap	Scan entire networks for various ports and the services running on them along with their status. The nmap utility can also be run as a GUI front end using the nmapfe command. This utility is primarily used to monitor remote network connections. There are a number of options for the nmap utility. These options help a user to get specific information about a network. The syntax of the nmap utility is nmap *[scan type] [options] {target specification}*.
tcpdump	Obtain packet information from a query string sent to the network interface. If the packet header matches the expression in the query, the packets are returned to the user. The syntax of the tcpdump utility is tcpdump *[option] {expression}*.
wireshark	Obtain packet information. It is a GUI-based utility. On running the wireshark command, the Wireshark Network Analyzer tool is displayed. Its functions are similar to the tcpdump utility.

The Intrusion Detection System

Definition:

The *Intrusion Detection System (IDS)* is a security sensor that protects portals, networks, and files from hackers. The IDS monitors system files, log files, and packets passed on the network. It also checks the network data stream for unauthorized signatures and attacks. IDS software can also analyze data and alert administrators to potential security problems. An IDS can comprise a variety of hardware sensors, intrusion detection software, and IDS management software. Each implementation is unique, depending on the security needs and the components chosen.

Example: Snort

Snort is an IDS that monitors each packet on the network. If a suspicious packet is detected, it passes an alert to the syslog file.

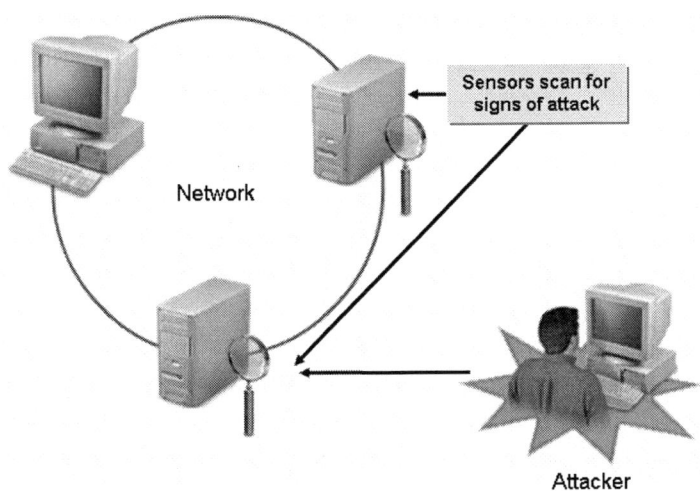

Figure 14-17: An IDS protecting a network from a hacker.

Passive and Active IDS

An IDS can be either passive or active. A *passive IDS* detects potential security breaches, logs the activity, and alerts security personnel. An *active IDS* does the same, and then takes the appropriate action to block a user from the suspicious activity. Some people consider the active IDS as a type of Intrusion Prevention System and not as a separate prevention system.

Tripwire

Definition:

Tripwire is an intrusion detection tool that compares the content of a file or directory with a database that contains the locations of the file or directory and the dates modified. It also monitors the attributes of the file such as the binary signature, size, or expected change of size. If the file has been changed, then the Tripwire tool passes an alert to the administrator by email.

Example:

Figure 14-18: Tripwire detects intrusion by comparing the content of a file and monitoring its attributes.

The Tripwire Database

The *Tripwire database* contains baselines, which are the snapshots of files and directories noted at a specific time. When usage becomes abnormal, problems can be easily detected by comparing the latest files and directories with the earlier snapshots. After a Tripwire is installed and configured, the database should be initialized. To initialize the Tripwire database, execute the following command: `/usr/sbin/tripwire --init`. While initializing the database, Tripwire creates a collection of filesystem objects based on certain specifications mentioned in the policy file. An integrity check should be done after initializing the database. To view the entire database, enter the command `/usr/sbin/twprint -m d --print-dbfile | less`.

The tw.cfg File

The tw.cfg file is the Tripwire configuration file. Before generating the tw.cfg file, you can modify the configuration options in the twcfg.txt file to suit your requirements. The following table lists some of the configuration options.

Use This Option	To Do This
POLFILE	Modify the location of the policy file, tw.pol.
DBFILE	Modify the location of the database file, [hostname].twd.
REPORTFILE	Modify the location of the report file, [hostname].[date].twr.
SITEKEYFILE	Modify the location of the site key file.
LOCALKEYFILE	Modify the location of the local key file.
EDITOR	Specify the editor called by Tripwire when the database is updated.
MAILPROGRAM	Specify the mail program used by Tripwire.
MAILMETHOD	Specify the mail protocol used by Tripwire.

 You cannot create the tw.cfg file if the Tripwire file locations are not properly specified in the twcfg.txt file.

Snort

Definition:

Snort is a network IDS that monitors network traffic. Snort monitors each packet on the network. If a suspicious packet is detected, it passes an alert to the syslog file and notifies the administrator through email or a pop-up window. It detects various network attack methods, including CGI attacks, denial-of-service, buffer overflow, and SMB probes.

Example:

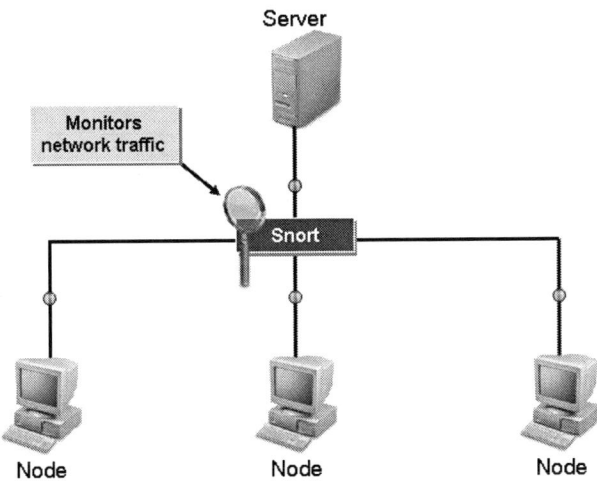

Figure 14-19: Snort monitoring traffic on a network.

Snort Options

Some frequently used `snort` command options are listed in the following table.

Use This Option	To Do This
`-v`	Run Snort in the verbose mode.
`-i interface`	Listen to packets on a specific interface.
`-l directory`	Specify the output logging directory.
`-n number of packets`	Specify the number of packets to be processed before exiting.
`-D`	Run Snort in the daemon mode and log all messages in the /var/log/snort/alert directory.

Portsentry

Definition:

Portsentry is an IDS that detects and responds to port attacks. It is run as a daemon on TCP and UDP sockets to detect port scans on the system. If a port attack is detected, portsentry generates a log entry that contains the details of the hostname, the time of attack, the attacking host's IP address, and the TCP or the UDP port. It reports to the syslog daemon and alerts the administrator through email.

 Portsentry is generally used to drop the route to the scanning host. This prevents the attacking host from using any information it gained from the port scan.

Example:

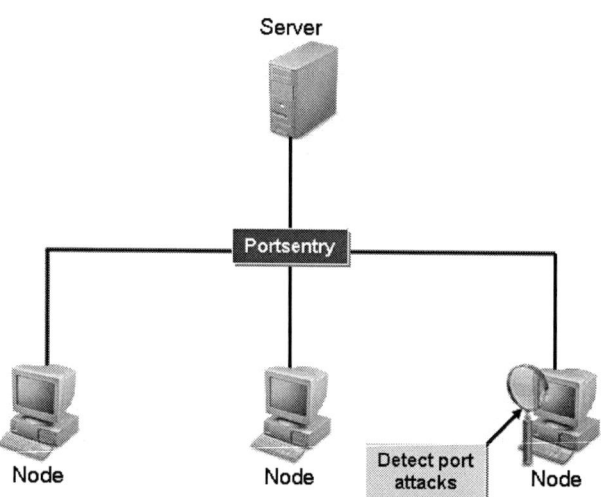

Figure 14-20: Portsentry detecting intrusion in a network.

Nessus

Definition:

Nessus is an IDS that audits the security of remote hosts and the services running on the network. Nessus performs vulnerability checks on the network and generates reports, listing all the security flaws and the possible ways to counter them. It consists of two parts, a server and a client. The server uses the nessusd daemon to maintain a vulnerability database for implementing security checks. The client uses this database and performs the security checks.

Example:

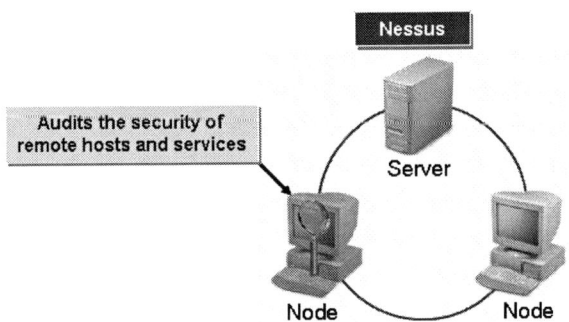

Figure 14-21: Portsentry auditing security in network systems.

How to Detect an Intrusion

Procedure Reference: Install Tripwire

To install Tripwire on a Linux server:

1. On the Linux server, log in as root
2. Download the tripwire-2.4.1.2-src.tar.bz2 file from **http://sourceforge.net/projects/ tripwire/files/.**
3. Copy the downloaded file to the /etc/ directory.
4. Enter `bunzip2 tripwire-2.4.1.2-src.tar.bz2` to extract the file.
5. Enter `tar -xvf tripwire-2.4.1.2-src.tar` to untar the file.
6. Navigate to the `/etc/tripwire-2.4.1.2-src` directory.
7. Enter the command `sed -i -e 's@TWDB="${prefix}@TWDB="/var@' install/install.cfg && ./configure --prefix=/usr --sysconfdir= /etc/tripwire && make` to install the Tripwire database and reports in the `/var/lib/tripwire` directory.
8. Enter `make install && cp -v policy/*.txt /usr/doc/tripwire` to create the Tripwire security keys and install the binaries and copy the Tripwire sample policy files in the documentation directory of the program.
9. View and accept the agreement to continue with the installation.

Procedure Reference: Configure Tripwire

To configure Tripwire:

1. Navigate to the /etc/tripwire directory.
2. If necessary, edit the twcfg.txt file to modify the location of the Tripwire files and customize its settings.
3. If necessary, edit the twpol.txt file.
    *   Comment the names of files or programs that do not require monitoring or that do not exist on your system.
    *   If you want to send an email message to users when a rule is violated, add a comma after the "severity=" line in the rule's directive section and then add the `emailto` parameter with the email addresses of users.

        `emailto = [email address 1], [email address 2].....]`

4. Run the /usr/sbin/tripwire-setup-keyfiles command.

    a. At the command prompt, enter `/usr/sbin/tripwire-setup-keyfiles`.

    b. When prompted, enter the passwords to create cryptographic keys for signing Tripwire files.

    c. When prompted, enter the local and site key passwords to sign the Tripwire files with the keys.

5. Back up a copy of the twcfg.txt and twpol.txt files.

6. Change the permissions of the twcfg.txt and twpol.txt files so that only the root user can read and modify the files.

```
chmod 600 twcfg.txt twpol.txt
```

7. Initialize the Tripwire database, which contains information about critical system files that have to be monitored based on the rules specified in the policy file. When prompted, enter the local password.

```
/usr/sbin/tripwire --init
```

8. Verify that the Tripwire database has been created.

```
/usr/sbin/twprint -m d --print-dbfile | less
```

Cryptographic Keys

Tripwire encrypts the configuration, policy, database, and report files by using cryptographic keys. You can modify the Tripwire files only if you provide the local and site passwords. The cryptographic keys are stored in the site.key and [domainname]-local.key files in the /etc/tripwire directory. Usually, these keys are generated when you run the twinstall.sh configuration script.

Procedure Reference: Check File Integrity

To check the integrity of files monitored by Tripwire:

1. Run an integrity check to find if there have been any changes in the files monitored by Tripwire.

```
/usr/sbin/tripwire --check
```

 By default, a shell script named tripwire-check is placed in the /etc/cron.daily directory. This script performs an integrity check every day.

2. View the report created by the integrity check.

```
/usr/sbin/twprint -m r --twrfile /var/lib/tripwire/report/file name.twr
```

Procedure Reference: Update the Tripwire Database

To update the Tripwire database:

1. Use the `tripwire` command with the latest report.

```
/usr/sbin/tripwire --update --twrfile /var/lib/tripwire/report/latest
report.twr
```

2. The report is displayed in the default text editor. Add or remove the "x" character to the file names you want to include or exclude from the Tripwire database.

3. Save and close the file.

4.   When prompted, enter the password for signing the database file.

Procedure Reference: Update the Tripwire Policy File

To update the Tripwire policy file:

1.   Regenerate the twpol.txt file.

```
/usr/sbin/twadmin --print-polfile > /path/twpol.txt
```

2.   Generate a new policy file.

```
/usr/sbin/twadmin --create-polfile -S site.key /path/twpol.txt
```

3.   Delete the existing Tripwire database and create another one.

```
rm /path/domainname.twd
```

```
/usr/sbin/tripwire --init
```

4.   Run the integrity check manually and view the report to verify that the database has been created.

```
/usr/sbin/tripwire --check
```

```
/usr/sbin/twprint -m r --twrfile /var/lib/tripwire/report/file name.twr
```

Updating Tripwire

You can access the **http://sourceforge.net/projects/tripwire** website to get information about the latest security updates and bug fixes.

Procedure Reference: Implement Portsentry

To implement Portsentry:

1.   Obtain the Portsentry source files from the Internet.

2.   Uncompress the source file.

```
gunzip portsentry-{version}.{release}.tar.gz
tar xvf portsentry-{version}.{release}.tar
cd portsentry_beta
```

3.   Read the README.install file.

4.   Install the source.

```
make
make install
```

5.   If necessary, in the `/usr/local/portsentry/portsentry.conf` file, specify the TCP or UDP ports you want to scan.

```
TCP=comma separated list of TCP ports
UDP=comma separated list of UDP ports
```

 The default configuration works fine with Portsentry. If required, in the portsentry.ignore file, you can add the hosts that you do not want to block.

Procedure Reference: Implement Snort

To implement Snort:

1.   In the Linux server, log in as root.

2. Mount the Linux installation media that contains the Snort RPM.

3. Navigate to the /media/[name of the media]/Packages directory.

4. Install the Snort RPM.

   ```
   rpm -ivh snort-{version}.{release}.rpm
   ```

5. Start the Snort IDS.

   ```
   service snortd start
   ```

6. Use the `snort` command options to detect network intrusion.

   ```
   snort Snort options
   ```

Updating Snort

You can access the **http://www.snort.org/vrt/** website to download the latest Snort rules that defend your system against newly discovered vulnerabilities.

Procedure Reference: Scan Ports Using nmap

To scan ports using nmap:

1. Install the nmap RPM file.

   ```
   rpm -ivh nmap-{version}.{release}.rpm
   ```

2. Use the `nmap` command to view information about open ports.

   ```
   nmap IP address
   ```

Options for the nmap Command

Some frequently used `nmap` command options are given in the following table.

Use This Option	To Do This
sT	Scan TCP ports
sU	Scan UDP ports
p *range of ports*	Scan specific ports
F	Search only in the nmap-services file, which contains information about ports

Procedure Reference: Implement Nessus

To implement Nessus:

1. Log in as root.

2. Download the nessus-{version}.{release}.rpm package from **http://www.nessus.org/download/.**

3. Install the Nessus RPM.

   ```
   rpm -ivh nessus-{version}.{release}.rpm
   ```

4. Create a Nessus user.

    1. Enter `/opt/nessus/sbin/nessus-adduser` to create a Nessus user.

    2. At the **Login** prompt, enter a user name.

    3. At the **Authentication** prompt, press **Enter.**

    4. At the **Login password** prompt, enter a password.

    5. At the **Login password** prompt, retype the password to confirm it.

    6. Press **Ctrl+D** to exit the prompt.

    7. Enter **y** to confirm and exit.

5. If necessary, make changes to the /opt/nessus/sbin/nessus/nessus.conf file to configure Nessus.

6. Start the Nessus service.

    - Enter `service nessusd start`

    - Or, enter `/opt/nessus/sbin/nessusd/ -D`

ACTIVITY 14-7

Detecting Intrusion Using Tripwire

Data Files:

tripwire-2.4.1.2-src.tar.bz2

Before You Begin

1. On srvA, you have logged in as root in the CLI.

2. The first terminal is displayed.

3. At the command line, enter `cp /085039Data/Securing_Linux/tripwire-2.4.1.2-src.tar.bz2 /etc` to copy the tripwire-2.4.1.2-src.tar.bz2 file to /etc directory.

4. Enter `cd /etc` to change to the etc directory.

5. Enter `bunzip2 tripwire-2.4.1.2-src.tar.bz2` to extract the file.

6. Enter `tar -xvf tripwire-2.4.1.2-src.tar` to untar the file.

7. Enter `cd tripwire-2.4.1.2-src` to change to the /etc/tripwire-2.4.1.2-src directory.

8. Enter the command `sed -i -e 's@TWDB="${prefix}@TWDB="/var@' install/install.cfg && ./configure --prefix=/usr --sysconfdir=/etc/tripwire && make` to install the Tripwire database and reports in the /var/lib/tripwire directory.

9. Enter `make install && cp -v policy/*.txt /usr/doc/tripwire` to create the Tripwire security keys and install the binaries and copy the tripwire sample policy files in the documentation directory of the program.

10. Press **Enter** to view the agreement.

11. Enter *accept* to accept the agreement.

12. Type *y* and press **Enter** to continue with the installation.

13. If necessary, enter `site#1` as the site key password.

14. If necessary, enter `loc@11` as the local key password.

15. Enter `site#1` as the site key password two times. Type *y* to overwrite the policyguide.txt file.

16. Clear the terminal screen.

Scenario:

You need to protect the configuration files, such as inittab, fstab, passwd, and shadow, in the /etc directory. Any incorrect modification done to these files can corrupt your server because they contain critical information about your server. Therefore, you want to take special care to protect these files from being modified by intruders.

What You Do	How You Do It
1. Customize the Tripwire configuration and policy files.	a. Navigate to the /etc/tripwire directory.
	b. Open the twpol.txt file.
	c. Locate the line beginning with "HOSTNAME."
	d. Press **O** to switch to the insert mode and move to a new line.
	e. Type **SIG_HI = 100;** to define a new variable and assign a value to it.
	f. Press **Esc** to switch to the command mode.
	g. Search for the text rulename = "Tripwire Data Files"
	h. Press **O** to switch to the insert mode and move to a new line.
	i. On the new line, enter **severity = $(SIG_HI),**
	j. Type `emailto = root` ,
	k. Press **Esc** to switch to the command mode.
	l. Save and close the file.
	m. Clear the screen.

2. Run the configuration script.

a. Enter `twadmin --create-polfile --site-keyfile /etc/tripwire/site.key /etc/tripwire/twpol.txt` to create policy file and key file.

b. Enter *site#1* as the site key password.

c. If necessary, enter the site key password again.

d. If necessary, enter the local key password again.

e. If necessary, enter the site key password two times to sign the configuration and policy files.

f. Observe that the policy file is created.

g. Change the permissions of the twcfg.txt and twpol.txt files so that only you can read and modify the files.

3. Initialize the Tripwire database.

a. Enter `tripwire --init` to start initializing the database.

b. Enter *loc@l1* as the local password.

c. Enter `/usr/sbin/twprint -m ⇒ d --print-dbfile` to create the database.

This will take more than ten minutes. Wait for the prompt to be displayed.

4. Check the integrity of your system files using Tripwire.

a. Run the `tripwire` program with the `--check` option to create a report.

b. Enter **ls /var/lib/tripwire/report** to check if the report has been created.

c. Observe that file with extension twr is displayed.

d. Enter **/usr/sbin/twprint -m** ⇒ **r --twrfile /var/lib/tripwire**⇒ **/report/srvA-<yyyymmdd>**⇒ **-<hhmmss>.twr | less** to view the report.

e. After viewing two pages, press **q** to return to the command line.

f. Clear the screen.

Lesson 14 Follow-up

In this lesson, you examined various options available to secure a Linux system connected to a network. You configured encryption; secured user accounts; implemented iptables and security auditing; and detected intrusion. You will now be able to allow or restrict user access to network resources and safeguard your network by effectively protecting confidential data.

1. **Which encryption method will you use to secure data? Why?**

2. **How will you detect intrusion on a network?**

15 | Managing Hardware

Lesson Time: 2 hour(s), 10 minutes

Lesson Objectives:

In this lesson, you will manage hardware associated with Linux machines.

You will:

- Identify common hardware components and resources.
- Configure power management.
- Configure removable hardware.
- Configure mass storage devices.
- Manage logical volumes.
- Configure disk quotas.

Introduction

You configured various services and ensured the security of your network. While working with Linux, hardware-related issues will arise. In this lesson, you will manage hardware.

As a Linux administrator, you will need to upgrade hardware components regularly. By adding, removing, managing, and troubleshooting hardware, you can ensure the efficient working of your system.

This lesson covers all or part of the following CompTIA Linux+ (2009) certification objectives:

- Topic A
  - Objective 2.7
- Topic C
  - Objective 1.11
  - Objective 2.7
- Topic D
  - Objective 1.2
- Topic E
  - Objective 1.2
- Topic F
  - Objective 2.7

TOPIC A
Identify Common Hardware Components and Resources

There are various computer hardware and peripheral components available in the market. However, not all are compatible with Linux. In this topic, you will identify common hardware components and resources for Linux.

Before you install any operating system, you need to have all your hardware and peripheral components in place. However, not all hardware is compatible with all systems. Thorough knowledge of each component, and how it works within a Linux system, is critical for its successful installation.

Hardware Components

Basic hardware components of a Linux system include Central Processing Unit (CPU)/Floating Point Unit (FPU) processors, hard drives, memory, network adapters, and video cards. Additional components include CD-ROM drives, sound cards, modems, USB devices, FireWire devices, PCMCIA/Cardbus cards, printers, and scanners.

Hardware Resources

Hardware resources, such as IRQs, DMA, memory addresses, and *Small Computer Systems Interface (SCSI)* IDs, can cause system configuration conflicts in a Linux system. To prevent such conflicts check the documentation to see what the device resource should be set to. You cannot always change this, but if possible, change the settings so that the devices do not conflict with each other.

Types of SCSI

SCSI, pronounced as "skuzzy," is a set of standards for connecting peripheral devices to a computer. It is a popular format for hard disks and CD-ROM drives. It has a fast transfer rate and can handle multiple devices. There are many SCSI types, each with their own specifications.

Type of SCSI	Bus Width and Maximum Throughput
SCSI-1	8 bits at 5 MB/sec
Wide SCSI	16 bits at 10 MB/sec
Wide Ultra SCSI	16 bits at 40 MB/sec
Fast SCSI	8 bits at 10 MB/sec
Fast Wide SCSI	16 bits at 20 MB/sec
Ultra SCSI	8 bits at 20 MB/sec
Ultra2 SCSI	8 bits at 40 MB/sec
Ultra3 SCSI	16 bits at 160 MB/sec
Ultra 320 SCSI	16 bits at 320 MB/sec
Ultra-640 SCSI	16 bits at 640 MB/sec

SCSI IDs

Each SCSI device has a unique SCSI ID, also known as a SCSI address, assigned to it so that the host adapter will be able to identify the device it is communicating with. The lowest SCSI ID is 0 and the highest is 7 or 15; 0 to 7 for narrow SCSI and 0 to 15 for wide SCSI. Priority is given based on the drive ID, 7 being the highest priority.

Normally, the host bus adapter (HBA), which provides the interface between the system and SCSI, is assigned the ID of 7. Slower devices should have higher-priority IDs so that faster devices do not monopolize the bus. So, the primary hard drive should be assigned a lower number and a slow device, such as a tape drive, should be assigned a higher ID number. Priority for narrow SCSI is 7, 6, 5, 4, 3, 2, 1, 0; for wide SCSI, it is 7, 6, 5, 4, 3, 2, 1, 0, 15, 14, 13, 12, 11, 10, 9, 8. SCSI IDs are set using jumpers or DIP switches on the SCSI device.

IRQ Device Description

Check the IRQ address for non-plug-and-play devices to ensure that there are no conflicts. The following table shows IRQ and I/O addresses for floppy drives, printer ports, and COM ports.

Device	IRQ	I/O Address
fd0 (floppy disk drive 1)	6	3f0–3f7
fd1 (floppy disk drive 2)	6	3f0–3f7
fd2 (floppy disk drive 3)	10	370–377
fd3 (floppy disk drive 4)	10	370–377
lp0 (LPT 1)	7	378–37f
lp1 (LPT2)	5	278–27f
ttyS0 (COM 1)	4	3f8
ttyS1 (COM 2)	3	2f8
ttyS2 (COM 3)	4	3e8
ttyS3 (COM 4)	3	2e8

Disk Space Tracking

The df and du commands facilitate disk space tracking. The disk free command (df) enables you to view free disk space. This includes the filesystem, total size, disk space used and available, percentage value of space, and the mount point. The disk usage command (du) displays how a disk is used including the size of directory trees and files within. It also enables you to track space hogs, which are directories and files that consume large amounts of space on the hard disk.

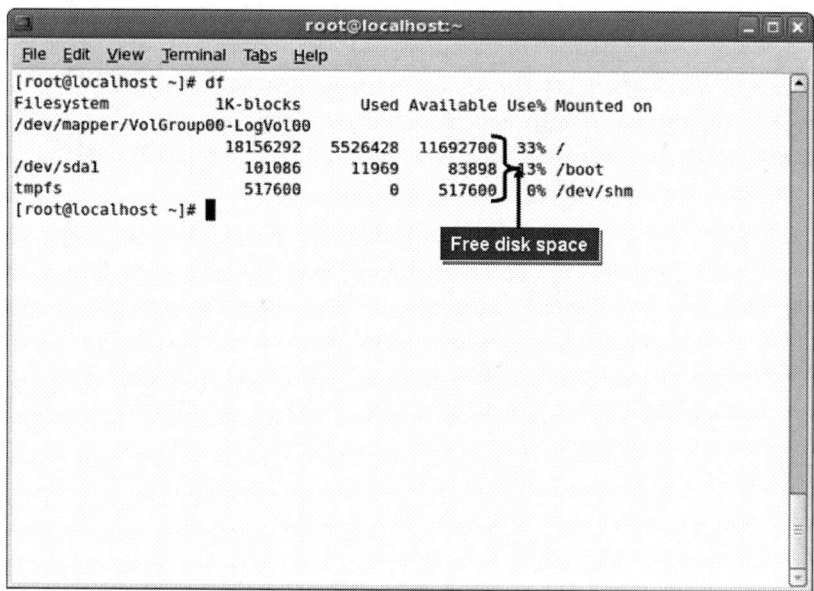

Figure 15-1: The df command displaying free disk space.

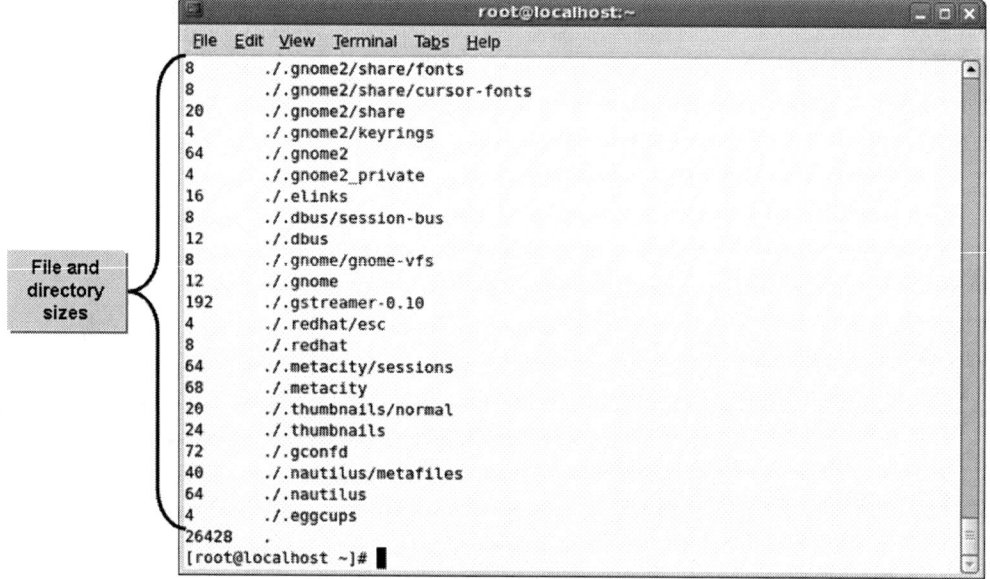

Figure 15-2: The du command displaying the size of directories and files on the disk.

How to Identify Common Hardware Components and Resources

Procedure Reference: Identify Hardware Components and Resources

To identify hardware components and resources:

1. Log in as root.
2. Switch to the /proc directory.
3. Document the hardware components for future reference.
   - Display CPU information using the `cat cpuinfo` command.
   - Display device information using the `cat devices` command.
   - Display partition information using the `cat partitions` command.
   - Display current hard disk size and usage using the `df -h` command.
   - Display current IRQ resources using the `cat interrupts` command.

ACTIVITY 15-1
Determining Hardware Components and Resources

Before You Begin:
1. On srvA, you logged in as root in the CLI.
2. The first terminal is displayed.

Scenario:
Your manager, Jane, wants all team members to switch to Linux systems. She is planning to finalize the additional hardware requirements with the Systems Manager. She would like you to document the resources that the current Linux systems are using so that she can decide on the system requirements.

What You Do	How You Do It
1. Document CPU information.	a. At the command line, enter `cat /proc/cpuinfo` to view the details about the CPU. b. Document the model name, processing power (in MHz), and cache size.
2. Document device information.	a. Enter `cat /proc/devices` to view the list of current character and block devices. b. Document the current character and block devices.
3. Document the number of hard drive partitions and the current usage statistics.	a. Enter `cat /proc/partitions` to view the list of partitions. b. Document the number of hard drive partitions. c. Enter `df -h` to view the amount of free space in each hard drive. d. Document the details about the total hard drive size, the amount of space used, and the amount still available.

4. Document the IRQ resources.

    a. Enter `cat /proc/interrupts` to view the IRQ list for various devices.

    b. Document the IRQs for each device listed.

    c. Clear the terminal screen.

TOPIC B
Configure Power Management

You identified hardware components and resources that can be utilized in a Linux system. By having the necessary hardware, you cannot ensure a fully functional system. You need to keep your hardware components operational and ensure a safe shutdown in the event of a power outage. In this topic, you will configure power management options.

A voltage drop or an abrupt power shutdown can cause your system to crash. Although the risks of unexpected power shutdown are less than what they once were, ensuring a clean shutdown is a valuable contribution to any system administrator's peace of mind.

Power Management

Efficient power management requires a combination of hardware and software solutions.

Solution	*Description*
Advanced Power Management (APM)	APM reads the /proc/apm file, where the battery status information is provided. APM allows the machine to be either in the standby or suspend mode. It is useful in APM BIOS laptops. The *apmd* package can be installed to enable user-friendly output.
Advanced Configuration and Power Interface (ACPI)	The ACPI specification provides an alternative to APM. It is a BIOS-based power management system that provides power to the CPU and devices. ACPI establishes industry-standard power management on laptops, desktops, and servers.
	The ACPI specification is a key component in Operating System–directed Power Management (OSPM).
	The ACPI OS takes over power management and plug-and-play functions from the legacy BIOS interfaces.
Uninterrupted Power Supply (UPS)	UPS performs three main functions:
	1. It acts as a power filter, smoothing out voltage fluctuations such as potentially damaging spikes.
	2. It provides a limited dwell time in the event of sudden short power failures, such as brownouts.
	3. It prevents or minimizes filesystem damage by allowing you to shutdown your computer in the correct manner.

apmd

The Advanced Power Management Daemon (apmd) is a monitoring daemon that controls the APM system.

ACPI Functional Areas

The ACPI specification covers various functional areas. Some of them are listed in the table below.

Functional Area	Description
System power management	ACPI defines mechanisms for setting up a computer in and out of system sleeping states. It also provides a general mechanism for any device to wake the computer.
Device power management	ACPI tables describe motherboard devices, their power states, the power planes the devices are connected to, and controls for setting up the devices in different power states. This enables the OS to set up the devices in low-power states based on application usage.
Processor power management	While the OS is idle but not sleeping, it will use commands described by ACPI to set up the processors in low-power states.
System events	ACPI provides a general event mechanism that can be used for system events such as thermal events, power management events, docking, device insertion and removal, and so on. This mechanism is very flexible in that and it does not specifically define how events are routed to the core logic chip set.

ACPI Battery Management

The battery management policy covers APM BIOS and ACPI OS. An ACPI-compatible battery device needs either a Smart Battery subsystem interface, which is controlled by the OS directly through the embedded controller interface, or a Control Method Battery interface. A Control Method Battery interface is completely defined by ACPI Machine Language (AML) control methods, allowing an OEM to choose any type of battery and any kind of communication interface supported by ACPI. The battery must comply with the requirements of its interface, as described either therein or in other applicable standards.

Altering Battery Behavior

The OS may choose to alter the behavior of a battery, for example, by adjusting the Low Battery or Battery Warning trip point. When there are multiple batteries present, the battery subsystem is not required to perform any synthesis of a composite battery from the data of the separate batteries. In cases where the battery subsystem does not synthesize a composite battery from the separate battery's data, the OS must provide that synthesis.

The apcupsd Package

The apcupsd package is a package that provides UPS power management functions. During a power outage, it allows the computer to run for a specific period with the support of a UPS. However, the user should save all changes made to the files and shutdown the system before the specified period expires. If the time does expire, then the package automatically performs a controlled shutdown of the system automatically.

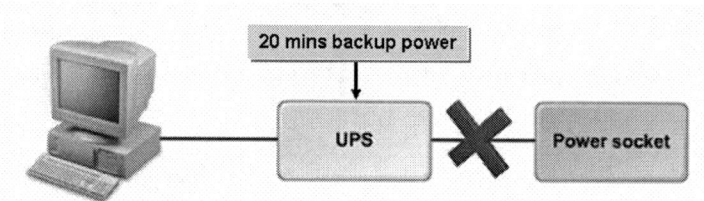

Figure 15-3: *UPS providing power to a system during a power outage.*

The apcupsd.conf File

The apcupsd.conf file is a configuration file that is required by the apcupsd package to communicate with the UPS. It contains directives that include configuration details about the UPS, which are added to a system. All the directives listed in the following table should be specified in the configuration file.

Directive	Description
UPSTYPE <type of UPS>	Specifies the name of the driver. The values could be dumb, apcsmart, net, usb, snmp, or test.
UPSCABLE <type of UPS cable>	Specifies the type of the cable used by the system.
DEVICE <name of the device>	Specifies the device that is used for UPS communication. Usually a serial port or a USB device is used for communication.
LOCKFILE <path of the lock file>	Specifies the path of the directory where the lock file for the USB or serial port needs to be created.

System Power States

A Linux system may support several states of power. Some of the power states are listed in the following table.

Power State	Description
Working	The system is fully usable.
Sleeping	The system appears to be off. Power consumption is reduced depending on how the system power is allocated.

Power State	Description
Soft Off	The system appears to be off and has very low power consumption.
Mechanical Off	The system is switched off and there is no power consumption. The system needs a full reboot to be fully usable.

How to Configure Power Management

Procedure Reference: Configure CPU Power Management

To configure CPU power management:

1. Switch to the /proc/acpi/processor/CPU{CPU Number} directory.
2. Verify that power management and throttling are turned on by using the `cat info` command.
3. Display the current power settings by using the `cat power` command.
4. Verify that the appropriate states for your machine are available.
   - If you have a desktop computer, verify that the first two C1 and C2 states are available.
   - If you have a laptop, verify that all three states are available.
5. Display the current throttle settings by using the `cat throttling` command.
6. Enter the `echo -n [throttle state] > throttling` command to adjust the throttle.

Throttling Technique

It is a technique by which a system is made to run at a capacity less than the maximum capacity it is capable of, with the intent of saving power.

ACTIVITY 15-2
Configuring CPU Power Management

Before You Begin:
1. On srvA, you have logged in as root in the CLI.
2. The first terminal is displayed.

Scenario:
Your manager would like you to check whether the new Linux systems support power management and configure power management on the systems to conserve power.

What You Do	How You Do It
1. Verify that power management and throttling are turned on for your CPU.	a. On the terminal, enter **cd /proc/acpi/processor/CPU0** to change to the CPU0 directory.
	b. Enter **cat info** to view the current settings of the CPU.
	c. Verify that power management and throttling are listed.
2. Display the current power and throttling settings.	a. Enter **cat power** to view the current power setting.
	b. Verify that C1 is available.
	c. Enter **cat throttling** to view the current throttling setting.
	d. Verify that eight states (T0 to T7) are listed and that the asterisk (*) is next to T0, the active state.

3. Adjust the throttling state.

    a. Enter **echo -n 7 > throttling** to set T7 as the active state.

    b. Enter **cat throttling** to view the new throttling setting.

    c. Verify that the asterisk (*) is next to the T7 state.

    d. Enter **echo -n 0 > throttling** to set T0 as the active state.

    e. Enter **cat throttling** to view the new throttling setting.

    f. Verify that the asterisk (*) is next to the T0 state.

    g. Enter **clear** to clear the terminal screen.

TOPIC C
Configure Removable Hardware

You addressed the necessary power management options. As a Linux+ administrator, you may need to add additional hardware devices to your system, based on user requirements. In this topic, you will configure removable hardware.

Advancement in technology may require you to constantly upgrade the hardware configuration of your Linux system. Removable devices are a convenient and efficient way to upgrade your Linux machine.

Removable Hardware

Linux systems allow you to utilize removable devices. Some of these devices are described in the following table.

Device	Example
Input	Keyboard, pointing device, joystick, scanner, webcam, digital tablet, and digital camera
Network	Modem and NIC
Output	Printer, sound card, and speakers
Storage	CD, DVD, tape drive, floppy disk, zip drive, flash drive, and hard drive

The PC Card

The PC card, formerly known as the PCMCIA, is of the size of a credit card and can be used for storage space, network cards, modems, and other purposes. Its standards and specifications are defined by the Personal Computer Memory Card International Association (PCMCIA).

The PCMCIA Organization

The PCMCIA organization is an alliance of members who promote interchangeability and compatibility among portable computers. The alliance defines the standards for the PC card.

Card and Socket Services

Card and socket services are loaded into memory when a portable computer is booted. This software comes with the PC and with the cards. These two layers of software detect and support a PC card when it is inserted into the portable computer. They also manage hot-swapping and pass changes in events to higher-level drivers written for specific cards.

Socket services interact with the BIOS to identify the number of sockets available. It can be built into the BIOS or added through software. When the system is turned on, it detects when a PC card is inserted or removed. Socket services work with card services above it, and communicate directly with the PC card's controller chips.

Card services automatically assign system resources when socket services identify that a PC card has been inserted. Card services manage system resources required by PC cards such as IRQs, memory, and I/O addresses. This software management interface also works in conjunction with upper-level software, such as hardware drivers, that may need to be loaded to work with the PC card.

The cardmgr Utility

The cardmgr utility monitors PCMCIA sockets for card insertion and removal events. When a card is inserted, the utility looks up the card in a database of known cards. If the card is identified, appropriate device drivers are loaded and bound to the card. When the card is ejected, the card's drivers will be unloaded if possible.

The /var/run/stab file contains identification and device driver information for PCMCIA cards. It is created by the cardmgr utility. Device driver lines comprise a series of tab-separated fields. These fields are described in the following table.

Field	Description
1	Socket number
2	Device class (identifies which script in /etc/pcmcia is used to configure or shutdown the device)
3	Driver name
4	Used to number devices when a single card has several devices associated with the same driver
5	Device name
6	Major device number, if required
7	Minor device number, if required

Arbitrary commands

Based on the contents of the PCMCIA card configuration database, the cardmgr utility may also execute arbitrary commands when appropriate cards are either inserted or removed. All insertion and removal events, device driver loads and unloads, startup and shutdown commands, and warnings and errors are reported in the system log file. Current card and device information for each socket is recorded in the /var/state/pcmcia/stab or /var/lib/pcmcia/stab file.

Normally, when a card is identified, the cardmgr utility will send a beep to the console. A beep is also generated when a card is successfully configured. A beep of lower pitch is generated if either of these steps fails. Ejecting a card produces a single beep. When the cardmgr utility receives a SIGHUP signal, it will reload its configuration file. When the cardmgr utility receives a SIGTERM signal, it will shutdown all sockets that are not busy and then exit, but drivers for busy sockets will stay loaded. If the PCMCIA_OPTS environment variable is set, its contents will be parsed after the main card configuration file is read.

The pcmcia File

The pcmcia file stored in the /etc/pcmcia/config directory is a card configuration database. It is read at startup by the cardmgr utility. It defines the resources that are available for use by the card services, explains how to load and initialize device drivers, and describes specific PCMCIA cards.

Stab File Update

The stab file is updated by the cardmgr utility whenever a card is inserted or ejected and when the cardmgr utility receives a signal. The stab file will normally be created in either the /var/state/pcmcia or /var/lib/pcmcia files, but if neither directory is available, it will be found in the /var/run file.

The pccardctl Utility

The pccardctl utility replaces the cardctl utility. It is used to monitor and control the state of PCMCIA sockets. If pccardctl is executed by the root user, all commands are available. If it is executed by a user with limited access rights, only the informational commands are accessible. The card control commands are listed in the following table.

Command	Description
status	Displays the current socket status flags.
config	Displays the socket configuration, including power settings, interrupt and I/O window settings, and configuration registers.
ident	Displays card identification information, including product identification strings, manufacturer ID codes, and function codes.
suspend	Shuts down and then disables the power for a socket.
resume	Restores power to a socket and reconfigures it for use.
eject	Notifies all client drivers that the PC card will be ejected and then cuts power to the socket.
insert	Notifies all client drivers that the PC card has just been inserted.

 If the command is to be applied to just one socket, the socket number should be specified; otherwise, all sockets will be affected.

Selecting PCMCIA Configuration Schemes

You can use the cardctl utility to select from among multiple PCMCIA configuration schemes. The current scheme name is passed to the device option scripts as part of the device address so that the scripts can use it to choose from among different setups.

USB

Universal Serial Bus (USB) is a hardware interface standard, designed to provide connections for numerous peripherals. *USB devices* are peripheral devices that communicate with a host computer. Some common USB devices include flash drives, memory card readers, and digital cameras.

USB Standards

USB 2.0 is the most commonly implemented standard. It can communicate at a rate of up to 480 Mbps. The original USB 1.1 standard is still commonly found in devices and systems. It can communicate at a rate of up to 12 Mbps. A USB 2.0 device connected to a USB 1.1 hub or port will communicate at only USB 1.1 speeds, even though it may be capable of faster speeds. Generally, the operating system will inform you of this when you connect the device.

USB 3.0, also called SuperSpeed USB, is the latest USB standard released and features a maximum transfer rate of 5.0 Gbit/s. It is 10 times faster than the USB 2.0 standard, has enhanced power efficiency, and is backward compatible with USB-enabled devices currently in use.

USB cables have a maximum distance before performance suffers. To work around this, one or more hubs can be used to create a chain to reach the necessary cable length. USB 1.1 has a maximum cable length of 3 meters, while USB 2.0's maximum length is 5 meters. In each case, a maximum of five hubs can be used to extend the cable length.

USB Plug and Play Capabilities

USB devices also incorporate plug-and-play technology that allows devices to self-configure as soon as a connection is made.

Kernel Support

While using USB devices, make sure that you have a kernel that includes USB support. Limited USB support was added in kernel 2.2.18, but it's best to run the 2.4.0 test kernel and any applicable patches for the next kernel. Be diligent in keeping up to date with new versions, because they tend to change frequently.

USB in Linux

Linux treats USB devices like SCSI disks, registering the first device as /dev/sda, where "sda" means the first partition of the first device.

FireWire

FireWire is an IEEE 1394-standard, high-speed serial bus, much like USB, which can run up to 30 times faster than USB. FireWire's higher bandwidth makes it ideal for devices such as digital video cameras and high-speed hard disk drives.

FireWire Cables

In FireWire cables, the electrical contacts are inside the structure of an IEEE 1394 cable connector. This helps protect the user from electric shocks. These cables are easy and safe to use. Users can blindly insert them into the systems. Terminators are not required and manual IDs do not have to be set.

The 1394 Subsystem Core

The core of the 1394 subsystem is a module that manages high- and low-level drivers, handles transactions, and triggers events. Subsystem high-level drivers, or routines, register themselves with the IEEE 1394 module by calling the function `hpsb_register_highlevel`.

The Loopback Device

The loopback device in the Linux system allows you to access a file or a set of files as a block device. It allows you to mount filesystem images, such as ISO, CD images, and floppy disk images, on the hard disk. You can create a floppy disk or CD, complete with the filesystem and files, on your Linux filesystem without actually copying or burning it onto the media. A copy of the floppy or CD can be taken later. Loopback devices are also used for filesystem encryption.

How to Configure Removable Hardware

Procedure Reference: Configure USB Hardware

To configure USB hardware:

1. Verify that the kernel version of your system is 2.4 or above.
2. Verify that the /proc/bus/usb directory has been created.

 The /proc/bus/usb directory contains subdirectories with information about the USB devices connected to the system.

3. Install the drivers for the device.
4. Plug in the device.

Procedure Reference: Configure PCMCIA Hardware

To configure PCMCIA hardware:

1. Check to see if the PCMCIA module is compiled in the kernel.
2. Verify that the /etc/pcmcia/config.opts file has been created.
3. Install any necessary drivers for the device.
4. Plug in the device.
5. Configure the device by using the `cardmgr` utility.

DISCOVERY ACTIVITY 15-3

Discovering Removable Hardware

Scenario:

Your manager, Linda, is pleased with the ease and success of the Linux setup. She would like to expand the use of Linux to the business laptops and other desktops with removable devices. Check the use of removable hardware with Linux and report the results to your manager.

1. **Which of these statements are true? Select all that apply.**

   a) USB is an IEEE 1394-standard, high-speed serial bus.

   b) A loopback device allows you to mount filesystem images, such as ISO, on the hard disk.

   c) FireWire is ideal to connect a digital video camera to a system.

   d) PCMCIA was formerly known as PC card.

   e) The cardmgr utility is used to monitor and control the state of PCMCIA sockets.

2. **Which is the earliest kernel that supported USB?**

   a) 2.2.18

   b) 2.4.16

   c) 2.6.22

   d) 2.2.13

3. **True or False? USB device information is located in the /proc/usb directory.**

   ___ True

   ___ False

TOPIC D
Configure Mass Storage Devices

You added removable hardware to the Linux system. As a Linux administrator, you may need to add storage devices that can store large volume of data. In this topic, you will configure mass storage devices.

In large organizations, the number of users accessing the file server increases steadily. Due to this overload, performance decreases and the server hangs. If the server shuts down abruptly because of some problem, systems crash and data is lost. If data is maintained using multiple mass storage hard disks, loss of data can be prevented.

Mass Storage Devices

Hard drives, or fixed disks, are a type of storage devices that provide fast access to large amounts of data in a small, reasonably reliable, physical package.

Device	Description
Zip	Portable storage device that precedes the flash drive.
Flash drive	Portable storage device that offers the same advantages as a CD-ROM.
Optical disc	CD-RW is a re-writeable compact disc (CD) format that allows repeated recording.
	DVD-R is a recordable DVD format that can record data once, where it becomes permanent on the disc.
	DVD-RW is a re-recordable DVD format, where data can be erased and recorded numerous times.

ATAPI

AT Attachment Packet Interface (ATAPI) is a protocol for controlling mass storage devices. ATAPI provides commands that are used for hard disks, CD-ROM drives, tape drives, and other devices.

RAID

Definition:

Redundant Array of Independent Disks (RAID) is a method that is used to store the same data in different locations on multiple hard disks of a server or a standalone disk storage system. Disk arrays are made fault tolerant by implementing RAID. Enabling RAID on hard disks increases their performance and reliability. RAID uses data striping and disk mirroring techniques to prevent loss of data due to hard disk crash. It breaks data into equal sized chunks and then each chunk is written onto the hard disk based on the RAID level. RAID can be implemented either by the operating system or by the RAID disk controller card.

 RAID is also referred to as Redundant Array of Inexpensive Disks.

Example:

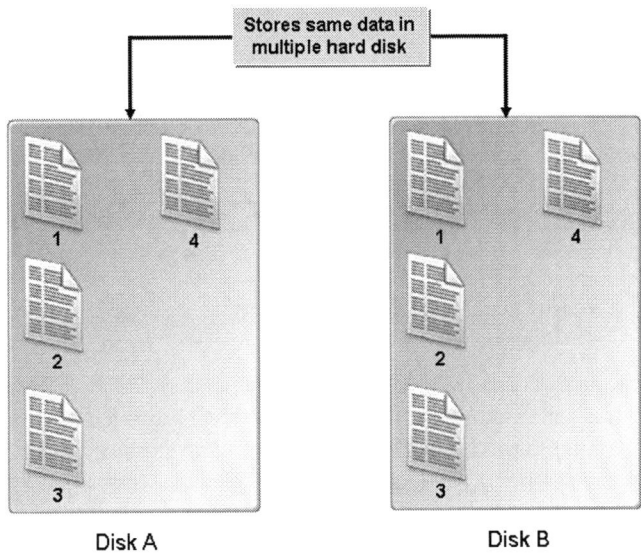

Stores same data in multiple hard disk

Disk A   Disk B

Figure 15-4: Same data stored on two hard disks using RAID.

RAID Levels

RAID can be implemented in different levels based on system requirements. Frequently used RAID levels are 0, 1, and 5.

RAID Level	Description
RAID 0	RAID 0 is commonly referred to as Data Striping. RAID 0 stores data across multiple devices by avoiding data redundancy. The operating system that implements RAID 0 will consider multiple disks as a single device. The advantage of RAID 0 is an increase in data access speed. It is suggested that when implementing RAID 0, the disks be of equal size. The disadvantage of RAID 0 is that if any hard disk crashes, then the entire data is lost.
RAID 1	RAID 1 is commonly referred to as Disk Mirroring. RAID 1 stores copies of the same data on multiple disks. The server has to write the same data onto more than one disk, which can saturate data buses and CPU utilization. RAID 1 leads to data redundancy and does not speed up data access.

RAID Level	Description
RAID 5	RAID 5 is an improved level of RAID 4. RAID 5 stripes the parity data among all disks in the RAID set. The advantages of RAID 5 are many. This speeds up multiple small writes. Multiple small reads are faster, because data resides on all drives in the array. It is possible to get all drives involved in the read operation. RAID 5 is the most commonly used RAID level.

 There are other RAID levels such as RAID 2, 3, 4, and 6. Disk tolerance increases with increase in the RAID level, and so does disk requirement.

Software RAID

Definition:

Software RAID is RAID implemented using software that is applied to the kernel disk code. It depends on the performance and the load of the server's processor. Software RAID is inexpensive because it works even with less expensive disks, such as IDE and SCSI. In addition, software RAID has higher fault tolerance levels that enable you to diagnose and fix problems on the system easily. Software RAID offers features such as kernel-based configuration, threaded OS rebuild, portable arrays among Linux machines without reconstruction, array reconstruction using idle system resources, automatic CPU detection, and hot-swappable drive support.

 When software RAID features are upgraded, they can be implemented on the system without any hardware upgrade.

Example:

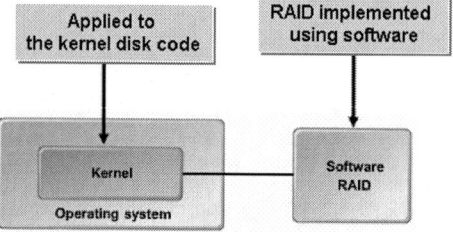

Figure 15-5: Implementation of software RAID.

Hardware vs. Software RAID

Hardware RAID system is implemented using a disk controller card. The hard disks that are connected to the RAID disk controller are configured as part of a RAID array. The disk controller will hide the array of disks and present it as a single logical storage unit or drive to the system. The operating system will not be able to identify the difference in the hardware.

Software RAID is an inexpensive way of implementing RAID. It is applied to the kernel disk code, and can be implemented on all types of hard disks. The software-based array is dependent on server CPU performance and load.

The mdadm Tool

The mdadm tool is used to manage RAID devices. This tool is used to create, remove, and monitor the RAID devices. It operates in multiple modes such as build, create, assemble, monitor, and manage.

 The mdadm tool is otherwise called the multiple disk administration tool.

The mdadm tool has various options. Some of them are listed below.

Option	Used To
-A	Assemble components of a previously created array.
-B	Build an array without superblocks.
-C	Create a RAID array.
-F	Switch to the monitor mode to track arrays.
-G	Increase or decrease the size or shape of an active array.
-h	Print help options.

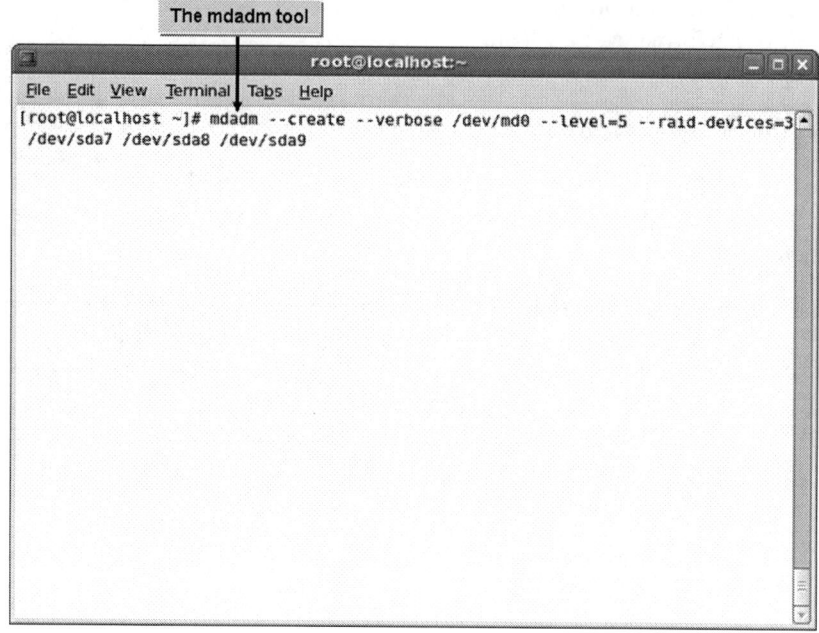

Figure 15-6: Creating a RAID device with the mdadm tool.

Syntax

The syntax of the `mdadm` tool is `mdadm {mode} {raid device} [options] {component devices}`.

mdadm Operation Modes

There are several modes of operation for the `mdadm` utility.

Mode	Function
Create	Creates and configures a new array.
Assemble	Starts and activates an existing array.
Manage	Adds or removes disks in an active array or marks a disk as failed.
Follow or monitor	Configures `mdadm` to send alerts when there are array errors or disk failures, and allows sharing of spare disks.
Build	Builds a legacy array without superblocks.
Misc	Performs any other operation on arrays, from getting information about devices to removing old superblocks and stopping active arrays.

How to Configure Mass Storage Devices

Procedure Reference: Configure Software RAID

To configure software RAID:

1. Log in as root in the CLI.

2. Enter `rpm -qi mdadm` to make sure that the RAID package is installed.

3. Create a software RAID.

    a. Create a RAID 0 array.

    - Enter `mdadm --create --verbose /dev/md{device number} --level=0 --raid-devices=2 /dev/{device name}{device number} /dev/{device name}{device number}` to create a RAID 0 array.

    - Or, enter `mdadm -Cv /dev/md{device number} -l0 -n2 /dev/{device name}{device number} /dev/{device name}{device number}`.

    b. Create a RAID 1 array.

    - Enter `mdadm --create --verbose /dev/md{device number} --level=1 --raid-devices=2 /dev/{device name}{device number} /dev/{device name}{device number}` to create a RAID 1 array.

    c. Create a RAID 5 array.

    - Enter `mdadm --create --verbose /dev/md{device number} --level=5 --raid-devices=3 /dev/{device name}{device number} /dev/{device name}{device number} /dev/{device name}{device number}` to create a RAID 5 array.

    - Or, enter `mdadm -Cv /dev/md{device number} -l5 -n3 /dev/{device name}{device number} /dev/{device name}{device number} /dev/{device name}{device number}`.

4. Enter `mdadm --detail --scan > /etc/mdadm.conf` to create the RAID configuration file with RAID array information.

5. Enter `vi /etc/mdadm.conf` to open the /etc/mdadm.conf file and specify device information.

6. Enter `mkfs -t {filesystem type} /dev/md{device number}` to create a filesystem on the RAID disk.

7. Create a mount point and mount the RAID disk.

8. Enter `cat /proc/mdstat` to verify that the RAID disk has been created.

9. Enter `mdadm -S /dev/md{device number}` to stop or deactivate the RAID service.

10. Enter `mdadm -AS /dev/md{device number}` to start or activate the RAID service.

11. Enter `mdadm -E /dev/{device name}{device number}` to examine device name information.

ACTIVITY 15-4
Configuring RAID Level 5

Before You Begin:

1. On srvA, you logged in as root in the CLI.

2. The first terminal is displayed.

3. Enter `cd /root` to change to the root directory.

Scenario:

You allocated 3 GB memory on your system to store sensitive transaction details. You want to effectively use the space and build fault tolerance in the hard disk so that you can recover data if the hard disk crashes.

What You Do	How You Do It
1. Create three logical partitions in the hard disk.	a. Enter **fdisk /dev/sdb** to invoke the `fdisk` utility for the /dev/sdb device.
	b. Enter **n** to create a new partition.
	c. Press **Enter** to accept the default first cylinder size.
	d. Enter **+1024M** to set the partition size.
	e. Enter **t** to change the partition type.
	f. Enter **7** to set the partition number.
	g. At the **Hex code (type L to list codes):** prompt, enter **fd** to change the partition from type 83 (Linux partition) to type fd (Linux raid auto).
	h. Create two logical partitions with size 1 GB each and type **fd**
	i. Enter **w** to write the changes onto the partition table.
	j. Enter **reboot** to reboot the system.
	k. Enter **ourglobalcompany** as the passphrase for starting the httpd server.
	l. Switch to the first terminal of the CLI and log in as **root.**

2. Create the software RAID 5.

   a. Enter **rpm -qa | grep mdadm** to check if the **mdadm** package is installed on your system.

   b. Observe that the mdadm package is listed with the version and release number indicating that it is installed.

   c. Enter **mdadm⇒ --create --verbose /dev/md0⇒ --level=5 --raid-devices=3⇒ /dev/sdb7 /dev/sdb8 /dev/sdb9** to create a RAID 5 array.

   d. If necessary, at the prompt, enter **y** to continue creating the array.

   e. Observe that the details about RAID are displayed and the array /dev/md0 is started. Press **Enter** to continue.

   f. Enter **mdadm --detail --scan > /etc/mdadm.conf** to create the RAID configuration file /etc/mdadm.conf with the RAID array information.

3. Specify the device information in the mdadm.conf file.

   a. Enter **vi /etc/mdadm.conf** to open the /etc/mdadm.conf file.

   b. On a new line, type **DEVICE /dev/sdb7 /dev/sdb8 /dev/sdb9** to specify the device information.

   c. Press **Esc** to exit the command mode.

   d. Save and close the file.

   e. Enter **clear** to clear the terminal screen.

4. Create a filesystem on the RAID device and mount the RAID device on a mount point called /raid.

   a. Enter **mkfs.ext3 /dev/md0** to create an ext3 filesystem on the RAID device /dev/md0.

   b. Observe that the inode tables are written and the journal is created.

   c. Enter **mkdir /raid** to create a mount point for RAID in the /raid directory.

   d. Enter **mount /dev/md0 /raid** to mount the RAID device /dev/md0 on the/raid mount point.

5. Check whether a new RAID device is created.

   a. Enter `cat /proc/mdstat` to verify that the RAID device has been created.

   b. Observe that the list of active RAID devices is displayed.

   c. Enter `clear` to clear the terminal screen.

DISCOVERY ACTIVITY 15-5

Configuring Mass Storage Devices

Scenario:

Your company has recently changed all the system-critical servers to Linux and your manager, Mike, wants you to back up data. He would like you to check the setup of a mass storage device with redundancy.

1. **Which file contains information on setting up your RAID arrays?**

    a) /etc/raid/raidtab

    b) /etc/mdadm.conf

    c) /etc/raid/raidtab.conf

2. **True or False? RAID is a method that is used to store the same data across multiple hard disks to provide improved performance and data security.**

    ___ True

    ___ False

3. **Which of these devices are mass storage devices? Select all that apply.**

    a) CD-RW drive

    b) Floppy disk drive

    c) DVD-RW drive

    d) Hard drive

TOPIC E

Manage Logical Volumes Using the Logical Volume Manager

You added new storage devices to store huge amounts of data on the Linux system. Now, you want to manage the storage area when the system runs out of space. In this topic, you will manage disk space with the help of the logical volume manager.

Consider a scenario where you are downloading source files from a website, to install new software. While downloading, an error is displayed stating that there is insufficient memory in your home directory. You want to increase the storage space, without disrupting the download. To manage the current situation, you decide to move the memory allocated to the swap filesystem to the home directory. Learning about LVM will enable you to accomplish this task.

LVM

Definition:

Logical Volume Manager (LVM) is a software tool that is used to manage disk storage on a computer system. LVM creates an abstraction layer over the storage area on the system so that details about where data is stored are hidden. It hides the storage details by completely separating the hardware storage from the software management, so that any changes made to the hardware do not affect the software during runtime. The volume manager organizes hard disks into volume groups and the partitions in the storage area are referred to as the *Logical Volumes (LV)*.

Example:

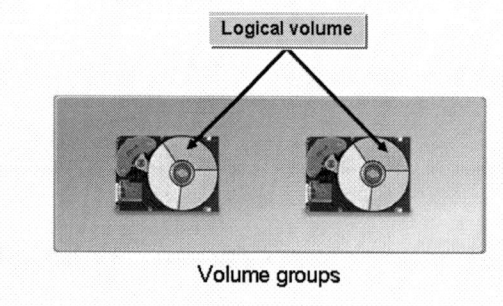

Figure 15-7: Logical volumes on a hard disk.

LVM Components

LVM comprises five main components.

Component	Description
Volume Group (VG)	VG component is the highest level of abstraction in LVM. The physical drives or hard disks are organized into VGs. The partition type of the disk or partition should be set to Linux LVM.
Physical Volume (PV)	PV is a physical medium with additional data that is used for administrative purposes. The `pvcreate` command is used to create a VG that contains one or more PVs.
Physical Extents (PEs)	Each physical volume is divided into blocks of data referred to as PEs. The size of PEs is the same as the size of logical extents for the volume group. PE is the smallest unit that can be addressed by LVM on physical storage.
Logical Volumes (LVs)	Actual data is stored in the logical volume. LV is referred to as a standard block device. It contains a filesystem, which is set using the `mkfs` command. For example, /home, /var.
Logical Extents (LEs)	Each logical volume is divided into blocks of data referred to as LEs. The size of LEs is the same for all logical volumes in the volume group.

LVM Architecture

In a storage drive, each PV is divided into equal sized PEs. Each PE is given a number, which is unique within the PV. In each PV, metadata information is stored in an area known as *Volume Group Descriptor Area (VGDA)*. VGDA includes a PV description, a VG description, an LV description, and several PE descriptions, which are stored at the beginning of each PV. Each LV is divided into LEs. LEs are of the same size as the PEs of that VG. Every LE is mapped to one PE on a PV.

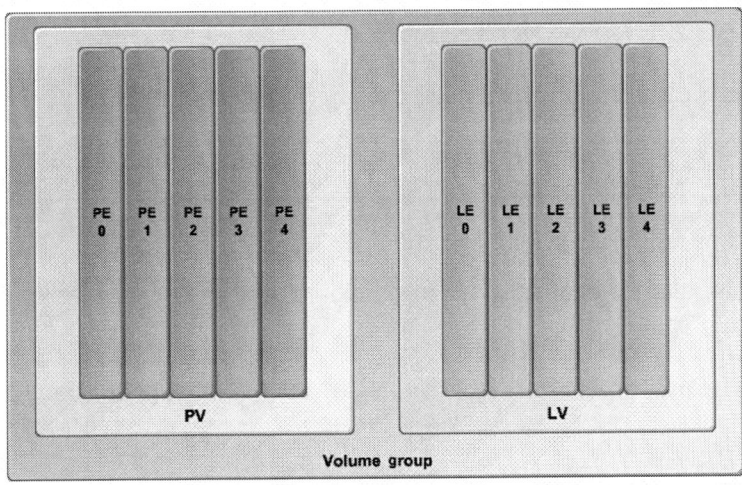

Figure 15-8: A volume group showing LVM architecture

LVM Management Tools

LVM contains a number of tools that perform a variety of functions.

The most frequently used LVM tools are listed in the following table.

Tool	Used To
lvcreate	Create an LV.
lvdisplay	Display information about an LV.
lvextend	Add space to an LV.
lvreduce	Reduce the size of an LV.
lvremove	Remove LVs from the system.
lvscan	List all LVs in all VGs.
pvcreate	Initialize PVs for use by LVM.
pvdisplay	Display various attributes of PVs.
pvmove	Move extents from one PV to another.
pvscan	List all PVs.
vgcreate	Create a VG.
vgdisplay	Display VG information.
vgextend	Add PVs to a VG.
vgreduce	Remove a PV from a VG.
vgremove	Remove a VG.
vgscan	Search for all VGs.
resize2fs	Resize ext2/ext3 filesystems.
vgcreate	Create a VG.
vgdisplay	Display VG information.
vgextend	Add PVs to a VG.
vgreduce	Remove a PV from a VG.
vgremove	Remove a VG.
vgscan	Search for all VGs.
resize2fs	Resize ext2/ext3 filesystems.

Syntax

The syntax for using the LVM tools is: *{Tool name} {disk partition}*.

LVM Snapshots

In the event of a system crash, LVM snapshots can be used to recover filesystems. LVM snap-shots are similar to copies of LVs. A user can create multiple copies of LVs in the form of block devices. LVs store the changes that are made to filesystems, instead of storing the entire filesystems. They can be created using the `lvcreate` tool.

Snapshot Volumes

A snapshot volume is a volume containing a record of data that was present in the volume at the time the snapshot was taken. Snapshot volumes enable you to take backups of the filesystem even when the filesystem is running and changes are being made to it. These may be mounted as an LV, to track changes that have been made to the filesystem because the snapshot volume was created.

How to Manage Logical Volumes Using the Logical Volume Manager

Procedure Reference: Create Logical Volume Using the Logical Volume Manager

To create logical volumes using the logical volume manager:

1. Log in as root in the CLI.
2. Enter `fdisk /dev/{device name}{device number}`.
3. Create a partition with type LVM.
   a. Type `n` and press **Enter.**
   b. Type `p` and press **Enter.**
   c. Type `1` and press **Enter.**
   d. Press **Enter** two times.
   e. Type `t` and press **Enter.**
   f. Type `8e` and press **Enter.**
   g. Type `w` and press **Enter.**
   h. Enter `partprobe` to update the partition table.
   i. Enter `vgscan` to enable LVM to locate partitions of type Linux LVM.
   j. Enter `pvcreate /dev/{device name}{device number}` to create physical volumes on each hard disk.

 You must create physical volumes on each hard disk that contains the Linux LVM partition. This is because a physical volume cannot span more than one hard disk.

   k. Enter `vgcreate {volume group name} /dev/{device name}{device number 1} .... /dev/{device name}{device number n}` vgcreate `{volume group name} /dev/{device` name}{device number 1} .... /dev/{device name}{device number n} to create volume groups by merging the physical volumes.

l. Enter lvcreate -L {size of logical volume} {volume group name} -n {logical volume name} to create logical volumes in the volume groups you created.

m. Enter reboot to reboot the system.

n. Enter mkfs -t {filesystem type} /dev/{volume group name}/{logical volume name} to assign a filesystem to the logical volumes you created.

Procedure Reference: Resize Logical Volume Using LVM Tools

To resize logical volumes using LVM tools:

1. Log in as root.

2. Enter pvcreate /dev/{device name}{device number} to create a physical volume.

3. Enter vgextend {volume group name} /dev/{device name}{device number} to add the partition to the existing volume group.

4. Enter lvextend -L +{size} /dev/{volume group name}/{logical volume name} to extend the filesystem.

5. Enter resize2fs /dev/{volume group name}/{logical volume name} to resize the filesystem.

6. View the changes you have made.

   - Enter vgdisplay to view volume group information.

   - Enter pvdisplay to view physical volume information.

   - Enter lvdisplay to view logical volume information.

Procedure Reference: Manage LVM Snapshots

To manage LVM snapshots:

1. Log in as root.

2. Enter lvcreate -L {size} -s {snapshot volume name} /dev/{volume group name}/{logical volume name} to create a snapshot of the volume.

3. Enter mount /dev/{volume group name}/{snapshot volume name} {mount point} to mount the snapshot volume.

4. Remove the snapshot volume.

   a. Enter umount {mount point} to unmount the snapshot volume.

   b. Enter lvremove /dev/{volume group name}/{snapshot volume name} to remove the snapshot volume.

ACTIVITY 15-6
Managing Disk Space Using LVM

Before You Begin:

1. On srvA, you have logged in as root in the CLI.

2. The first terminal is displayed.

Scenario:

While planning to set up a file server in your organization, you decide to allocate disk space according to the following requirements:

- Development team-1 GB

- Marketing team-1 GB

- Hardware team-1 GB

You have been provided with a hard disk that has a capacity of 80 GB.

What You Do	How You Do It
1. Create three logical partitions on the hard disk.	**a.** Enter **fdisk /dev/sdb** to invoke the fdisk utility for the /dev/sdb device.
	b. Enter **n** to create a new partition.
	c. Press **Enter** to accept the default first cylinder size.
	d. Enter **+1024M** to set the partition size.
	e. Enter **t** to change the partition type.
	f. Enter **10** to set it as the partition number.
	g. At the **Hex code (type L to list codes):** prompt, enter **8e** to change the partition from type 83 to type 8e.
	h. Observe that the system type of partition 10 is changed to **8e (Linux LVM).**
	i. Enter **w** to write the changes onto the partition table.
	j. Observe that the system displays a message that indicates that the new partition table will be applied only on rebooting the system.
	k. Create two logical partitions of size 1 GB each and partition type **8e**
	l. Enter **reboot** to reboot the system.
2. Create physical volumes on the LVM partitions.	**a.** Press **Ctrl+Alt+F1** to switch to the CLI.
	b. Log in as **root** in the CLI.
	c. Enter **vgscan** to enable LVM to locate partitions of type Linux LVM.
	d. Enter **pvcreate /dev/sdb10 /dev/sdb11 /dev/sdb12** to create physical volumes for each hard disk on the LVM partitions.
	e. Observe that the system has created the three physical volumes.

3. Create logical volumes on the hard disk.

a. Enter **vgcreate Myvolume /dev/sdb10 /dev/sdb11 /dev/sdb12** to create a volume group named Myvolume on the /dev/sdb device.

b. Observe that the system has created the Myvolume volume group.

c. In the **Myvolume** volume group, enter **lvcreate -L 1024 Myvolume -n Development** to create a logical volume with a size of 1 GB for the development team.

d. Observe that the system has created a logical volume named Development.

e. Enter **lvcreate -L 1024 Myvolume -n Hardware** to create a logical volume with a size of 1 GB for Hardware.

f. Enter **lvcreate -L 1024 Myvolume -n Marketing** to create a logical volume with a size of 1 GB for Marketing.

g. Enter **mkfs -t ext3 /dev/Myvolume/Development** to assign the ext3 filesystem to the logical volumes you created.

h. Observe that the inode tables are written and the journal is created.

i. Enter **mkfs -t ext3 /dev/Myvolume/Hardware** to assign ext3 filesystem to the logical volumes you created.

j. Observe that the inode tables are written and the journal is created.

k. Enter **mkfs -t ext3 /dev/Myvolume/Marketing** to assign ext3 filesystem to the logical volumes you created.

l. Observe that the inode tables are written and the journal is created.

4. Create mount points for the LVM partitions.

    a. Enter `mkdir /Development` to create the Development directory.

    b. Enter `mount /dev/Myvolume/Development /Development` to mount the volume group on the /Development mount point.

    c. Create mount points for the **Hardware** and **Marketing** groups.

    d. Enter `mount /dev/Myvolume/Hardware /Hardware` to mount the volume group on the /Hardware mount point.

    e. Enter `mount /dev/Myvolume/Marketing /Marketing` to mount the volume group on the /Marketing mount point.

    f. Enter `mount` to verify that the volume groups are mounted.

    g. Observe that the volume groups have been mounted on the /Development, /Hardware, and /Marketing mount points.

    h. Enter `clear` to clear the terminal screen.

TOPIC F
Configure Disk Quotas

You managed disk space on the file server. You will also need to ensure that all users have access to disk space for storing individual files on the file server. In this topic, you will configure disk quotas.

One of the tasks that a system administrator must undertake is limiting disk space usage. Users may need to store files and data in a common location. By configuring disk quotas, you can ensure that all users have adequate storage space in that common location.

Disk Quotas

Definition:

A *disk quota* is the disk space that is allotted to a user for file storage on a computer. Disk quotas need to be configured for each user. Every filesystem for which disk quota has been implemented will have a default grace period of seven days. This means that when a user has reached the soft limit, the grace limit feature gets activated. The soft limit is the quota value beyond which disk space usage is allowed only during the grace period. Once the grace period expires, the soft limit will be enforced as the hard limit, or a maximum limit will be set on disk usage and users cannot exceed this limit.

Example:

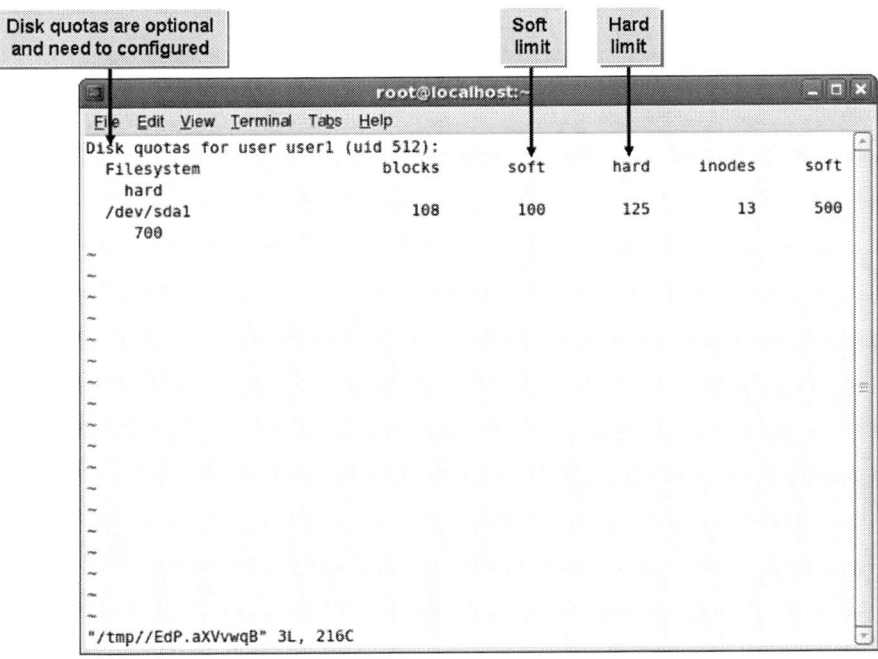

Figure 15-9: The disk quota for a user.

Quota Management Commands

Quota management is the effective allotment and monitoring of quotas for all users. Quotas should be assigned in such a way that users are able to maximize the utilization of disk resources without data overflow. Linux has various commands that help ease the job of quota management for the system administrator.

Command	Used To
edquota -u {user name}	Edit quotas for a specific user.
edquota -g {group name}	Edit quotas for a specific group.
setquota -u {user name}	Set quotas for a specific user.
setquota -g {group name}	Set quotas for a specific group.

Quota Reports

Quota reports are created by the system to view the usage of disk space by each user. These reports enable the system administrator to check which user is taking up maximum disk space. There are the two types of quota reports: user quota reports and group quota reports. A quota report contains the following details:

- The name of the user.
- The total number of blocks (in kilobytes) that have been utilized by the user on a partition.
- The *soft limit,* which is the maximum amount of disk usage that a quota user has on a partition.
- The *hard limit,* which is the absolute limit on disk usage that a quota user has on a partition.
- The *grace period,* which is the time limit before the soft limit is enforced for a filesystem with quota enabled.
- The total number of inodes that have been used on a partition by a user.
- The soft limits on inodes.
- The hard limits on inodes.

The quotacheck Command

The quotacheck command examines filesystems for which you enabled quotas, builds a table of current disk usage, and updates the aquota.user file. The quotacheck command has various options.

Option	Used To
-g	Create group quotas.
-u	Create user accounts.
-a	Specify all filesystems for which the usrquota mounting option is enabled.

Option	Used To
-b	Back up the quota file before writing new data.
-c	Perform a new scan.

Quota Reports Generation Commands

A number of commands are available for the generation of effective quota reports.

Command	Enables You To
repquota -a	Display the quota reports for all users.
repquota -u {filesystem name}	Display the quota report for a particular filesystem.
quota -uv {user name}	Display the quota report for a particular user.
warnquota -u {user name}	Check if a user is not exceeding the allotted quota limit.
warnquota -g {group name}	Check if a group is not exceeding the allotted quota limit.

How to Configure Disk Quotas
Procedure Reference: Set Disk Quota for a Filesystem

To set disk quota for a filesystem:

1. Log in as root in the CLI.
2. Specify user quota for the partition you want to allocate to users.
   a. Enter vi /etc/fstab.
   b. In the fourth field of the partition entry, change the default values.
      - Change defaults to defaults,usrquota to define user quota for the specified partition.
      - Change defaults to defaults,grpquota to define group quota for the specified partition.
      - Change defaults to defaults,usrquota,grpquota to define user and group quota for the specified partition.
   c. Save and close the file.
3. Enter mount -o remount {mount point} to remount the partition.
4. Enter quotacheck -c {Mount point of the partition} to scan for the disk usage and create a quota file.

Procedure Reference: Manage Quota Service on a System

To manage quota service on a system:

1. Log in as root in the CLI.

2. Manage the quota service on the system.

- Enter quotaon *[command option] {mount point}* to turn on the quota.
- Enter quotaoff *[command option] {mount point}* to turn off the quota.

Procedure Reference: Set Quota for Users

To set quotas for users:

1. Log in as root in the CLI.
2. Set quotas for users.
   - Use the edquota command to set user quota.
      a. Enter edquota *[command options] {user or group name}*.
      b. Specify the soft and hard limits for blocks and inodes.
      c. Save and close the file.
   - Enter setquota *[command option] {user or group name} {soft block limit} {hard block limit} {soft inode} {hard inode} [command option]* /dev/*{device name}{partition number}* to set quotas for users using the setquota command.

Procedure Reference: View Quota Reports

To view the quota report:

1. Log in as root in the CLI.
2. View the quota report.
   - Enter quota *[command option] {user or group name}* to display the quota report for the user or group.
   - Enter repquota *[command option] {mount point}* to display the quota report for the specified mount point.
   - Enter warnquota *[command option] {mount point}* to send the quota report as a mail message to the user as configured in /etc/warnquota.conf.

ACTIVITY 15-7
Configuring User Quota

Before You Begin:

1. On srvA, you have logged in as root in the CLI.

2. On the terminal, create a new user account named *user2*

3. Set *myp@$$w0rd* as the password for the user2 account.

4. Clear the terminal screen.

Scenario:

Your company has a common server that is used by all employees to store and share files within the company. You received complaints from users on the network about low disk space on the common server because some employees have excessive amounts of data on it. You decide to assign disk quotas to limit disk space usage for users according to the following details:

Space to be allocated to user1 and user2:

- Block soft limit=100

- Block hard limit=125

- Inode soft limit=500

- Inode hard limit=700

The quota has to be set for user1 and user2.

What You Do	How You Do It
1. Configure the user quota for the partition /.	a. On the terminal, enter **vi /etc/fstab** to open the /etc/fstab file.
	b. Press **I** to switch to the insert mode.
	c. On the line **LABEL=/ / ext3 defaults 1 1**, after the word "defaults," add ", usrquota" to set user quota for the / partition.
	d. Press **Esc** to switch to the command mode.
	e. Save and close the file.
	f. Enter **reboot** to restart the system.
	g. Enter *ourglobalcompany* as the passphrase for starting the httpd server.
	h. Log in as **root** in the GUI.
	i. Choose **Applications→Accessories→Terminal** to display the terminal window.
	j. Enter **quotacheck -cum /** to scan for the disk usage and to create a quota file.
2. Specify the disk space usage.	a. Enter **edquota -u user1** to edit the user1 quota.
	b. Press **I** to switch to the insert mode.
	c. Specify the hard and soft limit values for user1 as given in the scenario.
	d. Press **Esc.**
	e. Save and close the file.
	f. Specify disk space usage for user2 and save the file by following steps from (a) to (d).
	g. Enter **clear** to clear the terminal window.
	h. Enter **quotaon -u /** to apply the changes.
	i. Enter **clear** to clear the terminal window.

Lesson 15 Follow-up

In this lesson, you managed hardware associated with Linux machines. This will enable you to safely and efficiently replace, upgrade, manage, and troubleshoot hardware whenever the need arises.

1. **What are the benefits of implementing RAID on a network?**

2. **What are the advantages of assigning disk quotas? Why?**

16 | Troubleshooting Linux Systems

Lesson Time: 1 hour(s)

Lesson Objectives:

In this lesson, you will troubleshoot Linux system issues.

You will:

● Use the Linux rescue environment for troubleshooting the Linux system issues.

● Troubleshoot hardware.

● List the guidelines for troubleshooting network connection and security issues.

Introduction

While working with the Linux operating system, users may experience unexpected technical issues. To provide uninterrupted services to the users, you need to be able to solve the problems that arise while functioning. In this lesson, you will troubleshoot Linux-related issues.

As an administrator managing multiple systems on a network, you would have installed various services and packages required by users. However, when several users start using the system, there may be instances when the applications and services do not function as desired. As the administrator, you will be expected to determine and resolve the problems related to the system.

This lesson covers all or part of the following CompTIA Linux+ (2009) certification objectives:

● Topic A
  ■ Objective 1.10
  ■ Objective 5.2
● Topic B
  ■ Objective 1.10
● Topic C
  ■ Objective 3.5
  ■ Objective 4.5

TOPIC A
Troubleshoot System-Based Issues

You managed hardware devices that comprise a Linux system. While working with Linux, you may experience issues that may prevent you from using the system or its services. In this topic, you will troubleshoot system-based issues to recover the system.

As an administrator managing multiple systems on a network, you will experience various issues with the Linux operating system. Without proper identification and analysis, finding a solution will take lots of time and effort. Therefore, you must familiarize yourself with the procedures required to identify these issues and solve them efficiently.

Troubleshooting Strategies

A troubleshooting strategy is a plan of action for identifying the causes and resolving the effects of a system-related issue. There are various guidelines that need to be considered while troubleshooting.

Guideline	Description
Analyze the problem	Before attempting to troubleshoot an issue, try to identify the problem through its symptoms, such as error messages, and other available information such as log files and configuration files. Also, check if the relevant services are working properly.
Back up data	Before experimenting with issues in configuration files, log files, or any other important data, it is recommended to make a backup to avoid loss of information and further complication of the issues.
Eliminate possible causes	Observe whether the issue is related with the hardware, an application, a process, or any other service. Try to choose one or more symptoms and drill down to the root cause. Eliminating the root cause will rectify all the related issues.
Adopt fundamental problem-solving approaches	After identifying the underlying causes, try out fundamental methods of resolving the issue before proceeding to complicated problem solving procedures.

A Basic Troubleshooting Model

Some companies developed troubleshooting processes that are systematic and logical. Following these guidelines will help you find and correct problems on your network quickly and efficiently. One troubleshooting model divides the troubleshooting process into four steps:

1. Gather basic information.
2. Develop a plan of action.
3. Execute the plan and isolate the problem.
4. Document the solution.

Troubleshooting can be a difficult process. It is not likely that anyone can develop a complete and accurate approach to troubleshooting, because troubleshooting is often done through intuitive guesses based on experience.

The Linux Rescue Environment

The *Linux rescue environment* is a stand-alone Linux program for troubleshooting a corrupt Linux installation. It serves as an external environment through which errors in the Linux system can be fixed without the help of the existing installation files. The rescue environment mounts the standard Linux system directories in the /mnt/sysimage directory. These directories are mounted either in read-write mode or read-only mode, depending on the kinds of issues.

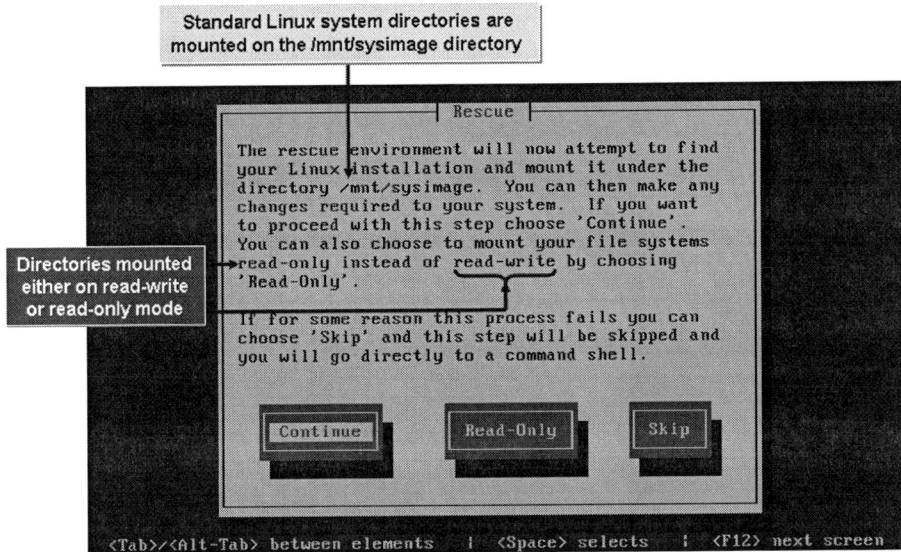

Figure 16-1: The rescue environment for troubleshooting Linux issues.

 In some cases, when system directories cannot be mounted on the /mnt/sysimage directory, the prompt will be available for troubleshooting.

The chroot Mode

The `chroot` mode shifts the /root directory to a different location for recovery. It is also known as jail mode because a user will not be able to access any other file or directory except this directory and its subdirectories.

Rescue Environment Utilities

A set of utilities is available in the rescue environment to troubleshoot different issues.

Category	*Utility*
Disk Maintenance Utilities	• LVM utilities such as `lvcreate`, `lvresize`, and `lvremove`. • Software RAID utility such as `mdadm`. • Disk partitioning and swap utilities such as `fdisk`, `sfdisk`, `mount`, `umount`, and `mkswap`. • Filesystem utilities such as `mkfs`, `tune2fs`, `fsck`, and `e2fsck`.
Networking Utilities	• Network debugging utilities such as `ifconfig`, `route`, `dig`, `netstat`, `traceroute`, `host`, and `hostname`. • Network connectivity utilities such as `ssh`, `ftp`, and `scp`.
Other Utilities	• Shell commands such as `chroot` and `bash`. • Process management tools such as `ps` and `kill`. • Editors such as `vi` and `nano`. • File management commands such as `cd`, `ls`, `cp`, `rm`, and `mv`. • Kernel management utility such as `sysctl`. • Package management tools such as `rpm` and `yum`. • Archiving and compression utilities such as `tar` and `gzip`.

Environment Configuration Problems

Configuration problems could prevent a user from logging in to the system and accessing the services provided by the server. Other problems could also be caused due to the system variables or due to user and group accounts. The symptoms, causes, and solutions for common configuration problems are provided in the following table.

Symptom	*Cause And Solution*
The user is unable to create a user or a group account.	**Cause:** The user does not have admin privileges; or the system is unable to allocate memory to the user account due to insufficient memory. **Solution:** Check whether the required privileges are granted to the user. Also, check for free space in the memory that can be allocated to the user account.

Symptom	Cause And Solution
The user is unable to log in.	**Cause:** The settings in the user account or the group account could be wrong.
	Solution: Check the user or group account settings, including the permission to log in to the system, the shell, and the path of the home directory.
The user is unable to access files and directories.	**Cause:** The required permission is not granted to the user.
	Solution: Check the user or group quota and the privileges granted to the user.
The user is unable to execute basic commands or applications.	**Cause:** The environmental variable is not properly set.
	Solution: Check the environmental variables and the library files of the application.
The scheduled jobs are not executed.	**Cause:** The `crond` daemon has not started or stopped due to the invalid configuration.
	Solution: Check whether the `crond` daemon is running. Otherwise, check whether the configuration set in the crontab file is correct.
The user is unable to switch between the runlevels.	**Cause:** The PATH variable is not set properly or permission is not granted to the user to switch between runlevels.
	Solution: Check whether the user is granted the necessary privileges required to change the runlevel or if the path of the sbin directory is set in the PATH variable.

Core System Variables

Core system variables affect the behavior of applications and commands. Some of the system variables and their functions are given in the following table.

Use This Variable	If You Need To Specify
HOSTNAME=*Hostname*	The hostname of the system.
SHELL=*Shell path*	The shell path for the system.
MAIL=*Mail path*	The path where mail will be stored.
HOME=*Home directory*	The home directory of the user.
PATH=*User path*	The path in which the user needs to operate.
HISTSIZE=*Number*	The number of entries to be stored in the history.
USER=*User name*	The name of the user.

The Single-User Mode

The single-user mode in Linux can be initialized by changing the runlevel to 1. It is used when the system does not allow you to log in after booting. The networking feature is disabled in the single-user mode, which makes it an ideal mode to troubleshoot network problems. It can even be used to recover the root password. Because most of the partitions are not mounted in runlevel 1, the single-user mode can be used for filesystem checks.

```
sh-3.2# passwd
Changing password for user root.
New UNIX password:
Retype new UNIX password:
type=1108 audit(1248939967.762:16): user pid=3699 uid=0 auid=4294967295 msg='PAM
: chauthtok acct="root" : exe="/usr/bin/passwd" (hostname=?, addr=?, terminal=co
nsole res=success)'
type=1108 audit(1248939967.763:17): user pid=3699 uid=0 auid=4294967295 msg='op=
change password id=0 exe="/usr/bin/passwd" (hostname=?, addr=?, terminal=console
 res=success)'
passwd: all authentication tokens updated successfully.
sh-3.2# _
```

Figure 16-2: Changing the root user password in the single-user mode.

Boot Disks

Definition:

A *boot disk* is a disk that contains the operating system files, such as init, klogd, and syslogd, to startup a system. It can be a hard disk, floppy disk, CD-ROM, DVD-ROM, or USB drive. The boot disk contains configuration files, startup files, and programs. The boot disk is used to boot a system following a hard disk crash. Some distributions use the first CD in the installation set as the boot disk. Other distributions allow you to create a floppy disk that can be used to boot the system.

Example:

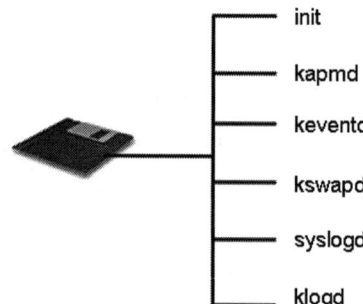

Figure 16-3: Contents of a boot disk.

Ramdisk

A ramdisk is a portion of memory that is allocated and used as a partition. The memory allocated as ramdisk is treated as a hard drive. Frequently accessed files can be placed in the ramdisk, which in turn will increase the performance of the system.

The ramdisk word Keyword

The `ramdisk word` keyword is a keyword that specifies the location of the root filesystem. The `ramdisk word` can be set and accessed using the `rdev` command.

The boot.iso File

The boot.iso file is an ISO–9660 image that is used to create bootable CD- or DVD-ROMs. This image file can be burned on to a CD-ROM, which can then be used for installing Linux, just like the original installation media itself. The boot speed of CD-ROMs is also an added advantage.

The diskboot.img File

The diskboot.img file is a VFAT filesystem image that is used to create bootable USB pen drives. Once the image is written onto the USB, it can then be used as a media for Linux installation. However, using a USB to boot a system depends on the BIOS settings. The diskboot.img image file should be written onto the USB using the dd command.

Root Disks

Definition:

A *root disk* is a disk that contains directories, such as etc, bin, home, and so on, which contain files required to run a Linux system. It need not contain a kernel or a bootloader. After the kernel is booted, the root disk can run a system without depending on any other disks.

Example:

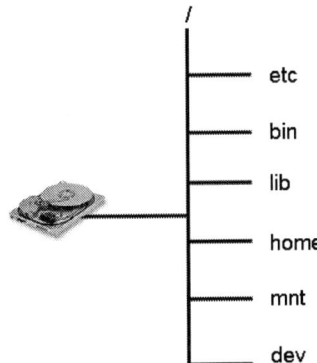

Figure 16-4: Various components of the root disk.

The Zero-Filled File

You need to create a filesystem that does not contain any data or partition tables to build a compressed root filesystem. To do this, you need to create a zero-filled file, partition, or ramdisk. The dd command can be used to create a zero-filled file or partition. This command erases data and partition tables, if any. It fills the specified number of blocks with zeros. By creating the zero-filled file or partition, you will be able to compress a filesystem to the maximum.

Bootloader Problems

If a user is unable to boot a system, it may be due to disk errors caused by the bootloader or hardware devices.

 RHEL5 does not support LILO.

Symptom	Cause And Solution
An error message "L" is displayed.	**Cause:** LILO is unable to load the /boot/boot.b file. **Solution:** Use the boot disk to boot the system and reinstall LILO.
An error message "LI" is displayed.	**Cause:** LILO is unable to locate the /boot/boot.b file or it could be any disk error. **Solution:** Log in to the rescue mode and reinstall LILO.
An error message "LIL" is displayed.	**Cause:** LILO is unable to locate the /boot/map file. **Solution:** Log in to the rescue mode and reinstall LILO.
An error message "LILO" is displayed with scrolling zeros and ones.	**Cause:** The hard disk is not supported by BIOS. **Solution:** Update BIOS or change the motherboard or the hard disk.
The Kernel Panic message is displayed.	**Cause:** The filesystem is corrupted or inaccessible. **Solution:** Log in to the rescue mode and perform the integrity check on the filesystem.

How to Troubleshoot Linux-Based Issues
Procedure Reference: Analyze the Problem by Gathering Data

To analyze the problem by gathering data:

1. Log in as root in the CLI.

2. Gather data about the issue using appropriate commands and files.

    ● Enter `history` to analyze the history of commands run by the user.

    ● Enter `grep {keyword} {log file name}` to find the specified keyword in the log file while troubleshooting.

    ● Enter `diff {current file} {backed up file}` to view if there are any changes in the file compared with the last backed up state.

    ● Enter `find {location of the directory to search} -cmin -{time in minutes}` to find all files that have been modified within a specified timing.

    ● Enter `strace {command}` to collect more information when the specified command is run.

    ● Enter `tail -f {log file name}` to view the log file as and when it is updated.

    ● Configure system logs to log all debug messages.

       a. Enter `vi /etc/syslog.conf` to open the system log configuration file.

       b. Type `{Facility} {Level of severity} {File where the log messages will get stored}` to set the type and level of severity to be logged in the specified file.

       c. Save and exit.

       d. Enter `service syslog restart` to restart the system log service and apply the changes.

Troubleshooting the Boot Process

Cause	Solution
If the bootloader screen does not appear, then GRUB may not be properly configured.	Configure the /boot/grub/grub.conf in the rescue mode.
If the **grub>** prompt appears, then GRUB may be corrupted.	Install GRUB again in the rescue mode.
If the kernel does not load, then the kernel image may be corrupted.	Install a new kernel in the rescue mode.
If the kernel does not load, then the parameter passed during the system start up may be wrong.	Specify the correct parameter by editing GRUB in the bootloader screen.
If there is a kernel panic, then: 1. The bootloader may have been misconfigured. 2. The /etc/inittab file is misconfigured. 3. Or, the root filesystem is misconfigured.	1. In the rescue mode, configure the bootloader configuration. 2. In the rescue mode, define the parameters in the /etc/inittab file correctly. 3. In the rescue mode, run a filesystem check on the filesystem.
If the kernel loads, but /etc/rc.d causes an issue, then the /etc/fstab file may have an error.	In the rescue mode, fix the /etc/fstab file.
If the kernel loads, but /etc/rc.d causes an issue, then the `fsck` utility may have failed.	In the rescue mode, run the `fsck` command manually.

Cause	Solution
If the services do not start correctly, then they may not have been configured properly.	Configure the services properly.

Procedure Reference: Use the Linux Rescue Environment

To use the Linux rescue environment:

1. Modify the BIOS settings to boot from the recovery disc.
2. Insert the first Red Hat installation CD into the CD-ROM drive and boot the system.
3. At the boot prompt, enter `linux rescue` to enter the rescue mode.
4. If necessary, specify settings necessary to access the installation files.
   a. Specify the language and keyboard settings.
   b. On the **Setup Networking** page, select **Yes.**
   c. On the **Network Configuration** page, specify the networking parameters or **eth0** and then select **OK.**
5. A message is displayed, stating that the root partition will be mounted in the **/mnt/sysimage** directory. Select **Continue** to mount the filesystem with read and write permissions.
6. Select **OK** to continue with the boot process.
7. The root directory is now mounted on the ramdisk. Enter `chroot /mnt/sysimage` to change the root directory to the one mounted in the **/mnt/sysimage** directory.
8. Troubleshoot to find the cause of system failure and make the necessary changes to recover the system. For example, if the system failed to boot due to inaccuracies in the LILO configuration file, modify the file and then reinstall LILO.
9. Enter `exit` to exit the chroot environment.
10. Enter `sync` so that the changes you made are reflected in the filesystem on the hard disk.
11. Enter `exit` to exit from the rescue mode. The system will now reboot.

ACTIVITY 16-1
Troubleshooting GRUB

Before You Begin:
1. On srvB, you have logged in as root in the CLI.
2. At the command line, enter `cd /boot/grub` to open the GRUB directory.
3. Enter `cp grub.conf grub1.conf` to back up the existing GRUB configuration file.
4. Enter `vi grub.conf` to open the current GRUB configuration file.
5. Comment all the lines.
6. Save and close the file.
7. Enter `reboot` to apply the settings.

Scenario:
Your system boots with the **grub** prompt rather than booting from the GUI prompt. Even after reboot, the situation remains the same. This indicates that there is an issue with the GRUB configuration. You require the system to boot through the GUI.

What You Do	How You Do It
1. Correct the GRUB settings.	a. At the **grub** prompt, enter *root*
	b. Enter **cat /grub/grub.conf** to view the current bootloader settings.
	c. Make a note of the kernel and module settings and press **Enter** to return to the **grub** prompt.
	d. Enter **clear** to clear the terminal screen.
	e. Enter **kernel /vmlinuz-2.6.18-128.el5 ro root= LABEL=/ rhgb quiet**
	f. Enter **initrd /boot/initrd-2.6.18-128.el5.img**
	g. At the **grub** prompt, enter **boot** to reboot the system.

2. Check the corrected grub.conf file to ensure that the settings are correct.

    a. Press **Ctrl+Alt+F1** to switch to the CLI.

    b. Log in as **root** in the CLI.

    c. Enter `cd /boot/grub/` to navigate to the grub directory.

    d. Enter `rm grub.conf` to delete the current GRUB configuration file.

    e. Enter `y` to confirm the remove action.

    f. Enter `mv grub1.conf grub.conf` to replace the correct GRUB configuration file.

    g. Enter `cat grub.conf` to view the current grub.conf file.

    h. Enter `clear` to clear the terminal screen.

ACTIVITY 16-2
Troubleshooting Partitions

Before You Begin:
1. On srvB, you have logged in as root in the CLI.
2. Enter `cd /root` to change to the root directory.
3. Enter `e2label /dev/sda2 /boo` to change the filesystem label.
4. Enter `reboot` to apply the settings.

Scenario:
A new employee, Jim, accidentally manipulated some files. When he tried booting the machine, he gets the error message "Checking filesystems. fsck.ext3: Unable to resolve 'LABEL=/boo'."

What You Do	How You Do It
1. Troubleshoot the partition label issue.	a. At the command prompt, enter the root password.
	b. At the **Repair filesystem** prompt, enter `cat /etc/fstab` to view label entries of all partitions.
	c. Enter `fdisk -1` to view the boot device information.
	d. Observe that the boot device partition is **/sda1.**
	e. Enter `e2label /dev/sda1` to check if the label name is the same as that in the /etc/fstab file.
	f. Observe that the boot directory information is specified as **/boo** instead of **/boot.**
	g. Enter `e2label /dev/hda1 /boot` to rectify the mistake in labeling.
	h. Press **Ctrl+D** to reboot the system.
2. Check whether the system recovered.	a. Verify that the system reboots and the GUI login screen is displayed.
	b. Log in as **root** in the GUI.

ACTIVITY 16-3

Troubleshooting Runlevels

Before You Begin:

1. On srvB, you logged have logged in as root in the GUI.

2. Switch to the CLI terminal.

3. Log in as root in the CLI.

4. Enter `vi /etc/inittab` to access the inittab file containing runlevel information.

5. Comment the line that starts with "si::sysinit:/etc/rc.d/rc.sysinit."

6. Save and close the file.

7. Enter `reboot` to apply the settings.

Scenario:

You are requested to troubleshoot a system that is unable to boot and throws an error message, "/etc/rc5.d/S00microcode_ctl: microcode device /dev/cpu microcode does not exist." You identify that there is a system initialization error with the rc.d settings.

What You Do	How You Do It
1. Troubleshoot runlevels using the RHEL boot CD-ROM.	a. Insert the RHEL 5 Rescue CD in the CD/DVD drive and reboot the system.
	b. At the **boot** prompt, enter **linux rescue** to switch to the Linux rescue mode.
2. Select the language and keyboard configuration options.	a. On the **Choose a Language** page, in the **Language Selection** list box, verify that the **English** option is selected and select **OK**.
	b. On the **Keyboard Type** page, in the **Keyboard** section, verify that the **us** option is selected and select **OK**.

3. Configure network settings and enter the rescue mode.

a. In the **Setup Networking** message box, select **Yes.**

b. In the **Configure Network Interface** message box, select **Yes** to configure the eth0 network interface on the system.

c. On the **Network Configuration for eth0** page, select the **Enable IPv4 support** option.

d. On the **IPv4 Configuration for eth0** page, select the **Manual address configuration** option.

e. In the **IP Address** text box, type the IP address of your system.

f. In the **Prefix (Netmask)** text box, type *255.255.255.0* and click **OK.**

g. On the **Miscellaneous Network Settings** page, press **F12** to move to the next page.

h. On the **Error With Data** page, select **Continue** to ignore the error.

i. On the **Error With Data** page, select **Continue** to ignore the error.

j. On the **Rescue** page, select **Continue.**

k. On the **Rescue** page, select **OK.**

4. Troubleshoot inittab settings.

a. At the **sh** prompt, enter `chroot /mnt/sysimage` to mount the rescue environment files.

b. Enter `vi /etc/inittab` to go to the inittab file.

c. Enter */#si* to go to the sysinit line.

d. Press **I** to switch to the insert mode.

e. Observe that the cursor is at the beginning of the line **# si::sysinit:/etc/rc.d/rc.sysinit.**

f. Delete the # symbol at the beginning of the line to remove the comment declaration.

g. Press **Esc** to exit to the command mode.

h. Save and close the file.

 Eject the rescue CD manually from the CD-RW drive before rebooting the system.

i. Enter `exit` to exit the chroot environment.

j. Enter `reboot` to reboot the system.

k. Observe that the system boots correctly and the login prompt is displayed.

l. Log in as **root** in the GUI.

TOPIC B
Troubleshoot Hardware Issues

You rectified system-based issues in a Linux system. Hardware devices may get corrupted and may not work properly. In this topic, you will troubleshoot hardware issues.

Systems may be connected to external devices such as speakers or modems. Sometimes, these devices may not work properly. Finding the cause of the problem will help you solve hardware issues.

Troubleshooting Tools

There are many troubleshooting tools that you can use, depending on the type of problem you are facing and the environment in which you are working. Some of these tools are described in the following table.

Tool	Description
dmesg	A system administration command that is used to examine and control the kernel initialization process. It is used to print messages about the status of various hardware devices on the system during kernel initialization. Status messages can also be accessed from the /var/log/dmesg file.
/dev	A file that is used to create a boot or recoverable disk.
GNU Parted	A program that allows you to create, destroy, resize, move, and copy hard disk partitions.
HardDrake	A service that provides hardware detection in a graphical interface.
KNOPPIX	A bootable CD (or DVD) that contains GNU/Linux software, which includes automatic hardware detection and support. KNOPPIX can be used as a rescue system.
ifconfig	A file that is used to view the IP address and subnet mask and verify that they are allocated. It can also be used to debug or tune a system.
/proc	The proc filesystem is a pseudo-filesystem that is used as an interface to the kernel data structures. Each process contains a subdirectory in the /proc directory.

LNX-BBC

LNX-BBC is a Linux distribution that is small enough to fit in a CD-ROM, which is the size and shape of a business card. LNX-BBCs can be used to rescue damaged machines or as a temporary Linux workstation. More information regarding LNX-BBC can be found at **http://www.lnx-bbc.org.**

Starting and Stopping Processes to Locate and Correct Problems

As discussed earlier in the course, both services and processes can be stopped and restarted. This can sometimes be used to fix problems. You can use the ps command along with the grep command to locate processes that you need to check on. You can then kill the processes if necessary.

The `pgrep` command is used to look up or signal processes based on their names or other attributes. It looks through the currently running processes and lists PIDs that match the criteria you specify. For instance, the `pgrep -u root sshd` command lists only processes called sshd and that are owned by the `root` user. The command `pgrep -u root,daemon` lists all processes owned by root or daemon.

The `pkill` command can be used in conjunction with the `pgrep` command to stop processes. Starting and stopping processes is just one more way to troubleshoot problems. When you see a certain symptom, such as a process taking too long, you should first check on the process using the `ps` or `pgrep` command; then if necessary, end the process using the `kill` or `pkill` command. Then, you should examine the process (the script or other command sequences associated with that process) and check for any problems. After fixing the problems, you should try running the command or script again. Check on it periodically to see if it is working properly.

Hardware Problems

Hardware devices may experience failures anytime while the system is being used.

Symptom	Cause And Solution
The user is unable to hear from the speakers.	**Cause:** The speaker or the sound card is not functioning properly.
	Solution: Check the speaker and its corresponding driver. If you still have a problem, then you need to check the sound card.
The modem is unable to dial in or out.	**Cause:** There is a mismatch between the modem configuration and the modem settings, or there could be a modem failure.
	Solution: Check the modem and serial port settings. If the problem continues, check the corresponding drivers.
When the system boots, the monitor switches to the power save mode or the power light flickers.	**Cause:** The CPU is unable to establish a link with the monitor.
	Solution: Check if the monitor cable is connected to the system and then check the functionality of the VGA card.
The dumb terminal device is unable to boot. It just stops with the display screen.	**Cause:** The dumb terminal is unable to connect with the server.
	Solution: Check the serial ports and cables.
A system connected to the UPS shuts down abruptly.	**Cause:** The UPS is malfunctioning, or there is a mismatch between the UPS settings and the configuration file.
	Solution: Check the serial ports, the cable, and the configuration file.
The user is unable to switch to the GUI mode.	**Cause:** The mouse does not function properly due to the configuration settings or there could be a problem in the device.
	Solution: Unplug and reconnect the mouse, then restart the system.

Symptom	Cause And Solution
The user is unable to access the floppy or the CD drive.	**Cause:** The driver is not mounted or there is some problem with the driver. **Solution:** Check whether the read/write indicator is on. Otherwise, check the power cable connected to the floppy.

Viewing Hardware Details

Some commands that are frequently used for viewing hardware details are listed in the following table.

Command	Used To
dmesg	View bootup messages.
/sbin/lspci	View information about PCI cards.
_lsdev	View information about the installed hardware.
/sbin/lsmod	View a list of loaded modules.
/bin/uname	View system information such as the kernel name, release and version numbers, hardware platform, and operating system.

How to Troubleshoot Hardware Issues

Procedure Reference: Troubleshoot Sound Card Problems

To troubleshoot the sound card issues:

1. Verify that the speaker is connected, switched on, and is functioning.

2. If the speaker is functioning but the problem persists, verify that the sound card is detected while booting.

   a. Verify that the sound card is listed in the output of the lspci command.

   b. If the sound card is not detected, contact your hardware engineer to resolve the sound card issue.

3. If the sound card is detected and the problem still persists, verify that the sound card module is loaded.

   a. Verify that the sound card module details are listed in the output of the lsmod command.

   ```
   lsmod module name
   ```

   b. If the sound card module is not loaded, add an entry for the sound card in the /etc/modprobe.conf file. To add an entry in the file, you need to know the slot number and the name of the module used for the sound card.

   ```
   alias sound-slot-{slot number} {module name}
   ```

The /lib/modules/[kernel version]/kernel/sound directory contains modules for the sound card.

c. Reboot the system to load the module automatically.

You can also load the module using the `modprobe` or `insmod` command. If you want to use the `modprobe` command, run the `depmod` command to build or update a module database.

Procedure Reference: Troubleshoot Modem Issues

To troubleshoot the modem issues:

1. Verify that the modem is connected properly to the system and powered on.
2. Check your telephone line and verify that it is connected properly to the modem.
3. Verify that the modem speed is set properly.
   a. Verify that the modem speed specified in the /etc/mgetty+sendfax/mgetty.config file is equal or less than your modem speed.
   b. If the modem speed is not set, modify the `speed` parameter in the file.

   `speed speed in bps`
4. Verify that the serial port settings are correct.
   a. Verify that the settings listed in the output of the `setserial -a /dev/ttyS0` command matches with your modem specifications.
   b. If the serial port settings are not proper, change them.

   `setserial /dev/ttyS{port number} {spd_normal | spd_hi | spd_vhi}`

   `setserial /dev/ttyS{port number} baud_base {baud rate}`
5. If you are still unable to dial using the modem, then the issue is hardware related. Contact your hardware engineer to resolve the issue.

Procedure Reference: Troubleshoot LCD Panel Issues

To troubleshoot the LCD panel issues:

1. Verify that the LCD panel is connected to the system properly and is powered on.
2. Verify that the VGA card module is configured correctly.
   a. Verify that all parameters in the Screen section in the /etc/X11/xorg.conf file are entered correctly.
   b. If necessary, modify the parameters according to your LCD panel specifications.
3. Verify that the monitor parameters such as DefaultDepth, Viewport, and Depth are configured correctly.
   a. In the /etc/X11/xorg.conf file, verify that the `DefaultDepth`, `Viewport`, and `Depth` parameters are set properly.
   b. If necessary, modify the parameters according to your LCD panel specifications.
4. If the LCD monitor is still not working properly, then the issue is hardware related. Contact your hardware engineer to resolve the issue.

Procedure Reference: Troubleshoot Dumb Terminal Issues

To troubleshoot the dumb terminal issues:

1. Verify that the dumb terminal device is connected properly to the server.
2. Verify that the serial port is configured correctly.

    a. Verify that the settings listed in the output of the `setserial -a /dev/ttyS0` command matches your device specifications.

    b. If necessary, change the serial port settings.

    ```
    setserial /dev/ttyS{port number} {spd_normal | spd_hi | spd_vhi}

    setserial /dev/ttyS{port number} baud_base {baud rate}
    ```

3. If the dumb terminal is still not working properly, then the issue is hardware related. Contact your hardware engineer to resolve the issue.

Procedure Reference: Troubleshoot Issues Related to UPS Devices

To troubleshoot issues related to UPS devices:

1. Verify that the UPS device is connected properly to the server.
2. Verify that the serial port is configured correctly.

    a. Verify that the settings listed in the output of the `setserial -a /dev/ttyS0` command matches your device specifications.

    b. If necessary, change the serial port settings.

    ```
    setserial /dev/ttyS{port number} {spd_normal | spd_hi | spd_vhi}

    setserial /dev/ttyS{port number} baud_base {baud rate}
    ```

3. If the UPS device is still not working properly, then the issue is hardware related. Contact your hardware engineer to resolve the issue.

Procedure Reference: Troubleshoot Mouse Issues

To troubleshoot mouse issues:

1. Verify that the mouse is connected properly to the system.
2. Reboot the system.
3. If the mouse is still not working, then the issue is hardware related. Contact your hardware engineer to resolve the issue.

Procedure Reference: Troubleshoot Floppy Disk Problems

To troubleshoot floppy disk issues:

1. Verify that the power connector to the floppy drive is proper.

    If the connection is not powered on, then there is a problem with the power connector.

    a. Verify that the read-write indicator is glowing.

    b. If it is not glowing, the power connector needs to be checked and replaced.

2. If the power connector is working and the floppy issue persists, then there is a problem with the floppy drive or the floppy.

    a. With your hardware engineer's help, verify that the floppy drive is functioning properly.

    b. If the floppy drive is functional, verify that your floppy is functioning properly.

Procedure Reference: Troubleshooting X

To troubleshoot X:

1. Switch to runlevel 3.

2. Check that the required criteria for X are met.

   - Ensure that the quota value for the user has not been reached.

   - Enter `service xfs status` to check whether the `xfs` font server is running.

   - Enter `X -probeonly` to gather more information.

   - Make sure that the host name of the system is configured properly.

   - Enter `system-config-display` to check whether the display settings are configured properly.

DISCOVERY ACTIVITY 16-4

Troubleshooting Hardware Issues

Scenario:

Your company organized a trade show, where you set up several dumb terminals with LCD monitors to demonstrate your company's products. You are responsible for troubleshooting any hardware-related issues.

1. In which file will you change the LCD monitor parameters such as DefaultDepth, Viewport, and Depth?

    a) /etc/x11Config

    b) /etc/XF86

    c) /X11/XF86Config

    d) /etc/X11/xorg.conf

2. One of the LCD monitors is not displaying any output. What could be the problem? Select all that apply.

    a) The LCD panel is not connected properly to the system.

    b) The VGA card module is not configured properly.

    c) Serial port settings are not configured properly.

    d) Monitor parameters, such as DefaultDepth, Viewport, and Depth, are not configured properly.

3. True or False? In the /etc/X11/xorg.conf file, the section Screen contains parameters of the VGA card module for an LCD monitor.

    ___ True

    ___ False

4. In one of the terminals, users are not able to listen to the audio associated with the animation. What will be your first step to troubleshoot the issue?

    a) Verify that the sound card is detected while booting.

    b) Verify that the sound card module is loaded.

    c) Contact the hardware engineer to solve the issue.

    d) Verify that the speaker is connected, switched on, and working properly.

5. **Which command will you use to verify serial port settings?**

    a) setserial -q

    b) setserial -v

    c) setserial -a

    d) setserial -z

TOPIC C
Troubleshoot Network Connection and Security Issues

You identified and solved system- and hardware-based issues in Linux. In a networking environment, Linux systems will be prone to connection and security-related issues. You need to continually identify and prepare for vulnerabilities. In this topic, you will troubleshoot network connection and security issues.

Security encompasses a number of different aspects; from passwords and permissions to data encryption, firewalls, and even physical security. Despite all this protection, if you are not aware of the symptoms that lead to security breaches, or if you are not familiar with steps required for repairing corrupted files, your network will remain open and vulnerable to potential attacks.

Network Issues

If users are unable to connect to a network, then they will not be able to log in to their system or access the services or shared resources. Network problems can be categorized as hardware-related issues and service-related issues. Hardware-related network issues can be solved by checking the network devices, including the network cable and the network card. Service-related network issues can be fixed by checking the network settings of a system or the server.

Network Troubleshooting Utilities

The `traceroute`, `ping`, and `arp` utilities are very useful in troubleshooting issues related to remote network services.

Utility	Description
traceroute	You can use the `traceroute` utility to track the route data takes to get to its destination. Utilizing the TTL field of the IP protocol, `traceroute` attempts to obtain an ICMP Time_Exceeded response from each gateway encountered on the path between the sender and the final destination.
	UDP probe packets are sent with a short TTL. The `traceroute` utility then listens for an ICMP Time_Exceeded reply from a gateway. This continues until you can get an ICMP Port_Unreachable response, which means that you either got to the host or reached the default maximum number of hops (30). The address of each system that responds (each gateway you pass through) is printed to your screen; if no response is received within five seconds, an asterisk (*) is printed for that probe.

Utility	Description
`ping`	You can use the `ping` utility to verify that a system can be reached on a network. It checks the host name, the IP address, and whether the remote system can be reached.
	`Ping` uses the ICMP Echo_Request datagram to check connections among hosts, by sending echo packets and then listening for reply packets.
`arp`	You can use the `arp` utility to display information, such as the hardware address, the hostname, and the network interfaces, about the *Address Resolution Protocol (ARP)* cache.

ARP

ARP is a network protocol that is used by IP to map network addresses to MAC addresses.

Symptoms of Network Security Problems

There are a variety of ways that security can be compromised on a system. It is recommended that you check the Linux log files before troubleshooting. Some symptoms that indicate potential security problems include:

● Disruption or Denial-of-Service (DoS)

● Unauthorized system use for processing data

● Unexplained system hardware changes

● Theft (data information and vandalism)

● Unusual software characteristics

● Suspected virus outbreak

Security Tips

Avoid using authentication methods based solely on IP addresses. Keep network packages up to date, and be aware of new versions of programs such as BIND, Postfix, and SSH. Disable unnecessary network services.

System Security Monitoring Tools

Various tools can be used to effectively monitor a system for any security issues and identify symptoms.

Tool	Description
System Log Files	There are three types of system log files that can help in monitoring system security:
	Log: This file contains information about connections established and files transferred.
	Stats: This file lists file transfer statistics.
	Debug: This file contains debugging information and login and password information for remote system connections.
Central Network Log Server	The reports generated from the server contain useful information on server logs and online alerts, which can be analyzed for identifying security breaches or threats.
chkconfig	This utility can be used to check configuration files and update and query runlevel information for system services.

Network Security Vulnerabilities

Although Linux is considered a secure operating system, a network of systems can still have unauthorized users gaining access. Once an attacker gains access to a system, almost any security system can be compromised.

Vulnerabilities include:

- Proliferation of worms and viruses via email messages.
- Malicious execution of programs by a user with root privileges.
- Potential hole in the Linux kernel.
- Passwords that can be easily deciphered.
- Services running on the system such as FTP, SMB, Sendmail, and SNMP.
- Domain spoofing.
- DNS servers running vulnerable versions of BIND.
- Remote Procedure Calls (RPCs).

IP Spoofing

IP spoofing is a technique for changing, or spoofing, your IP address in order to fool the target system into believing that your IP identity is actually another system with the spoofed address.

Software Vulnerabilities

Software vulnerabilities account for many successful attacks because attackers are opportunistic. They exploit well-known flaws using the most effective and widely available attack tools. They also count on organizations that do not fix the problems and scan the Internet for vulnerable systems.

BIND Attack

In a BIND attack, an intruder can erase your system logs and install tools to gain administrative access. In addition, once the attacker has gained access, he or she uses the attacked system to scan for and attack other network systems running vulnerable versions of BIND. In effect, the intruder uses the compromised system to attack hundreds of remote systems, resulting in additional successful compromises.

Sendmail Flaws

Flaws have been found in Sendmail over the years. In one of the most common intrusions, the attacker sends a crafted mail message to a machine running Sendmail. Sendmail, in turn, interprets the message as instructions requiring it to send the password file to the attacker's machine.

SNMP Flaws

SNMP uses an unencrypted community string as an authentication mechanism, and the default community string used by many SNMP devices is public. Sniffed SNMP traffic can reveal information about the structure of your network, as well as the systems and devices attached to it.

Honeypot System

A system designed to attract attackers is known as a *honeypot*. If an attacker managed to get past your packet filter and starts scanning for options, the honeypot should be the system configured to look like it is vulnerable to known attacks. A honeypot system should not be too easy to spot because a savvy intruder will be tempted to look further on the network.

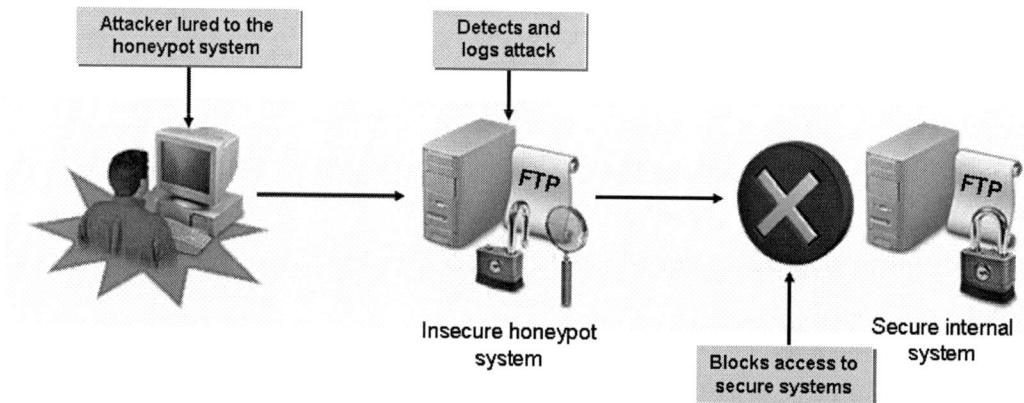

Figure 16-5: The functioning of a honeypot.

Goals of a Honeypot

There are several goals for a honeypot:

- To provide a lure so that attackers stay away from other equipment. You want the attackers to see a vulnerable system that they know they can exploit and gain access to. This system needs to be such that the attacker focuses his or her energy on exploiting the system, as opposed to the server with important data that is sitting right next to it.

- To know that the honeypot system will be attacked, so you can take extra measures when logging in to it. These logs should be moved off the system frequently—perhaps hourly or daily if your network is a high-profile target.

- To increase the ability to detect and respond to incidents. The theory is that if you are aware of what the attacker is doing to your honeypot, you can be better prepared to defend or, if possible, prevent the attack on your production systems.

Legal Issues Regarding Honeypots

Be aware that there may be legal issues surrounding the use of honeypot technology. The intentional setup of a honeypot may be considered entrapment, and therefore the same rules apply as in the real world.

Another issue is that of privacy. If an attacker were to set up an IRC server on the honeypot, it will be possible to log all conversations on that server. There is currently no defined law explicitly regarding this subject. However, it should be noted that an attorney could make privacy a viable defense argument.

Guidelines for Troubleshooting Network Issues

When troubleshooting a network problem, well-established guidelines help you narrow down the cause of the problem and map steps toward its resolution.

Guidelines

To troubleshoot a network problem:

1. Define the problem and gather the facts.

2. If possible, re-create the problem.

3. Consider all possibilities.

4. Create and implement an action plan.

5. Observe and document results.

6. Provide feedback.

Example: Troubleshoot a Network Problem

You have a client system that is unable to access a server. As the first step, you `ping` the server and realize that you do not receive a response. After that, you use `traceroute` to determine how far down the line, the problem is occurring. You discover that the problem is in the router. You take corrective action, document the results, and inform the user that the server is once again accessible.

How to Troubleshoot Network Connection and Security Issues

Procedure Reference: Troubleshoot Network Issues

To troubleshoot network issues:

1. Verify that the network cable is plugged properly.

2. View the /var/log/messages file to find out more information about the error.

3. Verify that the network service is available for the runlevel you are currently in.

   a. Verify that the network file is present in the /etc/rc.d/rc{runlevel}.d directory.

   b. If the file is not present, then enter chkconfig --level {runlevel} network on to enable the network service in the runlevel.

4. Verify that the network service is started.

   a. Enter service network status to view the status of the network service.

   b. If the service is stopped, then enter service network start to start it.

5. Verify that the IP address and subnet mask are allocated by viewing the output of the ifconfig command.

   a. Enter ifconfig to view the IP address and subnet mask.

   b. If no entries for IP address and subnet mask are displayed, determine if the IP addresses are allocated manually or through a DHCP server.

      1. If IP addresses are allocated through a DHCP server, change the **BOOTPROTO** parameter to **dhcp** in the /etc/sysconfig/network-scripts file.

      2. If IP addresses are allocated manually, verify that the **IPADDR** and **NETMASK** parameters are set in the /etc/sysconfig/network-scripts file.

      3. Restart the network service.

   c. Ping the network gateway to verify that you are able to connect to the network. /bin/ping {IP address}

6. Verify that the default gateway and routing table are configured properly.

7. Verify that the name-to-IP address resolution on your network is proper.

   • If you implemented DNS on your network, verify that the DNS entries are correct.

      a. Using the host, dig, or nslookup commands, verify that the name-to-IP address mapping is correct in the DNS configuration files.

      b. dig {host name or FQDN}

      c. host {host name or FQDN}

      d. nslookup {host name or FQDN}

   • Or, if you have not implemented DNS on your network, verify that the /etc/hosts file has correct name-to-IP address mapping information.

8. Verify that IP forwarding is enabled.

   a. Verify that the /proc/sys/net/ipv4/ip_forward file has the value 1.

   b. If the file contains 0, change the value to 1.

      1. In the /etc/sysctl.conf file, modify the value of the **net.ipv4.ip_forward** parameter to 1.

      2. Run the sysctl command to apply the changes in the sysctl -p /etc/sysctl.conf file.

9. Verify that the ports of the service you are trying to access are open at the destination host.

    a. Use Telnet to access the service through a specific port, `telnet {host name} {port number}`.

    b. In the /etc/hosts.allow and /etc/hosts.deny files and iptables, verify that you are allowed to access the ports.

    c. If the port is not open, start the service by using the `service {service name} start` command or by adding an entry for the startup script in the rc.local file.

10. Verify that the host name is set.

    a. Display the host name by using the `hostname` command.

    b. If the host name is not set, modify the /etc/sysconfig/network file to add an entry for the host.

Procedure Reference: Troubleshoot Security Issues

To troubleshoot security issues:

1. Check your newly created /var/log/iptables log file for intrusion attempts.
2. Check the /var/log/messages file for errors.
3. Check the /var/log/secure file for errors.

DISCOVERY ACTIVITY 16-5
Troubleshooting Network Issues

Scenario:
You recently received a lot of trouble tickets, all of which are related to network connections. You need to check the cause of these network issues and troubleshoot them.

---

1. One of your network users is unable to connect to the FTP server, which is located on a different network. The error message indicates that the other network is unreachable. You verified that the network cable is intact and that the FTP server is up. What could be the probable cause of the error? Select all that apply.

   a) The network service is not up.

   b) The resolv.conf file does not contain entries for the nameserver.

   c) Network parameters, such as the IP address, the subnet mask, or the default gateway, are not set correctly.

   d) The firewall is disabled.

---

2. You verified that the network service is running and that the network parameters are properly set. However, the user is still unable to connect to the network. What will be your first step to troubleshoot the network issue?

   a) Verify that the hostname is set.

   b) Verify that the DNS entries are correct.

   c) Verify that IP forwarding is enabled.

   d) Verify that the ports of the service you are trying to access are open at the destination host.

---

3. True or False? To set the hostname permanently, you need to modify the /etc/sysconfig/network file.

   ___ True

   ___ False

Lesson 16 Follow-up

In this lesson, you acquainted yourself with various troubleshooting strategies in Linux. This will enable you to effectively tackle most of the issues that arise while working with Linux-based systems.

1. **When will you troubleshoot the bootloader? Why?**

2. **Under what circumstances will you troubleshoot the system environment? Why?**

17 | Installing Linux

Lesson Time: 1 hour(s), 20 minutes

Lesson Objectives:

In this lesson, you will install the Linux operating system.

You will:

- Prepare for a Linux installation.

- Identify the phases of the Linux boot sequence.

- Configure the GRUB bootloader.

- Install the Linux operating system.

- Perform post-installation tasks.

Introduction

You have knowledge about all elements and services in the Linux operating system. Getting acquainted with the services and working of the Linux operating system will enable you to recognize your requirements while installing Linux. In this lesson, you will install the Linux operating system.

As a Linux+ professional, one of your basic competencies will be to install the Linux operating system. Before installing it, you have to ensure that the settings and hardware configuration of the computer targeted for installation are sufficient to host the Linux operating system. Also, you need to determine the features that have to be installed to suit your requirements.

This lesson covers all or part of the following CompTIA Linux+ (2009) certification objectives:

- Topic A
  - Objective 1.1
  - Objective 1.11
- Topic C
  - Objective 1.7
- Topic D
  - Objective 2.7
- Topic E
  - Objective 2.5

TOPIC A
Prepare for Installation

You troubleshot devices to ensure the smooth operation of the Linux system. To optimize the performance of the Linux system, you need to select devices that are fully supported by Linux. In this topic, you will perform the preparation tasks necessary for a successful installation of Linux.

Preparing for a new Linux installation is much like setting out to cook a fine meal. You need to gather all the necessary ingredients to accomplish the task. Thorough preparation will help prevent failure when attempting to boot your system for the first time.

Hardware Compatibility

The first thing you should do before purchasing any hardware component is to check whether it is on the hardware compatibility list (HCL) for Linux. Before you install Linux, you should gather information about your system. Much of this information is available in your system documentation. Some of the questions that you should address before purchasing a hardware component are listed in the table below.

Component	Questions to Address
Hard drive	• How may devices are installed? • Is it IDE or SCSI? • How large is the drive? • How many cylinders are contained on the drive?
Hard disk controller	• Is it IDE or SCSI? • Who is the manufacturer?
Memory	How much RAM is installed?
CD-ROM	Is the interface type IDE, SCSI, or other? (If it is not IDE or SCSI, you will need to record the make and model.)
SCSI adapter	Who is the manufacturer? What is the model?
Network card	Who is the manufacturer? What is the model?
Mouse	What type is it? (If serial, record the port to which it is connected.)
Monitor	• Who is the manufacturer? • What is the model? • What are the horizontal and vertical refresh rate ranges of the monitor?
Display adapter	• What chipset is used in the display adapter? • How much video RAM does the display adapter use?

Linux Distributor Testing

Distributors, such as Red Hat, Inc., test whether Linux operates correctly with specific hardware. After testing, they produce HCLs for each supported version. The lists include information about the hardware, but because the computer system configurations vary between what you may have and what they tested, the variations in manufacturing specifications aren't guaranteed to be compatible with any hardware. HCL is a list of hardware that has been tested under specific conditions (usually under many conditions) and should be used as a guide, not as an absolute testament that the hardware will work perfectly straight out of the box (because your system is probably configured in a slightly different way than the test systems).

Hardware Compatibility Websites

The following Linux hardware compatibility sites will assist you in determining if your hardware will work with Linux:

- Red Hat hardware compatibility list—**https://hardware.redhat.com/**
- Mandriva hardware compatibility list—**http://hcl.mandriva.com/**
- SuSE hardware compatibility list—**http://en.opensuse.org/Hardware**
- Fedora hardware compatibility list—**http://fedoraproject.org/wiki/HCL**
- Ubuntu hardware compatibility list—**http://www.ubuntuhcl.org**
- Linux Mint hardware compatibility list—**http://www.linuxminthcl.org**

CPU Compatibility

It is also important to determine if your CPU is compatible with Linux. Certain distributions of Linux are tailored to different CPU types.

Installation on New Systems

On newer systems, the Linux installation program often automatically identifies your hardware. It is still a good idea to gather information ahead of time, just in case the program does not figure out what you have.

Gather Installation Information

Depending on your installed equipment, you may have to look for information in a variety of resources.

- One way to gather information is to view CMOS or diagnostic information available at system boot time. Cold-boot your system and display setup or diagnostic information. This is displayed in different ways on different systems. For example, on most Compaq systems, when the block cursor moves to the upper-right corner of the screen, press **F10**. On some systems, when the View Setup message (or a similar message) is displayed, you press **Delete** (or the key indicated in the message).
- Access to manuals that came with the equipment can often be one of the best ways to find out about components. Manufacturers' websites also often contain valuable information about equipment.
- If you don't have the documentation and you don't have an application or a utility to provide this information, you will need to open the hood and look inside. Many cards, boards, and components have manufacturer and model information printed on them. However, they probably will not have a guide to interpreting the jumpers' settings.

● If your workstation is to be connected to a network, you will also need information about the network address to be assigned to your computer. Some systems will have a permanent network address and others will obtain a network address each time they access the network. Contact the system or network administrator to find out how to set up your system.

Linux Installation Methods

Linux installation can be done for servers and workstations. There are different methods by which Linux can be installed.

Installation Method	Description
Local CD/DVD-ROM Installation	Linux can be installed from a set of installation CD/DVD-ROMs. It requires the system's BIOS settings to support booting from CD/DVD-ROMs. This is like a local installation and is the easiest way to install Linux.
Local Hard Drive Installation	Linux installation can be done by staging the installation files on the local hard drive.
USB Drive Installation	Linux can also be installed through USB drives if CD/DVD-ROMs or other modes of installation are not supported by the system. To enable booting from USB drives, the diskboot.img file has to be copied from the images folder of the installation CD/DVD-ROM to the USB drive. This mode of installation also requires the BIOS to support booting from USB drives.
Network-Based Installation	Linux installation can be done on networked computers by staging all the installation files on a separate server and installing it on clients' systems. The network installation server shares the installation directory with the clients via NFS, FTP, or HTTP. This method is often faster than CD/DVD-ROM-based installations. The network installation server is necessary for all network-based Linux installations.

Preinstall Checklist

To ensure that your system is ready for Linux to be installed:

1. Collect basic system information about your computer.
2. Check the available hardware with HCL.
3. Verify that the minimum system requirements are met for the distribution you wish to install.
4. Plan the hard disk partitioning layout and the corresponding filesystems, including the size of the swap drive, depending on the physical RAM.
5. If necessary, check the installation media using the **Test the Media** option available on the Linux Installation CD.

The Anaconda Installer

The *Anaconda installer* is an installation program that enables installation of Linux through the text mode or the graphical mode. It provides step-by-step instructions to guide installation. It also enables you to partition and organize hard disks and manage RAID and LVMs. The installer provides various options to choose and add different packages based on your operating requirements.

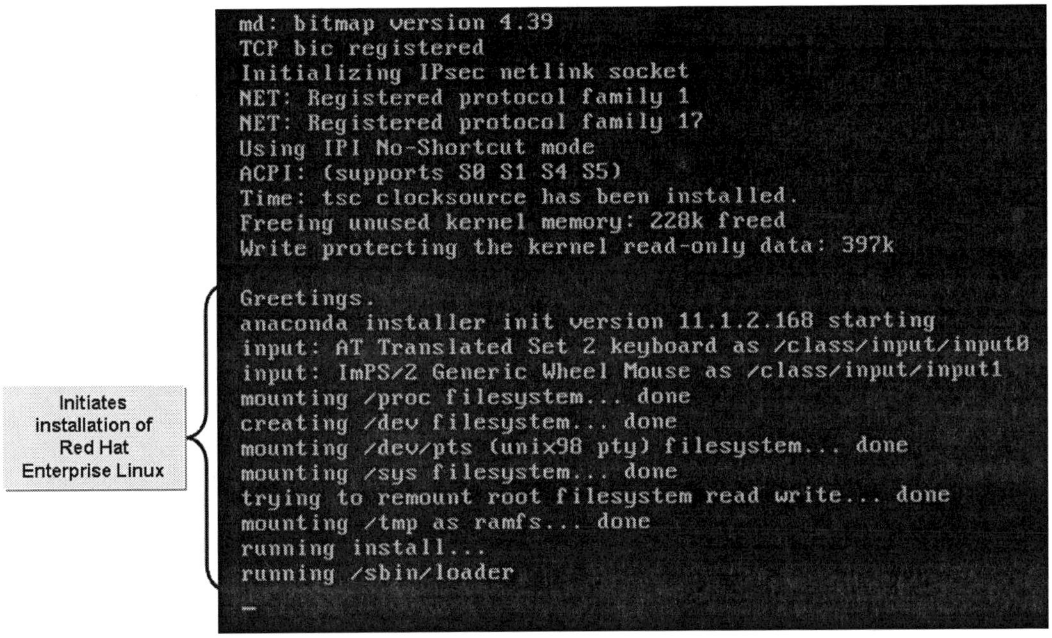

Figure 17-1: The Anaconda installer in Red Hat Enterprise Linux 5.

Partitioning Utilities

Definition:

The Linux operating system is usually installed on a partition of the hard disk. A *partition utility* is a program that is used to manage partitions on the hard disk. A partition utility enables you to create a new partition, modify the attributes of an existing partition, assign a filesystem to a partition, and delete a partition. The utility also enables you to specify the size of a partition and indicate whether the partition is a primary or a logical partition. The most frequently used partition utility is `fdisk`.

Example: Disk Druid

Disk druid is a program that is used to partition disk drives during the installation process.

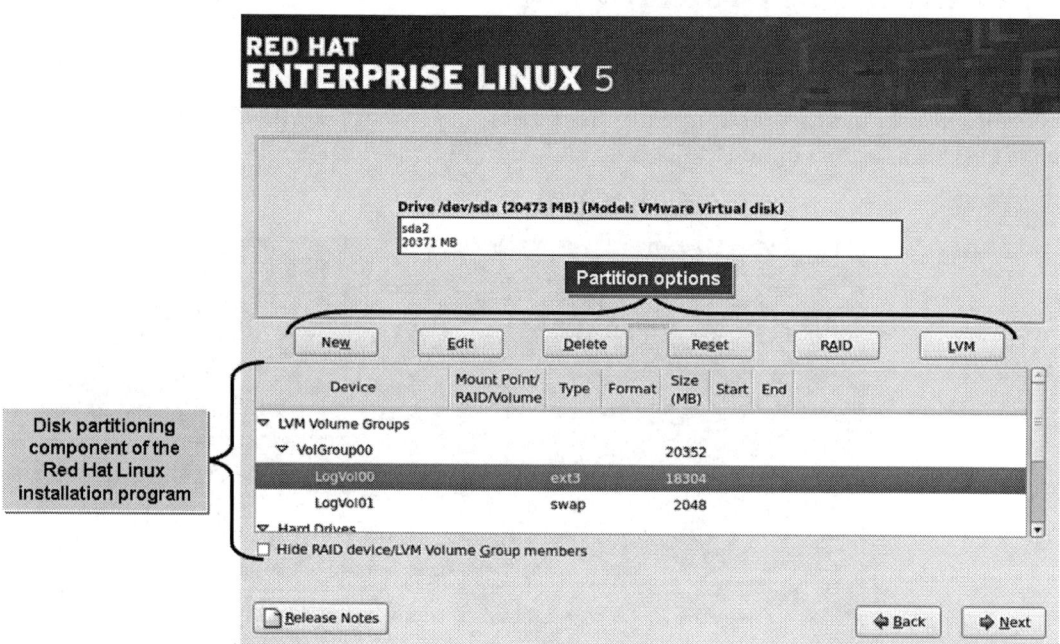

Figure 17-2: The disk partitioning component of the Red Hat Linux installation program.

Partition Device Name

The partition device name is often /dev/hda1 or /dev/hda2 for IDE disks and /dev/sda1 or /dev/sda2 for SCSI disks.

Repartitioning Strategies

If you have neither enough free space nor a partition to spare, then you can either add another drive to install Linux or repartition your existing drive. Most DOS-based systems have a single partition that includes the entire drive. This leaves you with no space to install Linux. You can either delete the existing partition and make it smaller to accommodate Linux, or use a partitioning utility to resize it.

Unless you use a special utility, you will have to delete and then re-create partitions of appropriate sizes. In recent years, several utilities have been developed that can move partition boundaries without destroying your data.

Destructive Repartitioning

Destructive repartitioning is a traditional method. You use the `fdisk` utility to delete the existing partition, and then re-create partitions. This means that you lose all the data saved on the partition when it is deleted. Therefore, before deleting the partition, if you want to retain any information, you will need to back it up, delete and re-create the partitions, and then restore the information.

Nondestructive Repartitioning

Several third-party utilities are now available that allow you to move the partition boundaries without destroying the data currently stored in the partition. This is referred to as nondestructive repartitioning. You still have to be extremely careful, and follow the utilities' documentation directions exactly, to avoid inadvertently destroying your data. Partition Magic and Partition-It are third-party utilities that can be purchased for this purpose.

Partitionless Installation

The partitionless installation option is available for users who want to try out Linux without installing it completely. All it requires is a formatted DOS FAT partition with enough free space for a workstation installation. However, it doesn't have all the options available that a full workstation installation would have, and you need to use a boot disk every time you want to run Linux. It is popularly known as Live CD.

The FIPS Program

The *First nondestructive Interactive Partition Splitting program (FIPS)* is a free utility that comes with some Linux distributions. It can be used to resize File Allocation Table (FAT) partitions. When running FIPS, two partitions are created: the one you resized and the one FIPS creates.

 FIPS is included on the Red Hat Linux CD-ROM in the dosutils directory.

FIPS Limitations

FIPS only works on DOS partitions with disk sector sizes of 512 bytes. Twelve-bit FATs will not be split by FIPS. Therefore, a partition will not be reduced below 4,085 clusters because this will require writing the 16-bit FAT as a 12-bit FAT. It also does not currently work with extended DOS partitions. If you already have four partitions, you cannot use FIPS to further split the partitions; FIPS requires a free partition entry with which it can work. Because of the wide variety of hardware and software configurations under which it must run, FIPS may not work properly on all systems.

How to Prepare for Installation

Procedure Reference: How to Prepare for Installation

To prepare for installation:

1. Gather information related to your system.
   - Hardware
   - Software
   - Network environment
2. Verify that your hardware is compatible with Linux.
3. Verify that the software you want to use after installing Linux will work.
4. Determine the purpose of the system.
5. Verify that your system hardware can handle the space and workload required for the purposes you need it for.

DISCOVERY ACTIVITY 17-1
Preparing to Install Linux

Scenario:

The final approval to implement Linux has been granted. Your manager, Peter, requested you to perform a company-wide implementation of Linux. Peter would like you to develop a procedure to prepare all systems for a Linux installation.

1. **What is the default bootloader in new versions of Red Hat Enterprise Linux?**

   a) LILO

   b) GRUB

   c) System Commander

2. **True or False? FIPS is used to resize FAT partitions.**

   __ True

   __ False

3. **When is it the best time to gather information about your Linux system?**

   a) Just after installing Linux.

   b) During the Linux installation.

   c) Before installing Linux.

   d) You do not have to gather system information.

TOPIC B

Identify Phases of the Linux Boot Sequence

You identified Linux compatible hardware and types of installation. To understand how Linux is loaded on your system, you need to learn about the boot process. In this topic, you will identify the phases of the Linux boot sequence and its components.

The boot process is the most important process in system startup, and it is essential for the proper loading of the operating system and all its applications. While installing Linux on multiple computers, it is important that you have sound knowledge of the boot process because it will help you identify and troubleshoot any issues related to system startup or the operating system.

BIOS

The *Basic Input/Output System (BIOS)* is a low-level firmware that acts as the interface between the hardware (chip set and processor) and the operating system on a computer. The BIOS settings can be modified according to the needs of a user. BIOS plays an important role in starting the boot process and determining the boot device settings. When your computer is powered on, BIOS is loaded into the memory and it initiates the *Power-On Self Test (POST)*.

 The BIOS size varies among vendors and has a maximum size of 8 MB.

ROM BIOS

There are several BIOSes in your computer. When people say BIOS, they are generally referring to the main system BIOS. However, there are also BIOSes to control peripherals. Typically, the video card has its own BIOS, which contains hardware-driving instructions for displaying video information. SCSI host adapters, hard drives, and other peripherals can also contain their own BIOS instructions.

Plug and Play

When the main BIOS looks for the video card and other peripheral BIOSes, it will look for and configure plug-and-play devices if your BIOS supports the plug-and-play standard. When a plug-and-play device is found, BIOS displays a message on the screen prompting user input and action.

POST

POST takes an inventory of your system's hardware components in a specific order. The following table lists the components in the order in which they are tested.

Component	Description Of Test
Processor	If this test fails, the system halts without displaying any message.

Component	Description Of Test
ROM BIOS	A series of checksums are computed; if they don't match, the system halts.
DMA controller	If this test fails, the system halts.
Interrupt controller	If this test fails, you will hear a long beep followed by a short beep; the system then halts.
Timing chip	If this test fails, the system halts.
Video card	If this test fails, you will hear a long beep followed by two short beeps; if the test succeeds, ROM BIOS gets copied into RAM memory.
Expansion boards	Boards are initialized and, if necessary, the expansion board's ROM gets copied into upper memory.
RAM memory	Counts and tests RAM by writing a bit to each memory bit.
Keyboard	Presence of keyboard and any stuck keys.
Floppy disk drive	Signal is sent to the adapter to activate the floppy disk drive's motor.
Other resources	Parallel and serial ports are queried; the system looks for an operating system to load.

CMOS

The *Complementary Metal Oxide Semiconductor (CMOS)* is a memory area with battery backup that is used to store system configuration settings. Prior to the use of CMOS, settings were configured with jumpers and switches. CMOS was introduced with the AT system boards. It allows more configuration options when compared to switches and jumpers. Some of the things you can configure through CMOS are:

- Password: You can specify whether a password is required following POST.

- Drive order: The order in which POST checks drives for the operating system.

- Memory: Some systems require you to specify in CMOS how much RAM is installed on the system.

- Drive type: Specifies the type of hard drive attached to the system.

- Display: Specifies the monitor type.

Bootloaders

Definition:

A bootloader is a program that loads the kernel from a hard drive or boot disk and then starts the operating system. It is also referred to as the *boot manager.* Boot managers can load more than one operating system into the computer's memory. A user is then allowed to select the desired operating system. The bootloader interacts with BIOS and utilizes subroutines to load the operating system. Boot managers can also protect the boot process with a password.

Example:

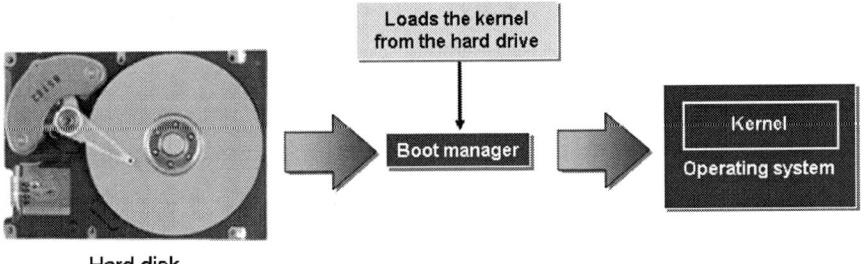

Hard disk

Figure 17-3: The function of a bootloader.

Bootloader Components

The bootloader uses three main components that work together to systematically load the operating system in stages.

Component	Description
Boot sector program	It is the first component of the bootloader. It is loaded by BIOS on startup and has a fixed size of 512 bytes. Its main function is to load the second stage bootloader; however, it can also load another sector or a kernel.
Second stage bootloader	It loads the operating system and contains a kernel loader.
Bootloader installer	It controls the installation of disk sectors and can be run only when booting from a disk. It coordinates the activities of the boot sector and the bootloader.

Types of Bootloaders

There are different types of bootloaders in Linux. Some of the bootloaders are described in the following table.

Bootloader	Description
GRUB	A popular Linux bootloader that allows you to place specific instructions in MBR.
LILO	A Linux bootloader that enables you to boot from up to 16 different configuration images, including DOS, OS/2, Windows NT, UNIX, and Linux partitions.
ELILO	A bootloader for Unified Extensible Firmware Interface (UEFI) machines. It supports flexible local booting from a FAT-32 filesystem and a wide variety of boot options via network booting over DHCP/TFTP.

Bootloader	Description
Loadlin	A bootloader that provides an alternative to LILO for users with hardware configurations incompatible with LILO. Unlike LILO, loadlin is a DOS application program that requires the user to first boot into DOS (or Windows) to run Linux. Loadlin starts a logical reload of your system, causing DOS to be completely overlaid with the Linux operating system.
System Commander	A third-party bootloader that can also be used as a boot manager. This utility enables you to control the environment you boot into, similar to LILO and loadlin. It has a full-featured boot manager and partitioning software.
SysLinux	An MS-DOS program that is similar to loadlin, although not as suitable as a general purpose bootloader. It is sometimes used to simplify a first-time installation of Linux and for creating a rescue boot disc.

GRUB Loading Order

GRUB loads in the following order: the primary bootloader is loaded, followed by the secondary bootloader and finally, the operating system is loaded. After receiving the correct instructions for the operating system to start, GRUB locates the boot file and hands off control of the machine to that operating system.

The LILO Boot Process

LILO boots itself in two stages, each of which is composed of several smaller processes. As the boot process progresses, additional letters of the four-letter prompt are displayed. When LILO has fully loaded itself, it displays the LILO prompt.

During the first stage of boot, LILO moves itself into a memory address and sets up the stack. It then loads the secondary bootloader and transfers control to it. Once the secondary bootloader starts, it continues with the boot process and displays the LILO: prompt.

If LILO does not successfully load, it will freeze at a certain point in its display. The following table shows each step of the display and boot process.

LILO Display	First Stage Bootloader	Second Stage Bootloader	Description
L error	Loaded	Cannot be loaded.	A two-digit error code is displayed.
LI	Loaded	Loaded but could not execute.	This is often caused by a geometry mismatch.
LIL	Loaded	Started but cannot load descriptor table.	This is often caused by a media failure or geometry mismatch.

Benefits of LILO

LILO does not depend on a specific filesystem. It can boot Linux kernel images from floppy disks and hard disks and can even boot other operating systems. One of up to 16 different images can be selected at boot time. Various parameters, such as the root device, can be set independently for each kernel.

LILO can even be used as MBR. MBR is the first sector of your hard disk. The computer's BIOS looks up to MBR for instructions on how to load an operating system. If you just had Windows 95 or DOS installed, it will only contain instructions to load that one operating system.

LILO Configuration File

Settings for LILO are saved in the /etc/lilo.conf file. When you boot your system, LILO uses the information in this file to determine how to boot your system.

UEFI

Earlier known as Extensible Firmware Interface (EFI), UEFI specifies an interface that operates between the operating system and the platform firmware. It is an alternative to BIOS for initiating a system, but does not completely replace BIOS.

The Boot Process

The *boot process* is a process that is repeated each time your computer is started, by loading the operating system from your hard drive. It involves a series of sequential steps. The boot sequence can be divided into the BIOS initialization, bootloader, kernel and init initialization, and boot scripts.

The boot process consists of the following stages:

1. The processor checks for the BIOS program and executes it.

2. BIOS checks for peripherals, such as floppy disk drives, CD-ROMs, and the hard disk, for bootable media. It locates a valid device to boot the system.

3. BIOS loads the primary bootloader from the MBR into the memory. The bootloader is a program that contains instructions required to boot a machine. It also loads the partition table along with it.

4. The user is prompted with a graphical screen that displays the different operating systems available in the system to boot from. The user should select an operating system and press **Enter** to boot the system. If the user does not respond, then the default operating system will be booted.

5. The bootloader determines the kernel and locates the corresponding kernel binary. It then uploads the respective initrd image into the memory and transfers the control of the boot process to the kernel.

6. The kernel configures the available hardware, including processors, I/O subsystems, and storage devices. It decompresses the `initrd` image and mounts it to load the necessary drivers. If the system has implemented any virtual devices such as LVM or software RAID, then they are initialized. The components that are configured by the kernel will be displayed one by one on the screen.

7. The kernel mounts the root partition and releases the unused memory. To set up the user environment, the `init` program is executed.

8. The init program searches for the `inittab` file, which contains the details of the runlevel, that has to be started. It sets the environment path, checks the filesystem, initializes the serial ports, and runs background processes for the runlevel.

9. If the graphical mode is selected, then `xdm` or `kdm` is started and the login window is displayed on the screen.

10. The user enters the user name and password to log in to the system.

11. The system authenticates the user. If the user is a valid user, then the profile, the `.login`, the `.bash_login`, and the `.bash_profile` files are executed. The shell is started and the system is ready for the user to work on.

 `xdm` refers to the X Window Desktop Manager. Users who use GNOME or KDE, use either `gdm` or `kdm`, respectively. In RHEL 5.3, `gdm` is the default desktop manager.

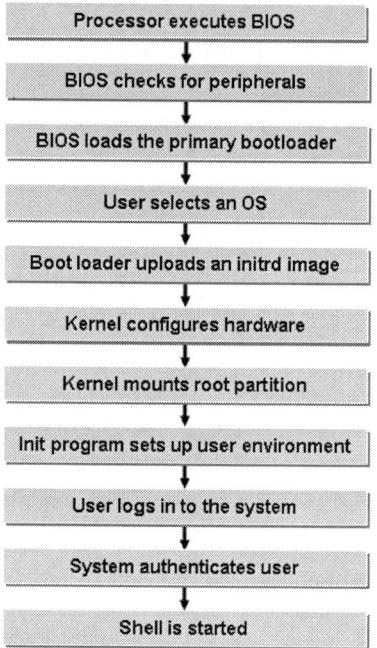

Figure 17-4: *Stages in the boot process.*

Superblocks

Definition:

A *superblock,* often called sb, is a data structure that is stored on a disk and contains control information for a filesystem. Linux partitions are discussed in terms of blocks. The superblock comprises the first 512 bytes of a partition. It contains information about the block size used by the filesystem, the location of the root directory, and the time it was last checked.

 Each partition on a disk is identified by a number. The number 1, is assigned to the first partition, number 2, to the second partition, and so on.

Example:

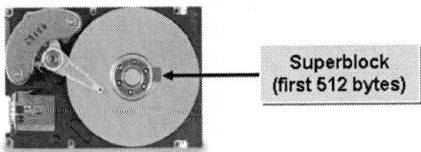

Figure 17-5: A superblock on a hard disk.

Sectors

Definition:

A *sector* is the smallest unit of storage, read or written onto a disk. A sector stores 512 bytes of data by default. A collection of sectors is called a track. The number of sectors in a track may vary, and so does their capacity to hold data. The size of the sector can be altered when formatting the hard disk.

Example:

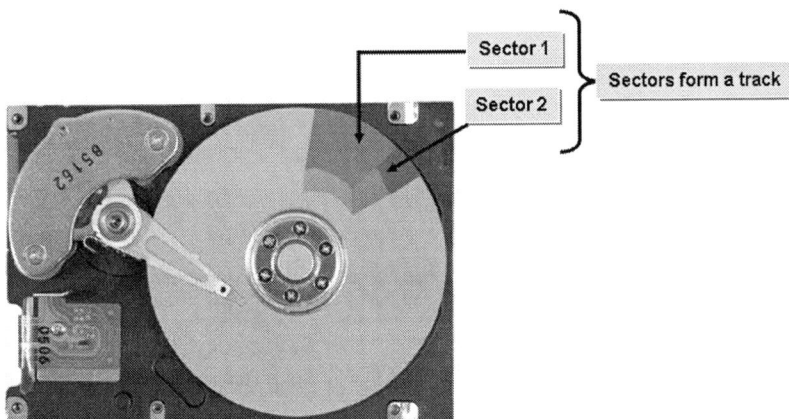

Figure 17-6: A hard disk showing sectors and tracks.

MBR

Definition:

MBR is the first physical sector on a hard drive, which contains the code that is used to load the operating system or bootloader into memory. It also contains the partition table of the hard drive. The MBR helps determine the partition that is currently active.

Example:

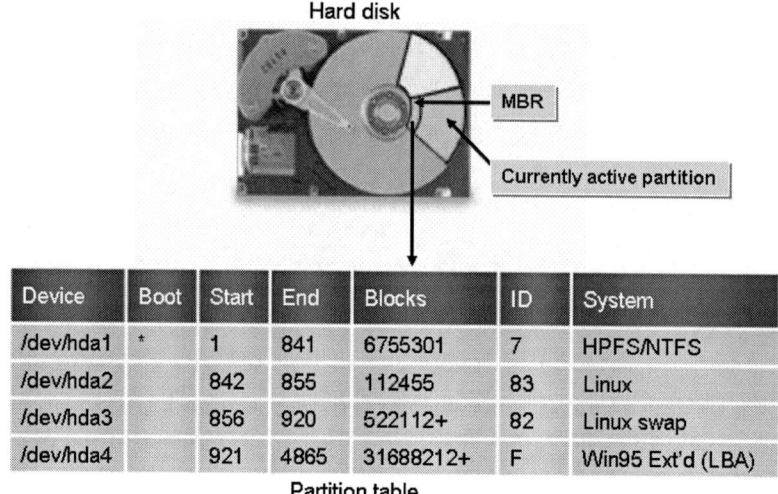

Figure 17-7: A hard disk showing MBR and the partition table loaded by it.

ACTIVITY 17-2
Discussing the Boot Process

Scenario:
As a junior administrator in your company, you are instructed to acquaint yourself with the boot sequence components because it will help you troubleshoot any issues that may arise when loading the operating system.

1. What enables you to choose the operating system to load from the hard disk?

    a) The number of sectors on the hard disk

    b) MBR

    c) The number of tracks on the hard disk

    d) BIOS

    e) The bootloader

2. What is true of MBR?

    a) MBR contains the partition tables.

    b) MBR contains a number of sectors.

    c) MBR contains the code to load the operating system into the memory.

    d) MBR determines the boot device settings.

    e) MBR determines the currently active partition.

3. True or False? The bootloader installer contains a kernel loader.

    ___ True

    ___ False

TOPIC C
Configure GRUB

You discussed the boot sequence. To manage the boot process, you must understand how to use and configure the components involved in it. By configuring GRUB, you can modify the system to run according to your requirements. In this topic, you will configure the GRUB bootloader and understand its functions.

The boot sequence listed the steps involved in the boot process. As a Linux+ administrator, you may be assigned the task of running multiple operating systems on the same system. In such a case, you must know how to add new kernels and boot the correct operating system. To accomplish this task, you should know about GRUB and how to configure it.

GRUB

Definition:

GRUB is a program that is used to install a bootloader in MBR. GRUB allows you to place specific instructions in MBR that loads a GRUB menu or environment command. This enables you to start the operating system of your choice, pass instructions to the kernel when booting, or check for system parameters before booting.

Example:

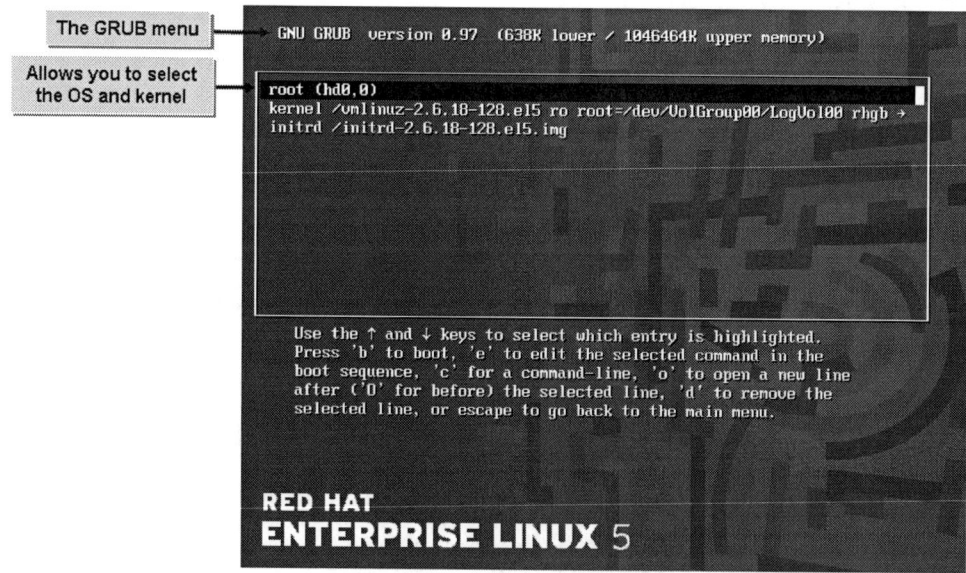

Figure 17-8: The grub bootloader menu screen with its various functions.

The grub.conf File

The grub.conf file found in the /boot/grub directory is the configuration file for the GRUB boot manager. It contains various configuration options for configuring and troubleshooting the boot manager.

Option	Enables You To
default=*Number*	Specify the default booting kernel number if multiple kernel images are found.
timeout=*Number*	Specify the time limit for the login screen to be displayed.
Splashimage=(hdx,y)/grub/*image location*	Specify the location of the login screen image.
title *user desired name*	Specify a title to differentiate between the kernel images in the login screen.
root (hdx,y)	Specify the location of MBR.
kernel *{Location}* *[option]*	Specify the location of the kernel.
initrd *Kernel image*	Specify the location of the kernel image.

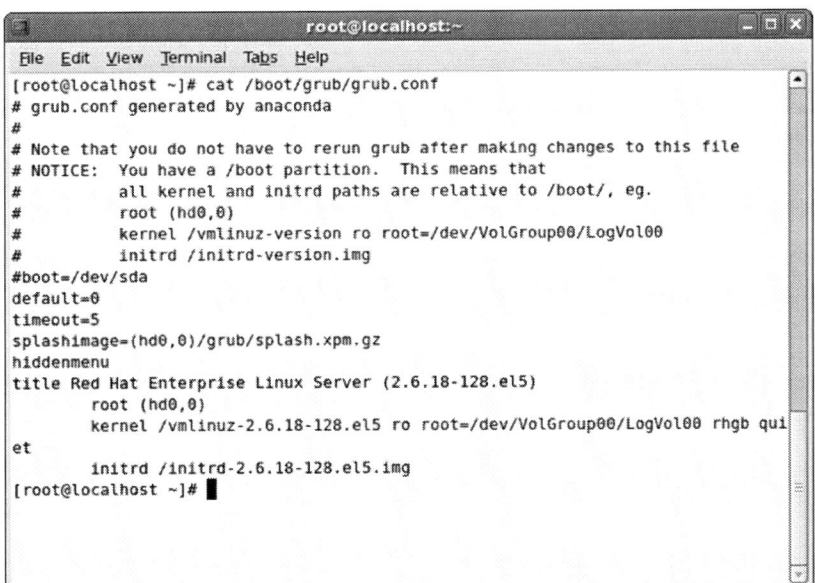

Figure 17-9: The grub.conf file that is used to configure the GRUB boot manager.

The GRUB Menu Configuration File

The configuration file, /boot/grub/grub.conf, is used to create a list of operating systems to boot from. This allows a user to select a group of commands to execute, which will launch the desired operating system.

The menu.lst File

The *menu.lst* file is a GRUB configuration file that lists all the kernels available on the system along with their partition numbers, boot information, and details of which kernel is booted. The menu.lst file is stored in the /boot/grub/ directory.

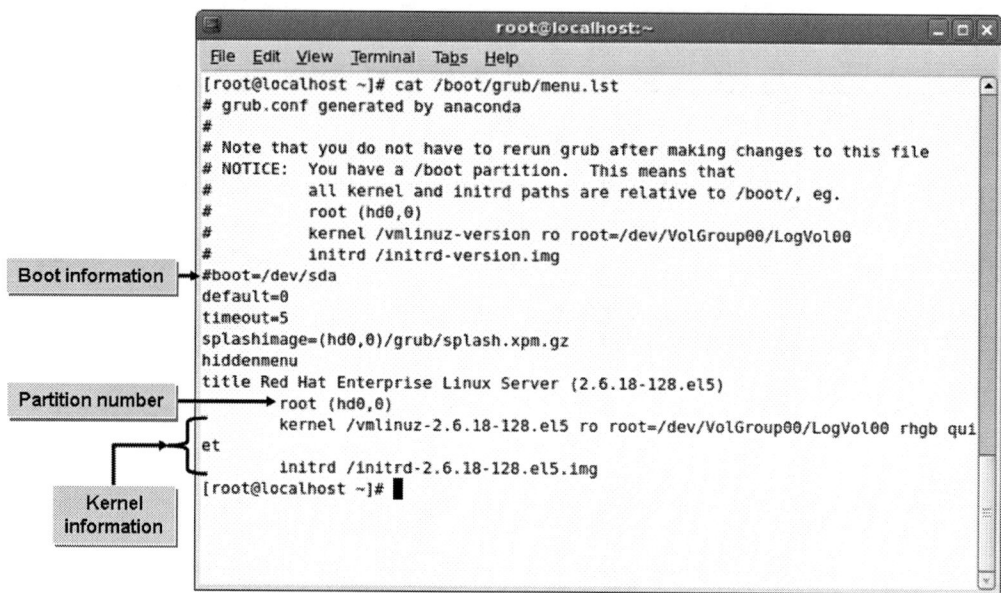

Figure 17-10: The menu.lst file displaying the system's kernel details.

GRUB Commands

GRUB commands enable a user to configure and modify the GRUB settings in each runlevel based on user requirements. General commands and CLI commands can be used anywhere on the menu and can be accessed from the CLI.

General Command	Enables You To
bootp	Use the BOOTP protocol to initialize a network device.
device	Create a disk image, and specify a file as a BIOS drive. This command is also used to troubleshoot GRUB in case of drive errors.
dhcp	Use the DHCP protocol to initialize a network device.
password	Set a password for the menu files. The locked files will not have the edit property set to them.
ifconfig	Configure a network manually. The gateway, IP address, subnet mask, and server address can be configured using this command.
terminal	Specify the terminal settings. Serial ports can be used only if this command is specified.

General Command	Enables You To
serial	Configure settings for various serial devices and serial ports.

CLI Command	Enables You To
boot	Load the operating system into the computer from the CLI.
cat *file name*	Display the content of a file.
find	Search for a file.
setup	Install and configure various services such as authentication, firewalls, and system services.
install	Install GRUB and other utilities.
kernel	Load a kernel boot image.
Lmodule	Load a kernel module.
halt	Shutdown your system.
reboot	Reboot your system.
exit	Exit from the GRUB shell.

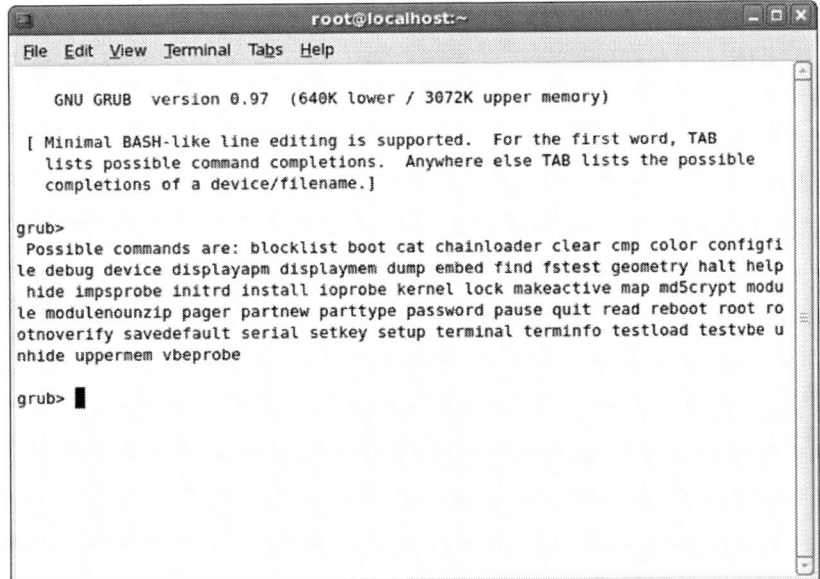

Figure 17-11: The commands that can be executed at the GRUB prompt.

GRUB Menu-Specific Commands

Menu-specific commands are used to configure GRUB from the configuration file. They can be enabled in the global section of the grub.conf configuration file.

Command	*Enables You To*
default	Set the default entry for the entry number NUM, which is used by GRUB in case of boot entry errors.
fallback	Set the fallback entry, allowing GRUB to override any errors in the boot entry.
hiddenmenu	Hide the menu control from a user at the control terminal. This does not affect the boot entry.
timeout	Set the timeout value before booting into the default boot entry. The hiddenmenu command can be disabled here by pressing **Esc** before timeout elapses.
title	Start a new boot entry, which is displayed on the menu interface.

How to Configure GRUB

Procedure Reference: Configure the GRUB Bootloader

To configure the GRUB bootloader:

1. Log in as root in the CLI.
2. Enter vi /boot/grub/grub.conf to open the grub.conf file.

 You can also use the softlink /boot/grub/menu.lst file to configure the GRUB boot manager.

3. Make the necessary changes.
4. Save and close the file.

Procedure Reference: Protect GRUB with a Password

To protect GRUB with a password:

1. Log in as root in the CLI.
2. Enter grub-md5-crypt to create an MD5 encrypted password.
3. Enter cd /boot/grub to navigate to the /boot/grub directory.
4. Enter vi grub.conf to open the grub.conf file.
5. Press **I** to switch to the insert mode.
6. On a new line below the **hiddenmenu** option, type password --md5 to specify your password.
7. Save and close the file.

Procedure Reference: Install the GRUB Bootloader

To install GRUB as the bootloader:

1. Log in as root in the CLI.
2. Enter `cat /boot/grub/device.map` to identify the boot device of the system.
3. Enter `grub-install {boot device}` to install the GRUB bootloader.
4. Enter `reboot` to check if the system boots with the specified bootloader.

Procedure Reference: Set up GRUB Manually

To set up GRUB manually:

1. Log in as root.
2. At the command prompt, enter `grub` to open the GRUB shell.
3. Enter `root` *(boot device node, partition)*.
4. Enter `setup` *(boot device node, partition)*.
5. Enter `quit` to close the GRUB shell.
6. Enter `reboot` to reboot the system.

Procedure Reference: Boot from the Menu Editing Mode

To boot from the menu editing mode:

1. Start the system.
2. On the GRUB graphical splash screen, press **Esc.**
3. Select an entry and press **E** to enter the menu editing mode.
   - Select a line and press **E** to edit the line.
   - Select a line and press **D** to delete the line.
   - Select a line and press **O** to add a line.
   - Select a line and press **C** to open the GRUB shell.
4. Press **B** to boot the system.

ACTIVITY 17-3
Configuring GRUB

Before You Begin:
1. On srvB, you have logged in as root in the GUI.
2. Switch to the CLI terminal.

Scenario:
The system administrator is receiving many complaints from users that their systems are not booting properly. As a junior administrator, you are assigned the task of troubleshooting the systems. You find that the bootloader is not installed properly, and that someone has modified the settings in the bootloader because there is no password protection. You decide to reinstall GRUB and protect it with a password.

These are your login details:

- Your login id is root.
- Your password is p@ssw0rd.

What You Do	How You Do It
1. Install the GRUB boot manager.	a. Log in as **root** in the CLI.
	b. Enter `grub-install /dev/sda` to install GRUB.
	c. Verify that the "Installation finished. No error reported" message is displayed. This indicates that GRUB has been installed successfully.
2. Generate an MD5 encrypted password for GRUB.	a. Enter `grub-md5-crypt` to generate an MD5 password for GRUB.
	b. At the **Password** prompt, enter *p@ssw0rd*
	c. Enter the password again at the **Retype password** prompt.
	d. Write down the MD5 password that is generated.

 This MD5 password will be used in the activity to protect GRUB with a password.

3. Enable password protection for GRUB.

a. Enter **cd /boot/grub** to navigate to the /boot/grub directory.

b. Enter **vi grub.conf** to open the grub.conf file.

c. Enter */hid* to go to the **hiddenmenu** line.

d. Press **O** to switch to the insert mode and move to a new line.

e. On the line below the **hiddenmenu** option, type **password --md5 password**

 In the password section, students must type the md5 password that they have generated.

f. Press **Esc** to switch to the command mode.

g. Save and close the file.

4. Check whether password protection is enabled for GRUB.

a. Enter **reboot** to restart the system.

b. On the **GRUB** graphical splash screen, press **A.**

 Unless you specify the password, you will not be able to edit the GRUB from the splash screen. Thus, password protection is enabled for the GRUB bootloader.

c. Press **P** to enter the password, to edit the GRUB configuration.

d. At the **Password** prompt, enter *p@ssw0rd*

e. Press **E** to edit the GRUB configuration.

f. Press **B** to boot with the default setup.

TOPIC D
Install the Operating System

You may have installed various operating systems previously. However, installation techniques do not apply universally to all operating systems, and you need to familiarize yourself with such information pertaining to Linux. With a clear understanding of the boot process, you will be prepared to begin the installation of Linux. In this lesson, you will install Linux on a computer after ensuring that the computer is suitable to host it.

Installation is perhaps the most important aspect in using of the Linux operating system. It involves many major tasks such as creating and configuring partitions and configuring devices. Also, Linux can be installed in different ways. As a Linux+ administrator, you may be required to install and reinstall Linux on a number of systems. Knowing how to administer Linux installation will enable you to utilize the potential of the features packed into Linux to the optimum.

How to Install the Operating System

Procedure Reference: Install Linux from a CD-ROM

To install Linux from a CD-ROM:

1. At the boot prompt, choose the mode of installation either as text or graphical mode.
2. If necessary, check the boot media and start the installation.
3. Click **Next** to begin the installation.
4. Choose the desired language.
5. Choose the desired key board type.
6. Enter the installation number and click **OK** or **Skip** the step.
7. A warning message will be displayed if you are using a new hard disk; click **Yes** to continue.
8. From the partition layout drop-down list, choose the desired partition layout and click **Next.**
9. If a warning message is displayed, click **Yes** to continue.
10. If necessary, review the partition table and click **Next.**
11. On the bootloader installation page, choose the type of bootloader and its location and then click **Next.**
12. On the network configuration page, configure the network and click **Next.**
13. Choose the desired time zone for the machine and click **Next.**
14. Enter the root password and click **Next.**
15. Accept the default package list or choose **Customize now** and click **Next.**
16. Select the necessary package and click **Next.**
17. On the installation complete page, click **Reboot** to finish the installation and reboot the system.

Procedure Reference: Install Linux on a Network

To install Linux on a network:

1. At the boot prompt, enter `linux askmethod` to view the boot medium options.

2. Select the appropriate network installation medium and press **Enter.**

3. Choose the desired language.

4. Choose the desired key board type.

5. Choose the type of installation method.

6. Configure the network settings.

7. Specify the remote install server information.

8. If necessary, check the boot media and start the installation.

9. Click **Next** to begin the installation.

10. Enter the installation number and click **OK** or **Skip** the step.

11. A warning message will be displayed if you are using a new hard disk; click **Yes** to continue.

12. From the partition layout drop-down list, choose the desired partition layout and click **Next.**

13. If a warning message is displayed, click **Yes** to continue.

14. If necessary, review the partition table and click **Next.**

15. On the bootloader installation page, choose the type of bootloader and its location and then click **Next.**

16. On the network configuration page, configure the network and click **Next.**

17. Choose the desired time zone for the machine and click **Next.**

18. Enter the root password and click **Next.**

19. Accept the default package list or choose **Customize now** and click **Next.**

20. Select the necessary package and click **Next.**

21. On the installation complete page, click **Reboot** to finish the installation and reboot the system.

Procedure Reference: Configure the Post-Installation Settings

To configure the post-installation settings:

1. On the post installation welcome screen, click **Forward.**

2. Accept the license agreement and click **Forward.**

3. If necessary, customize the **Firewall** settings and click **Forward.**

4. If necessary, customize the **SELinux** settings and click **Forward.**

5. If necessary, enable **kdump** and click **Forward.**

6. If necessary, customize the **Date and Time** settings and click **Forward.**

7. Set up software updates with RHN and click **Forward.**

8. Create a user and click **Forward.**

9. If necessary, customize the sound card settings and click **Forward.**

10. If necessary, install software from additional CDs.

11. Click **Finish** to complete the installation.

12. Log in to the system using the user name and password.

Procedure Reference: Access the Network Installation Server

To access the network installation server:

1. Log in as root.

2. Insert the installation CD into the CD-ROM and mount it using the command `mount /dev/cdrom /{mount point}`.

3. Enter `cp -R /{mount point}/* /{destination directory}/` to copy the installation image into the destination folder.

4. Replace the CD with the next installation CD and perform steps 2 and 3.

5. Configure the server to be used during the remote installation.

    a. Configure the NFS server for network installation.

        1. Enter `vi /etc/exports` to open the exports file.

        2. Type `/{destination directory} [options]` to specify the destination directory for obtaining installation files.

        3. Save and close the file.

        4. Enter `service nfs start` to start the NFS server.

        5. Enter `exportfs -r` to export the directory.

    b. Configure the FTP server for network installation.

        1. Ensure that the `/{destination directory}` is/var/ftp/pub for FTP-based installation.

        2. Type `/{destination directory} [options]` to specify the destination directory for obtaining installation files.

        3. Save and close the file.

        4. Enter `service vsftpd start` to start the FTP server.

    c. Configure the HTTP server for network installation.

        1. Ensure that the `/{destination directory}` is/var/www/html for HTTP-based installation.

        2. Type `/{destination directory} [options]` to specify the destination directory for obtaining installation files.

        3. Save and close the file.

        4. Enter `service httpd start` to start the httpd server.

Procedure Reference: Create a Boot Media

To create a boot media:

1. Log in as root.

2. Create a boot media.

    a. Create a boot CD.

        1. At the command prompt, enter `cp /media/images/boot.iso {destination directory}` to copy the boot image to the specified location.

        2. Enter `cd {destination directory}` to navigate to that location.

        3. Enter `cdrecord -v boot.iso` to create the boot CD.

    b. Create a boot USB drive.

        1. At the command prompt, enter `cat /media/images/bootdisk.img > /dev/{device name}{device number}` to redirect the bootdisk.img content to where the USB device node is located.

INSTRUCTOR ACTIVITY 17-4

Installing Linux

Before You Begin:

1. On srvB, the GUI login screen is displayed.
2. Insert the Red Hat Enterprise Linux CD 1 in the CD-ROM drive and reboot the system from the CD-ROM.

Scenario:

A Linux system needs to be allocated to a new employee of your organization. You have been assigned the task of installing the Linux operating system and configuring the basic network settings to connect to the organization's network.

What You Do	How You Do It
1. Initiate the Red Hat Enterprise Linux 5 installation process for a server system.  Ensure that the Red Hat Enterprise Linux CD 1 is inserted in the CD-ROM drive and boot the system from the CD-ROM.	a. On the **Boot** page, press **Enter** to install Linux in the graphical mode. b. On the **Welcome To Red Hat Enterprise Linux Server** page, in the **CD Found** dialog box, select **Skip** to skip the media test and start the installation process. c. On the **Red Hat Enterprise Linux 5** page, click **Next**. d. On the Language Selection page, in the **Language Selection** list box, verify that the **English (English)** option is selected and then click **Next**. e. On the Keyboard Configuration page, verify that the **U.S. English** option in the **Keyboard** section is selected and then click **Next**. f. Observe that the **Installation Number** dialog box is displayed. Select the **Skip entering Installation Number** option and click **OK**. g. In the **Skip** message box, click **Skip.** h. On the **Installation Option** page, verify that the **Install Red Hat Enterprise Linux Server** option is selected and click **Next**.

2.	Partition the hard disk manually.	a.	Verify that the **Remove linux partitions on selected drives and create default layout** option is selected and click **Next**.
		b.	In the Warning message box, select **Yes** and click **Next**.
3.	Set the network configuration.	a.	In the **Network Devices** section, click **Edit**.
		b.	In the **Edit Interface eth0** dialog box, select the **Manual Configuration** option and uncheck the **Enable IPv6 support** check box.
		c.	In the **IPv4** section, in the **Address** text box, type *192.168.0.2* and then press the **Tab** key.
		d.	In the **Prefix (Netmask)** text box, type *255.255.255.0* and click **OK.**
		e.	On the Network Configuration page, verify that in the **Hostname** section, in the **manually** text box, the text **localhost.localdomain** is displayed and then click **Next**.
		f.	In the **Error With Data** message box, click **Continue** to proceed with the installation without specifying the IP address of the gateway system.
		g.	In the **Error With Data** message box, click **Continue** to proceed with the installation without specifying the IP address of the primary DNS system.
4.	Set the time zone and root password.	a.	On the Time Zone Selection page, in the **Location** section, verify that the **America/ New_York** option is selected and then click **Next**.
		b.	On the Set Root Password page, in the **Root Password** text box, click and enter *p@ssw0rd*
		c.	In the **Confirm** text box, enter *p@ssw0rd* and click **Next**.

5.	Select the required software packages for the system.	a.	On the Software Selection page, in the Include Support section, check the **Software Development** and **Web server** check boxes.
		b.	In the **Customize** section, select the **Customize now** option and then click **Next.**
		c.	On the Package Selection page, in the first list box, verify that the **Desktop Environments** option is selected and in the adjacent list box, check the **KDE (K Desktop Environment)** check box.
		d.	In the first list box, select the **Servers** option, and in the adjacent list box, check the **DNS Name Server, FTP Server,** and **Network Servers** packages.
		e.	In the first list box, select the **Base System** option, and in the adjacent list box, check the **System Tools** check box and then click **Next.**
6.	Perform installation.	a.	On the Begin Installation page, click **Next.**
		b.	In the **Required Install Media** dialog box, click **Continue.**

 The required set of CDs, as displayed on the Required Install Media dialog box, must be kept ready before proceeding with the installation process.

		c.	When prompted, insert Red Hat Linux CD-02, CD-03, and CD-04 into the CD drive and click **OK.**
		d.	On the Congratulations page, click **Reboot.**

7. Configure the post installation settings.

a. On the **Welcome** page, click **Forward.**

b. On the **License Agreement** page, verify that the **Yes, I agree to the License Agreement** option is selected and then click **Forward.**

c. On the **Firewall** page, from the **Firewall** drop-down list, select **Disabled** and then click **Forward.**

d. In the confirmation message box, click **Yes.**

e. On the **SELinux** page, from the **SELinux Setting** drop-down list, select **Disabled** and then click **Forward.**

f. In the confirmation dialog box, click **Yes.**

g. On the **Kdump** page, click **Forward.**

h. On the **Date and Time** page, verify that the date and time is set to the current date and time and then click **Forward.**

i. On the **Set Up Software Updates** page, select the **No, I prefer to register at a later time** option and click **Forward.**

j. In the Red Hat network connection dialog box, click **No thanks, I'll connect later.**

k. On the **Finish Updates Setup** page, click **Forward.**

l. On the **Create User** page, click **Forward.**

m. In the confirmation message box, click **Continue.**

n. On the **Sound Card** page, click **Forward.**

o. On the **Additional CDs** page, click **Finish.**

p. In the confirmation dialog box, click **OK** to reboot the system.

TOPIC E
Perform Post-Installation Tasks

You successfully installed Linux. Now, you need to begin using the operating system. In this topic, you will perform post-installation tasks.

Before you begin working with your new Linux system, you need to perform certain basic tasks. To begin with, if you want to use the GUI environment you must configure X Windows. Secondly, you must document your settings. Documentation is the key to solving future problems, getting equipment upgrades, and preventing financial losses from network troubles. Documenting changes to setups, configurations, topologies, and histories can help you troubleshoot problems that arise later.

The X Windows Configuration

X Windows, also known as *X* or *X11,* is a client/server, multiuser system that resides on top of the operating system. The X Window system configuration option provides a choice of a graphical or text-based interface. The primary configuration file defines hardware devices and other critical components of the X server environment. Configuration options include monitor, video card, keyboard, pointing device, and many more.

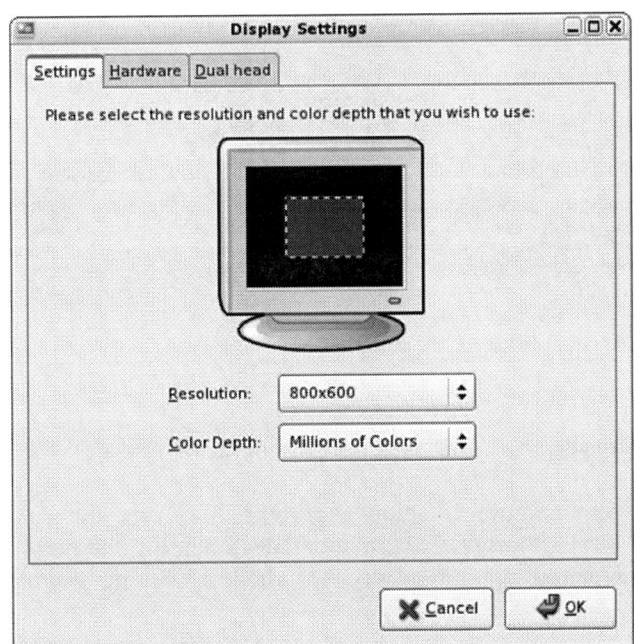

Figure 17-12: The Display Settings dialog box that is used to configure X Windows.

Red Hat Runlevel

If you configure the X Window system during the Red Hat Linux installation program, you have the option of choosing a graphical or text login screen. If you choose a text login screen, you will be operating in runlevel 3. If you choose a graphical login screen, you will be operating in runlevel 5.

Virtual Desktops

Consider a situation where you have multiple windows open on your desktop. In this case, you have three options:

- Leave all windows open, which may result in a cluttered desktop.
- Minimize those windows that you do not need at present and use the taskbar or press **Alt+Tab** to switch between them. This approach could still be a bit confusing.
- Or, use virtual desktops.

The default configuration provides two or four desktops depending on the distribution. For example, Ubuntu provides two desktops by default and RHEL provides four. You can switch between the virtual desktops by clicking one of the desktop buttons on the panel at the bottom of the desktop screen.

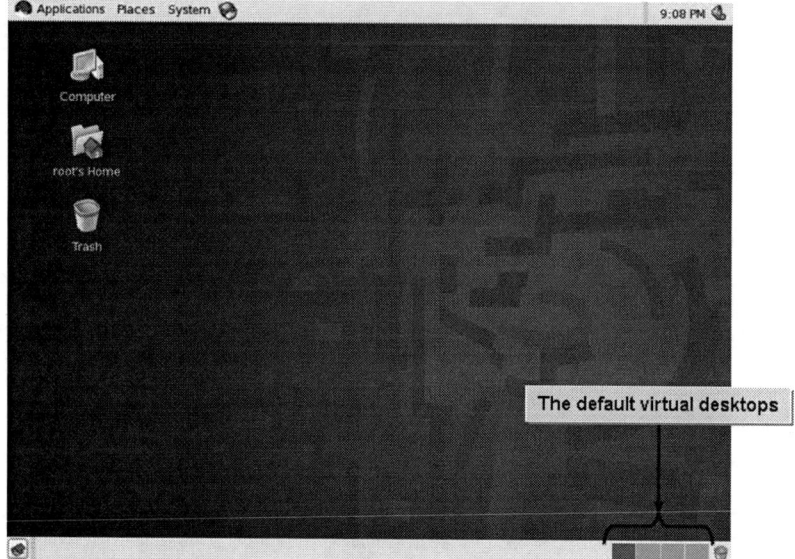

Figure 17-13: Virtual desktop buttons on the panel.

Documentation

Sufficient and proper documentation of setups, configurations, topologies, and histories can prove valuable while troubleshooting. This includes documenting the hardware and software components installed, why and when they were installed, by whom, and other important and specific information.

Include Log File Information

Check the log files:

- /var/log/messages
- /var/log/dmesg
- /tmp/install

These files contain information captured during the installation. You may want to include hard copies of these files in your installation documentation.

How to Perform Post-installation Tasks

Procedure Reference: Configure X Windows

To configure X Windows:

1. Log in to GNOME.
2. Choose **Applications→System Settings→Display.**
3. If necessary, adjust the **Display** settings.
    *   Resolution
    *   Color Depth
4. Select the **Hardware** tab to adjust the hardware settings.
    *   Monitor Type
    *   Video Card
5. Select the **Dual Head** tab to adjust settings for multiple monitors.

ACTIVITY 17-5

Configuring X Windows

Before You Begin:

The GUI login screen of srvB is displayed.

Scenario:

Because your manager would like even novice users to be able to use Linux, you should familiarize yourself with configuring X Windows. This will allow novice users to work in a GUI environment, which is more comfortable.

What You Do	How You Do It
1. Log in to GNOME and view the display settings.	a. At the login screen, type **root** and press **Enter.**
	b. For the password, type **p@ssw0rd** and press **Enter.**
	c. Choose **System→Administration→ Display.**
2. Adjust the resolution.	a. Change the resolution to **800x600.**
	b. To accept the changes, click **OK.**
	c. In the message box, click **OK.**
	d. Press **Ctrl+Alt+Backspace** to restart the X server.
	e. Log in as **root** in the GUI.
	f. Choose **System→Administration→ Display.**
	g. Verify that the resolution has changed.

3. Verify that the video card and monitor type are set correctly.

a. Select the **Hardware** tab.

b. Verify that the monitor is set to the monitor you are currently using.

c. Verify that the video card is set to the one you are currently using.

d. In the **Display Settings** dialog box, click **OK.**

e. In the message box, click **OK.**

Lesson 17 Follow-up

In this lesson, you installed the Linux operating system. You also performed pre-installation and post-installation tasks and documented your actions. These steps ensured your successful installation of the Linux operating system.

1. **How does the boot process affect the applications installed on a system? Why?**

2. **Which is the best runlevel to boot a system? Why?**

18 | Configuring the GUI

Lesson Time: 1 hour(s)

Lesson Objectives:

In this lesson, you will configure the GUI.

You will:

● Implement X.

● Customize the display manager.

● Customize the window environment.

Introduction

You used the CLI to perform tasks in Linux. However, for those who are not comfortable with the CLI, Linux also provides a more user-friendly GUI. In this lesson, you will configure the GUI.

Linux provides the flexibility of switching back and forth between the CLI and the GUI. While the command line allows you to perform an action with speed, the GUI is more user-friendly and allows you to find options and functions easily when you cannot remember the corresponding commands.

This lesson covers all or part of the following CompTIA Linux+ (2009) certification objectives:

● Topic A

■ Objective 2.5

● Topic B

■ Objective 2.5

● Topic C

■ Objective 2.5

TOPIC A

Implement X

You performed post-installation tasks. Sometimes, when you are guiding users through a process, they may not understand the commands you tell them to type in the CLI. In such situations, you can choose the GUI because it is more user-friendly. Combining the GUI and CLI in Linux provides users greater control and options. In this topic, you will implement X to work with the GUI.

Because Linux provides both the CLI and GUI, users can choose to work in either one of them or both. Some users may not like the blank screen of the command line. They may prefer working with more user-friendly icons and windows. Also, they may not always remember the commands to carry out a task. In such cases, they can use the GUI to accomplish the task.

X.Org

X.Org is a free version of the X Window GUI system for some Linux distributions. It provides an interface between input hardware, such as the mouse and the keyboard, and the desktop environment. It is platform independent and extensible because it can be modified by changing or adding new features.

X Servers

Definition:

An *X server* is a program that implements the GUI provided by the X Window system. It runs on the local machine and manages the keyboard, mouse, and display device. It converts the X Windows protocol commands to machine language commands. It also converts the GUI commands to X Windows protocol commands for clients. It draws pictures and displays text on the screen.

Example:

Figure 18-1: The GUI desktop.

The X Protocol

The *X protocol* is the standard protocol used by clients and servers in the X Window system. Using this protocol, requests for window operations can be exchanged.

X Clients

Definition:

An *X client* is an application that is written with the aid of the Xlib library, which gives programs access to any X server. An X client sends requests to the X server for a certain action to take place, for instance, to create a window. The X server sends the event that the X client is expecting, in response to the request. An X client also receives errors in requests from the server. There can be more than one X client sending requests to the X server.

Example:

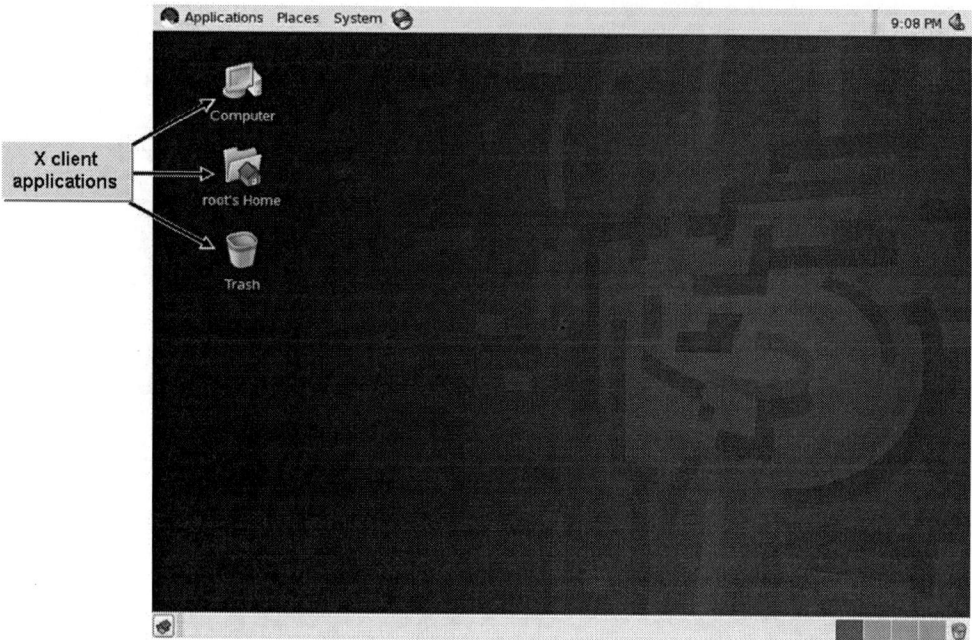

Figure 18-2: X client applications on the desktop.

X Font Servers

Definition:

An *X font server (Xfs)* is a service that provides fonts to the X server and X client applications that connect to the X server. The /etc/init.d/xfs script starts the Xfs server. The *font path,* which is a collection of paths in the filesystem where font files are stored, can also be edited using Xfs. Fonts may be stored on one machine acting as a networked font server. Multiple X servers can share these fonts over the network. Xfs supports the TrueType, Type1, and bitmap fonts.

Example:

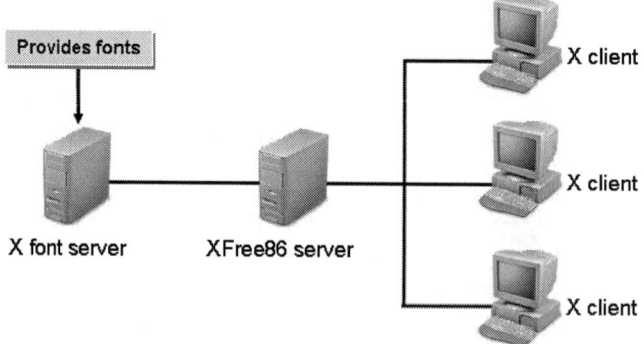

Figure 18-3: The X font server providing fonts to clients.

XOrg Runlevels

The X Window system boots in two main runlevels: runlevel 3 and runlevel 5. When you start a machine, it boots in the graphical mode, which is runlevel 5. You can also boot the machine in the CLI or text mode, which is runlevel 3. Runlevel 3 is the full multiuser mode. The X server is started from runlevel 3 using the `startx` or `xinit` command.

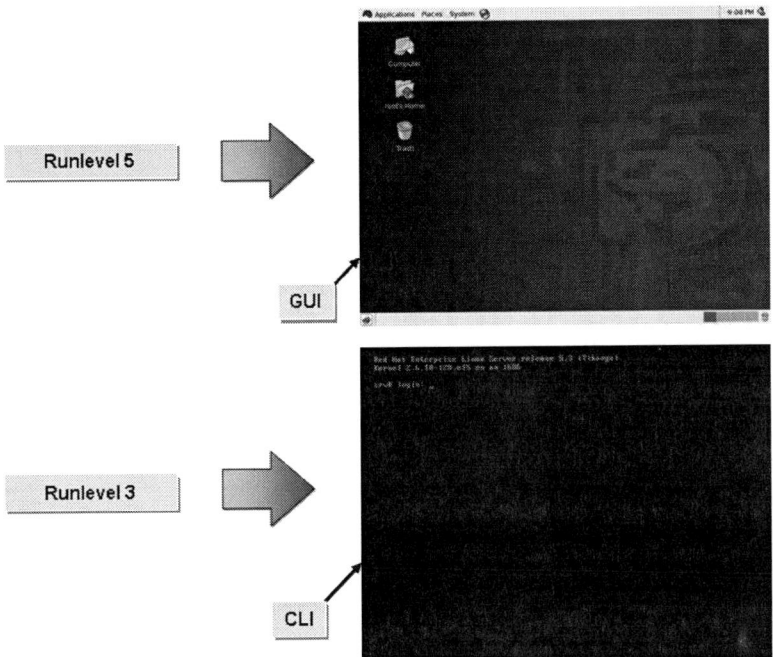

Figure 18-4: Booting in different runlevels results in different displays.

Remote X Sessions

Definition:

Remote X sessions are sessions where a user on a remote workstation is able to view the X Window of the host and run the host's applications. These sessions can run on local and TCP/IP networks. Remote X sessions can either be host based or user based. Host-based sessions are implemented by invoking the `xhost` command, which allows the user to add or remove hosts. User-based sessions are implemented by the `xauth` utility, which authorizes users who can access the remote X host using keys.

Example:

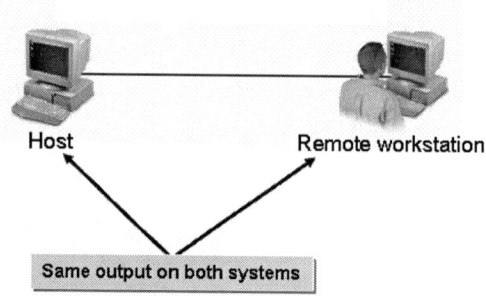

Host   Remote workstation

Same output on both systems

Figure 18-5: Remote X session over a network.

Commands Used in Remote X Sessions

The xhost and xauth commands are used to manage remote X sessions. A number of options are provided for effective session management.

Option	Enables You To
xhost - help	Display a usage message.
xhost +{name}	Add a name to the list of hosts or users connecting to the X server.
xhost -{name}	Remove a name from the list of hosts or users connecting to the X server.
xauth -f authfile	Set the authority file to be used by xauth.
xauth -i	Let xauth bypass authority file locks.
xauth -v	Let xauth print status messages.

X-Stations

Definition:

An *X-station* is a terminal or diskless workstation that is connected to a network and engineered to run the X Window system remotely. An X-station is not directly connected to a computer's CPU. All X-station systems on a network are connected to a central workstation. The central workstation provides the terminals with the operating system, memory, programs, and CPU cycles.

Example:

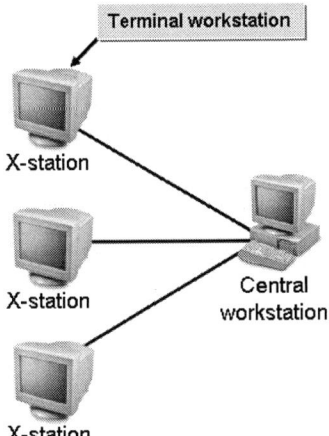

Figure 18-6: *X-station systems connected to a central workstation on a network.*

How to Implement X

Procedure Reference: Customize X for the Monitor Automatically

To customize X for the monitor:

1. Log in as root in the GUI.

2. In the warning box that appears, click **Continue.**

3. Choose **Applications→Accessories→Terminal** to display the terminal.

4. Enter `system-config-display` to open the **Display Settings** window.

5. Select the **Hardware** tab.

6. Customize the monitor settings.

    a. In the **Monitor Type** section, click **Configure.**

    b. To expand the **Monitor** section, click the triangle.

    c. Select the appropriate monitor model and click **OK** to save the settings in the /etc/ X11/xorg.conf file.

7. Click **OK** to close the **Display Settings** window.

8. At the prompt, click **OK.**

9. Choose **System→Log Out root** to log out of the GUI.

10. Log in for the changes to take effect.

 The X Window automatically detects the type of monitor and its settings. If you need to customize the monitor type, refer to the corresponding monitor's product manual to learn its type and optimum settings. Monitor type refers to the different models, sizes, and whether it's a generic or laptop display.

The system-config-display Command

The `system-config-display` command displays the **Display Settings** dialog box to set the system resolution, color depth, and other advanced display settings.

Procedure Reference: Customize X for the Monitor Manually

To customize X for the monitor manually:

1. Log in as root in the CLI.
2. Enter `cd /etc/X11` to navigate to the /etc/X11 folder.
3. Enter `vi xorg.conf` to open the X configuration file.
4. Under the **Section "Screen"** column, make necessary changes to the monitor settings.
5. Save and close the file.
6. Log out and log in for the changes to take effect.

Procedure Reference: Change Default Bitplanes for the Display Manager

To change the default bitplanes for the display manager:

1. Log in as root in the GUI.
2. Choose **Applications→Accessories→Terminal** to display the terminal.
3. Enter `system-config-display`.
4. From the **Resolution** drop-down list, select the desired resolution.
5. From the **Color Depth** drop-down list, select the desired color depth.
6. Click **OK** two times to save the settings.
7. Choose **System→Log Out root.**
8. In the **Log out of this system now?** dialog box, click **Log Out.**
9. Log in again to verify the applied settings.

 Bitplanes refer to the display resolution.

Refresh Rate

Refresh rate or vertical scan rate is the speed at which a screen is refreshed. Normally, color displays are refreshed 60 times per second.

Resolution and Color Depth

Resolution is the number of pixels that a computer monitor is capable of displaying. It is described in terms of Width x Height. The most common resolutions are 640 x 480, 800 x 600, and 1024 x 768.

Color depth refers to the number of colors used to display an image. The values can range from 256 colors to millions of colors. The size of a file increases with the increase in color depth value.

Procedure Reference: Customize X for the Video Card

To customize X for the video card:

1. Log in to the terminal as root.
2. Enter `system-config-display`.
3. Select the **Hardware** tab.

4. Customize X for the video card.

    a. In the **Video Card** section, click **Configure.**

    b. Select the appropriate video card and driver settings.

    c. Click **OK** two times to save the settings.

 The X Window automatically detects the type of video card and its driver settings. You can also refer to the product manual to learn the type and optimum settings of the video card.

 Every video card comes with a default memory requirement in the form of RAM, which is required for the video card to perform optimally. For normal graphics support, the default memory requirement is 32 MB RAM. If you use graphic-intensive applications, you may need to allocate higher RAM space for optimal performance, provided your video card supports it. You need to check the product manual of the video card for configuration details.

The xvidtune Command

The `xvidtune` command displays the **xvidtune** dialog box to configure the horizontal and vertical display settings.

 This command, when wrongly used, may cause permanent damage to the monitor or video card. Therefore, you must ensure that you do not change any settings without fully understanding the purpose of the setting.

Procedure Reference: Install Fonts

To install fonts:

1. Log in as root in the GUI.

2. Choose **Applications→Accessories→Terminal** to display the terminal.

3. Create a directory and copy the font into the directory.

    a. Enter `mkdir /{Directory name}` to create the font directory.

    b. Enter `cp /{Directory containing fonts}/{Font name}.ttf /{Directory name}.`

    c. Enter `cd /{Directory name}.`

4. Create the files fonts.scale and font.dir in the new directory.

    a. Enter `ttmkfdir -d /{Directory name} -o /{Directory name}/fonts.scale.`

    b. Enter `mkfontdir /{Directory name}.`

5. Enter `chkfontpath -a /{Directory name}` to add the new directory to the default font server configuration file, /etc/X11/fs/config.

6. If necessary, enter `chkfontpath --list` to view the newly added font path.

7. Enter `service xfs restart` to restart the xfs service.

8. Choose **System→Preferences→Fonts** to display the **Font Preferences** dialog box.

9. Click the menu button next to **Application font.**

10. In the **Pick a Font** dialog box, from the **Family** list, select the installed font.

11. Click **OK** and click **Close.**

The xorg.conf File

The xorg.config file is a configuration file for XOrg. This file is used for configuring different X Window parameters and is located in the/etc/X11/xorg.conf directory.

Procedure Reference: Configure X to Use the Font Server

To configure X to use the font server:

1. Log in as root in the CLI.

2. Enter `service xfs restart` to restart the X font server.

3. If necessary, enter `chkconfig xfs on` to make Xfs available at system startup.

4. Enter `startx` to start the X Window.

Procedure Reference: Configuring XOrg in Runlevel 3

To configure XOrg in runlevel 3:

1. Log in as root in the CLI.

2. Enter `init 3` to boot in runlevel 3.

3. Enter `xinit`, `startx`, or `init 5` to start the X server from the command line.

Procedure Reference: Configuring XOrg in Runlevel 5

To configure XOrg in runlevel 5:

1. Log in as root.

2. At the command prompt, enter `vi /etc/inittab` to open the inittab file.

3. Ensure that the line `id: runlevel: initdefault` reads `id:5:initdefault` to boot in runlevel 5.

4. Save and close the file.

5. Restart the computer.

Procedure Reference: Export X Sessions

To export X sessions:

1. Log in as root in the GUI.

2. At the terminal, enter `DISPLAY=Client IP Address:0.0` to set the display variable.

 DISPLAY is an environment variable that is used to specify where to export the X display.

3. Log in as root in the client machine in the GUI.

4. Enter `xhost +Server IP address` to add the server to the list of hosts.

ACTIVITY 18-1

Configuring X Font Servers

Data Files:

MalOtf.ttf

Before You Begin:

1. You have logged in as root in the GUI of srvA.

2. The terminal window is displayed.

3. On the terminal window, enter `rpm -qi libFS` to check if the libFS-1.0.0-3.1.i386.rpm package is installed.

4. Enter `rpm -qi xorg-x11-xfs` to check if the xorg-x11-xfs-1.0.2.4.i386.rpm package is installed.

5. Enter `rpm -qi chkfontpath` to check if the chkfontpath-1.10.1-1.1.i386.rpm package is installed.

6. Copy the MalOtf.ttf file from /085039Data/Graphical_User_Interface to the /root directory.

7. Enter `clear` to clear the terminal window.

Scenario:

You are setting up computers for new employees in various divisions of your organization. A new employee in the graphics department requires Linux GUI with high resolution and color settings. The employee also wants the MalOtf.ttf font installed in the system.

What You Do	How You Do It
1. Install the new font.	a. Enter `mkdir /usr/share/fonts/local` to create a font directory.
	b. Enter `cp /root/MalOtf.ttf /usr/share/fonts/local` to copy the font file to the /usr/share/fonts/local directory.
	c. Enter `cd /usr/share/fonts/local` to navigate to the local directory.
	d. Enter `ttmkfdir -d /usr/share/fonts/local -o⇒ /usr/share/fonts/local/fonts.scale`
	e. Enter `mkfontdir /usr/share/fonts/local`
	f. Enter `chkfontpath -a /usr/share/fonts/local`
2. Configure the new font.	a. Enter `service xfs restart` to restart the `xfs` service.
	b. Enter `clear` to clear the terminal window.
	c. Choose **System→Preferences→Fonts** to display the **Font Preferences** dialog box.
	d. Click the menu button next to **Application font.**
	e. In the **Pick a Font** dialog box, in the **Family** list, scroll up and select **MalOtf** and click **OK.**
	f. Click **Close.**

ACTIVITY 18-2

Configuring XOrg Server

Before You Begin:
1. You logged in as root in the GUI.
2. The terminal window is displayed.

Scenario:
Kevin, a user on your network wants to view the X Window of his system on the environment system, which is on the same network. You are assigned the task of setting up his system. You decide to configure the X server and check if it is in the proper runlevel. You decide to export the X session to the environment system.

What You Do	How You Do It
1. Configure the boot runlevel.	a. Enter `vi /etc/inittab` to open the inittab file.
	b. Verify that the line **id:{runlevel}:initdefault:** reads **id:5:initdefault:** to boot in runlevel 5.
	c. Close the file.
2. Export X sessions.	a. Enter `DISPLAY=192.168.0.2:0.0` to export the X session.
	b. Enter **exit** to close the terminal window.
	c. Choose **System→Log Out root** to log out of the system.
	d. In the message box, click **Log Out** to log out of the system.

TOPIC B

Customize the Display Manager

You implemented X to work with the Linux GUI. Now, you want to customize the GUI environment. In the GUI, the desktop is one of the first screens that a user interacts with. Therefore, it is necessary that the desktop be appealing and easy to use. In this topic, you will customize the display manager to manage the desktop environment.

The desktop is an important part of any GUI. Users may want to customize their desktop environments according to their own preferences. They can keep applications that they access frequently and shortcuts to different programs on the desktop. This will enable easy access to various applications and options.

Display Managers

Definition:

A *display manager*, or *window manager*, is a program that controls the look and feel of a desktop environment. The display manager provides a graphical login screen and manages a collection of X servers. These servers may be on the local host or on remote systems. These managers can be customized to run every time the system boots. The most popular desktop environments that are used by users are GNOME and KDE.

You can customize any of the applications present in the **Applications**, **Places**, or **System** folders for KDE and GNOME. After saving the settings, they will then be applied to the desktop environment. Most of the applications are common to both KDE and GNOME, while some are specific to the individual environment, such as **Control Center** in KDE.

Example:

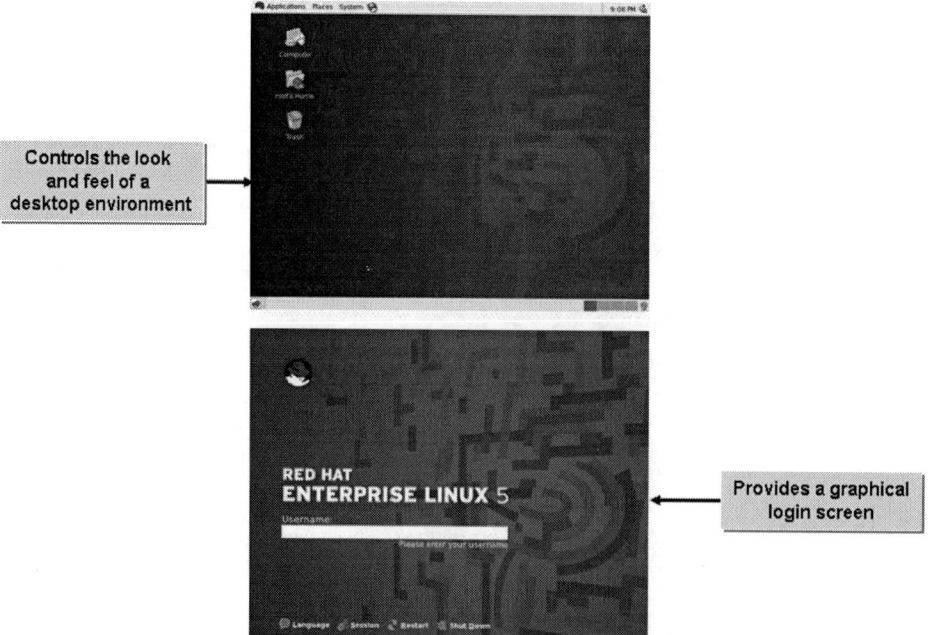

Figure 18-7: Output of the display manager.

Display Managers for Linux

Common display managers for Linux are as follows:

● The *GNOME display manager (GDM)* is the default display manager for Red Hat Linux. GDM allows users to configure language settings and log in to, shutdown, or reboot the system.

● The *KDE display manager (KDM)* is the display manager for KDE, or K Desktop Environment. It allows users to log in, shutdown, or reboot the system.

The GNOME Desktop Environment

The GNOME desktop environment (GDE) is the default desktop environment in most Linux distributions. The GNOME desktop initially displays three icons: **Computer, root's Home,** and **Trash.** There are two horizontal panels, one at the top and one at the bottom of the desktop. A user can customize these panels with shortcuts to applications that are frequently used. The GDM is used to customize the GDE.

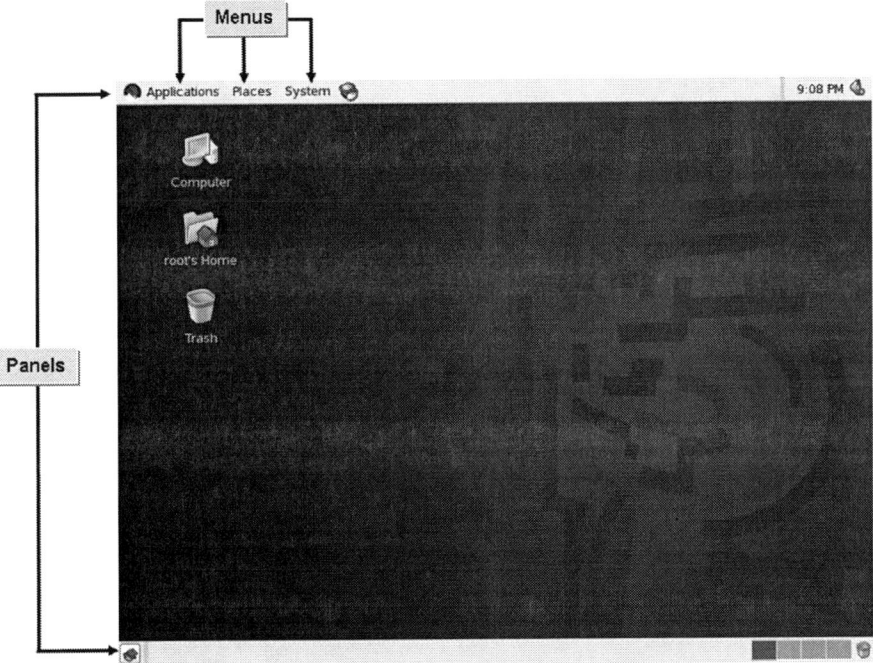

Figure 18-8: The GDM with its various components.

The KDE Desktop Environment

The KDE desktop environment is installed along with GDE in some distributions such as RHEL 5. In KDE, there is only one horizontal panel at the bottom. In RHEL 5, the main menu can be accessed by clicking the Red Hat logo at the bottom-left corner of the KDE panel. KDE can be customized to suit users' needs.

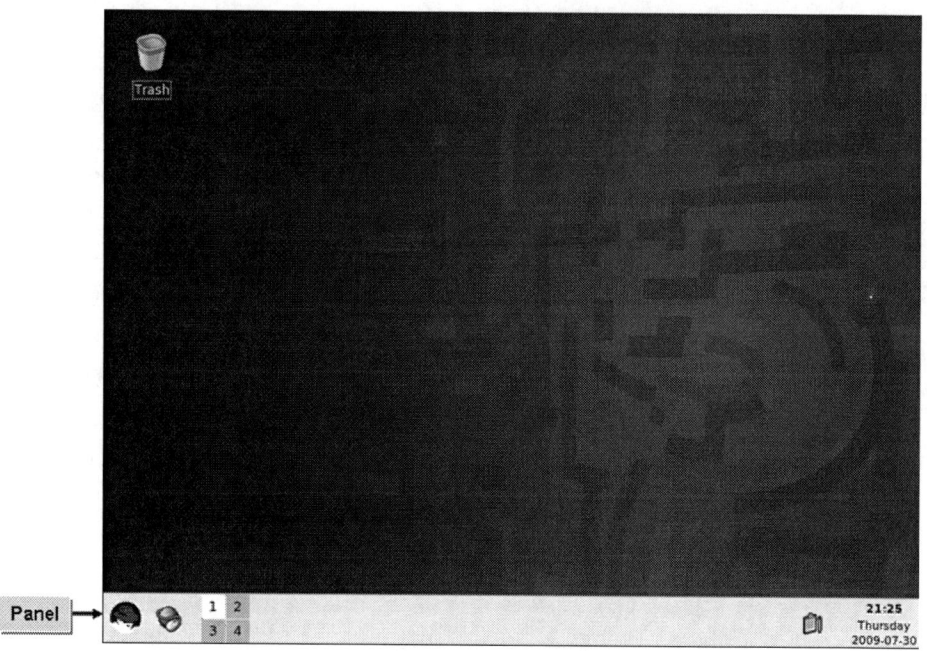

Figure 18-9: The KDE display manager, displaying only one panel.

Configure KDM

The **Configure - KDesktop** window enables you to customize the appearance of KDM. The options that are available in the **Configure - KDesktop** window are provided in the following table.

Configure - KDesktop Options	Used To
Display	Configure the resolution and other display settings.
Behavior	Configure the behavior of the desktop, such as enabling icons on the desktop and the action to be performed on clicking the right, left, or middle mouse button.
Multiple Desktops	Configure the number of virtual desktops. For example, you can specify up to 20 virtual desktops in RHEL.
Background	Change the background settings such as wallpaper and background.
Screen Saver	Set a screen saver and its timing options.

KDE Panel Configuration Options

The **Add Applet, Add Application,** and **Add New Panel** options are used to access and configure different applications that are categorized under **Applet, Application Button,** and **Panel.** Some of the options in each menu are provided in the following table.

Add Applet	Add Application	Add New Panel
Clock	The Internet	Panel
Lock/Logout Buttons	Office	Dock Application Bar
Quick Launcher	Find Files/Folders	External Taskbar
Trash	Control Center	KasBar
System Monitor	Help	Universal Sidebar

The switchdesk Command

The switchdesk command provides a simple method of switching among various desktop environments. To enable the switchdesk command, the packages switchdesk-4.0.8-6.noarch.rpm and switchdesk-gui-4.0.8-6.noarch.rpm have to be installed after the installation of the Linux operating system is complete. On running the switchdesk command from the terminal, the **Desktop Switcher** dialog box is displayed.

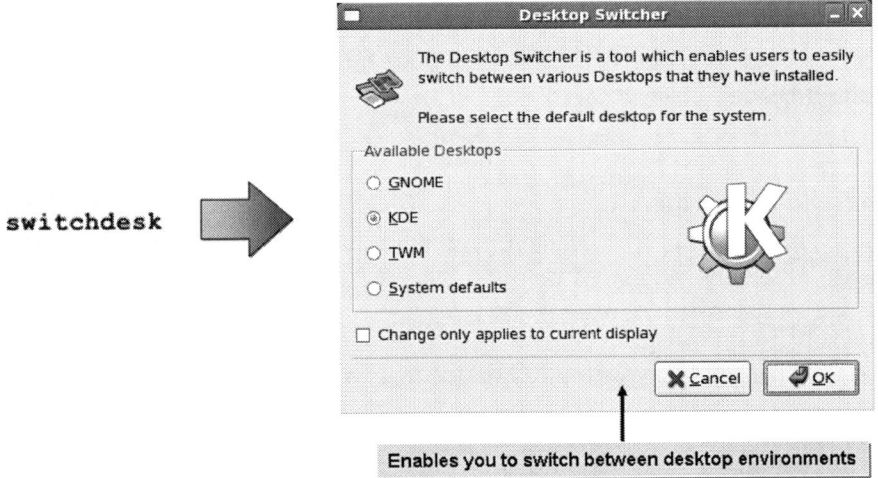

Figure 18-10: The Desktop Switcher dialog box used to switch between desktops.

How to Customize the Display Manager
Procedure Reference: Switch Between Desktop Environments

To switch between KDM and GDM:

1. Log in as root in GUI.
2. Display the terminal window.
3. To enable the switch desk feature, verify that the packages, switchdesk-{version}.{release}.rpm and switchdesk-gui-{version}.{release}.rpm are installed.
4. Enter `switchdesk {Desktop type}` to display the **Desktop Switcher** window.
5. Choose the desired desktop environment.
6. Click **OK** two times to apply the changes.
7. Log out and log in to verify the applied changes.

Procedure Reference: Configure GDM

To configure GDM:

1. Log in as root in the GNOME desktop environment.
2. Choose **Applications→System Tools→Terminal.**
3. Enter `gdmsetup` to open the **Login Window Preferences** dialog box.
4. Make the necessary changes.
5. Click **Close.**

Configure GDM Using the CLI

To configure GDM using the CLI, navigate to the /etc/X11/gdm/gdm.conf file. You can manually change the necessary settings, which will then be applied to the desktop after you save and exit the file and start the X Window service.

Procedure Reference: Configure KDM Using the Configure - KDesktop Window

To configure KDM using the **Configure - KDesktop** window:

1. Log in as root on the KDE desktop.
2. Right-click the desktop and choose **Configure Desktop.**
3. In the **Configure - KDesktop** window, configure the settings.
    - Select **Background** to modify the background settings.
    - Select **Behavior** to configure the desktop behavior.
    - Select **Multiple Desktops** to configure multiple virtual desktops.
    - Select **Screen Saver** to modify the screen saver settings.
    - Select **Display** to modify the display settings.
4. In the **Configure - KDesktop** window, click **Apply** and then click **OK.**

Procedure Reference: Configure Display Managers for Use by X Stations

To configure the desired display managers for use by X stations:

1. Log in as root in the GUI.
2. Enter `switchdesk` to display the **Desktop Switcher** window.
3. Choose the desired desktop environment.

4. Click **OK** two times to apply the changes.

5. Reboot the system to verify that the system boots in the specified desktop.

Procedure Reference: Change the GDM Greeting Page

To change the GDM greeting page:

1. Log in as root on the GNOME desktop environment.

2. Choose **Applications→Accessories→Terminal.**

3. Enter `gdmsetup` to display the **Login Window Preferences** dialog box.

4. In the **Login Window Preferences** dialog box, select the **Local** tab.

5. In the **Themes** section, choose the desired greeting page.

6. Click **Close.**

7. Enter `exit` to close the terminal window.

8. Choose **System→Log Out root.**

9. In the **Log out of this system now** dialog box, click **Log Out.**

Instead of using the `switchdesk` command to switch between desktops, you can switch between desktops from the welcome screen. Click the **Session** button at the bottom of the welcome screen and select the appropriate desktop.

ACTIVITY 18-3
Configuring KDM

Before You Begin:
1. You have logged in as root in the GUI of srvB.
2. Log out of the root user account.

Scenario:
Robin, an employee working in the graphics department wants to create a customized desktop environment. His requirements include changing the default background, having six desktop windows, and adding the menu bar at the top of the screen. You are assigned the task of changing Robin's background. You find that Robin presently has GDM configured on his system.

What You Do	How You Do It
1. Switch from GNOME to KDE.	a. On the welcome screen of the GUI, click **Session.**
	b. In the **Sessions** dialog box, select the **KDE** option and click **Change Session.**
	c. In the **Username** text box, type *root* and press **Enter.**
	d. In the **Password** text box, type *p@ssw0rd* and press **Enter.**
	e. In the message box that allows you to make the selected session as default, click **Just For This Session.** to retain the current default session.
2. Change the desktop background image.	a. On the KDM desktop, right-click and choose **Configure Desktop.**
	b. In the **Configure - KDesktop** window, in the left pane, verify that **Background** is selected.
	c. In the right pane, in the **Background** section, click the **Picture** drop-down list.
	d. From the **Picture** drop-down list, scroll up and select **Kubical.**

3.	Add the menu bar at the top of the screen.	a.	In the left pane, select **Behavior.**
		b.	In the **Menu Bar at Top of Screen** section, select the **Desktop menu bar** option.

4.	Configure virtual desktops.	a.	In the left pane, select **Multiple Desktops.**
		b.	In the **Number of desktops** spin box, double-click and type *6*

5.	Apply new settings.	a.	In the **Configure - KDesktop** dialog box, click **Apply** to apply the settings.
		b.	Click **OK** to close the **Configure - KDesktop** dialog box.

TOPIC C
Customize the Window Environment

In the previous topic, you customized the display manager to manage the desktop environment. In addition to the desktop, windows and icons form an important part of a user's interaction with the GUI. In this topic, you will customize the window environment.

While working in the GUI, users will need to work with windows. They may need to manipulate the size and placement of windows to suit their needs. This makes it essential for users to know how to customize the window environment in Linux.

The Window Environment

Definition:

The window environment is the GUI screen with which users interact. It allows users to control and manipulate the appearance of windows by modifying their size and placement. It also provides users with icons, taskbars, title bars, and other desktop objects.

Example:

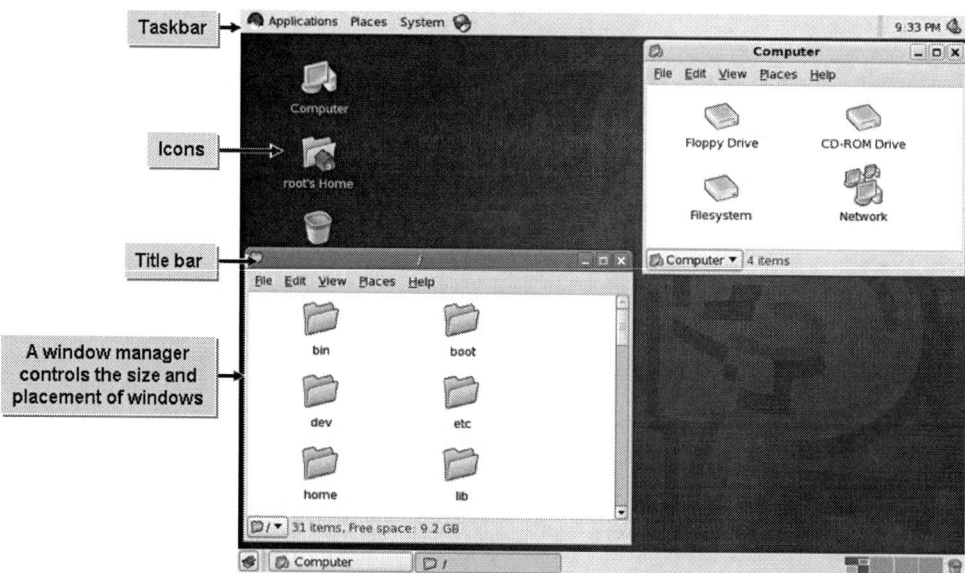

Figure 18-11: Desktop objects of a window environment.

The XTerm

Definition:

The *XTerm* is a screen for typing system commands for the X Window system. It is also known as the shell prompt, console, or terminal. It requires an X Server running on the local or remote system. It combines the advantages of the shell and the window manager user interfaces.

Example:

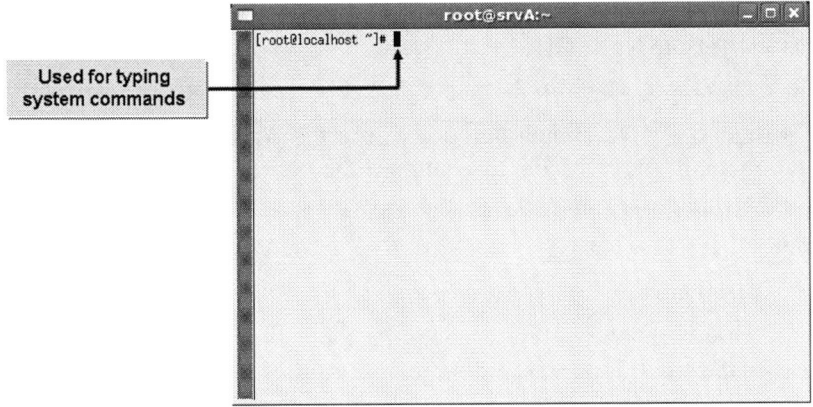

Figure 18-12: The XTerm window.

How to Customize the Window Environment

Procedure Reference: Customize a System-Wide Desktop Environment

To customize a system-wide desktop environment for KDE or GNOME:

1. Log in as root in the GUI.

2. On the desktop, click the **Start Here** icon in KDE to access the menu.

3. Click the **Applications, Places,** or **System** folder to access the respective contents and applications in GDE.

4. Make the necessary changes and save the settings.

Procedure Reference: Customize the Window Manager Menus

To customize the window manager in GNOME:

1. Customize the window manager menu in GNOME.

    a. Log in as root in the GNOME GUI.

    b. To add an application to the panel, right-click the empty space in the panel, which is located at the bottom of the screen, and choose **Add to Panel.**

    c. Choose the desired application and click **Add.**

    d. Click **Close** to close the **Add to Panel** dialog box.

    e. To move an application icon in the panel, right-click the icon, choose **Move** and then move the cursor to the desired location in the panel and click on the panel.

    f. If necessary, to delete an application icon in the panel, right-click the icon and choose **Remove From Panel.**

2. Position the panels in GNOME.

   a. Right-click the empty space in the panel, which is located at the bottom of the screen.

   b. Choose **New Panel** and choose the desired options.

   c. Right-click the panel and choose **Properties** to change the orientation, size, and color of the panel.

Procedure Reference: Configure a Panel in KDE

To configure a panel in KDE:

1. Log in as root in the KDE GUI.

2. Right-click the empty space in the panel and choose **Configure Panel.**

3. In the **Configure – KDE Panel** dialog box, use the **Arrangement, Appearance,** and **Taskbar** buttons in the left pane to configure the panel.

- The **Arrangement** option is used to change the position, length, and size of the panel.

- The **Appearance** option is used to change the appearance of the panel.

- The **Taskbar** option is used to configure the actions that need to be performed when clicking the right, left, and middle mouse buttons. It is also used to configure the taskbar.

4. Click **Apply** to apply the settings and click **OK** to close the **Configure – KDE Panel** dialog box.

Procedure Reference: Customize the Window Manager Menu for KDE

To customize the window manager menu for KDE:

1. Log in as root in the KDE GUI.

2. To add an application to the panel, right-click the empty space in the panel, and choose **Add Application to Panel** and then choose the desired application. The application icon is added to the panel.

3. To move an application icon in the panel, right-click the icon, choose the **Move [Application name]** button, and move the cursor to the desired location in the panel and then click to reposition the panel in the new location.

4. If necessary, to delete an application icon in the panel, right-click the icon and choose the **Remove [Application name]** button.

 You can add, move, or delete icons used applications in the KDE desktop.

Procedure Reference: Configure xterm

To configure xterm:

1. Log in as root in the GUI.

2. Display the terminal window.

3. Change the location of the xterm window in the screen.

   a. Enter `vi /etc/X11/xinit/xinitrc`.

   b. Scroll down and change `xterm -geometry 80x50-50+150`, which sets the location of the xterm window in the screen, to `xterm -{Parameter} {Value}`.

   c. Save and close the file.

The etc/X11/xinit directory contains the xinitrc file, which is used to start the window manager.

4. Log out from the current session.

5. Reboot the system to verify that the system boots on the specified desktop.

6. Click **Session,** choose **Failsafe Terminal** and click **OK.**

7. Enter the user name and password to display the xterm X terminal. Ensure that the cursor is within the xterm window.

8. Enter `exit` to log out and return to the login screen.

There are different types of terminals, such as xterm, rxvt, and aterm. The rxvt and aterm are X terminals that are intended as a replacement for xterm. Because they use less swap space than xterm, they are an advantage on any machine serving many X sessions.

Procedure Reference: Verify and Resolve Library Dependency Issues for X Applications

To verify and resolve dependency issues for X applications:

1. Enter `rpm -qpR {X application package name}` to identify the library files and the dependent packages needed for the installation of the X package.

2. Enter `locate {Library file}` to verify that the library files are present in the system.

3. Enter `rpm -ivh {X application package name}` to install all the dependencies and then install the required X application packages.

Importance of Library Files

During the installation of certain X applications, the application will search for library files and some dependent packages needed for the X application package to be successfully installed on a system. In case the library files are not installed on the system, you need to first identify the library files and then install the packages containing them along with the dependent packages required for the X application.

ACTIVITY 18-4

Customizing Desktop Panel Menus

Before You Begin:
1. You have logged in as root in the KDE GUI of srvA.
2. Display the **File Browser** window.
3. In the **File Browser** window, copy the data files from srvA to srvB using the FTP program.
4. Close the **File Browser** window.

Scenario:
A new user on your network, Paul, who is just getting familiar with Linux, wants to relocate the edge panel on the desktop to the left and make it compact. Moreover, the user finds it time consuming to access frequently used applications, such as the terminal window and the KWrite application, and also feels that the default panel background color does not suit the panel icons. He requested you to assist and guide him through the task of modifying the desktop.

What You Do	How You Do It
1. Position the panel at the top-left edge of the desktop.	a. In the panel located at the bottom of the screen, right-click the empty space and choose **Configure Panel.**
	b. In the **Configure - KDE Panel** dialog box, verify that **Arrangement** is selected.
	c. In the right pane, in the **Position** section, click the **Top left** button.
2. Resize the panel.	a. In the **Length** section, in the **Length** spin box, double-click and type *50*
	b. In the **Size** section, from the **Size** drop-down list, select **Small.**

3.	Change the panel background.	a. In the left pane, click **Appearance.**
		b. In the right pane, in the **Panel Background** section, check the **Enable background image** check box.
		c. Click the **Open file dialog** icon.
		d. In the **Select Image File - KDE Panel** dialog box, in the **Location** combo box, double-click and type */usr/share/wallpapers* and press **Enter.**
		e. Select **blue_angle_swirl.jpg** and click **OK** to close the **Select Image File - KDE Panel** dialog box.
		f. Click **OK** to apply the changes and close the **Configure - KDE Panel** dialog box.
4.	Add frequently used applications to the panel.	a. In the panel located at the top-left corner of the screen, right-click the empty space and choose **Add Application to Menubar→System→Terminal.**
		b. In the panel, right-click the empty space and choose **Add Application to Menubar→Utilities→Editors→KWrite.**
		c. Choose **K Menu→Log Out.**
		d. Click **End Current Session** to log out of the KDE session.

Lesson 18 Follow-up

In this lesson, you configured the GUI. Working with the GUI of Linux can be useful when recalling commands becomes difficult. The GUI is user-friendly and easy to understand. As a Linux+ administrator, it will help you direct users to configure their systems.

1. **Do you think using the Linux GUI in conjunction with the CLI will yield better results? Why?**

2. **In what way do you think customizing window managers is useful?**

Follow-up

In this course, you acquired the essential skills and information you will need to install, configure, troubleshoot, and perform preventative maintenance of the Linux operating system. If you are getting ready for a career as an entry-level Linux administrator or a computer support technician, and if your job duties require you to work with Linux servers and workstations on day-to-day basis, this course presented you with the background knowledge and skills you will require to be successful. Taking this course was also an important part of your preparation for the CompTIA Linux+ certification examination, 2009 objectives (Exam Code: XK0-003) in order to become a CompTIA Linux+ Certified Professional.

What's Next?

The material in *CompTIA® Linux+™ Certification* provides foundational information and skills required to pursue a career as a Linux administrator or support technician. It also assists you in preparing for the CompTIA® Linux+™ certification examination, 2009 objectives (Exam Code XK0-003), in order to become a CompTIA® Linux+™ Certified Professional. Once you have completed *CompTIA® Linux+™ Certification,* you may wish to continue your certification path by taking any one of the other Element K CompTIA certification courses, *CompTIA® Network+® (2009 Objectives), CompTIA® Security+® (2008 Objectives),* or *CompTIA® A+® Certification (2009 Objectives),* each of which prepares you for the associated CompTIA certification exam.

Mapping Course Content to the CompTIA Linux+ 2009 Exam Objectives

The following tables will assist you in mapping the Linux+ Certification course content to the CompTIA Linux+ certification exam objectives.

Domain 1.0—Installation and Configuration

Exam Objective	Linux+ Certification Lesson and Topic Reference
1.1: Compare and contrast installation sources	
● Physical installation media	Lesson 17 Topic A
■ CD-ROM	Lesson 17 Topic A
■ DVD	Lesson 17 Topic A
● Network Types	Lesson 17 Topic A
■ HTTP	Lesson 17 Topic A
■ FTP	Lesson 17 Topic A
■ NFS	Lesson 17 Topic A

Exam Objective	Linux+ Certification Lesson and Topic Reference
1.2: Implement partitioning schemes and filesystem layout using the following tools and practices	
● LVM	Lesson 15 Topic E
● RAID	Lesson 15 Topic D
● fdisk	Lesson 3 Topic A
● parted	Lesson 3 Topic A
● mkfs	Lesson 3 Topic A

Exam Objective	Linux+ Certification Lesson and Topic Reference
1.3: Explain the purpose for using each of the following filesystem types	
● Local	Lesson 3 Topic A
■ EXT2	Lesson 3 Topic A
■ EXT3	Lesson 3 Topic A
■ Reiser	Lesson 3 Topic A
■ FAT	Lesson 3 Topic A
■ NTFS	Lesson 3 Topic A
■ VFAT	Lesson 3 Topic A
■ ISO9660	Lesson 3 Topic A
● Network	Lesson 12 Topic E
■ NFS	Lesson 12 Topic E
■ SMBFS/CIFS	Lesson 12 Topic E

Exam Objective	Linux+ Certification Lesson and Topic Reference
1.4: Conduct routine mount and unmount of filesystems	
● mount	Lesson 3 Topic C
● unmount	Lesson 3 Topic C
● /etc/fstab	Lesson 3 Topic A Lesson 3 Topic C

Exam Objective	Linux+ Certification Lesson and Topic Reference
1.5: Explain the advantages of having a separate partition or volume for any of the following directories	
● /boot	Lesson 3 Topic B
● /home	Lesson 3 Topic B
● /tmp	Lesson 3 Topic B
● /usr	Lesson 3 Topic B
● /var	Lesson 3 Topic B
● /opt	Lesson 3 Topic B

Exam Objective	Linux+ Certification Lesson and Topic Reference
1.6: Explain the purpose of the following directories	
● /	Lesson 3 Topic B
● /bin	Lesson 3 Topic B
● /dev	Lesson 3 Topic B
● /etc	Lesson 3 Topic B
● /mnt	Lesson 3 Topic B
● /proc	Lesson 8 Topic B
● /root	Lesson 3 Topic B
● /sbin	Lesson 3 Topic B
● /usr/bin	Lesson 3 Topic B
● /usr/local	Lesson 3 Topic B
● /usr/lib	Lesson 3 Topic B
● /usr/lib64	Lesson 3 Topic B
● /usr/share	Lesson 3 Topic B
● /var/log	Lesson 11 Topic B

Exam Objective	Linux+ Certification Lesson and Topic Reference
1.7: Configure the boot process including the following	
● GRUB	Lesson 17 Topic C
■ /boot/grub/grub.conf	Lesson 17 Topic C
■ /boot/grub/menu.lst	Lesson 17 Topic C
■ grub-install	Lesson 17 Topic C
■ grub	Lesson 17 Topic C

Exam Objective	Linux+ Certification Lesson and Topic Reference
1.8: Perform the following package management functions	
● Install, remove and update programs	Lesson 7 Topic A
	Lesson 7 Topic B
	Lesson 7 Topic C
	Lesson 7 Topic D
	Lesson 7 Topic E
	Lesson 7 Topic F
	Lesson 7 Topic G
■ rpm	Lesson 7 Topic A
	Lesson 7 Topic B
	Lesson 7 Topic C
	Lesson 7 Topic D
	Lesson 7 Topic E
rpm -Uvh	Lesson 7 Topic C
rpm -qa	Lesson 7 Topic A
rpm -e	Lesson 7 Topic A
yum	Lesson 7 Topic E
■ deb	Lesson 7 Topic F
dpkg -i	Lesson 7 Topic F
dpkg -r	Lesson 7 Topic F
apt-get	Lesson 7 Topic F
apt-cache search	Lesson 7 Topic F
■ source	Lesson 4 Topic D
	Lesson 7 Topic G
./configure	Lesson 7 Topic G
make	Lesson 7 Topic G
make install	Lesson 7 Topic G
make uninstall	Lesson 7 Topic G
tar	Lesson 4 Topic D
	Lesson 7 Topic G
make clean	Lesson 7 Topic G
autoconf	Lesson 7 Topic G
make test	Lesson 7 Topic G
tar.gz	Lesson 7 Topic G
INSTALL	Lesson 7 Topic G

Exam Objective	Linux+ Certification Lesson and Topic Reference
1.8: Perform the following package management functions	
bzip	Lesson 4 Topic D
gzip	Lesson 4 Topic D
• Resolve dependencies	Lesson 7 Topic A
• Add and remove repositories	Lesson 7 Topic D

Exam Objective	Linux+ Certification Lesson and Topic Reference
1.9: Configure profile and environment variables system-wide and at the user level	
• PS1	Lesson 9 Topic C
• PS2	Lesson 9 Topic C
• PATH	Lesson 9 Topic C
• EDITOR	Lesson 9 Topic C
• TERM	Lesson 9 Topic C
• PAGER	Lesson 9 Topic C
• HOME	Lesson 9 Topic C
• PRINTER	Lesson 9 Topic C

Exam Objective	Linux+ Certification Lesson and Topic Reference
1.10: Troubleshoot boot issues using the following tools	
• Kernel options	Lesson 16 Topic A Lesson 8 Topic B
• Single-user mode (including recovering the root user)	Lesson 16 Topic A
• Rescue - live CDs, DVDs and USB keys	Lesson 16 Topic A
• dmesg	Lesson 16 Topic B

Exam Objective	Linux+ Certification Lesson and Topic Reference
1.11: Manage devices using the following tools	
• lsusb	Lesson 8 Topic E

Exam Objective	Linux+ Certification Lesson and Topic Reference
1.11: Manage devices using the following tools	
● lspci	Lesson 8 Topic E
● lsmod	Lesson 8 Topic B
● /sys	Lesson 8 Topic D
● /proc/usbinfo	Lesson 15 Topic C
● modprobe	Lesson 8 Topic B
● /proc	Lesson 8 Topic B
● /etc/modules.conf	Lesson 8 Topic B
● /etc/modprobe.conf	Lesson 8 Topic B
● Hardware Compatibility List (HCL)	Lesson 17 Topic A

Domain 2.0—System Maintenance and Operations

Exam Objective	Linux+ Certification Lesson and Topic Reference
2.1: Given a scenario, use the following fundamental Linux tools, techniques and, resources	
● Directory navigation (cd, ls, pushd, popd, pwd)	Lesson 3 Topic B
● File commands	Lesson 1 Topic B
	Lesson 3 Topic B
	Lesson 4 Topic B
	Lesson 4 Topic C
	Lesson 8 Topic D
	Lesson 9 Topic B
▪ file	Lesson 3 Topic B
▪ test	Lesson 9 Topic B
▪ find	Lesson 4 Topic B
▪ locate	Lesson 4 Topic B
▪ slocate	Lesson 4 Topic B
▪ which	Lesson 1 Topic B
▪ whereis	Lesson 4 Topic B
▪ ln	Lesson 4 Topic C
▪ ls-F	Lesson 3 Topic B
▪ mknod	Lesson 8 Topic D

Exam Objective	Linux+ Certification Lesson and Topic Reference
2.1: Given a scenario, use the following fundamental Linux tools, techniques and, resources	
■ touch	Lesson 3 Topic B
■ mkdir	Lesson 3 Topic B
■ mv	Lesson 3 Topic B
■ cp	Lesson 3 Topic B
■ rm	Lesson 3 Topic B
■ cd	Lesson 3 Topic B
■ file types	Lesson 3 Topic B
hardlinks, softlinks, directory, device file, regular file, named pipe	Lesson 3 Topic B Lesson 4 Topic C Lesson 8 Topic D
● File editing with vi	Lesson 4 Topic A
● Process management	Lesson 10 Topic A Lesson 10 Topic B Lesson 8 Topic F
■ ps	Lesson 10 Topic B
■ kill	Lesson 10 Topic B
■ top	Lesson 10 Topic B
■ iostat	Lesson 8 Topic F
■ pstree	Lesson 10 Topic B
■ nice	Lesson 10 Topic B
■ renice	Lesson 10 Topic B
■ signals	Lesson 10 Topic B
■ PID	Lesson 10 Topic A
■ PPID	Lesson 10 Topic B
● I/O redirection	Lesson 9 Topic D
■ <	Lesson 9 Topic D
■ >	Lesson 9 Topic D
■ =	Lesson 9 Topic D
■ = =	Lesson 9 Topic D
■ |	Lesson 9 Topic D
■ ;	Lesson 9 Topic D
■ tee	Lesson 9 Topic D

Exam Objective	Linux+ Certification Lesson and Topic Reference
2.1: Given a scenario, use the following fundamental Linux tools, techniques and, resources	
■ xargs	Lesson 9 Topic D
■ STDIN	Lesson 9 Topic D
■ STDOUT	Lesson 9 Topic D
■ STDERR	Lesson 9 Topic D
● Special devices	Lesson 8 Topic D
■ /dev/null	Lesson 8 Topic D
■ /dev/random	Lesson 8 Topic D
■ /dev/zero	Lesson 8 Topic D
■ /dev/urandom	Lesson 8 Topic D
● System documentation	Lesson 1 Topic C
■ Man pages	Lesson 1 Topic C
man#	Lesson 1 Topic C
apropos	Lesson 1 Topic C
makewhatis	Lesson 1 Topic C
whatis	Lesson 1 Topic C
■ Info pages	Lesson 1 Topic C
■ /usr/share/docs	Lesson 1 Topic C
● Virtual consoles	Lesson 1 Topic B
● Kernel / architecture information	Lesson 1 Topic B Lesson 8 Topic A Lesson 8 Topic B Lesson 8 Topic F
■ cat	Lesson 1 Topic B
■ /proc/version	Lesson 8 Topic B
■ uname	Lesson 8 Topic F
■ common sysctl settings	Lesson 8 Topic B
■ /etc/sysctl.conf	Lesson 8 Topic B

Exam Objective	Linux+ Certification Lesson and Topic Reference
2.2: Conduct basic tasks using BASH	
● Basics of scripting (only: execute permission, #!/bin/bash, sh script)	Lesson 9 Topic B Lesson 9 Topic E
● Shell features	Lesson 9 Topic A
■ history	Lesson 9 Topic A
■ tab completion	Lesson 9 Topic A

Exam Objective	Linux+ Certification Lesson and Topic Reference
2.3: Given a scenario, analyze system and application logs to troubleshoot Linux systems	
● Common log files	Lesson 11 Topic B Lesson 14 Topic B
■ /var/log/messages	Lesson 11 Topic B
■ /var/log/syslog	Lesson 11 Topic B
■ /var/log/maillog	Lesson 11 Topic B
■ /var/log/secure	Lesson 14 Topic B
■ /var/log/lastlog	Lesson 11 Topic B
● Rotated logs	Lesson 11 Topic B
● Searching and interpreting log files	Lesson 11 Topic B
■ grep	Lesson 4 Topic B Lesson 11 Topic B
■ tail -f	Lesson 11 Topic B
■ awk	Lesson 11 Topic B
■ sed	Lesson 11 Topic B

Exam Objective	Linux+ Certification Lesson and Topic Reference
2.4: Conduct and manage backup and restore operations	
● Copying data	Lesson 12 Topic E
■ rsync and ftp	Lesson 12 Topic E
● Archive and restore commands	Lesson 4 Topic D
■ cpio	Lesson 4 Topic D

Exam Objective	Linux+ Certification Lesson and Topic Reference
2.4: Conduct and manage backup and restore operations	
■ tar	Lesson 4 Topic D
■ dump	Lesson 4 Topic D
■ restore	Lesson 4 Topic D
■ dd	Lesson 4 Topic D
● Write to removable media (CD-RW, DVD-RW)	Lesson 3 Topic C

Exam Objective	Linux+ Certification Lesson and Topic Reference
2.5: Explain the following features and concept of X11	
● Starting and stopping X11	Lesson 18 Topic A
● Difference between the X11 client and server	Lesson 18 Topic A
● Window managers (KDM, GDM)	Lesson 18 Topic B
● Multiple desktops	Lesson 17 Topic E Lesson 18 Topic B
● X11 configuration file (xorg.conf)	Lesson 18 Topic A
● Terminal emulators (xterm, etc)	Lesson 18 Topic C

Exam Objective	Linux+ Certification Lesson and Topic Reference
2.6: Explain the difference in runlevels and their purpose	
● Command: init	Lesson 1 Topic D
● Runlevels	Lesson 1 Topic D
■ 0 – Halt	Lesson 1 Topic D
■ 1 – single-user mode	Lesson 1 Topic D
■ 2 – multi-user mode without networking	Lesson 1 Topic D
■ 3 – networked multi-user mode	Lesson 1 Topic D
■ 4 – user configurable	Lesson 1 Topic D
■ 5 – X11 multi-user mode	Lesson 1 Topic D
■ 6 – reboot	Lesson 1 Topic D

Exam Objective	Linux+ Certification Lesson and Topic Reference
2.7: Manage filesystems using the following	
● Check disk usage (df, du)	Lesson 15 Topic A
● Quotas	Lesson 15 Topic F
■ edquota	Lesson 15 Topic F
■ repquota	Lesson 15 Topic F
■ quotacheck	Lesson 15 Topic F
● Check and repair filesystems (fsck)	Lesson 3 Topic D
● Loopback devices (ISO filesystems)	Lesson 15 Topic C
● NFS	Lesson 12 Topic E Lesson 17 Topic D
■ configuration	Lesson 12 Topic E Lesson 17 Topic D
■ mount	Lesson 12 Topic E
■ exportfs	Lesson 12 Topic E
■ fstab	Lesson 3 Topic A Lesson 12 Topic E
■ /etc/exports	Lesson 12 Topic E
■ showmount	Lesson 12 Topic E
● Swap	Lesson 3 Topic A Lesson 3 Topic C
■ mkswap	Lesson 3 Topic C
■ swapon	Lesson 3 Topic C
■ swapoff	Lesson 3 Topic C

Exam Objective	Linux+ Certification Lesson and Topic Reference
2.8: Implement task scheduling using the following tools	
● cron (cron.allow, cron.deny)	Lesson 10 Topic D
● crontab command syntax	Lesson 10 Topic D
● crontab file format	Lesson 10 Topic D
● at (atq)	Lesson 10 Topic D

Exam Objective	Linux+ Certification Lesson and Topic Reference
2.9: Utilize performance monitoring tools and concepts to identify common problems	
● Commands	Lesson 8 Topic F
▪ sar	Lesson 8 Topic F
▪ iostat	Lesson 8 Topic F
▪ vmstat	Lesson 8 Topic F
▪ uptime	Lesson 8 Topic F
▪ top	Lesson 8 Topic F
● Load average	Lesson 8 Topic F

Domain 3.0—Application and Services

Exam Objective	Linux+ Certification Lesson and Topic Reference
3.1: Manage Linux system services using the following	
● /etc/init.d	Lesson 11 Topic A
▪ start	Lesson 11 Topic A
▪ stop	Lesson 11 Topic A
▪ restart	Lesson 11 Topic A
● inetd	Lesson 11 Topic A
● xinetd	Lesson 13 Topic E
● chkconfig	Lesson 11 Topic A

Exam Objective	Linux+ Certification Lesson and Topic Reference
3.2: Implement interoperability with Windows using the following	
● rdesktop – client	Lesson 12 Topic G
● vnc – server and client	Lesson 12 Topic G
● Samba – server and client	Lesson 6 Topic D Lesson 12 Topic E
▪ smb.conf	Lesson 12 Topic E
▪ winbind	Lesson 12 Topic E
▪ lmhost	Lesson 12 Topic E

Exam Objective	Linux+ Certification Lesson and Topic Reference
3.2: Implement interoperability with Windows using the following	
● Security and authentication (Kerberos)	Lesson 14 Topic A

Exam Objective	Linux+ Certification Lesson and Topic Reference
3.3: Implement, configure and maintain Web and FTP services	
● Apache	Lesson 13 Topic A Lesson 13 Topic B
■ Maintain PHP settings (php.ini)	Lesson 13 Topic A
■ Edit Apache configuration files	Lesson 13 Topic A
Enable and disable modules	Lesson 13 Topic A
■ Containers	Lesson 13 Topic A
Virtual hosts	Lesson 13 Topic B
Directories	Lesson 13 Topic A
■ Access control (.htaccess)	Lesson 13 Topic A
■ CGI (ExecCGI, ScriptAlias)	Lesson 13 Topic B
■ Commands: apachectl (-t, -S, graceful, restart)	Lesson 13 Topic A
■ Configuring apache logs	Lesson 13 Topic A
● FTP services	Lesson 12 Topic E
■ Configure FTP users	Lesson 12 Topic E
/etc/ftpusers	Lesson 12 Topic E
chroot	Lesson 12 Topic E
■ Configure anonymous access	Lesson 12 Topic E

Exam Objective	Linux+ Certification Lesson and Topic Reference
3.4: Given a scenario, explain the purpose of the following web-related services	
● Tomcat	Lesson 13 Topic A
● Apache	Lesson 13 Topic A
● Squid	Lesson 13 Topic C

Exam Objective	Linux+ Certification Lesson and Topic Reference
3.5: Troubleshoot web-related services using the following utilities	
● Commands	Lesson 12 Topic E
	Lesson 13 Topic A
	Lesson 16 Topic C
■ curl	Lesson 13 Topic A
■ wget	Lesson 13 Topic A
■ ftp	Lesson 12 Topic E
■ telnet	Lesson 13 Topic E
	Lesson 16 Topic C

Exam Objective	Linux+ Certification Lesson and Topic Reference
3.6: Given a scenario, troubleshoot common FTP problems	
● Active vs. passive	Lesson 12 Topic E
● ASCII vs. binary	Lesson 12 Topic E

Exam Objective	Linux+ Certification Lesson and Topic Reference
3.7: Given a scenario, perform the following MySQL administrative tasks	
● Locate configuration file	Lesson 4 Topic E
● Starting and stopping	Lesson 4 Topic E
● Test the connection	Lesson 4 Topic E

Exam Objective	Linux+ Certification Lesson and Topic Reference
3.8: Explain the purpose of each of the following mail services, protocols and features	
● Protocols	Lesson 13 Topic D
■ SMTP	Lesson 13 Topic D
■ IMAP	Lesson 13 Topic D
■ POP3	Lesson 13 Topic D
● MTA	Lesson 13 Topic D
■ Postfix	Lesson 13 Topic D

Exam Objective	Linux+ Certification Lesson and Topic Reference
3.8: Explain the purpose of each of the following mail services, protocols and features	
■ Sendmail	Lesson 13 Topic D
● Email aliases	Lesson 13 Topic D
■ /etc/aliases	Lesson 13 Topic D
■ newaliases	Lesson 13 Topic D

Exam Objective	Linux+ Certification Lesson and Topic Reference
3.9: Deploy and manage CUPS print services	
● Enable and disable queues	Lesson 6 Topic C
● Web management interface (port 631)	Lesson 6 Topic A
● Printing commands	Lesson 6 Topic B
■ lpr	Lesson 6 Topic B
■ lp	Lesson 6 Topic B
■ lpq	Lesson 6 Topic B
■ lpstat	Lesson 6 Topic B
■ cancel	Lesson 6 Topic B

Exam Objective	Linux+ Certification Lesson and Topic Reference
3.10: Set up, install, configure and maintain a BIND DNS server and related services	
● DNS utilities	Lesson 12 Topic D
■ named	Lesson 12 Topic D
■ rndc	Lesson 12 Topic D
● Config file locations (/var/named)	Lesson 12 Topic D
● Forward zones, reverse zones, root hints	Lesson 12 Topic D

Exam Objective	Linux+ Certification Lesson and Topic Reference
3.11: Perform basic administration of the DHCP server	
● /etc/dhcpd.conf	Lesson 12 Topic C

Exam Objective	Linux+ Certification Lesson and Topic Reference
3.11: Perform basic administration of the DHCP server	
● dhcpd.leases	Lesson 12 Topic C

Exam Objective	Linux+ Certification Lesson and Topic Reference
3.12: Given a scenario, troubleshoot NTP related issues	
● /etc/ntp.conf	Lesson 10 Topic E
● ntpdate	Lesson 10 Topic E
● date	Lesson 10 Topic E
● ntpq -p	Lesson 10 Topic E

Domain 4.0—Networking

Exam Objective	Linux+ Certification Lesson and Topic Reference
4.1: Identify common networking ports and the associated service	
● 20	Lesson 12 Topic A
● 21	Lesson 12 Topic A
● 22	Lesson 12 Topic A
● 23	Lesson 12 Topic A
● 25	Lesson 12 Topic A
● 53	Lesson 12 Topic A
● 80	Lesson 12 Topic A
● 110	Lesson 12 Topic A
● 123	Lesson 12 Topic A
● 143	Lesson 12 Topic A
● 443	Lesson 12 Topic A
● 631	Lesson 12 Topic A
● 3306	Lesson 12 Topic A
● /etc/services	Lesson 12 Topic F

Exam Objective	Linux+ Certification Lesson and Topic Reference
4.2: Execute network interface configuration using the following	
● dhclient	Lesson 12 Topic C
● dhcpcd	Lesson 12 Topic C
● ifconfig	Lesson 12 Topic A
● iwconfig	Lesson 12 Topic A
● route	Lesson 12 Topic B
● ifup	Lesson 12 Topic A
● ifdown	Lesson 12 Topic A
● network configuration files	Lesson 12 Topic A

Exam Objective	Linux+ Certification Lesson and Topic Reference
4.3: Implement configurations and/or configuration changes for the following	
● Packet filtering: iptables	Lesson 14 Topic C
● Hostname lookup	Lesson 12 Topic D
■ /etc/hosts	Lesson 12 Topic D
■ /etc/nsswitch.conf	Lesson 12 Topic D
■ /etc/resolv.conf	Lesson 12 Topic D

Exam Objective	Linux+ Certification Lesson and Topic Reference
4.4: Explain the different DNS record types and the process of DNS resolution	
● Local resolution	Lesson 12 Topic D
● TTL/caching	Lesson 12 Topic D
● Root name servers	Lesson 12 Topic D
● A	Lesson 12 Topic D
● MX	Lesson 12 Topic D
● PTR	Lesson 12 Topic D
● CNAME	Lesson 12 Topic D
● NS	Lesson 12 Topic D
● TXT	Lesson 12 Topic D

Exam Objective	PDI+ Certification Lesson and Topic Reference
4.5: Troubleshoot basic connectivity issues using the following tools	
● netstat	Lesson 12 Topic B
● ping	Lesson 12 Topic A
	Lesson 16 Topic C
● traceroute	Lesson 12 Topic B
	Lesson 16 Topic C
● arp	Lesson 16 Topic C
● telnet	Lesson 13 Topic E
	Lesson 16 Topic C
● route	Lesson 12 Topic B

Exam Objective	PDI+ Certification Lesson and Topic Reference
4.6: Troubleshoot name resolution issues using the following tools	
● dig	Lesson 12 Topic D
● host	Lesson 12 Topic D
● nslookup	Lesson 12 Topic D
● hostname	Lesson 1 Topic B
	Lesson 12 Topic D

Domain 5.0—Security

Exam Objective	PDI+ Certification Lesson and Topic Reference
5.1: Manage and monitor user and group accounts using the following	
● Tools	Lesson 1 Topic B
	Lesson 2 Topic A
	Lesson 2 Topic C
■ useradd	Lesson 2 Topic A
■ userdel	Lesson 2 Topic C
■ usermod	Lesson 2 Topic C
■ groupadd	Lesson 2 Topic A
■ groupdel	Lesson 2 Topic C
■ groupmod	Lesson 2 Topic C

Exam Objective	PDI+ Certification Lesson and Topic Reference
5.1: Manage and monitor user and group accounts using the following	
■ lock	Lesson 2 Topic C
■ who	Lesson 1 Topic B
■ w	Lesson 1 Topic B
■ last	Lesson 1 Topic B
■ whoami	Lesson 1 Topic B
● Files	Lesson 2 Topic A Lesson 2 Topic B
■ /etc/skel	Lesson 2 Topic B
■ /etc/passwd	Lesson 2 Topic A
■ /etc/shadow	Lesson 2 Topic A
■ /etc/group	Lesson 2 Topic A

Exam Objective	PDI+ Certification Lesson and Topic Reference
5.2: Given a scenario, select the appropriate file permissions and ownership and troubleshoot common problems	
● Tools	Lesson 5 Topic A Lesson 5 Topic B Lesson 5 Topic C Lesson 5 Topic D Lesson 16 Topic A
■ chmod	Lesson 5 Topic A
■ chown	Lesson 5 Topic C
■ chroot	Lesson 16 Topic A
■ chgrp	Lesson 5 Topic C
■ lsattr	Lesson 5 Topic D
■ chattr	Lesson 5 Topic D
■ umask	Lesson 5 Topic B
● Special Permissions	Lesson 5 Topic D
■ setuid	Lesson 5 Topic D
■ setgid	Lesson 5 Topic D
■ sticky bit	Lesson 5 Topic D

Exam Objective	PDI+ Certification Lesson and Topic Reference
5.3: Explain the basics of SELinux	
● Running modes	Lesson 11 Topic C
■ Enabled	Lesson 11 Topic C
■ Disabled	Lesson 11 Topic C
■ Permissive	Lesson 11 Topic C

Exam Objective	PDI+ Certification Lesson and Topic Reference
5.4: Given a scenario, implement privilege escalation using the following	
● sudo	Lesson 14 Topic B
● su	Lesson 14 Topic B
● /etc/sudoers	Lesson 14 Topic B

Exam Objective	PDI+ Certification Lesson and Topic Reference
5.5: Explain the appropriate use of the following security related utilities	
● namp	Lesson 14 Topic E
● Wireshark	Lesson 14 Topic E
● NESSUS	Lesson 14 Topic E
● Snort	Lesson 14 Topic E
● Tripwire	Lesson 14 Topic E

Exam Objective	PDI+ Certification Lesson and Topic Reference
5.6: Use checksum and file verification utilities	
● md5sum	Lesson 14 Topic A
● sha1sum	Lesson 14 Topic A
● gpg	Lesson 14 Topic A

Exam Objective	PDI+ Certification Lesson and Topic Reference
5.7: Deploy remote access facilities using the following	
● SSH	Lesson 12 Topic G
■ Secure tunnels	Lesson 12 Topic G
■ SFTP	Lesson 12 Topic E
	Lesson 12 Topic G
■ X11 forwarding	Lesson 12 Topic G
■ Keygen	Lesson 12 Topic G
● VNC	Lesson 12 Topic G

Exam Objective	PDI+ Certification Lesson and Topic Reference
5.8: Explain the methods of authentication	
● PAM	Lesson 12 Topic E
● LDAP	Lesson 12 Topic A
● NIS	Lesson 12 Topic F
● RADIUS	Lesson 14 Topic A
● Two-factor authentication	Lesson 14 Topic A

B | CompTIA Linux+ Acronyms

Introduction

The following is a list of acronyms that appear in the CompTIA Linux+ exam, covering 2009 objectives. Candidates are encouraged to review the complete list and attain a working knowledge of all listed acronyms as part of a comprehensive exam preparation program.

Acronym	Associated Term
ASCII	American Standard Code for Information Interchange
ACPI	Advanced Configuration and Power Interface
APT	Advanced Package Tool
ACL	Access Control List
APM	Advanced Power Management
ACPI	Advanced Configuration and Power Interface
ATAPI	AT Attachment Packet Interface
AML	ACPI Machine Language
BASH	Bourne Again Shell
BIND	Berkeley Internet Naming Daemon
BIOS	Basic Input/Output System
CD	Compact Disc
CA	Certificate Authority
CLI	Command Line Interface
CGI	Common Gateway Interface
CIFS	Common Internet File System
CUPS	Common Unix Printing System
CPU	Central Processing Unit
CNAME	Canonical Name
CHAP	Challenge Handshake Authentication Protocol
CMOS	Complementary Metal Oxide Semiconductor
DAC	Discretionary Access Control
DHCP	Dynamic Host Configuration Protocol

Acronym	Associated Term
DMA	Direct Memory Address
DNS	Domain Name Service
DVD	Digital Versatile Disc
ESMTP	Extended SMTP
EHLO	Extended HELLO
FAT	File Allocation Table
FTP	File Transfer Protocol
FHS	Filesystem Hierarchy Standard
FQDN	Fully Qualified Domain Name
FIPS	First nondestructive Interactive Partition Splitting Program
GB	Gigabyte
GUI	Graphical User Interface
GDM	GNOME Display Manager
GNU	GNU is not Unix
GMT	Greenwich Mean Time
GPG	GNU Privacy Guard
GPM	Group Policy Management
GRUB	Grand Unified Bootloader
GUID	Globally Unique Identifier
GPL	General Public License
GCC	GNU Compiler Collection
HAL	Hardware Abstraction Layer
HDD	Hard Disk Drive
HTTP	Hyper Text Transfer Protocol
HTTPD	Hypertext Transfer Protocol Daemon
HTTPS	Hyper Text Transfer Protocol-Secure
IMAP	Internet Message Access Protocol
ISC	Internet Software Consortium
ISO	International Standards Organization
IRQ	Interrupt ReQuests
ICMP	Internet Control Message Protocol
JVM	Java Virtual Machine
KDM	KDE Display Manager
L2TP	Level 2 Transfer Protocol
LDAP	Lightweight Directory Access Protocol
LILO	Linux Loader
LV	Logical Volumes
LE	Logical Extents
LVM	Logical Volume Manager
LPD	Laser Printer Daemon

Acronym	*Associated Term*
LMTP	Local Mail Transport Protocol
MAC	Mandatory Access Control
MB	Megabyte
MBR	Master Boot Record
MTA	Mail Transport Agent
MUA	Mail User Agent
MX	Mail Exchanger
MSP	Message Send Protocol
MPM	Multiprocessing Modules
MIME	Multipurpose Internet Mail Extensions
NFS	Network File System
NIC	Network Interface Card
NIS	Network Information Service
NAS	Network Access Server
NMAP	Network Mapper
NNTP	Network News Transfer Protocol
NSCD	Name Service Cache Daemon
NTFS	NT File System
NTP	Network Time Protocol
OS	Operating System
PV	Physical Volume
PE	Physical Extents
PAM	Pluggable Authentication Module
PAP	Password Authentication Protocol
PRNG	Pseudo Random Number Generation
PHP	Personal Home Pages
PID	Process ID
POP	Post Office Protocol
PPC	Power PC
PPID	Parent Process ID
PPP	Point to Point Protocol
PDL	Page Description Language
PPD	PostScript Printer Definitions
POST	Power-On Self Test
RADIUS	Remote Authentication Dial-in User Services
RAID	Redundant Array of Independent Disks
RAM	Random Access Memory
RDP	Remote Desktop Protocol
RHEL	Red Hat Enterprise Linux
RPM	RedHat Package Manager

Acronym	Associated Term
RTC	Real Time Clock
RJE	Remote Job Entry
RFC	Request for Comments
SAN	Storage Area Network
SOA	Start Of Authority
SCP	Secure Copy
SCSI	Small Computer System Interface
SELinux	Security-Enhanced Linux
SFTP	Secure File Transfer Protocol
SH	Shell
SMBFS	Samba File System
SMTP	Simple Mail Transport Protocol
SNMP	Simple Network Management Protocol
SSH	Secure Shell Login
SSL	Securer Socket Layer
SSID	Service Set Identifier
SUID	Set User ID
SGID	Set Group ID
SMB	Server Message Block
STDIN	Standard Input
STDOUT	Standard Output
STDERR	Standard Error
SFTP	Simple File Transfer Protocol
TTL	Time to Live
TFTP	Trivial File Transfer Protocol
TLS	Transport Layer Security
UID	User ID
USB	Universal Serial Bus
UDP	
UPG	User Private Group
UPS	Uninterrupted Power Supply
UTC	Universal Time Coordinated
VG	Volume Group
VFAT	Virtual File Allocation Table
VNC	Virtual Network Computer
VGDA	Volume Group Descriptor Area
XDR	eXternal Data Representation
YUM	Yellow dog Updater, Modified

C | Syntax

Introduction

The following is a list of the most frequently used commands with their syntax. Candidates are encouraged to review the complete list and attain a working knowledge of all listed commands as a part of a comprehensive exam preparation program.

Command	Syntax
alias	alias {command}='{command} [options]'
apachectl	apachectl start|stop|restart|status|configtest
apt-get	apt-get [options] {command}
aspell	aspell [options]
at	at [options] {time}
awk	awk [options] {file}
bunzip2	bunzip2 {file name}
bzcat	bzcat {file name}
bzdiff	bzdiff {file name}
bzip2	bzip2 {file name}
bzip2recover	bzip2recover {file name}
bzless	bzless {file name}
bzmore	bzmore {file name}
cal	cal {month} {year}
cancel	cancel [command options]
cat	cat [command options] {file name}
cd	cd {Absolute or Relative path}
cp	cp [command options] {Absolute or Relative path of the file or directory to be copied}/{file or directory name} {Absolute or Relative path of the destination}

Command	Syntax
chown	chown {user name} {file name} OR chown {user name.group name} {file name} OR chown {user name.} {file name} OR chown {.group name} {file name}
chattr	chattr [-RV] [-v version] { mode } files
command --help	command -options
count	operator [count] {motion}
chmod	chmod [option] {mode} {file name}
createrepo	createrepo [options] <directory>
cron	cron [option] {mail command}
chkconfig	chkconfig [option] {service name} {on|off|reset}
curl	curl [options] {URL...}
dd	dd [operand]... OR dd [option]
dump	dump {-level #} {dump file} {filesystem/file/directory}
dhcpd	dhcpd [options]
date	date +[format]
dumpe2fs	dumpe2fs [options] {block size} {device name}
diff	diff {file name 1} {file name 2}
dig	dig [command options] {query options} {Fully Qualified Domain Name | IP address}
dpkg	dpkg [option] {action}
echo	echo {"string"}
e2label	e2label /dev/{device name} {partition number}
export	export variable
finger	finger [user name]
fdisk	fdisk [option] {device name}
fsck	fsck -t {filesystem type} [options] OR fsck -r /dev/{filesystem}
find	find [options] {search locations} {search criteria} {actions}
ftp	ftp [command options] {hostname}
gzip	gzip [command options] {file name}
groupdel	groupdel {group name}

Command	Syntax
groupmod	groupmod [-g gid [-o]] [-n new group name] [old group name]
groupadd	groupadd [options] {group name}
parted	parted [option] device {command [argument]}
grep	grep [command options] {keyword} {file name}
gpg	gpg [options] {command} {arguments}
history	history [options]
host	host [command options] {FQDN | IP address}
hostname	hostname [options] {hostname}
inetd	inetd [option] [configuration file]
info	info {command}
insmod	insmod {file name} {module options}
ifconfig	ifconfig {interface name} {options or address}
iwconfig	iwconfig {interface name} {options or address}
iptables	iptables [-t table] {commands} {chain/rule specification} [options/parameters]
kill	kill [signal option] {PID}
killall	killall [signal option] {command}
klogd	klogd [options]
last	last [options]
lastlog	lastlog [options]
lp	lp [command options] {file name}
ln	ln [option] [-T] {target link name}
ls	ls [command options] [Absolute or Relative path of the directory]
logrotate	logrotate [options] {configuration file}
lsmod	lsmod
lpr	lpr [command options] {file name}
lpq	lpq [command options] {print queue name}

Command	Syntax
lprm	lprm {print job id}
lpc	lpc [parameter]
lpstat	lpstat [command options]
links	links [options] {URL}
lsattr	lsattr [-RVadv] [files...]
locate	locate [options] {string}
mv	mv {Absolute or Relative path}/{file or directory name} {Absolute or Relative path}/{new file or directory name}
modinfo	modinfo {module options}
man	man topic
mkinitrd	mkinitrd [options] {image name} {kernel version}
mkfs	mkfs [options] {filesystem}
mke2fs	mke2fs [options] {filesystem name}
mkdir	mkdir {directory name}
mount	mount [options] {device} {mountpoint}
mkswap	mkswap [option] device {size}
modprobe	modprobe [option] {module name}
mknod	mknod [option]... Name Type [major minor]
md5sum	md5sum --check {file name}
make	make {key file/digital certificate}
mdadm	mdadm {mode} {raid device} [options] {component devices}
netstat	netstat [options]
nice	nice -n {priority} {command}
nohup	nohup {command}
nslookup	nslookup {host name or FQDN}
nmap	nmap [scan type] [options] {target specification}
openssl	openssl {command} [options] {arguments}
pr	pr [command options] {file name}
passwd	passwd [user name]
pwd	pwd [option]
ps	ps [options]
pstree	pstree [options]

Command	Syntax
pidof	pidof *[command options] {string}*
pgrep	pgrep *[command options] {process name}*
pkill	pkill *[signal option] {command}*
renice	renice *{priority} [options]*
restore	restore *[options] {file}*
rm	rm *[command options] {Absolute or Relative path of file or directory}/{file or directory name}*
rmdir	rmdir *{directory name}*
rpm -q	rpm -q *{what_packages} {what_information}*
rpm -V	rpm -V *package_name*
rndc	rndc *[rndc options] {rndc command}*
rsync	rsync *{source file or folder} {destination file or folder}*
rdesktop	rdesktop *[options] server[:port]*
sleep	sleep *{time}*
shutdown	shutdown *[-t seconds] [-options] time [warning message]*
sfdisk	sfdisk *[options] device*
swapon	swapon *-e* OR swapon *-a*
swapoff	swapoff *-a*
sysctl	sysctl *[command options] {kernel parameter}={value}*
syslogd	syslogd *[options]*
system-config-services	system-config-services
ssh-keygen	ssh-keygen *[options]*
sed	sed *'address/pattern/action' file name*
smbclient	smbclient *//machine/service*
sftp	sftp *hostname*
sha1sum	sha1sum --check *{file name}*
sudo	sudo *command-name command-options*
tail	tail *[options] {file name}*
tar	tar *[archiving command options] {destination file}.tar {source directory}*
tee	tee *[options] {file}*

Command	Syntax
test	test {expressions}
telinit	telinit {runlevel}
top	top [options]
tr	tr {'character 1'} {'character 2'} < {file name}
traceroute	traceroute [options] {hostname|ip address}
touch	touch {file name}
tune2fs	tune2fs [options] {device name}
tmpwatch	tmpwatch [options] {hours}
tcpdump	tcpdump [option] {expression}
uname	uname [options]
uptime	uptime OR uptime [-V]
useradd	useradd [command options] {user name}
userdel	userdel [command options] {user name}
usermod	usermod [command options] {user name}
umount	umount [options] {directory|device}
uniq	uniq [command options] {file name}
unzip	unzip [command options] {file name}
umask	umask number
vim	vim [options] {file}
vncserver	vncserver {:display number} {-option}
vncviewer	vncviewer [options] {hostname|ipaddress}{:display}
w	w [options] {user name}
wc	wc [command options] {file name}
whatis	whatis command
which	which {file name}
whereis	whereis [-bmsu] [-BMS directory... -f] file name ...
who	who [options]
whoami	whoami [option]...
wireshark	wireshark [options]
wget	wget [command options] http://{hostname or IP of the destination}

Command	Syntax
xargs	xargs [options] {commands}
yum	yum [options] {command} {package name}

Lesson Labs

Due to classroom setup constraints, some labs cannot be keyed in sequence immediately following their associated lesson. Your instructor will tell you whether your labs can be practiced immediately following the lesson or whether they require separate setup from the main lesson content.

Lesson 1 Lab 1

Discussing the Evolution of Linux

Scenario:

You are preparing a presentation on the evolution and benefits of Linux. You decide to initiate a discussion about the advantages of using Red Hat Enterprise Linux as the operating system for all users in the organization.

1. What are the benefits of releasing software under GPL?

2. Identify the advantages of using open source software.

3. Compare free software and proprietary software.

4. List the features of Linux that make it competitive as an operating system.

Lesson 1 Lab 2

Performing Basic Tasks in Linux

 You can find a suggested solution for this activity in the Lesson 1 Lab 2 solution.html file in the Familiarizing_Linux\Solution folder in the student data files.

Before You Begin:
Ensure that you are logged in as the root user to perform all lesson lab activities.

Scenario:
You recently joined OGC and are required to add your email address and telephone number to the organization's database. You also have to prepare a report on the Linux server for which you need to determine how long the server is running and the number of users logged in to the server.

1. Check the uptime of the Linux server.

2. Determine the users currently logged in to the server.

3. Check the login and logout details of the Linux server for the last month.

4. Check the details of the failed logins.

Lesson 2 Lab 1

Managing User and Group Settings

 You can find a suggested solution for this activity in the Lesson 2 Lab 1 solution.html file in the Managing_Users_and_Groups\Solution folder in the student data files.

Scenario:

A contract employee, Mike, joined your organization. You need to create a user account for him based on the following details:

- Username: contractor01
- Password: myp@$$w0rd
- Period until which the user account needs to be valid: November 16, 2011
- The directory to be set as the default home directory: /home/oncontract/contractor01
- Password should expire in: 60 days
- Number of days to issue a warning before the password expires: 7 days
- Group to which the new user needs to belong: Contract

---

1. Create a user account, contractor01, and configure the user profile.

---

2. Modify the password expiration settings.

---

3. Create a group, Contract, and add the user, contractor01, to it.

Lesson 3 Lab 1

Managing Partitions

 You can find a suggested solution for this activity in the Lesson 3 Lab 1 solution.html file in the Managing_Partitions\Solution folder in the student data files.

Scenario:

As a system administrator, you will need to set up systems for new employees. You are required to configure their hard disks and separate the user accessible areas on the disk from the sensitive ones that contain system and software information. You must also populate the partitions with filesystems and ensure easy identification of the partitions. The users requirements are as follows:

Size of partition usr: 1024 MB

Size of partition root: 1024 MB

You are also required to create a filesystem labeled company policies and place it in the usr partition.

1. Create partitions.

2. Create two logical partitions within the extended partition.

3. Set logical partitions for the ext2 filesystem.

4. Verify that the new partition has the ext2 filesystem.

5. Add labels to the newly created partitions.

6. Apply a label to the partition.

7. Verify the label applied to the partition.

8. Mount the partition using its label.

Lesson 3 Lab 2

Organizing Files in Linux

 You can find a suggested solution for this activity in the Lesson 3 Lab 2 solution.html file in the Managing_Partitions\Solution folder in the student data files.

Data Files:

Software_Rules.txt, Hardware_Inventory.txt

Before You Begin:

Ensure that the required data files are copied into the /root directory.

Scenario:

As the junior administrator of your organization, you are required to perform the following tasks:

- Move the Software_Rules.txt file from the /root directory to the /home directory.
- Copy the Hardware_Inventory.txt file from the /root directory to the /home directory.
- Check if the Hardware_Inventory.txt file contains information that the list of contents has been updated in January 2009.
- Remove the Hardware_Inventory.txt file from the /root directory.
- Set the Nautilus Browser to open in the Spatial mode.

---

1. Move the Software_Rules.txt file to the /home directory.

---

2. Copy the Hardware_Inventory.txt file into the /home directory.

---

3. Remove the Hardware_Inventory.txt file from the /root directory.

---

4. Change the Nautilus Browser's view from the Browser mode to the Spatial mode.

Lesson 4 Lab 1

Finding Files

 You can find a suggested solution for this activity in the Lesson 4 Lab 1 solution.html file in the Managing_Files\Solution folder in the student data files.

Scenario:

You work on a multiuser system and you want to search for files you own, which are located in different directories on the system. You regularly back up important files and directories on your system. You also want to locate the unnecessary files and directories that are more than two years old so that you will able to delete them later.

1. Open the GNOME search tool and search for files owned by the root user.

2. Refine the search to include only empty files owned by the root user.

3. Refine the search to include only empty files owned by the root user that are older than 730 days.

Lesson 4 Lab 2

Managing Files in Linux

 You can find a suggested solution for this activity in the Lesson 4 Lab 2 solution.html file in the Managing_Files\Solution folder in the student data files.

Data Files:

Leave_Log.txt, Hardware_Report_09.txt, Empclaimfeb.txt, Empclaimjan.txt, Policies.txt

Before You Begin:

Ensure that the required data files are copied into the /root directory.

Scenario:

You want to clean up unused files in your Linux system. Before the clean up, you decide to archive important work-related files and create links to those files in the root directory.

---

1. Remove the Leave_Log.txt file from your home directory.

---

2. Create a zip archive of the Empclaimfeb.txt, Empclaimjan.txt, and Policies.txt files in your home directory.

---

3. Create a hard link for the Hardware_Report_09.txt file in the / directory.

Lesson 5 Lab 1

Modifying File Permissions and Ownership

 You can find a suggested solution for this activity in the Lesson 5 Lab 1 solution.html file in the Linux_Permissions\Solution folder in the student data files.

Data Files:

Leave_Log.txt, Stationery_List.txt

Before You Begin:

Ensure that the required data files are copied in the /root directory.

Scenario:

As a junior system administrator, you are responsible for managing user permissions for the administration team. In this role, you need to perform the following tasks:

1. Audit on the number of existing users and groups on the system.

2. Change the permissions of certain files.

1. View the users and groups on your Linux system.

2. Modify the permission of the Leave_Log.txt file to be read-only for all users.

3. Modify the permission using the character method and verify the change.

4. Modify the permission of the Stationery_List.txt file, using Nautilus browser to be writable by all users.

5. Modify the permission of the Stationery_List.txt file using the **Properties** dialog box.

Lesson 6 Lab 1

Configuring System Settings

 You can find a suggested solution for this activity in the Lesson 6 Lab 1 solution.html file in the Printing_Files/Solution folder in the student data files.

Data Files:

Onsite_Training_Policy.txt

Before You Begin:

1. If necessary, connect the USB printer to the system. Ensure that the necessary drivers are downloaded and the printer is ready for use.

2. Copy the required data file into the /root directory.

Scenario:

You have been transferred on-site for training. You want to configure a printer for your laptop, which is running the Linux operating system. You also want to apply text formatting and print the training policy document.

---

1. Configure a generic Postscript printer on srvB.

---

2. Select the make and model of the printer to be configured.

---

3. Check whether **printer2** has been added to the **Local Printers** list and make it the default printer of your system.

---

4. Apply text formatting on Onsite_Training_Policy.txt to print 30 lines per page.

---

5. Preview the document after specifying a header "The Onsite Training Policy" and applying double-spacing for the document.

Lesson 7 Lab 1

Managing Packages

 You can find a suggested solution for this activity in the Lesson 7 Lab 1 solution.html file in the Managing_Packages\Solution folder in the student data files.

Before You Begin:

1. Ensure that all the five CDs of the RHEL 5.3 installation are available.
2. Perform the steps on srvA. To perform this lab on srvB, you need to configure the yum package manager to disable gpgcheck.

Scenario:

You have been assigned the task of managing a few systems on the network. You need to update all the systems with php packages. You decide to set up a centralized repository.

---

1. Copy the installation files from all the five setup discs to /setup directory.

---

2. Define /setup directory as a private repository.

---

3. Install the php packages using the YUM package manager.

Lesson 8 Lab 1

Exploring the Kernel Services and Configuration

 You can find a suggested solution for this activity in the Lesson 8 Lab 1 solution.html file in the Managing_Kernel_Services\Solution folder in the student data files.

Before You Begin:

Copy the grub.conf file as grub.conf.bak to make a backup of the grub.conf file.

Scenario:

The system administrator is responsible for monitoring the performance of kernels to ensure smooth running of the systems. Therefore, you decide to acquaint yourself with various kernel services and how to configure them.

1. Create a new initrd image.

2. Update the GRUB configuration with the new initrd image.

3. View the new initrd image and boot the system using it.

4. View all peripheral devices that are connected to the system.

5. View all hardware devices that are connected to the system using the HAL device manager.

6. Monitor the processes currently running on the system.

Lesson 9 Lab 1

Managing Files Using Basic Bash Shell Operations

 You can find a suggested solution for this activity in the Lesson 9 Lab 1 solution.html file in the Working_with_Bash_and_Shell_scripts\Solution folder in the student data files.

Data Files:

Software_List.txt, Software_Rules.txt, Software_Audit_Report_08.txt, Software_Audit_Report_09.txt

Before You Begin:

Ensure that the required data files are copied into the /root directory.

Scenario:

You want to search for documents that you created several months ago. You remember that the names of the files begin with the word "Software." You want to find them and create a backup of the files in the /mybackup directory.

1. Search for file names beginning with "Software."

2. Create a backup of the files in the /mybackup directory.

Lesson 9 Lab 2

Use Variables to Configure the Shell Environment

 You can find a suggested solution for this activity in the Lesson 9 Lab 2 solution.html file in the Working_with_Bash_and_Shell_scripts\Solution folder in the student data files.

Scenario:

Your colleague asked you to set up his Linux system with the following requirements.

- Write a script to remind him to fill the effort tracking sheet everyday.
- Assign the /root directory to the local path in the system.
- The command prompt should reflect the company name, "Our Global Company."
- Customize the history file size to display only 500 entries on running the `history` command.

---

1. Write a script named Reminder to remind the user to fill his effort tracking sheet whenever he logs in.

---

2. Save and convert the file into an executable script.

---

3. Test the script.

---

4. Customize the environment variables in the ~/.bashrc script file to suit your colleague's needs.

---

5. Check the changes.

Lesson 9 Lab 3

Applying Basic Scripting Techniques

 You can find a suggested solution for this activity in the Lesson 9 Lab 3 solution.html file in the Working_with_Bash_and_Shell_scripts\Solution folder in the student data files.

Scenario:

You want to track your daily tasks so that you can fill your weekly timecard easily. You decide to maintain a list, daily work-done, in a text file with unique names. You decide to name each file with the current date, and also add the date as the first line of each file. You want to write a script named dailyupdate to automate this process.

1. Create a script file named dailyupdate using Vim.

2. Write the code to create text files redirecting the date input from the user.

3. Write the code to confirm file creation with a unique file name.

4. Test the script.

Lesson 10 Lab 1

Performing Process Management

 You can find a suggested solution for this activity in the Lesson 10 Lab 1 solution.html file in the Managing_Jobs_and_Processes\Solution folder in the student data files.

Scenario:

As a system administrator, you have to monitor the processes running on your system and their usage of system resources. You will perform the following tasks everyday.

- List all background jobs.
- Suspend or terminate unnecessary processes.

1. Execute three commands as background processes.

2. Terminate the last job.

3. Bring the second job to the foreground and suspend it.

4. Enter jobs to view the list of processes running in the background.

5. View your current running processes and all other running processes.

Lesson 10 Lab 2

Multitasking in Linux

 You can find a suggested solution for this activity in the Lesson 10 Lab 2 solution.html file in the Managing_Jobs_and_Processes\Solution folder in the student data files.

Scenario:

You received several complaints about processes taking longer than usual to complete. There are certain commands that are running with high priority, which can be lowered. Practice altering the command priority and delaying jobs to run at different times. This should free up some processing power so that critical processes can be run.

1. View the processes on your system.

2. Issue the command to copy installation files as a background process.

3. Renice the copy process by using the top command.

4. Issue a command to run in the background and log out of the system.

5. Log in as root and verify that the job is complete.

Lesson 11 Lab 1

Configuring System Services

 You can find a suggested solution for this activity in the Lesson 11 Lab 2 solution.html file in the Configuring_System_Services\Solution folder in the student data files.

Scenario:

You are a system administrator in OGC systems. Your organization has many branches and has already enabled system and network services on the server to allow employees from different branches to communicate and share information. You need to monitor the activities that take place on the server.

1. Enable SELinux on srvA.

2. Configure syslogd to set up the system to act as a central network log server.

3. Configure alerts and warning on logs.

Lesson 12 Lab 1

Implementing DNS Service

Before You Begin:

1. On the system labeled srvB, using the vi editor, open the /etc/sysconfig/selinux file.

2. Change **SELINUX=permissive** to **SELINUX=disabled.**

3. Switch to the command mode. Save and close the file.

4. Reboot the system. Switch to the CLI. Log in as root.

5. Enter `iptables -F` to flush the IP tables. Enter `iptables -F -t nat` to flush the NAT IP table. Enter `service iptables save` to save the IP tables' settings.

6. Reboot the system. Switch to the CLI. Log in as root.

7. Enter `yum localinstall /rhelsource/Server/bind*` to install the BIND packages. Enter `y` to continue with the installation. Clear the screen.

Scenario:

Your organization opened a new branch. The marketing department uses a server srvB and 50 systems to manage its functions. To facilitate communication and efficient administration, you want to bring all systems under a common domain, **ourglobalcompany.com.**

The parameters for the forward and reverse zones are given in the table:

Parameters	Forward Zone	Reverse Zone
TTL value	86400 seconds	86400 seconds
Serial number	1001	1001
Length of the refresh cycle	28800 seconds	28800 seconds
Length of the retry cycle	7200 seconds	7200 seconds
Duration for the slave server to respond to queries	3600000 seconds	604800 seconds
The default TTL value for negative caching servers	86400 seconds	86400 seconds

 You can find a suggested solution for this activity in the Lesson 12 Lab 1 solution.html file in the Configuring_Network/Solution folder in the student data files.

1. Configure the DNS server for the **ourglobalcompany.com** domain on srvB.

2. Enter the NS and A records for the forward zone.

3. Create a zone file for the reverse domain resolution.

4. Specify global configuration options and zone statements for the root and loopback domains in the named.conf file.

5. Add zone statements for the forward and reverse zones.

6. Start the named service.

7. Add DNS name server data to the /etc/resolv.conf file on srvA.

8. Check whether the DNS server resolves hostnames and IP addresses.

Lesson 12 Lab 2

Configuring FTP Services

Data Files:

software-1, software-2, software-3, sourcecode-1.pl, sourcecode-2.pl, sourcecode-3.pl

Before You Begin:

To complete this lab activity, you need to perform the following tasks on srvB:

1. Create the users laura, linda, and miller.

2. Create a directory named /mnt/software_files and copy the files software-1, software-2, and software-3 from the /085039Data/Configuring_Network directory to the /mnt/software_files directory.

3. Create a directory named /sourcecode and copy the files sourcecode-1.pl, sourcecode-21.pl, and sourcecode-3.pl from the /085039Data/Configuring_Network directory to the /sourcecode directory.

Scenario:

You are a network administrator in OGC Systems. You want to enable teams in various locations to transfer files among each other. You need to ensure that only the required number of users can access the service.

 You can find a suggested solution for this activity in the Lesson 12 Lab 2 solution.html file in the Configuring_Network/Solution folder in the student data files.

1. On srvB, create a directory named files_uploaded in the /var/ftp directory and grant full permission to it.

2. In the /etc/vsftpd/user_list file, add the users laura and linda.

3. In the /etc/vsftpd/vsftpd.conf file, set the value of the directives `userlist_enable` to `YES` and `userlist_deny` to `NO`, to allow the users listed in the user_list file to access the FTP server.

   Start the FTP service and set the service to start whenever the system boots.

4. On srvA, access the FTP server and upload a specific file using the `put` command.

5. At the end of the /etc/vsftpd/ftpusers file, add the user miller, to deny FTP server access for miller.

Lesson 12 Lab 3

Configuring Network Sharing Services

 You can find a suggested solution for this activity in the Lesson 12 Lab 3 solution.html file in the Configuring_Network/Solution folder in the student data files.

Scenario:
You are a network administrator in OGC Systems. You want to enable teams in various locations to frequently share files and folders. You want to enable file sharing across a network from a central remote server. But this can result in confidential files being shared, and so you want to ensure that all client requests are filtered.

1. On srvB, export the /sourcecode directory.

2. Activate the nfs service. Add csmith and wwalters as Linux users using the `useradd` command and assign *myp@$$w0rd* as password.

3. On srvB, at the end of the /etc/samba/smb.conf file, define the share section named source and set the following parameters:

```
path = /sourcecode
public = no
browseable = yes
valid users = csmith, wwalters
```

4. Add csmith and wwalters as samba users.

5. Start the smb service and set the service to start whenever the system boots.

6. Reboot srvA into Windows and verify that the user is able to access the /sourcecode directory from a Windows workstation.

Lesson 13 Lab 1

Configuring Web Services

Data Files:

english.html, English, german.html

Setup:

To complete this lab activity, you need to perform the following tasks on srvB:

1. Copy the English directory and the english.html file from the /085039Data/Web_Services to the /var/www/html directory.

2. Create a new directory, /var/www/german, and copy the german.html file from the /085039Data/Web_Services directory to the new directory.

3. Add a CNAME entry for the german website in the forward zone file.

4. Add the nameserver entry as 192.168.0.3.

5. Modify the web browser setting to turn off the proxy.

Scenario:

Your organization wants to keep all its stakeholders updated on all upcoming developments. To update stakeholders including customers, investors, and employees on recent developments, management decided to host an interactive website, www.ourglobalcompany.com. After discussing the requirements with management, the web design team plans to implement the following:

1. Support for PHP pages should be configured to enable customers to buy products online.

2. Only the authenticated webusers will be allowed to access the website.

3. A german version of the website will be created to support your company's marketing activities in Germany. The German version will be called german.ourglobalcompany.com.

4. The contents of accessed web pages will be cached locally to improve the web access speed within the organization.

5. The Internet access will be restricted during weekends according to the regulations stated in the Internet policy.

 You can find a suggested solution for this activity in the Lesson 13 Lab 1 solution.html file in the Web_Services\Solution folder in the student data files.

1. Install httpd on srvB.

2. Enable PHP support on the system.

3. Specify alias names for the web server in the forward zone.

4. Configure the web server to allow web hosting.

   In the /etc/httpd/conf/httpd.conf file, set the `ServerName` directive to `www.ourglobalcompany.com:80`.

   Set the `DirectoryIndex` directive to `english.html`.

5. Start the httpd service to apply the configuration changes.

6. Specify alias names for the web server in the httpd.conf file.

7. Add `VirtualHost` directives to the English and German websites.

   At the end of the httpd.conf file, specify the IP address of the web server (192.168.0.3) using the `NameVirtualHost` directive.
   1. Define the `VirtualHost` directive for the website with the `ServerName` directive set to `192.168.0.3`, `DocumentRoot` directive set to `/var/www/html`, and `DirectoryIndex` directive set to `index.html`.
   2. Define the `VirtualHost` directive for the German website with the `ServerName` directive set to `192.168.0.3`, `DocumentRoot` directive set to `/var/www/german`, and `DirectoryIndex` directive set to `german.html`.

8. Save and close the file.

9. Create users who can access your website.

10. Configure Apache to authenticate users. In the .htaccess file, define the `Authname`, `Authuserfile`, and `Authtype` parameters. Also, specify that all valid users can access the website using the `require valid-user` parameter.

11. Check that you are able to access the English and German versions of the website.

12. On srvA, access the sites using the links `http://www.ourglobalcompany.com` and `http://german.ourglobalcompany.com`.

13. In the /etc/squid/squid.conf file, uncomment the line `http_port 3128`.

14. In the `INSERT YOUR OWN RULE` section, define the myhosts ACL, admin ACL, and lunch-time ACL. Also, set the `http_access` directive to provide access rights to myhosts ACL and lunch ACL, and deny access rights to the admin ACL.

15. Create the `restricted_site` ACL and deny the ACL to reject access to pornographic sites.

16. Start the squid service.

Lesson 14 Lab 1

Securing Linux

 You can find a suggested solution for this activity in the Lesson 14 Lab 1 solution.html file in the Securing_Linux\Solution folder in the student data files.

Scenario:

An employee, Pat, asked your manager, John, to make his password more secure. John requests you to make Pat's password more secure and add additional rules to the firewall to allow Samba to communicate with the system. Update Pat's password and adjust the firewall rules.

1. Using the `passwd` command, update the password of **Pat.**

2. View the existing rules and add three new rules to the iptables firewall.

   ```
   iptables -A INPUT  -p udp  -s 192.168.0.0/255.255.255.0 -d
   192.168.0.1/32 --dport 137 -j ACCEPT
   iptables -A INPUT  -p udp  -s 192.168.0.0/255.255.255.0 -d
   192.168.0.1/32 --dport 138 -j ACCEPT
   iptables -A INPUT  -p tcp  -s 192.168.0.0/255.255.255.0 -d
   192.168.0.1/32 --dport 139 -j ACCEPT
   ```

Lesson 15 Lab 1

Verifying Hardware Compatibility

Scenario:

Your manager wants to put in an order for 50 new Linux computer systems, but is not sure what hardware to choose in each system. Visit the Red Hat hardware compatibility site and determine which hardware will work with Red Hat Enterprise Linux. Report your findings to your manager.

 This activity can be performed on Linux systems with Internet connectivity or on Windows systems with Internet connectivity.

1. Log in to the GUI and launch a web browser.

2. Access the Linux hardware compatibility article at **https://hardware.redhat.com/.**

3. Select the **Systems** link for **Version 5** to view the Hardware Catalog. Browse the Hardware Catalog to check the hardware that are compatible with Linux.

4. Return to **https://hardware.redhat.com/** and select the **Components/ Peripherals** link for **Version 5** to view the list of components and peripherals that are compatible with Linux.

5. Close the web browser window.

Lesson 16 Lab 1

Troubleshooting Linux System Issues

Scenario:

As a system administrator, you may encounter many system issues that have to be rectified to restore the system or its services. So, you decide to refresh your knowledge on troubleshooting Linux systems.

1. What is the first step in troubleshooting a corrupt X Window system?

   a) Switch to runlevel 3 to fix the issue.

   b) Switch to runlevel 0 to fix the issue.

   c) Switch to runlevel 6 to fix the issue.

   d) Switch to runlevel 5 to fix the issue.

2. The _____ command is used to check the display settings.

3. In which file should the name server entry be defined to enable the domain name server to resolve the domain name to IP address?

   a) /etc/hosts

   b) /etc/host.conf

   c) /etc/resolv.conf

   d) /etc/sysconfig/network

4. Which of these commands is used to repair a broken filesystem?

   a) e2fsck

   b) mkfs

   c) fsck

   d) dump2fs

5. You need to edit the _____ file to configure the system log information.

6. Which of these files is used to define the label /boot for the device /dev/sda2?

   a) e2label /dev/sda2 /boot

   b) e2label /boot /dev/sda2

   c) e2label /boot

   d) e2lable /dev/sda2

Lesson 17 Lab 1

Installing Linux

 You can find a suggested solution for this activity in the Lesson 17 Lab 1 solution.html file in the Installing_Linux\Solution folder in the student data files.

Before You Begin:
Ensure that the five installation CDs of RHEL 5.3 are available.

Scenario:
Your manager would like you to install a fresh version of Linux on a system so that it can be duplicated and installed throughout the company. Install Linux on a system that most of the users in the company are using, to ensure that the drivers will work across the board.

1. Initiate the Red Hat Enterprise Linux 5 installation process for a server system.

2. Partition the hard disk manually.

3. Set the time zone and root password.

4. Select the required software packages for the system.

5. Perform installation.

6. Configure post installation settings.

Lesson 18 Lab 1

Configuring the Linux GUI

 You can find a suggested solution for this activity in the Lesson 18 Lab 1 solution.html file in the Graphical_User_Interface\Solution folder in the student data files.

Data Files:

A.D. MONO.ttf

Setup:

If students are going to perform this lab activity immediately after Lesson 18, they need to copy the data files from the 085039Data/Graphical_Interface/ directory in the student data CD, to the user's root directory. However, if they are going to perform it outside the classroom environment, they need to have the following setup:

1. A system running Red Hat Enterprise Linux 5 with the CLI components installed.

2. Data files extracted from the /085039Data/Graphical_Interface/ directory in the student data CD, to the user's root directory.

Scenario:

The system allocated to a new employee has the CLI but not the GUI. The employee requested you to configure the GUI based on the following specifications:

● Set the screen resolution as 1024x768 and color to millions of colors.

● Install the font A.D. MONO.ttf.

● Select the newly installed font and set the font size as 14 in KDM.

1. Enable the Linux GUI.

2. Adjust the resolution.

3. Log in as root in the KDE GUI.

4. Install the new font.

5. Configure the new font.

Solutions

Lesson 1

Activity 1-1

1. **Which of these statements about open source software are true? Select all that apply.**

   ✓ a) Its source code is accessible by all.

   ✓ b) Users have the right to modify and redistribute it.

      c) It is always available at zero price.

      d) It cannot be updated.

2. **Which of these statements apply to Linux? Select all that apply.**

   ✓ a) Increased security

      b) Proprietary in nature

   ✓ c) Customizable

   ✓ d) Easy licensing procedure

      e) High cost

3. **True or False? Software released under GPL can be modified and copyrighted by any user.**

   ___ True

   ✓ False

4. **What are the advantages of Linux? Select all that apply.**

   ✓ a) Enables software to be customized.

      b) Comes with strong single-vendor support.

   ✓ c) Increases the likelihood of bugs being detected because of increased numbers of programmers who can view code.

   ✓ d) Fosters a community among users and a sense of shared responsibility for the software.

5. **What are the potential disadvantages of using Linux? Select all that apply.**

    a) Licensing Linux is a difficult task and requires large amounts of money.

    ✓ b) Limited number of mainstream applications are available.

    ✓ c) Possible lack of comfort in believing that a single vendor can provide support.

    d) Mainstream Linux distributions come complete with a set of games and office, network, and graphics applications.

6. **True or False? There are a limited number of Linux distributions and that is why users have trouble when deciding which distribution to use.**

    ___ True

    _✓_ False

7. **True or False? Because of Linux's simple licensing terms, IT administrators do not have to spend a lot of time monitoring the number of installations or tracking licenses.**

    _✓_ True

    ___ False

Activity 1-4

5. **True or False? It is common practice to write a detailed report of exactly what is installed and changed on each Linux system in your environment.**

    _✓_ True

    ___ False

6. **What are the additional help options that may be installed on your Linux system?**

    ✓ a) --help

    b) helpme

    ✓ c) HOWTO

    ✓ d) Textinfo

7. **In what formats are HOWTOs available?**

    ✓ a) PostScript

    b) Email

    ✓ c) PDF

    ✓ d) HTML

Lesson 1 Follow-up

Lesson 1 Lab 1

1. **What are the benefits of releasing software under GPL?**

   Source code of the software will be freely available and can be modified by users. This feature enables users to customize the software to suit their requirements. GPL also prevents users from copyrighting the software after modifications, thus protecting the rights of the developer. The software will be constantly developed and improved by a community of users.

2. **Identify the advantages of using open source software.**

   Open source software allows users to modify the source code. Users can improve the code and redistribute it freely. Moreover, the software can be used and distributed without much restriction.

3. **Compare free software and proprietary software.**

   Free software can be freely distributed among users without any restriction. Proprietary software is bound by licensing agreements and cannot be distributed without an appropriate license. Source code of free software is freely available to users for modification and redistribution. Whereas, the source code of proprietary software is not accessible to users, because it is the legal property of the owner or company.

4. **List the features of Linux that make it competitive as an operating system.**

   Linux is available as various distributions to suit the requirements of different users. It can be downloaded free of cost or purchased at a low cost. Linux provides good security, performance, and stability.

Lesson 3

Activity 3-5

2. **At which runlevel can you perform disk maintenance without damaging the disks?**

   a) Runlevel 0

   ✓ b) Runlevel 1

   c) Runlevel 3

   d) Runlevel 5

3. **True or False? You can run the e2fsck command to perform a disk check on a mounted filesystem.**

   __ True

   ✓ False

Lesson 8

Activity 8-1

1. **Which function is associated with the SCI layer of the kernel?**

    a) Passing requests to device drivers

    ✓ b) Sending service requests to the kernel

    c) Processor time allocation for functions

    d) Process scheduling functions

    e) File organization

2. **What are the major functions performed by the kernel? Select all that apply.**

    a) Kernel initialization

    ✓ b) Process management

    ✓ c) Memory management

    d) Module installation

    e) Dependency management

3. **True or False? The kernel maintains a list of all devices in the /boot directory.**

    ___ True

    ✓ False

Lesson 15

Activity 15-3

1. **Which of these statements are true? Select all that apply.**

    a) USB is an IEEE 1394-standard, high-speed serial bus.

    ✓ b) A loopback device allows you to mount filesystem images, such as ISO, on the hard disk.

    ✓ c) FireWire is ideal to connect a digital video camera to a system.

    d) PCMCIA was formerly known as PC card.

    e) The cardmgr utility is used to monitor and control the state of PCMCIA sockets.

2. **Which is the earliest kernel that supported USB?**

    ✓ a) 2.2.18

    b) 2.4.16

    c) 2.6.22

    d) 2.2.13

3. **True or False? USB device information is located in the /proc/usb directory.**

___ True

✓ False

Activity 15-5

1. **Which file contains information on setting up your RAID arrays?**

   a) /etc/raid/raidtab

   ✓ b) /etc/mdadm.conf

   c) /etc/raid/raidtab.conf

2. **True or False? RAID is a method that is used to store the same data across multiple hard disks to provide improved performance and data security.**

   ✓ True

   ___ False

3. **Which of these devices are mass storage devices? Select all that apply.**

   ✓ a) CD-RW drive

   b) Floppy disk drive

   ✓ c) DVD-RW drive

   ✓ d) Hard drive

Lesson 16

Activity 16-4

1. **In which file will you change the LCD monitor parameters such as DefaultDepth, Viewport, and Depth?**

   a) /etc/x11Config

   b) /etc/XF86

   c) /X11/XF86Config

   ✓ d) /etc/X11/xorg.conf

2. **One of the LCD monitors is not displaying any output. What could be the problem? Select all that apply.**

   ✓ a) The LCD panel is not connected properly to the system.

   ✓ b) The VGA card module is not configured properly.

   c) Serial port settings are not configured properly.

   ✓ d) Monitor parameters, such as DefaultDepth, Viewport, and Depth, are not configured properly.

3. **True or False? In the /etc/X11/xorg.conf file, the section Screen contains parameters of the VGA card module for an LCD monitor.**

      ✓ True

      ___ False

4. **In one of the terminals, users are not able to listen to the audio associated with the animation. What will be your first step to troubleshoot the issue?**

      a) Verify that the sound card is detected while booting.

      b) Verify that the sound card module is loaded.

      c) Contact the hardware engineer to solve the issue.

      ✓ d) Verify that the speaker is connected, switched on, and working properly.

5. **Which command will you use to verify serial port settings?**

      a) setserial -q

      b) setserial -v

      ✓ c) setserial -a

      d) setserial -z

Activity 16-5

1. **One of your network users is unable to connect to the FTP server, which is located on a different network. The error message indicates that the other network is unreachable. You verified that the network cable is intact and that the FTP server is up. What could be the probable cause of the error? Select all that apply.**

      ✓ a) The network service is not up.

      b) The resolv.conf file does not contain entries for the nameserver.

      ✓ c) Network parameters, such as the IP address, the subnet mask, or the default gateway, are not set correctly.

      d) The firewall is disabled.

2. **You verified that the network service is running and that the network parameters are properly set. However, the user is still unable to connect to the network. What will be your first step to troubleshoot the network issue?**

      a) Verify that the hostname is set.

      ✓ b) Verify that the DNS entries are correct.

      c) Verify that IP forwarding is enabled.

      d) Verify that the ports of the service you are trying to access are open at the destination host.

3. **True or False? To set the hostname permanently, you need to modify the /etc/sysconfig/network file.**

      ✓ True

      ___ False

Lesson 16 Follow-up

Lesson 16 Lab 1

1. **What is the first step in troubleshooting a corrupt X Window system?**

    ✓ a) Switch to runlevel 3 to fix the issue.

    b) Switch to runlevel 0 to fix the issue.

    c) Switch to runlevel 6 to fix the issue.

    d) Switch to runlevel 5 to fix the issue.

2. **The** *system-config-display* **command is used to check the display settings.**

3. **In which file should the name server entry be defined to enable the domain name server to resolve the domain name to IP address?**

    a) /etc/hosts

    b) /etc/host.conf

    ✓ c) /etc/resolv.conf

    d) /etc/sysconfig/network

4. **Which of these commands is used to repair a broken filesystem?**

    a) e2fsck

    b) mkfs

    ✓ c) fsck

    d) dump2fs

5. **You need to edit the** */etc/syslog.conf* **file to configure the system log information.**

6. **Which of these files is used to define the label /boot for the device /dev/sda2?**

    ✓ a) e2label /dev/sda2 /boot

    b) e2label /boot /dev/sda2

    c) e2label /boot

    d) e2lable /dev/sda2

Lesson 17

Activity 17-1

1. **What is the default bootloader in new versions of Red Hat Enterprise Linux?**

    a) LILO

    ✓ b) GRUB

    c) System Commander

2. **True or False? FIPS is used to resize FAT partitions.**

   ✓ True

   ___ False

3. **When is it the best time to gather information about your Linux system?**

   a) Just after installing Linux.

   b) During the Linux installation.

   ✓ c) Before installing Linux.

   d) You do not have to gather system information.

Activity 17-2

1. **What enables you to choose the operating system to load from the hard disk?**

   a) The number of sectors on the hard disk

   ✓ b) MBR

   c) The number of tracks on the hard disk

   d) BIOS

   e) The bootloader

2. **What is true of MBR?**

   ✓ a) MBR contains the partition tables.

   b) MBR contains a number of sectors.

   ✓ c) MBR contains the code to load the operating system into the memory.

   d) MBR determines the boot device settings.

   ✓ e) MBR determines the currently active partition.

3. **True or False? The bootloader installer contains a kernel loader.**

   ___ True

   ✓ False

Glossary

/etc/group file
A file that contains a list of groups.

/etc/issue
The login banner that is displayed to local users.

/etc/issue.net
The login banner that users see when they make a network connection, such as Telnet or SSH, with the system.

/etc/syslog.conf
The file that controls the location where syslogd records system logs.

3DES
A block cipher algorithm that can encrypt and decrypt data using a single secret key.

absolute path
The specific location, including the domain name, irrespective of the working directory or combined paths.

ACL in Squid
(Access Control List in Squid) A set of entries that define the permissions to access a system and all resources within it.

ACL
(Access Control List) A list of permissions attached to an object.

active IDS
An IDS that detects a security breach according to the parameters it has been configured with, logs the activity, then takes the appropriate action to block the user from the suspicious activity.

algorithm
A procedure or formula for solving a problem using a finite set of well-defined instructions for accomplishing some task that, given an initial state, will terminate in a corresponding recognizable end-state.

alias command
Shorthand for a longer expression.

Anaconda installer
An installation program that enables installation of Linux through the text mode or graphical mode.

anacron
A daemon that executes commands at intervals, which are specified in days, without requiring the computer system to be running continuously.

Apache
An open source web server.

apmd
(Advanced Power Management Daemon) A monitoring daemon that controls the Advanced Power Management system.

application access controls
Daemons that are used to restrict access to certain important applications.

application server

A server program running on a computer connected to a distributed network.

archiving

A method of storing data for later use by copying data from a system disk drive on to a backup device.

argument

An argument is usually a file name or directory name that indicates on which files the command will operate.

ARP

(Address Resolution Protocol) A network protocol that is used by IP to map network addresses to MAC addresses.

Aspell

A utility that functions as a spell checker in Linux.

asymmetric encryption

An encryption type where a key pair is used for encryption.

at command

The command that is used to execute a given set of commands only once, at a specified time.

ATAPI

(AT Attachment Packet Interface) A protocol that is used to control mass storage devices.

authentication

A process which verifies the identity of users.

automatic rotation

A system of regular rotation of logs to maintain a minimum log file size.

average time

See "true time"

awk command

A command that performs pattern matching.

background process

A program that allows the Linux shell to execute a command that runs a job in the background, enabling processes to run simultaneously.

Bash shell

(Bourne-Again SHell) A default shell in Linux that facilitates command line editing, command history, and shell scripting.

BIND

(Berkeley Internet Name Domain) A domain name service that resolves hostnames to IP addresses.

BIOS

(Basic Input/Output System) Low-level software that acts as the interface between the hardware and the operating system on a computer.

block special files

Large files that are used for data storage.

Blowfish

A symmetric block cipher that provides strong encryption and uses key sizes up to 56 bytes.

boot disk

A disk that contains the operating system files to start up a system.

boot manager

See "bootloader"

boot process

The process of starting or restarting your computer by loading the operating system from your hard drive.

bootloader

A program that loads the kernel so that Linux and other operating systems can boot.

BOOTP

(Bootstrap Protocol) A network protocol that passes requests sent from a diskless workstation to a server node.

broadcast address

A special IP address that is used to send messages to all hosts with the same network address.

browser mode

The mode in the Nautilus browser that enables you to display the selected folder in the same window.

cd
The command that is used to change directories.

central network log server
A server that is used to implement centralized logging services.

Certificate Authority certificates
A digital certificate generated by a common and trusted Certificate Authority (CA) on receiving a certificate signature request (csr).

CGI
(Common Gateway Interface) A protocol that provides a way for the web server to communicate with external dynamic content created using CGI scripts or programs.

chains
A set of rules used by iptables to handle IP filtering.

CHAP
A security authentication protocol that encrypts the user name and password information using a key and transmits them over the network.

character special files
Small files that are used for streaming of data.

check for dependency
The first stage in the Debian Archive Package Installation process. In this stage, the package manager checks the specified Debian archive package for the numerous dependencies required.

child process
A process started by another process.

CIFS
(Common Internet File System) A standard Linux filesystem that is used to mount and access shared resources available on a heterogeneous network.

Class A addresses
A subnet scheme that provides 16,777,214 nodes per network.

Class B addresses
A subnet scheme that provides 65,534 nodes per network.

Class C addresses
A subnet scheme that provides 254 nodes per network.

CLI
(Command Line Interface) A textual interface based on the operating system, where a user typically enters commands at the command prompt to instruct the computer to perform a specific task.

clock drift
The gradual variation in time that sets between the hardware clock and the system clock.

CMOS
(Complementary Metal Oxide Semiconductor) Pronounced as "see-moss." The most widely used type of integrated circuit for digital processors and memories. Virtually everything is configured through CMOS today.

command line interpreter
A program that implements the commands entered in a text interface.

command mode
A mode in Linux that allows users to perform different editing actions using single keystrokes.

command prompt
A sequence of one or more characters in a CLI that is used to indicate the interpreter's readiness to accept commands.

command substitution
The ability to reassign the output of a command as an argument to another command.

configure
The last stage in the Debian Archive Package Installation process. In this stage, the unpacked files can be configured with the default values or customized to suit your requirements.

console

See "terminal"

control statement

An instruction that determines the direction a program takes depending on a condition.

controls statement

A statement that is used to configure various security requirements needed by the rndc command to administer the named service.

copyleft

A concept that emphasizes the enforcement of public ownership of creative works.

count

A number that multiplies the effect of key-strokes in Vim.

cpio

A command that copies files to and from archives.

createrepo command

A command that is used to create yum repositories.

cron job

A task scheduled via cron.

cron

A daemon that runs in the background and executes specified tasks at a designated time or date.

crontab

The file that contains instructions defining the tasks to be executed by a cron.

cryptographic hashes

An encryption method where arbitrary data is encapsulated within a fingerprint, which is a fixed string called the hash value, checksum, or message digest.

CUPS

(Common UNIX Printing System) A print management system designed for scheduling print jobs, processing administrative commands, and providing printer status information to local and remote programs.

curl

A command line tool that is used to transfer data to or from a server using the URL syntax.

cylinder

The aggregate of all tracks that reside in the same location on every disk surface.

daemon

A program that runs in the background without the need for human intervention.

database

An organized collection of information to facilitate easy storage and retrieval of data.

datagram

See "packet"

dd command

A command that copies and converts files to enable them to be transferred from one type of media to another.

default gateway address

The IP address assigned to the default gateway router.

default gateway

A gateway that acts as a network segment's access point to all other external networks and the Internet.

delayed job

A job that can be run at some specified time after you issued the command.

DES

(Data Encryption Standard) An encryption method developed by IBM in 1977, which uses a 56-bit private key applied to each 64-bit block of data.

detached job

A job that can be set to run after you log out of the system.

device driver

A software program that enables a computer's operating system to identify the characteristics and functions of a hardware device, communicate with it, and control it.

device management layer
A layer in the kernel that manages devices by controlling device access and interfacing between user applications and hardware devices of the computer.

device node
An access point to the device drivers that is used while mapping service requests with device access.

device tree
A structure that lists all hardware devices installed on the computer and assigns device nodes to them. It is auto generated by the computer's operating system.

DHCP
(Dynamic Host Control Protocol) A server that hands out IP addresses on an as-needed basis.

dhcpd.conf
A file that is used to configure the DHCP server.

diff command
A command that is used to compare individual text files or contents of directories.

digital certificate
A digital document that authenticates a specific public key belonging to an individual or a company.

directory service
A software system that stores and organizes information in a directory.

disk image
See "ISO image"

disk quota
The specific amount of disk space that is allotted to a user for file storage on a computer.

display manager
A program that controls the look and feel of a desktop environment.

DMA
(Direct Memory Address) A method by which hardware devices directly communicate with the memory to obtain memory allocation without going through the processor.

DNS resource record
A record that defines some parameters for a zone.

DNS
(Domain Name System) A distributed, hierarchical database system that maintains information about hostnames and their equivalent IP addresses on the Internet.

domain name
A label given to a domain.

domain namespace
A database consisting of information about the hierarchy of domains and the hosts under each domain.

domain
A node in the hierarchical structure of the data stored in DNS.

driver
A program that controls a device attached to a computer.

dump command
A command that dumps all the files in a filesystem on to a tape or another file.

dumpe2fs utility
A utility that is primarily used for managing an ext2-based filesystem.

editing operators
Powerful tools in the command mode that can be used to manipulate text using simple keystrokes.

ELILO
A bootloader for UEFI machines. It supports flexible local booting from a FAT-32 filesystem.

elinks
A non-GUI, text-based web browser.

Emacs
A flexible, powerful, and popular text editor used in Linux and Unix.

encryption
The process where user access to information is controlled by configuring the data to appear in the form of codes that cannot be interpreted by unauthorized users.

entropy
A measure of randomness collected by a device, application, or system.

environment variable
A storage location in the environment of the operating system's command shell.

execute mode
A mode in Linux that allows users to execute commands within the editor.

exports file
A configuration file that is used to export a filesystem.

extended partition
A partition that does not contain any data and has a separate partition table.

fdisk
A utility program that is used for creating, modifying, or deleting partitions on a disk drive.

FHS
(Filesystem Hierarchy Standard) A collaborative document that specifies a set of guidelines for the names of files and directories and their locations.

fields
Small segments of organized data in a database.

file owner
A user who creates a file or directory.

filesystem integrity
The correctness and validity of a filesystem.

filesystem management layer
A layer in the kernel that manages the filesystem, which involves storing, organizing, and tracking files and data on a computer.

filesystem
A method used by an operating system to store, retrieve, organize, and manage files and directories in various mass storage devices.

find command
A command that is used to search a specific location for files and directories.

FIPS
(First nondestructive Interactive Partition Splitting program) A utility that is used to resize the FAT partitions.

firewall
A software program or a hardware device that protects a system or a network from unauthorized access by blocking unsolicited traffic.

FireWire
A high-speed serial bus developed by Apple Computer, Inc. and Texas Instruments that allows various devices to be connected with a system. It was originally a trademarked term for IEEE 1394, but is now used interchangeably.

flash drive
A portable storage device.

font path
A collection of paths in the filesystem where font files are stored.

for loop
A loop that executes a part of the script for a specific number of times.

foreground process
The program that the user is interacting with currently.

forward zone
A DNS zone that is used for mapping hostnames to IP addresses.

FQDN

(Fully Qualified Domain Name) A method by which systems are uniquely identified in the worldwide network.

fsck command

The command that is used to check the integrity of a filesystem.

fstab

A configuration file that stores information about storage devices and partitions and where and how the partitions should be mounted.

FTP

(File Transfer Protocol) A protocol that is used to send and receive files from one system to another through the Internet.

gateway

A device, software application, or system that converts data between incompatible systems.

GCC

(GNU Compiler Collection) A compiler system that supports various programming languages.

GDM

(GNOME Display Manager) The default display manager for Red Hat Linux.

gedit

A simple yet powerful GUI-based text editor used in the GNOME desktop.

global user profile

A description of the settings, preferences, bookmarks, stored messages, attributes, permissions, and other user items that users have access to, on whichever system they log in to.

globbing

A function that expands file names using a pattern-matching behavior.

GMT

(Greenwich Mean Time) The time at the prime meridian at Greenwich, England.

GNOME search tool

A graphical utility used for searching files.

GNOME system monitor

A graphical utility that is used to monitor the system processes, resources, and filesystems.

GNU Parted utility

A utility that can be used to create, destroy, and resize partitions.

GNU project

(GNU's Not Unix) A project started by Richard Stallman to create a comprehensive computer operating system composed entirely of free software.

Gopher

A protocol that is used to search and retrieve documents from the Internet.

grace period

The time limit before the soft limit is enforced for a filesystem.

group database

The file named /etc/group, which contains a list of groups, each on a separate line.

group

A collection of system users having the same access rights.

GUI

(Graphical User Interface) A collection of icons, windows, and other graphical images on screen that help users interact with the operating system.

Gvim

The graphical version of the Vim editor.

gzip

(GNU zip) A compressing utility that reduces the size of the named files.

HAL

(Hardware Abstraction Layer) A logical interface that enables software applications of a system to interact with hardware devices at an abstract level through system calls.

hard limit

The absolute limit on disk usage that a quota user has on a partition.

hard link
A reference to another file; it allows the file's data to have more than one name in different locations in the same filesystem.

history command
A command that is used to view previously typed commands.

home directory
A directory where you are placed when you log in to a system.

honeypot
A system designed to attract attackers.

HTTP
(Hyper Text Transfer Protocol) A protocol that is used to transfer hypertext files across the World Wide Web.

I/O address
(Input/Output address) An address that is used to identify the requests sent to or from a hardware device.

ICMP
(Internet Control Message Protocol) A protocol that is used to handle error and control messages.

ICP
(Internet Cache Protocol) A protocol that is used for coordinating and communicating among web caches.

IDS
(Intrusion Detection System) A security sensor that protects portals, networks, and files.

ifconfig command
A command that is used for configuring network interfaces for Linux servers and workstations.

IMAP
(Internet Message Access Protocol) A protocol that is used to retrieve email messages over the TCP connection on port 143.

immutable flag
An extended attribute of a file that prevents the file from being modified.

include statement
A statement that is used to specify the file name that needs to be included in the named.conf file.

index node table
A data structure that contains information about individual files in a filesystem.

inetd command
A system service daemon that starts programs needed for accessing different Internet services.

init
The parent of all processes. It creates processes at system boot time from the /etc/inittab file.

initrd image
An archived file containing all the essential files that are required for booting the operating system.

initrd
The initial ramdisk that is temporarily mounted as the root filesystem for loading the start up programs and modules.

inittab
A file found in the /etc directory that stores details of various processes related to system initialization.

inode
(index node) A computer's reference for a file.

insert mode
A mode in Linux that allows users to insert text by typing.

insmod
A utility that installs a module into the currently running kernel.

IP address
A unique address that identifies a host on the Internet.

IP filtering
A mechanism employed for processing, dropping, logging, or forwarding data packets received by a system.

ipchains

A Linux tool for managing packet filtering on a Linux server.

IPng

See "IPv6"

iptables

A firewall program in Linux that provides protection to the internal network.

IPv4

(IP Version 4) An older version of IP, which is being replaced by IPv6 with extended features.

IPv6

(IP Version 6) A new version of IP, which is being implemented on the Internet. Also called IP Next Generation (IPng).

IRQ

(Interrupt ReQuests) A signal sent by a hardware device to the kernel to request for processing time for performing an operation.

ISO image

An archive file format for files that are to be written to optical discs like CDs and DVDs.

iwconfig command

A command that is used for configuring wireless network interfaces for Linux servers and workstations.

Java servlet

A Java object file that is developed as a component and can be run on the server.

jobs table

A table containing information about processes running in the background.

journaling filesystem

A method that is used by an operating system to quickly recover after an unexpected interruption, such as a system crash.

KDM

(K Display Manager) The display manager for KDE, or K Desktop Environment.

Kerberos

A network authentication service that is used by client/server applications.

kernel module

A system-level function that extends the functionality of the kernel.

kernel

The central core of the Linux (or Unix) operating system that manages all the computer's physical devices.

key

A block of information that authorizes users to access data.

klogd

(kernel logging daemon) A daemon that tracks kernel messages by prioritizing them.

KWrite

A flexible GUI-based text editor used in KDE.

LAN

(Local Area Network) A network that connects computers in a small geographical area such as a floor or a building.

lastlog command

A command that displays the latest login details of all users.

LDAP

(Lightweight Directory Access Protocol) A communication protocol that defines the transport and format of messages used by a client to access the directory service.

lease database

A database that stores information about leases.

lease

The amount of time given by the DHCP server to a client for using an IP address.

LED

(Light Emitting Diode) An electrical component frequently used as an indicator light on network adapters and other types of network equipment.

LILO

(Linux Loader) A program that is used to specify the operating system environment to boot to.

Linux documentation

The material that provides information on various Linux commands and blocks of code.

Linux kernel

The core constituent of the Linux operating system that manages all other resources on the system. It performs functions such as sharing resources and allocating of memory, input and output operations, security settings, and user access.

Linux rescue environment

A stand-alone Linux program for trouble-shooting a corrupt Linux installation.

Linux

An open source computer operating system derived from Unix.

ln command

A command that is used to create a link to a file.

load average

The average number of processes waiting to run on the system for the last 1 minute, 5 minutes, and 15 minutes.

Loadlin

A DOS application program that requires a user to first boot into DOS (or Windows) to run Linux.

local or private repositories

Repositories stored on your system.

locate command

A command that performs a quick search for any specified string in file names and paths stored in the mlocate database.

lock command

A command that is used to temporarily prevent a user from logging in to a Linux system.

log file analysis

The process of examining the messages generated by logging daemons in log files.

log file

A file that stores log messages.

logging service

A daemon used to track logs or errors that are created in a system or kernel.

logical partition

A partition created within an extended partition.

logrotate command

A command that is used to compress, delete, or mail log files.

logwatch utility

A utility that is used to monitor logs.

lpc command

The command that is used to manage print jobs.

LPD

(Line Printer Daemon) A Linux system service for network printing.

lpr command

The command that is used to submit files for printing.

lsmod

A utility that displays the currently loaded kernel modules, their size, usage details, and dependent modules.

LV

(Logical Volume) A partition in the storage area.

LVM

(Logical Volume Manager) A software tool that is used to manage the disk storage on a computer system.

MAC address

See "physical address"

mail protocol

A method of distributing email messages from a mail server.

mail queue
A waiting area for email messages that need to be processed by a computer.

major number
A number stored as part of the structure of a device node. It identifies the device driver that controls a particular device.

MAN
(Metropolitan Area Network) A network that connects computers in a broad geographical area such as a city and its suburbs.

manual pages
Pages containing the complete documentation that is specific to every command, presented in simple ASCII text format.

MBR
(Master Boot Record) The first physical sector on a hard drive that contains the code that is used to load the operating system or bootloader into memory.

MD5
(Message-Digest algorithm 5) A command-line utility that generates and verifies message digests.

MDA
(Mail Delivery Agent) A program that delivers an incoming email to the respective user's mailbox.

memory management layer
A layer in the kernel that manages the computer's memory.

menu.lst
A GRUB configuration file that lists all the kernels available in the system along with their partition numbers, boot information, and details of which kernel is booted.

message digest
A message digest is a compact digital signature for an arbitrarily stream of binary data.

MIME
A standard Internet format that supports ASCII character sets, non-ASCII character sets, non-text attachments, and multiple parts in a message body.

minor number
A number stored as part of the structure of a device node. It identifies a particular device installed on the computer.

mke2fs utility
A utility that is used to create both ext2 and ext3 filesystems.

mkfs command
A command that is used to build a Linux filesystem on a device, usually a hard disk partition.

mkinitrd command
A command that is used to create the initial ramdisk image for preloading the kernel modules.

mknod command
A command that allows you to create device files that are not present, using the major and minor node numbers of a device.

mkswap command
A system administration command that is used to create swap space on a disk partition.

modinfo
A utility that displays information about a particular kernel module such as file name of the module, license, description, author's name, module version number, dependent modules, and other parameters or attributes.

modprobe
A utility that is used to add or remove modules from a kernel.

modular kernel
A kernel in which only a minimal set of essential modules are built-in. It is also known as a micro kernel or a dynamic kernel.

monolithic kernel

A kernel in which all the required modules, such as device drivers or filesystems, are built-in.

motd

(Message of the day) The /etc/motd file that is displayed to all users after a successful login.

motions

Single-key shortcuts that are used to navigate through files in the command mode.

mount point

An access point to information stored on a local or remote storage device.

MRA

A retrieval agent that retrieves messages from the spool.

MTA

(Mail Transfer Agent) A mail transport program on the Internet that is used to send email messages through SMTP.

MUA

(Mail User Agent) A program that is used to read and compose email messages.

multitasking

The capability to perform more than one task at a time for each user.

MySQL

An open source RDBMS used for managing data.

mysqld

(mysql daemon) The MySQL server that manages the MySQL server service.

name server

A program or a server that implements the domain naming system on a network.

named.conf

A configuration file that is used to manage the BIND service.

namespace

The part of the name that must be unique for DNS to function.

nano

A small, user-friendly text editor that evolved from the Pico editor.

Nessus

An IDS that audits the security of remote hosts and services running on the network.

NetBIOS

A program that allows applications installed on different computers to communicate over a LAN.

netfilter

A framework that implements packet filtering in Linux for managing firewalls and securing data.

network interface

A point of connection between two systems.

network protocol

A set of rules that enable communication and data transfer among network devices.

network

A group of computers connected together to communicate with each other and share resources.

NFS

(Network File System) A networking protocol that allows a computer system to access files over a network or the Internet as though they were on a local disk.

NIC

(Network Interface Card) A small circuit board device that is installed in a computer to enable a computer to connect to a network.

nice command

A command that lets you run a command at a priority lower than the command's normal priority.

nice value

The priority of a process.

NIS

(Network Information Service) A service that manages network information about systems and users on a network.

nmbd
A daemon that is used to handle WINS requests and resolve NetBIOS names.

NSS
(Name Service Switch) A protocol that enables services to access databases to check for user accounts from various sources.

NTP
(Network Time Protocol) A standard Internet protocol for synchronizing the internal system clock with a server or network clock.

ntp.conf
A file containing the configuration options for the NTP server.

online repositories
Repositories found on the Internet.

open source software
Software that allows users to access and modify its source code.

OpenSSH
A free version of the SSH protocol that ensures secure communication by encrypting data transmitted over the Internet.

options statement
A statement that is used to define the global server configuration and set default values for other statements.

package integrity
The method of checking packages based on criteria, such as file structure, format, and checksum, along with verifying if packages are installed or not.

package manager
A tool that enables the installation, verification, upgrading, or removal of packages.

package
A collection of classes, functions, or procedures that can be imported as a single unit.

packet filtering
A process of passing or blocking incoming and outgoing packets after inspecting each packet for user-defined content.

packet
A formatted unit of data being sent across a network.

PAM
(Pluggable Authentication Modules) An interface that allows a Linux system administrator to provide different methods of user authentication to system applications in a method-independent manner.

PAP
A security authentication protocol for logging in to a network.

parent directory
A directory that is one level above your current working directory.

parent process
A process that creates another process.

partition management
The process of creating, destroying, and manipulating partitions to optimize system performance.

partition utility
A program that is used to manage partitions on the hard disk.

partition
A section of the hard disk that logically acts as a separate disk.

partprobe
A program that is used to update the kernel with changes in the partition tables.

passive IDS
An IDS that detects potential security breaches, logs the activity, and alerts security personnel.

password policy
A set of guiding principles that help form effective passwords.

patch command
A command that updates text files with changes according to instructions contained in a patch file.

PATH variable

A system variable that allows you to specify the directories that need to be searched while executing a command.

path

An address that specifies a location in the filesystem.

PATH

An environmental variable.

PDL

(Page Description Language) A computer language that is understood by a printer.

Perl

(Practical Extraction and Reporting Language) A programming language that is used to write scripts.

permissions

The security information that Linux uses to determine who is allowed to access a particular file and what they are allowed to do.

persistent configuration

A configuration where the kernel settings are permanent.

physical address

A globally unique hexadecimal number burned onto every NIC by the manufacturer.

physical network interface

An interface that is implemented using a hardware device.

PID

(Process ID) A unique number assigned by the operating system to each process started on the system.

ping

A command that is used to test network connectivity.

pipe

An operator that combines commands.

POP3

(Post Office Protocol version 3) A protocol that is used to retrieve email messages over the TCP connection on port 110.

port

An access point to a logical connection. It serves as a point of exit and entry for data channels on a network.

portmap

A daemon that dynamically assigns ports to RPCs for communication between clients and servers.

portmapper

A program that an RPC application uses to register the port numbers used by the application.

portsentry

An IDS that is used to detect and respond to port attacks.

POST

(Power-On Self Test) A series of built-in diagnostics that are performed when the computer is started. Proprietary codes are generated to indicate test results.

PostScript®

A Page Description Language (PDL) that tells a printer how to display text or graphics on a page.

PPID

(Parent Process ID) A number assigned to a process that spawns other processes.

primary partition

A partition in which the swap filesystem and the boot partition are normally created.

print queue

A temporary storage area that sorts incoming print jobs.

print server

A computer that provides users on a network access to a central printer.

printer software

The program that enables a printing device to print text or graphics on a page.

private key

The key retained on the local system and not transmitted to the destination server.

PRNG

(Pseudo Random Number Generation) The algorithm that governs random number generation.

process management layer

A layer in the kernel that handles different processes by allocating separate execution space on the processor and ensuring that the running of one process does not interfere with the other processes.

process monitoring

A mode of tracking the processes running on a system to determine the performance and reliability of the system.

process table

A record that summarizes the current running processes on a system.

process

An instance of a running program that performs a data processing task.

profile file

A file that contains the commands to tailor a user's login session according to the requirements of the user.

program

A set of instructions describing how to carry out a task.

proxy server

A server that acts as an intermediary between a web browser and a web server, containing data to which the user requires access.

public key

The key transmitted to the destination server along with the request.

pwd command

A command that is used to display the current working directory relative to the root directory.

quota report

A report created by the system to view the usage of disk space by each user.

RADIUS

(Remote Authentication Dial In User Service) A networking protocol that facilitates centralized authentication, authorization, and accounting over a network.

RAID

(Redundant Array of Inexpensive Disks) A method that is used to store the same data in different locations on multiple hard disks of a server or a stand-alone disk storage system.

random number generation

A method of encrypting data where the kernel is used to generate random numbers that are assigned to files before transfer.

RDBMS

(Relational Database Management System) A system that enables you to store and organize logically related data.

redirector

An operator that redefines the standard input or the standard output.

relational database

A database that stores logically related data consistently in the form of related tables.

relative path

The path relative to the current working directory.

remote X session

A session where a user on a remote workstation is able to view the X Window of the host.

renice command

A command that enables you to alter the scheduling priority of a running process.

repomd

The XML metadata based on the rpm.

repository

The name of the database that holds the source code and compilations.

resolver

Client-based software that sends a request to DNS name servers for translating a domain name to its IP address or vice versa.

restore command

A command that enables you to restore files or filesystems from backups made with the dump command.

reverse zone

A DNS zone that is used for mapping IP addresses to hostnames.

RMON

(Remote Monitoring) A network management protocol that allows network information to be gathered at a single workstation.

rndc utility

A BIND utility that allows command line administration of the named daemon from the local or remote host.

root disk

A disk that contains directories, which contain files required to run a Linux system.

root user

A user who has access rights to all files and resources on the system.

router

A networking device that connects multiple networks together.

routing table

A table of network addresses that is used by routers to forward packets over networks.

routing

The process of selecting the best route for moving a packet from its source to destination on a network.

RPC

(Remote Procedure Call) A package that contains a collection of tools and library functions.

RPM

(RPM Package Manager) A tool for maintaining packages.

rsync utility

A utility that is used to synchronize files among systems.

RTC

(Real Time Clock or the hardware clock) The clock that keeps track of the time when the system is turned off and not when the system is on.

runlevel

A setting that specifies which group of processes runs on your system. Levels include single user, multiuser, reboot, and halt, among others.

Samba

A suite of network sharing tools that help in the sharing of files and printers on a heterogeneous network, which consists of computers running on different operating systems.

SASL

(Simple Authentication and Security Layer) A framework that provides authentication and data security to Internet protocols.

SCI layer

(System Call Interface) An abstraction layer that handles function calls sent from user applications to the kernel.

SCSI

(Small Computer Systems Interface) A set of standards for connecting peripheral devices to a computer.

search path

A sequence of various directory paths that is used by the shell to locate files.

sector

The smallest unit of storage read or written onto a disk.

sed command

A command line program that can modify text files according to command line parameters.

self-signed certificates

A certificate generated by a user and contains the public key of the user as the signature.

SELinux
(Security-Enhanced Linux) A security enhancement feature that implements various security policies on the Linux operating system.

service access controls
Daemons that are used to restrict access to certain important services.

service
A set of applications that perform tasks in the background.

sfdisk utility
A utility that is used to manipulate partitions.

shell
A component that interacts directly with users and functions as the command interpreter for the Linux system.

shutdown command
The command that is used to shutdown or restart a system. This closes files and performs other tasks necessary to safely shutdown a system.

signals
Messages sent to a process to perform a certain action.

skel directory
The location where the default files and directories that need to copied to the new user's home directory is stored.

slapd
(Stand-alone LDAP Daemon) An LDAP directory service, which allows users to create and provide their own directory service that can be connected to the global LDAP directory service.

SMBFS
(Samba File System) A standard Linux filesystem that is used to mount and access shared resources available on a heterogeneous network.

SMTP
A protocol that defines a set of rules to enable interaction between a program sending an email message to a server and a program receiving an email message from a client.

SNMP
(Simple Network Management Protocol) A network management protocol that enables you to remotely monitor and configure network components such as bridges, routers, network cards, and switches.

snort
A network IDS that monitors the network traffic.

soft limit
The maximum amount of disk usage that a quota user has on a partition.

software RAID
RAID implemented using software that is applied to the kernel disk code.

spatial mode
The default mode of the Nautilus browser.

spool
A temporary storage space for files waiting to be printed.

spooler
A component that temporarily stores files waiting to be printed.

spooling
The procedure by which print jobs can be temporarily stored.

Squid
A proxy server that is used for caching Internet data.

ssh-keygen command
A command that generates, manages, and converts authentication keys.

SSH
(Secure Shell) A network protocol that controls the secure flow of data among computers on a network.

SSL

(Secure Socket Layer) A protocol that ensures secure transactions between web servers and browsers.

standard error

A stream in Linux that is used as the destination for error messages.

standard input

The source for command input.

standard output

The destination for command output.

statement

A collection of options that define the domain name settings.

static host

A host that receives the same IP address from the DHCP server.

STDERR

The symbol that is used to refer to the standard error file.

STDIN

The symbol that is used to refer to the standard input file.

STDOUT

The symbol that is used to refer to the standard output file.

sticky bit

A permission bit that provides protection for files in a directory.

su command

(substitute or switch user command) A command that allows you to change the ownership of a login session without logging out.

subnet mask

A filter that tells the server whether an IP address is on the local network or a remote network.

subnets

A logical subsection of a single large network.

sudo command

(super user do command) A command that allows users to run programs with the security privileges of the root user.

superblock

A data structure that is stored on a disk and contains control information for a filesystem.

swap space

A portion of the hard disk that is used in situations when Linux runs out of physical memory and needs more of it.

symbolic link

A reference to a file or directory that allows you to access mounted filesystems from a different directory.

symmetric encryption

An encryption type where only a single key is used to authorize information during encryption and decryption.

syslogd utility

A utility that tracks system logs.

system initialization

The first process that starts when the system is booted.

system load

A measurement of the amount of work done by a computer over a given period of time.

system logs

Records of system activities that the syslogd utility keeps track of.

system time

The time maintained by a computer's internal clock.

tab completion

A feature that facilitates auto completion of commands and file names by pressing the Tab key.

tar command

A command that creates archives of data.

TCP/IP

(Transmission Control Protocol/Internet Protocol) A protocol that is used to transfer packets of data from one system to another on a network.

Telnet

A terminal emulation protocol that enables a user on a site to simulate a session on a remote host.

terminal

A computer interface for text entry and display, where information is displayed as an array of preselected characters.

text editor

An application that allows you to view, create, or modify the contents of text files.

text stream

Data flowing between an application and an operating system entity such as a keyboard, screen, file, or other object in the form of text.

text-based web browser

An application that is used to access web pages in the CUI mode.

TFTP

(Trivial File Transfer Protocol) An unauthenticated version of FTP that runs over UDP.

TLS

(Transport Layer Security) A protocol that provides secure communication channel between servers and clients. It is the third version of SSL.

tmpwatch command

A command that is used to delete files, which have not been accessed for some time.

tr

(translate command) A command that is used to translate strings from the standard input to the standard output.

traceroute

The command that is used to print the route that packets take to reach their destination.

transactional configuration

A configuration where the kernel setting are updated for a required service.

Tripwire

An intrusion detection tool that compares the content of a file or a directory with a database that contains the locations of a file or directory and the dates modified.

true time

The average time on a number of high accuracy clocks around the world.

tune2fs utility

A utility that helps tuning parameters associated with a Linux filesystem.

tunneling

A protocol in which one protocol is layered over the other, for a layered model.

udev

A device manager that manages the automatic detection and configuration of hardware devices.

UDP

(User Datagram Protocol) A connectionless transport protocol that transports data by switching packets.

UID

(User ID) A unique ID number assigned to every user when an account is created.

umask command

A command that automatically alters the default permissions on newly created files and directories.

uniq command

A command that is used to display duplicated lines in a sorted file.

Unix

A well-known operating system originally developed by AT&T's Bell Labs in the 1970s.

unpack

The second stage in the Debian Archive Package Installation process. In this stage, the Debian archive package and its dependant packages are unpacked into the filesystem of the hard disk.

UPG

(User Private Group) A unique group created by default whenever a new user account is created.

USB device

(Universal Serial Bus device) A peripheral devices that can communicate with a host computer.

USB

(Universal Serial Bus) A hardware interface standard designed to provide connections for numerous peripherals.

user account

A collection of information that defines a user on a system.

user profile

A description of the settings, preferences, bookmarks, stored messages, and other user items that characterize a user.

UTC

(Universal Time Coordinated) A time scale that forms the official measure of time in the world.

variable

A symbolic name that represents a value.

verbose

A mode that displays varying levels of status messages as the program is processed.

VGDA

(Volume Group Descriptor Area) An area in a PV where metadata information is stored.

Vi

The standard Unix text editor.

Vim

A default Linux text editor especially meant for programming.

virtual host

A system that manages more than one domain.

virtual network interface

An interface that is implemented through software support.

visual mode

A mode in Linux that allows users to highlight or select text for copying, deleting, and so on.

VNC

(Virtual Network Computing) A platform-independent system through which a user can control a remote system.

VSFTPD

(Very Secure File Transfer Protocol Daemon) A daemon used for sending and receiving files from one computer to another through the Internet.

WAN

(Wide Area Network) A network that connects computers in a wide geographical area such as across the country or around the world.

wc

(word count command) A command that is used to count the number of lines, words, and characters of text files.

web server

A software application that is run on a system to provide world wide web services.

whereis command

A command that is used to locate the details associated with a command.

while loop

A loop that enables you to repeat a set of instructions for a fixed number of times till a specific condition is met.

wildcard

A special character that is used to substitute characters in a string.

window manager

See "display manager"

WINS

(Windows Internet Naming Service) A service that implements the Windows-specific method of name of resolution.

X client

An application that is written with the aid of the Xlib library.

X protocol

The standard protocol used by clients and servers in the X Window system.

X server

A program that implements the GUI service provided by the X Window system.

X Windows

A client/server, multiuser system that resides on top of the operating system.

X-station

A terminal that is connected over a network and engineered to run the X Window system remotely.

X

See "X Windows"

X.Org

A free version of the X Window GUI system for Linux.

X11

See "X Windows"

XDR

(eXternal Data Representation) A format that allows systems to communicate across a network, especially across heterogeneous networks.

Xfs

(X font server) A service that provides fonts to the X.Org server and the X client applications that connect to it.

xinetd

A daemon that controls system services on a network.

XTerm

A screen for typing system commands for the X Window system.

YUM

(Yellow dog Updater, Modified) A package manager similar to RPM.

zip

A portable storage device that precedes the flash drive.

zone file directive

A file that specifies the task to be performed by the name server and the settings of the zone.

zone file

A file that contains information about a particular namespace.

zone statement

A statement that is used to define the characteristics of a zone.

zone

A point of delegation in a DNS tree structure.

Index

085039 S3PB rev 1.0
ISBN-13 978-1-4246-1310-6
ISBN-10 1-4246-1310-8

90000